LAW, THE STATE, A]
THE INTERNATION
COMMUNITY

VOLUME ONE

A Commentary on the Developm
Legal, Political, and International

LAW, THE STATE, AND THE INTERNATIONAL COMMUNITY

By JAMES BROWN SCOTT

Trustee and Secretary, Carnegie Endowment for International Peace and Director of its Division of International Law; Professor of International Law and Foreign Relations, Roman Law and Jurisprudence, Georgetown University

IN TWO VOLUMES

VOLUME ONE

A Commentary on the Development of Legal, Political, and International Ideals

GREENWOOD PRESS, PUBLISHERS
WESTPORT, CONNECTICUT

Originally published in 1939
by Columbia University Press

First Greenwood Reprinting 1970

SBN 8371-2809-9 (SET)
SBN 8371-2807-2 (VOL. 1)

PRINTED IN UNITED STATES OF AMERICA

To GEORGE A. FINCH

In appreciation of more than thirty years of association and coöperation both in the Department of State of the United States and in the Carnegie Endowment for International Peace.

HOW SMALL a fraction of mankind is eloquent or proficient in the law, even if we include those who are ambitious to be so.—CICERO, *Pro Cnaeo Plancio* xxv. 62.

O PHILOSOPHY, thou guide of life, o thou explorer of virtue and expeller of vice! Without thee what could have become not only of men but of the life of man altogether? Thou hast given birth to cities, thou hast called scattered human beings into the bond of social life, thou hast united them first of all in joint habitations, next in wedlock, then, in the ties of common literature and speech, thou hast discovered law, thou hast been the teacher of morality and order: to thee I fly for refuge, from thee I look for aid, to thee I entrust myself, as once in ample measure, so now wholly and entirely:—CICERO, *Tusculan Disputations*, V. ii. 5–6.

THE LAW disposes of sharp practices in one way, philosophers in another: the law deals with them as far as it can lay its strong arm upon them; philosophers, as far as they can be apprehended by reason and conscience. Now reason demands that nothing be done with unfairness, with false pretence, or with misrepresentation.—CICERO, *De officiis* III. xvii. 68.

WHAT MAN is there who can claim that in the eyes of every law he is innocent? But assuming that this may be, how limited is the innocence whose standard of virtue is the law! How much more comprehensive is the principle of duty than that of law! How many are the demands laid upon us by the sense of duty, humanity, generosity, justice, integrity—all of which lie outside the statute books!—SENECA, *De ira* II. xxvii. 2.

MAN IS by nature a political animal. And therefore, men even when they do not require one another's help, desire to live together all the same, and are in fact brought together by their common interests in proportion as they severally attain to any measure of well-being. This is certainly the chief end, both of individuals and of states.—ARISTOTLE, *Politics*, III. vi. 3–4.

THE CIVIL LAW and the Law of Nations are divided as follows. All peoples that are governed by laws and customs make use of the law which is partly peculiar to themselves and partly pertaining to all men; for what each people has established for itself is peculiar to that State, and is styled the Civil Law; being, as it were, the especial law of that individual commonwealth. But the law which natural reason has established among all mankind and which is equally observed among all peoples, is called the Law of Nations, as being that which all nations make use of.—*Institutes of Justinian* I. ii. 2.

PREFACE

For nearly half a century, from the time of entering Harvard College until the present day, I have been deeply interested in the fundamental conceptions of law and of the state; and in later years it has been my good fortune to have had practical experience with the law of the state, and especially with the law of the international community.

The present work, the result of long and constant interest in both theory and practice, has the somewhat ambitious purpose of examining the leading contributions to jurisprudence, the theory of the state, and the law of nations from the classic days of Greece to the youthful contribution of the great Grotius at the beginning of what is generally considered the modern era of legal and political philosophy.

But in order that this examination might have a sure and firm foundation, it seemed desirable to begin by assembling what might be termed the essence of these contributions in the form of quotations from outstanding philosophers, moralists, and jurists to whom the world is indebted for its conceptions of law and government. As the quotations thus assembled—for the most part comparatively brief statements of theory and principle—grew in number, it became apparent that if they were grouped in more or less logical order, such an arrangement of them would in itself strikingly demonstrate the nature of our legal and political heritage and the process of its development. The quotations, therefore, in English translation, have been grouped as articles under various captions, and these captions fall into three main divisions, "Jurisprudence," "The State," and "The Law of Nations." The articles, thus grouped and arranged in ideological rather than in chronological order, are in effect a codification of the fundamentals of political science and jurisprudence, both national and international. They represent what is believed to be the best thought of admitted masters in these fields during a period of some twenty centuries, from the golden days of Plato and of Aristotle to the masterpieces of the sixteenth and seventeenth centuries which ushered in the political and legal conceptions of our modern world. This codification, if I may so call it without in any way implying by that term the fixity and finality of a hard and fast code, constitutes the second volume of the present work.

In bringing together these quotations no attempt has been made to include extracts from all of the innumerable statements of legal and political doctrine, but rather to select passages from those which form, as it were, the main current of development through the centuries, thus enabling the reader to acquire a background of the ages and a comprehension of the birth and growth of the great principles without which it is difficult to understand the world in which we live. Even within those limits more quotations—and better ones—doubtless could and should have been chosen for the purpose. It is hoped that others, noting the omission of many a splendid passage which I have overlooked, will be led to add to the considerable nucleus here assembled and thus throw an ever-stronger light on the growth of our legal, political, and international ideals.

It may be thought, however, that a lesser number of extracts on some topics would have sufficed, and indeed I am conscious of frequent reiterations or restatements of certain principles; but it has seemed advisable for the present purpose thus to indicate and emphasize the importance attributed to these very principles by successive writers through more than two thousand years. Such a consensus of opinion is not lightly to be rejected.

Obviously the extracts do not purport, in the case of each one of the writers quoted, to indicate his legal and political theories in anything like a full and complete manner. This failure to present their theories in full is of course inevitable in the preparation of any compendium of quotations, especially in view of the fact that the authors not infrequently cast their argument in a form which does not readily lend itself to the selection of brief quotations. And while some of the chapters in the first volume might be considered as in a measure remedying this defect, I am regretfully aware that the remedy is inadequate. It should be added that considerable care has been taken, however, not to reproduce passages which, when separated from their context, would misrepresent the author's views.

Where the quotations contained matter which seemed irrelevant, it has been omitted, and the omission is indicated in the text. If, on the other hand, it has been essential to insert a word or two in order to complete the meaning of an abbreviated passage, the insertion has been placed in square brackets. While it has been necessary in some instances to prepare English versions for the occasion, the majority of the quotations from ancient and medieval authors in both volumes of the work have been drawn from more or less familiar translations. As regards passages from the Scriptures, a Scotch Presbyterian upbringing inclines me to favor the phraseology of the King James version upon which I have been, so to speak, nourished from childhood. Hence that version has usually been employed rather than the admittedly more accurate Douay text, or those several "modern" versions which have appeared in our own day. In spirit and in substance they are, after all, the same, and I trust that readers, whatever their faith, will bear with a preference for phrases familiar to me for more years than I like to count.

A few further comments on the quotations are perhaps advisable. Many headings pertaining to the older law of war, such as hostages, safe-conduct, rights and duties of vassals, ransoms, and so forth, are entirely omitted, while others include but few extracts. One reason for this is my belief that the so-called law of war is not true law. The late Andrew Carnegie rightly condemned war as the "foulest blot upon our civilisation," and the idea that the rules and regulations applying to that "blot" should be raised to the dignity of law seems little if anything less than an absurdity. Law is one of the highest expressions of civilization: war is, for the most part, the negation of law; and to speak of the law of war is to bestow the name of law upon the very rules by which it is either silenced or destroyed. Nevertheless, custom has so long sanctioned the paradox of considering the so-called rules of war as a part of the law of nations, that quotations on a number of the more important of them have been included.

A second reason is that not a few of the topics which were considered important by the older writers *de iure belli* have today but an academic interest, while on the other hand certain subjects—like that of neutrality—assumed the importance with which we now credit them only in comparatively recent times and hence, if dealt with at all, they were touched upon only in passing by the authors included in the present survey.

It may also seem, especially to those who are not familiar with Francisco Suárez, that the number of quotations from his writings is disproportionately large. And it is quite true that more passages have been drawn from Suárez than from any other writer.[1] Readers may wonder, and very properly, why this should be so. My own explanation would be that Suárez' large representation among the extracts is due, not to partiality (though I freely confess to a deep admiration for the great Spanish Jesuit and "last of the Schoolmen"), but to the fact that in certain of his writings, especially in his great *Tractatus de legibus ac Deo legislatore,* there is summed up and blended into a philosophic whole the best of our legal and our

---

[1] Many more passages might have been drawn from Suárez, however, had it not been decided to quote only from the *Selections* from his works which have been translated into English and are now being published by the Carnegie Endowment for International Peace in "The Classics of International Law."

political heritage from the ancient and the medieval worlds. A profound thinker, thoroughly familiar with the learning of antiquity and of the Middle Ages, he gathered together and systematically restated the great conceptions of the past. And being also a devout Christian and a great theologian, he restated those conceptions in the light of Christian morality.

But important as Suárez' contribution is, it was based on—indeed grew out of—the many contributions of his predecessors. And the nature and extent of those contributions is demonstrated, it is believed, in the compendium of quotations or—as I prefer to regard it—codification of the legal and political principles which are fundamental to the existence of both the state and the international community. The conceptions of law and of political science emerging from these quotations are a composite of the ideals of philosophers, jurists, statesmen, and theologians. They are not of one country and not of one time. They are of Greece when it was in its greatest glory, and of Rome when it also was in its greatest glory, as well as in its later days, when the harvest of antiquity was garnered by Justinian. They are of the Middle Ages following the decline of the old order, when the new order was being slowly but surely molded by the Christian philosophy of the Man of Nazareth, and Christian ideals of life and of conduct, of law and of government, based on the wisdom of the past, were being developed into an acceptable system, especially by St. Thomas Aquinas in his *Summa Theologica*. And finally, these conceptions are of the beginning of our modern era, when Erasmus and St. Thomas More became the prophets of a better life and when, in consequence of the discovery of the New World, the international conceptions, slowly matured through centuries, were given their practical form by Francisco de Vitoria, of the University of Salamanca, and their theoretical presentation by Francisco Suárez, of the University of Coimbra—the one the founder, in the opinion of many, of the modern law of nations, and the other declared by a competent authority to be the "prince of modern jurists."

The first volume is in the nature of a historical commentary on the principal contributors to the second. In the course of preparation this commentary has, it must be confessed, far outgrown the original outline. In order to keep it within reasonable bounds, certain limitations of scope and treatment were found to be necessary. Thus the field of study has been restricted to written contributions which have come down to us from the beginning of what is called the "historical era." Behind that era lies a vast and as yet little explored world, shrouded in what once seemed to be an impenetrable mist, a mist which is even now but faintly penetrated by light from long and arduous investigations. In years to come history will doubtless be pushed further and further back into this No Man's Land of the past, until much more of the endless highway along which humankind has advanced will become visible, stretching far back and growing narrower and fainter, yet running ever true to the line of human development.

Although the period of the survey ends with the opening years of the seventeenth century, that limitation does not apply in the case of the introductory chapter. The purpose of the "Introduction" is to bring to the reader's attention certain conceptions of law and society which are at once fundamental and almost universally accepted, albeit oftentimes overlooked because of their very familiarity. Fortunately, though our perception of it may grow dim, truth does not wear out. We may fail to notice it—may even forget it, to our sorrow—but a reminder brings it before us again, as solid and enduring as ever. The introductory chapter, then, is a reminder of certain legal and political truths which, I believe, we cannot ignore without great peril to ourselves and to posterity.

How much the present work owes to many writers, both ancient and modern, will be clear from the text itself, from the footnotes, the list of acknowledgments, and from the bibliographies. In certain instances, however, more than a formal acknowledgment of such indebtedness must be made. The collection of quotations forming the second volume has been greatly facilitated by use of translations in "The Loeb Classical Library." The editors have kindly permitted the reproduction of innumerable passages from that admirable series, to which the modern world is under great and increasing obligation for a knowledge of classical literature. The passages from the law of Rome have been taken from Samuel P. Scott's English version of the *Corpus Iuris Civilis*. While it must remain a matter of regret that this American scholar did not live to complete the revision of the text, his monumental translation stands as a landmark in the modern history of Roman law. Without attempting here to acknowledge indebtedness' to all of the many other translations which have been drawn upon, appreciative reference should be made to the late Dr. Jowett's masterly English rendering of Plato's dialogues and Aristotle's *Politics,* to the careful translation of the *Summa Theologica* of St. Thomas Aquinas by the Fathers of the English Dominican Province, and to the English versions of classic works on the law of nations published in the "Classics of International Law."

I am deeply indebted also to many writers of our own day who have contributed much to our present knowledge of legal and political theory. To list all of these writers here would be to repeat a considerable portion of the bibliography printed elsewhere in these pages. But a special acknowledgment of obligation must be made to the brothers R. W. and A. J. Carlyle, whose *History of Mediaeval Political Theory in the West* (the sixth and final volume of which was recently published by Dr. A. J. Carlyle, the surviving brother) is at once rich in learning and ripe of thought; to the various authors, the editors (under the chairmanship of Col. John H. Wigmore), and the translators who are responsible for the "Modern Legal Philosophy Series"; to Professor Ernest Barker, who in many a learned chapter and profoundly penetrating essay has ranged the history of political thought from Greece to the present day; and to Professor Charles McIlwain, whose *Growth of Political Thought in the West* is a modern classic.

To the members of the Division of International Law of the Carnegie Endowment for International Peace I am likewise under great obligation, for without their helpful interest and coöperation the preparation of the commentary and the compilation of quotations could never have been undertaken. Mr. George A. Finch, Assistant Secretary of the Endowment and Assistant Director of its Division of International Law, by largely taking over the burden of administrative routine, has made it possible for me to devote time to the present volume. Mr. Alan T. Hurd, by research, suggestions, and revision, has shared in both the preparation of the chapters and the compilation of quotations. In the verification of references and the editing of the manuscript Mr. Walter H. Zeydel has rendered indispensable services. Miss Gwladys L. Williams has supplied numerous admirable translations and has verified others, and Mr. Francis Crane Macken has likewise given valuable assistance in the preparation of translations and in special research.

Finally, the text owes much to the faithful care of Miss Mary Emily King, who has typewritten the manuscript, and has copied and recopied many parts of it, each time with omissions, additions, or suggestions which have improved the text not only in appearance but also in expression and meaning.

To readers of the volume, if any there are to be, I shall be grateful if they will point out errors in the text and offer suggestions which will render the collection of quotations more useful and acceptable.

James Brown Scott

WASHINGTON, D. C.
April 1, 1939

ACKNOWLEDGMENTS

Grateful acknowledgment is made to the following publishers and authors for their generous permission to use selections from their copyrighted works:

Librairie Félix Alcan (Paris), for quotations from *Histoire de la science politique dans ses rapports avec la morale* by Paul Janet.

George Allen and Unwin, Ltd., for quotations from *Essays and Addresses* by Gilbert Murray.

American Bar Association Journal, for quotations from the article "Our Common Inheritance of Law" by Sir John Simon.

American Book Company, for quotations from *Selections from the Public and Private Law of the Romans* by James J. Robinson.

American Historical Review, for quotations from the article "International Calvinism through Locke and the Revolution of 1688" by Herbert D. Foster.

The American Scholar, for quotations from the article "Erasmus, Enemy of Pedantry" by Preserved Smith.

G. Bell and Sons, Ltd., for quotations from *A Defence of Liberty against Tyrants* (a reprint of the 1689 translation of the *Vindiciae contra Tyrannos* by Junius Brutus, with an introduction by Harold J. Laski), and from *The Chief Works of Benedict de Spinoza* translated by R. H. M. Elwes.

A. and C. Black, Ltd., for quotations from *Historical Introduction to the Private Law of Rome* by James Muirhead (3d ed. by Grant).

Wm. Blackwood and Sons, Ltd., for quotations from *A History of Mediaeval Political Theory in the West* by R. W. Carlyle and A. J. Carlyle;[1] *The Institutes of Law* by James Lorimer (2d ed.); and *The Sovereignty of the Sea* by Sir Thomas Wemyss Fulton.

Burns, Oates and Washbourne, Ltd., for quotations from *The Catholic Tradition of the Law of Nations* by John Eppstein, and *The "Summa Theologica" of St. Thomas Aquinas* translated by Fathers of the English Dominican Province.

Calmann-Lévy, Editeurs (of Paris), for quotations from *Discours et conférences* by Ernest Renan.

Chatto and Windus, for quotations from *Cicero, a Study* by George Chatterton Richards.[2]

---
[1] See also under G. P. Putnam's Sons, *infra*.
[2] See also under Houghton Mifflin Co., *infra*.

ACKNOWLEDGMENTS

The Clarendon Press, for quotations from *The Age of Erasmus* and *Erasmus, Lectures and Wayfaring Sketches* by P. S. Allen; *Sir Thomas More, Selections from His English Works and the Lives by Erasmus and Roper*, edited by P. S. Allen and H. M. Allen; *Studies in History and Jurisprudence* by Viscount Bryce; *The Legacy of the Middle Ages*, edited by C. G. Crump and E. F. Jacob; *Institutes of Roman Law by Gaius* translated by Edward Poste (4th ed. by Whittuck); *Studies in International Law* by Sir Thomas Erskine Holland; *Of the Laws of Ecclesiastical Polity* by Richard Hooker (Book I), edited by R. W. Church; *Dante's Convivio* translated by William Walrond Jackson; *The Politics of Aristotle* and *The Dialogues of Plato* translated by B. Jowett; *The Legacy of Greece*, edited by R. W. Livingstone; *The Modern State* by Robert Morrison MacIver; *Essays by the Late Mark Pattison*, collected by Henry Nettleship; *Sir Thomas More's Utopia*, translation by Ralph Robynson (1551) edited by J. Churton Collins; *The Earliest Latin Commentaries on the Epistles of St. Paul* by A. Souter; *The Prince by Niccolò Machiavelli* translated by Ninian Hill Thomson; *Outlines of Historical Jurisprudence* by Sir Paul Vinogradoff; and *The Praise of Folly* by Erasmus, translation by John Wilson (1668), edited by Mrs. P. S. Allen.

P. F. Collier and Son Corporation, for quotations from John Henry Newman's essays as printed in "The Harvard Classics" (Vol. xxviii).

Columbia University Press, for quotations from *The Education of a Christian Prince by Desiderius Erasmus* translated, with an Introduction, by Lester K. Born; *Hellenic Civilization*, edited by G. W. Botsford and E. G. Sihler; *The Equality of States* by Julius Goebel, Jr.; and *The Genius of the Common Law* by Sir Frederick Pollock.

"Columbia Studies in History, Economics, and Public Law," for quotations from *An Encyclopedist of the Dark Ages, Isidore of Seville* by Ernest Brehaut (permission also granted by the author).

F. S. Crofts and Company, for quotations from *The Statesman's Book of John of Salisbury* translated by John Dickinson.

Desclée, de Brouer et Compagnie (Paris), for quotations from *Erasme* by Th. Quoniam.

The Dial Press, for quotations from *Plato, the Man and His Work* by A. E. Taylor.

The Dolphin Press, for quotations from *Canon Law* by Archbishop Cicognani (authorized English version by Joseph M. O'Hara and Francis Brennan).

E. P. Dutton and Company, for quotations from *The State and the Nation* by Edward Jenks; *Machiavelli and His Times* by D. Erskine Muir; *Greek Ethical Thought from Homer to the Stoics* by Hilda D. Oakley; and from the following works in Everyman's Library: *Sesame and Lillies* and *Unto This Last* by John Ruskin, and *The Oxford Reformers* by Frederic Seebohm.

The *Encyclopaedia Britannica*, for quotations from the article "Roman Law" by Henry Goudy in Vol. XXIII of the Eleventh Edition.

ACKNOWLEDGMENTS

Eyre and Spottiswoode (Publishers), Ltd., for quotations from *A Portrait of Thomas More, Scholar, Statesman, Saint* by Algernon Cecil.

Librairie de Firmin-Didot et Compagnie (Paris), for quotations from *Excursions historiques et philosophiques à travers le moyen âge* by Charles Bréchillet Jourdain.

Fordham University Press, for quotations from *De laicis or the Treatise on Civil Government by Robert Bellarmine* translated by Kathleen E. Murphy.

Paul Geuthner (Paris), for quotations from *Etudes d'histoire juridique offertes à Paul-Frédéric Girard . . .* , by his students.

W. Green and Son, Ltd., for quotations from *Studies National and International* by James Lorimer, and from *Roman Law in Modern Practice* by James Mackintosh.

The Grotius Society, for quotations from *A Treatise on the Law of Prize* by Constantine John Colombos.

Harcourt, Brace and Company, for quotations from *Thomas More* by R. W. Chambers.

George C. Harrap and Company, Ltd., for quotations from the series of volumes on "Social and Political Ideas" edited by F. J. C. Hearnshaw.

Harvard Law Review, for quotations from the article "Rome and Law" by A. H. F. Lefroy.

Harvard University Press, for quotations from the Loeb Classical Library; *The Defensor Pacis of Marsiglio of Padua* by Ephraim Emerton; *The Laws and Liberties of Massachusetts,* reprinted from the 1648 ed. with an Introduction by Max Farrand; the Introduction by Carl Joachim Friedrich to the *Politica Methodice Digesta* by Joannes Althusius (reprint of 1614 ed.); and *The Chief Sources of English Legal History* by Percy H. Winfield.

W. Heffer and Sons, Ltd., for quotations from *The History of Political Science from Plato to the Present* by Robert H. Murray.

William Hodge and Company, Ltd., for quotations from *An Outline of Roman Law* by John Spencer Muirhead.

The Hogarth Press, for quotations from *Politics and Morals* ("Day to Day Pamphlets," No. 30) by George Peabody Gooch (permission also granted by the author).

Houghton Mifflin Company, for quotations from *Cicero, a Study* by George Chatterton Richards.[3]

Jefferson Medical College (co-assignee of copyright), for quotations from *The Civil Law* translated and edited by S. P. Scott.[4]

The Johns Hopkins Press, for quotations from *Primitivism and Related Ideas in Antiquity* by Arthur O. Lovejoy and George Boas.

[3] See also under Chatto and Windus, *supra.*
[4] See also under Elizabeth W. Scott, *infra.*

ACKNOWLEDGMENTS

The Journal of Comparative Legislation and International Law, for quotations from the article "The Function of Law in Society" by Edward Jenks.

The Law Faculty of the University of Leyden, for quotations from the essay "An Unpublished Work of Hugo Grotius" (in Bibliotheca Visseriana, Vol. V) by Robert Fruin.

Little, Brown and Company, for quotations from *Spain, a Short History* and *In Praise of Gentlemen* by Henry Dwight Sedgwick.

Longmans, Green and Company (New York), for quotations from *The Place of Sir Thomas More in English Literature and History* by R. W. Chambers; *The Political Aspects of S. Augustine's "City of God"* by John Neville Figgis; *History of the Rise and Influence of the Spirit of Rationalism in Europe* by W. E. H. Lecky; and *Historical Sketches* by John Henry Newman.

Longmans, Green and Company, Ltd. (London), for quotations specified under their New York house, above, and from the article "Luther and Henry VIII" by Preserved Smith, in *The English Historical Review.*

The Macmillan Company (New York), for permission to translate passages from C. W. Previté-Orton's edition of *The Defensor Pacis of Marsilius of Padua* (published in England by the Cambridge University Press); and for quotations from *Church, State and Study—Essays* and *The Citizen's Choice* by Ernest Barker; Barker's Introduction to his translation of Otto Gierke's *Natural Law and the Theory of Society, 1500–1800; Roman Law and Common Law, a Comparison in Outline* by W. W. Buckland and Arnold D. McNair; *The Cambridge Ancient History* (Vols. VII and IX) and *The Cambridge Medieval History* (Vol. V); *Studies of Political Thought from Gerson to Grotius* by John Neville Figgis; *Historical Introduction to the Study of Roman Law* by H. F. Jolowicz; *Constitutional History of England* by F. W. Maitland; *The Influence of the Roman Law on the Law of England* by Thomas Edward Scrutton; *Chapters on International Law* by John Westlake; *Desiderius Erasmus Concerning the Aim and Method of Education* by William Harrison Woodward (all published in England by the Cambridge University Press); and from *The Cambridge Modern History* (Vols. I, II and XII); *Readings in Political Philosophy* (rev. ed., 1938) by Francis William Coker; *A Survey of English Literature, 1780–1880* by Oliver Elton; *The Growth of Political Thought in the West* by Charles Howard McIlwain; and *Modern Legal Philosophy Series* (Vols. II, V, VII and X).

Macmillan and Company, Ltd. (London), for quotations from *Lectures on Modern History* by Lord Acton; *Essays in Criticism* (First Series) by Matthew Arnold; *Greek Philosophy, Part I: Thales to Plato* by John Burnet; *History of Federal Government in Greece and Italy* (Bury ed.) by Edward A. Freeman; *The English Legal Tradition—Its Sources and History* by Henri Lévy-Ullmann (trans. by M. Mitchell); *Miscellanies* (Fourth Series) by John Morley; the article "Ius Gentium" by Henry Nettleship in *The Journal of Philology; The International Law and Custom of Ancient Greece and Rome* by Coleman Phillipson; *Essays in Jurisprudence and Ethics* and *Essays in the Law* by Sir Frederick Pollock.

ACKNOWLEDGMENTS xvii

P. Maglione, successore di E. Loescher e compagnia (Rome), for quotations from *Ricerche sulla storia e sul diritto pubblico di Roma* by Ettore Pais.

Marshall Jones Company, for quotations from *The Spirit of the Common Law* by Roscoe Pound.

D. B. Updike—The Merrymount Press, for quotations from *Erasmus Against War*, edited by J. W. Mackail.

Methuen and Company, Ltd., for quotations from *Greek Political Theory— Plato and His Predecessors* by Ernest Barker (permission also granted by the author); *The History of the Decline and Fall of the Roman Empire* (Bury ed.) by Edward Gibbon; *A History of English Law* by Sir William Holdsworth; *Sir Thomas More* by William Holden Hutton; *A History of Europe from 1198 to 1378* by C. W. Previté-Orton; and *Aristotle* by W. D. Ross.

J. B. Metzlersche Verlagsbuchhandlung (Stuttgart), for quotations from Pauly-Wissowa: *Real-Encyclopädie der classischen Altertumswissenschaft*.

John Murray, for quotations from *The Constitutional History of England* (7th ed.) and *Introduction to the Literature of Europe* (4th ed.) by Henry Hallam; *The New Jurisprudence* by Edward Jenks; *Ancient Law* (new ed., 1930, with Pollock's notes and Introduction) and *Village Communities in the East and West* (7th ed.) by Sir Henry Maine.

Martinus Nijhoff (The Hague), for quotations from *La Guerre comme instrument de secours ou de punition* by D. Beaufort, and *Der Gedanke der Internationalen Organisation in seiner Entwicklung, 1300–1800* by Jacob Ter Meulen.

The Norwegian Nobel Institute, for quotations from *Histoire de l'internationalisme* by Christian L. Lange.

W. W. Norton and Company, for quotations from *The Greek Way* and *The Prophets of Israel* by Edith Hamilton.

Philip Nutt, for quotations from Walter Raleigh's Introduction to his edition of *The Book of the Courtier from the Italian of Count Baldassare Castiglione* translated by Sir Thomas Hoby.

The Ohio State University Press, for quotations from the Introduction by George Holland Sabine and Stanley Barney Smith to their translation, *Cicero: On the Commonwealth*.

The Oxford University Press, for quotations from *Thomas Aquinas* by M. C. D'Arcy; *European Civilization, Its Origin and Development*, edited by Edward Eyre; *Progress and History*, edited by F. S. Marvin; *On Liberty, Representative Government, The Subjection of Women* ("World's Classics" ed.) by John Stuart Mill; *Sir Thomas More and His Friends* by E. M. G. Routh; *The Lyfe of Sir Thomas Moore, Knighte* by William Roper, edited by Elsie Vaughan Hitchcock and published for the Early English Text Society; *The Lives of John Donne, Sir Henry Wotton, Richard Hooker, George Herbert and Robert Sanderson* ("World's Classics" ed.) by Izaak Walton.

ACKNOWLEDGMENTS

Librairie Plon (Paris), for quotations from *La Doctrine politique de Saint Augustin* by Gustave Combés.

Roscoe Pound, for quotations from a rewriting of the portion of the article "Theories of Law" (22 *Yale Law Journal*, 114) having to do with Greek law, which will be contained in section 38 of a forthcoming treatise on jurisprudence by Roscoe Pound.

G. P. Putnam's Sons, for quotations from *The Political Thought of Plato and Aristotle* by Ernest Barker; *A History of Mediaeval Political Theory in the West* by R. W. Carlyle and A. J. Carlyle,[5] and *Outlines of Roman Law, Comprising Its Historical Growth and General Principles* (rev. ed.) by William C. Morey.

Aurelia Henry Reinhardt, for quotations from *The De monarchia of Dante Alighieri* translated by Aurelia Henry (Reinhardt).

George Routledge and Sons, Ltd., for quotations from Hugh Goitein's Introduction to his edition of *Sir Thomas More, The Utopia ... Francis, Lord Bacon, The New Atlantis* ("Broadway Translations").

Royal Historical Society, for quotations from the *Transactions of the Royal Historical Society*.

Elizabeth W. Scott (co-assignee of copyright), for quotations from *The Civil Law* translated and edited by S. P. Scott.[6]

Charles Scribner's Sons, for quotations from *The Dawn of Conscience* by James Henry Breasted; *History of England* (ed. of 1870) by J. A. Froude; *Greek Thinkers, a History of Ancient Philosophy* by Theodor Gomperz (trans. by Laurie Magnus and G. G. Berry); *Erasmus* by J. Huizinga; *Latin Literature* by J. W. Mackail; and *A Select Library of the Nicene and Post-Nicene Fathers of the Christian Church*, edited by Philip Schaff.

Sheed and Ward, for quotations from *The Spirit of Medieval Philosophy* by Etienne Gilson.

Charles P. Sherman, for quotations from *Roman Law in the Modern World* (3d ed.) and *Epitome of Roman Law* by Charles P. Sherman.

Simon and Shuster, Inc., for quotations from *Biography of the Bible* by Ernest Sutherland Bates.

Librairie du Recueil Sirey (Paris), for quotations from *Académie de Droit international de La Haye: Recueil des cours.*

Société de Législation Comparée (Paris), for quotations from the article "Le Droit ecossais" by Henri Lévy-Ullmann in the *Bulletin de la Société de législation comparée.*

The Society for Promoting Christian Knowledge and The Sheldon Press, for quotations from *Erasmus and Luther: Their Attitude to Toleration* by Robert

---

[5] See also under Wm. Blackwood and Sons, Ltd., *supra.*
[6] See also under Jefferson Medical College, *supra.*

ACKNOWLEDGMENTS

H. Murray, and *Illustrations of the History of Medieval Thought and Learning* (2d rev. ed.) by Reginald Lane Poole.

Verlagsbuchhandlung Julius Springer (Berlin), for quotations from *Römisches Privatrecht* (based on work of Paul Jörs) by Wolfgang Kunkel.

Stevens and Sons, Ltd., for quotations from the article "The Crisis of the State" by Giorgio Del Vecchio in *The Law Quarterly Review*.

Tulane Law Review Association, for quotations from the article "The Crisis of the Science of Law" by Giorgio Del Vecchio in the *Tulane Law Review*.

The United Lutheran Publication House, for quotations from the *Works of Martin Luther*.

The University of Chicago Law Review, for quotations from the article "This Thing Called Law" by Joseph C. Hutcheson, Jr.

The University of Chicago Press, for quotations from *Sociological Study of the Bible* by Louis Wallis.

The University of Wisconsin Press, for quotations from *The Genossenschaft-Theory of Otto von Gierke* by John D. Lewis.

Società Anonima Vallecchi (Florence), for quotations from *Da Bartolo all' Althusio* by Francesco Ercole.

Giorgio Del Vecchio, for permission to quote from any or all of his writings.

Vier Quellen Verlag (Leipzig), for quotations from *Moralphilosophie* by Viktor Cathrein.

The Viking Press, Inc., for quotations from *Erasmus of Rotterdam* by Stefan Zweig (trans. by Eden Paul and Cedar Paul; copyright 1934 by the Viking Press, New York).

West Publishing Company, for quotations from *Handbook of Roman Law* by Max Radin.

John H. Wigmore, for quotations from the "Continental Legal History Series" and the "Evolution of Law Series."

Yale University Press, for quotations from *The Growth of Law* by Benjamin Nathan Cardozo; *The High Court of Parliament and Its Supremacy* by Charles Howard McIlwain; *An Introduction to the Philosophy of Law* by Roscoe Pound; and *Marcus Aurelius* by Henry Dwight Sedgwick.

CONTENTS

Volume One

I. Introduction 3

The Greek Background

II. The Contributions of Ancient Greece 43
III. Socrates (*c.* 469–400 b. c.) 61
IV. Plato (428–348 b. c.) 68
V. Aristotle (384–322 b. c.) 85
VI. The Stoics 92

The Roman Heritage

VII. The Law of Rome 107
        Appendix I: The Stoic Philosophy and the Later *Jus Gentium* 133
        Appendix II: The *Jus Gentium* in Roman Jurisprudence 137
VIII. Marcus Tullius Cicero (104–43 b. c.) 143
IX. Seneca (4 b. c.—a. d. 65) 158

The Christian Heritage, Ancient and Medieval

X. The Hebrew Prophets and Christianity 165
XI. St. Augustine (a. d. 354–430) 184
XII. St. Isidore of Seville (*c.* 560–636) and Gratian's *Decretum* 196
XIII. John of Salisbury (*c.* 1115–1180): *Policraticus* 206
XIV. St. Thomas Aquinas (*c.* 1225–74) 213
XV. Dante Alighieri (1265–1321) 223
XVI. The Church as an Institution: Its Influence on Law and Politics 228

The Transition from Medieval to Modern Thought

XVII. The Survival and Influence of Roman Law and Jurisprudence 241
        Appendix: The Law of Nature in the Modern World 264

CONTENTS

XVIII. MARSIGLIO OF PADUA (*c.* 1275–1343): *Defensor Pacis* 271
XIX. NICCOLÒ MACHIAVELLI (1469–1527): THE PRINCE 278
XX. BALDASSARE CASTIGLIONE (1478–1529): THE COURTIER 295
XXI. CHRISTOPHER ST. GERMAIN (1460–1540): DOCTOR AND STUDENT .. 301
XXII. FRANCISCO DE VITORIA (*c.* 1483–1546) 310
XXIII. JEAN BODIN (1530–96) 324
XXIV. BALTHAZAR AYALA (1548–84): *De Jure et Officiis Bellicis et Disciplina Militari* 353
XXV. ALBERICO GENTILI (1552–1608) 363
   Appendix: Pierino Belli (1502–75): His Relation to Vitoria and Gentili 387
XXVI. TYRANNY VERSUS LIBERTY 393

The Era of Reform

XXVII. ST. THOMAS MORE (1478–1535) 425
XXVIII. CALVINISM 452
XXIX. MARTIN LUTHER (1483–1546) 468
XXX. DESIDERIUS ERASMUS (*c.* 1466–1536) 484

The Beginning of the Modern Age

XXXI. HUGO GROTIUS AND THE *Mare Liberum* 521
XXXII. ST. ROBERT BELLARMINE (1542–1621) 546
XXXIII. FRANCISCO SUÁREZ (1548–1617) 558
XXXIV. RICHARD HOOKER (*c.* 1553–1600) 570
XXXV. EPILOGUE 591

VOLUME TWO

Jurisprudence

THE NATURE OF JURISPRUDENCE, 3: Right (*ius*), 4; Law and the human being, 5; Reason and law, 6; Morality and law, 10; Conscience and law, 16; Justice, 18; Justice and law, 27; LAW DEFINED, 29: Purpose and function, 34; Promulgation, 38; General application, 39; Interpretation, 41; Binding force, 44; Obedience to law, 46; Ignorance of law, 48; Alteration or cessation of law, 49; ETERNAL LAW: Defined, 52; Scope, 54; As the source of all law, 55; Promulgation and binding force, 57; Human knowledge of, 58; Divine law, 59; NATURAL

LAW: Defined, 60; Relation to eternal law, 64; Relation to divine law, 64; As right reason, 65; Immutability, 68; Scope and purpose, 72; Human knowledge, 77; As a standard for human law, 79; Obligations imposed by, 80; Interpretation, 84; CUSTOM: Defined, 85; Introduction of, 87; Private, 88; Scope and limitations of, 89; Relation to natural law, 89; The law of nations and, 90; Custom and written law, 90; Subject matter and form of custom, 92; Voluntary nature of custom, 93; Custom as creating law, 93; As confirming and interpreting law, 95; In opposition to law, 96; Law in opposition to custom, 100; Binding effect of custom, 102; Tests applied to custom, 102; Its interpretation, 105; Its alteration and cessation, 105; HUMAN LAW: Its origin and nature, 106; Its purpose, 111; Positive law, 112; EQUITY: Definition of, 113; Its relation to natural law, 115; Its application, 116; BEFORE THE COURT, 120: The qualifications of the judge, 121; His duties, 122; Failure in performance of his duties, 126; Judgment, 128; Appeals, 129; *Res iudicata,* 130; Precedents, 130; Penalties and punishment, 130; Purpose of punishment, 131; Authority to inflict punishment, 134; Measure of punishment, 135; Condemnation, 137; Remission or relaxation of penalties, 137; Exile, 138; JURISDICTION, 138; EQUALITY, 140; PRIVILEGE, 143; LIBERTY, 144; AGREEMENTS AND CONTRACTS, 147: Good faith, 151; Obligations, 155; Fraud, 157; INJURY, 157; ACCESSORIES TO CRIME, 158; PROPERTY, 158: *Ius* and property, 159; Public and private property, 159; Division of common into private property, 161; *Res nullius,* 164; Possession of property, 164; Prescription, 165; Usucaption, 167; *Uti possidetis,* 167; Transfer, 167; Religion does not affect ownership, 168; Alluvion, 169

The State

MAN AS A SOCIAL BEING, 173; AS A POLITICAL BEING, 176; ORIGIN AND NATURE OF THE STATE, 179: The state as a well-ordered and perfect community, 184; As a union based on agreement, 186; The purpose of the state, 187; NATIONALITY AND DOMICILE, 190: The state and the citizen, 191; Foreigners, 193; THE NATURE OF POWER, 195: Necessity for public authority, 196; Vesting of public authority, 198; NATURE AND KINDS OF GOVERNMENT, 202: Aim and purpose of government, 205; Will of the majority, 206; Lèse majesté, 206; THE QUALIFICATIONS AND DUTIES OF THE CHIEF MAGISTRATE, 207: The tyrant, 218; Rebellion against tyrannical magistrates, 223; LEGISLATION OF THE STATE—ITS NATURE AND FUNCTION, 225: The power to make laws, 232; Approval of legislation by the people, 237

The Law of Nations

ANCIENT JUS GENTIUM AND THE LAW OF NATIONS, 241: LAW OF NATIONS AND NATURAL LAW, 243; NATURE AND SCOPE OF THE LAW OF NATIONS, 249: Changes in the law of nations, 252; INTERNATIONAL COMMUNITY, 254: International agreements, 258; Arbitration and judicial settlement, 263; Ambassadors, 267; Freedom of the seas, 272; Freedom of travel and trade, 274; Discovery, possession, and occupation, 275; Dominion, 276; Mandates, 277; Postliminium, 278; VIOLATIONS OF THE LAW OF NATIONS, 281; PEACE AND WAR, 282: Definitions of peace, 283; Definitions of war, 284; Effect of war on law, 285; War condemned, 286; Self-defense, 288; Private war condemned, 289; Right to wage war, 290; Sedition and rebellion, 292; Whether Christians may engage in war, 294; War as a force suit, 296; Steps which should precede war, 299; Just war, 301; Just causes of war, 303; Unjust war, 308; Unjust causes of war, 309; Religion and war, 310; Missionaries, 313; Whether soldiers and subjects should inquire into the justice of war, 314; Conscientious objectors, 316; The law of war, 316; Declaration of war, 317; Wanton destruction condemned, 318; Noncombatants, 318; Immunity in war, 320; Allies in time of war, 321; Enemy aliens, 321; Neutrals, 322; Right of capture, 323; Treatment of captives, 325; Pirates, 326; Mercenaries, 328; Craft and stratagems in war, 328; Arms and munitions, 329; Peace should be the aim of war, 330; Peace conditions imposed by victor, 331

BIBLIOGRAPHIES 337
   General Bibliography 339
   Bibliography of Source Materials 354
INDEX 363

INTRODUCTION

A complete end is one whose attainment wholly satisfies us; while the attainment of a partial end leaves us longing for something more. If we attain Justice, there are still many things we desire; but if we attain Happiness, we are wholly content. Happiness, then, is that best of human goods which is the object of our inquiry.

ARISTOTLE, *Magna moralia* I. ii. 7.

Peace and liberty . . . belong in their entirety to all men just as much as they belong to each individual.

SENECA, *Epistulae morales* LXXIII. 8.

Chapter I

INTRODUCTION

The aim of the present survey is to examine in some detail the development of our legal, political, and international ideals, but since the subject is of vast extent it has been necessary to impose arbitrary boundaries upon the field to be covered. Therefore the survey goes no further than the opening years of the seventeenth century, years marking not only the end of the transition from the medieval to the modern era but also the beginning of the turbulent period of great wars which long scourged Europe and which ushered in certain dubious legal conceptions and political policies. For obvious reasons, fifth-century Greece has been chosen as the starting point for the survey,[1] thus confining it to the historical period, with but a glance in passing at that dim yet fascinating era which precedes the dawn of history.

Of the prehistoric phases of the subject it may be observed that while man must exist in the present he seems always to have sought to comprehend that present against the background of a more-or-less-distant past. This endeavor to understand himself and his surroundings has therefore led him from very early times to evolve various theories concerning the course of human development—theories which modern scholars have grouped under the general term "primitivism." Now if man regards the past or some period of it as embodying the best of which humanity is capable, he is likely to take a somewhat gloomy view of the future or, at best, to consider it as holding forth only the possibility of recovering what has been lost. If, on the other hand, he sees in the past a record of gradually mounting achievements, he will look to the future with optimism—tempered, perhaps, by the realization that civilization does not really "march" but rather climbs a rugged path haltingly, slipping back a pace for each two painful steps forward.

The first of these two attitudes is related to what is technically known as cultural primitivism, a term which has been defined in a recent authoritative volume[2] as

---

[1] This statement should perhaps be slightly qualified, for in chap. viii a brief excursion is made into an earlier period.

[2] *Primitivism and Related Ideas in Antiquity*, by Lovejoy and Boas, with supplementary essays by Albright and Dumont, p. 7. This is the initial volume of a series to be issued under the general title, "A Documentary History of Primitivism." The volumes will be accompanied by a collateral series consisting of critical editions of texts which are important in the history of modern primitivism. Several of these collateral texts have already been published.

the discontent of the civilized with civilization, or with some conspicuous and characteristic feature of it. It is the belief of men living in a relatively highly evolved and complex cultural condition that a life far simpler and less sophisticated in some or in all respects is a more desirable life. Its temper, when combined, as it very commonly has been, with chronological primitivism is summed up in the words of the Preacher, which, indeed, in the history of Judaism and Christianity seemed to give it a definite biblical sanction: "God hath made man upright; but they have sought out many devices."

This discontent with things as they are is, of course, no new thing.

To men living in any phase of cultural development it is always possible to conceive of some simpler one and usually possible to point to other men, past or present, in whose life it is exemplified. Cultural primitivism has thus had enduring roots in human nature ever since the civilizing process began. It is a not improbable conjecture that the feeling that humanity was becoming over-civilized, that life was getting too complicated and over-refined, dates from the time when the cave-man first became such. It can hardly be supposed—if the cave-men were at all like their descendants—that none among them discoursed with contempt upon the cowardly effeminacy of living under shelter or upon the exasperating inconvenience of constantly returning for food and sleep to the same place instead of being free to roam at large in the wide-open spaces.[3]

Primitivism, again, is related to—indeed is a part of—a larger human tendency which has profoundly affected philosophy in general, including legal philosophy. To quote another passage from the same volume:[4]

The history of primitivism is in great part a phase of a larger historic tendency which is one of the strangest, most potent and most persistent factors in Western thought—the use of the term "nature" to express the standard of human values, the identification of the good with that which is "natural" or "according to nature."

The word "nature," however, has been endowed by theorists with a variety of meanings and shades of meaning, with the result that he who would examine its rôle in the development of human thought must read warily and discriminatingly. But in subsequent pages we shall need to consider only that one of its principal meanings which has exercised the greatest influence on legal and political theory, namely, the conception which credited to "nature" those general truths universally known and accepted by human beings. On this conception, as we shall see, were founded the law of nature of Aristotle, of Cicero, and of the Schoolmen, and its Anglo-Saxon equivalent, "right reason."

But without attempting to enter further into the prehistoric phases of man's development and his theories concerning that development—subjects

---

[3] Lovejoy and Boas, *op. cit.*, p. 7.   [4] *Ibid.*, pp. 11–12.

which would lure us far from the field of the present work—it is nevertheless advisable to deal at some length in certain preliminary generalizations on the cause and origin of both law and political institutions which, as we now know, prevailed in more or less rudimentary form far back in the prehistoric era. And in setting forth these generalizations it will be necessary to draw heavily upon the writings of the most enlightened and, in the opinion of many, the most acceptable authorities of our own day.

It may safely be asserted that human beings have for untold centuries existed in some form of society. Why? The answer to the question, given more than twenty centuries ago and still accepted, is that man is a social animal, a gregarious being, and that his social needs make him likewise a political being, for he cannot permanently associate with others of his kind, in groups large or small, without some form of social organization. What may have been the first form of social organization we do not know, and it is not within the present field to speculate on the subject. The admitted fact of that organization, developed by the use of human reason, is our starting point. Now an organization cannot be established, or once established cannot continue to exist, without rules, however rudimentary they may be; and therefore, spurred by their social needs, human beings began to evolve rules. What does this imply? That, in the language of a distinguished German scholar and jurist, the late Josef Kohler,[5] "law is not the chance product of profitable and unprofitable hours; but is the result of an innately reasonable impulse of humanity, a sociological process pushed forward by necessity through the coexistence of reasonable beings with material and spiritual wants."

What, then, of law?

The law here referred to is the fundamental law. It is not the law made by legislators (which is a thing of yesterday and of today), but a long development, prehistoric in its beginning, historic in at least part of its long growth, and immeasurable in its future possibilities growing out of its immeasurable past.

The question which inevitably confronts us and to which there are many answers—although the question is still outstanding in the world at large—is: What is law? And no answer may be given without further questions. How did it originate and how did it develop? What are the elements which

[5] In his article on the evolution of law, quoted from trans. by Kocourek, in *Primitive and Ancient Legal Institutions,* pp. 4–5. Taking this opportunity to acknowledge his personal indebtedness to Professor Kohler, of the Law School of the University of Berlin, the present writer recalls with great pleasure that when he entered the Law School in the fall of 1891, Josef Kohler extended to him the right hand of fellowship, as he did to every student who presented himself.

constitute law? What is its purpose? What are the fundamental kinds of law and their interrelations? And here we are face to face with jurisprudence, which Justinian[6] defines as "the knowledge of matters divine and human, and the comprehension of what is just and what is unjust."

Now if law, as Professor Kohler says, is a "sociological process," then it grows out of human association. And if law depends upon organization, that is, upon the establishment of some form of state, the state also depends upon the law.[7] This fact, which is fundamental, was set forth in classic language by the late Sir Paul Vinogradoff, Corpus Professor of Comparative Law in the University of Oxford.[8] First, of the dependence of law on the state:

Although from a wider aspect the function of law may be attributed to all forms of social organization, it cannot exist anywhere without leaning directly or indirectly on some kind of political union acting as a safeguard of social order. In this sense law requires the State as a condition of its existence.

Now for the reverse of the picture: "On the other hand, neither the State, nor any other political or quasi-political body, can exist apart from Law, in the sense of a set of rules directing the relations and conduct of their members."[9] Yet the distinguished author does not here conceive of the state as a creature of might rather than right, for he immediately continues:

The individuals who appear in the last resort as the component elements of these political bodies are not welded together by physical forces, and have therefore to be united by psychical ties ranging from occasional agreement to more or less permanent rules of conduct; and in the case of any society organized as a political union these ties are bound to take the shape of laws, customary or enacted, complete or imperfect, but all tending to establish order and to apportion rights and duties.[10]

There is another aspect of the subject, already touched upon, but so important that it requires further consideration. It has been remarked that the state developed from the social needs of reasonable beings. So also law consists of rules of conduct for reasonable beings in association. The individual in isolation does not require law, because he is a law unto himself and has no relation to other beings. But if he wearies of isolation and enters into relations with a group of individuals, he finds that he is expected to conform in these relations to certain rules recognized by others in the group.

[6] *Institutes*, I. i. 1. Unless otherwise indicated, all translations of references to the *Corpus iuris civilis* are taken from S. P. Scott, *The Civil Law*.

[7] "There is complete agreement among all thinkers, that Law and the State are inseparably intertwined, if not as cause and effect, at least as inevitable concurrents in the stream of political and social evolution."—Jenks, "Recent Theories of the State," *The Law Quarterly Review*, XLIII (1927), 186.

[8] *Outlines of Historical Jurisprudence*, I, 85.   [9] *Ibid.*   [10] *Ibid.*

In a word, law depends upon human relationships and comes into being only when those relationships are established. A learned German scholar of more than a century ago, both philosopher and patriot, has thus stated this fundamental and world-wide principle:[11] "The concept of law is the conception of a relation between rational beings." What is the consequence of this? Simply that law "exists, therefore, only on the condition that such beings are thought of in relation to each other."

Now the origin of law is veiled by the mists of time, but, whenever it may have emerged and whatever form it first assumed, it contained an ethical element. Human beings are reasonable beings, and reason, whether primitive or modern, is always as a lamp distinguishing right from wrong. And law, rooted in the hidden past though it be, is inextricably involved in human conceptions of good as distinguished from evil by the light of reason. There is ample support for this view of the relationship between law and ethics, but two authorities must here suffice, both of whom are distinguished Italians of the present day. "The supreme dictates of conscience," says the Most Reverend Archbishop Amleto Giovanni Cicognani, Apostolic Delegate to the United States, in his admirable volume on *Canon Law*,[12] "are the same for all mankind and consequently must derive from some common source which is the property of all. And that source is nothing else than the light of reason manifesting to us what is good and what is evil—in a word, the natural law." The second and lay authority is Professor Giorgio Del Vecchio, until recently Dean of the Law School of the University of Rome, formerly Dean of its faculty of Political Sciences and later its Rector:[13] "Morals and law are correlated ethical categories, presupposing a common base," he declares. Admitting that "however far back we trace the development of life, we cannot find the moment when law first appeared," he immediately adds that "some system of ethical thought, perhaps rudimentary and ill-defined, is found in every stage of human life."

What is this ethical element in all law, whether primitive or modern, upon which the Italian jurist lays such emphasis in his contributions to the philosophy of law? We shall have to return to this question later, but for the moment it will suffice to say that while the ethical element may have many names and various manifestations, its essential characteristic is justice.

[11] Fichte, *Grundlage des Naturrechts*, I, 53, cited by Del Vecchio, *The Formal Bases of Law*, p. 166.
[12] This authoritative work was first published in Latin under the title *Jus canonicum* when the author was Professor of Canon Law in the Pontifical Institute of Canon and Civil Law, at Rome. The present quotation is from the authorized English version by the Rev. O'Hara and the Rev. Brennan, p. 25.
[13] *The Formal Bases of Law*, pp. 162–63, 167.

Here again we encounter man in society; for is not justice the bond of commonwealths, as Cicero says, and also of human beings whenever and wherever associated? In this connection there is a magnificent sentence from another Italian authority:[14] "The idea of justice develops in man when he comes in contact with other men, and can be called the architectural idea of human society."

Future investigators of humanity's distant past may find, in examining ancient records, the concrete evidence of the truths which these eminent writers have divined. But the fact remains that for the most part the latter have had to rely in their investigations upon the fragmentary chronicles of the early historical era, those of Greece and particularly those of Rome, which contain records of the earliest well-developed political and legal systems of which we have adequate knowledge. Yet even these records can be traced but a few centuries into the pre-Christian era before they merge into the legends and myths of a heroic age.[15] The early development of society, of law, and of justice goes far back into a more remote past, of which our knowledge is as yet based more upon surmise and analogy than upon discovered facts.[16]

These general observations concerning the origin of law, the state, and justice open the way to a consideration of the development of law, a topic which also pertains to the prehistoric past, but in the discussion of which modern jurists and publicists feel themselves on surer ground. We may begin with a premise stated by a learned French authority,[17] that "every man bears within himself the principle of law," a principle which emerges, when men group themselves into society, as rules of law. As Cicero happily expresses it, *Ubi societas, ibi ius:* not simply law but justice, for *ius* is, as we shall see, essentially a compound term, in that it includes the conception of right as well as that of law.

Now as man is the product of his past—remote as well as immediate—so the law of each age is likewise the product of its past. Again to quote M. Tarde:[18]

---

[14] Carle, *La vita del diritto,* p. 510. Cited by Del Vecchio in *The Formal Bases of Law,* p. 168.

[15] "The traditions of Roman law, and the monuments of the Latin language go back to a time covered by night and mist; and not even the most acute vision will be sufficient to penetrate this veil, and look upon the facts and forces which lie in the depths of the past." Kohler, *op. cit.,* II, 3, 4.

[16] Students of the prehistoric development of law and society owe much to anthropology, and their debt in the future will doubtless be vastly increased. For an illuminating discussion of the relationship between the two fields of study, see Cairns' "Law and Anthropology," in *The Making of Man, an Outline of Anthropology,* ed. by Calverton, pp. 331–62.

[17] Tarde, "The Imitation Theory," being a translation of the Introduction and chap. vii of Tarde's *Les Transformations du droit,* in *Primitive and Ancient Legal Institutions,* pp. 36, 65.

[18] *Ibid.,* p. 64.

INTRODUCTION 9

The law of any people in all stages retains the signs and residues of precedent phases of growth, however remote. Juridical rules and beliefs of the ages past survive in some sort in the present; they are never completely lost.

Law, then, is a thing of consistent development—not merely from the physical past of man, but above all from his spiritual past. It is, in short, a result of the nature and dignity of the human being. "Law," declares M. Tarde,[19] "is not an isolated fact which alone is encountered among this people or in that epoch; but everywhere that men are found, there are discovered traces of an ethical system, and of a law which reflects a common activity of man's spirit."

What is the consequence of such a spiritual factor in the development of law? The answer of M. Tarde must be stated in his own words:[20]

Thus, whether by the internal elaboration which goes on in the bosom of the law of each people, or whether by the borrowings which occur among different peoples, we arrive degree by degree at a realization of universal juridical criteria sufficient to govern all humanity. In a word, there is established and perfected an ensemble of common principles, a *societas humani generis* based on laws inherently natural to all persons.

These principles are common because of the spiritual kinship of human beings—a kinship based essentially upon the ethical or moral element already referred to as an attribute of law.[21]

---

[19] *Ibid.*, p. 65.   [20] *Ibid.*, pp. 68–69.

[21] In a series of lectures, entitled "La Société des nations au point de vue de la philosophie du droit international," which he delivered at the Hague Academy of International Law in 1931, Professor Del Vecchio spoke at some length on this phase of the subject: "Tout homme porte en lui le principe du droit; toute conscience a en elle les éléments pour s'élever au-dessus de sa propre personnalité empirique et la coordonner éthiquement avec celle d'autrui. Il est nécessaire de ne pas perdre de vue ce principe, ou *semence éternelle* de la justice, comme disait Vico, qui est au fond de l'esprit de l'homme, pour bien comprendre la nombreuse série des faits qui en procèdent et que l'observation vient de découvrir.

"Ainsi, nous reconnaissons tout d'abord que l'aptitude psychologique à distinguer dans une certaine mesure le juste et l'injuste, à sentir et à concevoir la vérité juridique, n'est pas le propre de quelques hommes seulement, mais essentiellement de tous. Encore, le droit n'est pas un fait particulier, qui se rencontre seulement chez tel peuple et à telle époque, mais partout où il y a des hommes, il y a trace d'un ordre éthique établi, d'un droit dans lequel se reflète une activité commune de leur esprit.

"D'autre part, de même que l'esprit humain va lentement des formes les plus obscures de la conscience aux plus claires, de même le droit naît d'une manière presque inconsciente, et ce n'est que peu à peu qu'il s'élève à une connaissance réfléchie. L'instinct obscur, l'intuition vague de leurs fins propres, est suffisante à produire chez les hommes des organisations et des institutions, qui sembleraient dénoter, tant est complexe leur structure, l'étude la plus profonde et la plus mûrie; elles n'en sont past même toutefois un produit de l'esprit et de l'intelligence, bien que nées spontanément et comme inconsciemment. Il n'est pas possible de perdre de vue cette idée, sur laquelle Vico fonda sa *Scienza nuova*, il y a deux cents ans: le monde civilisé est certainement *l'oeuvre des hommes*, et ses principes doivent se retrouver *dans notre propre esprit*. Le droit positif est bien un phénomène naturel; cela n'empêche pas qu'il soit aussi un produit de l'esprit, précisément parce que, comme l'écrit Vico, les *hommes* le firent avec *intelligence*.

This, however, leads to the question: How did the moral element enter into law? When it may have effected its entry is a matter of conjecture. But for present purposes the question is, not when, but how. An answer is supplied by a distinguished Frenchman:[22]

> Among the Greeks and Romans, as among the Hindus, law was at first a part of religion. The ancient codes of the cities were a collection of rites, liturgical directions, and prayers, joined with legislative regulations. The laws concerning property and those concerning succession were scattered about in the midst of rules for sacrifices, for burial, and for the worship of the dead.
>
> What remains to us of the oldest laws of Rome, which were called the Royal Laws, relates as often to the worship as to the relations of civil life.

Two additional and equally interesting examples are cited by the same author:

> The work of Solon was at the same time a code, a constitution, and a ritual. . . . At Rome it was a recognized truth that no one could be a good pontiff who did not know the law, and, conversely, that no one could know the law if he did not understand questions relating to religion.

The conception of the threefold relationship of law, religion, and morality endured for many centuries; doubtless it existed in the prehistoric world and certainly in the ancient and medieval world. And although today attempts have been made to solve in an arbitrary fashion the problem of this relationship, it still confronts us, as an eminent English publicist has pointed out:[23]

> Even the educated man, who happens to be neither a theologian nor a trained jurist, is often puzzled by what he conceives to be a confusion of boundaries between religion and law. He is faced by the obvious fact that a very large number of important rules are common to both; and he is inclined to doubt, with much justice, whether the term "law" can rightly be claimed as the exclusive property of secular tribunals, such as police and county courts. He realises, for example, that the precepts: "Thou shalt do no murder," "Thou shalt not steal," "Thou shalt not bear false witness," are common both to

---

"L'unité de l'esprit humain, dans lequel le droit a sa source, ne ressort pas seulement, en général, de la continuité et de l'universalité du droit; une série d'identités et de ressemblances, qui se rencontrent dans le droit de tous les peuples, en est une autre confirmation particulière. Le préjugé qui domina pendant un certain temps, spécialement sous l'influence de *l'Ecole historique,* selon lequel tout peuple aurait nécessairement un droit particulier, qui lui appartiendrait en propre et ne s'appliquerait qu'à ses conditions particulières de vie, et qui, en conséquence, serait toujours différent de celui des autres peuples, a dû céder devant une étude plus large des phénomènes juridiques. Cette étude a désormais démontré d'une manière certaine qu'une grande partie des principes et des institutions juridiques fondamentaux est le patrimoine commun de toute l'humanité à toute époque. Les modernes maîtres du droit comparé insistent sur cette similitude, parce qu'ils comprennent bien, même sans le dire expressément, que cette science tire sa véritable raison d'être de l'unité substantielle de l'esprit humain, qui se révèle aussi dans le droit."—*Recueil des cours,* Vol. 38, pp. 590–91.

[22] Fustel de Coulanges, "Religious Origin of Ancient Law," being a translation of a part of Fustel de Coulanges's *La Cité antique,* in *Primitive and Ancient Legal Institutions,* pp. 104–5.

[23] Jenks, *The State and the Nation,* pp. 71–72.

religious and secular systems; even if there are others, such as: "Thou shalt not covet," which are peculiar to religion, and: "Thou shalt not omit to register the birth of thy child," which are peculiar to secular law.

The truth is, that there is much excuse for this state of bewilderment; and it is by no means easy to find a test which will disperse it in all cases. The origin of the difficulty is obvious. It lies in the fact that, as we have seen, in primitive communities, religion and law are the same thing. When once Primitive Man has come to the conclusion that an act is Wrong, he has reached the end of his short chain of reasoning. To ask him whether it was forbidden by religious or by secular authority, or how he knew it to be wrong, or why it should be wrong, or how the offender was to be punished, or to what extent, would be to beat the air. These are questions which much more highly developed minds have been long struggling to solve, by no means with complete success. For they really involve an understanding of that complex, mysterious, and yet all-important thing, human society.

It is only because of the so-called "enlightenment" of the modern world that an effort has been made to separate law from religion and morality and place it, so to speak, in a water-tight compartment, where it may not be "tainted" by the spiritual standards and aspirations of man. The result is that law and politics have been too long without a standard; and that law, government, and international relations are founded upon expediency instead of upon the bedrock of principle.[24]

The basic absurdity of those who would exalt the status of force and expediency is revealed by an Italian authority on natural law whom Mr. Del Vecchio invokes in behalf of his concept of law:[25]

The idea of law implies conformity to the moral order of reason. On the contrary, not only just but unjust acts enter the sphere of the so-called law of might, which has no regard for norm, law or regulation. The predication of law, which essentially includes a controlled force and excludes by definition all violence, is opposed to the arbitrary use of force. The law of the strongest is, therefore, both morally absurd and a contradiction in terms.

On this phase of the matter Mr. Del Vecchio[26] himself postulates:

The truth of the alleged antinomy between morals and law is this: that an act can be the object of diverse judgments; and it can be weighed by individual

---

[24] Those who founded the United States of America were much less disturbed than their descendants have been over the relationship between religion and law. Unlike their descendants, they discerned that relationship clearly and approved it as both fitting and natural. And one of their number, James Wilson, deeply versed in jurisprudence and political science, expressly declared that "far from being rivals or enemies, religion and law are twin sisters, friends, and mutual assistants. Indeed these two sciences run into each other. The divine law, as discovered by reason and the moral sense, forms an essential part of both."—*Works of James Wilson, . . .* ed. by Andrews, I, 94.

[25] Giovanni Domenico Romagnosi, *Assunto primo della scienza del diritto naturale,* sec. XIX. Cited by Del Vecchio, *The Formal Bases of Law,* p. 156 n.

[26] *Ibid.,* pp. 162–63.

criteria, different from those moulded in positive institutions. The antinomy does not exist between morals and law, but between different ethical criteria. . . . A natural law, that is, a system of juridical demands founded on simple human nature, cannot fail to admit corresponding natural duties. The same degree of certainty and naturalness enters morals and law. Whoever, therefore, denies the existence of natural law, should reach, to be consistent, an analogous denial of morality and duty.

It would be much easier to deal with these and related problems if law could be defined in simple terms. But to find a definition of law which would be universally accepted is a task which has baffled the best minds throughout the ages. A German philosopher has stated the difficulty in one sentence:[27] "noch suchen die Juristen eine Definition zu ihrem Begriffe vom Recht." (The jurists are still looking for a definition for their conception of law.) And a commentator on Del Vecchio's legal philosophy, Hans Reichel,[28] an authority on Roman law and legal philosophy, remarks:

Nothing in any science, one would suppose, should be freer from controversy, and more settled, than its fundamental principles. But this expectation is deceptive. The historical development of knowledge often leads far away from a logical arrangement of the objects of knowledge. The reason for this, easy to see, is psychological. According to logic (or, as it were, "de jure") general ideas assume a leading importance, while from the standpoint of experience (or "de facto") sensible things have priority; for experience, first of all, deals with particulars. . . .

Logically, of course, "quid jus" always precedes "quid juris"; for before one can determine what is lawful, he must first know what is law. Actually, however, the situation is reversed. There is widespread and thoroughgoing agreement as to particular questions of law—the "quid juris"; the most complicated problems of detail have been in part exhaustively investigated and treated. On the contrary, the higher we climb toward the general and fundamental, the darker and more thorny becomes the path. The summit of this ascent, the question "quid jus?" is surrounded, so it would appear, by a heavy fog.

And no less an authority on the history of law and political theory than the late Professor Otto von Gierke[29] declares that "the science of law is neither more nor less fortunate than its sister sciences; after centuries of labor, it has not attained a satisfactory and unobjectionable answer to this question (sc., what is law?) upon a solution of which an understanding of this science itself depends."

[27] Kant, *Kritik der reinen Vernunft* (Transcendentale Methodenlehre), Kerbach ed., p. 560; or Meiklejohn trans., p. 445.
[28] Review of Del Vecchio's *I presupposti filosofici della nozione del diritto*, in *Kritische Vierteljahresschrift für Gesetzgebung und Rechtswissenschaft*, Dritte Folge, XI (1907), 209–24, a translation of which forms Appendix I to Del Vecchio's *The Formal Bases of Law*, pp. 339–40.
[29] *Naturrecht und deutsches Recht*, p. 4.

INTRODUCTION

It is not the purpose here to undertake the laborious task of repeating the definitions which have been attempted throughout the ages,[30] many of which will be found in their appropriate place in the second part of this work.[31] Nevertheless, he who would deal with law cannot ignore certain definitions. He may choose, however, to define, not law in its detailed manifestations, but the philosophy of law. The term "philosophy of law" is preferred here, rather than the more formal expression "jurisprudence," for the reason that "jurisprudence" is often used, especially in the English-speaking world,[32] in the sense of the formal science of law rather than of legal philosophy; in other words, it is practical rather than philosophical jurisprudence that the term thus used implies. The important distinction between these two fields is pointed out by a modern German jurist and philosopher.

"Leaving to practical jurisprudence," says Dr. Fritz Berolzheimer, "the determination of what is lawful, the philosophy of law proposes the problem of the nature of the law itself."[33] And he adds on the following page a further statement of the distinction he has in mind: "The jurist considers the structure and function of law; the philosopher, its underlying principles and causes."

A learned American judge, a chief justice of the supreme court of Missouri, has suggested in felicitous and somewhat whimsical terms the scope of the philosophy of law:[34]

---

[30] "Les jurisconsultes romains, malgré leur supériorité indéniable, n'ont aucunement pu réussir, même à la dernière époque, à léguer à ceux qui les suivirent une bonne définition du droit." Lévy-Ullmann, *Eléments d'introduction générale à l'étude des sciences juridiques: I. La Définition du droit*, p. 7.

For one of the best modern attempts to formulate an adequate definition of law, Professor Lévy-Ullmann's book from which this quotation is taken, is to be strongly recommended.

[31] Because law itself is essentially an abstract conception, resort has often been had to figures of speech by those who sought to define it. One of the most interesting examples of this in our own day is the definition by an English jurist and statesman, Sir John Simon. Of those "influences," he says in an address on "Our Common Inheritance of Law," "which make for the reconciliation of mankind and the saving of humanity from the unspeakable horrors of armed conflict, Law, in its highest and broadest sense, is one of the chief. It is the instrument of Justice; it is the handmaid of Order; it is the guarantor of Individual Right; it is the arbiter of Dispute and the reconciler of Difference; it is the Cement which binds together the fabric of human institutions; it is the standard which society erects to guide those that are tempted, to recall to the true path those who are led astray and to symbolize the fact that each one of us cannot live for himself but must serve and work for the common good."—Address delivered at the Forty-fourth Annual Meeting of the American Bar Association, Cincinnati, August 31, 1921. Printed in the *American Bar Association Journal*, VII (Sept., 1921), 450.

[32] For a learned discussion of the Anglo-Saxon conception of jurisprudence as contrasted with the Continental conception, see Salmond, *Jurisprudence*, 8th ed.

[33] Berolzheimer, *The World's Legal Philosophies*, pp. 1–2.

[34] Lamm, in Introduction to von Jhering, *Law as a Means to an End (Der Zweck im Recht*, trans. by Husik), p. xxvii.

To know anything well, one must know it by its cause and by its reason. True philosophy consists in looking with a piercing and discriminating eye beneath mere surfaces and appearances, the shell of things, to the real heart, the kernel, of the matter. Religion has its philosophy, nature has its philosophy, the mind has its philosophy, morality has its philosophy, history has its philosophy. Philosophy surrounds man as water does an island. As Sir John Culpepper said of monopoly in the Long Parliament, it sups in our cup, it dips in our dish, it sits by our fire. It would be strange indeed, then, if Law did not have its philosophy. It emphatically has. And it levies tribute on all other philosophies, —on ethics, logic, metaphysics, morals, nature, history, as well as on experience— which latter is a school of philosophy all to itself, withal having a bitter teacher. The philosophy of the law overlaps them all, even as Aaron's rod swallowed the magicians' rods.

And a somewhat briefer but no less felicitous definition of the scope of legal philosophy has been furnished by the late Justice Cardozo, whose death was a grave loss to American jurisprudence:

A philosophy of law will tell us how law comes into being, how it grows, and whither it tends. Genesis and development and end or function, these things, if no others, will be dealt with in its pages. To these it will probably add a description of the genesis and growth and function, not only of law itself, but also of some of those conceptions that are fundamental in the legal framework.[35]

Dealing with the development of legal philosophy in a discussion of what he terms the "crisis of the philosophy of law," Professor Del Vecchio says:[36]

A glorious crisis marked its beginning, when in the daybreak of the human mind,—Hellenic civilization—the intellectual volt of Sophic scepticism gave birth to the philosophies of Socrates and Plato. From that day, the history of the philosophy of law has never been separated from that of the serious revolts which have changed the conditions of human society. There is no doubt that this philosophy will be preserved in the future, and far from being weakened or overthrown, will gain new dignity and strength in the struggle in which it will be called upon to intervene.

And he concludes this admirable comment on the history of legal philosophy with the remark that "while the occasions, and even the methods and forms of the crises change with the years, yet crises remain the constant law of its development, the surest sign of its life and the chief ground for its necessity."

For present purposes a famous definition, already referred to, may be adopted as a guide. It is contained in the *Institutes* of Justinian, where jurisprudence is defined as "the knowledge of matters divine and human, and the comprehension of what is just and unjust."[37] To this classical definition

---
[35] Cardozo, *The Growth of the Law*, p. 24.
[36] *The Formal Bases of Law*, p. lii.
[37] *Institutes*, I. i. 1.

INTRODUCTION 15

may be added a passage from the *Digest:* "It is characteristic of human jurisprudence to be always indefinitely extending."[38]

These passages indicate something of the nature of the philosophy of law. But what of its purpose? In nontechnical terms, the purpose of the philosophy of law is to trace law to its sources; to follow its development from age to age; to analyze the nature and fundamental purpose of law and therefore to examine its relation to the human being in society—which in turn would involve, if time permitted, a consideration of its relationship to other phases of human activity;[39] and finally, to criticize its application and to discover the ultimate ideals toward which law should aim.[40]

Here it must be noted that legal philosophy and political philosophy are closely related—so closely that they inevitably overlap. Observing that political theory must "borrow its material largely from law," and that it "must ultimately rise into a philosophy of political values and a doctrine of the ultimate ends of organized society," Professor Ernest Barker adds[41] that

here the philosophy of law may join hands with political philosophy; and though the legal philosopher will talk of the ends of law, and the political philosopher

---

[38] Second Preface of Justinian to the *Digest*, sec. 18.

[39] Macdonell, in his Introduction to Berolzheimer's volume, *The World's Legal Philosophies* (previously cited), states (p. xxxv) that "the law is not a robe or dress changeable at will; it is very part of the body social. Even the composers of Utopias are circumscribed and are the creatures of their circumstances. In the 'Republic' and the 'Laws' are imbedded much of the Athenian Law of Plato's age. More and Campanella are unconsciously in their political romances thinking of their own time. All hangs together—law, ethics, religion, economics."

[40] This latter conception of the aim of legal philosophy is admirably stated by August Geyer in his *Geschichte und System der Rechtsphilosophie in Gründzügen* (Innsbruck, 1863), as quoted by Berolzheimer, *op. cit.*, pp. 1-2: 'The philosophy of law proposes an ideal which the actual order is to attain, not the law as actually prevailing."

In the same footnote Berolzheimer also quotes the works of the distinguished German publicists, Heinrich Ahrens and Felix Dahn: "*Ahrens*, 'Naturrecht,' Sixth edition, Vienna,—1870 (Vol. I, p. 1): 'The philosophy of law or natural law is the science which derives the supreme principle or conception of law from the nature and destiny of man and of human society, and develops a system of legal principles for all the divisions of private and public law.' Ahrens, 'Cours de droit naturel,' VIII, Leipzig, 1892 (Vol. I, p. 1): 'The philosophy of law or natural law is the science that sets forth the first principles of law as conceived by reason and, as based upon the nature of man considered in itself and in its relations with the universal order of things.' . . . *Dahn*, 'Über Werden und Wesen des Rechts' (II), in Z. f. v. Rechtsw., Vol. III, 1881, pp. 3 seq., § 6, designates the problem of the philosophy of law as that 'of establishing the idea of law and the several products and manifestations of legal activity as a mode of manifestation of the absolute law. Legal philosophy thus attempts to determine and present the inherent logical element in the law.' ('Rechtsphilosophischer Historismus.')"

To these statements may be subjoined the comment, in the form of an analogy, by an eminent moral philosopher: "Just as it would be incorrect to divide the theory of drawing into the art of drawing and perspective, so it is wrong to divide moral philosophy into ethical rules of conduct and the science of law. The philosophy of law is part of moral philosophy." —Cathrein, *Moralphilosophie*, I, 585.

[41] In the Introduction to his translation of Gierke's *Natural Law and the Theory of Society, 1500–1800*, I, xxvii–xxviii.

will speak of the ends of the State, there will be little difference between them. For the State is essentially law, and law is the essence of the State.

This may appear at first sight to be an overstatement, and therefore Professor Barker's brief but adequate justification of it must be quoted:

The State is essentially law in the sense that it exists in order to secure a right order of relations between its members, expressed in the form of declared and enforced rules. Law, as a system of declared and enforced rules, is the essence of the State in the same sort of sense as his words and acts are the essence of a man.

As the characteristics of the state depend, in the final analysis, upon the characteristics of its inhabitants, so the nature of law, it may fairly be said, is determined by the nature of the human being. To refer again to Professor Del Vecchio, this time to one of his most recent works, "La crisi della scienza del diritto,"[42] "We can find the law in our own nature, *ex interiore homine*." The learned philosopher of the law vouches as his authority a historian and philosopher of his own country, but of an earlier century, Giambattista Vico,[43] whose view it was that "this civil world was made certainly by men and its principles must be found in the human mind." To this far-reaching statement Professor Del Vecchio adds a comment which is as a light to him who would understand the nature of law:[44] "All the positive juridical institutions, all laws, all customs, are nothing more than

[42] English trans., "The Crisis of the Science of Law," *Tulane Law Review*, VIII (1934), 329.

[43] Of Vico it may be said that he was a founder of the modern conception of history and its philosophy.

[44] *Tulane Law Review*, VIII, 329.

Lest it be thought that these are isolated expressions of Professor Del Vecchio's fundamental beliefs, it should be added that they appear again and again in his published works; thus, to speak only of the most recent, in his "Il problema delle fonti del diritto positivo" (*Rivista internazionale di filosofia del diritto*, XIV [1934], 4, 17), he observes: "In un senso molto generale, può dirsi (e ciò tutti, o almeno quasi tutti, gli studiosi dovrebbero essere d'accordo) che il diritto ha la sua fonte essenziale nella natura umana . . . affermiamo semplicemente che per natura umana non si deve intendere un qualsiasi motivo empirico, ma la stessa costituzione dell'essere umano come soggetto. . . . [La] prima, assoluta ed inesauribile fonte del diritto . . . è, in un senso più alto, lo spirito umano nella sua universale natura."

In his "Sulla statualità del diritto (*Rivista internazionale di filosofia del diritto*, IX [1929], 21), he says: "Il diritto nel suo principio . . . è coevo all'uomo: perchè il sentimento e l'idea del diritto sono elemento costitutivo ed indefettibile della coscienza umana."

In "The Crisis of the State" (*The Law Quarterly Review*, LI [1935], 625), Professor Del Vecchio administers a rebuke to the "dogmatizers on law": "The dogmatizers on law, who state as axiomatic the exclusive derivation of law from the State, and denounce as a heresy the conception of law which does not derive from the State, should settle their account with history even before that of the philosophy of law."

As an example of another school of thought concerning the origin of law—that is, the conception of war and constant struggle as the source of law—see the small but classic volume of Dr. Rudolf von Jhering, the distinguished German Romanist and jurist, *The Struggle for Law* (*Der Kampf ums Recht*), trans. by Lalor.

manifestations or reflections of sentiments, of thoughts, and of beliefs, no matter how variously expressed and imperfectly fused, since they emanate from a multitude of subjects and the succession of generations."

The application of the law, like its nature, is human. Such application depends ultimately upon the people who have made the law or who have consented thereto; and if the law is not applied as they desire, it is their privilege, indeed it is their right and their duty, to secure its proper application—even by force, if necessary.

In one of his later and most elaborate masterpieces—*Der Zweck im Recht*, translated into English under the title, *Law as a Means to an End*[45]—the German jurist Rudolf von Jhering, who shares with Savigny the primacy among German masters of Roman law and jurisprudence, says:

> The security of right depends in the last instance entirely upon the moral force of the national sense of right. *Not* upon the form of government; you may think it out as skilfully as you please, yet we can imagine no form which would as a matter of fact take away from the State authorities the possibility of trampling the law under foot. *Not* upon the oaths, by which we think it is secured; experience shows how often these are broken. *Not* upon the nimbus of holiness and inviolability with which theory clothes the law; despotism is not overawed by it. The only thing that impresses it is the real power which stands behind the law the people, who recognize in the law the condition of their existence, and feel an injury done to it as an injury done to themselves; the people, from whom it may be expected that in case of necessity they will fight for their rights. I do not mean to say that this low motive of fear is the only thing which induces the State authorities to observe the law. I mean only that it is the last and extreme motive which does not deny its services even when the higher motive of respect for the law for its own sake fails. The security of the law in the upward direction is situated similarly with its security in the downward direction. The fear of the law must be replaced by respect for it. But where this is not the case there still remains fear as the last resort. . . . The security of the law is everywhere the work and the merit of the people itself.

Another passage in the same chapter completes von Jhering's thought on this phase of law and its application:

> Where the national morality consists in accommodating and subordinating oneself to others, in a policy of cunning, craft, dissimulation and doglike submissiveness, no characters can be formed. A soil of this kind produces only slaves and servants. Those of them who conduct themselves as masters are only servants in disguise, domineering and brutal toward their inferiors, cringing and cowardly toward their superiors. For the development of character man needs from the beginning the *feeling of security*. But this inner, subjective

---

[45] Trans. by Husik (previously cited), pp. 285-86.

feeling of security presupposes an external objective security in society; and this man possesses through the law. Man on the law is as firm and unshaken in his confidence in it as the believer in his confidence in God. Or, more precisely, both of them put their trust not merely in something outside of them, but rather they feel God and the law within them as the firm ground of their existence, and as a living part of themselves; which therefore no power on earth can deprive them of, but can only destroy in and with them. This is in both of them the source of their power.[46]

On the question of the purpose and aims or ideals of law, volumes might be written, and indeed have been written, but for present purposes the view of an eminent English writer of the present day may be adopted:

The difference between a mere crowd and a society is just the difference between body and spirit; and Justice, whatever else it may be, is a spiritual force without which no society can live. And as a mere crowd is converted into a society by the pursuit of a common aim, so the Law, by directing the energies of mankind towards the pursuit of Justice, has before it the ideal of welding mankind into a great and noble society. That is the historic function of Law in building up Society.[47]

This is the conception of law as a constructive force in society. But as von Jhering points out, law is a means, not an end in itself:

Law exists for the sake of society, not society for the sake of law. Hence, it follows that when in exceptional cases . . . the relations are such that the government finds itself facing the alternatives of sacrificing either the law or society, it is not merely empowered, but in duty bound, to sacrifice law and save society. For higher than the law which it violates stands the consideration for the preservation of society, in the service of which all laws must stand, the "lex summa," as Cicero ("De Legibus" III, 3) calls it in his well-known saying, "Salus populi summa lex esto."[48]

No consideration of the purpose of law would be worthy of the name unless it were devoted in large part to the conception and application of justice.

Of justice [observes an American writer],[49] it has been said that its seat is in the bosom of God. Finite justice, as it is administered under human law, has its seat in the enlightened conscience of mankind.

[46] Von Jhering, *Law as a Means to an End,* pp. 287–88.
Modern legal philosophers may not subscribe wholeheartedly to all of the views propounded by von Jhering, but this should not keep us from recognizing the great contributions which von Jhering made to legal and political thought, especialy in his classic but unfinished *Geist des römischen Rechts.*
[47] Jenks, "The Function of Law in Society," *The Journal of Comparative Legislation and International Law,* 3d series, V (1923), 169, 177.
[48] *Law as a Means to an End* (previously cited), p. 317.
[49] Hutcheson, "This Thing called Law," *The University of Chicago Law Review* (December, 1934), 2.

INTRODUCTION

But he who deals with justice must first of all have some knowledge of its nature and its place in the preservation of society. There are, according to another American writer (whose chief field was geology, but who strayed into many bypaths and on one occasion into the field of jurisprudence, with magnificent results),

> five fundamental principles of justice; that is, to secure justice, five fundamental purposes must be considered: Justice is the establishment of peace. Justice is the establishment of equality. Justice is the establishment of liberty. Justice is the establishment of equity; and justice is the establishment of truth. In all law, primitive and modern alike, these principles are recognized, and all institutions are organized for these purposes.[50]

From this definition it is clear that justice, like law, is a creature of human reason and morality. The great natural laws of the physical world—meaning those which govern alike atoms and planets in their courses—are independent of the moral conception of justice. It is to the moral nature of man that we must look for the spring from which justice flows, and it is with the conception of justice that legal philosophy, properly speaking, must inevitably concern itself; for without justice there could be no law in our sense of the term, and without law there could be no philosophy of law. This is, of course, tantamount to declaring that an unjust law is not law.

Justice, again, is both the substance and the ideal of law. As the substance of law it is a constant element. As the ideal of law, however, it is an element ever expanding to meet the needs of an onward and upward-marching humanity.[51] In this latter sense justice is the fundamental principle of that law of nature which was the guiding star of the philosophers of the ancient and medieval worlds. A French writer, Joseph Charmont,[52] has stated tersely the need for a revival of the conception of the natural law: "The confirma-

---

[50] Powell, "On Regimentation," *Fifteenth Annual Report of the American Bureau of Ethnology* (1893–94), p. cxi.

[51] Del Vecchio, in his pamphlet entitled *Giustizia e diritto,* says: "La giustizia si afferma allora non come sinonimo di diritto positivo, ma come suo paradigma e modello ideale, sempre valido nella sua sfera, anche se solo parzialmente o difettosamente attuato; così come l'ideale della virtù e l'imperativo del dovere ('non fare ad altri ciò che non vorresti fosse fatto a te stesso', ecc.) valgono sempre, anche se innumerevoli volte materialmente violati. . . . Abbiamo così ancora una volta sperimentato che oltre le leggi scritte ve ne sono altre, più alte, non scritte; e che la giustizia si riflette bensì variamente in tutte le leggi, ma non si esaurisce in nessuna; onde essa sola può, nelle grandi ore, imporre come dovere e sacrificio supremo di infrangere e oltrepassare l'ordine giuridico positivo, quando esso sia irreparabilmente corrotto, affinchè con un ordine nuovo prosegua e si perfezioni quel processo di avveramento e di rivendicazione della stessa giustizia, che ha per teatro la storia e per fonte inabolibile e inesauribile lo spirito umano."—Reprint from *Rivista internazionale di filosofia del diritto,* Anno XIV, fasc. iii.

[52] "Recent Phases of French Legal Philosophy" (trans. of chaps. v–xii of Charmont's *La Renaissance du droit naturel),* in *Modern French Legal Philosophy,* p. 145.

tion of natural law, or more exactly of juridical idealism, has appeared to us to offer the only solution for the crisis in legal philosophy."[53]

Perhaps it will not be inappropriate to close the discussion of this phase of the matter with a few words from a Justice of the Supreme Court of the United States, Mr. Justice Moody[54] "It is sufficient to say," he declares, quoting Mr. Justice Brown, "that there are certain immutable principles of justice which inhere in the very idea of free government"; and these principles, he adds by way of warning, "no member of the Union may disregard."

So much for the law in its relationship to justice and morality.

But what of the state? The determination of its genesis should be left to the investigations of those who specialize in the vast and still partially unexplored domains of ethnology and the related sciences. One theory advanced in that particular field, however, must be met, namely, that the state is fundamentally a product of war and of conquest. To adopt such a theory and to carry it to its logical conclusion would be to admit that the political progress of humanity culminating in the state depends upon the form of murder which we call war, and this admission leads to what is (to most of us, at least) the absurd conclusion that human beings are fundamentally antisocial rather than social and that force is the supreme cohesive element in society.

It must be admitted, of course, that force in the form of war or conquest has profoundly affected the development of political organization. Nevertheless, an increasing number of investigators and political scientists, discarding the theory of conquest as the unique element in state-making, hold that the political development and progress of humanity have been the result of various factors, some external and some innate in human nature.[55] The rôle of force in society has been admirably described by Professor Robert Morrison MacIver,[56] formerly of McGill, now of Columbia University, who, after having demonstrated "that the emergence of the state was not due to force, although in the process of expansion force undoubtedly played a part," adds certain penetrating conclusions:

---

[53] A significant emphasis is placed on the moral nature of man by another French jurist, M. Alfred Fouillée, who declares that "the charter of conscience and nature should not be the gift of a sovereign, but the natural property of every man."—"Synthesis of Idealism and Naturalism" (trans. of Book IV of Fouillée's *Idée moderne du droit*), in *Modern French Legal Philosophy*, p. 164.

[54] *Twining* v. *New Jersey*, 211 U.S. 78, 102, quoting *Holden* v. *Hardy*, 169 U.S. 366, 389.

[55] See on this interesting subject Lowie, *The Origin of the State*, pp. 11-17; MacLeod, *The Origin and History of Politics*, chaps. iii-viii, pp. 39-111.

[56] *The Modern State*, p. 222.

INTRODUCTION 21

Force holds nothing together. Force is a substitute for unity. So far as it rules, there is no unity and no development. Force as the servant of intelligence at times prepares the way for unity, but the credit belongs more to the master than to the servant. Force always disrupts unless it is made subservient to common will. The only justification for the doctrine which attributes social origins to force is simply this, that men learn by experience the inefficacy of mere force and then learn to modify or supersede it. Thus looking backwards we perceive that force once played a greater rôle than now belongs to it. "The good old rule, the simple plan" is proved to have serious drawbacks. To take and to hold by force wastes the energies of those who take and those who resist, which might have been profitably applied to their co-operative endeavour.

What then is the actual status of force as a social and political implement?

Within a society it is only the clumsy and the stupid who seek to attain their ends by force. Brute strength earns little reward. It enables a bully to beat his wife. It earns a pittance in the humblest forms of manual labour. But it is the least prized of human possessions, the poorest servant of intelligence. It is put under the yoke, because if suffered to go free it breaks the order of life and habit, and tramples down the amenities and satisfactions which spring from the responsive and unrepressed activity of social man. It is an intruder felt and resented and chained. If suffered to prevail, it would destroy not only material goods but also the cultural gains, the spirit of truth, the work of the mind, the fertility of thought.[57]

But whatever origin or origins the state may have had, the fact remains that it emerged as a community[58] consisting of a group of human beings having certain common interests, and that the formation of such communities, rudimentary or advanced in form, is a universal phenomenon.[59] The principle laid down by Aristotle, which soon became a truism of political philosophers, that man is a social animal, that he has a natural, innate tendency to associate with his kind, is beyond argument, for it is evidenced in every record of the history of mankind. Von Jhering, although not averse to force under certain conditions, accepted and restated this Greek conception.[60]

Human life and social life are synonymous. The ancient Greek philosophers recognized this perfectly; there is no saying which expresses the social nature of man more concisely and more fittingly, than the designation of man as ζῷον πολιτικόν, *i.e., social* being.

---

[57] *Ibid.*, p. 223.
[58] "The fact of *Community*, i.e., the fact that human beings can, and do, combine to further common ends, is the cardinal fact in the history of civilization, and pre-eminently in the history of politics."—Jenks, *The State and the Nation*, p. 1.
[59] See Lowie, *op. cit.*, especially chap. vi.
[60] *Law as a Means to an End* (previously cited), p. 67.

Now it must be granted that every group or association of human beings is not a state; for within the state are smaller associations and beyond the state are larger ones culminating in what we of today call the international community. In truth, the various associations of humanity are as rings within rings. This conception of society (of circles within circles) has been expressed by Professor Del Vecchio:[61]

> Le défaut de "autarchia," c'est-à-dire l'impossibilité pour l'individu de se suffire à lui-même, sur laquelle Aristote faisait reposer la raison fondamentale de la société politique, se traduit, en réalité, en une sorte de propulsion permanente, qui pousse les hommes à élargir peu à peu le cercle de leurs relations sociales, et cela déjà avant que se manifeste l'État proprement dit, et même après sa formation.

The authority upon which Professor Del Vecchio here relies is the distinguished French publicist M. Gabriel Tarde,[62] from whom he quotes the following passage:

> Une belle, une admirable progression, qu'on n'a pas pris la peine de remarquer, et qui accompagne néanmoins toutes les évolutions juridiques, c'est l'élargissement continuel des relations de droit: d'abord restreintes au groupe étroit et serré des parents, qui s'est agrandi tant qu'il a pu par l'adoption, par la légende, s'annexant toutes sortes de parents fictifs ou imaginaires, elles se sont etendues ensuite, soit par le contrat féodal, soit par le contrat d'association corporative, au cercle plus vaste des voisins, des confrères, des concitoyens locaux; plus tard, par l'idée de patrie, à des millions de compatriotes, et par l'idée de chrétienté, d'Islam, de communauté religieuse quelconque, à des centaines de millions d'étrangers même; enfin, par l'idée d'humanité, de droit de gens, de droit naturel, à tous les hommes.

It is necessary, however, to distinguish between society—which includes humanity as a whole, and thus embraces all of the various forms of grouping or association—and the state, which for the moment may be defined[63] as a political organization or unit of society, characterized by territorial delimitation. In this definition of the state, we are confronted by a matter which is fundamental to the conception of the state. The term "political organization" involves the element of status, but the status is to be political by definition. Now a word about the term "political." The Greece of ancient times, as we shall see,[64] was a very small group of Greek-speaking communities, the principal unit being the city. The state was therefore appropriately known as the "city-state." In Greek *polis* means town or city-state,

---
[61] *Recueil des cours*, vol. 38, pp. 541, 589, cited *supra*, p. 9.
[62] *Les Transformations du droit*, p. 59; *Recueil des cours*, vol. 38, pp. 589–90, n. 1.
[63] See *infra*, pp. 28 ff., for a discussion of Ernest Renan's conception of the state.
[64] *Infra*, pp. 43 ff.

that is, a community in which human beings were associated in a group. The term, therefore, implies first of all the union of people within a small district; it is, however, the people who unite, the district being, so to speak, merely incidental.[65] Union alone, however, was not sufficient to establish order; therefore the need for organization; and out of organization develops government—the union becomes political, the *polis* is on the way to statehood.

But what is the meaning of the second characteristic of the state, territorial delimitation? In its simplest definition, "territorial delimitation" means that beyond certain physical limits the state may not exercise its functions. It is fundamentally a limitation of jurisdiction. Ancient Greece, however, would not have been the glory of the ancient world but for its people; for that which made the greatness of Greece was the people who inhabited the territory—not the territory itself, nor even the status of organization as separate and distinct from the people. Until we can reverse the order of nature so that the territory generates the inhabitants instead of human beings generating their offspring, we shall have to look upon the state as people politically organized and exercising jurisdiction within certain territorial boundaries. Neither the organization nor the boundaries can be considered as constituting the state. Remove both and you would still have the people; but remove the people and you have nothing. The state, in a word, is simply the people organized for political purposes within certain arbitrary geographical limits. It is not a "person" with aims and purposes independent of those shared by the people to whom it owes its origin and continued existence.

"What constitutes a state?" asked Sir William Jones, excellent lawyer and occasional writer of exquisite verse, and his answer, in a few happy lines, should be memorized by every schoolboy:[66]

> What constitutes a state?
> Not high-raised battlement or labour'd mound,
>   Thick wall or moated gate;
> Not cities proud with spires and turrets crown'd;
>   Not bays and broad-armed ports, . . .
>   No:—Men, high minded men, . . .
>   Men, who their duties know,
> But know their rights, and knowing, dare maintain; . . .
>   These constitute a state.

---

[65] We may and do, of course, speak of a union of territories, but a mere joining of two or more physical portions of land into one portion does not constitute a union in the sense in which the word is here used—a human and spiritual union.

[66] "An Ode in Imitation of Alcaeus," *Poems of Sir William Jones*, Vol. LXXIV, "The British Poets Including Translations" (Cheswick, 1822), pp. 106–7.

INTRODUCTION

One of the smallest so-called "states" of the world is Andorra, part of which is south of the dividing line between France and Spain, the other part to the north.[67] In all it contains but a few square miles—175, to be exact—within which a few thousand inhabitants dwell and exercise their jurisdiction through appropriate agents of their own choice, constituting a government of their own making, and without interference from the outer world. What would happen to the "state" of Andorra if a cyclone coming from the south should blow the inhabitants northward into France and leave the entire territory of Andorra a vacant lot? Again what would happen if a cyclone from the north should blow these inhabitants southward and restore them to their deserted territory? In the first case, what had formerly been the state of Andorra would be nothing but an uninhabited strip of land. In the second case, the Andorrans would be in possession of their land,

---

[67] For those to whom Andorra is but a name, I quote two excerpts from the *New York Times* on this small but ancient state. The first is from the *Times* "Review of the Week" (Section 4, p. E 2, May 16, 1937):

"Times change, but only imperceptibly in Andorra, tiny semi-independent State perched atop the Pyrenees between Spain and France. Across the border crackle the guns of the Spanish civil war, but the lean and taciturn Andorrans go about their immemorial occupations of agriculture, stock raising and smuggling.

"Charlemagne is said to have established an independent Andorra as a buffer between his realm and the aggressive Moors. Since 1278 the Andorrans have been under the joint suzerainty of French rulers and the Spanish Bishops of Urgel. The Bishop receives tribute every Christmas time of twelve fine cheeses, twelve fat chickens and six wood-smoked hams. The French co-Prince—now the President of France—receives annual tribute of 960 francs (currently $43), a sum ceremoniously presented last week at Perpignan by a delegation of leading Andorrans.

"In 1806 Napoleon gave Andorra a republican Constitution, but its ancient government defies classification. It is ruled by a Council General of twenty-four elected for four years and presided over by a President, whose real title is 'Most Illustrious Sindic and Procurator General of the Valleys.' Only patriarchs or heads of families may vote; much grazing and forest land is held in common."

The second excerpt from the *Times* (Section 4, p. E 9, May 23, 1937) proves that journalistic mistakes are possible about even so tiny a republic. It must be admitted, however, that not often—indeed this is the first time within my knowledge—has Andorra been the subject of a "letter to the *Times*."

"I hope you won't take it in the wrong way if I correct some of your statements in the Review Section last Sunday concerning the tiny republic in the Pyrenees, Andorra. You err as to the yearly contribution of Andorra to the Bishop of Urgel; the latter receives 849 French francs every two years, at least this was the amount before the last French devaluation. But that is not all. The contributions in kind are also wrongly stated in your article. The Bishop's tribute consists of 12 chickens, 6 hens and 24 cheeses. If the Andorrans were to deliver only 12 cheeses, this would probably be the long awaited spark exploding the European powder barrel. Your brief statement contains further a slur on the Andorran character. It is true that there is some smuggling, but less than usual, and the place of smuggling has been taken by fleecing of foreign visitors who flock into the valley and look at the last bulwark of medieval feudalism tainted now by democratic principles. I expect that you will publish this correcting statement in order to avoid serious diplomatic difficulties between the United States and Andorra.—Professor Karl Loewenstein, Amherst, Massachusetts."

INTRODUCTION 25

exercising jurisdiction: the state would again exist. That is the truth of the matter and no amount of argument can endow the territorial state with real personality.

Indeed, however we may define the state—and the definitions are many and various—we can only pretend that it is a person. Such pretense has been stripped away in a few sentences by Léon Duguit, whose recent death the scholars of the world deplore. After examining the contentions of those who insist that the state is a person, the distinguished French publicist sweepingly declared that these doctrines of state personality are "fictions":[68]

All these doctrines, whatever the authority and ingenuity of their defenders, are mere hypotheses and fictions—when they do not run in a vicious circle. . . . Is not the assertion of the existence of a collective personality behind the actions and the practical life of individuals, an affirmation of a thing-in-itself, the creation of hypostases, the personification of what is only the manifestation of a force? Only on condition of keeping within the world of reality can a science exist. And the realities are men,—men who have common needs, who have different talents, who exchange services, who have always lived in common and have always exchanged services; who, because of their physical nature, can only live in common and by exchange of services; men some of whom are stronger than others, of whom the stronger have always used compulsion on the weaker; men who act and who act knowingly. These are the facts, beyond them are nothing but fictions. Men in groups form, it is said, a living organic being, thinking, willing, and distinct from the individuals who compose it. But no one has seen it. Volumes have been written in an unsuccessful attempt to prove its existence.[69]

[68] "Theory of Objective Law Anterior to the State," being a trans. in part of *L'État: Le droit objectif et la loi positive*, in *Modern French Legal Philosophy*, pp. 241–42.

[69] In law, the corporation, like the state, is also termed a "person," and there have been many who regarded it as having an existence wholly distinct and apart from that of the incorporators by whom the organization was formed and who direct its destinies. The fallacy of this view, however, is gradually coming to be recognized. The corporation may properly be termed a creature of law, but as such it is no more than a legal fiction set up in order that the law may endow it with certain capacities and functions. If we strip away the fiction and look at the facts, we find ourselves confronted with human beings in the persons of the incorporators, who actually control the corporation.

In a famous case—the *Daimler Co., Ltd., v. Continental Tyre and Rubber Co. (Great Britain), Ltd.*, appealed to the House of Lords—Lord Parker of Waddington ([1916] 2 A.C. 307, 340, 341, 344–45) stated that in deciding the question of the enemy character of a corporation, an important fact was that of "control." Observing that the acts of a company's organs and officers within the limits of their authority may determine its character, his Lordship continued: "It seems to me that similarly the character of those who can make and unmake those officers, dictate their conduct mediately or immediately, prescribe their duties and call them to account, may also be material in a question of the enemy character of the company. If not definite and conclusive, it must at least be prima facie relevant, as raising a presumption that those who are purporting to act in the name of the company are, in fact, under the control of those whom it is their interest to satisfy."

Referring with approval to the opinion of Chief Justice Marshall—in the case of *Bank of United States v. Deveaux*, 5 Cranch 61, 81—Lord Parker remarked that "his actual decision

Therefore, when we speak of states, we really mean men and women and children, without whom there would be nothing but an uninhabited world. If we must have the term "state," let us have the state a humanized organization, a creation of human and therefore moral beings, an agency to meet human necessities.[70]

The state exists *for* the people, and its prime function is—or should be—to provide them with what the Greeks termed "the good life," or, in the modern phrase of Professor Ernest Barker, "a better moral life." Discussing various views on "human betterment and the purpose of the State," Professor Barker says:[71]

There is still another view of the nature of human betterment and the purpose of the State. This is the view which is held by the votaries of the State ethical—the State which is based not on biological, nor economic, nor psychological, but on moral foundations. . . . The primary fact about man, and the fact which constitutes the ultimate foundation of any political community, is the fact that he is a moral being. . . . Moral claims, and their answering moral responsibilities—these are the foundations of politics. The better life which the State seeks to produce among its members by the agency of law is a better moral life. . . . Not that the legal obligation supersedes the moral obligation. It is a reinforcement, and not a supersession. Moral obligation always remains—the permanent rock; the abiding foundation. . . . The moral foundations of politics, in the last resort, are superior to politics. There have always been martyrs to this truth, from the days of Socrates to the days of Sir Thomas More, and even to our own troubled days. Indeed there will always be martyrs to it, so long as law is made by fallible men who are liable to forget the rock of its foundation.

Now the fundamental purposes of the state are to supply human needs, to protect human rights and to require the performance of human duties,

---

proceeds upon the assumption that for certain purposes a Court must look behind the artificial persona—the corporation—and take account of and be guided by the personalities of the natural persons, the corporators."

And in summarizing the law on the case his Lordship laid down a principle which is of prime importance:

"A company incorporated in the United Kingdom is a legal entity, a creation of law with the status and capacity which the law confers. It is not a natural person with mind or conscience. To use the language of Buckley L. J., 'it can be neither loyal nor disloyal. It can be neither friend nor enemy.'"

[70] "Philosophical criticism dissolves state idolatry," says Professor Del Vecchio, "while it assigns and defends the right of the state to its own mission, from the fulfilment of which alone it may attract a superior consecration of its authority. This mission consists (it is worth while repeating this) in the realization of justice, or of that supreme law which no arbitrary will is capable of suppressing, which shines and governs in every conscience and which imposes on all people respect for the sacred dignity of the human being."—"Ethics, Law, and the State," *The International Journal of Ethics*, XLVI (October, 1935), 47.

[71] *The Citizen's Choice*, pp. 127-29.

and it is for these purposes that the inhabitants of the state create the agency of government. As they make their government, so they may unmake it, for if this agency does not respond to their needs, or fails in the protection of rights and in requiring the performance of duties, it is a faulty structure and should be replaced by a new one.

In their creation of the agency of government, the individuals who make up the state renounce not their rights but the individual exercise of them, in order that the rights in question may be exercised by the agency in behalf of and for the good of the community as a whole. Thus prior to the organization of the state, the individual would himself exercise the right to protect himself, his family, and his property, but in a status of organization (in other words, in a state) he renounces the exercise of this right—except in cases of the gravest emergency—in order that it may be exercised by the agency which he and his fellows have duly created and constituted. It is a popular conception that the distinguishing feature of the government of a state is that it exercises control. It is true that the agency of government is endowed with certain powers by its principal, the people, and that among these is the power of control to insure justice; but the control is fundamentally that of the people who granted it and not a power which comes from above and is imposed upon the people without their consent.

The question of control naturally leads to a consideration of the means by which such control is to be exercised, and this means is nothing more nor less than law, without which there can be no justice, for justice depends upon law and in its absence the government of the state is but tyranny. "The due administration of justice," wrote George Washington, "is the firmest pillar of good government."[72]

Now there are, broadly speaking, two general divisions of law within the state. There is the constitutional law, which is, so to speak, above the government of the state, in that it contains the very provisions by which the government is authorized and formed by the people, and under which it functions as an agency of the people. Indeed in many instances, a constitution is drawn up by the representatives of the people and submitted to the people themselves for their approval and ratification.[73] To say, therefore, that the government of a state or the head of the government of a state is above the law is manifestly to ignore the principle that the source of law

---

[72] Letter to Edmund Randolph, Sept. 27, 1789. *The Writings of George Washington*, col. and ed. by Worthington Chauncey Ford (14 vols., New York and London, 1891), XI, 432.
[73] In the case of the United States, the Constitution was drawn up by duly chosen representatives of the states, and the Constitution was submitted for ratification to the representatives of the people of the separate states.

is in the people. It is obvious of course that the government of a state—or certain organs of it—is also in one sense the source of law. Legislatures of states do formulate and pass laws, but the legislators are representatives of the people, chosen by the people, and acting under their mandate.

It is difficult to understand, in this thirty-ninth year of the twentieth century, the conception—often stated as incontrovertible and unfortunately widely accepted—that law is a command of the so-called sovereign state. That view is here rejected, as it has been rejected generally by the enlightened of our day. A statement of this rejection which might well be termed classic has been made by Professor MacIver[74] and it is quoted *in toto*, because it seems to demolish so completely the theory of law as a command:

> Law is the very antithesis of command, as that term is usually understood, for command separates the giver and the receiver, separates their status always and sometimes their interest as well. But law unites, for it applies no less to the legislator than to those for whom he has authority to legislate. When an army officer issues a command, he does not have to obey it himself, any more than an employer who gives instructions to his *employé*. Besides, command belongs properly to the sphere of administration and not of legislation. It is concerned with ways and means, with specific occasions, usually with details that do not admit of a rule. It is a means of execution, not a form of enactment. Law is permanent and fundamental as compared with command. Every new law has to be fitted into a system, to be adjusted to, and made to consist with, the whole body of pre-existing law. The confusion of law and command destroys the very order of the state. Even in extreme despotisms mere command leaves intact the major realm of law—otherwise the state would break into chaos. The rule of law, the very criterion that a state exists, is possible only in so far as law is distinguished and set apart from command. And it is a mark of the modern state, in fact of the developing state at all times, that it extends the rule of law so that no classes (like the medieval clergy) and no individuals, not even the "monarch," are withdrawn from its authority.

On a previous page[75] the state was tentatively defined in terms of political organization and territorial delimitation. Such a definition, however, is but partial and therefore inadequate. In truth, the state, like law, is difficult of definition. Nevertheless, a great French historian, critic, and man of letters of the last century, Ernest Renan, was courageous enough to attempt to define the state,[76] and his definition amply repays study.

He begins by pointing out that "the forms of human society are extremely varied."[77] Referring to the great masses of people in China, in ancient Egypt

---

[74] *The Modern State* (previously cited), pp. 257–58.   [75] *Supra*, p. 22.
[76] "Qu'est-ce qu'une nation?"—a lecture delivered at the Sorbonne, March 11, 1882; published in *Discours et conferences*, pp. 277–310.
[77] *Ibid.*, p. 277.

and Babylon, to tribes like the Hebrews and Arabs, to the city-states of Athens and Sparta, to great unions like the Roman Empire and the empire of the Carlovingian monarchs, to religious communities like the Israelites and the Parsees, to modern nations like France and England, to confederations like Switzerland and the United States, to the kinship established by race and language, as among the Germanic and Slavic peoples—M. Renan warns us that these numerous different kinds of human association must not be confused one with another.

In the ancient world, he observes, there were no nations in the modern sense. Egypt and ancient Chaldea were in truth but multitudes led by a monarch who claimed relationship to the sun or proclaimed himself "a son of heaven."[78] Nor can the early city-states of the Mediterranean lands be termed states as we understand that term. So it was with other groups of peoples, whether they were large or small. It was not until the time of the Roman Empire, which was "synonymous with order, peace and civilization,"[79] that something approaching the conception of the modern state began to emerge. Yet, as Renan points out, an empire a dozen times as large as France of the present day did not constitute "a state in the modern acceptance of that term."[80]

With the break up of the Roman Empire the first seeds of modern statehood were sown. Yet it was not a process of separation but rather one of fusion which characterized the period following the Empire's dissolution. The various fragments into which the domain of Rome was shattered eventually became linked by a common religion, Christianity; by a common language (Latin) super-imposed, as it were, upon the various local languages of Europe; and by the gradual admixture of races produced by conquest and intermarriage. In the course of time many of the formerly sharp distinctions between racial elements originally separate were forgotten. The peoples which emerged from this process of fusion developed a sense of unity, although in so doing they may be said to have committed the historical error of ignoring their separate origins.

"Forgetfulness, and I would say even historical error," observes Renan, "constitute an essential factor in the creation of a nation."[81] Too much attention, he adds, to historical investigation may on this account be dangerous to nationality, because it brings to light violent deeds and historical distinctions which a people have long since forgotten.

But what is it that produces a state? Numerous theories have been advanced to answer this question and Renan considers them at length. Certain

---

[78] *Ibid.*, p. 280.   [79] *Ibid.*, p. 281.   [80] *Ibid.*   [81] *Ibid.*, pp. 284-85.

political theorists, for example, seemed to feel that a dynasty was essential for the establishment of a state. These theorists have in mind the days when government was a personal prerogative of monarchs who enlarged the boundaries of their princedoms to the full extent of their power. But Renan points out that in spite of numerous examples of dynastic expansion which history affords, the existence of dynasties is not necessary for the establishment of states. Otherwise, as he observes, there would have been no nation of Switzerland, no nation of the United States of America, which states certainly cannot be said to have had a dynastic foundation.

It must therefore be admitted [continues Renan] that a nation can exist without a dynastic beginning, and even that those nations which were established by dynasties can separate themselves from dynastic elements without thereby ceasing to exist. The ancient principle, which took no heed of anything except the right of princes, can no longer be upheld.[82]

Today, instead of the royal right there is the national right. But if dynasties are not essential to the establishment of states, what *is* the determining factor in their origin and development? Various answers to this question had been proposed—race, language, religion, community of interests, geography—and Renan considers these factors one by one.

It was true, he granted, that in the ancient world the fact of race played and important rôle, but that rôle lost much of its significance with the formation of the Roman Empire. The universal adoption of Christianity still further diminished the importance of the part played by race in national development. The result was that political boundaries were for centuries drawn without consideration of ethnographic factors (and indeed, it may be added, only in recent times have racial considerations begun again to influence conceptions of the state).

Pointing to the fact that the population of modern nations is in every instance made up of a mixture of races, Renan concludes that ethnographic considerations are not fundamental in the establishment of states. "The truth is," he declares, "that no pure race exists and that to base political conceptions upon an ethnographic analysis is to found them upon a chimera."[83] And his conclusions are that the matter of race, however significant originally, is steadily losing its importance, that "human history differs essentially from zoology,"[84] and that "while the study of racial questions is important for the savant concerned with the history of humanity," it is "without application in matters political."[85]

---

[82] *Discours et conférences* (previously cited), p. 290.
[83] *Ibid.*, 293–94.   [84] *Ibid.*, p. 297.   [85] *Ibid.*, p. 296.

INTRODUCTION 31

As for the effect of language, Renan declares that it must be considered in much the same light as the subject of race.

Language induces unification but does not impose it by force. The United States and England speak the same language, as do also Spanish-America and Spain, yet in neither case do these peoples form a single nation. On the other hand Switzerland, which is so well established because it was founded with the consent of its different parts, includes three or four languages. There is something in man superior to language, and that is his will.[86]

Speech after all is but the expression of thought and feeling. "Can we not have," Renan pertinently asks, "the same feelings and the same thoughts, love the same things, in different languages?"[87] There are, he concludes, perils and disadvantages in giving too much weight to the effect of languages. And chief among the perils is that of considering nationality in too narrow a sense. He who commits this error "quits the open air which he breathes on the vast field of humanity" in order to shut himself up in what Renan calls "conventicles of compatriots." There is, he assures us, "nothing worse for the spirit, nothing more unfortunate for civilization." And he continues:

Let us not abandon this fundamental principle, that, prior to being penned in by this or that language, prior to being a member of this or that race, an adherent of this or that culture, man is a reasonable and moral creature. Preceding French culture, German culture, Italian culture, there is human culture. Consider the great men of the Renaissance; they were not French, nor Italian, nor German. They had re-discovered, through their intercourse with antiquity, the secret of the true education of the human spirit, and they devoted themselves to it body and soul. How splendidly they wrought![88]

So much for language. Renan next considers religion, which, he says, could not "offer a sufficient foundation for the establishment of a modern nationality."[89] He concedes that religion was originally of great importance to the existence of the social group. But absolute religious uniformity is no longer to be found within the groups of our own day. Instead, there is an almost infinite variety in kinds and shades of religious belief. The state religion as such no longer exists. According to the observations of Renan, the inhabitants of most countries might be Catholics, Protestants, Jews, agnostics, or atheists, without their religious belief affecting in any way their status as citizens. "Religion has become an individual matter; it has to do with the conscience of each person. The classification of nations as Catholic or Protestant is no longer employed."[90]

[86] *Ibid.*, pp. 298–99.　　[87] *Ibid.*, p. 299.　　[88] *Ibid.*, pp. 300–1.
[89] *Ibid.*, p. 301.　　[90] *Ibid.*, p. 303.

Next, of community of interests. On this subject, Renan's comments are brief and to the point.

Community of interests is assuredly a powerful bond among men. But do interests suffice to create a nation? I do not think so. Community of interests creates commercial agreements. But nationality is in part a matter of sentiment; it is body and soul at one and the same time. A *Zollverein* is no one's fatherland.[91]

But what of geography? Does it not, by means of rivers and mountains, furnish so-called "natural frontiers?" It is true that rivers and mountains have frequently marked the boundaries of states, both ancient and modern. But mountain ranges and river channels there are in vast numbers which have never constituted an international boundary. To Renan, the fact that a frontier was marked by a certain mountain or river did not cause it to be any more natural than if it had been marked by some other mountain or river. Indeed, it seemed to him that the whole doctrine of natural boundaries was one both arbitrary and dangerous. If a country were free to determine its own "natural" boundaries, there would be no end to pretexts for expanding frontiers and for violent seizures. Hence, as regards geography, Renan declares:

No, it is no more land than it is race which makes a nation. The land furnishes the *substratum,* the field of struggle and of labor; it is man who furnishes the soul. Man is everything in the formation of the sacred thing which we call a people. Merely material elements do not suffice. A nation is a spiritual principle produced by the profound complexities of history; it is a spiritual family, not a group determined by the configuration of the soil.[92]

Renan's definition has thus far progressed negatively, so to speak, by a process of elimination. He now undertakes a statement of his conception of the state in positive terms:

A nation is a soul, a spiritual principle. Two things which, truth to tell, are but one, go to make up this soul, this spiritual principle. The one is in the past, the other in the present. The first is the possession in common of a rich legacy of memories; the second is a matter of actual consent, of desire to live in a body, to make the most of a heritage jointly received. Man, gentlemen, has not been suddenly improvised. The nation, like the individual, is the outcome of a long past full of stress, of sacrifices and of devotion.[93]

The state being so largely a product of a people's past, Renan feels that there is some justification for the worship of ancestors since, as he observes, "our ancestors have made us what we are."[94] The foundation of the national

---

[91] *Discours et conferences,* p. 303. [92] *Ibid.,* p. 305. [93] *Ibid.,* p. 306. [94] *Ibid.*

INTRODUCTION 33

conception is to be discovered in a heroic past and the common desire to build upon that past.

> To share common glories in the past, to share a common will in the present; to have done great things together, to desire to do them again—such are the essential conditions for the establishment of a people. . . . To have shared in suffering, in joy, in hope—that is of greater worth than the establishment of customs duties and of frontiers adapted to strategic ideas. . . . I have just said "to have shared in suffering," and indeed suffering in common is more unifying than joy. When it comes to national memories, sorrows are more important than triumphs, for they impose duties and they require efforts in common.[95]

Renan is now ready to expand his definition of the state:

> A nation, therefore, is a vast solidarity formed as a result of the consciousness of the sacrifices which the people have made and of those they are ready to make again. It implies a past; and in the present it is summed up, moreover, in a tangible fact: the consent, the clearly expressed desire, to continue life in common.[96]

In such a conception of the state, the theory that might makes right has no place. This was implicit in the statement which Renan had made, and he now proceeds to render it express:

> A nation has no more right than a king to say to a province: "You belong to me, I am going to take you." For us a province consists of its inhabitants; and if any one has a right to be considered in such a matter, it is the inhabitant.[97]

Renan here pauses to glance toward the future. States, as he had shown, had not always existed. Are they to be a permanent human institution hereafter? Since man had chosen to establish states, might he not eventually choose some other form of political organization?

> Human wills change—but what does not change here below? Nations are not eternal things. They have had their beginning, they will have their end. They will be replaced, probably, by a European Confederation. But that is not the order of the century in which we live. At the present time the existence of nations is advantageous, is necessary. Their existence is the guarantee of liberty, which would be lost if the world had but one law and one lord.[98]

And finally, summing up his entire doctrine of nationality, Renan says:

> Man is not the slave of his race, of his language, of the courses of rivers, nor of mountain chains. A large group of men, sane of mind and warm of heart, creates a moral conscience which is called a nation. In so far as this moral conscience demonstrates its strength by sacrifices which require a renunciation

---

[95] *Ibid.*, pp. 306–7. [96] *Ibid.*, p. 307. [97] *Ibid.*, p. 308.
[98] *Ibid.*, pp. 308–9.

on the part of the individual for the sake of a community, it is legitimate, it has the right to exist. If doubts arise with respect to its frontiers, consult the populations in the disputed areas. They have a right to their own opinion in such a question.[99]

Renan himself supplies a measured judgment on the views which he sets forth. In the preface to the volume in which his essay on nationality is published, he informs the reader that it is this essay to which he attaches the most importance.

I have weighed each word in it with the greatest care; it is my profession of faith in those matters which pertain to human affairs; and when modern civilization shall have foundered in consequence of the fatal ambiguity of the words nation, nationality, race, I desire that these twenty pages may be remembered. I believe them to be entirely accurate. Wars of extermination are embarked upon because the salutary principle of free adherence is abandoned, because to nations, as to dynasties in former times, the right is granted of annexing provinces against their will.[100]

Alluding to the politicians who jeered at the principle which he advanced, that a people should have a right to decide whether or not it should be annexed by a neighboring state, Renan continues:

Let them triumph at their ease. It is we who are right. This fashion of grasping peoples by the throat and saying to them: "You speak the same language as we, therefore you belong to us"—such a fashion is indeed an evil one. Poor humanity, if treated too much like a herd of sheep, will in the end weary of such treatment.[101]

And Renan completes his noble conception of the human being in a passage which must be quoted in full:

Man does not belong either to his language or to his race: he belongs only to himself, for he is a free being, a moral being. We no longer admit that it is permissible to persecute peoples in order to make them change their religion; and to persecute them in order to make them change their language or their country seems to us equally wrong. We believe that it is possible to express noble feelings in all languages and, while speaking in various tongues, to follow the same ideal. Above and beyond language, race, natural frontiers, geography, we place the consent of populations, whatever may be their language, their race, their creed. Switzerland is perhaps the most justly established nation in Europe. But within its jurisdiction there are three or four languages, two or three religions, and Heaven knows how many races. For us a nation is a soul, a spirit, a spiritual family, arising, as regards the past, from memories, from sacrifices, from glories, often from sorrows and common regrets; and as regards the present, from a desire to continue living together. What consti-

---

[99] Renan, *Discours et conférences*, pp. 309–10.   [100] *Ibid.*, pp. ii–iii.   [101] *Ibid.*, p. iii.

INTRODUCTION 35

tutes a nation is not speaking the same language or belonging to the same ethnographic group; a nation is the result of having in the past performed great deeds together and of wishing to perform them again in the future.[102]

The preceding pages have been concerned chiefly with the state as a separate unit, with its inhabitants and the bonds which link them together—in short, with relationships within the state. There is, however, an external relationship, that among the governments of different states. Of such relations among states there are unfortunately two categories, one of peace and one of war. It is the hope of humanity that the relations of the future will be those of peace based upon justice, and that these will outlaw those of war based on force. There is no essential difference between the law that the states—meaning thereby governments and not "personified" states—should apply in their relations with one another and the law which they apply within their own jurisdictions. Justice is universal, whether applied between individuals, or between groups of individuals. What leads to unspeakable tragedies is the separation, in the relations of states, of the moral and spiritual element from the rules of their intercourse. Within the state there are organs of justice; for the settlement of disputes among the states there must also be organs of justice, if civilization is to endure. Fortunately, a twofold demonstration has been made of the possibility of the administering of justice among two or more states in controversy. Thus the Supreme Court of the United States adjudicates cases arising among states of the American Union (cases which are in fact if not in form international), and its decisions are accepted by the states as they are by individuals.[103] Thus also the Permanent Court of International Justice is a living proof of that justice which is the "bond of commonwealths." In very truth, the mere existence of these two international courts marks the beginning of a new era in which the conception of the state as a distinct, self-willed, and irresponsible personality will vanish from the scene and international law will be recognized as binding among politically organized groups of human beings, even as national laws are binding within those groups.

But it may be said—indeed it has been said and will doubtless continue to be said by the conservatives of the future—that controversies between

---

[102] *Ibid.*, pp. iii–iv.

[103] "The usual remedies between nations, war and diplomacy, being precluded by the federal union [i. e., the United States], it is necessary that a judicial remedy should supply their places. The Supreme Court of the Federation dispenses international law, and is the first great example of what is now one of the most prominent wants of civilized society, a real International Tribunal."—Mill, "Considerations on Representative Government," in *On Liberty, Representative Government, The Subjection of Women*, p. 395.

states are primarily political and, such being the case, that they should not and therefore will not be submitted to an international tribunal, any more than they would be submitted to a tribunal of one of the states in controversy.

Admitting for the purposes of argument that a specified controversy between states may be termed political, must we accept that terminology as unchangeable? There is excellent judicial authority for an answer in the negative. In the first attempted union of the erstwhile British Colonies, the Articles of Confederation[104] contained a provision in the ninth article for the arbitration of disputes among the American states through temporary tribunals of arbitration. A few years later the Constitution of the United States[105] provided that the jurisdiction of the Supreme Court of the United States was to extend—as it actually has extended—to controversies among states of the "more perfect union." It was inevitable that an objection should be made sooner or later to the exercise of this jurisdiction by the Supreme Court, on the ground that a particular dispute between the states in controversy was political and hence that the Supreme Court, being a judicial tribunal, could not accept jurisdiction and decide the controversy. In the course of time such an objection was made, and the Supreme Court was obliged to consider at length the origin and nature of political questions. The simple way in which the so-called political question might become a judicial one was shown in one of the long-drawn-out series of decisions of the Supreme Court of the United States. In the leading case of the *State of Rhode Island and Providence Plantations* v. *The Commonwealth of Massachusetts*,[106] the counsel who had made the objection to the jurisdiction of the Court was none other than Daniel Webster, then the leader of the American bar, who appeared for Massachusetts. The Supreme Court took the objection under consideration and its opinion, delivered by Mr. Justice Baldwin, is, it is believed, the most far-reaching decision that has been pronounced by that august tribunal—and in all likelihood the most profound opinion that it ever will pronounce, because the principle stated is applicable not merely to the particular case arising between two states of the American Union but to every question which might arise both between states of the American Union and between states of the international community. Mr. Justice Baldwin said in substance that controversies which arose

---

[104] Adopted in Philadelphia on Nov. 15, 1777, and ratified by the last of the thirteen states (Maryland) on March 1, 1781.
[105] Adopted Sept. 17, 1787; in effect from and after March 4, 1789.
[106] 12 Peters 657, 737, 738.

INTRODUCTION 37

between states were indeed political questions when the governments of such states decided them by political authority or through diplomatic negotiations, whereas an agreement of the states in controversy to submit the question to a court made of it a judicial question to be decided by the law applicable to the controversy. The learned Justice's opinion delivered in behalf of the Supreme Court of the United States will well repay a meticulous reading; but for present purposes the quotation of a few passages must suffice.[107]

The first passage deals with the status of the various American states, their independence of one another, and their subsequent agreement as to the settlement of disputes arising among them:

> In the declaration of independence, the states assumed their equal station among the powers of the earth, and asserted, that they could of right do, what other independent states could do: "declare war, make peace, contract alliances"; of consequence, to settle their controversies with a foreign power, or among themselves, which no state, and no power, could do for them. They did contract an alliance with France in 1778; and with each other, in 1781 [the Articles of Confederation of the Union]: the object of both was to defend and secure their asserted rights as states; but they surrendered to congress, and its appointed court, the right and power of settling their mutual controversies; thus making them judicial questions, whether they arose on "boundary, jurisdiction or any other cause whatever."

The second passage distinguishes political from judicial power:

> We are thus pointed to the true boundary line between political and judicial power and questions. A sovereign decides by his own will, which is the supreme law within his own boundary (6 Pet. 714; 9 Ibid. 748); a court or judge decides according to the law prescribed by the sovereign power, and that law is the rule for judgment.

But what happens if the sovereign powers in controversy should decide to use not political means but judicial means for the settlement of their disputes; in a word, how is the question converted from a political to a judicial status?

> The submission by the sovereigns, or states, to a court of law or equity, of a controversy between them, without prescribing any rule of decision, gives power to decide according to the appropriate law of the case (11 Ves. 294); which depends on the subject-matter, the source and nature of the claims of the parties, and the law which governs them.

---

[107] For a further discussion of this classic case, see especially the following volumes by J. B. Scott: *The United States of America: a Study in International Organization*, pp. 420-24; *Sovereign States and Suits before Arbitral Tribunals and Courts of Justice*, pp. 141-50; and *The Judicial Settlement of International Disputes*, pp. 29-37.

It may here be observed that the law which governs states in the international community is the law of nations, whether it be in the form of custom or of treaties. To continue, however, with Mr. Justice Baldwin's masterly analysis:

From the time of such submission, the question ceases to be a political one, to be decided by the *sic volo, sic jubeo,* of political power; it comes to the court, to be decided by its judgment, legal discretion and solemn consideration of the rules of law appropriate to its nature as a judicial question, depending on the exercise of judicial power.

Now for the conclusion, which gives to this decision its international application:

These considerations lead to the definition of political and judicial power and questions; the former is that which a sovereign or state exerts by his or its own authority, as reprisal and confiscation (3 Ves. 429); the latter is that which is granted to a court or judicial tribunal. So, of controversies between states; they are in their nature political, when the sovereign or state reserves to itself the right of deciding of it; makes it the "subject of a treaty, to be settled as between states independent," or "the foundation of representations from state to state." This is political equity, to be adjudged by the parties themselves, as contradistinguished from judicial equity, administered by a court of justice, decreeing the *equum et bonum* of the case, let who or what be the parties before them.

The process by which a controversy between states, political in its nature, was to become a judicial question was, in the case of the United States, an agreement on the part of the states in the Articles of Confederation, and subsequently in the Constitution of the United States, to submit their controversies to a tribunal of their own making: under the Confederation, a temporary court of arbitration; under the Constitution, a permanent tribunal—the Supreme Court of the United States. The first phase of this process the world at large is familiar with through the practice of entering into treaties—technically called *compromis*—by which the parties agree to submit their disputes to a court of arbitration of their own creation. As to the second phase, the international counterpart of the Supreme Court of the United States may be seen in the establishment in The Hague of a tribunal of their own creation by some fifty-odd powers of the world, which have agreed to submit their disputes of an international character to the Permanent Court of International Justice, stipulating in general terms the law to be applied to their settlement, and thus converting many erstwhile difficult political questions into simple judicial cases. The transforming agent giving to a political quarrel the dignity of a cause at law, to be decided judicially, is the agreement of the parties—in this case the statute of the Permanent Court of International Justice.

But the conservative of the future, like the conservative of today, may argue: What are you going to do with the decision of the international court when it is rendered? The court has no power to enforce it and no agency to call upon for its enforcement; hence, the conservative may continue, as the decision is unenforceable it is, in his opinion, futile.

The answer is that during the past century the Supreme Court of the United States has been rendering decisions from time to time in controversies arising between the states of the American Union. There is no provision for the enforcement of such decisions, yet every one has been complied with. The Permanent Court of International Justice at The Hague occupies, in effect, the same position in the world at large that the Supreme Court of the United States occupies in the American Union. The question, therefore, is one which history seems already to have answered. It is for the future to confirm that answer.

According to the original plan proposed by the commission for the establishment of the Permanent Court, the contracting parties were to agree to submit all their disputes of an international character to that tribunal. This proposal was objected to by some of the Powers, the reason apparently being that they had, or anticipated having, controversies which they did not wish to submit to judicial decision. In a word, these Powers seemed to be insuperably opposed to a process whereby all questions political in origin would have been transformed in advance into judicial questions, to be settled by due process of law. Therefore this provision was stricken from the draft, but by means of the so-called "optional clause"—by which the court shall assume jurisdiction of any and all disputes which the nations themselves designate in signing the clause—the provision has in great part been restored. At some future date the "Supreme Court" of the world will doubtless have unquestioned jurisdiction over all international disputes, just as the Supreme Court of the United States has jurisdiction over the disputes between the states of the United States.

From all of which the conclusion may fairly be drawn that in their external activities the so-called "sovereign states" of the international community are, from the standpoint of legal philosophy, in no way superior, before justice and before the law, to the individuals within the states who lay their disputes before courts established by governments of their own making, under laws to which they have assented.

If the state is to respond to the needs of a progressive humanity, it must not look backward to the ancient shibboleths of might and force, of irresponsible power, lawlessness, and oppression; nor can it remain static. It must be forward-looking, or, to use a term of the day, "dynamic." Otherwise it cannot measure up to humanity's ever advancing standard of justice and will fail of its purpose, which, in the language of the schoolmen, is the "common good," or in the language of the American Declaration of Independence, "Life, Liberty and the pursuit of Happiness." As progress is fundamental and inherent in our conception of civilization, so must it be also in our conception of the temporal state, the greatest of human social and political institutions.

The state has no finality, can have no perfected form. What we name democracy is a beginning and not an end. The state is an instrument of social man. Its changes are a record alike of his experience with it and of his own changing needs. But long ages have shaped it, and as we follow the process we learn something of the true nature of the instrument, alike of its potentialities and of its limitations.[108]

[108] MacIver, *The Modern State* (previously cited), Preface.

THE GREEK BACKGROUND

Chapter II

THE CONTRIBUTIONS OF ANCIENT GREECE

BEFORE EXAMINING THE POLITICAL AND LEGAL CONTRIBUTIONS OF GREECE TO the past, the present, and the future, it will be well to consider for a moment the Greek world of the fifth century before the Christian era. First of its physical extent. Ancient Greece was a small country, smaller in fact than Scotland, and, like Scotland, mountainous, with deeply indented coasts. It was a land suitable only for hardy inhabitants who could wrest a living from its thin soil or brave the sea in search of profits and adventure.

Politically considered, ancient Greece was not a unit; rather it was a series of units, of city-states varying in size and power and form of government, but all of them small communities which in the modern territorial sense could hardly be considered states at all. In this respect they were in striking contrast with the vast empires of the East, and with rapidly growing Rome, dominated by imperial ambitions. And as their size was insignificant when measured by modern standards, so also were their populations small as compared with the great cities of other lands and other times. In the middle of the fifth century before Christ, Athens, the most populous of the states of Greece, is said to have had some 300,000 residents, of whom possibly half were citizens and their families, the remaining population consisting of resident aliens and slaves. Many of the states were much smaller, a few thousand inhabitants dwelling in areas of a few square miles.

Of the historical reasons for such a minute division of political groups this is not the place to attempt an explanation. It must suffice to say that to the Greek the separate and independent status of his own particular community was fully as important as is the independence of his country to the citizen of the modern state. But where the citizens of our day too often display a lamentable indifference to political matters, the Greeks prized highly the opportunity afforded by the small size of their states to take an active and personal part in affairs of government. Moreover, they looked upon their own small communities as having not only a historical continuity but a distinct individuality, an individuality which they were ready to defend to the utmost. The city-state was on the whole a self-sufficient state, often democratic in form, always proud of its independence and of its special characteristics as compared with other states.

Professor Coleman Phillipson has admirably described the Greek conception of the state, and contrasted it with the Roman conception:[1]

> In the Hellenic world, where the science of politics advanced so rapidly, we have a remarkable illustration of the ancient conception of the State as a city-commonwealth. The State was co-extensive with the city—ἡ πιόλs. The city-state was an organized community enjoying independence, autonomy, αὐτονομία and dwelling usually within a walled town. Each city had its surrounding territory, large enough—but not unnecessarily extensive—to allow of the convenient assembly of its free citizens, for the purpose of exercising the rights and discharging the obligations incidental to citizenship. Thus Aristotle[2] insisted that a State should not be so large as to make it impossible or difficult for its free citizens to have ready access to each other, and be acquainted with one another. . . .
>
> Perfection within the circle, rather than extension of empire or territorial aggrandisement, was the Greek ideal. "Les Grecs n'ont jamais eu la pensée d'étendre leur domination sur le monde: leur idéal n'est pas la monarchie universelle, mais la cité."[3] This is a remarkable contrast to the Roman policy. To the Greek the mother-country was self-sufficient, it was considered an adequate sphere for the realization of his ideals, for the cherishing of metaphysical abstractions, for the worship of the beautiful, for the attainment of philosophic culture. The Roman, no less patriotic, chafed against territorial limitations, and thirsted for constant expansion of power and rule. For the Greek, intensity of the inner life and development was the aim; for the Roman, extension of the outer circle of life and material supremacy (of which aspiration towards universal dominion is an inevitable corollary) formed the object to be attained.

Yet this is not to say that the inhabitants of the city-state were without a feeling of unity with their Greek neighbors. On the contrary, all Greeks were keenly aware that they were of one race, language, religion and culture. This unity is perhaps best exemplified in two of their common possessions.

The first was the sanctuaries of Delphi and Olympia. At Delphi all of the states of ancient Greece aided in building the temple. At Delphi, too, their representatives met in the Amphictyonic League[4] each spring; and to

---

[1] *The International Law and Custom of Ancient Greece and Rome*, I, 28–9, 30.
[2] *Politics* VII. iv. 13.
[3] François Laurent, *Etudes sur l'histoire de l'humanité—Histoire du droit des gens et des relations internationales*, II, 3.
[4] On the objects and functions of the Amphictyonic Council, see Phillipson, *op. cit.*, II, 5–11.

Delphi also came individuals, as well as officials, from all of the Greek world to consult the oracle of Apollo. At Olympia were held, every four years, the Olympic Games, which drew contestants and audiences from every Greek city.[5]

The second of their common possessions was Homer, whose immortal writings were the legacy of all Greece.

His supreme genius was at once the inspiration of the poets and his verses the universal task of the schoolboy wherever Greek was spoken. But more than this: he wrote of Greeks as a whole, not of separate states, before indeed those states had crystallized into separate units; he belonged not to one district or section of the people but to all, his poems a common legacy to the Greek world, making for unity and fusion amid the variety and sharp divisions and quarrels of later times: the possession of all, as the Greek and Roman cultures are to modern Europe; the classics, but not the Bible, of the Greeks.[6]

As in Greece, so perhaps in a future still to be realized, the unity of the peoples may depend upon their greatest literature—the common heritage of civilization.

There was one manifestation of unity in Greece which was highly important in the development of Greek thought as well as in the maintenance of the Greek people as a distinct and, for centuries, an unmixed race. This was their attitude toward foreigners, whom they considered not merely as foreigners in our sense, but as barbarians. With other Greek states they might quarrel, enter into treaties, and have other relations, but they did so with a sense of dealing with their own kind.[7] Not so in relations with alien peoples. Foreigners were regarded as being for the most part on a

---

[5] While the Olympic was the chief of the festivals which the Greeks celebrated in common, there were several others which were regarded as belonging to all Greece, such as the Pythian Games (held at Delphi), the Isthmian (at the Isthmus of Corinth), and the Nemean (at Nemea in Argolis). For an account of these festivals, see Blümmer, *The Home Life of the Ancient Greeks* (trans. from the German by Alice Zimmern), chap. XI.

[6] Gomme, "The Greeks," in *European Civilization, Its Origin and Development*, ed. by Eyre, I, 544.

[7] In their relations with one another, it should be said, the Greek city-states developed something in the nature of international law. Thus Professor Phillipson (*op. cit.*, I, 30) says: "Though the Greeks spoke a common language, took part in the common games, consulted the same oracles and worshipped the gods in common, yet their separation into independent city-states rendered possible the evolution of law governing the relationships between them in their capacity of sovereign powers." In a subsequent passage (*ibid.*, I, 63–64), which may astonish those who regard the law between states as being wholly an invention of the modern world, the learned author describes at length the scope of this interstate law of Greece, showing that it was similar in content to our modern law of nations. Unfortunately this body of rules applicable between the Greek states was destined to fade with the development and conquests of imperial Rome.

lower plane of civilization—as indeed they usually were—and the Greek in their presence was ever conscious of pride in his superiority of race and culture.

The preference of the Greeks for small political communities, rather than for imperial domains like those of the despotic potentates on their eastern horizon, had numerous important consequences for the world of our day,[8] but none was more important than the fact, previously mentioned, that the small communities made it possible for each and every one of their inhabitants to feel an immediate and personal interest in the government of his state and to take a direct part in it. Government in the democratic states especially—and it is with those that political philosophy is chiefly concerned —became a matter for discussion not by a few but by all citizens.

This, so far as the records of history inform us, was something new in the world. Hitherto government had meant the rule of one—one in whose hands all the reins of power were gathered, who might be benevolent or cruel according to his nature, but whose will was supreme and unquestionable law for his subjects. He was himself the government, and in such a scheme of things subjects were not merely powerless but voiceless.

It was otherwise with the Greeks. Something, it may be, in their sharply sculptured land—seagirt and rugged, sun-lit for so many months of the year, beautiful to the eye though productive of but meager crops—endowed them with a great zest for living and with alert and curious minds. The problems of man and nature, of dwelling together in society, of understanding human relations, of discerning and protecting common interests—all these problems aroused in them an eager curiosity. *How* and *why* were questions which confronted them at every turn, and the tremendous task of finding answers was a challenge to their singularly clear and balanced minds. For tradition, blind faith, and apathetic acceptance they substituted an eternal questioning, lucid thinking, and courageous reasoning. "They attempted," says Professor Ernest Barker,[9] "to conceive of the universe in the light of reason." And because they were keenly interested in humanity, in human beings living in groups, and especially those in their own particular group, they were seldom content to leave to one or to a few the exclusive management of their

---

[8] "The greatest legacy which the Greeks have left to the after-world is their City State patriotism. The City State was the centre and inspiration of all their most characteristic achievements, culminating in the great outpouring of literature and art and practical energy, of great men and great deeds, in fifth-century Athens. The world has seen nothing comparable to it either before or since."—Alfred Zimmern, *The Greek Commonwealth, Politics and Economics in Fifth-Century Athens*, p. 58.

[9] *Greek Political Theory—Plato and His Predecessors*, p. 1.

common affairs.[10] What was the business of one should be the business of all. In the language of a distinguished authority on fifth-century Athens, "The State is in fact, as the Greeks called it, τὸ κοινόν, 'the common interest,' or, as the Romans said, 'Res publica,' 'everybody's business.'"[11] Imperfections, even absurdities, may become apparent in the strict application of such a theory, but it is at any rate far more in keeping with human dignity than abject and unquestioning submission to the despot, be he never so benign. The Greek recognition of the truth that man is not only a social but a political being lighted a great beacon for the future and revealed the complementary truth that it is the right and indeed the duty of men to take part in political life. These truths the Greeks saw with their accustomed clearness, and having seen them they boldly set their speculative minds to seeking the principles of government, principles with which they built the permanent foundations of political science.

The first valuable contribution the Greeks made to political study [says Sir Alfred Zimmern] [12] was that they invented it. It is not too much to say that, before fifth-century Greece, politics did not exist. There were powers and principalities, governments and subjects, but politics no more existed than chemistry existed in the age of alchemy. An imitation of an idea, as Plato has taught us, is not the same as an idea; nor is the imitation of a science the same as a science. Rameses and Nebuchadnezzar, Croesus the Lydian and Cyrus the Persian, ruled over great empires; but within their dominions there were no politics because there were no public affairs. There were only the private affairs of the sovereign and his ruling class. Government and all that pertained to it, from military service and taxation to the supply of women for the royal harem, was simply the expression of the power and desire of the ruler. The great advance made by Greece was to have recognized that public or common interests exist and to have provided, first for their management, and secondly for their study.

This was, as has been said, a radical departure from the past. Yet the Greeks were not radicals in the sense of breaking with tradition and established custom. Indeed, they felt a deep reverence for their traditions and for

---

[10] Thus Euripides has Theseus rebuke the herald from the autocratic king of Thebes for having sought a "despot" in Athens:
"First, stranger, with false note thy speech began,
Seeking a despot here. Our state is ruled
Not of one only man: Athens is free.
Her people in the order of their course
Rule year by year, bestowing on the rich
Advantage none; the poor hath equal right."
Suppliants, ll. 403-8.

[11] Alfred Zimmern, *op. cit.*, p. 63.

[12] "Political Thought," in *The Legacy of Greece,* ed. by Livingstone, pp. 331-32.

those unwritten laws which had claimed their obedience and respect for long centuries. They had the courage to look forward, to build for the future, but they built upon the past and with an eye always to the circumstances of their own day. What they built has endured; and being designed for a small city which was at the same time a state, the political principles which they set forth are still the foundation for the governing of villages, of cities, and of states.

It will be necessary later to examine these principles at some length. But for the moment it is more important to see them in actual use, and for this purpose no better summary description can be found than a passage from the funeral oration delivered by the great statesman and orator, Pericles:

> We live under a form of government which does not emulate the institutions of our neighbours; on the contrary, we are ourselves a model which some follow, rather than the imitators of other peoples. It is true that our government is called a democracy, because its administration is in the hands, not of the few, but of the many; yet while as regards the law all men are on an equality for the settlement of their private disputes, as regards the value set on them it is as each man is in any way distinguished that he is preferred to public honours, not because he belongs to a particular class, but because of personal merits; nor, again, on the ground of poverty is a man barred from a public career by obscurity of rank if he but has it in him to do the state a service. And not only in our public life are we liberal, but also as regards our freedom from suspicion of one another in the pursuits of every-day life; for we do not feel resentment at our neighbour if he does as he likes, nor yet do we put on sour looks which, though harmless, are painful to behold. But while we thus avoid giving offence in our private intercourse, in our public life we are restrained from lawlessness chiefly through reverent fear, for we render obedience to those in authority and to the laws, and especially to those laws which are ordained for the succour of the oppressed and those which, though unwritten, bring upon the transgressor a disgrace which all men recognize.[13]

Thus was the city-state, as exemplified by Athens, depicted in the year 431 B. C. in a description which, fortunately for us, was recorded by Pericles' contemporary, Thucydides, whose narrative of the Peloponnesian War ranks him, in the opinion of many, as the greatest historian of all time. There was no despotism in the city-state of Pericles, but there was democracy: government by politically trained citizens,[14] equality before the law, preferment

---

[13] Thucydides II. xxxvii.

[14] "The Athenian Democracy made a greater number of citizens fit to use power than could be made fit by any other system. No mistake can be greater than to suppose that the popular Assembly at Athens was a mob such as gathers at some English elections, or such as the Assembly of the Roman Tribes undoubtedly became in its later days. It was not an indiscriminate gathering together of every male human being to be found in the streets of Athens.

for merit instead of wealth and rank, and respect for duly constituted authorities, for enlightened laws, and for those fundamental rules which were universally recognized. Small though the city-state was, "few States," says Professor Barker,[15] "have occupied as large an area of the kingdom of the mind, and few have unfolded so much the dignity of the human spirit, as some of the cities of ancient Greece."

What manner of people was it, we of a later age may wonder, who could have given to the world so lofty and so permanent a standard? An anecdote as true in spirit as it is charming in form, which is narrated by Miss Edith Hamilton,[16] may serve to answer this question.

Once upon a time—the exact date cannot be given but it was not far from 450 B. C.—an Athenian fleet cast anchor near an island in the Ægean as the sun was setting. Athens was making herself mistress of the sea and the attack on the island was to be begun the next morning. That evening the commander-in-chief, no less a one, the story goes, than Pericles himself, sent an invitation to his second in command to sup with him on the flag-ship. So there you may see them sitting on the ship's high poop, a canopy over their heads to keep off the dew. One of the attendants is a beautiful boy and as he fills the cups Pericles bethinks him of the poets and quotes a line about the "purple light" upon a fair cheek. The younger general is critical: it had never seemed to him that the color adjective was well chosen. He preferred another poet's use of rosy to describe the bloom of youth. Pericles on his side objects; that very poet had elsewhere used purple in the same way when speaking of the radiance of young loveliness. So the conversation went on, each man capping the other's quotation with one as apt. The entire talk at the supper table turned on delicate and fanciful points of literary criticism. But, none the less, when the battle began the next morning, these same men, fighting fiercely and directing wisely, carried the attack on the island.

The literal truth of the charming anecdote I cannot vouch for [says Miss Hamilton], but it is to be noted that no such story has come down to us about the generals of any other country except Greece. No flight of fancy has ever

---

Citizenship was something definite; if it was a right, it was also a privilege. The citizen of Athens was in truth placed in something of an aristocratic position; he looked down upon the vulgar herd of slaves, freedmen, and unqualified residents, much as his own plebeian fathers had been looked down upon by the old Eupatrids in the days before Kleisthenês and Solôn. The Athenian Assembly was an assembly of citizens, of ordinary citizens without sifting or selection; but it was an assembly of citizens among whom the political average stood higher than it ever did in any other state."—Freeman, *History of Federal Government in Greece and Italy*, ed. by Bury, pp. 29–30.

It may be added that according to the democratic theories obtaining in Athens, all citizens were presumed to be properly qualified to hold the majority of state offices, and appointments to such offices were therefore made by lot. In the case of certain offices, however, it was recognized that qualifications of an exceptional order were needed, and hence these positions were filled by election.

[15] *Greek Political Theory* (previously cited), p. 20.   [16] *The Greek Way*, pp. 78–80.

conceived of a discussion on color-adjectives between Cæsar and the trusty Labienus on the eve of crossing the Rhine, nor, we may feel reasonably assured, will any soaring imagination in the future depict General Grant thus diverting himself with General Sherman. That higher truth which Aristotle claimed for poetry over history is here perfectly exemplified. The little story, however apocryphal, gives a picture true to life of what the Athenians of the great age of Athens were like. Two cultivated gentlemen are shown to us, of a great fastidiousness, the poets their familiar companions, able the evening before a battle to absorb themselves in the lesser niceties of literary criticism, but, with all this, mighty men of action, soldiers, sailors, generals, statesmen, any age would be hard put to it to excel. The combination is rarely found in the annals of history. It is to be completely civilized without having lost in the process anything of value.

But the small states of Greece, like small states throughout much of the long narrative of history, were doomed to lose their independence. The tiny communities on the peninsula and on the adjacent islands of the Aegean Sea were unable to live long at peace with one another, or with the foreign empires bent on conquest and the unification of the world under the rule of might. There was, however, a fundamental difference between war among the Greek communities and war with invaders. The interstate conflict consisted of battles and campaigns within the Greek world, not precisely a family affair, but one in which the parties shared a common racial, religious, and cultural heritage; and the consequences, whether in victory or defeat, were likely to be of a more or less temporary nature. But war against invading hordes was a vastly more serious matter. To suffer defeat in a conflict with a neighboring state would be a misfortune, but the conquerer would seldom be inclined to disrupt a manner of living and of government similar to his own. Life would go on much the same as before. To suffer conquest by foreign legions, however, meant not merely material destruction but the imposition of "barbarian" government and the loss of all that the Greeks valued most highly. It is not surprising, therefore, that in the face of a common danger from foreign invasion most of the Greek states submerged their differences and presented a united front against the enemy from without. More than once they fought stubbornly and successfully against what seemed to be overwhelming odds, and the tales of their courageous struggles will ring down the ages as long as humanity endures. But whether they submitted to the superior forces of neighbors or whether they successfully asserted their superiority over other Greek states, only to find themselves confronted by powerful foreign enemies, in the end they yielded to the inevitable and became subject peoples. The cities, to be sure, remained civic units whose inhabitants felt for them a loyalty quite different from their personal allegiance to a distant king or emperor. But the old independence and the pride in democratic liberty were gone.

The story of bitterly fought wars, of heroic resistance, and final surrender belongs to the great sagas of history. Here they have been touched upon only because they affected profoundly the heritage of political thought which ancient Greece passed on to posterity.

As the necessity for unity in the face of a common danger became evident to the Greeks, their exclusiveness gradually diminished; and in the course of time they lost much of their sense of superiority to all other peoples. Slowly, with the passing of the independent city-states, a new conception of humanity began to dawn upon them, a conception which eventually rejected the narrow limitations of race and geography and revealed a universal society made up, so the Stoics taught, not of Greeks and barbarians, but of human beings as citizens of the world.[17]

Meanwhile the civilization of Greece had already begun to spread. Trade and travel were the first channels through which Hellenism seeped into other lands. Colonization continued the process, and later the irresistible armies of the Macedonian Empire spread Hellenism far and wide, although mingling with it strange elements and leaving it often as a veneer so thin that it soon vanished. Later still, and most important of all for the modern world, the Romans found much to admire in Greek civilization and, as was their nature, they took what they wanted. Through Rome and subsequently through the Byzantine Empire, the Greek heritage descended to the medieval world, to be born afresh, as it were, in all its classical strength during the Renaissance, when the thought and the ideals of the ancient Greeks became a dominant force in our modern civilization.

[17] The Greeks' "pride of race," said Sir Paul Vinogradoff, "begins to undergo a remarkable transformation towards the end of the classical age. Instead of the racial, it is the cultural aspect that is thrust into the foreground, and hereby a transition is provided to a different world in which Hellenism appears not as a national peculiarity, but as a badge of civilization. One of the forerunners of the Hellenistic age, Isokrates, has expressed this in as many words [Isokr. iv. 50]: 'Our city has so far surpassed the rest of mankind in power of thought and speech that her disciples have become the teachers of the rest; she has made the name of Hellene seem to belong no longer to the race, but to the mind, so that the name is given to those who share in our culture more than to those who share the common blood.' "—*The Collected Papers of Paul Vinogradoff*, II, 269; this passage is also contained in Vinogradoff's *Outlines of Historical Jurisprudence*, II, 164.

"The political conception of ancient society was the apotheosis of the state, while Stoicism proclaimed that conscience and spirit are superior to the state. The essential idea of ancient society was to confine civilization within the limits of a single city, while Stoicism extended the bounds of that city to the very ends of the earth. The ancient world was to vanish under the influence of this idea, opening the way to a vaster and more human world."—Castelar, *La civilización en los cinco primeros siglos del Christianismo*, III, 59.

The nature and extent of our debt to Greece can be adequately summarized only by one who is an indisputable authority on the subject. Such an authority is Gilbert Murray, for many years Regius Professor of Greek in the University of Oxford. In a few illuminating sentences he reveals how much we owe to the people who, some twenty-five centuries ago, faced the fundamental problems of human life with a clear and level vision and thought them straight through to logical and still unassailable conclusions.

The seeds of almost all that we count best in human progress [says Professor Murray[18]] were sown in Greece. The conception of beauty as a joy in itself and as a guide in life was first and most vividly expressed in Greece, and the very laws by which things are beautiful or ugly were to a great extent discovered there and laid down. The conception of Freedom and Justice, freedom in body, in speech and in mind, justice between the strong and the weak, the rich and the poor, penetrates the whole of Greek political thought, and was, amid obvious flaws, actually realized to a remarkable degree in the best Greek communities. The conception of Truth as an end to pursue for its own sake, a thing to discover and puzzle out by experiment and imagination and especially by Reason, a conception essentially allied with that of Freedom and opposed both to anarchy and to blind obedience, has perhaps never in the world been more clearly grasped than by the early Greek writers on science and philosophy. One stands amazed sometimes at the perfect freedom of their thought. Another conception came rather later, when the small City States with exclusive rights of citizenship had been merged in a larger whole: the conception of the universal fellowship between man and man. Greece realized soon after the Persian war that she had a mission to the world, that Hellenism stood for the higher life of man as against barbarism, for Aretê, or Excellence, as against the mere effortless average. First came the crude patriotism which regarded every Greek as superior to every barbarian; then came reflection, showing that not all Greeks were true bearers of the light, nor all barbarians its enemies; that Hellenism was a thing of the spirit and not dependent on the race to which a man belonged or the place where he was born: then came the new word and conception ἀνθρωπότης, *humanitas,* which to the Stoics made the world as one brotherhood. No people known to history clearly formulated these ideals before the Greeks, and those who have spoken the words afterwards seem for the most part to be merely echoing the thoughts of old Greek men.

Certain preliminary observations are advisable before attempting an examination of the great Greek contributions to the sciences of government and law. The inhabitants of the city-states, as has been said, were keenly interested in the management of their public affairs. Their direct participa-

---

[18] "The Value of Greece to the Future of the World," in *The Legacy of Greece,* ed. by Livingstone, pp. 21–22.

tion in various phases of government was possible because the communities were small in size. But that alone will not account for an interest in public matters so strong that it often demanded the sacrifice of personal rights. In our modern conception of government the rights of individuals play an important part, so much so that we are forever seeking a compromise between the demands of individual rights and the public interests of the community. We proceed in building our political institutions from the individual to the state. The Greeks, on the other hand, gave the common interests first consideration, placing them above individual rights.[19] To them, therefore, the administration of the government, affecting as it did the common welfare and the very life of the state for which they felt so strong a patriotic attachment, was a matter of supreme importance. This does not mean that the individual was ignored by the Greeks as he so often was by the rest of the ancient world. But to us of a later age, accustomed to the creeds of individualism, Greek political philosophy seems prone at times to underemphasize the rights of the man in considering the duties of the citizen.

Yet this defect—from our point of view—is largely compensated by the fact that to the Greeks in their Golden Age government was, with some exceptions, a constitutional procedure, with the citizens in public assembly as the ultimate authority, with an administration of the state by chosen officials with specifically limited powers, and with law supreme over both lawmaking and law-enforcing agencies.

It is fitting [says Hypereides[20]] that not the threats of a man but the clear tones of the law should be master of the happy. . . . The safety of the citizens should not rest upon those who flatter the powerful and deceive the people, but upon confidence in the laws.

Therefore it is but natural that the city-states, holding to such a conception of government, seldom suffered for long the rule of despots, and that they proved to be fertile fields for the development of political thought.

Much as they respected law, however, the Greeks showed little interest in it as a formal science. The philosophical bases of jurisprudence—morality, justice, and equity, and later equality and liberty—they pondered deeply and discussed at great length, and their views on these matters are and must

---

[19] "While modern thought starts from the rights of the individual, and conceives the State as existing to secure the conditions of his development, Greek thought starts from the right of the State to a self-governing and self-sufficing existence, and conceives the individual as existing to further that existence."—Barker, *Greek Political Theory*, p. 27.

[20] *Funeral Oration*. Trans. by Wallace E. Caldwell, in *Hellenic Civilization,* ed. by G. W. Botsford and E. G. Sihler (New York, 1915), p. 612. This volume is one of a series edited by James T. Shotwell under the general title, *Records of Civilization: Sources and Studies.*

always be fundamental to an enlightened legal science.[21] But when the Greek philosophers theorized about law, they usually thought of it as a branch of political science, of the art of governing human beings in society. Thus, even when Plato wrote *The Laws,* he made that masterpiece of his old age more a political than a legal treatise. There is much to be said for such a conception, especially if we consider the tendency, so frequently encountered, to separate law from life and to exalt it as an end in itself. The Greeks had a strong sense of measure and proportion. They were not specialists in the modern sense[22] because they were always aware of the interrelation of all of the factors of life, and of the necessity for harmonizing those factors. They saw the larger whole, and they lacked the specialists' enthusiasm for isolating the parts—a laudable enthusiasm for the most part, but one which sometimes leads to overemphasis and unfortunate distortions of the truth. To them law was not an end, but a means for promoting goodness and justice among citizens as a part of the larger purpose of the state, which was not "life only," but "a good life."[23] The Greeks, it must never be forgotten, considered politics to be an ethical science because their state was essentially a moral society directed toward a moral end, the "good life" of its inhabitants. The political thought produced by the city-state, Professor Barker observes,[24] "conceived the State as a moral association, and, as a result, approached its subject from an ethical point of view." The law which they recognized as their sovereign in the state was therefore "a complex of ethical rules,"[25] based firmly upon fundamental and universally recognized principles of morality, and it was from these principles that law derived its binding force. Law, in short, was a means of applying these principles to the multitudinous relations of human beings dwelling together in society for the sake of the "good life."

[21] "The philosopher, the theorizer, influenced the statesman and the legislator more in Greece than elsewhere. It could scarcely have been otherwise, as the Hellenic temperament was marked by an untiring curiosity and yearning to experience the unknown, to apply at once in practice the abstract constructions of the intellect."—Phillipson, *op. cit.,* I, 33.

[22] See, however, mention of Plato's theory of division of labor, *infra,* p. 78.

[23] Aristotle *Politics* III, 9, 6. See also Plato's *Crito* 48, where the same thought is brought out by Socrates:
Socrates. . . . I should like to know whether I may say . . . that not life, but a good life, is to be chiefly valued?
Crito. Yes, that also remains unshaken.
Socrates. And a good life is equivalent to a just and honourable one—that holds also?
Crito. Yes, it does.

[24] *Greek Political Theory,* p. 11. The term morality is used here and throughout the present volume in the sense of ethics, as that word was employed by the Greeks.

[25] Vinogradoff, *Outlines of Historical Jurisprudence* (previously cited), II, 19.

CONTRIBUTIONS OF ANCIENT GREECE

Therefore, it is not surprising that to the Greeks the spirit of the law was more important than the letter. They felt no need, in their courts, for judges learned in all the fine points of the law, since the important element in the settlement of legal disputes was simply to distinguish between right and wrong and to administer justice. Thus it was that in Athens cases were decided by arbitrators (who might be any citizens of the age of sixty) or were heard and decided by juries of citizens, who not only rendered a verdict but assessed the penalty.[26] Professional advocates there were, but they were experts in persuading juries, not jurists in the Roman or the modern sense. This does not mean that the Greeks had established no systems of law. They devoted much attention to legislation,[27] and they had, for example, well-defined branches of law relating to property and heredity, to contracts, and especially mercantile matters; but the development of jurisprudence as such was left to the Romans, who were interested, as the Greeks never were, in law as a science.

A perfect summary of the growth of law in Greece, and its relation to the development of Roman law, has been given by one of the greatest jurists of our day—who is, indeed, the acknowledged "prince" of legal

[26] "The Greeks did not allow their law to lapse into abstruse technicality and to become a tool of professional jurists. Greek law in its application was meant to be a frame for public opinion. In Athens, at any rate, the remarkable experiment was made of handing over the administration of justice and the application of legal rules to batches of 201, 401, 1,001 jurors. The principle on which heliasts were called to decide cases was the same as that which has made the institution of the jury the usual device for deciding questions of fact in modern criminal procedure. It is the view that justice should be administered to the members of a community in accordance with the standards of morality and common sense prevailing in this community. But the Greeks went much further than we do, and entrusted to their many-headed juries not only questions of fact and responsibility, but questions of law which affected the distribution and enforcement of rights. . . . on the whole, I confess that the wonder seems to be not that the heliasts should have been sometimes led astray or that they proved unable to analyse doctrine in the same way as this was done by Roman jurists, but rather that they should have grappled with their task as well as they did. These large tribunals were admittedly free from corruption, and, what is more, they were well able to appreciate the acute dialectics of Isaios or the refined literary skill of Hypereides. Apart from that, although learned jurisprudence in the sense of the Romans could not arise on such soil, the courts succeeded in treating problems of property, possession, obligation, association, etc., in the light of advanced notions of justice, fairness, and social expediency. This explains why Greek legal rules, instead of disappearing before the more strict and technical doctrines of Roman jurists, came to modify the latter in many ways: the more we study Roman Law, the larger is the share we have to assign to the influence of Greek custom and Greek legislation."—*Ibid.*, II, 11, 12.

[27] "Apart from certain wilfully backward cities like Sparta, the Greek world was a world of adventure, migration, commercial intercourse; the psychology of the race was marked by definite and ever-recurring traits—by a highly sensitive, artistic spirit, by eager exploration both on the theoretical and on the practical side, by a sense of harmony and measure. Starting from common family arrangements, the various cities carried out the process of law-making on analogous lines."—*Ibid.*, II, 6.

philosophers in the United States—Dean Roscoe Pound, of the Harvard Law School. Observing that[28] "the definition of law has been one of the battlegrounds of jurisprudence," and that it is therefore advisable to "look into the history of that definition," Dean Pound continues:

But there is a special reason for so doing in that definitions set forth strikingly and concisely the ideas of law held by jurists at different times and places. Thus when we examine their formulas we are in fact investigating the history of the idea of law.

While it might be expected that in such an examination we should turn first to the Roman formulas, since it was in Rome that "a strict law and a legal profession" were first developed, Dean Pound reminds us that "the first Roman definitions of law are founded upon Greek originals." Hence he begins "by looking at Greek law and Greek definitions of law as determined thereby."

Greek law is the law of city-states. But social control in the city-states was still largely that of kin-organized societies. Legal institutions lag behind political institutions, and Greek legal institutions were in transition from what Vinogradoff calls tribal law to the law of a politically organized society. It was at most tending toward but by no means had attained a stage of strict law. At Rome after the Twelve Tables, the pontifical college went on with its function of custody of the legal tradition and developed a function of interpretation of the written law. Following the secularization of law, what had been a monopoly of priests became a monopoly of professional lawyers. At Athens the official interpreters ceased for practical purposes to be more than advisers as to procedure. There were professional speech writers (one cannot quite say advocates), but not professional lawyers. Hence there was no juristic development either of tradition or of enacted precepts. There was only legislative development, and for want of a uniform logical interpretation legislative precepts were much at large.[29] The customary law was codified and there was at least the beginning of conscious legislative lawmaking on matters of private law. Indeed, in cities of a highly democratic polity conscious legislative lawmaking was carried a long way. Hence to understand Greek thinking about law we must remember four points: (1) It is the thinking of philosophers or of orators, not of jurists.[30] (2) It is influenced by the contrast of politically

---

[28] A rewriting of the portion of the article "Theories of Law," 22 *Yale Law Journal*, 114, having to do with Greek law, published with the permission of the author in advance of sec. 38 of a forthcoming treatise on jurisprudence.

[29] "Bonner puts this well. *Lawyers and Litigants in Ancient Athens*, 104 ff. But it was not so much that enactments were not well drafted as that there were no means of developing and fixing their meaning. No text can be self-sufficient."

[30] "The nearest to a law book is the treatise of Theophrastus (372–287 B. C., the successor of Aristotle) on laws. Cf. the earliest Roman books. The glossary to the orators by Harpocration (not earlier than the second century A. D.) cites the opinion of a Roman jurist of the time of Hadrian or Antoninus Pius on a question as to the scope of a Greek action discussed by Isaeus, Lysias, and Demosthenes."

CONTRIBUTIONS OF ANCIENT GREECE

declared or politically made law and tribal ethical custom in what was still an undifferentiated social control. (3) Enacted law was in origin declared custom and was largely felt to be declared custom, and yet in cities of a democratic polity was felt to be consciously enacted. (4) There was a growing sense of law as a conscious product of wisdom.

After discussing briefly the nature of Greek definitions of law, Dean Pound states that after the time of Solon, Athenian law "purported to be a conscious product of human wisdom." But by this time the philosophers had become interested in the relations of such law "to the ideas of right and wrong," and they gave much attention to the problem.

Was an act right, they asked, because it conformed to law, or were both the act and the law right if and in so far as they coincided with an absolute and eternal standard above the law.[31] One answer was that what corresponded to the latter standard was natural, but what corresponded only to the humanly imposed customary or legal standard was conventional right.[32] Others held that justice rested on convention or enactment rather than upon nature.[33]

The consequence is, as the learned jurist points out, that in Greek thought two ideas developed concerning law.

On the one hand there is the idea of law as human wisdom, ascertained and promulgated through the state. On the other hand there is the idea of law as the manifestation of an immutable and eternal right and justice. In other words, there is the idea of *lex* and the idea of *ius*. This double aspect of Greek thinking about law is due in part to the peculiar problem of social control in the Greek city-state involved in the perennial conflict between oligarchies, hewing to the old traditions, and the *demos* seeking to use political power as a means of maintaining a standard of life.[34] But it is largely due to the circumstance that Greek law in the classical period was in form a body of enactment and yet had become a subject of philosophical speculation instead of a subject of exposition by lawyers. Greek jurists did not arise to develop the law by legal reasoning. Instead Roman jurists put the ideas of the Greek philosophers into practical effect.

In our appreciation of the remarkable legal ability of the Romans, however, we may all too easily minimize the debt of Roman jurisprudence to

---

[31] "Compare Socrates in Xenophon *Memorabilia* IV. ii. 5–15 (e. g., IV. ii. 12: 'for I say that which is legal is just') with Aristotle *Nicomachean Ethics* V. vii. 1: 'Of the politically just, one part is natural and the other legal. The natural is that which everywhere is equally valid, and does not depend on being or not being received. But the legal is what originally was indifferent, but having been enacted is so no longer.'"

[32] "Aristotle *Rhetoric* I. xiii. 1; Aristotle *Nicomachean Ethics* V. vii. 1. See also the Stoic doctrine as stated by Diogenes Laertius VII. 128: 'They say that the just exists by nature and not by enactment.'"

[33] "Aristippus, quoted by Diogenes Laertius II. 93: 'that nothing is just or good or base by nature, but by law and convention.' Justice is not transgressing any of the enactments of the state in which one is a citizen.' Antiphon, the Sophist, in *Oxyrynchus Papyri* XI. 1364."

[34] "See Pound, *Introduction to the Philosophy of Law*, pp. 20–26."

58   CONTRIBUTIONS OF ANCIENT GREECE

the Greeks. As will be seen in a subsequent chapter,[35] the Stoic doctrine greatly influenced the conception of the *ius naturae,* which penetrated and profoundly altered the law of Rome. Greek legislation, too, as well as Greek theory, contributed much to Roman law. When the Twelve Tables were to be drawn up, for example, it is said that a Roman embassy was sent to Greece and to the Greek settlements in southern Italy to study their legislation. How much of Greek law was actually included in the Tables it is difficult to determine, but we know that Greek definitions were included in the *Digest* and we have it on good authority that the Romans borrowed to some extent from the laws of Solon.[36] In any event it may be safely assumed that Rome laid Greek law under contribution, just as it did Greek literature and art.[37]

Finally, it must not be overlooked that in developing their political theories the Greek philosophers had before them two examples of government in particular, which differed in important respects. The first was the government of Athens, where, to quote again from Professor Barker,[38] "there was a highly developed political life, with its appropriate and regular organs, which had attained to full self-consciousness." There freedom was

[35] *Infra,* chap. VII.

[36] The three most famous of the Greek definitions in the *Digest* are those of Demosthenes, Chrysippus, and Theophrastus (I. iii. 2, 3, 6). On the provisions borrowed from the laws of Solon, see the statements of Gaius in *Digest* X. i. 13 and XLVI. xxii. 4; also Cicero's remarks in his *Laws* II. xxiii. 59 and xxv. 64.

[37] "It is through the Romanization of the Hellenes," Professor Rudolph Sohm tells us in his admirable volume on Roman law, "that the Hellenization of the Roman Empire and Roman law was promoted. Within the large area covered by Greek civilization, Greek law had attained to full development and, at the same time, to a strong unity. With the discovery of the papyri, whose value in legal history is being daily more appreciated, the legal life of the Egyptian nation, of Greece and of Rome, has during the last generation emerged vividly and freshly before our eyes from the desert sands of Egypt—a legal life remarkable for its creative power and the abundance of its content. It was obvious that so highly developed a legal system could not be set aside by Caracalla by a mere stroke of the pen. The Greek and likewise other oriental national law survived in the practice of the mass of the people, in spite of the Roman imperial law. But this was not all. It was precisely through Pan-romanism, which brought the entire Hellenic world under the sway of the Roman imperial law, that Greek legal ideas were given free scope to react, in their turn, on the further development of Roman law. After the fourth century the center of gravity of the Empire shifted more and more decidedly to the Greek East. Hellenism with its cosmopolitan character came to be the victor over old Romanism. It was no longer the traditions of Rome and Italy, but the views and requirements of Greek provincialism that surrounded and influenced the emperor of Constantinople. The provinces had ousted the old premier country and Hellenism had displaced Romanism. And so, too, it came to pass that the *jus gentium* finally displaced the old *jus civile.* Under the influence of Greek law the development of Roman law was completed: from the law of the city there was created a universal law."— Sohm, *Institutionen, Geschichte und System des Römischen Privatrechts,* ed. by Mitteis, pp. 118–20.

[38] *Greek Political Theory,* p. 13.

claimed [he continues] as a birth-right; and by freedom men understood the right of "living as one liked" in social matters, and the sovereignty of the majority in political affairs. Equality was a watchword; and equality meant "Isonomy, or equality of law for all; Isotimy, or equal regard paid to all; and Isagoria, or equal freedom of speech."

Nor was culture forgotten, for "Athens prided herself on being a *Kulturstaat*." The second example was Sparta, whose cultural ideals were much narrower and whose consuming interest was war.

None the less Sparta had a great attraction for the philosopher, because almost alone of Greek States, she enforced a "training" (ἀγωγή) which preserved the "tone" of her constitution, and because by this means she was able to teach each individual Spartan to regard himself as a part of the social organism. Here there was a principle carried to its conclusion with what seemed a thorough and remorseless logic; and the philosopher could not but admire the philosophic State. Here the sense of "limit," which meant so much to the Greek, was a living and active thing: if Athens boasted of εὐτραπελία Sparta could boast of her εὐνομία; while the stability of a constitution which had stood secure for hundreds of years was something to which the versatile Athenian was entirely strange. No wonder therefore that the *Republic* is, to some extent, a "Laconising" pamphlet—a critique of Athens, and a laudation of Spartan logic, Spartan training, and Spartan subjugation of the individual to the State.[39]

There was a further reason, adds Professor Barker, for thus holding up Sparta as an example:

Athens had sinned, in Plato's eyes, in the want of training for politics which disfigured her politicians: she had sinned still more because the spirit of self had invaded her politics, and the individual, in his claim for a false freedom and a false equality, had set himself up in arms against the State. Her salvation, and that of Greece, was to be found in following Spartan example, so far at any rate as to train the citizen for his work and to inculcate upon him his duty to the State. But Sparta too had her faults, of which Plato is not unaware, and which Aristotle trenchantly exposes. The principle she had adopted was of the narrowest: she had made success in war the end and aim of her existence. Her training only produced a limited and stunted type of character; and underneath a fair show of ascetic loyalty to the State there lurked not a little self-indulgence. The width of Athenian and the concentration of Spartan character needed to be blended to form the ideal Greek; and the ideal city must reconcile the expression which the individual attained in Athens with the order and the unity which the State enforced in Sparta.[40]

Fortunately the political thinking of the Greeks was not limited by the political facts of their day. They planned for the future, and for something

[39] *Ibid.*, pp. 13–14. [40] *Ibid.*, p. 14.

better. Their thought "is made of the stuff of general humanity, and the ideals which it attained will always remain ideals for humanity at large."[41]

The political power of Athens waned and disappeared; kingdoms rose and fell; centuries rolled away,—they did but bring fresh triumphs to the city of the poet and the sage. There at length the swarthy Moor and Spaniard were seen to meet the blue-eyed Gaul; and the Cappadocian, late subject of Mithridates, gazed without alarm at the haughty conquering Roman. Revolution after revolution passed over the face of Europe, as well as of Greece, but still she was there,—Athens, the city of mind,—as radiant, as splendid, as delicate, as young, as ever she had been.[42]

[41] Barker, *Greek Political Theory*, p. 15.
[42] Newman, "The Idea of a University," in *Essays English and American*, p. 41.

Chapter III

SOCRATES (c. 469–400 b. c.)

The Greeks as individuals were not fond of solitude. They were sociable people who enjoyed mingling in company, whether in small groups or in large gatherings. And it is not surprising that, in a land where good fellowship was the rule and taciturnity the exception, there was also a spirit of equality abroad which, although it did not eliminate social distinctions, made for free intercourse among all classes and an absence of that reserve which in northern peoples stifles a natural and friendly interest in the affairs of others. No doubt the climate of Greece had much to do with this habit of sociability. During many months of the year it was decidedly pleasanter to be in the open than to remain indoors, and therefore Greek men spent comparatively little time around their own hearthstones—although it must be admitted that they expected the women of their families to stay at home. Xenophon's Athenian "gentleman" declares: "I certainly do not pass my time indoors." That was his wife's place, for woman's nature, he considered, was adapted "to the indoor and man's to the outdoor tasks and cares."[1] Therefore, leaving his wife with her household cares, "he went out cheerfully," Professor Zimmern observes,[2] "to spend his day in the fields, or the market-place, or the wrestling-ground, or the law-courts, or the assembly, or wherever else duty or pleasure called him." And whatever his destination might be, he was most likely to fall in with acquaintances or friends en route; and that meant discussion about matters of common interest, for the Greeks were notable talkers with an appreciation of leisure that enabled them to develop to a high degree the art of conversation.

The city was not only a unit of government, it was also a club. It was not only politically self-governed: it had also (what made its self-government possible) a large freedom of social discussion. The home meant much less to the Greeks than it does to us: the open life of the market-square meant much more. In the frequent contact of such a life men of all classes met and talked with one another; and the democratic ideals of equality and of freedom of speech found their natural root.[3]

---
[1] *Oeconomicus* vii. 3, 22.   [2] *The Greek Commonwealth* (previously cited), p. 60.
[3] Barker, *Greek Political Theory* (previously cited), p. 19.

What were the matters of common interest about which they conversed? Farming, art, commerce—these would hold the attention of some. Others might talk of athletic sports, the great festivals, or the latest war news. But there was one topic, as has been intimated, of perpetual interest to all, and that was the conduct of public affairs—in a word, politics. It must be remembered that there were no newspapers in ancient Greece. People did not read about current political questions, and absorb their opinions about them from editorials; nor did they have news concerning problems of the day interpreted for them by radio commentators. Instead, they talked about such problems in small groups here, there, and everywhere. And they talked freely, discussing questions from every angle and saying exactly what they thought or felt. Thus was public opinion developed, directly, spontaneously, without benefit of editor or columnist.

It was such a society which furnished the rich soil out of which Greek philosophy grew. It was in such a society, in fifth-century Athens, that Socrates moved, seeking to discover knowledge and to disclose the truth to his fellow men.

Of Socrates the man we know but little. He wrote no books and left no material records by which posterity might remember him. Socrates the philosopher, a literary Socrates, has been immortalized for us in the dialogues of his friend and admirer, Plato.[4] Other admirers and disciples added to the Socratic literature, but unfortunately their contributions have been lost except for the dialogues of Xenophon, a chapter in the famous *Lives of Eminent Philosophers* by Diogenes Laertius, and occasional refences by Aristotle and other writers. How much the real Socrates resembled the wise, unselfish, and noble philosopher of Plato's dialogues, or the Socrates of Xenophon, we do not know. Where scholars are at variance, it is not for the layman to express an opinion. The fact remains, however, that it is the Socrates of Plato and, to a lesser degree, of Xenophon, who has come down through the ages and who, with his simple but pithy questions, inexorably exposing error and pursuing the truth, is still the guide and counselor of philosopher and student.

Socrates, born about the year 469 B. C., lived during the great age of Pericles and the troubled period of the Peloponnesian War. As a youth he is said to have worked at the craft of his father, an Athenian sculptor, and later in life he served his state in more than one military campaign in which he exhibited both courage and extraordinary endurance in the

[4] The Socrates of Plato's dialogues is admirably presented by the late Professor Burnet in his scholarly work, *Greek Philosophy*, Part I: *Thales to Plato*, chaps. viii-x.

face of hardship. In these activities he was, save perhaps for his indifference to physical discomforts and pleasures, a typical Athenian of his day. But he was soon to become a marked man in the city, admired by some, an enigma to others, and regarded by many with more or less suspicion.

It is more than probable that he found the sculptor's craft uncongenial. The necessity for constant attention to minute detail could not but be irksome to a mind powerfully impelled toward speculation. A sculptor cannot lose himself in meditation—and Socrates was subject to fits of abstraction while his mind pursued some elusive thought—without risk of damage to the marble upon which he is at work. At any rate the philosopher soon overcame the sculptor, and Socrates laid down his tools to devote himself to the discovery of truth and wisdom.

Apparently he first sought to find them in the physical sciences. "When I was young," he says in Plato's *Phaedo*,[5] "I had a prodigious desire to know that department of philosophy which is called the investigation of nature; to know the causes of things, and why a thing is and is created or destroyed appeared to me to be a lofty profession." But his intellect was too original, too ardently concerned with the truth that lies deeper than concrete facts, to remain content with the investigation of material nature. Hence his study of the scientific theories of his day left him dissatisfied and indeed "grievously disappointed." The truth he was seeking must deal with ultimate causes, not with what seemed to him the superficial phenomena of the physical world. Thus it was that he reached the conclusion—a conclusion which justifies Cicero in calling him "the father of philosophy"[6]—that he "had better have recourse to the world of mind and seek there the truth of existence."[7] Henceforth he was to devote himself to the great problems of humanity—not the material problems, but those of the spirit. Philosophy as he conceived it was not merely a human but an ethical, a moral, science.[8]

There can be little doubt that Socrates was preëminently fitted for his chosen calling. Nature, it would seem, had endowed him with a strong personality, a generous heart and one of the clearest and most profound minds ever born into the world. If we add to these qualities fearlessness,

---

[5] Page 96. [6] *De finibus* II. i. 1. [7] *Phaedo* 99–100.

[8] "From the ancient days down to the time of Socrates, who had listened to Archelaus the pupil of Anaxagoras, philosophy dealt with numbers and movements, with the problem whence all things came, or whither they returned, and zealously inquired into the size of the stars, the spaces that divided them, their courses and all celestial phenomena; Socrates on the other hand was the first to call philosophy down from the heavens and set her in the cities of men and bring her also into their homes and compel her to ask questions about life and morality and things good and evil."—Cicero, *Tusculan Disputations* V. iv. 10–11.

disregard of narrow conventions, and serenity of spirit, we have a summary, however inadequate it may be, of Socrates' mental and spiritual equipment. But one further quality must be added, without which he could never have attained tranquility nor the constant preservation of a remarkably balanced and impartial judgment in the face of any and all circumstances. That further quality was a strong will.

That a powerful nature like this must have been originally endowed with a host of strong impulses, and could only have attained serenity of soul by a process of self-education, is so probable in itself that we cannot refuse credence to the ancient traditions which point that way. The Syrian soothsayer and physiognomist, Zopyrus, as reported in the dialogue bearing his name and written by Phædo of Elis, a favourite disciple of the master, saw in the countenance of Socrates the imprint of strong sensuality. Loud protests were raised by the assembled disciples, but Socrates silenced them with the remark, "Zopyrus is not mistaken; however, I have conquered those desires." Insufficiently attested, but not in itself improbable, considering the fiery temperament of the man, is the statement that he was subject to occasional outbursts of violent rage. Such outbursts cannot have been frequent, for nothing is better established than the masterful dominion which the powerful will was wont to exercise over every emotion. Self-command, indeed, was an indispensable qualification for the calling of his choice.[9]

Socrates was in himself an exemplar of that balance and harmony in life for which the Greeks strove.

In his character seemingly opposite tendencies were held in lightly balanced harmony. His rationalism found the key to goodness in clear thinking, and claimed for the individual an autonomy over-riding every recognized authority, divine or human. It was not clear to his contemporaries why this assertor of individual freedom should not be antinomian; why he should be indifferent to his own interests and pleasures; why he should not repudiate, or try to subvert, social institutions. Yet he challenged no conflict with received religion or with the demands of the State. He conformed to the established cult, and his accusers could find no more damaging charge than that he sometimes spoke of warnings received from a "divine sign." He did not, like the later Cynics, insult the decencies of common life, or exalt a state of nature above the civilization of Athens. Though he kept aloof from politics, he fulfilled the duties of a citizen, held office, married, and brought up children. . . . He was content to find in Athenian society freedom enough to go about his chosen business, avoiding any serious breach without the least compromise of principle. Regarding pleasure, and even comfort, with complete indifference, he had not that fear of pleasure which makes the ascetic. He could take pleasures when they came; when they did not come, he never missed them.[10]

[9] Gomperz, *Greek Thinkers, A History of Ancient Philosophy*, II, 48.
[10] Cornford, "The Athenian Philosophical Schools," *The Cambridge Ancient History*, VI, 309-10.

The Greeks, as we have said, had a great and innate gift for conversation. Therefore it was natural that Socrates, intent on the study of the human mind, should seek the company of his fellow citizens of Athens and should pursue his studies by means of conversation with them. Apparently discussion with any who cared to talk with him—and their number grew through the years—became his chief occupation, so much so that he neglected his home and material interests (at least according to conventional standards) and lived the remainder of his life in poverty. For though he gained wide recognition as a teacher both in Athens and abroad, he would accept no fees, Xenophon tells us, from those who came to hear him.

He would not make money himself out of their desire for his companionship. He held that this self-denying ordinance insured his liberty. Those who charged a fee for their society he denounced for selling themselves into bondage; since they were bound to converse with all from whom they took the fee. He marvelled that anyone should make money by the profession of virtue, and should not reflect that his highest reward would be the gain of a good friend.[11]

Indeed, the Socrates portrayed by Plato declared that he would "even pay for a listener."[12] Certain it is that for many years he spent his days in the city overlooked by the stately temples of the Acropolis, talking to men wherever he found them, not in order to reveal his own knowledge—for he asserted that his only wisdom lay in the admission that he knew nothing —but in order to question those who themselves claimed to be wise, or to arouse the interest of others in fundamental human problems.

We may, if we choose, imagine him issuing from one of the narrow, crooked streets of Athens into the market place, where in the morning sunlight he strolls at a leisurely pace past busy booths and stalls and the tables of the money changers. Or, if it should chance to be raining, he may seek shelter under the crowded colonnades. To many he is merely the well-known Socrates to whose peculiar ways they have long since grown accustomed, but a stranger, let us say from Corinth, is likely upon encountering him to pause and stare for a moment. He sees a short, strongly built figure, inclined to corpulence with the approach of age, barefooted and clad in a threadbare cloak which, according to Xenophon, was "never changed summer or winter."[13] But the attention of the Corinthian stranger lingers more over the face than over the rather comic figure. For at first glance there is something still more comic, even grotesque, about the features. It is a face "like that of a satyr," the "carved head of the Silenus,"

---

[11] *Memorabilia* I. ii. 5–7.   [12] *Euthyphro* 3.   [13] *Memorabilia* I. vi. 2.

according to Alcibiades.[14] The nose is upturned, with flaring nostrils, the mouth large and thick-lipped, the eyes prominent. Coarse, almost clownish features, our stranger may at first conclude, until he looks into the eyes that gaze so steadily at him. Then, being a discerning man, he becomes suddenly aware of a strange dignity about this quaint individual, a something in the eyes that reflects the calm soul, the generous heart, and the powerful mind within.

As the Corinthian possesses the lively curiosity with which most Greeks were endowed, he turns and follows Socrates, until the latter is hailed by a little group of wealthy young Athenians lounging in a portico. The mixture of respect and affectionate raillery with which the elder man is greeted, and his good-humored responses, still further excite the curiosity of the stranger. Who can this odd person be who consorts on such familiar terms with young aristocrats?

Drawing nearer, the Corinthian leans idly against a column and listens to the conversation. It is at first little more than a series of jests, some of them concerning Socrates' appearance and habits, to which he replies with the utmost good nature, tinged with a gentle irony. But one of the group, a handsome, thoughtful youth in his early twenties, who is addressed by his companions as Plato, chances to refer to a trial held on the preceding day in the law courts. Socrates professes ignorance of it and asks the views of the company on the decision. There is a division of opinion, some holding that justice had been done, others asserting that the decision was unjust. Apparently Socrates is interested, for he makes further inquiries. These questions are simple in themselves—so simple, indeed, that the listening stranger is a good deal astonished to discover after a time that they have somehow converted what began as a trivial conversation into an earnest discussion of the foundations of justice. Presently he gives up all pretense of idling and openly joins the group, deeply interested in the swift play of question and answer and admiring the skill with which Socrates, probing ever deeper into his subject, leads the discussion from one acknowledged truth to another, often by means of homely examples of cobblers or cooks or even animals.

Frequently passers-by pause, the Corinthian notes, to listen to the argument, occasionally to join it. Others merely glance at the group with a

---

[14] Plato, *Symposium* p. 215 B. Xenophon comments, on the comparison of Socrates' features with those of a satyr, "Socrates, as fortune would have it, really resembled these creatures." —*Symposium* iv. 19.

tolerant smile. And still others stare into the portico with a frown that seems to imply both displeasure and suspicion.

The conversation is touched ever and again with Socrates' ironical humor, particularly in the case of those who are too sure of their own knowledge. These overconfident individuals, the Corinthian observes with amusement, are likely suddenly to find themselves unable to answer seemingly innocent questions without denying their positive assertions of a few minutes ago. Some take their discomfiture in good part, but two or three, feeling humiliated, withdraw in vexation.

The others, however, continue the discussion until, the noonday heat becoming too great for comfort, the whole group breaks up, some resuming neglected business, others turning homeward or going to the baths, and a few of the more energetic to the gymnasia. Socrates is invited by several to join them, but he jestingly protests that if he favors one the others will be jealous. With a word of farewell he goes his way alone, seeking others who are in a mood for conversation. And the Corinthian stranger, left alone in the portico, watches him depart with the feeling that he will not soon forget this morning's curious experience in Athens.

Wholly imaginary though this incident is, we know that something not unlike it must have occurred countless times during Socrates' years of search after wisdom. We know, too, that his investigations were always of such fundamental subjects as goodness, beauty, justice and injustice, government and law, the state and the statesman. But to attempt a realistic sketch of his life or a detailed account of his theories (as distinct from those of Plato) would be impossible, in the absence of any records or writings left by him. And it would be equally futile, in view of the immortal description of Plato, to attempt a narration of his trial—perhaps the most momentous trial, with a single exception, in human history—and of the circumstances of his noble death in obedience to the laws of his country. It is best to leave him, in the market place of Athens where, with reason for his guide, he spent so much of his life in the endless quest for truth, and turn to Plato, the greatest of his successors.

Chapter IV

PLATO (428–348 B.C.)

The great and enduring contributions of Plato to the entire field of philosophy have been universally acknowledged for many centuries. If he was not the founder of philosophy, it cannot be gainsaid that in his works are to be found the tenets upon which nearly all of our modern philosophical thought is based. So true is this that Plato the philosopher seems destined always to overshadow that other Plato who, gifted with supreme poetic and dramatic powers, was one of the literary glories of Greece.

In the conception of Plato, philosophy was the guiding star for human beings; it constituted a means by which men in society might attain—or at least approach—their goal of happiness. To him, as to many Greeks, philosophy was essentially a way of life, a way in conformity with the highest ideals which enlightened human intelligence was capable of conceiving.

Now Plato realized that all men are not philosophers and, indeed, that the truly philosophically minded are comparatively few in number. How, then, was philosophy to benefit the multitude, the mass of the people who make up political groups? How, in a word, was it to become political? Plato's answer to this question was, as we shall see, that government should be placed in the hands of philosophers. Only thus, he felt, could politics be changed from a thing of expediency, at the mercy of human passions and weakness, into a science endowed with the loftiest ethical standards. The statesman who was a philosopher would be able, in Plato's view, both to comprehend and to attain the aims and purposes of the state as no mere politician ever would or could.

The conception of the philosopher-king lies at the core of Plato's entire political system. To be sure, this conception underwent changes in the course of his long life; but though he altered it both in form and in application, it is fair to say that his purpose from first to last was to unite philosophy with government and law, in order to raise the state to the philosophic ideal of the "good life." Fortunately, though we know comparatively little of Plato's life, it is possible to trace briefly the train of circumstances which influenced him in the development of his political theories.

Of his association with Socrates we need say but a word or two, since the potent effect of the elder man's teachings upon his youthful friend is magnificently evidenced in the dialogues, which are in themselves a homage unparalleled in the entire history of literature. "The monument of Socrates is that he is the spirit of philosophy for Plato."[1]

Whether their relationship was that of master and disciple may perhaps be doubted, since Plato himself refers to Socrates, not as a master but as a friend. Be that as it may, it appears that the friendship began very early in Plato's life, probably in his boyhood during the association of his relatives, Charmides and Crito, with Socrates. There is good reason to believe, however, that in his youth Plato, like so many sons of well-to-do Athenians, was chiefly attracted by political life, and that during his association with Socrates he gave little thought to philosophy as a vocation. Nevertheless, during this early period his mind was absorbing the Socratic doctrines so that, unconsciously perhaps, he was preparing himself for a life to be devoted to philosophical speculation, in which the influence of Socrates was to be paramount for many a year.

What was it that turned the interest of the young Athenian from a political career to philosophy? On this point Plato himself furnishes the best of evidence in the seventh of his *Epistles*—provided we consider it genuine, as many scholars of recent years have done. This letter was written late in life to the friends and associates of the recently murdered Dion, a statesman, patriot, and philosopher of Syracuse, who had been associated with Plato in his ill-fated attempts to realize in Sicily his dream of a state ruled by a philosopher-king. In the epistle Plato says:

In the days of my youth my experience was the same as that of many others. I thought that as soon as I should become my own master I would immediately enter into public life.[2]

Certain important changes, however, which occurred in the political situation, profoundly affected Plato. A revolution took place in Athens and an oligarchic government was set up under the "Thirty Tyrants," among whom were "connexions and acquaintances" of his. Doubtless knowing of the young man's political ambitions, they invited him "at once to join their administration, thinking it would be congenial." What happened thereafter is described in the epistle in a few revealing sentences: "The feelings I then experienced, owing to my youth, were in no way surprising: for I imagined

---
[1] Oakeley, *Greek Ethical Thought from Homer to the Stoics*, p. xxi.
[2] *Epistles* VII.

that they would administer the State by leading it out of an unjust way of life into a just way, and consequently I gave my mind to them very diligently, to see what they would do." But what he actually observed, failed entirely to measure up to his expectations:

> I saw how these men within a short time caused men to look back on the former government as a golden age; and above all how they treated my aged friend Socrates, whom I would hardly scruple to call the most just of men then living, when they tried to send him, along with others, after one of the citizens, to fetch him by force that he might be put to death—their object being that Socrates, whether he wished or no, might be made to share in their political actions; he, however, refused to obey and risked the uttermost penalties rather than be a partaker in their unholy deeds. So when I beheld all these actions and others of a similar grave kind, I was indignant, and I withdrew myself from the evil practices then going on.[3]

Before long, however, the Thirty Tyrants were overthrown and a democratic form of government restored. Plato's youthful political ambitions revived, "though less urgently," he tells us. Nevertheless, he felt again a "desire to take part in public and political affairs." But his reawakened ambitions were to be short-lived, for he soon witnessed "many deplorable events" which doubtless made him hesitate to assume any active part in the administration of government. It was not, however, until Socrates was again subjected to political pressure—this time through the accusation and trial which had such tragic consequences—that his disillusionment concerning political affairs was completed.

Of the trial and death of Socrates he had written long ago in dialogues that were destined to become immortal. Now, years afterward, his comment in the letter, brief though it is, reëchoes the sorrow and indignation of his youth.

> Certain men of authority summoned our comrade Socrates before the law-courts, laying a charge against him which was most unholy, and which Socrates of all men least deserved; for it was on the charge of impiety that those men summoned him and the rest condemned and slew him—the very man who on the former occasion, when they themselves had the misfortune to be in exile, had refused to take part in the unholy arrest of one of the friends of the men then exiled.

The effect of these events on Plato was to throw, as it were, all the faults of politics and government into strong relief. His attitude at that time, with more than a hint of its subsequent development, he has revealed in a single sentence:

[3] *Epistles* VII. The instance here related is referred to also in Plato's *Apology*.

When, therefore, I considered all this, and the type of men who were administering the affairs of State, with their laws too and their customs, the more I considered them and the more I advanced in years myself, the more difficult appeared to me the task of managing affairs of State rightly.[4]

Difficult, indeed, the task was—so difficult that more than two thousand years later mankind is still struggling with it. Plato, no longer stirred by political ambitions, might well have been excused if he had turned his back in despair upon the formidable problems of government which he came so clearly to perceive against the background of an Athens already drifting into its long decline. Instead, he faced the problems and devoted himself, year in and year out, to seeking their solution by means of permanent reforms based, not upon political expediency nor a multitude of laws, but upon the enduring foundations of a philosophy of government, of the state and of law itself—a philosophy in which human reason, as embodied in the philosopher-king, should be supreme.

Nor were his political and legal reforms of the "closet" variety. True, he kept apart from the political activities of Athens and gave himself almost wholly to a life of reflection, of occasional writing, and of teaching in the famous Academy which he founded about the year 387 B. C. But the theories of law and government which he developed were not merely academic exercises. Based upon the supremacy of human reason, they were intended for practical application whenever and wherever rulers might be found who were enlightened enough to apply them. We must not suppose, however, that Plato labored under illusions on this point. Whether from direct observation (for according to some authors he had traveled extensively while still a young man) or from hearsay, he knew the world of his day and was well aware that nowhere had kings yet become philosophers or philosophers kings. Still it was within the realm of possibility that the metamorphosis might take place. At any rate it offered the only permanent cure he could discover for the ills afflicting political societies.

It is probable that he never expected, when he wrote the *Republic,* that he himself would have an opportunity to test his theories. Yet an opportunity of a sort did occur in Sicily, when Plato was sixty years of age. Some twenty years before he had visited Sicily and had gained a convert to his views in Dion, brother-in-law of Dionysius I, the reigning tyrant. When the latter was succeeded by Dionysius II, Dion persuaded Plato to come to Sicily in order to instruct his nephew, the new ruler, and thus put into practice the Platonic theories concerning government by a philosopher-king.

[4] *Ibid.*

Plato, it appears, was not altogether sanguine as to the success of the experiment. And subsequent events justified his misgivings. For Dionysius, unfortunately, was not of the stuff from which true philosophers are made. The plan of education which Plato laid out for him was pursued only fitfully and was soon wrecked by personal and political jealousies.

Plato was reluctant to abandon his plan, and indeed he returned to Sicily five years later in the hope that Dionysius might still be made a philosopher. But again he was unsuccessful. And though he continued for some years to keep in touch with Sicilian affairs,[5] he seems at length to have become resigned to the failure of his plan.[6]

Not that he relinquished his lofty ideal of the philosopher-king. But the failure to realize that ideal in Sicily led him to the consideration of another and, as it were, a secondary method for achieving the political reforms which he advocated—a method which might be said to represent a compromise between the ideal and the practicable.

He had gone to Sicily with high hopes of founding the city of his dreams, and of training a king to become a philosopher wise enough to regulate human affairs by that living play of Reason, which he held to transcend so greatly the dead letter of the Law. He had begun by believing in the supremacy of Reason and in monarchy: he ended by believing in the rule of Law and the mixed constitution—not indeed as ideals, but as things practicable; not as the Best of which thought was capable, but as that second best which may sometimes be better than the Best.[7]

In the *Laws*, the work of his old age, he set forth in detail this "second best" plan in which, as the late Professor Jowett observes, "the legislator has taken the place of the philosopher."[8] Yet philosophy, if it seems to play a lesser rôle in the *Laws* than in the *Republic*, is still supreme in Plato's conception of government. For while law rather than the philosopher-king was to be sovereign in the state described in this, his posthumously issued work,

---

[5] See the *Epistles* previously cited. An excellent brief account of the ill-fated Syracusan experiment is given by Barker, *op. cit.*, pp. 112–17. See also Burnet, *Greek Philosophy*, Part I: *Thales to Plato* (previously cited), pp. 294–301.

[6] Plutarch has an interesting comment on the Sicilian enterprise: "Surely the teachings of philosophers, if they are firmly engraved in the souls of rulers and statesmen and control them, acquire the force of laws; and that is why Plato sailed to Sicily, in the hope that his teachings would produce laws and actions in the government of Dionysius; but he found Dionysius, like a book which is erased and written over, already befouled with stains and incapable of losing the dye of his tyranny, since by length of time it had become deeply fixed and hard to wash out. No, it is while men are still at their best that they should accept the worthy teachings."—"That a Philosopher Ought to Converse Especially with Men in Power," *Moralia*, p. 779 B C.

[7] Barker, *Greek Political Theory* (previously cited) p. 116.

[8] *The Dialogues of Plato*, Jowett trans., V (Intro.), xxxiv.

law itself was to be philosophic. The rules of law were to have preambles setting forth the theory and principles which justified them.

We shall perhaps come nearest to Plato's own mind if we conceive these preambles as the bridge by which he passes from the rule of the trained philosophic mind to the rule of law. They represent the principles which would have inspired the ideal ruler untrammeled by law; the law, as far as its power can reach, represents the detailed application of these principles which such a ruler would have made. Taken together, the two are the nearest possible approach to philosophic monarchy. It is not the rule of bare law which Plato advocates: it is the rule of a law which trails a cloud of glory, and recalls the philosophic home from which it has come.[9]

In a word, if philosophers were not to be kings, then the next best thing was to have philosophic legislators.

In the development of Plato's political philosophy the various circumstances described in the preceding pages were of the first importance. But there was another event which must have exercised a profound influence upon the entire range of his philosophic thought during the latter half of his life. This was the establishment, already referred to, of his school of philosophy.

The founding of the Academy is the turning-point in Plato's life, and in some ways the most memorable event in the history of Western European science. For Plato it meant that, after long waiting, he had found his true work in life. He was henceforth to be the first president of a permanent institution for the prosecution of science by original research.[10]

The idea of founding such an institution did not, of course, originate with Plato. He was familiar, for example, with the school of Euclides of Megara, while in Athens Isocrates had already established his successful school of rhetoric. The latter was, in a sense, a rival to Plato's institution, for the views of these two Athenian teachers on the subject of education were decidedly at variance. Both aimed at training young men for public life, but where Plato felt that such training, to be of any permanent value, must consist of scientific study with its constant stimulation towards profound thinking, Isocrates could see little use in the study of abstract sciences.

He professed to teach "opinions," as we should say, to provide the ambitious aspirant to public life with "points of view," and to train him to express his "point of view" with the maximum of polish and persuasiveness. This is just the aim of "journalism" in its best forms, and Isocrates is the spiritual father of all the "essayists," from his own day to ours, who practise the agreeable and

---

[9] Barker, *op. cit.*, p. 305.   [10] Taylor, *Plato, The Man and His Work*, p. 5.

sometimes beneficial art of saying nothing, or saying the commonplace, in a perfect style.[11]

The scheme of teaching adopted by Plato, on the other hand, required the practical application to education of his conviction that "political power and genuine science" must be united.

This is why the pure mathematics—the one department of sheer hard thinking which had attained any serious development in the fourth century B. C.—formed the backbone of the curriculum, and why in the latter part of the century the two types of men who were successfully turned out in the Academy were original mathematicians and skilled legislators and administrators. . . . It is this, too, which makes the Academy the direct progenitor of the mediaeval and modern university: a university which aims at supplying the State with legislators and administrators whose intellects have been developed in the first instance by the disinterested pursuit of truth for its own sake is still undertaking, under changed conditions, the very task Plato describes as the education of the "philosopher-king." [12]

In the Academy Plato apparently lectured without notes, and while it may be assumed that his students took down the gist of his discourses, the lectures are lost to us save for a few casual references. Yet, though the courses of instruction which he gave and even their very subject matter are for the most part unknown, the influence of Plato as a teacher has remained dominant throughout the centuries. The Academy itself continued, more or less under the traditions which he had established, for over nine hundred years, until it was closed by Justinian in the year 529. Generation

---

[11] Taylor, *op. cit.*, p. 5. Equally illuminating is a passage by Burnet, *Greek Philosophy* (previously cited), p. 217: "Where Plato and Isokrates differed was in their conception of education. Isokrates was what we call a humanist, and the rivalry between him and Plato was really the first chapter in the long struggle between humanism and science. It must be remembered, however, that Greek humanism was of necessity a far shallower thing than what we call by the name. In the first place, modern humanism has gained immeasurably from having to deal with the language and literature of other peoples, and especially with those of classical antiquity. An exclusive preoccupation with the literature of one's own country always tends to shallowness. That is why even Roman humanism, as we know it in Cicero, for instance, is a far deeper thing than the contemporary Greek rhetoric. It has Greek antiquity as well as Roman behind it, and that gave it strength. The humanism of the Renaissance, again, was saturated with the results and spirit of Greek science, and so prepared the way for the scientific discoveries of the sixteenth and seventeenth centuries, while Greek humanism inherited from the Sophists of the fifth century a rooted distrust of science and scientific methods. The humanism of Isokrates had, therefore, hardly any real content, and tended to become little more than the art of expressing commonplaces in a perfect form.

"At the same time, the form invented by Isokrates really was perfect in its way, and he has, directly or indirectly, influenced every writer of prose down to the present day. Even commonplace thinking may have its value, and it is a very good test of that to express it in an artistic way. If one has to utter one's thoughts in accordance with a prescribed scheme, they will at least gain in lucidity and coherence, so far as they are reasonable at all."

[12] Taylor, *ibid.*, pp. 5-6.

after generation of students attended it, not only from Greece but from Asia Minor, from Northern Africa and (like Cicero[13]) from Rome. And if its teachers became less and less creative in their thought and methods, failing sadly as the centuries passed to measure up to the lofty standards of the founder, nevertheless the Academy kept alight the torch of learning and became the model for the universities of later ages.[14]

It is beyond the scope of the present chapter to attempt a detailed analysis of Plato's works. That task has, in any event, been competently performed again and again.[15] For the purpose in hand, therefore, it will suffice to examine briefly certain of the principal subjects which Plato treated in the development of his legal and political theories.

Mention has already been made of his advocacy of the philosopher-king, or—failing that—the philosophic legislator. Philosophy, in a word, he conceived of as the guide of the state. But what was Plato's conception of philosophy? To attempt a simple definition of a complex subject, it was a way of life based on truth discovered by human reason. And it was the duty of the philosopher not merely to discover the truth, but to make it known, to put it into action. Professor Burnet[16] has aptly described this twofold function of Plato's philosophy. "In the first place, it is the conversion of a soul, and in the second place, it is the service of mankind." The discovery of truth means the recognition of truth, i. e., the conversion of the discoverer. But the process should not end there, however much the philosopher (and even Plato himself) might prefer a life of contemplation, of seeking knowledge for its own sake. No one insisted more than he "on the necessity of disinterested scientific study, freed from all merely utilitarian preoccupations, but at the same time no one has maintained more firmly that such study is only justified in the last resort by the service it can render to human life."[17] And since human beings live in political groups, it is but natural that Plato should consider that one of the chief services of philosophy to humanity should be the guiding and directing of those groups.

[13] "I confess," says Cicero, "that as an orator . . . I have come forth, not from the workshops of the rhetoricians but from the porticoes of the Academy; for those porticoes wherein the footsteps of Plato were first impressed are the channels through which there now flows abundant and varied discourse. . . . An orator derives his chief inspiration and support from the discussions of Plato as well as of other philosophers."—*Orator, ad M. Brutum,* iii. 12.

[14] On the nature of the Athenian Schools and their importance in the long tradition and development of universities, see Newman, "The Idea of a University" (previously cited).

[15] The fullest English analyses of all the dialogues are to be found accompanying the late Professor Jowett's admirable translation above cited; and in *Plato and the Other Companions of Sokrates* by Grote, the famous English historian of Greece.

[16] *Greek Philosophy* (previously cited), p. 218.

[17] *Ibid.*

It will be necessary here to consider for a moment Plato's views on the aim and purpose of the political group or—to call it by its accustomed name—the state. For if philosophy is to guide the state, it must comprehend both the goal toward which the state should be directed, and the means by which that goal is to be attained. Now the end of Plato's state was the "good life," which is synonymous with true happiness. The elements of this good life are not, however, material but spiritual: justice, temperance, courage, wisdom—all of which are but phases of the ultimate idea of good. It is the duty of philosophy, in guiding the state, to cause these elements or qualities to prevail over their opposites, and this can be brought about only by education; for in Plato's conception it is through knowledge alone that the qualities in question emerge and become operative.

The consequence is that the philosopher-king must be an educator and that the primary function of the state which he rules must be the education of its members, "the training of noble personality."[18]

Education exists for the sake of the initiation of the citizen into the spiritual life of his State; and conversely the government of the State exists for the sake of education. The *Republic,* according to one of its titles, a treatise "concerning the constitution" of the State, is concerned not with questions of political structure, but with questions of educational method; and indeed the only system of government which Plato suggests—the rule of philosopher-kings—is really the issue and consequence of his educational theory. Yet there is also another aspect of Plato's theory of education. Education is indeed a social process, and, as such, it is intended to adjust the individual to his society; but it is also the way to the vision of absolute truth, and that vision is a vision of the individual soul. Apart from society and from social values, education is good in itself and for its own sake: its ultimate goal is rather the contemplation of the reality which lies behind time and existence than a life of action among earth's vain shadows—though we must always, Plato bids us, play our part like men among the shadows, and refuse to forget our duty to our fellows in the ecstasy of contemplation. Here speaks the philosopher of the Academy, seeking through mathematics, and the studies that lie beyond mathematics, to attain to absolute truth; and on this ground Plato joins issue with the Sophists, and Isocrates, and all teachers who regard education as a way of social success. They are doubly wrong. Education, so far as it is social, is the way of social righteousness, and not of social success. And not only is it the way of social righteousness: it is also the way of truth itself.[19]

Only brief mention may here be made of another phase of Plato's political doctrine, which has long been subject to considerable criticism—his advocacy

---

[18] Taylor, *Platonism and Its Influence,* p. 64.
[19] Barker, *Greek Political Theory* (previously cited), p. 182.

of a system of communism. Of his various motives for advancing such a system the most important seems to have been the desire to remove the danger of the subordination of political to economic power—a danger, incidentally, which still troubles the political philosopher. To Plato, elaborating his plan of an ideal state in the *Republic,* the only solution for this problem appeared to be the abolition of private property, not for all the members of the state but for the members of his ruling class. This, it need hardly be pointed out, is not the modern conception of either socialism or communism. It is rather a means of insuring that those to whom the powers of government are entrusted shall be free from material temptations and thus able to devote themselves fully, impartially, and unselfishly to their appointed tasks. Whether it is the best means for attaining that end will no doubt continue to be questioned or denied by many. Yet we are bound to admit that thus far the world has discovered no other method of dealing satisfactorily with the problem.

In connection with his system of communism Plato advances certain theories concerning the position of women. This is not the place to discuss his scheme for a community of wives and of children,[20] but his views on the liberation of women from domestic bondage require brief comment. In the Greece of his day women were supposed to "belong in the home," to be inferior to men in every way. Plato swept all such suppositions aside. He refused to believe that there was any actual difference in ability between men and women. A physical difference, a difference in strength and capacity, yes, but otherwise they were the equals of men and should have the same education as that given to men and an opportunity to participate in the same work.

That Plato should have emancipated himself from the ideas of his own country and from the example of the East shows a wonderful independence of mind. He is conscious that women are half the human race, in some respects the more important half (Laws vi. 781 B); and for the sake both of men and women he desires to raise the woman to a higher level of existence. He brings, not sentiment, but philosophy to bear upon a question which both in ancient and modern times has been chiefly regarded in the light of custom or feeling.[21]

---

[20] Plato's plans for improving the human race lie, of course, wholly outside the scope of the present work. But it may be observed in passing that, though certain specific methods advocated by him for bringing about such improvement have long been severely criticized, the general principles which he advanced are finding expression in our own day in the new science of eugenics founded by Sir Francis Galton. For recent advanced views on the subject, see the statements of the noted British biologist, Julian Huxley, in an interview with William I. Lawrence published in the *New York Times* of Sept. 6, 1937, under the caption "Huxley Envisages the Eugenic Race."

[21] *The Dialogues of Plato,* Jowett trans., III (Intro.), clxxx.

But there was a further attribute of Plato's state, of the utmost importance to the political system which he advocated. The Greek mind, as has already been intimated, was blessed with what we may call a sense of unity and harmony, and this sense pertained to all phases of life, including the state and the multifarious relationships which characterize it as an association of human beings. If the state were to be a unit, those varied relationships must be harmonious. What was the guiding principle of such harmony? Plato found it in justice—not, it should be stated at once, the legal justice of the courts so familiar and so dear to the lawyers, but a moral, a social justice. When, in the *Republic,* he recounts the search of Socrates and his companions for a definition of justice, we see how one by one the wellworn theories are discarded: justice as giving to each his due, as the interest of the stronger, as the result of fear and the product of convention. Probing deeply, Plato arrived at a more fundamental conception of justice which, briefly stated, is to do one's duty. The *Republic's* division of labor, to which Plato applies the definition, is still regarded as a utopian ideal, but the definition itself is fundamentally sound. If man is a social being, he must have social duties as well as social rights, and justice, as Plato conceived it, lay in his complete and whole-hearted performance of those duties. This is the principle underlying the unity and harmony of the state. What, precisely, the individual finds his duties to be will depend upon two factors: the rules of the social organization or state of which he is a member, and his own individual sense of duty, i. e., of justice. And as justice in the state signifies the harmony which arises from the universal performance of social duties, so justice in the individual signifies the harmonious functioning of his entire being. Only when his nature is, so to speak, fully in tune will he be able to attain that high sense of duty which will enable him to distinguish unerringly the just from the unjust.

We must recollect [says Socrates in the *Republic*[22]] that the individual in whom the several qualities of his nature do their own work will be just. . . . But in reality justice . . . [is] concerned, however, not with the outward man, but with the inward, which is the true self and concernment of man: for the just man does not permit the several elements within him to interfere with one another, or any of them to do the work of others,—he sets in order his own inner life, and is his own master and his own law, and at peace with himself; and when he has bound together the three principles within him, which may be compared to the higher, lower, and middle notes of the scale, and the intermediate intervals—when he has bound all these together, and is no longer many, but has become one entirely temperate and perfectly adjusted nature,

---

[22] IV. 441 and 443-44.

then he proceeds to act, if he has to act, whether in a matter of property, or in the treatment of the body, or in some affair of politics or private business; always thinking and calling that which preserves and co-operates with this harmonious condition, just and good action, and the knowledge which presides over it, wisdom, and that which at any time impairs this condition, he will call unjust action, and the opinion which presides over it ignorance.

One phrase in this noble passage—that in which the just man "sets in order his own inner life"—demands a further word of comment. It was not an empty phrase, for Plato, speaking through Socrates, had already described in detail this process of setting in order the "inner life"—a process in which justice becomes almost synonymous with temperance. Reason, "the rational principle, which is wise, and has the care of the whole soul,"[23] should rule the inward man. It is the function of reason, "that little part which rules," to direct the other elements of man's nature and thus insure inward unity and self-control. "He is temperate who has these same elements in friendly harmony, in whom the one ruling principle of reason, and the two subject ones of spirit and desire are equally agreed that reason ought to rule."[24] In a word, the just man must be both a reasonable and a reasoning man, for "the sacred and golden cord of reason" is, as Plato tells us elsewhere, "the common law of the state."[25]

In speaking thus of a "common law" Plato does not, of course, mean human legislation, but rather a fundamental law—that "right reason" which, in a later era, was to become identified with the law of nature. It is, in a sense, but another aspect of the Platonic idea of good which is discoverable by the philosopher through the use of reason, and which "corresponds to a certain extent," says Professor Jowett, "with the modern conception of a law of nature, or of a final cause, or of both in one."[26] This is the fundamental credo which underlies all of Plato's political thought. It is true, as has been so often charged, that he does not distinguish politics and law from ethics as we of a later age pride ourselves on doing. But though we have gained in logic and definition by the separation, do we not run the risk of over-emphasizing distinctions—of locking ethics away, so to speak, in solitary confinement—with the consequent peril that the legislator will substitute the legal for the moral standard, while the politician will consider questions of right and wrong as merely rhetorical? That this risk has long been a real one must be obvious to any clear-sighted student of law and politics, whether national or international—and perhaps especially international. Fortunately there are indications that the passion for such distinctions is on the wane.

---

[23] *Ibid.,* IV. 441.   [24] *Ibid.,* 442.   [25] *Laws* I. 645.
[26] *The Dialogues of Plato,* Jowett trans., III (Intro.), ccvii.

We are today rediscovering that justice, law, politics, and government should be not merely legal but *social* conceptions, that their primary function is the social one of promoting what Plato many centuries ago called "the best life."[27] And the standards of the best life are, and must always be, moral standards. Only the most determined legalist would deny that law, after all, is a thing of the spirit as well as of the law courts.

Turning now to Plato's conception of man-made law, we find ourselves seemingly confronted by a curious contradiction. There is, in the first place, the traditional Greek attitude of respect and indeed reverence toward law displayed in the *Crito,* where he represents Socrates as choosing to die rather than disobey the laws of Athens. We are asked to imagine that the laws speak in their own behalf:

> Having brought you into the world, and nurtured and educated you, and given you and every other citizen a share in every good which we had to give, we further proclaim to any Athenian by the liberty which we allow him, that if he does not like us when he has become of age and has seen the ways of the city, and made our acquaintance, he may go where he pleases and take his goods with him. None of us laws will forbid him or interfere with him. Any one who does not like us and the city, and who wants to emigrate to a colony or to any other city, may go where he likes, retaining his property. But he who has experience of the manner in which we order justice and administer the state, and still remains, has entered into an implied contract that he will do as we command him. And he who disobeys us is, as we maintain, thrice wrong; first, because in disobeying us he is disobeying his parents; secondly, because we are the authors of his education; thirdly, because he has made an agreement with us that he will duly obey our commands.[28]

But later, when Plato was constructing his ideal state in the *Republic,* he viewed much of the field of human legislation as unworthy of attention. Concerning "business," "dealings between man and man," "agreements," "insult and injury," "impositions and exactions," "police, harbours and the like,"[29] he makes Socrates and his interlocutor agree that there will be no necessity for laws. And in the *Statesman* the Eleatic Stranger compares law to "an obstinate and ignorant tyrant, who will not allow anything to be done contrary to his appointment, or any question to be asked."[30]

These objections to law are, however, readily understandable in the light of the theories advanced by the author of the *Republic* and the *Statesman.* In the one case Plato would substitute education for legislation. He would have human beings educated beyond the need of what seemed to

---

[27] *Laws* IV. 707.
[28] *Crito* 51.
[29] *Republic* IV. 425.
[30] *Statesman* 294. Cf. *Protagoras* 337.

him petty laws and regulations. Give men true knowledge so that they may clearly perceive and understand right and justice, and they will have no need of rules to bind them to right doing. In the other case, Plato was viewing law from the standpoint of the philosopher-statesman. If, as he held, the latter should have a free hand in the guidance of the state, then the rigid rules of the law could be considered only as a hindrance to such guidance. The permanence of law and its very universality were, in this sense, its weaknesses, for it ignored changes brought by time and admitted of no "differences of men and actions."[31] The philosopher-statesman, on the other hand, if not bound by the tyranny of law, could take account of individual and temporal variations and provide for them.

These are still valid arguments, but in the world in which we live they can be overstressed. In the course of time Plato apparently realized this, and in the *Laws,* which summed up, we may assume, the views to which he had come at the end of a long life, he returned to some extent to the traditional Greek respect for the sovereignty of law. Indeed, he had already gone more than a step in that direction in later passages of the *Statesman*.[32] This is not to say that he gave way to any feeling of cynicism. The philosopher-king still remained his ideal, as he indicates more than once,[33] but the ideal could be realized, if ever, only in the dim future. Meanwhile, the political philosopher intent on a workable plan could but make the best of things as they are. He might endeavor to endow law with philosophy, but it would be law, and not philosophy, which was sovereign. "Mankind must have laws," he concedes in one of his preambles, "and conform to them, or their life would be as bad as that of the most savage beast."[34] And he then proceeds to indicate why laws are essential:

... no man's nature is able to know what is best for human society; or knowing, always able and willing to do what is best. In the first place, there is a difficulty in apprehending that the true art of politics is concerned, not with private but with public good (for public good binds together states, but private only distracts them); and that both the public and private good as well of individuals as of states is greater when the state and not the individual is first considered. In the second place, although a person knows in the abstract that this is true, yet if he be possessed of absolute and irresponsible power, he will never remain firm in his principles or persist in regarding the public good as primary in the state, and the private good as secondary. Human nature will be always drawing him into avarice and selfishness, avoiding pain and pursuing pleasure without any reason, and will bring these to the front, obscuring the juster and better; and so working darkness in his soul will at last fill with evils both him and the whole city.[35]

[31] *Statesman* 294. [32] *Ibid.,* 300 ff. [33] *Laws* IV. 709 ff. [34] *Ibid.,* IX. 875. [35] *Ibid.*

Ideally, of course, man should not need law, Plato continues, harking back to the theories he had developed in years gone by.

For if a man were born so divinely gifted that he could naturally apprehend the truth, he would have no need of laws to rule over him; for there is no law or order which is above knowledge, nor can mind, without impiety, be deemed the subject or slave of any man, but rather the lord of all. I speak of mind, true and free, and in harmony with nature.[36]

Could such "mind" be discovered, however, among human beings? Plato's answer is tinged with regret and resignation: "But then there is no such mind anywhere, or at least not much; and therefore we must choose law and order, which are second best."[37]

Now if law was to be sovereign, it must have no favorites. High and low alike, governors and governed, must be obedient to it. Indeed, obedience to law becomes an important test for fitness to hold office.

We must not entrust the government in your state to any one because he is rich, or because he possesses any other advantage, such as strength, or stature, or again birth: but he who is most obedient to the laws of the state, he shall win the palm; and to him who is victorious in the first degree shall be given the highest office and chief ministry of the gods; and the second to him who bears the second palm; and on a similar principle shall all the other offices be assignd to those who come next in order. And when I call the rulers servants or ministers of the law, I give them this name not for the sake of novelty, but because I certainly believe that upon such service or ministry depends the well- or ill-being of the state. For that state in which the law is subject and has no authority, I perceive to be on the highway to ruin; but I see that the state in which the law is above the rulers, and the rulers are the inferiors of the law, has salvation, and every blessing which the Gods can confer.[38]

Law, in a word, must be supreme, for it is to govern in the place of the philosophical mind. It must, therefore, have a philosophical justification (expressed, as we have already seen, in the form of preambles), and a philosophical purpose clearly perceived by the legislator. What was this purpose? Though Plato's methods may vary, his aim remains constant— the realization of the ideals of the good, of human happiness, of justice, temperance, courage, and wisdom. "The object of laws," he tells us, "is to make those who use them happy; and they confer every sort of good."[39] But what does Plato mean when he speaks of every sort of good? As if anticipating this question he supplies a definition in the sentences immediately following.

[36] *Laws* IX. 875.   [37] *Ibid.*   [38] *Ibid.*, IV. 715.   [39] *Ibid.*, I. 631.

Now goods are of two kinds: there are human and there are divine goods, and the human hang upon the divine; and the state which attains the greater, at the same time acquires the less, or, not having the greater, has neither. Of the lesser goods the first is health, the second beauty, the third strength, including swiftness in running and bodily agility generally, and the fourth is wealth, not the blind god [Pluto], but one who is keen of sight, if only he has wisdom for his companion. For wisdom is chief and leader of the divine class of goods, and next follows temperance; and from the union of these two with courage springs justice, and fourth in the scale of virtue is courage. All these naturally take precedence of the other goods, and this is the order in which the legislator must place them, and after them he will enjoin the rest of his ordinances on the citizens with a view to these, the human looking to the divine, and the divine looking to their leader mind.[40]

As might be expected, Plato here exalts the things of the spirit over "the lesser goods." Later he emphasizes his conviction on this point by a restatement of his views, ending with a question to which there is but one enlightened answer—an affirmative.

A State which would be safe and happy, as far as the nature of man allows, must and ought to distribute honour and dishonour in the right way. And the right way is to place the goods of the soul first and highest in the scale, always assuming temperance to be the condition of them; and to assign the second place to the goods of the body; and the third place to money and property. And if any legislator or state departs from this rule by giving money the place of honour, or in any way preferring that which is really last, may we not say, that he or the state is doing an unholy and unpatriotic thing?[41]

The state which Plato described had no counterpart in the world of his day. It was an ideal commonwealth—the first of a series which owe their inspiration to the Platonic model. But its influence on political thought bids fair to outlast that of any actual state in the annals of time. Empires which waxed powerful have waned, kingdoms have endured for a few centuries and vanished into history, despotisms and dictatorships have had their brief span of months or years before revolution swept them into the past. It may almost be said that the lessons of history are of a negative nature, for the records of nations which have disappeared teach us—if we would but heed them—what not to do. But Plato's state lives serenely on, furnishing positive ideals for countless generations of students. Many of the great thinkers who have contributed most to our political heritage owe an incalculable debt to his teachings: Aristotle, Cicero, the early theologians (and especially,

[40] *Ibid.*
[41] *Ibid.*, III. 697.

of course, St. Augustine), Sir Thomas More,[42] Rousseau, and a host of others—the doctrines of Plato have not only inspired them all but have entered into the development and substance of their own theories.

And today Plato still offers the same inspiration, the same wealth of ideas, to all who will become listeners, as it were, to those immortal discussions contained in his dialogues.

The echo of his words continues to be heard among men, because of all philosophers he has the most melodious voice. He is the inspired prophet or teacher who can never die, . . . in whom the thoughts of all who went before him are reflected and of all who come after him are partly anticipated. Other teachers of philosophy are dried up and withered,—after a few centuries they have become dust; but he is fresh and blooming, and is always begetting new ideas in the minds of men. They are one-sided and abstract; but he has many sides of wisdom. Nor is he always consistent with himself, because he is always moving onward, and knows that there are many more things in philosophy than can be expressed in words, and that truth is greater than consistency.[43]

[42] The greatest of modern utopias is unquestionably that of Sir Thomas More. See *infra*, pp. 434 ff.
[43] *The Dialogues of Plato*, Jowett trans., V (Intro.), ccxxxvii-ccxxxviii.

CHAPTER V

ARISTOTLE (384-322 B.C.)

It is a somewhat singular historical fact, and one interesting to reflect upon, that political philosophy—and indeed philosophy in general—should be so deeply indebted to the comparatively brief period of a century and a half which elapsed between the birth of Socrates in about the year 470 B.C. and the death of Aristotle in 322 B.C. It was, in a sense, a cumulative period, for the three minds of the first order which it produced were linked together not merely by common interests and ideals but by personal association and friendship. Socrates, as we have seen, passed on the torch to his youthful friend, Plato. And Aristotle in turn, coming to Athens from his birthplace at Stagira in Chalcidice in his eighteenth year, joined the Academy and for two decades studied under the dominant influence of its master. If his debt to Plato is less obvious to us than that of Plato to Socrates (since the latter speaks to posterity almost exclusively through the Platonic dialogues), it is none the less real and fundamental. "It is clear," says Professor W. D. Ross, "that in Plato's philosophy he found the master-influence of his life."[1] Aristotle in short, however much he subsequently departed in theoretical details from the doctrines taught by Plato, may fairly be said to have been the first and the greatest Platonist in the fullest sense of that term. As regards political theory, any one who troubles to make a close comparison of Plato's *Laws* with Aristotle's *Politics* will discover for himself how much the latter work owes to the former, in spite of obvious and sometimes exaggerated differences.[2]

Differences there were, of course, and important differences, for Aristotle's thought was not merely derivative. It was inevitable that his powerful mind should pursue its own course—a course which, as he grew older, withdrew him to some extent from the influence of Plato, just as the latter eventually drew away from Socratic doctrines. There was, moreover, some difference in particular fields of interest. While Plato's thought turned more and more to the abstract, to "ideas" and "numbers," Aristotle's interest shifted in the

---
[1] *Aristotle*, p. 2.
[2] The extent of this debt is shown in a brief but masterly comparison of the two works by Barker, *Greek Political Theory* (previously cited), pp. 380-82.

course of time from the abstract to the concrete, to the facts of history and of nature. The Greeks, as has been observed, had a lively curiosity concerning the world in which they lived; and in this respect Aristotle, with his enthusiasm for the observation and encyclopedic recording of facts, was but exhibiting what might be called a racial characteristic—a characteristic intensified in his case to an exceptional degree and guided by a remarkable intellect.

In a somewhat limited sense it may be said that with respect to political philosophy Plato was an idealist, Aristotle a realist. The dialogues of Plato bristle with innovations; he is the reformer who would "change this sorry scheme of things." Aristotle, on the other hand, to whom concrete facts made a strong appeal, felt the importance of institutions actually in existence. His mind was not given to conceiving radical changes and developing new institutions. Yet this tendency toward a "realistic" and conservative outlook can be overstressed. Aristotle, too, was an idealist in that he looked toward a better functioning of existing institutions. And the world needs, and will always need, both kinds of idealism.

Here as elsewhere in comparing Plato with Aristotle, a certain amount of caution is needed because the comparison is between two completely different types of work. For of Plato we have the published works (the *Dialogues*) but not his lectures at the Academy; and of Aristotle we have only lectures delivered at his school, and not his published literary writings. Thus we encounter difficulty, as Professor Burnet points out,[3] "in passing from Plato to Aristotle," so much so that "we seem to be in a different world altogether."

Of the lost works of Aristotle little need be said here. Some were dialogues which seem to have been much appreciated for their smoothness and lucidity of style. These were modeled on the Platonic dialogues both in thought and in form, but were apparently of a less dramatic nature. There were also numerous other works of a literary character, some of which would have been of immense value to the student of Aristotelian legal and political philosophy: particularly, for example, the essay on monarchy and the works dealing with constitutional law cases, colonies, barbarian customs, and the description of 158 *Constitutions*. Of the last-mentioned work we have at least a sample by reason of the fortunate discovery in Egypt, nearly half a century ago, of one of the *Constitutions,* that of Athens.

Most of our knowledge of Aristotle's philosophy is derived, of course,

[3] *Greek Philosophy* (previously cited), p. 215.

from his surviving works. These treatises were doubtless begun during what may be called the second period of his life in which, following the death of Plato, he spent some twelve years away from Athens, more than half of them in Macedonia, where for a time he was engaged by Philip of Macedon as tutor of the young prince and future conqueror, Alexander. But the treatises assumed the form in which we now have them after his return to Athens, where he opened a school in the Lyceum, a school to which the name "Peripatetic" was applied because of his custom of walking among his students while discussing philosophy with them. Lecturing in the school, Aristotle prepared extensive memoranda of the courses which he gave, and these—possibly supplemented occasionally by the notes of students—constitute the body of Aristotelian literature which was destined to survive.

Before undertaking a brief examination of Aristotle's great contributions to legal and political philosophy it is necessary to consider for a moment his conception of political science. To him, as Mr. Barker has observed, it is the "master science . . . from which all other practical sciences take their cue"[4] because it is concerned with the good which is the ultimate end of all human activities, i. e., happiness. But we of the modern world have grown accustomed to consider the question of the good as being an ethical and therefore an individual rather than a political matter. To be sure, we say that among man's political rights is the right to happiness, but we are for the most part thinking of happiness in a material, an economic, rather than an ethical and spiritual sense. This was not Aristotle's view. Ethics to him, as to Plato, was not a separate science. The supreme good of the state was also the supreme good of its individual members. It is significant that early in the First Book of his *Ethics* he describes "the end of the science of Politics" as "the Good of man," and adds that this "Good is the same for the individual and for the state."[5] Such being the case the study of ethics merges into that of politics, and "the subjects studied by political science are"—not merely government and statecraft, in accordance with the usual modern conception, but, to continue the quotation—"Moral Nobility and Justice."[6]

As has been intimated, there is more than a passing resemblance here between the views of Plato and Aristotle. Yet the fact remains that, while Plato made no attempt at a separate treatment of moral and political ideals, Aristotle wrote a treatise on each. To be sure, they overlap, and indeed the

---
[4] *The Political Thought of Plato and Aristotle*, p. 239.
[5] *Nicomachean Ethics* I. ii. 7–8.   [6] *Ibid.*, iii. 2.

Ethics is in more ways than one an introduction to the *Politics*. But before reaching the end of the latter work we find that political science has descended somewhat from the high plane on which it was introduced at the beginning of the *Ethics*. It has become more of a "practical" science in the narrower sense of the term, a science which deals with things as they are. The moral ideal shows a tendency to fade in the face of acute observation and analysis of existing institutions. The realist to some extent takes precedence over the idealist.

Nevertheless, it remains true that he who would understand Aristotle's political theories must be familiar with his *Ethics*.

Whatever the differences between the two, the *Ethics* are indispensable to the full understanding of the *Politics*. However much the argument may assume in its course a practical aspect, it still remains the fundamental characteristic of the *Politics,* that its author treats his subject ideally, from a moral point of view, in terms of ethics.[7]

Aristotle held, as has been stated, that the end of human life, and therefore of the state, is happiness. But what is happiness? His definition of it may be briefly paraphrased as the continuous functioning of man's faculties under the guidance of reason and in accordance with virtue. This is essentially a moral conception. And because the aim and purpose of the state is, in Aristotle's view, the promotion of happiness as thus defined, the conception forms the corner stone of his political theory, and is fundamental to his theories of law, of justice, of education.

Thus law becomes for Aristotle the embodiment of reason—a reason which, unlike that of individuals, is pure and dispassionate, and which therefore safeguards man against his passions and aids him in the attainment of happiness. The purpose of law, viewed in this light, is moral, and its primary rules are the moral code of the people.

If we thus conceive of law, and if we choose to define justice as action in obedience to law, then justice may be considered as "the chief of the virtues," indeed as "perfect virtue because it is the practice of perfect virtue," not merely by oneself, but "towards others."[8] Justice, in a word, becomes "virtue in action." It "means that each member of a community should so act in regard to his fellows, as to fulfil every moral obligation, because every moral obligation is enacted in the law, and to realise the Final Good, as the aim of the State expressed in its law."[9]

---

[7] Barker, *The Political Thought of Plato and Aristotle* (previously cited), p. 251.
[8] *Nicomachean Ethics* V. i. 15.
[9] Barker, *The Political Thought of Plato and Aristotle*, p. 322.

As for education, it is the royal road to wisdom, and "Wisdom produces Happiness."[10] Wisdom is, in fact, "a part of Virtue as a whole,"[11] and is therefore essential to the end both of the state and of the individual. Although his treatment of education is incomplete, the thesis of Aristotle, like that of Plato, seems to have been that, given a perfect system of education, a perfect state will be the inevitable result. Therefore education was considered to be a "political" matter in that its purpose was to fit the members of the state to attain that which is the end of the state—the good life, or happiness. For the state could never achieve its purpose if its members were unable to reach that goal. And since the goal is a moral one, education must deal not merely with the facts which constitute knowledge, but with the development of character and the training of the will. Education in Aristotle's view, therefore, was no mere cramming of facts. Nor was it to be concerned solely with the development of the powers of reason, important though that was. It must also develop physical and mental health, good habits, and sound characters. In twenty-odd centuries we have not gone beyond—if, indeed, we have reached—the ideals of education which Aristotle briefly and incompletely sketched in the last two books of his *Politics*.

Reference has already been made to one of Aristotle's definitions of justice: obedience to law, in which sense it is "coextensive with virtue in general."[12] He has a second definition, however, which has had no small influence on political philosophy. Justice also means "that which is equal or fair."[13] The first type of justice is "general" justice, the second "particular," the latter being divided into "distributive" justice and "corrective" justice.

The function of distributive justice is to render to each individual his due on the basis of merit, as determined by his contribution to the social group of which he is a member. Here equality is the guiding principle, but an equality tempered by proportion. It is also, but in a somewhat different sense, the principle underlying corrective justice, which relates to transactions between individuals. In all such transactions, of whatever nature, there should be a *quid pro quo,* a fair and equitable exchange from which neither party emerges as the loser. But in fact, the contrary frequently occurs, either as a result of breach of agreement, or of delict or tort. It is the business of corrective justice to redress the wrong and thus restore equality. Here the parties, whatever their merits may be otherwise, stand on an equal footing before the law.

---

[10] *Nicomachean Ethics* VI. xii. 5.
[11] *Ibid.*
[12] *Ibid.*, V. ii. 10.
[13] *Ibid.*, V. i. 8.

The law looks only at the degree of damage done, treating the parties as equal, and . . . asking whether one has done and the other suffered injustice, whether one inflicted and the other has sustained damage. Hence the unjust being here the unequal, the judge endeavours to equalize it: inasmuch as when one man has received and the other has inflicted a blow, or one has killed and the other been killed, the line representing the suffering and doing of the deed is divided into unequal parts, but the judge endeavours to make them equal by the penalty or loss he imposes, taking away the gain.[14]

Perhaps the most frequently repeated of Aristotle's pronouncements on the subject of justice is that relating to equity. It has had a profound influence on the development of juristic thought, and it is as pertinent today as it was in fourth-century Athens. In the *Rhetoric* Aristotle touched upon the subject, declaring that "equity is justice that goes beyond the written law,"[15] the reason being that legislation necessarily has "recourse to general terms," which cannot provide for the variations occurring in an "infinite number of cases." In the *Ethics*[16] he took up in greater detail the relation between equity and justice:

Equity, while superior to one sort of justice, is itself just: it is not superior to justice as being generically different from it. Justice and equity are therefore the same thing, and both are good, though equity is the better. . . . Equity, though just, is not legal justice, but a rectification of legal justice. The reason for this is that law is always a general statement, yet there are cases which it is not possible to cover in a general statement. In matters therefore where, while it is necessary to speak in general terms, it is not possible to do so correctly, the law takes into consideration the majority of cases, although it is not unaware of the error this involves. And this does not make it a wrong law; for the error is not in the law nor in the lawgiver, but in the nature of the case: the material of conduct is essentially irregular.

How, then, does equity provide for those cases which the general rule of law fails to fit?

When therefore the law lays down a general rule, and thereafter a case arises which is an exception to the rule, it is then right, where the lawgiver's pronouncement because of its absoluteness is defective and erroneous, to rectify the defect by deciding as the lawgiver would himself decide if he were present on the occasion, and would have enacted if he had been cognizant of the case in question. Hence, while the equitable is just, and is superior to one sort of justice, it is not superior to absolute justice, but only to the error due to its absolute statement. This is the essential nature of the equitable: it is a rectification of law where law is defective because of its generality.[17]

It is, however, Aristotle's conception of the state and of government which has penetrated most deeply into the thought of innumerable generations.

[14] Aristotle, *Nic. Ethics*, V. iv. 3–5.   [15] I. xiii. 13.   [16] V. x. 2–5.   [17] *Ibid.*, V. x. 5–6.

As man is not only a "social" but a "political" animal, so it is the nature of men, Aristotle taught, to associate in political groups; and therefore the state is not an artificial creature but a natural development responding to the needs of human nature. This does not mean that it is independent of man's control, that it may not be altered for the better by human "art." The progress of humanity is measured in large part not only by its recognition of, and adaptation of itself to, natural laws, but also by its control of those laws based upon right reason and knowledge. Aristotle, like Plato, would have us seek to understand not simply the nature of the state, but its purpose. Thus while the state is first of all the result of a process of organization for the sake of life, its purpose looks far beyond mere existence or even material welfare, for its ultimate end, as we have seen, is "a good life."[18] The state, therefore, is "not a mere society, having a common place, established for the prevention of crime and for the sake of exchange." Those are merely "conditions" without which the state could not survive; but "all of them together do not constitute a state, which is a community of well-being in families and aggregations of families, for the sake of a perfect and self-sufficing life."[19] Friendship, the natural desire of the individual to associate with his fellows, is the "motive" of social life; but "the end is the good life."[20] Now the good life means the practice of virtue, and since justice in the general sense is one with virtue, it follows that "justice is the bond of men in states."[21] Furthermore, if justice is the bond, it should be administered, not by men (whose hearts "passion must ever sway"),[22] but by law as the sovereign of the state—the law which "is passionless,"[23] which is "reason unaffected by desire,"[24] and whose rule is therefore "preferable to that of any individual."[25] This being the case, he who governs the state should not be a tyrant above the law, but "a good and wise man"[26] who is himself obedient to the law. And if he fails to observe the law and arrogates to himself tyrannical powers, the people of the state may call him to account.

These Aristotelian doctrines, so familiar to us as to seem truisms, have for centuries been the stock in trade of political philosophers. A varied and often painful experience in government and statecraft has added a thought to them here and there—not always, unfortunately, to their betterment—but the fact remains that through the long tapestry of history the political truths revealed by Aristotle run like threads of gold, threads still bright and untarnished in our own day.

[18] Aristotle, *Politics* III. ix. 6.   [19] *Ibid.*, 12.   [20] *Ibid.*, 13.   [21] *Ibid.*, I. ii. 16.
[22] *Ibid.*, III. xv. 5.   [23] *Ibid.*   [24] *Ibid.*, xvi. 6.   [25] *Ibid.*, 4.   [26] *Ibid.*, III. iv. 7.

Chapter VI

THE STOICS

The political and legal philosophy of Plato and Aristotle envisioned human society as divided into small, self-sufficient units—the city-states. But even in Aristotle's day, although apparently he was unaware of it, the city-state was doomed. His pupil, Alexander (356–323 B. C.) thought in terms of a vast empire and dreamed of a fusion of races. However one may assess the Macedonian conqueror's services, or disservices, to the world, it cannot be denied that he lowered (where he did not completely destroy) the ancient barriers behind which self-sufficiency and not a little contempt for the rest of the world had been nurtured. Men began to look beyond their old horizons. Indeed it was as though those horizons had been lifted like curtains, letting in the winds of the world and affording a view of another horizon so remote that it encompassed the earth.

Now the political and legal concepts built for the city-states were fundamentally sound, but if they were to be applied to a changing order of things, a certain amount of adaptation was necessary. It is this process which must now be considered.

For its beginnings we must turn back a hundred years to the latter part of the fifth century, when a strong patriotic attachment to small political units was common to all Greeks. Perhaps even then, however, there were exceptions—or at least occasional doubts as to whether there should not be some wider allegiance. Socrates was a patriotic citizen of Athens, yet (if we are to believe Plutarch[1]) he referred to himself on occasion as a citizen of the world. And Antisthenes, one of his disciples, founded the Cynic School, whose members rebelled against the theory and conventions of the city state, substituting for them the ideals of individual self-sufficiency on the basis of reason, and a vague cosmopolitanism. Diogenes, who was the greatest of the Cynics and one of the most picturesque of philosophers, carried even further his denial of the state and its institutions. His social ideal appears to have been "the removal of all barriers that divide man from man"[2] and perhaps the establishment of some kind of world state.[3]

[1] *De exilio.*   [2] Gomperz, *Greek Thinkers* (previously cited), II, 160.
[3] No writings of Diogenes have survived, but many anecdotes concerning his life and sayings are given by Diogenes Laertius, VI. 20 *et seq.*

THE STOICS

But the philosophy of the Cynics was largely materialistic and concerned with rebellion and denial rather than affirmation. Again, the members of the school were "radicals" in the lengths to which their revolt led them, and the fact that many of them carried their theories to extremes, rejecting even the accepted canons of courtesy and decency, tended to repel the more conventional-minded and to obscure under a cloud of eccentricities the nobler phases of their doctrines.

For present purposes, however, the importance of the Cynics lies less, perhaps, in their tenets than in the fact that they are a connecting link between the classical Greek philosophy of the city-state era and the doctrines of the Stoics.

The connection between Cynicism and Stoicism is direct and obvious, for Zeno, who founded the latter school of philosophy at the end of the fourth century, was a pupil of the Cynic teacher Crates. The school took its name from the colonnade or "porch" (*stoa*) where Zeno, according to Diogenes Laertius,[4] was accustomed "to discourse, pacing up and down." It is not without interest to note that the founder of the new philosophy was of Phoenician descent, and that more than one of his successors came from the Near East. It has been said of Zeno, indeed, that if he had not chanced to dwell "in a Greek trading city" but had lived instead in Judaea, "he would have been a prophet of Jehovah."[5] Hence Stoicism is not wholly of Greek origin but represents in part the beginning of that mingling of the West with the East which followed in the wake of Alexander's conquests.

Stemming as they did from the Cynic school, the Stoics adopted in some measure the tenets of Cynicism. And like their precursors, the Stoics were Socratics in the belief that knowledge is the basis of virtue, of moral conduct. But it was not knowledge derived from abstract speculation so much as from sense impressions which were coördinated by reason. To the Stoics, as to Socrates, reason was supreme, but in a somewhat different manner. Zeno conceived of reason as at once divine and all-pervading. It was his doctrine that

> God is mind, God is soul, God is nature:
> It is God that holdeth the universe together.
> The artificer and disposer of the universe
> Is the word, and the word is reason;
> He is fate.
> He is the determining cause of all things,
> He is Zeus.[6]

---

[4] VII. 5. The colonnade was adorned with frescoes by the artist Polygnotus. Hence it is sometimes referred to as the "painted porch."   [5] Sedgwick, *Marcus Aurelius*, p. 19.

[6] Quoted from Sedgwick, *op. cit.*, pp. 20–21, who translates fragments from Zeno collected by von Arnim in *Stoicorum veterum fragmenta*.

THE STOICS

Thus "the Stoics asserted," as the late Sir Frederick Pollock pointed out in his illuminating essay on "Stoic Philosophy,"[7] "that the world is a product of reason, and that all the laws of nature aim in the long run at reasonable ends." Reason here becomes identified on the one hand with a universal mind or soul, and on the other with a universal ruling principle, or law.

Thus Zeno proclaimed that:

> In all things is the divine;
> The law of nature is divine.
> The world and the heavens are the substance of God,
> And the divine power worketh in the stars,
> And in the years, in the months and in the seasons.[8]

Now man was a part of this divine and all-embracing system, and therefore it was his duty, Zeno taught, to live in harmony with it.

> The fulfillment of a man's life
> Is to live in accord with nature;
> So to live is to live in righteousness,
> For nature leadeth to righteousness,
> And the end of life is to live in accord with virtue.
> Follow the Gods.[9]

Such righteousness, according to the Stoic teacher, was man's true destiny.

> Man is born solely for righteousness,
> For righteousness draweth to itself the souls of men
> With no lure, no offerings from without,
> But of its own splendor.
> Virtue of itself is sufficient for happiness;
> Righteousness is the sole and only good,
> And nothing is evil save that which is vile and base.[10]

Zeno thus taught his followers that they should choose the good and reject the evil. But what of things that were "neither good nor evil?" These the Stoics classified as "indifferent":

> Of things that are, some there are
> Which are good and some which are evil,
> And some which are neither good nor evil.
> And the good are these:
> Wisdom, Sobriety, Justice and Fortitude.
> And the evil are these:
> Folly, Intemperance, Injustice and Cowardice.
> And things that are neither good nor evil are indifferent.
> And things indifferent are these:
> Life and death, good repute and ill repute,
> Pain and pleasure, riches and poverty,
> Sickness and health, and such like.[11]

---

[7] *Essays in Jurisprudence and Ethics*, pp. 314–51, 325.
[8] Sedgwick, *op. cit.*, p. 21.   [9] *Ibid.*   [10] *Ibid.*   [11] *Ibid.*, pp. 21–2.

But man himself could not be "indifferent." He must choose, as we have said, between good and evil, and by his choice he placed himself in one of the two categories into which the Stoics separated mankind.

> And of men there are two sorts,
> The upright man and the wicked man;
> And the upright man all his life
> Will do the things that are right,
> But the ways of the wicked are evil.[12]

It followed that, in the opinion of Zeno, the wicked were foolish folk, and that the good were wise.

> The wise man is blessed, the wise man is rich;
> Only the wise, however needy they be, are rich;
> Only the wise, however ill-favored, are beautiful;
> For the lineaments of the soul
> Are more beautiful than those of the body.[13]

Of all the Stoic maxims the most fundamental was that the life of man should be in harmony with nature. But that maxim, at least to us of a later age, is subject to more than one interpretation. To quote again from Sir Frederick Pollock's essay,[14] "'Live according to Nature,' is at first sight the most ambiguous of precepts." The Stoics, however, the learned jurist and philosopher pointed out, used the expression "with a definite meaning." They maintained, he continued by way of explanation of this meaning, that all things are subject to a "universal order," which is arranged by, or rather is conceived as being, a supreme and all-pervading intelligence.

This order being determinate and irresistible, every agent and event in some way or other fulfils it. Even those who think to hinder it are against their own conceit working for it. . . . On this ground there is obviously no foundation for ethical distinctions. But when we so far quit this universal point of view as to consider any particular species in relation to the whole, we see that it has certain constant relations to the rest of the world, which in fact determine its specific character, and which in the case of living creatures the life of the species is occupied in maintaining. Every creature has some normal function as part of the general order of the Kosmos; what those functions are for each kind is to be ascertained by experience. They must always include, however, the preservation of the species; otherwise it could not exist as a species.[15]

Here Sir Frederick introduced an example:

Thus the impulse of self-preservation, which the Stoics ascribed to every creature as the first spring of action, is not only common, as a matter of fact, to all active beings, but is an integral part of the common order of the world. Every act

---

[12] *Ibid.*, p. 22.   [13] *Ibid.*
[14] Pollock, *Essays in Jurisprudence and Ethics*, p. 333.   [15] *Ibid.*, pp. 333–34.

of an individual which belongs to the proper function of its species as thus understood is, in the Stoic language, *according to Nature* as regards that species —that is, according to its specific nature (ἰδία φύσις); and inasmuch as it is an instance of the general law which fixes the normal place and action of the species in the great concert of the Kosmos, it is also said to be in an eminent manner *according to Nature,* taken in the general sense as the universal order (κοινὴ φύσις).[16]

All creatures are part of this universal scheme of things, but the part of man, as a reasoning creature, differs from that of other animals.

Now man, as well as other creatures, has his specific function, or *nature* in the Stoic sense, as part of the cosmical plan. But, unlike other creatures, he can fulfil it with conscious intelligence and choice. He may know his station in the world, and know also that in maintaining it he is fulfilling the purpose of the supreme Reason. By the very fact of being addressed to an understanding agent the command "Live according to Nature" becomes "Live according to Reason." [17]

Reason is thus the guide or the standard for human life.

This reason, as expressed in the constitution of man and his relations to the world, his capacities, his achievements, and his aspirations, furnishes a type or pattern of life which may be sufficiently known by those who choose to model their conduct upon it. Actions conformable to this type are morally right, and rightmindedness is the conscious striving to attain it (we neglect for the moment the minuter points of Stoic doctrine); it is in this sense that moral goodness is the fulfillment of man's proper nature. . . . This then is the calling imposed upon man by the supreme Reason; a fact to be observed which implies a law to be obeyed. Righteousness consists in fulfilling the duties imposed by it with a cheerful obedience of discipline.[18]

Sir Frederick here raises an interesting question.

A modern reader [he observes] is tempted to ask where is the *sanction* in the Stoic scheme of morality? How does it answer the question which some regard as the very first that moral philosophy is bound to answer—why should I do right? [19]

His answer to this question is not without interest to a world considerably troubled over the topic of sanctions in one form or another.

It may seem strange to us, but so it is, that the Greek philosophers, and especially the Stoics, troubled themselves very little to find a direct reply. The question seems hardly to have occurred to them in that form; they rather assumed that a doctrine of ethics is addressed to learners who are in the main willing to be taught, and it is far from certain that they were wrong in so doing. It may be fairly doubted whether it is the business of moral philosophy to establish the existence of its own subject-matter.[20]

[16] Pollock, *op. cit.*, p. 334   [17] *Ibid.*   [18] *Ibid.*, pp. 334–35   [19] *Ibid.*, p. 335   [20] *Ibid.*, pp. 335–36.

THE STOICS

Such sanction as existed in the Stoic system was internal and made itself felt in the conscience of the individual. Sir Frederick quotes in this connection a passage from Marcus Aurelius[21] (whose *Meditations* will be dealt with at greater length on a subsequent page):[22]

When thou hast done a kindness, what more wouldst thou have? Is not this enough that thou hast done something in accordance with thy nature? Seekest thou a recompense for it? As though the eye should claim a guerdon for seeing, or the feet for walking! For just as these latter were made for their special work, and by carrying this out according to their individual constitution they come fully into their own, so also man, formed as he is by nature for benefiting others, when he has acted as benefactor or as co-factor in any other way for the general weal, has done what he was constituted for, and has what is his.

Such doctrines led to several interesting and important theories. For one thing, a reason which is divine can attain to a conception of perfection, of perfect virtue or goodness. Now since man, according to the Stoics, partakes of this divine reason, the completely "wise man" should and would be the perfect man. But what did the Stoics mean by "goodness"?

In his Moncure Conway Memorial Lecture on "The Stoic Philosophy,"[23] Professor Gilbert Murray has answered this question, in an admirable passage which must be quoted at some length. Analyzing Zeno's conception of goodness, he takes up first the Greek definition that "goodness is performing your function well."[24] This, however, is tantamount to defining goodness in its own terms. What is meant by saying that a thing is done "well"?

Here [says Professor Murray] the Greek falls back on a scientific conception which had great influence in the fifth century B. C., and, somewhat transformed and differently named, has regained it in our own days. We call it "Evolution." The Greeks called it *Phusis*, a word which we translate by "Nature," but which seems to mean more exactly "growth," or "the process of growth." It is Phusis which gradually shapes or tries to shape every living thing into a more perfect form. It shapes the seed, by infinite and exact gradations, into the oak; the blind puppy into the good hunting-dog; the savage tribe into the civilized city.[25]

It follows, therefore, that "if you analyze this process, you find that Phusis is shaping each thing towards the fulfilment of its own function—that is, towards the good."[26]

Professor Murray, passing over any consideration of the occasions when this process fails to attain its purposes (for these occasions are merely exceptions to the rule), again refers to "Phusis" as a force resembling in some

---

[21] Book IX, sec. 42.   [22] *Infra*, p. 100.
[23] Delivered at South Place Institute on March 16, 1915. Published in *Essays and Addresses*.
[24] *Ibid.*, p. 96.   [25] *Ibid*.   [26] *Ibid*.

degree our modern "evolution," a force "present in all the live world," and "always making things grow towards the fulfilment of their utmost capacity."[27] It then becomes clear that Greek goodness "is living or acting according to Phusis, working with Phusis in her eternal effort towards perfection."[28] This means more, Professor Murray points out, than our expression, living "according to nature."

It does not mean "living simply," or "living like the natural man." It means living according to the spirit which makes the world grow and progress.[29]

To the Stoics this Phusis was

at work everywhere. It is like a soul, or a life-force, running through all matter as the "soul" or life of a man runs through all his limbs. It is the soul of the world.[30]

But it has another aspect which Professor Murray thus explains:

In Zeno's time the natural sciences had made a great advance, especially Astronomy, Botany, and Natural History. This fact had made people familiar with the notion of natural law. Law was a principle which ran through all the movements of what they called the *Kosmos,* or "ordered world." Thus Phusis, the life of the world, is, from another point of view, the Law of Nature; it is the great chain of causation by which all events occur; for the Phusis which shapes things towards their end acts always by the laws of causation. Phusis is not a sort of arbitrary personal goddess, upsetting the natural order; Phusis is the natural order, and nothing happens without a cause.

A natural law, yet a natural law which is alive, which is itself life. It becomes indistinguishable from a purpose, the purpose of the great world-process.[31]

It is clear that these concepts contain important implications—implications which were developed into tenets of the Stoic doctrine. If man is to employ his reason in the attainment of his end (i. e., goodness or virtue), he must be free. Not only that, but under the universal law he is on a plane of equality with all other men. And again, since he is a reasoning creature possessed of freedom and a status of equality, he is individually responsible for his own development. In this sense each man stands alone and the Stoic is an individualist. Yet, on the other hand, he is also part, with all other human beings,

> . . . of one stupendous whole
> Whose body Nature is, and God the soul.

And in this sense, which deeply impressed itself upon the Stoics, he emerges as a citizen of the world. All men are individuals, they are free and equal:

[27] Gilbert Murray, *Essays and Addresses,* p. 96.   [28] *Ibid.*   [29] *Ibid.*, p. 97.   [30] *Ibid.*   [31] *Ibid.*

but they are also brothers in a common humanity knit together by the bonds of reason, of a purpose common to all, and of a universal law of nature. The idea of a universal community was set forth in Zeno's *Republic* (which unfortunately has not come down to us), as is shown by Plutarch's summary.

> The much-admired *Republic* of Zeno, the founder of the Stoic sect, may be summed up in this one main principle: that all the inhabitants of this world of ours should not live differentiated by their respective rules of justice into separate cities and communities, but that we should consider all men to be of one community and one polity, and that we should have a common life and an order common to us all, even as a herd that feeds together and shares the pasturage of a common field. This Zeno wrote, giving shape to a dream or, as it were, shadowy picture of a well-ordered and philosophic commonwealth.[32]

In their social relations the Stoics in different times and different places emphasized now individualism, now cosmopolitanism. As Professor Murray observes, there were two distinct types of Stoic, "one who defies the world and one who works with the world."[33] In the course of time, and particularly in Rome—where Stoicism was readily accepted and fundamentally affected not only philosophic but legal thought—the latter type of Stoic predominated. As it was adapted and developed by the Romans, Stoicism emphasized devotion to duty, the moral standard of the law of nature, and the community of mankind. It appealed, as an American humanist[34] has pointed out, "to the personal dignity of man, as a sharer in the divine dignity of God." And the same writer adds: "It is, perhaps, this appeal to a sense of personal dignity that gives to Stoicism its imperishable value."[35] The Romans accepted Stoicism as a philosophy, but in the course of time they endowed it with the attributes of a religion, so that in the words of Mr. Henry Dwight Sedgwick, the humanist to whom we have referred,

> even if we concede that Roman Stoicism in Cicero's time was still a matter of the intellect, within a few generations it had acquired the emotional coloring and spiritual significance that convert a philosophy into a religion. The austerity of early Stoicism had been softened by contact with life in the metropolis of the world, it had been tempered by other philosophies, especially by Epicureanism, it had loosed itself from the Hebraic dogmas of Zeno, and acquired a ripeness, a mellowness, that merely needed the saintliness of Marcus Aurelius to give it a religious spirit such as one can find elsewhere at that time only in Christianity.[36]

---

[32] "On the Fortune or the Virtue of Alexander," I. 6; *Moralia* IV. 329A-B.
[33] Murray, *Essays and Addresses* (previously cited), p. 99.
[34] Sedgwick, *op. cit.*, p. 34.   [35] *Ibid.*   [36] *Ibid.*, p. 31.

The Romans thus did much to "humanize" Stoicism, and they also stressed its practical application. It proved, indeed, peculiarly adaptable not only to their temperament but to their aims, as Professor W. S. Ferguson points out

> Rome's need for Stoicism was three-fold: to justify theoretically her dominion over the *orbis terrarum;* to guide her courts in the award of legal rights when political rights did not determine them; and to give her citizens a reason for doing their duty disinterestedly when patriotism proved not enough.[37]

In subsequent pages it will become apparent that both Cicero and Seneca responded to the influence of Stoicism, and that the Stoic conception of the law of nature became the guiding principle of Roman legal philosophy. But for the purpose of indicating the still later effect of the Stoic doctrines on Roman political thought, a few passages may be quoted from the *Thoughts* or *Meditations* of Marcus Aurelius, who as emperor came nearer than any other ruler to realizing Plato's ideal of the philosopher-king.[38]

To Marcus[39] "all things are mutually intertwined," in "one ordered Universe." There is "one God immanent in all things, and one Substance, and one Law, one Reason common to all intelligent creatures, and one Truth." To this conception there is a series of what we may call corollaries:

> That reason also is common which tells us to do or not to do. If so, law also is common. If so, we are citizens. If so, we are fellow-members of an organized community. If so, the Universe is as it were a state—for of what other single polity can the whole race of mankind be said to be fellow-members?—and from it, this common State, we get the intellectual, the rational, and the legal instinct.[40]

Next let us turn to Marcus' conception of the "end for rational beings." It is, we are told, "to submit themselves to the reason and law of that archetypal city and polity—the Universe."[41] For man is a "citizen" of that polity, of "the highest state, of which all other states are but as households,"[42] and it is the citizen's duty to obey the law.

But man is not only a rational being and therefore subject to universal law; he is also a "civic creature,"[43] with civic duties. These two phases of

---

[37] "The Leading Ideas of the New Period," in *The Cambridge Ancient History*, VII. i. 40.

[38] It is recorded of Marcus Aurelius that "The sentence of Plato was for ever on his lips: *Well was it for states, if either philosophers were rulers or rulers philosophers.*"—"Sayings" of Marcus Aurelius, 3.

It may not inappropriately be added that Thomas Jefferson came nearer than any other chief magistrate of modern times to the Platonic ideal of the philosopher-statesman.

[39] *Meditations*, VII. 9.

[40] *Ibid.*, IV. 4.   [41] *Ibid.*, II. 16.   [42] *Ibid.*, III. 11.   [43] *Ibid.*, III. 7.

man's nature were not inconsistent, as Marcus viewed them, and neither should be denied, or suppressed.

> My city and country, as Antoninus, is Rome; as a man, the world. The things then that are of advantage to these communities, these, and no other, are good for me.[44]

In a later passage Marcus affirms:

> I am a part of the whole Universe controlled by Nature; ... I stand in some intimate connexion with other kindred parts. ... As long then as I remember that I am a part of such a whole, I shall be well pleased with all that happens; and in so far as I am in intimate connexion with the parts that are akin to myself, I shall be guilty of no unsocial act, but I shall devote my attention rather to the parts that are akin to myself, and direct every impulse of mine to the common interest and withhold it from the reverse of this. That being done, life must needs flow smoothly, as thou mayest see the life flow smoothly of a citizen who goes steadily on in a course of action beneficial to his fellow-citizens and cheerfully accepts whatever is assigned him by the State.[45]

In the civic state justice should be the rule between its inhabitants. Now it is "in justice," so Marcus maintained, that "all the other virtues have their root."[46] But what does he mean by justice? It is clear that he conceives of justice as having its origin in the universal law, that it is, in the application of right reason.

> A property of the Rational Soul [he explains] is the love of our neighbour, and truthfulness, and modesty, and to prize nothing above itself—a characteristic also of Law. In this way then the Reason that is right reason and the Reason that is justice are one.[47]

Not justice alone, however, but its companions, truth and charity, were essential in social relationships. Marcus' exhortation is that we "live out our lives in truth and justice, and in charity with liars and unjust men."[48]

Like the older philosophers, Marcus seems to have dreamed of an ideal state, although he credits his "conception" of such a state to one Severus, a relative by marriage who was apparently a philosopher. The description of the ideal is brief in the extreme, yet it contains the fundamentals of all good government, for it presents to us "a state with one law for all, based upon individual equality and freedom of speech, and of a sovranty which prizes above all things the liberty of the subject."[49]

But the individual, as we have seen, was something more than a citizen of the state. He was a part of the larger, all-embracing whole with the laws

---

[44] *Ibid.*, VI. 44. [45] *Ibid.*, X. 6. [46] *Ibid.*, XI. 10.
[47] *Ibid.*, 1. [48] *Ibid.*, VI. 47. [49] *Ibid.*, I. 14.

of which, according to the Stoic ideal, he should aspire to be in complete harmony. In the noble and poetic words of the philosopher-Emperor,

All that is in tune with thee, O Universe, is in tune with me! Nothing that is in due time for thee is too early or too late for me! All that thy seasons bring, O Nature, is fruit for me! All things come from thee, subsist in thee, go back to thee. There is one who says *Dear City of Cecrops!* Wilt thou not say *O dear City of Zeus?* [50]

And finally one of Marcus' admonitions to himself must be quoted, an admonition which is at once the code of a good man, a good citizen, and a good ruler, and the essence of a humane and temperate Stoicism:

Keep thyself a simple and good man, uncorrupt, dignified, plain, a friend of justice, god-fearing, gracious, affectionate, manful in doing thy duty. Strive to be always such as Philosophy minded to make thee. Revere the gods, save mankind. Life is short. This only is the harvest of earthly existence, a righteous disposition and social acts.[51]

Of Marcus Aurelius it has justly been said:

He was the noblest of Romans,[52] and take him all in all, there has not been his like since. Between the Rome of his day and our modern world there rolls an ocean of tempest-tossed centuries; and he and we are far apart. It is true that in many respects our modern world is more like that ancient world than like any of the periods between, and yet great human movements, chief among them Christian theology, have so affected our moral atmosphere that at best we must be doubtful of our capacity to judge men of old with due moral appreciation. Nevertheless, his figure seems to stand clearly before us. He was a man of tender and heroic heart, with what one might call a romantic sentiment for self-sacrifice. There never was a great ruler, not even Abraham Lincoln, with less love of self. . . . His *Meditations* reveal his constant endeavor to keep himself unspotted by sin; and so religious are they in their holy purity, so akin in temper, if not in doctrine, to the thoughts of Thomas à Kempis, that one must keep firm hold of the fact that this was no anchorite, no monk, who had turned his back upon the world, but a valiant Roman, soldier and statesman, whose energy, wisdom, courage, and perseverance propped up a tottering world.[53]

The effect of Stoicism on Rome and, through Rome, on the medieval and modern world, is summed up by James Lorimer,[54] a great publicist, jurist, and internationalist of Scotland:

---

[50] Marcus Aurelius, *op. cit.*, IV. 23.   [51] *Ibid.*, VI. 30.

[52] Tributes to Marcus Aurelius' nobility of spirit and of character are indeed legion. To limit ourselves to one further and felicitous example, we may recall the statement of Matthew Arnold that Marcus "is perhaps the most beautiful figure in history. He is one of those consoling and hope-inspiring marks, which stand for ever to remind our weak and easily discouraged race how high human goodness and perseverance have once been carried, and may be carried again. . . . Marcus Aurelius was the ruler of the grandest of empires; and he was one of the best of men."—*Essays in Criticism*, First Series, pp. 354–55.

[53] Sedgwick, *Marcus Aurelius*, pp. 256–57.   [54] *The Institutes of Law*, pp. 151–52, 153.

It ruled Roman life unconsciously before it had any theoretical footing at all; during the period of bloom it held its own against Epicureanism amongst the better spirits; and when finally, as a rule of citizen life, it experienced the relaxing and deadening influences of the empire, it kept alive, as the prevalent theoretical opinion, the idea of virtue as the chief good, and the aspiration after liberty within the sphere of individuality, and the idea of universal charity and cosmopolitan benevolence, as the means to its attainment. Nor ought it to be forgotten that when social corruption and degeneracy had reached their culminating point, and the world of antiquity was about to expire, the last words which she addressed to her successor, the advice which guided the spirit of the middle age and moulded its institutions—its asceticism, its chivalry, and even its romance—consisted in the inculcation of Stoicism. The famous work of Boethius, like the system which it taught, owed very little either to the abilities of its author, or to the speculative value of its subject-matter; to us, it is a disappointing book; and yet, for nearly a thousand years, it enjoyed a reputation such as perhaps never fell to the lot of any other confessedly human production. . . . It was in imitation of these expiring efforts of Stoicism that the *Summa* of the schoolmen and casuists began to be composed—of which the *Summa* of Thomas Aquinas is the noblest specimen; and they in their turn gave rise to the Spanish Theological Jurists.

THE ROMAN HERITAGE

CHAPTER VII

THE LAW OF ROME

THERE ARE TWO IDENTIFICATIONS WHICH HAVE GREATLY AFFECTED ROMAN LAW and therefore its contribution to jurisprudence. The first identification, that of the *ius gentium* with the Roman civil law, resulted in the universal law of the ancient civilized world; the second identification, that of the *ius gentium* with the conception of natural law derived from the Greeks, and especially from the Stoics, eventually resulted in the formation of an international law.

The *ius gentium* is a term which has given rise to much discussion and difference of opinion. It is, however, safe to say that it was not originally regarded as a law universally existing; nor was it a theoretical law. It was a very practical law; it was—as far as Rome is concerned—the law applicable to foreigners living within Roman jurisdiction. The Roman citizen had a law of his own to which only a Roman citizen could appeal. If all the outlying regions of Rome which made up Italy had been inhabited by Roman citizens, and if foreigners had not crossed the Italian frontiers, there would have been a single and identical law of Rome and of Italy. But Rome, originally a small inland community on its Seven Hills in the valley of the Tiber, some thirteen miles from the Mediterranean, constantly enlarged its original territory by conquest of the neighboring Italian communities, so that before the end of the Republic it had not only annexed Italy but Sicily and Sardinia and vast territories encircling the Mediterranean. The little city of Rome had grown into the center and capital of an imperial domain before it expanded itself into an empire. With the growth of the city, however, it became necessary for Romans to have other than warlike relations with peoples beyond its spreading jurisdiction. An international commerce grew up, necessitated in part by the urgent requirements for supplies for Rome's conquering armies. Gradually the peoples with whom this commerce had developed were brought under Roman sway. The trade with the city on the Seven Hills continued, but now largely within the confines of Rome's expanded jurisdiction.

The earlier commerce with peoples beyond the Roman domain had brought many foreigners to Rome. Later, as conquest succeeded conquest, the trade originally with foreigners became a trade with Roman subjects who were not, however, citizens of Rome. Thus it was that as the years passed Rome's non-citizen population (originally consisting of genuine foreigners, but later largely of merchants from subject lands) grew to a considerable proportion as compared with those inhabitants of the city who were actually citizens. An equally important factor was the increasing number of outlying communities whose inhabitants were subject to Rome but were not Roman citizens and who, as their numbers grew, had an ever-swelling volume of business transactions of one kind or another with the citizens of Rome and with one another.

What was the law which should control these many and varied transactions, whether between citizens and foreigners in earlier times, or, in the later period, between citizens and non-citizen subjects, or between non-citizen subjects of different communities? It could not be the Roman law, because Rome was long disinclined to extend the privilege of its law either to a foreigner or to a non-citizen subject. Apparently the solution as regards the relationship between a Roman citizen and a non-Roman was the application to the transaction of the element common in the law of Rome and in the law to which the foreign litigant was subject in his own community. An instance of this is to be found in the conveyance of land to a foreigner by a Roman citizen. To have legal effect, the transaction would need to comply with the strict, rigid Roman law. But in the case of controversy over such conveyance by a Roman citizen to a foreigner, the settlement of the matter was through the mutual acceptance of the principles common to the laws of both. This was a practice to which occasional recourse was had, even before it became the recognized rule. In due course the practice of discovering what may be termed the common legal denominator was also applied to disputes between non-Romans or non-citizens which came up for legal settlement before Roman judicial authorities.

The office of the praetor[1]—whom we might call today, not a judge in the modern sense, but rather a minister of justice within the city, of consular rank and possessing the full power of Rome known as *imperium*—was established approximately 367 years before the Christian Era. Now the praetor as the chief officer of justice was bound to the administration of the Roman civil law—centered in the law of the Twelve Tables—the application of which was limited to cases involving Roman citizens. By his *imperium,* however, he was able to instruct the *iudex* to decide—or exception-

---

[1] On the office of the praetor, see especially Girard, *Histoire de l'organisation judiciaire des Romains.* Vol. I. *Les six premiers siècles de Rome,* pp. 167 *et seq.*

ally, to decide himself—by rules of his own making those cases between citizens which were not covered by the Twelve Tables, or other statutory law, thus legislating, as it were, by means of his *imperium,* in order to meet new conditions not contemplated by the old *ius strictum,* yet keeping always within the ostensible bounds of the civil law. In this way the *praetor urbanus,* for such was his title, did not abrogate the Twelve Tables, but added to them a new law to supply the defects of the old.

So much for cases affecting only Roman citizens. But what of cases involving non-citizens, whether foreigners or subjects? Such litigation, as has been intimated, occurred with increasing frequency in the city of Rome but still more frequently in the outlying Italian communities. This situation led eventually to the appointment of another praetor whose chief duty was to decide those controversies in which at least one of the two contending parties was not a Roman citizen.[2] The full title of this law officer was originally *praetor qui inter peregrinos ius dicit*—a term indicating clearly the nature of his duties—but in the course of time was shortened to *praetor peregrinus,* that is, the foreign praetor.[3]

Now the *praetor peregrinus,* dealing with cases to which the Roman civil law did not apply, was thrown, so to speak, upon his own resources. Appointed to relieve the *praetor urbanus* of an increasing number of cases in which one of the litigants at least was a non-citizen the *praetor peregrinus* was confronted by the question, what was the law which should apply in these cases? It could not be the Roman civil law, applicable only to Roman citizens. Before the establishment of the foreign praetor's office, it appears that the earlier city praetors had decided such cases as arbiters, that is, according to what they considered *aequum et bonum.* But the *praetor peregrinus* was free to go further afield, not merely figuratively but actually—indeed, he subsequently traveled from community to community within the borders of Italy—and it may not inaptly be said that he made his law where

[2] Later, with the rapid expansion of Rome's territorial possessions, additional praetorships were created for the provinces abroad.

[3] "The word *peregrinus,*" says Professor Phillipson (*The International Law and Custom of Ancient Greece and Rome,* previously cited, I, 214-15), "has strictly no precise equivalent in English. Such terms as 'alien' and 'foreigner' are only approximate renderings. It has a larger denotation than 'alien,' inasmuch as it implies not only the nationals of foreign States or of colonies, either autonomous or dependent, but also what the Greeks called ἀπόλιδες, individuals actually without a country, State, or city, those who could not be called *cives* at all,—such as the *dediticii,* subjugated by Rome and deprived of their civic organization, as well as exiles, outlaws. And, further, before the issue of Caracalla's constitution, the majority of the subjects of Rome in her provinces were even denominated *peregrini.* The expression 'non-citizen' is still more inadequate than 'alien' to indicate the position of the peregrine; for 'non-citizen' would, under the earlier Empire, include the Latini Iuniani, who were not *cives,* and yet were not regarded as *peregrini.*"

he found it; in any event he did not decide according to the Roman law as such, but sought his own law outside of the city on the Seven Hills. If the dispute brought before him were between two non-citizens of the same nationality, his decision would usually be in accordance with the law of their community. If they were non-citizens of different nationalities, however, the *praetor peregrinus,* after examining the laws of both, would endeavor to decide the controversy in accordance with a principle common to the laws of both. And finally, if one litigant were a Roman citizen and the other not, the *praetor* again sought a common principle to apply—common this time to the law of Rome and to that of the non-citizen. Thus he chose, in a conflict of two laws or systems of law, the element common to both. This he could do by a free use of his *imperium;* but it is important to note that the *praetor peregrinus* did not himself attempt at any time to interfere with the *ius civile* in its application to purely Roman affairs.

Nevertheless his procedure did affect the civil law of Rome. To return for a moment to the *praetor urbanus.* In the course of time he developed a mode of legislation peculiar to the praetorship—although he was not himself, strictly speaking, a legislator. At the beginning of his year of office, for such was the term of the praetor, it became the custom that he should issue an edict (*edictum perpetuum*) informing the Roman public how he would decide the concrete cases submitted to him and what remedies he would make available.[4] It was also the custom of each succeeding praetor to include in his edict what had proved to be acceptable in preceding edicts. This included matter was known as the *edictum tralaticium.*

The *praetor peregrinus,* as would be expected, likewise annually issued an

[4] "The praetor was entitled to issue edicts and, in fact, these edicts were a very important source of law, but the praetor was not a legislator; he could not alter the law directly and openly as could the sovereign assembly by a *lex* or a *plebiscitum,* and his edict consequently did not take the same form as a statute. It consisted, on the contrary, chiefly of statements by the praetor of what he would do in certain circumstances, of the way in which he would carry out his duty of jurisdiction, and it was the great freedom he had in this respect that made it possible for him to influence the law to such an enormous extent. He would thus say that in such and such a case he would give an action (*iudicium dabo*), i. e., if a man came to him with a complaint against another which did not, at civil law, give him any claim against that other for redress, the praetor might nevertheless allow him an action. Or the praetor might say that in certain circumstances he would put a man into possession of property (*possidere iubebo, bonorum possessionem dabo*), or that he would put a man back in his original position (*in integrum restituam*) i. e., account some transaction, say a contract into which the complainant had been induced to enter by fraud, as never having taken place, and so on. The praetor could also refuse to allow a plaintiff to proceed with his claim, though he did not as a rule announce his intention in exactly this way in the edict. The essence of the praetor's power lies, in fact, in his control over remedies. He does not give a right (as a law can), he promises a remedy, and once there is a remedy there is, by implication, a right also."—Jolowicz, *Historical Introduction to the Study of Roman Law,* pp. 96–97.

edict of his own, known as the *edictum praetoris peregrini*, in which, like the city praetor, he embodied the acceptable portions of his predecessor's edicts. In the course of time the city praetor apparently found it convenient to transfer from the foreign praetor's edict to his own such portions as met with his approval for the amelioration of hardships caused by the rigor of the Roman civil law. By this means the general principles adopted by the *praetor peregrinus* from the laws of many communities entered into Roman civil jurisprudence and became a part of the positive law of the Eternal City. Thus the spirit of common equitable principles triumphed year by year over the harsh letter of the law. In cases involving non-citizens this spirit had already been victorious to such an extent that in the years intervening between the creation of the foreign praetorships and the fall of the Republic, a system of law had grown up, based on the principles of law commonly accepted in the relations of Roman citizens with foreigners. This law was generally assumed to be the law common to all civilized communities. It was, so to speak, law reduced to the lowest common denominator. In other words, the principles of justice everywhere accepted were the basis of this broader all-embracing law, whose name (the *ius gentium*) has been familiar for centuries and centuries to all persons interested in law and jurisprudence. It should be observed, however, that at first this "common" law, as applied between citizens and non-citizens, was regarded as being of a positive nature, in that it was based upon principles drawn from the positive law of the various communities of which the parties in controversy were members. In this earlier and positive form, therefore, it may be said to have lacked a philosophic background.

It was the law of nature which supplied the needed philosophy. Now the law of nature, in its relation to the *ius gentium*, may be looked upon as both a standard rooted in the moral nature of human beings, and as a system of general and universally accepted rules revealed by human reason. This conception it was, of a law founded upon human nature and upon human reason, which ultimately found its place in the greatest of codifications the law has ever known—the *Digest* of Justinian.

But how did this philosophic conception, so fundamental in the development of law, make its entrance into Roman jurisprudence? An answer to this question requires a somewhat detailed consideration of the private law of Rome. It is generally agreed that this private law was developed through various forms of action. Thus in early times a legal remedy lay only when there was an existing *legis actio*—a term with the twofold meaning of a legal right of action, or of an accepted form of legal procedure.

What, however, was the origin of the concept of a legal remedy? At first, it may safely be assumed, the right of self-redress was claimed by the ancestors of the Romans; but in the course of time, as the development has been outlined by Sir Henry Sumner Maine,[5] the contestants for a parcel of land, let us say, adopted the practice of appealing to a bystander to settle their dispute, instead of resorting to the usual method of force. As a private person, the bystander had not the power of the community behind him in the settlement of the difference. He could only render an opinion (*sententia*). But if the parties accepted his opinion, the dispute was settled. If, however, the loser did not accept the *sententia,* then the right of self-redress had full sway. This *sententia* was the beginning, it is supposed, of the Roman judicial remedy, although it was as yet without the sanction of law. But gradually certain Roman officials were granted judicial functions. How did this happen? It may be assumed, as Sir Henry Maine assumes, that the praetor—originally a military officer—happened to pass as the disputants argued, and, being a person in whom they had confidence because of his standing, was called upon to arbitrate the controversy. It is not illogical, in view of later developments, to suppose that calling upon the praetor in such circumstances became a custom, and that gradually a customary procedure grew up, taking the form in due course of the *legis actio sacramenti,* the earliest of all forms of legal action, "out of which all the later Roman Law of Actions may be proved to have grown."[6] The primitive procedure emerges in its legal form in the pages of Gaius' *Institutes,* where he describes at length and with concrete detail the *actio sacramenti.*[7]

[5] *Ancient Law*, with introduction and notes by Pollock.   [6] *Ibid.*, p. 396.
[7] See *Gai Institutiones or Institutes of Roman Law by Gaius,* trans. and ed. by Poste, revised and enlarged by Whittuck, pp. 455–58.
Omitting for present purposes the fragmentary description of the *sacramentum* as a personal action, two sections are here quoted describing the *sacramentum* in the case of a real action and picturing what was once a dramatic legal procedure but which has long since developed into a humdrum process of the courts:
"When the sacramentum was a real action, movables and animals that could be brought or led into the presence of the magistrate were claimed before him in the following fashion. The vindicant held a wand, and then grasping the object itself, as for instance a slave, said: 'This man I claim as mine by due acquisition, by the law of the Quirites. See! as I have said, I have put my spear (vindicta) on him,' whereupon he laid his wand upon the man. The adversary then said the same words and performed the same acts. After both had vindicated him, the praetor said: 'Both claimants quit your hold,' and both quitted hold. Then the first claimant said, interrogating the other: 'Answer me, will you state on what title you found your claim?' and he replied: 'My putting my spear over him was an act of ownership.' Then the first vindicant said: 'Since you have vindicated him in defiance of law, I challenge you to stake as sacramentum five hundred asses': the opposite party in turn used the same words, 'I too challenge you.' That is to say, if the thing was worth more than a thousand asses, they staked five hundred asses or else it was only fifty. Then ensued the same ceremonies as in a personal action. The praetor then awarded to one or other of the

However, except in a few extraordinary cases, the praetor appears soon to have appointed to the arbitral function a private person as his proxy. This appointment might be in accordance with the choice of the parties to the dispute; or, if they failed to agree, the selection was made by the praetor himself. These arbiters, it would seem, were originally not men of law, nor did they need to be, inasmuch as their function was to apply the law which was either supplied to them by the praetors or available to them through the opinions of the jurisconsults. But it doubtless became evident, as litigation increased and the law became more complex, that suitable arbiters were not always easy to find, and hence a group of qualified persons was appointed who would be available to arbitrate disputes—a panel, so to speak, out of which subsequently developed the *album iudicium*. It should be stated, however, that the arbiter did not become a permanent judicial official, a judge in the full sense of the term, until the reign of Diocletian, 290 years after the beginning of the Christian Era. Thereafter he was a judge in law as well as in fact, with the power of the state behind him to enforce his *sententia*—which had developed from arbitral opinions into judicial sentences.[8]

As has been implied, the early arbiter was not required to be learned in the law. Therefore, with the law that was supplied to him, he might also need advice as to its application and interpretation. In due course this need was met by the jurisconsults of Rome, citizens of the "upper class" who were learned in the law but were not law officers or—as we would say—practitioners. It was an honor to be consulted as a legal adviser, just as it

---

claimants possession of the thing pending the suit, and made him bind himself with sureties to his adversary to restore both the object of dispute and the mesne profits or value of the interim possession, in the event of losing the cause. The praetor also took sureties from both parties for the stake (summa sacramenti) which the loser was to forfeit. Now the wand which they used represented a lance, the symbol of absolute dominion, for what a man had captured from the enemy was held to be most distinctly his own. Accordingly in Centumviral trials (where questions of inheritance are decided) a lance is set up in front as an ensign or symbol.

"If the object of dispute was such as could not conveniently be carried or led before the praetor, as for instance a column, or a herd of cattle, a portion was brought into court, and the formalities were enacted over it as if were the whole. Thus if it was a flock of sheep or herd of goats, a single sheep or goat, or even a single tuft of hair was taken before the magistrate; if it was a ship or column, a fragment was broken off and brought similarly; if it was land, a clod; or if it was a house, a tile; and if it was a dispute about an inheritance, then in the same way."—*Ibid.*, IV, secs. 16–17.

For a brief but very lucid discussion of the *legis actio* and its application, see Greenidge, *The Legal Procedure of Cicero's Time*, pp. 49–78.

[8] For a discussion of the development of international arbitration from its foundations in the early procedure of the Roman law, see Scott, *L'Evolution d'une juridiction internationale permanente*. This volume is an expanded version of the article "The Evolution of a Permanent International Judiciary," *The American Journal of International Law*, VI (1912), 316–58.

was an honor to the arbiter to render an opinion. Honor, indeed, was the only reward, for neither one nor the other was entitled to compensation for his services.

We shall see later how the opinions of the jurisconsults grew in weight and eventually assumed the force of law; but for the moment it is sufficient to note the fact that these opinions gradually became positive law, which was to be administered subject to the supreme law-making power of the emperor. Indeed the writings of the jurists, whether privileged or not to give opinions, were to be, after Diocletian, the repository of much of the law of the courts, and they were cited as authoritative. The question therefore arose as to which of the writings, in case of a divergence of views, should be the most authoritative and should be accepted as the written positive law to be applied by and administered in the courts. Early in the reign of Valentinian III, 426 years after Christ, a Law of Citations was issued, decreeing that the writings of Papinian, Paulus, Ulpian, Gaius, and Modestinus, as well as certain writings quoted with approval by those jurists, should be considered as having the effect and force of statutes, and as being, therefore, binding upon the judge, as in the case of other positive law. Justinian reënacted, in the first edition of his *Code,* Valentinian's Law of Citations, and shortly afterwards appointed the commission, the aim of which, in preparing his famous *Digest,* was "to do with thoroughness what the Law of Citations had attempted rudely."[9]

Such, in very brief summary, was the development of the concept of the legal remedy. Since it became associated at an early period, as has been indicated, with the forms of action, it will be necessary to give some attention to the background and development of those forms.

It is generally presumed that in the days of the older kings the College of Pontiffs, a priestly body which in early times appears to have elected its own members, acted in an advisory capacity to the king, giving *consilii* in matters of law as well as of religion.[10] Moreover, the College seems to have determined not only the days upon which legal actions might be brought,[11] but also the forms of procedure, the so-called *legis actiones*. It is probable that both of these matters were originally connected with or formed a part of religious ritual, and such ritual in all of its phases, religious or legal, long

---

[9] Radin, *Handbook of Roman Law,* pp. 90–91.

[10] On the law and procedure of Rome under the kings, see Girard, *op. cit.,* chap. i, and numerous authorities there cited; also Greenidge, "Historical Introduction" to Poste's *Institutes of Gaius* (previously cited), pp. xiv–xv; and James Muirhead, *Historical Introduction to the Private Law of Rome,* Part I.

[11] In this connection see Mommsen, *The History of Rome,* trans. by Dickson, I, 219–20. See also Jolowicz, *op. cit.,* p. 86, n.

remained a strictly guarded secret of the members of the College, who alone in early times were regarded as repositories of both religious and legal knowledge. Thus private law was in the beginning the patrimony, so to speak, of a closed corporation, to which both king and people would turn for instruction or an opinion concerning not only religious matters but also legal rights and duties. And the College, be it noted, was both a closed corporation and an aristocratic, that is to say, a patrician body.

Now how was the legal function of the College exercised? A party to a controversy, or a magistrate, desiring to invoke the law, must needs turn to the College or to an individual member—Pomponius states that one pontifex was designated annually to give counsel in such matters—for information as to the days when suits might properly be instituted and for advice as to the law and procedure applicable. With respect to the days appointed when suits could be brought, the response of the pontifex was not advisory but definitive, and indeed much the same might be said as to the earliest *responsa* in the matter of procedure or form of action and the law involved. But there was still a further element in the *responsa* of the pontifex—the application or adaptation of the form of action to the particular matter in controversy, an element both interpretative and advisory in its nature. The litigant might perhaps disregard this advisory element, but it may be assumed that he could do so only at his peril.

In the course of time, however, the College of Pontiffs underwent changes which profoundly affected its nature, with the result that its legal knowledge became less and less of a monopoly. The first change arose from the publication, about 450 B.C.,[12] of the Twelve Tables, with which it may be said that the real history of Roman law begins, and by which knowledge of the law itself became public property—so much so that for centuries all Romans with any pretense to education committed the law of the Tables to memory. It was statutory law, a codification,[13] so to speak, of traditional

---

[12] This is the date supplied by tradition for the publication of the Twelve Tables, although some modern writers on Roman law place the date of publication much later. See on this question, and on other historical problems pertaining to the Twelve Tables, Pais, *Ricerche sulla storia e sul diritto pubblico di Roma,* especially chaps. i-iv; also Girard, *Mélanges de droit romain,* Vol. I, *Histoire des sources,* chap. i, and appended note, regarding various writings on this question.

[13] It is questionable, however, whether the Twelve Tables should be regarded as a code in the modern sense of a permanent formulation. The Tables were, it is true, destined to have a long life, but it is doubtful if their authors conceived of them as any final and all-inclusive statement of the law. "The most typical and important utterance of the Tables," observes Mr. Greenidge in his "Historical Introduction" to Poste's *Institutes of Gaius,* pp. xxiv-xxv, "is to be found in the injunction that 'the last command of the People should be final.' It is an utterance which shows how little the Decemvirs regarded their own work as final, how little they were affected by the Greek idea of the unalterability of a Code, of a Code

and customary law as it existed at the time, and although it gave to Roman law a rigidity which long hindered its further development, its most important effect, when it was enacted and placed in the forum, was to render accessible to the Roman people as a whole a knowledge of the traditional law hitherto preserved, guarded, and interpreted by the patrician class. From the time of its publication, the pontifex was under obligation to bring his *responsa* within the terms of the Twelve Tables. Nevertheless the monopoly continued, although within narrower limitations, for nearly a century and a half. But as time passed the remaining elements of the monopolistic patrimony became more widely known to those interested in matters of law, so that it was possible for any who cared to do so to make more or less exhaustive notes regarding them, as an unofficial reporter might be minded to do. Apparently such notes were taken by Appius Claudius Caecus, or by his secretary Gnaeus Flavius. At any rate, the latter published, in 304 B. C., "a list of the days which were *fasti*"—when suits might be brought—and "the exact wording of all the *legis actiones.*"[14] This collection, known according to Pomponius as the *ius civile Flavianum,* thus made public not only the legal calendar but also the chief remaining element in the pontifical legal monopoly. A further step, however, remained to be taken—the admission of plebeians to the hitherto patrician college. With this admission the monopoly ceased.

Almost contemporaneous with Appius Claudius's publications is the Lex Ogulnia admitting plebeians and with them fresh air to the college. It is no accident that the first plebeian *pontifex maximus,*[15] Ti. Coruncanius (*cos.* 280 B. C.), was also the first *publice profiteri* (Pomponius, Dig. I. ii. 2, 35, 38), by which phrase we must understand at least that he argued and expounded the questions arising in his practice before those desirous of learning the law. Thereby he was disclosing the last secret, and completing the change from oracular to professional jurisprudence which the Twelve Tables had rendered inevitable in the long run.[16]

---

forming a perpetual background of a Constitution—in fact, by the idea of a fixed or written Constitution at all. It is an utterance that expresses the belief that law is essentially a matter of growth, and prepares us for the fact that Rome saw no further scheme of successful codification until nearly a thousand years had passed."

[14] Radin, *op. cit.,* p. 34.

[15] Jolowicz, *Historical Introduction to the Study of Roman Law* (previously cited), p. 86, n. 1, gives the date of the first plebeian *pontifex maximus* as 253 B. C. It may be added that Professor Jolowicz, in the fifth and sixth chapters of his book, furnishes an interesting and wholly admirable account of the sources of law in the Republic, and of the *jus gentium* and *jus naturale.*

[16] Zulueta, "The Development of Law under the Republic," in *The Cambridge Ancient History,* Vol. IX, chap. xxi, pp. 842, 847.

Thus was completed the laicization of Roman law, and curiously enough the last step in this important process was taken by a *pontifex maximus,* Tiberius Coruncanius, who was, however, not a patrician but a plebeian. He had been consul in 280 B. C. and military commander against Pyrrhus. Trained in the law and possessed of the secret learning of the College, he is also noted as having been the first to offer free public instruction in the use of the *legis actiones,* which is tantamount to saying that he was the first Roman to conduct a course in law open to the public.[17] Of Coruncanius Professor Paul Jörs says:

> He admitted every one to his consultations who showed an inclination for the profession of respondent and before such an audience he would discuss the legal cases submitted to him. It is in this sense that we must look upon *publice profiteri;* it must not be thought of in the light of theoretical instruction. . . . Thus the spell was completely broken by which the pontifices held sway over the development of jurisprudence; the art of the application of law, the tradition of the college, the knowledge of precedent [Vorentscheidung] had become common property. Public instruction in law, as given by C., is the turning point from pontifical to an independent jurisprudence.[18]

[17] It is impossible to overestimate the importance of the innovation of Coruncanius. For a short account of the development of Roman law subsequent to his throwing open, as it were, the last secrets of that law, see Robinson, *Selections from the Public and Private Law of the Romans,* Intro., pp. 19–21. To quote a few sentences from Mr. Robinson: "Tiberius Coruncanius (about 264 B. C.), announced himself as ready to give advice publicly regarding the mysteries of the law (*primus publice profiteri coepit*), not only to those interested as party in a particular case, but also to those seeking a theoretical knowledge of law. This was the beginning of a system of public legal instruction which led soon to the preparation of textbooks and eventually to a legal literature"; and this in turn led, as Mr. Robinson points out, to the "development of a trained legal profession" and the jurisconsults' practice of giving legal *responsa* which were to exert so profound an influence on the character of Roman law.

For a brief but interesting description of the subsequent development of legal education in Rome, see Sherman, *Epitome of Roman Law,* Preface, p. xv.

[18] Jörs in Pauly-Wissowa's *Real-Encyclopädie der classischen Altertumswissenschaft,* IV, 1664. For an extended account of Coruncanius, see Professor Jörs' *Römische Rechtswissenschaft zur Zeit der Republik,* pp. 73–79.

See also Pais, *op. cit.,* pp. 263, 292–93, 310, who says:

"Tiberius Coruncanius, in the period 255–252 B. C., [was] the first of the plebeians to attain the office of *pontifex maximus,* and he was likewise the first to begin the public teaching of law, and even made known his *responsa* in matters relating to the *jus pontificium.* . . .

"For a long time [before this] Rome had been governed by the pontiffs in matters relating to civil jurisdiction. Everything that was dealt with in the *comitia curiata,* that pertained to birth, adoption, adrogation, matrimony and wills, and finally to procedure, remained within the competence of the pontiffs. But the latter, relying upon tradition, were destined slowly to lose ground in the face of challenges or demands on the part of the people, especially with respect to the penal law.

"There is no reason to doubt the statements of the ancients to the effect that the pontiff was 'the arbiter' of all things human and divine, that to him belonged the interpretation of the law. Such was the situation not only in the most ancient times; it lasted indeed until

This admirable statement is confirmed by Professor Sohm:

The announcement made by Tiberius Coruncanius meant that he was prepared to go further and answer questions addressed to him by persons whose interest was purely theoretical, in other words, questions put by those whose object it was to know the law and to study the existing *jus civile*. The knowledge of law was to be opened up to all. Here, then, we have the first beginnings of a system of public legal instruction and—as its necessary consequence—the first beginnings of a juristic literature.[19]

It must not be supposed, however, that the laicization of law and its lay administration were sudden developments following the events just narrated.[20] In point of fact, as we have seen, the office of the praetor charged especially with litigation had been created some sixty-three years before the publication of Flavianus' collection. The earliest praetors, it may be assumed, turned as a matter of course to the College of Pontiffs for legal information and advice. But with the publication of the *ius Flavianum* the praetor was less dependent upon the College, for he had in his own possession the knowledge required for determining the forms, the procedure, and the law which the *iudex,* a praetorian appointee, was to apply to the facts of the case as he found them. The praetor had, however, no monopoly of this knowledge, for it was open also to the public, which would have been quick to resent any departure from the known and accepted legal practice.

In their earlier stage of development the *legis actiones* were rigid legal forms of action, apparently but five in number. They were obligatory upon litigants and were strictly enforced by the magistrates. In the course of time, however, the praetor found the *legis actio,* as such, inadequate for dealing with the great variety of cases which came before him.[21] In an attempt to

---

the end of the fourth and into the third century when through the actions of Tiberius Coruncanius, of Licinius Crassus and the two jurists Mucius Scaevola, there were laid the foundations of the *jus civile* which was later to be separated from the pontifical law.

". . . . The office of *pontifex maximus* was occupied about 255 B. C. by the plebeian Coruncanius who, following the tradition established by Gnaeus Flavius, divulged the secrets of pontifical jurisprudence, himself offering public instruction in the *jus civile* and giving *responsa* with respect to the sacred law."

[19] *Institutionen Geschichte und System des Römischen Privatrechts* by Sohm, trans. by Ledlie, under the title *The Institutes—A Textbook of the History and System of Roman Private Law,* p. 90.

[20] The Romans usually preferred to develop their institutions gradually. They were not given to sudden innovations and hasty changes and experiments, and this is nowhere more apparent than in the growth of the Roman law. For an excellent brief statement on this point see Schulz, *Prinzipien des Römischen Rechts,* p. 58.

[21] The *legis actio* procedure required that claims be strictly phrased in the words of the statute conferring the right of action. As transactions grew more complex and the cases arising out of them more complicated, it obviously became increasingly difficult, and often impossible, to comply with this requirement.

cope with this difficulty the forms were subjected to considerable adaptation, but their essentially ritualistic nature made them inadequate for a progressive amplification to meet new needs and conditions. What then was to be done? The praetor gradually adopted for the civil law the so-called formulary procedure, under which he drew up, after hearing the claims of the parties, a written document "formulating" the issue and indicating the mode of decision imposed upon the *iudex,* appointed for the occasion, which formula was accepted by both parties in controversy. Now the origin of the formulary procedure is to be found in the method adopted by the foreign praetor to settle disputes between non-citizens in which the *legis actio* of the civil law could not be applied. In this, as in many other instances, the city praetor took a leaf from the book of the foreign praetor, but in so doing he created a conflict between the new formulas and the rigid and formalistic *legis actio.*[22] It was probably because of this conflict that the *lex Aebutia* of approximately 130 B. C.[23] was enacted, by which the validity of actions by the formulary procedure was recognized, so that in due course they supplanted the *legis actio* in the city courts. Thus both in the city of Rome and abroad the flexible formulas of the praetors were legally recognized and contributed in no small measure to ameliorating the harsh formalism of the earlier Roman law and to rendering it more just and equitable. We have already seen how the *ius gentium* permeated the Roman civil law through the praetorian edicts, and it may be said that the formulary procedure was another highway by which the *ius gentium* entered Rome.

In following the practical development of Roman law and procedure, it must not be forgotten that there was also a development of theory. It is true that the law grew out of actual practice, and that it was molded and interpreted in response to the needs of daily life. But the theoretical and scientific element was destined to become of even greater creative import than was the influence of practitioners. Even in the earlier stages of the Roman law this element had not been entirely lacking, for there was more than a trace of it to be found in the *responsa* of the *pontifices.* Yet the pontiffs were not free agents as regards legal theory, being bound by patrician precedents and tradition. Moreover, they were disinclined to reveal to the public such theoretical reasoning as entered into their *responsa.* A new era began, however, when the plebeians were admitted to the College, and above

[22] For an interesting account of the formulary system, its nature, application, and origin, see Jolowicz, *op. cit.,* pp. 201–29.

[23] Authorities differ widely on the date of the *lex Aebutia,* but in any event it may safely be assumed that its enactment was some time subsequent to the establishment of the peregrine praetorship in about the year 242 B. C.

all when, as already mentioned, a plebeian became *pontifex maximus* and offered free instruction in the mysteries of the law.

It was inevitable thereafter that legal learning should spread rapidly and should attract an increasing number of laymen, many of whom eventually became sufficiently learned in the law to give opinions on cases brought to their attention by litigants or magistrates. But whereas the *responsa* of the *pontifices* had been binding upon the judges, the opinions of the learned laymen, however respected they might be, had not at first any official standing. Nevertheless, the custom of seeking lay opinions grew, and it became evident that if the practice of giving such *responsa* were not eventually to fall into disrepute, they must be endowed with an official status. Such status they were given by the Emperor Augustus, who decreed that certain of the lay jurisconsults were to have the right to give *responsa*, which thus gained authority because given under his imperial sanction. And later a rescript of Hadrian further strengthened the authority of the opinions of patented jurists, making them in effect binding upon the *iudex*.[24]

Thus the opinions of these jurisconsults became, in due course, a source of positive law.[25] The right to give the authoritative *responsa*—termed the *ius respondendi*—was in fact the privilege of furnishing legal opinions which, when formally delivered, were to be considered authoritative by the *iudex*. At first each of the *responsa*, handed down in writing and under seal, was applicable only to the particular case for which it was delivered. But there

---

[24] For a good brief treatment of the *responsa prudentium*, see Jolowicz, *op. cit.*, pp. 365–68.

[25] "Wer mit diesem Vorrecht ausgezeichnet war, durfte seine Rechtsgutachten im Namen des Kaisers (*ex auctoritate principis*) erteilen. Seine juristische Praxis gewann damit die Autorität, die der Kaiser für sich selbst im ganzen Bereich des staatlichen Lebens beanspruchte, und wie die unmittelbare Äusserung der kaiserlichen Macht im Laufe der Zeit Gesetzesgeltung erlangte, so musste auch das Gutachten eines vom Kaiser privilegierten Juristen schliesslich für den Richter schlechthin verbindlich werden. Es konnte ferner nicht ausbleiben, dass man sich im Rechtsstreit auf derartige Gutachten auch den berief, wenn sie für einen anderen Fall ergangen waren, und dass die Rechtsauffassung, die unter den Trägern des *ius respondendi* herrschte, geradezu als geltendes Recht behandelt wurde. Auf diese Weise hob sich aus der Menge der kaiserzeitlichen Juristen eine Reihe von Persönlichkeiten heraus, denen es kraft kaiserlichen Willens vorbehalten war, in besonderem Masse schöpferisch in den Bestand der Rechtsordnung einzugreifen."—Kunkel, *Römisches Privatrecht* (based on work of Jörs), pp. 24–25.

On the action of Augustus and its consequence, a noted Romanist thus comments: "Whatever may have prompted his action in the matter, its beneficial consequences for the law can hardly be over-rated. For the powers with which they were invested enabled the patented counsel to influence current doctrine not speculatively merely but positively (*jura condere*), and so to leaven their interpretations of the *jus civile* and *jus honorarium* with the principles of natural law as to give a new complexion to the system."—Goudy, late Regius Professor of Civil Law at Oxford, in the article on Roman Law in the *Encyclopedia Britannica*, XXIII, 563.

See also James Muirhead, *op. cit.*, pp. 281–83; Girard, *Manuel elémentaire de droit Romain*, pp. 72–73; Sohm, *op. cit.*, pp. 93–95; and *Imperatoris Iustiniani institutionum libri quattuor*, with Introductions, Commentary, and Excursus by Moyle, Intro., pp. 51–52.

THE LAW OF ROME

seemed no valid reason why an opinion prepared for one case should not apply to like cases in the future, and indeed the practice of citing previous *responsa* soon developed.

Now what was the significance of the *ius respondendi*, apart from the fact that it was, in effect if not in form, a species of judicial interpretation[26] and legislation? The answer to this question involves a consideration of the controlling elements which entered into the formulation of the opinions of the jurisconsults. Obviously the first element must be the existing civil law—and for present purposes that term may include the *ius honorarium*, the expression used to designate the body of law developed through the edicts of the praetors and certain other magistrates.[27] But in the multitude of cases upon which their advice was sought the jurisconsults inevitably found a considerable number to which the civil law was inapplicable in greater or less degree, not to speak of unforeseen situations for which no law of the state existed. And here theory came to the aid of practice. New legal principles, upon which to base new rules and new interpretations, were sought and found, for which principles a philosophical justification was necessary. Whence were these principles derived, and whence their justification? They were drawn from the law of nature and the *ius gentium*, and justified by human reason. This does not mean that the jurisconsults were merely speculators in the realm of philosophy. They were in fact practical and hardheaded, as were most Romans, but legal necessities obliged them to resort to legal theories in search of practical solutions for real and hypothetical questions which presented themselves. The result of their "practical" theorizing was a jurisprudence firmly founded upon general principles which were fundamental in the customs and legislation of enlightened peoples.

The *responsa* of the privileged jurisconsults were not, it should be added,

---

[26] Without attempting here more than a passing reference to the subject, it may be said that the process of interpretation was of vast importance in the development of Roman law. There were in general two types of interpretation: that of the magistrate, growing out of his need to fit the law to new or changing circumstances; and the more theoretical interpretation of the jurisconsults. See the short but admirable discussion of this subject by Greenidge in his "Historical Introduction" to Poste's *Institutes of Gaius* (previously cited), pp. xxxi-xl.

[27] The Roman *ius civile* as such was, of course, statutory law (enlarged in no small measure by interpretation), and therefore to be distinguished from magisterial law. But the two were eventually commingled to such a degree that despite certain differences they may be regarded as a single system. "From the edicts of those whose duty included jurisdiction," says Professor Jolowicz (*op. cit.*, pp. 95-96), "especially from that of the *praetor urbanus*, there arose the *ius honorarium* or magisterial law, which came to be placed side by side with the *ius civile* arising from statute and interpretation, and was interwoven with it in a way which, in spite of important differences, may be compared with the manner in which the common law and equity have combined to make up the English legal system."

the sole juristic literature of Rome. Apart from the formal opinions prepared for their clients, the jurisconsults composed many commentaries and other legal works of a theoretical as well as a practical nature. Then, too, there were distinguished men of law both in the Eternal City and in the provinces who did not possess the *ius respondendi,* but who nevertheless were eminently qualified to write with learning and authority on law, its principles, its interpretation, and its application.[28] They did write, and their works enjoyed an ever-increasing respect, with the result that, when the *ius respondendi* was discontinued at the close of the third century after Christ, the writings of certain of the non-privileged jurists gradually assumed an authority equal to that of the opinions of the privileged jurisconsults.[29] And, like the possessors of the *ius respondendi,* the unofficial jurists were "practical" philosophers in the realm of law, developing fundamental legal theories with an eye always to the actual application of these in the world about them, for many of them were engaged in the practice and teaching of law.

It may not improperly be said that the Roman legal writers, whether "official" or "unofficial," were interested in abstract principles, not as abstractions, but as applicable to concrete questions confronting them. They were not closet philosophers, but they were nevertheless deeply concerned with theories of right and wrong, because they discovered that those theories were essential to the development of law in the form of acceptable rules of action. The jurisprudence of Roman writers, in the words of Ulpian, was the "science which discriminates between the just and the unjust."[30] It was therefore an ethical science, a science of law based upon morality. And finally the law of the jurists was an equitable law, since one of the purposes, if not the chief purpose, of the *responsa* and the accepted writings of other jurists was to temper the harshness of the civil law with the equity derived from natural justice, which is the ideal justice of reasonable human beings. Just, moral, and equitable, the contribution of Roman legal writers was a jurisprudence of universal significance.

But how did the conceptions which formed the philosophic bases of their

[28] Thus Gaius, whose works were destined to exert a vast influence on Roman legal literature, is generally conceded to have been an "unofficial" jurist.

[29] The extent of the authority enjoyed by Roman juristic writings generally has been the subject of no little controversy. For a recent statement on this topic, see *Roman Law and Common Law, a Comparison in Outline,* by Buckland and McNair, pp. 10–14, in which the learned authors indicate how large a part conjecture plays in our knowledge of certain phases of this question.

[30] *Digest* I. i. 10.

responsa, treatises, and disquisitions become a part of the Roman legal heritage?

At a comparatively early period the Romans came into contact with the Greeks, especially in the Greek colonies on the large island of Sicily and in the southern part of the Italian peninsula. But with the definitive conquest of Greece itself and its annexation to the Roman domain, intercourse with the Hellenic world was not occasional nor merely commercial; it was administrative as well. The influence of Greece on Roman legal institutions may, of course, have been antecedent to these events.[31] Tradition has it that the law of the Twelve Tables was drawn up by the decemvirate under Greek influence; indeed the decemvirs charged with drafting the Tables are said to have been directed to put themselves into contact with the Greeks. But without relying upon this tradition, which many authorities question, we know as a fact that with the annexation of Greece, Greek civilization greatly influenced the Romans. If Rome conquered Greece materially, Greece conquered Rome spiritually. In the legal domain that conquest was twofold, resulting in the Roman acceptance of both the conception of the law of nature and the fundamental ethical doctrines of the Stoics.

It was the elite of Rome who first submitted to the Greek influence, and as the jurisconsults of Rome were largely of the patrician class, they soon became acquainted with and accepted Greek theories. But with the Roman jurists the acceptance of a theory meant the putting of that theory into practice. Thus, although they were not originally philosophers, they were destined to become jurists with a philosophic background. And Greece it was which supplied this philosophic background for Roman legal thought. What was the result? The jurisconsults, when confronted by important legal questions, examined them not merely under the existing civil law, not merely in accordance with the edict of the praetor, but in the light of the fundamentals of the Greek law of nature which, in the course of time, had permeated the opinions of one Roman jurisconsult after another.

As has already been indicated, the problem which confronted the jurists was twofold: that of finding principles of law applicable to cases not covered by the increasingly inadequate Roman civil law; and that of ameliorating the Roman law when its application would have resulted in hardship and therefore in injustice. They found the needed principles as well as the ameliorating influence in the Stoic doctrine of a universal and reasonable

---

[31] For an interesting study of Greek elements in the law of the Twelve Tables, see Pais, *op. cit.,* chap. v.

law,[32] equally applicable to all human beings and based upon the essential nature of the human being.[33]

What was this expanding Roman law as it had developed under the all-pervasive influence of Greek philosophy? It may be roughly classified as falling into two general groups, with the same influence operative in both. There was the civil law of Rome (which through the influence of the law of nature was destined to become an equitable law), and there was the *ius gentium* (which from its beginnings as rules based upon the common positive laws of different communities had become largely, if not entirely, identified with the law of nature itself).[34]

[32] "The jurisconsult," Dean Roscoe Pound points out, "had no legislative power and no *imperium*. The authority of his *responsum*, as soon as law ceased to be a class tradition, was to be found in its intrinsic reasonableness; in the appeal which it made to the reason and sense of justice of the *iudex*. In Greek phrase, if it was law, it was law by nature."—*An Introduction to the Philosophy of Law*, p. 29.

[33] "In the main," says Lefroy, ("Rome and Law," *Harvard Law Review*, XX [1906–7], 614–15, 616), "this development of law at Rome in a right and true direction was not the result of any scientific theory of what private law should be, but rather the outcome of circumstances, and of the absolute necessity of devising rules of law applicable to the transactions of trade and the affairs of the numerous transient or permanent non-citizen residents at Rome. The praetors' edict is evidence of the way in which the Roman magistrates met the necessities of the situation with the practical ability which characterized them; but law was still in its empirical stage, nor was the praetors' edict capable of fully meeting the necessities of legal development, any more than legislation by parliament would be in our own day. In order that the expansion and liberalization of the law should advance uniformly towards the building up of a perfect system, it was necessary that some theory, or ideal, as to the true nature of law in general, should establish itself, and this we shall now see was destined in the fullness of time to come to pass.

"This ideal was found, apparently about the beginning of the Empire, in the Stoic conception of a law of nature, which the Roman jurists adopted in their speculations, and applied to matters legal in a way in which the Stoics themselves had never done. The contribution of the Stoics to legal studies 'consisted more in the informing spirit than in any definite conceptions which were borrowed' (W. W. Capes, *Stoicism*, pp. 239–240).

". . . it is to be observed that the semi-official position of the Roman certificated jurists, and the *jus respondendi* which they possessed, and the authoritative force of their legal opinions when produced before the *judices* to whom lawsuits were remitted by the praetor, enabled them in large measure to secure the embodiment of their views in the actual law of the land. As it has been concisely expressed, the bar gave the law to the bench at Rome, not the bench to the bar, as with us. The only objection to the phrase is that, strictly speaking, there was no bar and no bench."

[34] "The theoretical *ius naturale* and the practical *ius gentium* interact, refining and enlarging each other,—the former representing the ideal, what ought to be established, the latter representing the real, what is universally established. And as the two have a very large portion of their respective contents in common and converge towards the same goal, there is a tendency, especially in minds of what may be called a practical nature, to call one by the name of the other. Hence the jurisconsults, whilst using the two expressions as practically synonymous, generally speak of *ius naturale, ius naturae,* or *naturalis ratio,* in order to emphasize the *raison d'être* of some particular rule; and, on the other hand, speak of *ius gentium* when they desire to point out its practical application."—Phillipson, *The International Law and Custom of Ancient Greece and Rome* (previously cited), I, 92.

Now this *ius gentium* may be called, as has been observed, the common denominator of the various systems of law then prevailing in civilized communities. By some authorities it is Englished as the "law of nations." A better rendering of the *ius gentium,* especially in its older Roman significance, would seem to be the common elements of the various systems of domestic law; or better still, the "law common to peoples of different cities," as Messrs. Sabine and Smith put it, in the introduction to their English translation of Cicero's *Commonwealth.*[35] These authors appropriately add that the process of development of this *ius gentium* was "essentially similar to that by which the law merchant was formed and later incorporated with the English common law."[36]

This *ius gentium,* as it was ultimately developed by the Roman jurists, was in essence justice freed from technical requirements. At times identified with the *ius naturale,* so that the two terms were often used indifferently as meaning approximately the same thing, the *ius gentium* may be described as differing from the *ius naturale* largely in the fact that it contained a positive element derived from those positive local laws which were more or less similar among all civilized communities. The *ius naturale,* on the other hand, was in the nature of an ideal and therefore abstract justice, the ideal which the Stoics had held up before the world and which ultimately penetrated the rude and hard law of Rome, contributing to it a quality synonymous to a great extent with the "equity" of our own day.

To consider their contribution from a somewhat different angle, it may be said that what the Roman jurists really did was to give positive form and effect to abstract conceptions and principles. This aspect of their great achievements is stressed by a learned Scots jurist, the late James Muirhead.[37] Citing with approval the views of Voigt,[38] a German authority on the

---

In the view of Mr. Greenidge ("Historical Introduction" to Poste's *Institutes of Gaius,* previously cited, p. xxxvi), the identification of the *jus gentium* and the *jus naturale* "seems to be complete except in one important point. According to the view finally adopted by the jurists, the Jus Naturale implies personal freedom; for all men are born free in a state of nature. But the Jus Gentium (the law of the civilized world) admits the institution of Slavery. In this point, therefore, the two are in conflict, and the Jus Naturale presents an even higher ideal of society than the Jus Gentium. The relation between the three types of Jus, known to the theory of Roman jurisprudence, may be expressed by saying that the Jus Civile is the Right of man as a member of a state, the Jus Gentium the Right of the free man, the Jus Naturale the Right of man."

[35] *On the Commonwealth,* Marcus Tullius Cicero. Trans. with Notes and Introduction by Sabine and Smith, p. 36.
[36] *Ibid.*
[37] *Historical Introduction to the Private Law of Rome* (previously cited), pp. 272–73.
[38] *Die Lehre vom jus naturale, aequum et bonum und jus gentium der Römer.*

law of nature, Muirhead declared that the acceptance of the opinions of the jurists made them in effect the "legislative organs of the state; so that in introducing principles of the *jus naturale* or of *aequum et bonum,* they at the same moment positivised them and gave them the force of law."

The contribution of the jurists, from whatever angle it be considered, is of profound importance to the philosophy of law in general, and in particular to those who believe that law should neither rest insecurely on the sands of expediency nor remain fast in the bog of tradition, but should grow from age to age toward advancing ideals. The significance in this respect of the development of the Roman law has been admirably summarized by an eminent American jurist in a brief page or two:[39]

> It must be borne in mind that "nature" did not mean to antiquity what it means to us who are under the influence of the idea of evolution. To the Greek, it has been said, the natural apple was not the wild one from which our cultivated apple has been grown, but rather the golden apple of the Hesperides. The "natural" object was that which expressed most completely the idea of the thing. It was the perfect object. Hence the natural law was that which expressed perfectly the idea of law and a rule of natural law was one which expressed perfectly the idea of law applied to the subject in question; the one which gave to that subject its perfect development. For legal purposes reality was to be found in this ideal, perfect, natural law, and its organ was juristic reason. Legislation and the edict, so far as they had any more than a positive foundation of political authority, were but imperfect and ephemeral copies of this jural reality. Thus the jurists came to the doctrine of the *ratio legis,* the principle of natural law behind the legal rule, which has been so fruitful both of practical good and of theoretical confusion in interpretation. Thus also they came to the doctrine of reasoning from the analogy of all legal rules, whether traditional or legislative, since all, so far as they had jural reality, had it because and to the extent that they embodied or realized a principle of natural law.
>
> Natural law was a philosophical theory for a period of growth. It arose to meet the exigencies of the stage of equity and natural law, one of the great creative periods of legal history. Yet . . . even the most rapid growth does not permit the lawyer to ignore the demand for stability. The theory of natural law was worked out as a means of growth, as a means of making a law of the world on the basis of the old strict law of the Roman city. But it was worked out also as a means of directing and organizing the growth of law so as to maintain the general security. It was the task of the jurists to build and shape the law on the basis of the old local materials so as to make it an instrument for satisfying the wants of a whole world while at the same time insuring uniformity and predicability. They did this by applying a new but known technique to the old materials. The technique was one of legal reason; but it was a legal reason identified with natural reason and worked out and

---

[39] Pound, *An Introduction to the Philosophy of Law* (previously cited), pp. 31-34.

applied under the influence of a philosophical ideal. The conception of natural law as something of which all positive law was but declaratory, as something by which actual rules were to be measured, to which so far as possible they were to be made to conform, by which new rules were to be framed and by which old rules were to be extended or restricted in their application, was a powerful instrument in the hands of the jurists and enabled them to proceed in their task of legal construction with assured confidence.

In this way the theory of an ideal justice as contained in the natural law began to pass into practice in the administration of law in Rome and throughout its outlying possessions. If the theory did not entirely pass into the practice of the Romans, neither, we may add, has the theory of today become the practice of today. Indeed it is the hope of the future that the entry of theory into practice may never be complete, that theory may always lead and illumine the way in a never-ending process.

"Ideals," in the words of Messrs. Sabine and Smith,[40] "are not important solely because they triumph, but rather because they furnish some principle of rational guidance, some factor of intelligent control, in a society which, lacking them, would scarcely rise above the instinctive, the habitual, and the brutal." If the ideal of justice embodied in the natural law never became in its full extent the justice administered through the *ius gentium* and the Roman law, nevertheless, largely because of the responses of the jurisconsults, the law of nature did permeate and guide the *ius gentium* and the *ius civile* which Rome handed down to posterity.

Of the Roman understanding of the interrelation between the law of Rome and the *ius gentium,* made up of universal laws and customs and supplemented by the law of reason, no better example can be given than a masterly and familiar passage from the *Institutes* of Gaius:

All peoples who are ruled by laws and customs partly make use of their own laws, and partly have recourse to those which are common to all men; for what every people establishes as law for itself is peculiar to itself, and is called the Civil Law, as being that peculiar to the State; and what natural reason establishes among all men and is observed by all peoples alike, is called the Law of Nations [*ius gentium*], as being the law which all nations employ. Therefore the Roman people partly make use of their own law, and partly avail themselves of that common to all men.[41]

And perhaps there is no more concise statement of the function of the Roman jurists in exercising the *ius respondendi* than Gaius' brief sentence: "The answers of jurists are the decisions and opinions of those who are authorized to define the law."[42]

---

[40] In their "Introduction" to Cicero, *On the Commonwealth* (previously cited), p. 38.
[41] I. i. 1; trans. by S. P. Scott, *The Civil Law*.   [42] I. i. 7.

Ulpian, another famous Roman jurist, defined the natural law and the *ius gentium* (in somewhat different terms):[43]

Natural law is that which nature teaches to all animals, for this law is not peculiar to the human race, but affects all creatures which deduce their origin from the sea or the land, and it is also common to birds. From it proceeds the union of male and female which we designate as marriage; hence also arises the procreation of children and the bringing up of the same; for we see that all animals, and even wild beasts, appear to be acquainted with this law.

The Law of Nations [*jus gentium*] is that used by the human race, and it is easy to understand that it differs from natural law, for the reason that the latter is common to all animals, while the former only concerns men in their relations to one another.

These definitions are of the two great branches of what may for the moment be called non-Roman law, in that it did not originate in Rome. Among the best definitions of the strictly Roman or civil law is that Papinian:[44] "The Civil Law is that which is derived from statutory enactments, plebiscites, decrees of the Senate, edicts of the Emperors, and the authority of learned men."

In this connection Papinian also deals with the praetorian law, defining it[45] as "that which the Praetors introduce for the purpose of aiding, supplementing, or amending the Civil Law, for the public welfare."

No appreciation of the fundamentals of Roman jurisprudence would be possible without the quotation of two or three additional definitions from Ulpian. The first is on the subject of freedom. "According to the natural law," he declares,[46] "all persons were born free."

Next of justice: "Justice is the constant and perpetual desire to give to every one that to which he is entitled."[47] This is the justice not only of the market place and the forum but of the inner conscience, for it implies a full and continuous recognition of the rights of others, accompanied by a scrupulous respect for those rights. If it be true that such definition may apply to a static condition of society in which rights are rigidly graded, is it not equally true that it may apply also in a progressive society in which rights and duties are constantly expanding? At any rate, it may safely be said that civilization has not yet outgrown Ulpian's definition, although conceptions of human rights and duties have advanced from age to age.

There is another definition in which Ulpian combines in a single sentence the essence of the law natural and of its progeny, equity, with

---

[43] *Digest* I. i. 1, secs. 3–4 (Ulpianus, Book I, *Institutes*).
[44] *Ibid.*, 7.   [45] *Ibid.*, sec. 1.   [46] *Ibid.*, 10.   [47] *Ibid.*, 4.

justice: "The precepts of the law are the following: to live honorably, to injure no one, to give to every one his due."[48]

Ancient Rome—the Republic and the Empire in all their material grandeur—lives only in the pages of history. But its law, like the City of Rome, is eternal. In the words of an Italian Romanist, Roman law "dominò le persone per secoli e domina tuttora il pensiero giuridico per merito dei suoi giuristi."[49]

The value of our political and legal heritage from the ancient world has been assessed with remarkable lucidity in Professor McIlwain's *The Growth of Political Thought in the West*:[50]

The philosophic basis of Roman law is Greek and it was laid in the Republican period, but the particular principles of the law itself are Roman, worked out step by step with patient thoroughness by generations of magistrates and jurists. As the poet says of the English constitution they were "broadening down from precedent to precedent," slowly expanding to meet changing social and economic needs in a sure and gradual development scarcely matched in the whole history of human institutions for the length of the process or the permanence and solidity of the result.

After quoting from an admirable French exposition of the juridicial institutions of the Romans,[51] the statement "that the Romans have fixed for all time the categories of juristic thought," Professor McIlwain continues:

Cato might have boasted of the permanence of Roman private law with even more justice than he did of the Roman Republic and for the same reason: it was established not by the genius of one man but of many, nor for the life of one but for ages.

Contrasting the Greek and Roman contributions to political and legal science, Professor McIlwain says:

The Greek genius produced a theory of the state and of law, Rome above all developed a scientific jurisprudence. . . . A permanent legal system such as Rome's or England's must be a gradual evolution, a conservative development based on precedent, and the work of innumerable hands, the product not so

---

[48] *Ibid.*, 10, sec. 1.
[49] Perozzi, *Istituzioni di diritto Romano*, I, 48.
So too, the great historian, Gibbon, pays his respects to the law of Rome: "The vain titles of the victories of Justinian are crumbled into dust; but the name of the legislator is inscribed on a fair and everlasting monument. Under his reign, and by his care, the civil jurisprudence was digested in the immortal works of the CODE, the PANDECTS, and the INSTITUTES; the public reason of the Romans has been silently or studiously transfused into the domestic institutions of Europe; and the laws of Justinian still command the respect or obedience of independent nations."—*The History of the Decline and Fall of the Roman Empire*, ed. by Bury, IV, 441.
[50] Pages 121–22.   [51] Cuq, *Les Institutions juridiques des Romains*, I, xxiv.

much of individual genius as of collective administrative ability, and of this the brilliant restless mind of Greece seemed impatient.

But, he warns us, "It is dangerous to generalize about racial characteristics, and Greece had little chance to develop the political solidarity necessary for a great permanent system of jurisprudence." It is true that individual states "like Athens, and probably others if we knew more of them and their institutions, had gone some distance in that direction." But the facts remain, Mr. McIlwain points out, that for one reason or another "Greece produced, and in the circumstances could produce, nothing comparable with the Praetor's edict," and that "Rome certainly produced no political philosopher comparable with Aristotle."

What is the learned writer's conclusion? "Greek political philosophy—whatever the reason may be—was largely the work of exceptional individuals." On the other hand, "the Roman constitution was the working system of a capable people; and naturally the former tended to emphasize aristocracy; the central principle of the latter was the sovereignty of the *populus*." This, however, is by no means to minimize the value of the Roman contribution, for while "Rome's influence upon the growth of political thought is thus radically different from that of Greece," it is, nevertheless, "in its way scarcely less important."

If the Roman Empire had survived as a unit, the civil law of Rome would have remained the law of the Roman world, just as the law of Justinian, in Greek translation, remained—with various modifications—the law of the Eastern Empire until its overthrow by the Turks in 1453. The history of the West, however, was different from that of the East; for the West succumbed to the repeated invasions of Germanic peoples from the north, and 476 years after Christ a Teutonic king (Odoacer) was installed in Rome. From that time the Empire of the West crumbled, and in crumbling gave way to various kingdoms and princedoms set up by different German tribes under their respective chieftains. The conquering invaders brought with them their laws, but the Romans and the Romanized inhabitants of the provinces which they had overcome endeavored to keep as much as possible of the Roman law with which they were familiar. In this endeavor they succeeded to such a degree that their conquerors permitted them for the most part to retain their own law. In some instances, it is true, the Teutonic rulers provided new codes for their Roman subjects,[52] but these were based largely upon Roman legal authorities. In general the whole question appears

---

[52] Such as the *Lex Romana Visigothorum* and the *Lex Romana Burgundionum*.

to have been settled in the manner indicated by the decree of Chlothar II: "We have ordained that the conduct of cases between Romans shall be decided by the Roman laws."[53] In dealing with their own people the invaders not unnaturally preferred their own law, but it was inevitable that the two systems of law, existing side by side, should influence each other. In the course of time, as will appear in a subsequent chapter, there was a compromise between the two systems. Here it will suffice to note that Roman law eventually triumphed, so much so as to become the source of the civil law, not merely in Italy but in Spain and in France. For the moment it is necessary to emphasize only the fact that the law of Rome continued to exist in many if not in all of the separate units which had formerly constituted the Roman Empire. It was no longer the universal law, but it was the one law which was common to many of the separate units or principalities. It was not the law of the Teutonic portion of the population, but on the other hand the fact that the invaders had settled within the area of, though not under, its jurisdiction, gave them an increasing familiarity with and respect for its rules and concepts.

What was the result? By way of reply to this question a single example will suffice; that of medieval Lombardy. An eminent authority on Roman law during the medieval period,[54] after a careful examination of the legal literature of the time, arrives at the conclusion "that the Lombard doctors considered Roman Law as the general or common law to which recourse must be made in all cases where Lombard enactments provided no ground of appeal." Apparently this was a well-established practice, and indeed was recognized as a rule and not as mere theory. "The rule is stated in so many words," we are told, "in the Exposition to Guido, c. 5: the ancients said that, as the law did not contain any precepts on certain questions, such cases must be decided according to Roman Law, which is the general law of all (*qui omnium est generalis*)."

Now the existence of numerous principalities or kingdoms gave rise to intercourse of various kinds between them. Here two factors of importance must be considered. The principalities in question became Christianized, and Latin was the language of the Christian Church. Again, the Roman law passed into the canon law of the Church as one of its chief constituents What was more natural, therefore, than that the law to be applied by these newly established principalities in their relations one with another should be the law common to them, that is to say, the Roman law? In other words,

[53] Quoted by Jenks in his *Law and Politics in the Middle Ages*, p. 15.
[54] Vinogradoff, *Roman Law in Medieval Europe*, pp. 52–53.

the common element in the law of each of these peoples became, as it were, a new *ius gentium*—the common law of the principalities in their external relations.

But why was it called the *ius gentium?* The answer will be clear if we consider the matter from a slightly different angle. The original *ius gentium* of Rome had consisted of the principles common to the laws of the various peoples which came into contact with Rome. After these peoples had been drawn into the Roman Empire, there was but one jurisdiction, and the law of the peoples became law in the empire; indeed, the *ius gentium* permeated the civil law, as has been observed, until the two were in fact, if not in terminology, largely identical. When, however, the Empire was dissolved and separate principalities came into existence, the *ius gentium* (which had almost become absorbed into the civil law of the Empire) again emerged as the common law of the peoples, in due course to become, in the language of our day, the law of nations or law international.

Obviously, if there was to be a law applicable to the mutual relations of the principalities, it would hardly be the law of one principality as distinct from that of others; there must be a common denominator. For this problem the natural solution, as has been implied, was the resurrection of the *ius gentium,* which had been applied almost from time immemorial to the relations both with foreigners and with the numerous inhabitants in those different parts of the Roman Empire to which the civil law of Rome had not yet been extended. In other words, the *ius gentium,* having been once the law applicable to relations with foreigners and other non-citizens, would logically and almost inevitably be chosen again as the law to be applied between groups of foreigners or the principalities which succeeded the Roman Empire. Now the *ius gentium,* as thus taken over and adapted to newer conditions, was for the most part—with the exception, of course, of its rules regarding slavery—identified with, or at least a logical development from, the natural law, which thus became the foundation of the law applied between the independent communities; or, to put it in more figurative language, the law of nature is the very root and trunk from which the law of nations has branched.

Fortunately the intimate relationship between natural law and the *ius gentium* was not overlooked by the Spanish schoolmen, of whom but one need be cited here. In 1532 Francisco de Vitoria, who was moved by the discovery of America to write on the status of the Indians, declared that the *ius gentium* "either is natural law or is derived from natural law." It will be shown in a later chapter how Vitoria, taking his text from the *Institutes* of Justinian, laid upon this relationship the foundations of the modern law of nations.[55]

And in our own day, the late Sir Frederick Pollock declared:[56] "We must either admit that modern International Law is a law founded on cosmopolitan principles of reason, a true living offshoot of the Law of Nature, or ignore our own most authoritative expositions of it."

APPENDIX I

The Stoic Philosophy and the Later Jus Gentium[1]

THE UNITY WHICH THE ROMAN LAW ACQUIRED BY BEING BROUGHT UNDER THE authority of the Emperor as supreme law-giver would have been merely formal and artificial had it not been supplemented by some more fundamental and rational principle of growth. A more important unifying influence than that due to political centralization was derived from the philosophical spirit that pervaded the legal thought of the time. It was this scientific spirit that distinguished the law of the Empire from that of the Republic.

During the Republican period, the law had advanced, for the most part, through empirical methods. Legal reforms had been brought about through the agency of the praetor, and in the actual process of administration. The rules of law had not been deduced from general principles of justice; but had been gathered together from local customs, or constructed by the extension of existing law to new cases as they might happen to arise. The praetorian law, like the old *jus civile,* had grown up through procedure. Under the Empire, however, the belief that law was founded upon ethics, that the specific rights and duties of men were derived from certain ultimate and universal principles of natural justice, furnished a new impulse and gave a new direction to legal development.

The effort to found civil law upon natural equity gave to Roman jurisprudence a breadth and liberality that it had not possessed under the Republic; and, in fact, resulted in the development of a body of universal legal principles applicable to all times and nations. The influences which thus furnished a scientific impulse to the legal reforms of the early Empire were derived, in great part, from the philosophy of the Greeks—especially that of the Stoics.

1. *The Stoic Philosophy at Rome.*—Since the conquest of Greece, this philosophy had been received with favor by the Romans, and was especially culti-

---

[55] *Infra,* p. 316. [56] *Essays in the Law,* p. 67.
[1] Reprinted from *Outlines of Roman Law, Comprising Its Historical Growth and General Principles,* by Morey, pp. 107-15.

vated by the more intelligent classes. Even under the later Republic it had been a formidable rival of the schools of Epicurus and Carneades. Cicero, though attached to the speculative doctrines of the New Academy, accepted with little change the ethical principles of the Stoics. After the establishment of the Empire, this philosophy attained a still greater influence; and although it was proscribed by a few despotic princes, it was the object of favorable regard on the part of nearly all the early emperors. Athenodorus was highly esteemed and often consulted by Augustus. Seneca was a Stoic as well as a statesman, and as long as he was the adviser of Nero, the imperial government was mild and judicious. Under Antoninus Pius, schools of Stoicism were supported at public expense. In the person of Marcus Aurelius, Stoicism ascended the throne of the Empire; and from the time of the Antonines to that of Alexander Severus this philosophy continued to be taught at Athens and Alexandria, the two great intellectual centres of the Roman world.

The Stoic philosophy thus became an important element in Roman education and culture, and received the almost uninterrupted support of the state during the period in which the influence of the Roman jurisconsults was most marked.

2. *The Stoic Theory of Natural Law.*—The prevalence of a philosophy so vigorous and elevating as that of Stoicism could not fail to affect the fundamental conceptions and the habits of thought of all those persons who were brought under its influence. It will not be difficult for us to find in this system certain doctrines, which, however vague and speculative they may appear in the writings of Greek theorists, were yet capable of a practical application in the hands of Roman jurists, in solving questions regarding the rights and duties of men in civil society.

The point of contact between the Stoic philosophy and Roman jurisprudence is to be found in the theory of the Law of Nature—which the Stoics had deduced from their conception of the universe, and which the Roman jurists employed, under the name *jus naturale,* to indicate the natural or ethical foundation upon which civil law must rest. With the Stoics, the universe was considered as imbued with an all-pervading soul or power, which was looked upon not only as a dynamical force producing motion, but as a rational principle producing order and perfection. This rational principle is a constituent element of all being. It is revealed not only in external nature as a law of the physical world, but also in the original nature of all men as a guide for human conduct. The great duty of man is, hence, to discover and conform to the highest law of reason, as this law is set forth in the essential constitution of his nature. "To live in harmony with nature" was thus the highest precept of the Stoic philosophy, and the ultimate principle which must guide men in all the relations of life. By his original constitution, man is a participant of the Universal Reason, and by the exercise of his rational faculties he can discover the law of nature, so far as it is necessary to control his own conduct. When looked at from a moral point of view, the law of nature is thus the highest rule of human conduct, and the ultimate standard by which all human actions, whether individual, social, or civil, must be judged.

3. *Acceptance of This Theory by the Jurists.*—This conception of natural law worked its way into Roman thought, and was used to explain, not only the foundation of individual and social morality, but also the basis of legal rights and duties. From the time of Cicero to that of Alexander Severus, the legal literature of Rome is pervaded with the idea that law has a more ultimate foundation than custom or convention—that it is founded in the very nature of things. The first important attempt made by the Roman writers to ground law upon nature we find in the "Laws" of Cicero, where the fundamental proposition is laid down "that man is born for justice, and that law and equity are not a mere establishment of opinion, but an institution of nature" ("De Leg.," Bk. I.). The specific application of this principle in determining legal rights and duties was reserved for the jurists of the Empire.

The influence of Stoicism upon the Roman lawyers is not to be judged—as was attempted by Cujacius and his followers—by any servile repetition of particular moral precepts. It is to be judged rather by the prevalent belief in natural law as the ethical basis of civil law; by the general recognition of the supremacy of reason as a guide in civil action; and by the common method which came to be employed of interpreting legal duties in the light of the higher principles of natural equity. It is sometimes claimed that the idea of natural law exercised very little influence upon these writers, on the ground that the term itself is rarely employed in their works; and that, when it is employed, it is not used in the sense of the Stoics. But as a matter of fact, not only is the term "natural law" specifically defined by the institutional writers in an ethical sense, but the method of reasoning which is used in their interpretation of the law is founded upon the theory that the civil law must be brought into harmony with natural justice—with what is right in the nature of things.

It is true that Ulpian gave a peculiar definition to natural law—as that which nature teaches all animals—which conception exercised little or no influence upon the legal thought of Rome. But even Ulpian in other forms of expression recognized, like his contemporaries, an ethical standard of law; for example, when he defines justice as the "constant desire to grant each one his right"; when he lays down as the fundamental precepts of the law, "to live right, to hurt no one, to give to each his due"; when he defines jurisprudence as "the science of what is just"; and when, in speaking of the duties of the jurists, he says: "We cultivate justice, and the knowledge of the right, distinguishing right from wrong, the lawful from the unlawful" (D., 1, 1, 1). But to cite from other jurists: Paulus refers definitely to the law of nature as a moral principle, when, in distinguishing the various meanings attached to the word *jus*, he says: "That which is always right and good is called *jus*, or rather *jus naturale*" (D., 1, 1, 11). The belief that all law is limited and determined by nature is expressly declared by Celsus in the words: "Things prohibited by nature can be justified by no law" (D., 50, 17, 188).

These few illustrations are sufficient, for the present, to show that the jurists of the Empire possessed certain philosophical conceptions concerning the moral basis of law which were closely related to the ethical system of the Stoics. The influence of these conceptions, and the method of reasoning which followed their adoption, will be more clearly understood as we proceed.

4. *New Meaning Attached to* Jus Gentium.—The influence of new ideas in changing the significance of existing phrases is seen in the way in which the term *jus gentium* came to be turned from its old meaning and brought into harmony with the new theory of natural law. This term was originally applied, as we have seen, to the body of customs common to Rome and the states subject to Roman dominion. As the Roman conquests came to be looked upon as universal, the *jus gentium* was considered to be the law common to all nations. But still there was attached to the term no philosophical meaning. It was simply the sum of the ingredients which were found in the actual laws of existing communities. When viewed, however, in the light of the "natural law," the *jus gentium* acquired a new significance. The common laws collected by the praetors were now believed to be based upon that natural law which the Universal Reason had instituted for all men. The fact that they were common seemed to prove that they were derived from universal principles inherent in the very nature of man. The tendency thus showed itself among the more philosophical jurists to identify the *jus gentium,* in its highest sense, with the *jus naturale.* Gaius says that "the law which natural reason has constituted for all men obtains equally among all nations, and is called *jus gentium*" (Gaius, Inst., 1, 1).

This higher interpretation of the *jus gentium* served to explain the practical superiority of the praetorian law over the ancient *jus civile.* It was now easy to see that the praetors in their efforts to develop a universal law had been unconsciously reaching after the perfect law of nature. But with the highest respect for the edictal law so far as it had been developed, it was yet believed that the perfect law of reason could best be discovered not through the empirical method of the praetors, but through the rational interpretation of the jurists; and these writers, when expounding the Edict, felt called upon to construe it as far as possible in accordance with the highest dictates of reason.

The gradual change in the meaning of the term *jus gentium* also explains the apparent ambiguity which is sometimes seen in its use during this period. For example, Florentinus says that "slavery is an institution of the *jus gentium,* by which one becomes subject to another contrary to nature" (D., 1, 5, 4, 1). This could hardly be true in the sense in which Gaius used the term, as being the law which is in conformity to natural reason. It is evident that while the old meaning of the word has survived in the former author, it has acquired its higher philosophical significance in the latter. Slavery was consistent with the older idea of *jus gentium* as a body of common usages, but it was inconsistent with the later idea of *jus gentium* as a body of principles founded upon the law of nature.

5. *The Later* Jus Gentium *Viewed as Equity.*—As the *jus gentium* received a higher significance when seen in the light of the theory of natural law, so too the conception of equity passed from that view in which it refers simply to the broader and more liberal portion of the positive law, to that view in

which it is looked upon as a rational standard to which all positive law must conform.

The old *jus gentium* by its incorporation into the praetor's edict, had become a part of the positive law of Rome. It possessed as definite a sanction as the *jus civile*, and was in the same way enforced by the public authority. As it was distinguished from the special and technical features of the *jus civile* by containing broader and more liberal rules, it was sometimes called *jus aequabile*, *jus aequum*, or *aequitas*. Equity, in its earlier sense, thus referred to the more general and impartial rules which the positive law had derived from the administration of the *praetor peregrinus*. But with the growth of more philosophical ideas regarding the *jus gentium*, it was believed that the superiority of the equitable portion of the positive law was due to its approximation to the perfect law of reason. That is, equity, in its highest sense, is identical with natural reason and justice. In this way the *positive equity* of the praetors, which had been derived from the observation of general customs, and had become actually incorporated in the existing body of law, was supplemented by the *natural equity* of the jurists, which was based upon the dictates of reason and regarded as a moral standard by which the character of the existing law must be judged, and to which it must as far as possible be made to conform.

It was by means of this higher conception of equity, which resulted from the identification of the *jus gentium* with the *jus naturale*, that the alliance between law and philosophy was made real and efficient. As the ethical system of the Stoics thus acquired a legal significance in the writings of the jurists, there was erected a moral standard of justice to which every expounder of the law felt obliged to appeal, and by a comparison with which the defects of the existing law were exposed and corrected. Paulus says: "In omnibus quidem, maxime tamen in jure, æquitas spectanda est" (D., 50, 17, 90), and the same jurist in interpreting a provision of the edict defends the position which he advocates by saying: "Hæc æquitas suggerit, etsi jure deficiamur" (D., 39, 3, 2, 5). According to the view of the classical jurists, law, though made compulsory by the state, derives its ultimate authority from the moral code of nature, and is itself regarded simply as a means for the administration of justice.

APPENDIX II

The Ius Gentium *in Roman Jurisprudence*

It is universally admitted that the natural law and the *ius gentium* penetrated the civil law of Rome, making that equitable in the highest degree which had hitherto been not only national and local but rigid and often inequitable. The significance of this relationship may, however, be overlooked unless recourse is had to the results of expert and authoritative investigation. A distinguished Latinist, Henry Nettleship, Corpus Professor of Latin in the University of Oxford, set himself the laborious task of searching the extant literary remains of Rome, in order to discover the meaning of the *ius gentium*, its relationship to the law natural, and the place of both in Roman jurisprudence. The task he found difficult indeed, for it led him, to quote his own words, "to examine all the passages" in which he could "find that the expression"—meaning *ius gentium*—"occurs." Certain passages in his article, *"Ius Gentium,"*[1] are of unusual interest and value.

He begins by laying before his readers three quotations: the first from Sir Henry Maine's *Ancient Law;* the second from Puchta's *Cursus der Institutionen;* and the third from Professor Clark's *Practical Jurisprudence.*

After referring to Maine's view "that the foreigners, who came in great numbers to Rome, could not have cases of their own decided by the Roman *ius civile*," Professor Nettleship proceeds to quote at length from the volume *Ancient Law,* to the effect that the Romans

set themselves to form a system answering to the primitive and literal meaning of *Ius Gentium,* that is, a Law Common to all nations. *Ius Gentium* was, in fact, the sum of the common ingredients in the customs of the old Italian tribes, for they were *all the nations* whom the Romans had the means of observing, and who sent successive swarms of immigrants to Roman soil. Whenever a particular usage was seen to be practised by a large number of separate races in common, it was set down as part of the Law Common to all Nations, or *Ius Gentium*. . . . The *Ius Gentium* was accordingly a collection of rules and principles, determined by observation to be common to the institutions which prevailed among the various Italian tribes. . . . The *Ius Gentium* was merely a system forced on his [the Roman's] attention by a political necessity. He loved it as little as he loved the foreigners from whose institutions it was derived and for whose benefit it was intended. A complete revolution in his ideas was required before it could challenge his respect, but so complete was it when it did occur, that the true reason why our modern estimate of the *Ius Gentium* differs from that which has just been described is, that both modern jurisprudence and modern philosophy have inherited the matured views of the later jurisconsults on the subject. There did come a time, when, from an ignoble appendage of the *Ius Civile,* the *Ius Gentium* came to be considered a great though as yet imperfectly developed model to which all law ought as far as possible to conform.[2]

Next of Puchta, whose exposition of the matter was somewhat different:

He starts from the *Ius Fetiale,* and assumes that in the ancient treaties between Rome and Carthage there must have been clauses regulating the relations arising from the intercourse of the private citizens of the allied states. Then, after discussing the institution of *recuperatores* and the appointment of the *praetor inter peregrinos* (B. C. 267), he goes on:[3]

"Es bildete sich aus jenen ersten beschränkten Anfängen des Fremdenverkehrs, aus den particulären Landesrechten der Peregrinen, die bei ihren Rechtstreitigkeiten zur

---

[1] Nettleship, "Ius Gentium," *The Journal of Philology,* XIII (1885), 172.

[2] *Ibid.,* p. 169; Maine, *Ancient Law* (5th ed., 1865), pp. 47–50.

[3] Nettleship, *op. cit.,* p. 170; Puchta, *Cursus der Institutionen,* Band I: *Geschichte des Rechts bei dem römischen Volk,* p. 206.

IUS GENTIUM IN ROMAN JURISPRUDENCE

Sprache kamen, und aus den Ansichten der Römer selbst über das, was unter den gegebenen Umständen als gerecht und passend erschien, ein allgemeines römisches Peregrinenrecht."

Interpolating a comment on this statement Professor Nettleship observes:

If, for instance, a *peregrinus* claimed a piece of property before the tribunal of a Roman praetor, he found that he could not, not being a Roman *civis*, use the *formulae* of the Roman *ius civile*: so that the case was decided according to universally accepted principles, or (if so be) according to the law recognized by the state or nation to which the *peregrinus* belonged.

The eminent Latinist[4] then continues his quotation from Puchta:

"Das römische *ius gentium* ist das Recht welches Rom den *Gentes*, also den Völkern ausser dem römischen, in ihren Gliedern, die vor den römischen Behörden Recht suchen, gewährt, Zugleich liegt in dem Wort, dass es ein allgemeines, nicht bloss für ein einzelnes Volk bestimmtes Recht ist. Es ist endlich auf dem Grund einzelner fremder Rechte entstanden, aber erst auf dem römischen Boden, unter dem Einfluss römischer Ansichten durch die Römer selbst zu diesem allgemeinen Character ausgebildet worden...

"War es doch in der That selbst römisches Recht, wenn auch aus nicht rein-römischen Principien gebildet... Es war nur ein kleiner Schritt, in dem *Ius Gentium* ein allgemeines Recht zu erkennen, und zu schliessen, *quod civile non idem continuo gentium, quod autem gentium, idem civile esse debet."*

And Puchta's conclusion, Professor Nettleship states, is summed up thus:

"Das *Ius Gentium* hat zwei Seiten: einmal ist es das allgemeine Peregrinenrecht, nach welchem die Römer die Rechtsverhältnisse von Personen beurtheilten, für die das *Ius Civile* keine Anwendung fand: die Grundlage dieses Rechtes waren wirkliche Peregrinenrechte, nur nach dem Bedürfniss allgemeiner Anwendbarkeit und unter dem Einfluss römischer Auffassung mannigfaltig modificirt und erweitert.

"Dann aber ist es das Recht, welches in den erweiterten allgemeinen Rechtsansichten des römischen Volks seinen Ursprung hat, das also nicht auf eine künstliche Art, durch Speculation oder gelehrte Forschung, gemacht, sondern durch die innere Macht des in seiner Bildung fortschreitenden Volksgeistes hervorgetrieben ist."[5]

As is to be expected, Professor Nettleship contrasts the views of Messrs. Maine and Puchta:

Sir Henry Maine regards the *Ius Gentium* as originally "the sum of the common ingredients in the customs of the old Italian tribes": Puchta regards it as a law essentially Roman, though formed partly out of non-Roman elements, administered to the *gentes* or non-Roman peoples. Both Sir Henry Maine and Puchta think that the idea expressed by *ius gentium* underwent a change, that from meaning the law of, or the law administered to, foreigners the expression came to connote universal law, or the law which lies at the foundation of all particular codes: but Puchta thinks this change easy and natural, while Sir Henry Maine supposes that it required "a complete revolution" in Roman ideas.[6]

---
[4] Nettleship, *op. cit.*, p. 170; Puchta, *op. cit.*, pp. 206–7.
[5] Puchta, *op. cit.*, p. 208.
[6] Nettleship, *op. cit.*, p. 171.

Professor Clark's account differed from that of the two authorities just quoted:

> Taken as a whole, Cicero's, which seems not improbably to have been the first, *ius gentium,* is in its origin a *ius naturae,* a philosophic ideal. . . . It is something which should rightly, but may not actually, form part of the law of a particular nation. Springing from the "partnership of all mankind," it forbids the sharp practice which a national law will often allow. It is in fact little removed from the theoretical law of the older Stoics. . . .
>
> The theoretical *Ius Gentium* becomes more and more identified with parts of existing systems in general, and in particular with that part of the Roman system which turned, from the old national rules, towards reasonableness and equity. It would perhaps be more correct to say that the former theory of the *ius gentium* was replaced by a new one, for the later classical jurists probably concerned themselves as little with the examination and comparison of different actual systems as did Cicero and his Stoic teachers.[7]

The views set forth in this passage are thus contrasted, in the comment which immediately follows it, with the theories expressed in the preceding quotations: "Professor Clark, therefore, supposes that a change took place in the application of the term, but in an opposite direction to that indicated by Puchta and Sir Henry Maine." [8]

Professor Nettleship next attempts, on the basis of his own elaborate investigations, to establish the following propositions:

(1) *Ius Gentium* is a popular, as well as a legal, phrase;

(2) Its legal usage is pre-Ciceronian, and is essentially the same as the popular usage;

(3) No essential change took place at any time in the application of the term;

(4) In its application to transactions between states or communities, there is no evidence that the *ius gentium* had any necessary connection with the *ius fetiale* or the institution of *recuperatores;*

(5) In the legal writers the phrase is mostly applied to certain simple cases of contract, of action, and of ownership;

(6) The word *gentium,* as Professor Clark says, bears the same meaning as in the phrases *nusquam gentium, minime gentium, ubi gentium,* and thus *ius gentium* means the common law or usage of the world;

(7) *Ius gentium* has certain points of agreement with, and certain points of difference from, *ius commune* and *ius* or *lex naturae. Ius gentium* is a Latin and popular, *ius naturae* a Greek and philosophical expression.

For present purposes Professor Nettleship's argument on the first five propositions—in which argument he cites chapter and verse at length—may be omitted, in order to present his discussion of the sixth proposition:

> We are now in a position to ask what was the original meaning of the expression. As I have said above, I believe that *ius gentium* meant *the usage of the world, of all mankind,* and that it was in all probability first employed as a quasi-technical expression by the lawyers of the second century B. C., Cicero's *maiores.* They originally

---

[7] Nettleship, in *The Journal of Philology,* XIII (1885), 171–72; Clark, *Practical Jurisprudence,* pp. 358–59.

[8] Nettleship, *op. cit.,* p. 172.

intended to express by it such customs or usages as the Romans found, in the experience which they would pick up away from Italy in war or commerce or travel, or in their intercourse with *peregrini* in Italy itself, to be universally observed. These usages would naturally be connected in the main with war and commerce, and thus *ius gentium*, when the term is applied to the dealings of Romans with foreigners, is used mostly of the laws of war and of transactions involved in a state of war, or of commerce and transactions connected with it, such as *obligationes* of various kinds. The sea, as being the property of no state or person in particular, is *iuris gentium:* in other words, at sea only such usages are considered binding as all states are agreed upon. So of the shore and alluvial deposits: they belong to no one and may be claimed by anyone, for all allow the claim.

I cannot agree with Puchta that the *ius gentium* was exclusively a product of Roman law applied to the dealings of the Romans with the *peregrini* who came to Italy. This theory seems to me too narrow, because it ignores the fact that while, after the first Punic war, many foreigners came to Italy and Rome, many Romans and Italians also went abroad, and came into constant contact with the inhabitants of Greece, Macedonia, Syria, and Africa. In the numerous details of commerce and general intercourse which would be brought across his path, the Roman would find some practices or usages universally prevalent, and these he referred to the category of *ius gentium*.[9]

What was the result? These universal practices and usages eventually assumed "such importance . . . in the eyes of the jurists of the second century B. C., that *ius gentium* was formally distinguished from *ius civile.*" Thus the former was, to the jurists, "universal, informal, often unwritten usage," while the latter consisted of "special, formal, recorded enactments."

The seventh and last proposition which Professor Nettleship laid down had to do, as we have seen, with the question of the relation of *ius gentium* to *ius commune* and *lex naturae*. From his answer to this question we lift certain passages:

In accordance with the meaning of the word *communis*, *ius commune* by itself should mean *the law or usage acknowledged by the speaker or writer in common with certain other persons whom he is addressing, mentioning, or thinking of:* and this is in fact the case, as will be seen by the following examples: . . .[10]

Of these examples only three need be quoted here:

Aut cum iure communi aut cum rebus iudicatis dissentire. (The standard of justice or right which you and I acknowledge.)[11]

Siculi neque suas leges neque communia iura tenuerunt. (The rules of law common to them and ourselves.)[12]

Totum ius fetiale et alia iura communia. (The rules observed by both of the contending parties.)[13]

Professor Nettleship then passes to the law of nature, saying: "*Lex* and *ius naturae* are philosophical phrases, imported from Greece." What, then, was the relationship of the *ius naturae* to the *ius gentium*? In his answer to this query he invokes a distinguished German Romanist:

[9] *Ibid.*, pp. 178–79. [10] *Ibid.*, p. 179. [11] Cornificius *Ad Herennium* 2, sec. 14.
[12] Cicero *Ad Verrem* Actio 1, sec. 13. [13] Cicero *De officiis* 3, sec. 108.

Voigt has, in my opinion, correctly conceived the difference between *ius naturae* and *ius gentium*, where they differ. *Ius gentium* is usage actually existing everywhere: *ius* or *lex naturae* is an ideal law, a law that may or may not exist in universal practice, but which is in any case to be wished for. Thus it may often coincide with *ius gentium*, but may sometimes differ from it.[14]

Referring now to Cicero, Professor Nettleship says: "Cicero, it must be observed, generally uses *lex naturae* in a context where he intends to give a philosophical tinge to his writing." [15]

He then quotes Cicero[16] as wishing to explain the less familiar *lex naturae* by the more familiar term *ius gentium*. And while Professor Nettleship grants that the *lex naturae* and the *ius gentium* were at times distinguished from one another, he adds by way of conclusion: "In most cases, however, in later Latin the two expressions are virtually synonymous."

[14] "Ius Gentium," *The Journal of Philology*, XIII (1885), 180.

[15] Nettleship adds: "Thus in the *De Inventione*, a treatise which, it must be remembered, is in great part a translation from the Greek, we have (2 161) *naturae quidem ius esse, quod nobis non opinio sed quaedam innata vis adferat*: ib. 67 *naturae quidem iura minus ipsa quaeruntur ad hanc controversiam: quod neque in hoc civili iure versantur et a vulgari intellegentia remota sunt: ad similitudinem vero aliquam aut ad rem amplificandam saepe sunt inferenda.* Tusc. Quaest. 1 sec. 30 *consensus omnium gentium lex naturae putanda est*: Rep. 1 sec. 27 *nec civili nexo sed communi lege naturae*. In the *De Legibus*, the phrase, it need hardly be said, occurs often."

[16] In *De Haruspicum responsis* xiv. 32: *lege naturae, communi iure gentium* and in *De officiis* iii. 23: *natura, id est iure gentium*.

CHAPTER VIII

MARCUS TULLIUS CICERO (106-43 B.C.)

For his countrymen, and for posterity throughout the civilized world, the writings of Cicero were the most important of the several channels through which Greek philosophy reached Rome. Lawyer and orator, statesman and politician, military commander (who was rewarded with a triumph), student and man of letters, Cicero was also one of the world's great philosophers. In our modern day, however, it has been the custom of certain critics to belittle his works, to dismiss his philosophical conceptions with the statement—which is, after all, but half true—that he was merely a transmitter, that he derived the whole of his philosophy from the Greeks. And here, as is so often the case, the half-truth is misleading. For while Cicero did translate, paraphrase, or otherwise incorporate in his treatises the leading doctrines of the Greek schools, he also freely adapted and modified his borrowed materials—even illustrating them copiously with Roman literary and historical examples—and thus rendered them more readily applicable to the life and institutions not only of Rome but of the medieval and modern world. In a word, Cicero transmuted as well as transmitted these great doctrines of the past.

Moreover, if his philosophy was not his own because it was based so largely upon the teachings of the Greek masters, none can deny that he exhibited an ability which amounted to sheer genius in presenting their theories in a classical Latin garb,[1] at once accessible and intelligible to his own and to later ages.[2] For not only did Cicero create, as a distinguished Classicist tells us, "a language which remained for sixteen centuries that of the civilised world," and "a style which nineteen centuries have not replaced,

---

[1] "Cicero's claim to originality, and it is a very real claim, consists in the fact that he alone saw the possibility of creating a philosophical literature in Latin."—Torsten Petersson, *Cicero, a Biography*, p. 585.

[2] Cicero it was, says Mr. George Chatterton Richards, "who first made his mother tongue into a magnificent vehicle of speech whether in oratory or writing, and he it was who preserved the best of Greek thought to the following ages by translating it into exquisite Latin. Thus during the long centuries when Greek was practically unknown to the western world, some tincture of Greek thought was preserved to it in the writings of Cicero."—*Cicero, a Study*, p. 2.

and in some respects have scarcely altered"; [3] he also enriched his mother tongue with a philosophical terminology which was to have a profound effect both on philosophy in general and on political and legal theory through the centuries during which Latin was the common language of Europe.[4]

Modern criticism has at times attacked Cicero from a somewhat different angle, accusing him of giving sonorous utterance to truisms and platitudes. The answer to this accusation is simply that many of the doctrines which Cicero stressed have been so universally accepted that they are now regarded as commonplace and self-evident truths. But they were not commonplace in the age of Cicero. That they are so considered today is merely proof that time has woven his doctrines into the tapestry of our civilization in a design grown so familiar that to us it appears trite and obvious. "If his philosophy seems now to have exhausted its influence, it is because it has in great measure been absorbed into the fabric of civilized society." [5]

It is not difficult to criticize Cicero as a man or as a philosopher, for he had his share of human weaknesses. In political life he was a "new man," an ambitious man, and the student of his career will discover that it was at times marred by faults and mistakes. Yet the just critic can but admit that Cicero's political virtues far outweighed his defects; that his influence as a statesman in his own and later ages was due to his genuine patriotism and to the loftiness of his motives and political ideals. Indeed it is the measured judgment of an American authority on the life and literature of Rome that "whenever government officials have been actuated by a high sense of responsibility and a genuine spirit of patriotism, they have consciously or unconsciously followed in the footsteps of Cicero." [6]

The real difficulty is to appreciate the importance of his contributions to our social conceptions and institutions. Perhaps the best answer to disparag-

---

[3] Mackail, *Latin Literature*, p. 62. "Ciceronian prose," adds Mr. Mackail (p. 63), "is practically the prose of the human race; not only of the Roman empire of the first and second centuries, but of Lactantius and Augustine, of the mediaeval Church, of the earlier and later Renaissance, and even now, when the Renaissance is a piece of past history, of the modern world to which the Renaissance was the prelude." For a discussion of the influence of Cicero's style through the centuries, see Sandys' lecture "The History of Ciceronianism," in his *Harvard Lectures on the Revival of Learning*, pp. 145–73.

[4] "Before the works of Cicero, no attempts worth considering had been made for using the Latin tongue in philosophical subjects. The natural stubbornness of the language conspired with Roman haughtiness to prevent this application. . . . Yet, with whatever discouragement his design was attended, he ultimately triumphed over the pride of an unlettered people, and the difficulties of a defective language."—Newman, "Marcus Tullius Cicero," *Historical Sketches*, p. 261.

[5] Mackail, *op. cit.*, p. 73.   [6] Rolfe, *Cicero and His Influence*, p. 27.

ing criticism is that, after all has been said that can be said by way of depreciation, the indisputable fact remains that Cicero's writings have stood the test of time. They have endured for two thousand years among that small group of permanent treasures of the spirit which humankind cherishes from age to age. It is more than doubtful if time will deal so charitably with his modern critics.

A statement by Mr. J. W. Mackail supplies what is perhaps the most accurate and measured estimate of the value of Cicero's contributions:[7]

Cicero represents a force that no historian can neglect, and the importance of which it is not easy to over-estimate. He did for the Empire and the Middle Ages what Lucretius, with his far greater philosophic genius, totally failed to do—created forms of thought in which the life of philosophy grew, and a body of expression which alone made its growth in the Latin-speaking world possible; and to that world he presented a political ideal which profoundly influenced the whole course of European history even up to the French Revolution. Without Cicero, the Middle Ages would not have had Augustine or Aquinas; but, without him, the movement which annulled the Middle Ages would have had neither Mirabeau nor Pitt.

At an early age Cicero became indoctrinated with Greek philosophy, studying under the great teachers of the day, first in Rome and subsequently abroad in Athens and elsewhere. Throughout an exceptionally active life he appears to have lost none of his youthful interest in the writings of Plato, Aristotle, Zeno, and other Greek masters. Thus it was natural that when, in later life, he was beset by personal or political troubles, he should turn to philosophy as a refuge and solace. During these periods of distress he occupied himself with writing, among other works, a series of what might be called manuals of philosophy in which, as we have seen, he incorporated the great conceptions of the Greeks. Now the Greek philosophers devoted no little attention to politics and law. It was therefore to be expected that Cicero—himself both a lawyer and a politician—would also deal with these subjects. This he did at length, writing on the state (*De re publica*) and on law (*De legibus*), as Plato had done some three centuries before. And not only did he write on the same subjects as the Greeks; he cast his discussions in the same literary form, the dialogue.

It is said that his dialogues were modeled on those of Aristotle, and it is certain that they are less dramatic in form than the Platonic dialogues. But it was perhaps to Plato even more than to the founder of the Peripatetic School that he was indebted for much of the substance of his philosophy.

[7] Mackail, *op. cit.*, pp. 73–74.

His tastes, however, were catholic, his culture broad; he did not, therefore, confine himself to any one school of thought, but chose from many what seemed to him the best.[8] In his own day the two leading systems of philosophy were the Stoic and the Epicurean. Most of the tenets of the latter Cicero rejected outright as being demoralizing. But Stoicism could not be so easily dealt with. Certain of its harsher features—its fatalism, its formalism, and its paradoxes—repelled him. Its ethical doctrines, on the other hand, its emphasis on morality, on reason, on the unity of mankind, attracted him more and more as he grew older. And at sixty he began to wonder if, after all, the Stoics were not "the only true philosophers."[9]

In a sense it was not strange that Cicero apparently found the ethical theories of the Greeks (which were political as well as individual) the most attractive part of their philosophy. For he was, after all, a Roman despite his familiarity with foreign culture, and the Roman's chief interest lay not in knowing, but in doing; not in profound speculation and the acquisition of wisdom for its own sake, but in action. It was because of this that the Romans were so deeply interested in regulations of action, i.e., in rules of conduct or law. And ethics was a guide to action; in that sense it was the most "practical" branch of philosophy. Himself a man of action, the leader of the Roman bar, Cicero thought most often in terms of conduct and rules of conduct, and it is for this reason that ethics bulks so largely in his treatises.[10]

[8] The truest description of Cicero, says Mr. Richards, "is that he was 'Father of Humane Letters,' the first parent of that international culture which strives to incorporate in one the best from every source, and which assuredly is the only hope for the future to-day."—Richards, *op. cit.,* p. 3. On a later page (p. 282) the author adds: "The Latin language has an untranslatable word *humanitas:* a Professor of Latin in Scotland has always borne the title 'Professor of Humanity.' Whether the word means unfailing sympathy with brother man, be he slave or noble, foreigner or fellow citizen, or kindliness and obligingness of disposition, or social *bonhomie* and acceptableness, or culture in its widest sense of the word, in each and all of its senses, it would be hard to find a better exponent than Cicero."

[9] Cicero *Tusculan Disputations,* IV. xxiv. 53.

[10] This is not the place to undertake a comparison of the intellectual and moral qualities of Cicero and Caesar. Yet the latter has been so long extolled (and his martial exploits imbibed by every schoolboy), while the former has been so often and unjustifiably denounced, that we cannot refrain from quoting at length the just comparison made by Mr. Richards, *op. cit.,* pp. 278–79:

"They [Cicero and Caesar] were in many ways extremely similar. Both were adepts at winning influence and untiring in doing personal favours, and both were lucky in having devoted friends. It is true that Caesar won his enemies by bribery, and did not always secure their good opinion when he had bought them . . .; but his personal qualities won for him the loyalty of a Matius. Both were generous and, as a rule, forgiving. There were exceptions in both cases. Both cared little for money in itself except as an instrument of power. Caesar's attitude to money was exactly that of Cecil Rhodes. Both may be acquitted of the sordid avarice which disgraced so many of their contemporaries. Finally, both were devoted to the culture of the mind.

Of the two treatises—*De re publica* and *De legibus*—which deal particularly with political science and law, the former was for many centuries accounted a lost work. The modern world's knowledge of it was limited to fragments preserved in various manuscripts until the year 1820, when Cardinal Mai, Prefect of the Vatican Library, discovered a considerable portion of it in a palimpsest which contained St. Augustine's Commentary on the Psalms. Two years later the Cardinal published the recovered manuscript, and *De re publica* thus at long last fulfilled its destiny by becoming, even in its incomplete form, one of the great source books for students of the history of political theory.

De legibus, too, is incomplete. But the portion which has survived (the first three books, forming perhaps half of the treatise) was long available in manuscript to the medieval world and appeared in print as early as 1498. Of the lost books no less a person than Professor McIlwain[11] has said that their discovery "would more than compensate for the lost books of Livy's history."

In the first book of the treatise *De re publica*[12] Cicero gives us his conception of the nature and origin of the state and, as we would expect, this conception is one inherited from the Greeks:

A commonwealth is the property of a people. But a people is not any collection of human beings brought together in any sort of way, but an assemblage of people in large numbers associated in an agreement with respect to justice and a partnership for the common good. The first cause of such an association is not

---

"But the differences between them were more numerous. Cicero was essentially a man's man and had no romantic side: to Caesar, even if one rejects the vulgar scandals about him, the society of women was an essential part of life.

"Cicero became a great figure in politics rather by accident than because he sought anything beyond the ordinary career of a Republican statesman. Caesar was ambitious of something that soared above that: he was a 'born dictator.' Thus there was this moral barrier between them. Cicero held with Plato that to do violence to one's fatherland was as bad as doing it to one's father: Caesar had no such scruples. Cicero hated bloodshed: Caesar did not seek it; but if he thought it necessary, had no pricks of conscience. Cicero's triumphs were won in peace: Caesar, at the age of over forty, suddenly became one of the few great generals of the world. He made no changes in the art of war, but he was a born leader. Cicero was saluted father of his country, for foiling an anarchic plot in 63 B. C.: Caesar for annihilating his fellow citizens in the battle of Munda, 45 B. C. Cicero permanently influenced the thought and expression of the Roman world, and through it the nations of modern Europe: Caesar inaugurated an imperial period which only ended in 1918. The world is anxiously asking itself at this moment [1935], 'What is to follow?' and hoping that it will not be the ruthlessness and *Schrecklichkeit* shown by our modern imitators of Caesar but the kindlier spirit of reconciliation which Cicero seems to have advocated in his works *On the Republic* and *On the Laws*."

[11] *The Growth of Political Thought in the West* (previously cited), p. 106 n.
[12] I. xxv. 39.

so much the weakness of the individual as a certain social spirit which nature has implanted in man.

This social spirit is innate in man; it is, as Cicero tells us, part of his nature. This view must later be considered at greater length, but it may here be remarked that it points to the doctrine of the brotherhood of man, a doctrine rooted in Stoic philosophy and approximated by Cicero in a passage in *De legibus*[13] where he refers to "our natural inclination to love our fellow-men," an inclination which is "the foundation of Justice."

What was to be the purpose of the state? Not merely that its inhabitants should be able to live, but that they should, as the Greeks said, "live well" and in happiness. "It is impossible," Cicero tells us, "to live well except in a good commonwealth, and nothing can produce greater happiness than a well-constituted State." [14]

But something more than association by agreement was necessary if the state was to be "well constituted." There must be provision for government: [15] "Nothing is so completely in accordance with the principles of justice and the demands of Nature (and when I use these expressions, I wish it understood that I mean Law) as is government, without which existence is impossible for a household, a city, a nation, the human race, physical nature, and the universe itself."

The form of such government was a matter to be settled by the choice of the people, though Cicero himself favored what he described as a mixed form. But whatever choice might be made, there were certain principles which were fundamental to all government. The first is that the unifying element in the state, the "bond" as Cicero termed it, is law, the purpose of which is to enforce justice between the citizens. A state, indeed, is "an association or partnership in justice." [16] And justice, in Cicero's opinion, was no mere product of devious legal definition; it was a primary element in all human relationships, for it was based on good faith. "The foundation of justice," he tells us elsewhere, "is good faith—that is, truth and fidelity to promises and agreements." [17]

Justice is impossible, however, unless there be equality between the citizens. Here again Cicero is indebted to the Greeks, and especially to the Stoics. But he does not advocate the absolute equality which would "equalize men's wealth" or require the false assumption of an "equality of innate ability." What he demands is equality of rights under the law: "The legal

---

[13] I. xv. 43. Cf. I. x. 29. [14] *De re publica* V. v. 7. [15] *De legibus* III. i. 3.
[16] *De re publica* I. xxxii. 49. [17] Cicero *De officiis* I. vii. 23.

rights . . . of those who are citizens of the same commonwealth ought to be equal."[18]

Again, there can be neither justice nor equality in a society whose members are slaves or serfs. Hence in Cicero's state there must be liberty. But liberty means, in the final analysis, that the people must be recognized as the source of power. Cicero maintains, indeed, that "liberty has no dwelling-place in any State except that in which the people's power is the greatest, and surely nothing can be sweeter than liberty; but if it is not the same for all, it does not deserve the name of liberty."[19]

Liberty, therefore, must be guarded. It cannot thrive—and in fact the entire welfare of the state is imperiled—if a people yields itself to the whims of a despot. "The fortune of any people is . . . a fragile thing," Cicero observes, "when it depends on the will or the character of one man."[20] Virtue, not power and wealth, should be the standard of government; and virtue in this sense implies reason embodied in law which is supreme over governor and governed alike.

What can be nobler than the government of the State by virtue? For then the man who rules others is not himself a slave to any passion, but has already acquired for himself all those qualities to which he is training and summoning his fellows. Such a man imposes no laws upon the people that he does not obey himself, but puts his own life before his fellow-citizens as their law.[21]

We have here referred to Cicero's conception of law as the embodiment of reason. It was a conception (derived from the Greek philosophers, especially from the Stoics) which became almost an obsession with him, and he dwelt upon it again and again in his writings. Thus we encounter it in a fragment of *De re publica* preserved for us by Lactantius:

True law is right reason in agreement with nature; it is of universal application, unchanging and everlasting; it summons to duty by its commands, and averts from wrongdoing by its prohibitions. And it does not lay its commands or prohibitions upon good men in vain, though neither have any effect on the wicked. It is a sin to try to alter this law, nor is it allowable to attempt to repeal any part of it, and it is impossible to abolish it entirely. We cannot be freed from its obligations by senate or people, and we need not look outside ourselves for an expounder or interpreter of it. And there will not be different laws at Rome and at Athens, or different laws now and in the future, but one eternal and unchangeable law will be valid for all nations and all times, and there will be one master and ruler, that is, God, over us all, for he is the author of this law, its promulgator, and its enforcing judge. Whoever is disobedient is fleeing from

---
[18] Cicero *De re publica* I. xxxii. 49.
[19] *Ibid.*, 47.   [20] *Ibid.*, II. xxviii. 50.   [21] *Ibid.*, I. xxxiv. 52.

himself and denying his human nature, and by reason of this very fact he will suffer the worst penalties, even if he escapes what is commonly considered punishment.[22]

Here Cicero is dealing in fact, if not in name, with the law of nature, universal, immutable, of divine origin yet identical with right reason and therefore manifest to and binding upon reasoning and reasonable beings. Through *De legibus* the same conception runs like a refrain. For present purposes, however, quotations from that treatise must be limited to but a few passages, of which three require no comment:

Let us investigate the origins of Justice. Well then, the most learned men have determined to begin with Law, and it would seem that they are right, if, according to their definition, Law is the highest reason, implanted in Nature, which commands what ought to be done and forbids the opposite. This reason, when firmly fixed and fully developed in the human mind, is Law. And so they believe that Law is intelligence, whose natural function it is to command right conduct and forbid wrongdoing. . . . Now if this is correct, as I think it to be in general, then the origin of Justice is to be found in Law, for Law is a natural force; it is the mind and reason of the intelligent man, the standard by which Justice and Injustice are measured.[23]

Since there is nothing better than reason, and since it exists both in man and God, the first common possession of man and God is reason. But those who have reason in common must also have right reason in common. And since right reason is Law, we must believe that men have Law also in common with the gods. Further, those who share Law must also share Justice; and those who share these are to be regarded as members of the same commonwealth.[24]

Justice is one; it binds all human society, and is based on one Law, which is right reason applied to command and prohibition. Whoever knows not this Law, whether it has been recorded in writing anywhere or not, is without Justice.[25]

From time to time mention has been made of the influence of Stoicism on Cicero's views. That influence is more than apparent in the fourth of the passages to be quoted:

It has been the opinion of the wisest men that Law is not a product of human thought, nor is it any enactment of peoples, but something eternal which rules the whole universe by its wisdom in command and prohibition. Thus they have been accustomed to say that Law is the primal and ultimate mind of God, whose reason directs all things either by compulsion or restraint.[26]

And finally a fifth passage supplies still stronger evidence of how completely the thought of Cicero was impregnated by the doctrines of the Stoics,

---

[22] Cicero *De re publica* III. xxii. 33; quoted by Lactantius in *Divine Institutes*, VI. viii. 6–9.
[23] *De legibus* I. vi. 18–19.
[24] *Ibid.*, vii. 23. [25] *Ibid.*, xv. 42. [26] *Ibid.*, II. iv. 8.

and consequently by the conception of reason as an essential and universal element of nature:

> What is more true than that no one ought to be so foolishly proud as to think that, though reason and intellect exist in himself, they do not exist in the heavens and the universe, or that those things which can hardly be understood by the highest reasoning powers of the human intellect are guided by no reason at all? In truth, the man that is not driven to gratitude by the orderly courses of the stars, the regular alternation of day and night, the gentle progress of the seasons, and the produce of the earth brought forth for our sustenance—how can such an one be accounted a man at all? And since all things that possess reason stand above those things which are without reason, and since it would be sacrilege to say that anything stands above universal Nature, we must admit that reason is inherent in Nature.[27]

But if Cicero owed to the Stoics his conception of law as a product of divine and universal reason pervading all nature, he was equally indebted to them for his thesis that there is an international community coextensive with the human race. His theory that a social spirit by which men are drawn together is one of the fundamental qualities of human nature, has already been mentioned. An examination of a few passages from several of his writings will show how far he developed this theory. Discussing in *De officiis* "the principles of fellowship and society that nature has established among men," he declares the "first principle" to be "that which is found in the connection subsisting between all the members of the human race; and that bond of connection is reason and speech, which by the processes of teaching and learning, of communicating, discussing, and reasoning associate men together and unite them in a sort of natural fraternity."[28]

This fraternity was not merely political, it was social; it was also moral because, as he explained elsewhere, it was the very foundation of justice. "The justice of mankind at large . . . is rooted in the social union of the race of men."[29] This is natural and universal justice, the justice of "mankind at large." Here it is necessary to return for a moment to Cicero's con-

---

[27] *Ibid.*, vii. 16. That this conception of reason as essential in nature became an integral part of Christian theology is evident from the writings of no less an authority than St. Thomas Aquinas, who declared that "every act of reason and will in us is based on that which is according to nature . . . for every act of reasoning is based on principles that are known naturally."—*Summa Theologica*, I–II, qu. 91, art. 2, ad 2. And again, "As, in man, reason rules and commands the other powers, so all the natural inclinations belonging to the other powers must needs be directed according to reason. Wherefore it is *universally* right for all men, that all their inclinations should be directed according to reason."—*Ibid.*, qu. 94, art. 4, ad 3. The italics are ours.

[28] Cicero *De officiis* I. xvi. 50.   [29] Cicero *Tusculan Disputations*, I. xxv. 64.

ception of a law for the community of mankind, which law, as we have seen, was the law of nature identified with right reason. In *De finibus*,[30] his treatise on ethics, he restates his conception in different terms: "The nature of man . . . is such, that as it were a code of law subsists between the individual and the human race, so that he who upholds this code will be just and he who departs from it, unjust."

And finally one of those purple passages which occur so frequently in Cicero's writings may be quoted from the same work:

> In the whole moral sphere of which we are speaking there is nothing more glorious nor of wider range than the solidarity of mankind, that species of alliance and partnership of interests and that actual affection which exists between man and man, which, coming into existence immediately upon our birth, owing to the fact that children are loved by their parents and the family as a whole, is bound together by the ties of marriage and parenthood, gradually spreads its influence beyond the home, first by blood relationships, then by connections through marriage, later by friendships, afterwards by the bonds of neighbourhood, then to fellow-citizens and political allies and friends, and lastly by embracing the whole of the human race. This sentiment, assigning each his own and maintaining with generosity and equity that human solidarity and alliance of which I speak, is termed justice.[31]

Of the many interpretations and evaluations of Cicero's contributions to political and legal philosophy, only three by authoritative writers of the present day may be considered here. The first is by Professor Charles Howard McIlwain of Harvard University, whose *The Growth of Political Thought in the West* must be considered a classic.

> The idea of the equality of men is the profoundest contribution of the Stoics to political thought, that idea has colored its whole development from their day to ours, and its greatest influence is in the changed conception of law that in part resulted from it. To Cicero law is coeval with man. Man as man shares it with God, and by nature he shares it equally with other men of whatever race or city, and this before the foundation of any state or the establishment of its *jus civile*. True, this in essence may be the same as the theory of Plato and Aristotle. The Stoics and the Roman jurists after them defended the objectivity and the natural character of law against their opponents much as Socrates and Plato and Aristotle had done against the Sophists, but the belief in equality has made in effect a new theory of it. . . .
>
> It is in this newer conception of law that the departure from the inequality of antique thought has had its greatest influence upon later ideas of the state. For to Cicero this law common to all men and to God and as old as time is

---

[30] III. xx. 67. [31] *Ibid.*, V. xxiii. 65.

also the source of the state itself,—a state is nothing else than "a partnership in law" (*juris societas*).[32]

Not only is Cicero's law different from Plato's or Aristotle's; his whole theory of the state is far more dependent on law than theirs, a theory of rights in a sense with which the Greeks were unacquainted; and this legalistic character, apparently of Roman and not Greek origin, confirmed by the later Roman jurists, was handed on by them to remain one of the distinguishing marks of western political thought almost to our own day, if it is not so still.

These observations led Professor McIlwain to the following conclusion:

> To Cicero, then, the state is not "prior" to the individual, not even in thought, as with Aristotle. Society and the state are no longer equivalent terms. He can speak of society as a wider thing than any political unit and an older, and he can think of man as something more than a mere "part" of a state, lifeless as a foot of stone if separated from it, and even inconceivable but in reference to it. Man may have a real existence before he enters into any state, he *has* had an existence before states were or any of their laws; and if so, it is possible to think of him as in some ways independent of a state's existence, and it is conceivable that he may have "rights" with which it has nothing to do. We are plainly in the presence of the beginnings of "modern" political thought.[33]

The second authority on Cicero is a learned German publicist, Dr. Hermann Rehm, who, at the time of the appearance of his tractate,[34] was Professor of Political Science at the University of Erlangen—although subsequently, it may be added, he was appointed to the University of Strasbourg. In his opinion, Cicero conceived of law as originating *ex intima philosophia,*

> which means to create it from reason, according to the thesis that true law is reason dwelling within nature. What should this mean other than that the general foundation of jurisprudence must be philosophy and not positive law?

Professor Rehm, in discussing the Hellenic view of the state, observes that "the Epicureans conceived it as a compact; the Stoics as a constitutional community, i. e., a community consisting of an order and distribution of state power." Turning then to Rome, he declares that to Cicero "the *res publica-civitas* is *juris societas*,[35] but after the phrase explaining this *jus,* i. e.,[36] (*cum*) *lex* (*sit*) *civilis sociatatis vinculum*,[37] it becomes a community of general law." But to Cicero, Professor Rehm observes, "*res publica* means

---

[32] McIlwain, *The Growth of Political Thought in the West*, pp. 115, 116, citing *De re publica* I. 32: "*Quid est enim civitas nisi juris societas?*"

[33] *Ibid.*, pp. 116, 117.

[34] *Geschichte der Staatsrechtswissenschaft*, pp. 148–49, 149–53.

[35] The state is an association in justice. See Cicero *De re publica* I. xxxii. 49.

[36] Which may here be translated as justice.

[37] Since law is the bond which unites the civic association. Cicero *De re publica* I. xxxii. 49.

... not *societas,* but *res populi,* i. e., the affair 'of all,' of 'the whole people,' the *constitutio populi,* the whole organized, united nation." But what is this *populus*? It is, in Cicero's language, *coetus multitudinis juris consensu et utilitatis communione sociatus,*[38] "a society of people united by their general interest in the common rights and good of all." Professor Rehm points out that the organization of the state, in Cicero's opinion, is fundamentally an organization "of the people themselves and (since *res publica* and *civitas* are considered identical) of free men capable of defending themselves." Declaring that "The Roman knows the state only as an organized community of citizens (organized in the assembly of the people), as a governing assembly of all citizens," the same author adds that to the Roman "the state in the legal sense coincides with the assembly of the people," and that therefore "the assembly of the people is the state, not merely the organ of the *populus,* but the *populus* itself." That this is the legal conception of the Romans is clear, he maintains, from the *Institutes*[39] of Justinian, where it is said that "when the *populus* so increased that it was difficult to have it meet in a place for the purpose of legislation, such legislation was announced *senatus vice populi consulto.*"

After a somewhat critical discussion of the relationship of the Roman chief magistrate to the people, Professor Rehm makes the following fundamental distinction and reveals the basic importance of Cicero's conception:

Politically, but not legally, the form of the state depends upon the establishment of state organs; politically, but not legally, there exists a distribution of the power of the state between people, consuls and senate. For the political question regarding the permanency of the character of the state, we must consider the actual participation in the power of the state, and not the question of the legal relationship of those who exercise that power. The legal conception of Cicero is found in all its clearness in Book III of *De legibus;*[40] there he gives the outline of the fundamental law of the state and in it the *populus* alone has *potestas;* the senate only *auctoritas,* i. e., *consilium;* the magistrate has *auspicium, judicium* and *imperium,* but in subordination to the *populus.*

As the third authority on Cicero we have chosen a distinguished publicist, Dr. A. J. Carlyle:

There is no change in political theory so startling in its completeness as the change from the theory of Aristotle to the later philosophical view represented by Cicero and Seneca. Over against Aristotle's view of the natural inequality of human nature we find set out the theory of the natural equality of human nature. There is no resemblance in nature so great as that between man and man, there

---

[38] *De re publica* I. xxv. 39. [39] *Institutes* I. ii. 5. [40] III. xii. 27, 28.

is no equality so complete. There is only one possible definition for all mankind, reason is common to all. . . . Nature has given to all men reason, that is, true reason, and therefore the true law, which is right reason commanding and forbidding.[41]

These generalizations were of vast importance, and they lay at the root of enlightened Roman doctrines of law and government. "It can scarcely be doubted," adds the author, "that we have here . . . the foundation of those dogmatic statements of the lawyers like Ulpian and Florentinus,[42] in which all men are presented to us as being by nature free, by nature equal." The true significance of this Roman adaptation of Greek theory is, in Dr. Carlyle's words, that here "We are indeed at the beginnings of a theory of human nature and society of which the 'Liberty, Equality, and Fraternity' of the French Revolution is only the present-day expression."[43] And what of Cicero's part in the development of this theory? "The 'Fraternity' of the Revolution is only a later form of Cicero's phrase,[44] 'By nature we are disposed to love men; this is the foundation of law.'"

"Cicero," continues Dr. Carlyle, "already speaks with the cosmopolitan accent of modern civilisation; to him the older conception of an absolute natural difference between the civilised man and the barbarian has become impossible."[45]

To Cicero, as we have seen, society was "a natural institution." Indeed, in Dr. Carlyle's interpretation of Cicero, "Man is naturally made for society,"[46] and the state is the outgrowth of the family. Now it is evident that in this respect at least Cicero is an Aristotelian. But more than this, he conceived of the state "as an organic growth in contradistinction to the conception of it as a mechanical product,"[47] a conception whose significance was not appreciated until it was recognized by Burke in the eighteenth century.[48] With Cicero the state is, in Dr. Carlyle's words, "the natural method of human life." It

---

[41] *A History of Mediaeval Political Theory in the West*, I, 8-9.
[42] *Digest* I. i. 4; I. v. 4; L. xvii. 32.
[43] The American expression of this ancient yet ever-new conception, which antedated the French Revolution by nearly a score of years, is to be found in the Declaration of Independence of the United States of America of July 4, 1776: "We hold these truths to be self-evident, that all men are created equal, that they are endowed by their Creator with certain unalienable Rights, that among these are Life, Liberty and the pursuit of Happiness.—That to secure these rights, Governments are instituted among Men, deriving their just powers from the consent of the governed.—That whenever any Form of Government becomes destructive of these ends, it is the Right of the People to alter or to abolish it, and to institute new Government, laying its foundation on such principles and organizing its powers in such form, as to them shall seem most likely to effect their Safety and Happiness."
[44] *De legibus* I. xv. 43.   [45] Carlyle, *op. cit.*, I, 10.
[46] *Ibid.*, p. 14.   [47] *Ibid.*   [48] See *infra*, p. 604.

is not a mere haphazard association, but is "founded upon justice, upon law," and its purpose is to promote "the common wellbeing of all its citizens."[49] Here we have, so to speak, an ancient version of Bentham's greatest good, not merely for the greatest number, but for all.[50]

Thus, as Dr. Carlyle points out, Cicero arrives at the conception of the state as a "multitude associated together under a common law,"[51] with, of course, the common welfare in view. Such an association under law means government of one form or another, but whatever its form justice must be its bond and the common good its end. Indeed to Cicero, as Dr. Carlyle indicates, an unjust government "whether it is that of the king or of the few or of the people . . . is not to be called corrupt, but rather . . . it is no State at all."[52]

Turning now to the question of liberty, the author says:

Cicero's identification of liberty with a share in political power is another of the indications of the essentially modern character of his political thought. We seem to be at the commencement of that mode of thought which has been so characteristic of modern democracy, that political liberty is identical with the possession of the franchise, that even the best government is unsatisfactory which is not directly controlled by the people as a whole.[53]

And at the end of his survey Dr. Carlyle gives in a paragraph or two his measured opinion of the political theory of Cicero:

We have thus seen how important in the political theory of Cicero are the three related conceptions of natural law, natural equality, and the natural society of

---

[49] Carlyle, op. cit., I, 14.

[50] It may be remarked in passing that Bentham's formula, in varying languages, runs through the ages from Aristotle down, and that in our modern era Bentham's statement of it was preceded by the statements of the English Hutcheson and the Italian Beccaria.

"*That Action* is *best*, which procures the *greatest Happiness* for the *greatest Numbers*."—Francis Hutcheson, *An Inquiry into the Original of Our Ideas, Beauty and Virtue*. This volume was first published in 1720. The quotation here given is from the "Fifth Edition, Corrected" (London, 1758), p. 185.

"*La massima felicità divisa nel maggior numero.*"—Cesare di Bonesana Beccaria, *Trattato dei delitti e delle pene* (1764), Preface.

"It is the greatest happiness of the greatest number that is the measure of right and wrong."—Jeremy Bentham, *A Fragment on Government*. The quotation is from the preface to the first edition, published in 1776.

Cf. also the statement of the French writer, Claude-Arien Helvetius: "*Si c'est dans le plus grand nombre que réside essentiellement la force, & dans la pratique des actions utiles au plus grand nombre que consiste la justice, il est évident que la justice est, par sa nature, toujours armée du pouvoir nécessaire pour réprimer le vice & nécessiter les hommes à la vertu.*"—*De l'esprit* (2 vols., Paris, 1758), I, 310–11.

[51] Carlyle, op. cit., I, 14.

[52] Ibid., I, 15, citing *De re publica* I. xxvi. 41, 42; and St. Augustine's reference to Cicero in *De civitate dei* II. xxi.

[53] Carlyle, ibid., I, 15, 16.

men in the State. Nature is the test of truth and validity in law, in social order, in organised society. We do not mean that Cicero has a very clear and precise conception of the meaning of nature; generally he seems to use it as expressing the true order of things, though once at least he seems to use it as equivalent to the primitive, undeveloped order. [*De officiis*, I. vii. 21.] But generally his conception of natural law is sufficiently distinct.[54]

In describing the Ciceronian conception of natural law, Dr. Carlyle declares that for Cicero "Behind all actual laws and customs of men there exists a supreme and permanent law, to which all human order, if it is to have any truth or validity, must conform." There is, in a word, an "ultimate principle," which "is the law and will of the power which lies behind all the external forms of the universe, and it is by it that all things live, while it also manifests itself, at least in part, to the rational consciousness of men."[55] And finally, Cicero appears to have repudiated "the traditional philosophical justification of slavery." For he maintained not only that "the State must be just," but that it "must also provide for liberty."[56]

[54] *Ibid.*, I, 17.   [55] *Ibid.*   [56] *Ibid.*, I, 18.

Chapter IX

SENECA (4 B.C.–A.D. 65)

Seneca, like Cicero, was not born in Rome. Indeed, he was not even an Italian, as was Cicero; he was a Spaniard and, strangely enough, we shall find that his contribution to posterity, like that of his later fellow countrymen, was in part theological. Thus he was, in a sense, the beginner of that Spanish influence upon the thought of Europe which has endured for centuries.

His political theories were inherited. They were largely those of the Greeks, and of the Stoics in particular. In many respects, therefore, they were similar to those of Cicero, although Cicero's is much the more complete and classic statement of them. In his writings, however, Seneca was concerned more with individual than with political ethics; he was a moralist, not a political scientist. Consequently his views on society and the state are not given in connected form but are to be found scattered through his essays and letters.

Of two phases of these views to be considered here, the first deals with familiar Stoic conceptions.

Man is a reasoning animal. Therefore, man's highest good is attained, if he has fulfilled the good for which nature designed him at birth. And what is it which this reason demands of him? The easiest thing in the world,—to live in accordance with his own nature.[1]

The Stoic influence is specifically acknowledged in another passage:

I follow the guidance of Nature—a doctrine upon which all Stoics are agreed. Not to stray from Nature and to mould ourselves according to her law and pattern—this is true wisdom.[2]

But man, even as a "reasoning animal," could hardly have survived in isolation, for he is also a social animal. "While other creatures possess a strength that is adequate for their self-protection, and those that are born to be wanderers and to lead an isolated life have been given weapons, the covering of man is a frail skin; no might of claws or of teeth makes him a terror to others, naked and weak as he is, his safety lies in fellowship."[3]

[1] Seneca *Epistulae morales* XLI. 8–9.
[2] Seneca *De vita beata* iii. 3.
[3] Seneca *De beneficiis* IV. xviii. 2.

Reason and fellowship, in Seneca's view, are what stand between man and destruction.

God has given to him two things, reason and fellowship, which, from being a creature at the mercy of others, make him the most powerful of all; and so he who, if he were isolated, could be a match for none is the master of the world. Fellowship has given to him dominion over all creatures; fellowship, though he was begotten upon the land, has extended his sovereignty to an element not his own, and has bidden him be lord even upon the sea; it is this that has checked the assaults of disease, has made ready supports for old age, has provided solace for sorrow; it is this that makes us brave, this that we may invoke as a help against Fortune. Take away this fellowship, and you will sever the unity of the human race on which its very existence depends.[4]

Yet, though man derives protection from fellowship, Seneca by no means believes that the motive impelling human beings to association is fear. On the contrary, he held that "human life is founded on kindness and concord, and is bound into an alliance for common help, not by terror, but by mutual love."[5]

Now society is made up of individuals, and since the welfare of the whole depends upon the welfare of its members, it is the duty of society to protect the individual: "As all the members of the body are in harmony one with another because it is to the advantage of the whole that the individual members be unharmed, so mankind should spare the individual man, because all are born for a life of fellowship, and society can be kept unharmed only by the mutual protection and love of its parts."[6]

But the individual also has duties. "No one can live happily who has regard to himself alone and transforms everything into a question of his own utility; you must live for your neighbour, if you would live for yourself. This fellowship, maintained with scrupulous care, . . . makes us mingle as men with our fellow-men and holds that the human race have certain rights in common."[7]

Seneca emphasized, as we have seen, the conception of a natural society coextensive with the human race. But this does not mean that he ignored the smaller "commonwealths" to which men were bound by political ties. Some men might serve only the larger society, some only the smaller, but Seneca apparently saw no reason why the individual should not acknowledge his allegiance to both:

Let us grasp the idea that there are two commonwealths—the one, a vast and truly common state, which embraces alike gods and men, in which we look

[4] *Ibid.*, 2–4.   [5] *De ira* I. v. 3.   [6] *Ibid.*, II. xxxi. 7–8.   [7] *Epistulae morales* XLVIII. 2–3.

neither to this corner of earth nor to that, but measure the bounds of our citizenship by the path of the sun; the other, the one to which we have been assigned by the accident of birth. This will be the commonwealth of the Athenians or of the Carthaginians, or of any other city that belongs, not to all, but to some particular race of men. Some yield service to both commonwealths at the same time—to the greater and to the lesser—some only to the lesser, some only to the greater.[8]

Regarding law Seneca had, as would be expected, much less to say than Cicero. It will suffice here to state that to him, as to the Greeks, law as the embodiment of reason was unswayed by passion. The ruler of the state was the "guardian of the law," but he was to administer it temperately and equitably. For to Seneca the spirit of the law was always more important than the letter; natural justice more fundamental than the justice of the courts. And as a moral force he ranked man's sense of duty above all the statute books.

How much more comprehensive [he exclaims] is the principle of duty than that of law! How many are the demands laid upon us by the sense of duty, humanity, generosity, justice, integrity—all of which lie outside the statute books![9]

Unhappily, a sense of duty seems not to be enough in this very human world, as Seneca recognized with deep regret. Conscience fails all to often in human transactions unless it be buttressed by the rules of contract, the promise under seal and signature, and the testimony of witnesses.

Would that I could persuade the lenders of money to accept payment only from those who are willing to pay! Would that no compact marked the obligation of buyer to seller, and that no covenants and agreements were safeguarded by the impress of seals, but that, instead, the keeping of them were left to good faith and a conscience that cherishes justice! But men have preferred what is necessary to what is best, and would rather compel good faith than expect it. Witnesses are summoned on both sides. One creditor, by having recourse to factors, causes the record to be made in the books of several people; another is not content with oral promises, but must also bind his victim by a written signature. O, what a shameful admission of the dishonesty and wickedness of the human race! More trust is placed in our seal-rings than in our consciences.[10]

A second important phase of Seneca's views on society has to do with theories which resemble certain conceptions in Christian theology. Like the learned of his day, he was familiar with the Roman poets, and apparently he was deeply interested in the Golden Age which they so often described in verse—an age of innocence in which there was no law because, in the

---

[8] *De otio* iv. 1–2.　　　[9] *De ira* II. xxviii. 2.　　　[10] *De beneficiis* III. xv. 1–3.

absence of wrong, law was unnecessary. It would seem that in Seneca's opinion such an age had really existed some time prior to the dawn of history, and he made it a part of his theory of the origin of society. In one of his letters he sets forth his views on the subject at length.[11]

Thus he tells us that in this long past era men had lived in peace and happiness, possessing all things in common. Order and harmony were theirs because they followed nature and were ruled by the best and wisest of their fellows. Nature supplied their simple needs with an abundance available to all alike. They were without guile, and their race was of a cleaner, fresher type than exists today.

Thus far we have a more or less conventional picture, similar to those depicted by "back-to-nature" enthusiasts in various ages. But Seneca has not completed his description, and in certain details which he adds we find him departing from those who would have us believe that the primitive "natural" condition was one of perfection.

In Seneca's golden age men were not perfect because "they were not wise men."[12] Happiness they possessed, in that they were innocent and uncorrupted, but theirs was the bliss of ignorance rather than of positive virtue. It was, in the fullest sense of the term, an era of innocence, but it was a static era. And it was no doubt because man's happiness in this golden age was founded upon ignorance instead of knowledge that in the course of time "vice stole in"[13] and humanity became heir to all the evils of avarice and selfishness, of poverty and war. Property became private, lust for wealth and power grew rampant. In such an unhappy condition of things there must be restraints and remedies based upon justice, and for this purpose laws and the many and varied institutions of society were needed. Life was no longer simple; it had become a complex mixture of good and evil, and consequently of worries and perplexities. Men required knowledge now in order to distinguish between right and wrong. They must have wise men to frame their laws and governments. In a word, they needed wisdom, the product of philosophy—not for the discovery or invention of the things that make up material wealth, not to teach "the use of keys and bolts,"[14] but in order to find the lost road to happiness. "Truth, and nature," the "law of life" with its "universal principles,"[15] and "the whole company of virtues,"[16] all that goes to make up the art of "living well"—such is "the gift of philosophy"[17] to man. Thus for Seneca, a Roman Stoic, philosophy becomes a means for rendering the highest form of service to a troubled

[11] *Epistle* XC.   [12] *Ibid.*, 44.   [13] *Ibid.*, 6.
[14] *Ibid.*, 8.   [15] *Ibid.*, 34.   [16] *Ibid.*, 3.   [17] *Ibid.*, 1.

world, and the true philosopher, while he should be self-sufficient, will recognize his duty to serve society.

Now if Christianity had not triumphed in the reign of Constantine and if the Christian religion had not replaced the inherited religion of the Greek and the Roman world, it may be that Seneca's conception of a golden age would have had even less authority than that of the poets and would have been looked upon as little more than the attempt of a moralist to invade the realms of phantasy. But there was something in the Old Testament which could be invoked in behalf of Seneca's "age of innocence." Adam, the progenitor of the human race, according to Christian theology had also experienced an age of innocence. Eve, his wife, was likewise created in that sinless and happy era, but the forbidden apple, which opened her eyes to a less innocent world than that in which she lived, was passed by her to Adam and eaten by him, and the consequence was the fall of both. Adam and Eve, because of their disobedience in partaking of the forbidden fruits of human knowledge, were expelled from the Paradise in which they were living, to begin life anew in the outer world in which the age of innocence was but a memory. In their fallen state, laws were necessary for Adam, for Eve, and for their descendants, just as in Seneca's opinion laws were passed because they were essential after the corruption of man. Thus the conception of Seneca, based upon the phantasy of the poets but interwoven by him with the philosophy of the Stoics, met and merged into the Christian conception of an unregenerate and lawmaking world whose salvation lies in the universal principles and the eternal verities set forth in the Christian philosophy of the New Testament.

THE CHRISTIAN HERITAGE,
ANCIENT AND MEDIEVAL

Chapter X

THE HEBREW PROPHETS AND CHRISTIANITY

It is impossible even to conjecture how great has been the contribution of the Bible to legal and political philosophy. Hence in treatises on our ideals of law and government it is customary to take that contribution more or less for granted and, foregoing any attempt to examine it as a whole, to turn at once to the individual contributions of the fathers and theologians of the church. It is easy to understand why this is so, for neither the Old Testament nor the New is concerned with the exposition of a system of law or politics—or, indeed, a system of any kind. The one is primarily the record of the religious experience and development of a people; the other the record of the birth and teaching, in simple, untechnical terms, of the noblest religion the world has ever known. In both, religious and therefore moral conceptions are paramount, but there is no attempt in either to construct a "system" of ethics, an abstract philosophy, such as the pagans built. The development of Christian theory and Christian philosophy was to come later, after the establishment of the Church Universal. Then, indeed, as we shall see, theology became an all-embracing science to which, as Francisco de Vitoria was to declare from his chair at the University of Salamanca, "no argument, no discussion, no text, seem alien"[1]—a science wherein law and politics were but parts of that larger whole which treats of all things divine and human pertaining to man as a moral being.

But in the Old Testament we do not find such a science; rather we have moral conceptions in action, morality developed by the long and often painful experience of a religiously minded people. In the New Testament, again, we do not find a science of ethics, but we do find a moral standard so universal and so lofty that it is for all men and for all ages. In both, however, we are dealing with individual rather than political morality. The question therefore arises, should not discussions of legal and political science omit, as foreign to their purpose, any attempt to deal with the moral conceptions of the Bible?

[1] *De potestate civili,* first paragraph.

The answer to this question is to be found in the fact that political groups are made up of individuals, and that—though many statesmen and politicians of the past and of the present have tried hard to convince us otherwise—the moral standard of the group is essentially that of its individual members because it is derived from those members. It cannot be higher than the standard of the individuals any more than a stream can rise above its source, and it can fall lower only when, through some fault or corruption in organization, the actions of the group fail to respond to the will of its members. When the individuals came together in association, they did not create something apart from themselves—something superhuman, a Frankenstein monster. Elsewhere this point will be dealt with at greater length,[2] but for the moment it will suffice to emphasize the fact that the political group consists simply of individuals in a status of organization, and that the moral standards of the group, like its powers, are derived directly from its members and from no other source.

If this be true (and certainly there seems to be no adequate evidence for a contrary view), then it becomes apparent that he who would treat of legal and political morality, of the moral standard of the state, must also consider the moral standard of the individual. And that standard, for the Christian world, is to be found in the Bible. It will therefore be necessary to consider at some length, but from a nontheological viewpoint, the moral conceptions of the Old and New Testaments which, when Christianity entered the stream of thought flowing from pagan sources, pervaded and modified legal and political theories.

As a preliminary step, however, certain observations should be made concerning what may be termed the material background of biblical conceptions. This background is today called Palestine. In ancient times, as in the present day, it was a small area, some 150 miles in length, unproductive in the southern portion and poor in natural resources. From the dawn of history it was crossed by important trade routes. From the dawn of history, too, it was overrun innumerable times by conquering armies. Around it the earliest civilizations flourished and fell—in Egypt, in the ancient city kingdoms of Sumeria and the empire of Babylon, in Crete, and in the bustling Phoenician ports.

Such was the home of the Hebrews, the land of Israel and Judah. With their long and interesting history we are not here concerned except to note that, though they exhibited an extraordinary capacity for retaining their

---

[2] *Infra*, pp. 457 ff.

cultural and racial integrity, they were constantly subject, in war and in peace, to the influence of neighboring peoples. Of these foreign influences the most potent was apparently that of Egypt, "the mother of civilization." For long periods Palestine was under Egyptian suzerainty and, according to biblical history, the Hebrews had once sojourned in Egypt in considerable numbers. We are told, moreover, that their great national hero and legislator, Moses, was not only born in the land of the Pharaohs, but was brought up as a member of the royal household. As such he was no doubt well educated, and indeed, according to St. Paul, he became "learned in all the wisdom of the Egyptians."[3] In view of this it is reasonable to believe that, tenaciously as the "children of Israel" clung to their own beliefs and habits of life, they absorbed not a little from Egyptian civilization.[4]

It will be advisable, therefore, to consider certain ethical and legal conceptions which were current in ancient Egypt, the influence of which may well have been felt in Palestine. These have become known to the modern world as a result of the tireless investigations of archaeologists, whose discoveries in recent years have thrown a flood of light on the culture and civilization which existed under the old dynasties.

The earliest conceptions which may usefully be considered here are to be found in the maxims of one Ptahhotep, a famous grand vizier in the twenty-seventh century before Christ. The maxims are admonitions to the vizier's son, and while they seek for the most part to inculcate a shrewd worldly wisdom derived from long official experience, they also insist upon a standard of right conduct. "If thou desirest that thy conduct be worthy," one of the maxims runs, "withhold thee from all evil, and beware of avarice."[5] Avoidance of evil, however, is but the negative side of virtue. What of its positive side?

Great is righteousness [declares the vizier]. Its dispensation endures, nor has it been overthrown since the time of its maker; for punishment is inflicted on the transgressor of its laws. . . . *Although misfortune may carry away wealth, . . . the power of righteousness is that it endures.*

Therefore he charges his son to "hold fast the truth (or 'righteousness') and transgress it not, even though the report (which thou art delivering) be not

---

[3] *Acts* vii: 22.
[4] In fact those who have made a study of the ancient records of Egyptian civilization incline to the belief that the debt of Hebrew culture to Egypt is much greater than has hitherto been supposed. See, for example, the late James Henry Breasted, *The Dawn of Conscience,* especially chap. xvii.
[5] This and the following quotations from Ptahhotep are taken from Breasted (*op. cit.,* pp. 129–39), who supplies a detailed analysis of the maxims.

one pleasing the heart." This points clearly to the necessity for an upright character. Accordingly, we find the further admonition: "Attain character . . . make righteousness to flourish and thy children shall live." The son, moreover, should "deal justly with all," holding fast to the standard of righteousness. *"Established is the man whose standard is righteousness, who walketh according to its way."* And the old vizier, who wrote down his maxims when he was full of years, closes by citing his own long experience, in order to emphasize his insistence upon right doing.

They [the years] are not few that I have spent on earth. I have attained one hundred and ten years of life, while the king gave to me rewards above those of the ancestors because *I did righteousness* for the king even unto the grave.

Some four hundred years later, in the twenty-third century before Christ, an unknown author, deeply interested in social reform, set forth his views in dramatic form in the "Story of the Eloquent Peasant." Interesting as are the details of the story, it must suffice for present purposes to summarize the facts by stating that the peasant, after suffering rank injustice at the hands of a minor official, makes a series of fluent and impassioned appeals for redress to the grand steward of the pharaoh. The significance of these appeals lies, not in the incident of cruel oppression which caused them, but in their revelation of a standard of justice and of official integrity which was clearly recognized by the author and his readers in spite of its violation. Thus the peasant, in addressing the grand steward, calls him a "leader free from avarice," a "great man free from littleness, who destroys unrighteousness and establishes righteousness."[6] "Respond to the cry which my mouth utters," he pleads. "When I speak, hear thou. Do justice." A later appeal exhorts the grand steward to "ward off the robber, protect the wretched, become not a torrent against him who pleads."

"Take heed," the peasant continues in a note of warning. "Eternity draws near." And he continues with a series of striking admonitions:

Prefer acting as it is (proverbially) said, "It is the breath of the nostrils to do justice" (or "right," Maat). Execute punishment on him to whom punishment is due, and none shall be like thy uprightness. Do the balances err? Does the scale-beam swerve to one side? . . . Speak not falsehood, (for) thou art great (and therefore responsible). Be not light, (for) thou art weighty. Speak not falsehood, for thou art the balances. Swerve not, for thou art uprightness.

---

[6] These quotations from the peasant's appeals are from Breasted (*op. cit.*, pp. 183–93), who discusses "The Story of the Eloquent Peasant" at some length.

And the plea for justice rises to a lofty conception in the final passage to be quoted:

> Do justice for the sake of the lord of justice whose justice has indeed become justice, thou (who art) Pen and Roll and Writing Palette, (even) Thoth, being far removed from doing evil; when right is (really) right, then is it (indeed) right. *For justice (Maat) is for eternity. It descendeth with him that doeth it into the grave, when he is placed in the coffin and laid in the earth. His name is not effaced on earth, but he is remembered because of right.*

There is more than an echo of this conception a century later, in a proverb found inscribed on the tomb of a noble: "A man's virtue is his monument (but) forgotten is the man of evil repute."[7]

From about the same period there has been preserved a set form of address which the pharaoh was accustomed to deliver to each new vizier or prime minister appointed to office. In it are certain principles which, though laid down some four thousand years ago, are still applicable to those who are entrusted with the affairs of government. Thus the vizier was warned that his office was no sinecure, and no gateway to selfish ends. It was one of the "bitter" things of life, not the "sweet." The duties and not the privileges of office were emphasized. And law and justice were to be the vizier's guides: "See thou to it," he is admonished, "that everything is done in accordance with law, that everything is done according to the custom thereof, [giving] to [every man] his right."[8]

The address contains numerous earnest exhortations:

> Forget not to judge justice. It is an abomination of the god to show partiality. This is the teaching. Therefore do thou accordingly. Look upon him who is known to thee like him who is unknown to thee; and him who is near the king like him who is far from [his house].[9]

If the vizier, as the representative of the ruler, thus renders justice impartially, men will have a wholesome respect for the government. They will be fearful of committing unjust deeds because of their knowledge that the ruler "does justice."

And lest the vizier mistake these admonitions for mere formalities, the pharaoh's address proceeds to reiterate them with solemnity and sternness:

> Behold, men expect the doing of justice in the procedure [of] the vizier. . . . Behold, when a man is in his office, let him act according to what is commanded him. [Behold] the success of a man is that he act according to what is said to him. Make no [delay] at all in justice, the law of which thou knowest.[10]

---

[7] *Ibid.*, p. 160.   [8] *Ibid.*, p. 209.   [9] *Ibid.*, pp. 209–10.   [10] *Ibid.*, p. 210.

It is not for the layman to attempt any estimate of the extent to which these Egyptian ideals may have influenced the conceptions of the Hebrews.[11] But it seems logical to assume that such influence was felt in greater or less measure, and entered into the epoch-making contributions of Palestine to our civilization.

The Hebrews were at once a poetic and a realistic people. And all the poetic side of their nature expressed itself in a sublime religious conception to which they turned for refuge from hard and often bitter realities. Yet at the same time they faced those realities with fortitude and exceptional good sense. Life, as most of them knew it, was none too pleasant, for though they enjoyed interludes of peace and prosperity, they had again and again to endure the hardships of defeat and conquest. Yet they sought always to learn by experience, and they valued wisdom above all human qualities because it taught them how to live. Praise of wisdom is sung over and over in some of the Old Testament books; in the Proverbs it is like a refrain. Those who gain wisdom shall "understand righteousness, and judgment, and equity; yea, every good path."[12] Again, in that magnificent chapter[13] where wisdom, personified, is pictured as calling from the high places, from the pathways of men, from the city gates, and in the very doors of the homes, she tells us that her "fruit is better than gold," that she leads "in the way of righteousness, in the midst of the paths of judgment." Prudence and counsel are hers, and just laws and government.

I wisdom dwell with prudence, . . . Counsel is mine. . . . By me kings reign, and princes decree justice. By me princes rule, and nobles, even all the judges of the earth.

In short, wisdom must be, according to the Hebrews, the very foundation of justice and law. Thus Moses, their great patriot and legislator, was not

---

[11] The importance of Egyptian influence on the culture of the ancient world generally has been a matter of some controversy. That the extent of that influence was considerable, however, cannot be doubted, for many Greeks and Romans, notable travelers, had visited Egypt from earliest times, not only for purposes of trade but to investigate the culture and learning of an older civilization. It is common knowledge that Herodotus, sometimes called the "father of history," found his way to Egypt, where he observed with keen eyes the customs and institutions of the country and conversed at length with the learned priests. Whether Plato is actually to be numbered among the visitors to the land of the Pharaohs is perhaps open to question, but there can be no doubt of his familiarity with certain aspects of Egyptian learning. The Romans, too—not to speak of Caesar and Mark Antony—were well acquainted with Egypt and its inhabitants; indeed, it may be said that in the course of time the civilization of Rome mingled with that of Egypt. And the Romanists of today are finding in Egyptian papyri many valuable and hitherto undiscovered records of the law which they profess.

[12] *Proverbs* ii: 9.   [13] *Ibid.*, viii.

only an inspired religious leader but a wise man, possessing as we have seen, all the learning of the Egyptians. And justice is inherent in the law which he gave to his people.

We are today perhaps rather prone to think of that law as belonging to a remote past and therefore as having but little interest for us of the modern world. Yet its influence, direct and indirect, upon the development of jurisprudence in the Christian world has been very great. "Anglo-Saxon Law, Norman Law, Roman Law and Canon Law," says a learned Scots writer,[14] "were all strongly influenced by the Mosaic Law." And this influence has been felt no less in the United States than elsewhere. Indeed some of our colonial forefathers turned directly to the Old Testament for guidance when they began to frame systems of laws. In the colony of Massachusetts Bay, for example, a "Body of Liberties," drawn up by one Nathaniel Ward (who had practiced law in England before becoming a clergyman) to serve as a foundation for the code of law which the colony needed, was distributed among the towns of the colony in 1641. This "Body of Liberties" is described, in an introductory "Epistle" prefixed to the alphabetical abridgment of laws subsequently published by the colony,[15] as "a modell of the Iudiciall lawes of Moses with such other cases as might be referred to them," and as intended for use "in composing our lawes." The provisions of this "modell" were "compiled from the Scriptures, Magna Charta, and the statutes and common law of England."[16] The abridgment itself, which was published in 1648 under the title, *The Book of the General Lauues and Libertyes concerning the Inhabitants of the Massachusets*, is based in part upon the "Body of Liberties," and directly incorporates, in its section on "Capital Lawes," some fourteen provisions from the Old Testament, with references to the various books from which they are taken.[17] Thus, while the law of England is the chief source from which the colonial legislators drew, the laws laid down in the Scriptures served them not only as a moral standard but as a supplementary source. And both the preliminary "modell" and the abridgment of 1648 were of importance in the legal history of New England.

[14] Gardner, "The Influence of the Law of Moses," in *An Introductory Survey of the Sources and Literature of Scots Law*, p. 235.

[15] *The Laws and Liberties of Massachusetts*, reprinted from the 1648 ed., with an Intro. by Farrand.

[16] *Ibid.*, p. vi.

[17] For further details concerning the influence of the Scriptures, and especially the Old Testament, on early Puritan legislation in New England, see historians dealing with that period, such as Laboulaye, *Histoire des Etats-Unis*, I, 173–77; Adams, *The Founding of New England*, pp. 207–11.

The Book of the General Lawes and Libertyes of 1648 is the next significant measure after the Body of Liberties in the legal development of Massachusetts. It is a more important work than its predecessor, standing as the basis of all Massachusetts legislation, and influencing as well the legislation of other colonies, notably Connecticut and New Haven. It is furthermore the first attempt at a comprehensive reduction into one form of a body of legislation of an English-speaking country.[18]

To return, however, to the law which Moses gave to his people. Justice, as has been said, was inherent in that law, yet it was in many respects, and especially in its provisions relating to crimes, an absolute and untempered justice based on the ancient principle of "eye for eye, tooth for tooth, hand for hand, foot for foot."[19] It did, of course, contain not a few humanitarian rules: "Ye shall not afflict any widow, or fatherless child";[20] "Thou shalt not oppress a stranger: for ye know the heart of a stranger, seeing ye were strangers in the land of Egypt";[21] and that sublime command which foreshadows the teachings of Christ: "Thou shalt love thy neighbour as thyself."[22]

But the spirit of the Mosaic law was, on the whole, harsh and uncompromising. Obedience to it, and to the countless rules of ritual and ceremony which it included, was due largely to fear of punishment, rather than to an understanding of and respect for the purpose of the law itself. And when, in the course of time, fear diminished, the Hebrews gradually fell into the habit of exalting the rules of ritual above the rules of law. Lip service was substituted for obedience, and the splendor of ceremonial for the spirit of the law which should govern human relations. It was a period which cried aloud for reform, for a profounder and truer conception of right and wrong. And that conception was supplied by the great prophets of the Hebrews.

Now the prophets were not, as their title might be taken to imply, mere diviners of the future. They were rather preachers of reform.

It has been taken for granted that the prophets were mostly talking about "things to come," and that their main value and significance lay in foretelling the birth and life of Jesus. But the primary meaning of the word "prophet," as well as of the Hebrew term *nabi*, does not relate to prediction, but simply to *preaching*. If, instead of saying, the "Book of the Prophet Amos," we should say, the "Book of the *Preacher* Amos," we should convey a more accurate impression of the facts. For the prophets were preachers, before everything else; and their attention was directed chiefly upon the conditions and problems of their own age.[23]

---

[18] *The Laws and Liberties of Massachusetts*, p. viii.
[19] *Exod.* xxi: 24; *Lev.* xxiv: 20; *Deut.* xix: 21.
[20] *Exod.* xxii: 22.   [21] *Ibid.*, xxiii: 9; see also *Lev.* xix: 33–34.
[22] *Lev.* xix: 18.   [23] Wallis, *Sociological Study of the Bible*, p. 147.

These problems were in part of a political nature. The Hebrews were threatened by danger of invasion from without, and were weakened by the evils of a moral decline from within.

In fact, it was the national peril that brought the Prophets on the scene. One and all, they strove to strengthen the morale of their people by bidding them abstain from the idolatries of the surrounding nations, by pleading with them to search their own hearts, by exhorting them to faith in Jehovah. The essence of their political message was that the Hebrews must look to themselves for salvation rather than to their ever-shifting alliances with this or that neighboring monarch.[24]

The first of the great prophets was Amos, who, appearing at a festival in the town of Bethel, lifted his voice against the shallow magnificence of his day and proclaimed certain immortal realities. Miss Edith Hamilton thus describes the scene in one of her admirable studies:[25]

We must imagine a priestly procession, splendid with "gold and blue and purple and scarlet and fine linen," a long line of slow-moving sacrificial animals, holy vessels of "cunning work in silver and gold and brass," deep voices chanting prayers, music of "trumpet, psaltery and harp"—all the ceremonial, solemn and stately, in which priests throughout the ages the world over have expressed themselves. But on that particular day in the little town, the order was suddenly interrupted. In front of the procession, bringing it to a halt, a wild-looking figure stepped forth, sun-scorched and weather-worn, a rough herdsman's cloak wrapped round him. The chief priest, assured that he had before him one of the foolish ravers who called themselves prophets and got food from simple people as being holy, bade him sternly, "Flee thee away into the land of Judah and there eat bread and prophesy there. But prophesy not any more at Bethel; for it is the king's chapel and the king's court."

But Amos was not to be thus easily silenced. Miss Hamilton continues, quoting from the Old Testament:

Then answered Amos, "No prophet I, neither a prophet's son, but an herdsman and a gatherer of sycamore fruit. And the Lord took me as I followed the flock and said unto me, Go, prophesy unto my people Israel. . . . Now therefore hear thou the word of the Lord: I hate, I despise your feast days and I take no pleasure in your solemn assemblies. Though ye offer me burnt offerings and your meat offerings, I will not accept them. . . . Take thou away from me the noise of thy songs; for I will not hear the melody of thy viols. But let justice well up as waters and righteousness as a mighty stream." And at that moment in the priest and the herdsman stood personified the pleasing, outward show and the difficult inward substance of religion, and for the first time on record, ritual and righteousness confronted each other.[26]

[24] Bates, *Biography of the Bible*, pp. 26–27.
[25] *The Prophets of Israel*, pp. 42–43.
[26] *Ibid.*, p. 43.

Amos, as Miss Hamilton tells us, was closely followed by three other prophets, Hosea, Micah, and Isaiah, and the common purpose of each was, "when life and worship had lost all connection," to call men "away from worship out into the streets, away from a ritual to fairness and kindness."[27]

Will the Lord be pleased [thunders Micah] with thousands of rams, or with ten thousands of rivers of oil? . . . He hath shewed thee, O man, what is good; and what doth the Lord require of thee, but to do justly, and to love mercy, and to walk humbly with thy God?[28]

Hosea, however, was the first of the prophets to see love instead of fear as the true motivating force that "could draw men away from evil to good."[29] And Isaiah, statesman as well as prophet of the Hebrews, continues and rounds out the message of his predecessors, insisting on righteousness, justice and mercy in place of "vain oblations" and "incense." What was important was to "cease to do evil" and to "learn to do well"; to "relieve the oppressed, judge the fatherless, plead for the widow."[30] And to tyrants, his warning is: "Woe unto them that decree unrighteous decrees," that "turn aside the needy from judgment" and "take away the right from the poor of my people, that widows may be their prey, and that they may rob the fatherless."[31]

Both Isaiah and Micah, looking far beyond their own day, saw a vision which the world has yet to realize—a vision of the day when the peoples of the earth "shall beat their swords into plowshares, and their spears into pruninghooks: nation shall not lift up sword against nation, neither shall they learn war any more."[32]

The prophets, as Miss Hamilton says, pointed the way to what should be:

They had a vision of what was possible for men, a vision at no time even approximately realized in the nearly three thousand years between them and us, yet so important for human life that it has never been dismissed. It has never been put in the category of the dream palaces men are always building to console themselves for things as they are. The prophets saw a world where no man was wronged by another, where the strong shared with the weak, where no individual was sacrificed for an end, where each individual was prepared to sacrifice himself for the end of making what God wished become a realized good. . . . They knew human nature. They wanted a different world but they knew the only way to get it was for men to be different. They never worked out a system or built up an organization—not until Ezekiel. Justice and mercy would prevail on the earth only if men wanted them.[33]

---

[27] Hamilton, *The Prophets of Israel*, p. 52. [28] *Mic.* vi: 7–8. [29] Hamilton, *op. cit.*, p. 77.
[30] *Isa.* i: 13, 16, 17. [31] *Ibid.*, x: 1–2. [32] *Ibid.*, ii: 4; *Mic.* iv: 3.
[33] Hamilton, *op. cit.*, pp. 192, 193.

HEBREW PROPHETS AND CHRISTIANITY

The prophets did not try to compel belief in their messages by means of miracles. Nor were they philosophers seeking to demonstrate and classify the truths they proclaimed.

Justice, mercy, all the truths of the spirit, could not be grasped by looking at them or thinking about them but only by acting upon them, by living them. Love, the central truth of the spirit, cannot be understood by the observation of the mind or by the perception of its spiritual beauty. It must be experienced; it will never be known otherwise. Nor can its presence be proved intellectually, or in any way except by living it. It is an experience of which the proof is unselfish action. . . . Justice and mercy—where will they be if men do not show them? Their truth, their reality on earth, depends upon the way men act. If men fail to be just and merciful there will be no justice and mercy.[34]

The message of the prophets was, in its essentials, a plea for men to build a better and more peaceful world. It is a timeless message, for though voiced more than two thousand years ago, it still has the power to arouse the desire and hope for a new order:

The prophets' ideal was conceived with the utmost simplicity and directness in terms of actual life. Men could bring it to pass; it was a goal they could attain to. "And they shall beat their swords into ploughshares and their spears into pruning hooks; nation shall not lift up sword against nation, neither shall they learn war any more, and none shall make them afraid." Through such words men catch a glimpse of a world they must try to create. Not centuries, but millenniums, have passed since those words were written, and yet they do not bring a sense of hopelessness that as they never have been made true, so they never will be. Fire is in them forever to kindle the desire that they shall be true. The excellent becomes the permanent, said the Greeks. When mankind have seen a good, they do not ever let it go. They are not able, as human beings it is not in them, to blot it out completely and forget it. What the prophets wanted for the world has never been dropped from men's consciousness. The possibilities they discovered we still must strive to realize. The desires of the best and greatest have a strange authority; they carry compulsion.

Only the outside of life changes. Within, the thing that hath been is that which shall be, and there is no new thing under the sun. The Old Testament is the great book of human experience, and the greatest experience in it is in the prophets.[35]

With the passing of centuries, however, the ideal of the prophets grew dim in the minds of the Hebrews. In that respect the people of Israel did not differ from other peoples, who, having listened to inspired voices, have heeded them for a time and then turned again to the half truths and the false prophets until gradually the outward form stifled the inner spirit. So

---

[34] *Ibid.*, pp. 199, 200.   [35] *Ibid.*, pp. 201–2.

it has been, unfortunately, throughout human history, and so it was in Palestine at the end of the pre-Christian Era. "Ye pay tithe of mint and anise and cummin, and have omitted the weightier matters of the law, judgment, mercy, and faith."[36] There was need for another and a greater prophet to bring back to the minds of men those "weightier matters of the law" and to reveal in universal terms the goal of humanity.

Yet He who came for this purpose—a man of the town of Nazareth, of humble station but with a vision of truth and light such as has been vouchsafed to no other—found few to heed Him among His people. The rich and the powerful, the scribes and the Pharisees, were like their brethren in all lands—ultraconservative, self-righteous, sticklers for outward form and ceremony, and jealous of the privileges which they claimed as rights. And the men of law were as bad, or worse, for as has happened only too often with members of that profession, they had sought to profit by insisting on the letter and hiding the spirit of the law:

Woe unto you also, ye lawyers! for ye lade men with burdens grievous to be borne, and ye yourselves touch not the burdens with one of your fingers.... Woe unto you, lawyers! for ye have taken away the key of knowledge: ye entered not in yourselves, and them that were entering in ye hindered.[37]

To these and to their followers the teachings of Christ seemed a menace to that potent idol of the market place and the court, "the established order of things." To be sure, He made no attempt to interfere in political affairs, bidding His listeners "render to Caesar the things that are Caesar's, and to God the things that are God's."[38] But it was inevitable, as perhaps it would be today, that one who constantly set at naught all the material rewards which the rich and powerful prized so highly, should be regarded with a suspicion that quickly grew into hostility. And so they incited the mob to crucify Him on the hill of Calvary, thinking thus to put an end to the truths which they could recognize only as being dangerous to their ways and their interests. But the teachings which they sought to destroy were immortal, and the crucifixion but hastened the recognition of their divine nature and their acceptance as the supreme law of human life.

All this is true, it may be said, but the law of the New Testament is not the law of the court room or the foreign office. In discussing it here, are we not confusing two quite different things? Is not the law of the Gospels a matter solely for the individual—something distinct and apart from the law of the lawyer, the statesman, and the politician? The answer is that the moral standard of the New Testament is not alone for individuals as

---

[36] *Matt.* xxiii: 23.   [37] *Luke* xi: 46, 52.   [38] *Mark* xii: 17.

such: it is for groups of individuals, whether these consist of a few gathered together, or of many, or indeed of the inhabitants of the wide world who make up the international community. It is the standard by which should be measured not only the individual actions of men and women, but also the actions of states and groups of states. Because it is universal, and is for all time, human beings, singly or in political groups, cannot fully attain it —at least in their present state of imperfection. But standards are not lowered by failure to reach them. If they were, the years of our civilization would indeed be numbered.

But how, it may be asked, does the New Testament apply to legal and political matters? The simplest and surest way to answer such a question is to examine a few of the teachings of Christ: "Ye have heard," He said in the Sermon on the Mount, referring to the ancient law of retribution, "that it hath been said, An eye for an eye, and a tooth for a tooth." This was not to be the rule of the New Testament:

But I say unto you, That ye resist not evil: but whosoever shall smite thee on thy right cheek, turn to him the other also. And if any man will sue thee at the law, and take away thy coat, let him have thy cloke also. And whosoever shall compel thee to go a mile, go with him twain. Give to him that asketh thee, and from him that will borrow of thee turn not thou away. Ye have heard that it hath been said, Thou shalt love thy neighbour, and hate thine enemy. But I say unto you, Love your enemies, bless them that curse you, do good to them that hate you, and pray for them which despitefully use you, and persecute you.[39]

In these few verses we have rules which, if they were followed, would close every court and put an end to all war. It is true that we have failed to follow them, but they are none the less an ideal. It is only when we reach the ideal that it ceases to be one. Some may say, however, that such an ideal is unsuited to the nature of men, for human beings and nations alike naturally resist any interference with their "rights." That they have done so in the past, with a few exceptions, must be admitted. So also have the beasts in the jungle. Unfortunately, moreover, privileges founded upon force—the right of the strongest—are often mistaken for true rights. And it is over rights, alleged or real, that most of the disputes and wars of humankind have arisen. But man, the reasoning creature, has a spiritual sense which, apparently, the lower animals lack—a sense of duty. Gradually there may dawn upon him the conception that duties are greater than rights, that love is an infinitely nobler emotion than jealousy and hatred and all the baser feelings aroused by the endless controversies over selfish questions of "mine

[39] *Matt.* v: 38–44.

and thine," of insult and injury, and of personal and national honor. And the greatest of all exhortations to duty is the Sermon on the Mount. We may, and often do, ignore it. As nations and as individuals we exalt our rights; we yield to selfish desires, to ambition for wealth and power. We may win them, though the spiritual sense of duty is only too likely to shrivel away in the process. But however great the victory, we stand face to face in the end with the inevitable question, "what is a man profited, if he shall gain the whole world, and lose his own soul? or what shall a man give in exchange for his soul?"[40] The alternative is that chosen by Christ in the wilderness:

The devil taketh him up into an exceeding high mountain, and sheweth him all the kingdoms of the world, and the glory of them; And saith unto him, All these things will I give thee, if thou wilt fall down and worship me. Then saith Jesus unto him, Get thee hence, Satan.[41]

On another occasion a certain questioner—who, it may be noted, happened to be a lawyer—sought to tempt Christ by asking him how to obtain "eternal life." Only two things were necessary, was the answer: to love God completely and wholeheartedly, and "thy neighbour as thyself." But the lawyer, as might be expected, demanded a definition: "Who is my neighbour?" And the reply was the immortal parable of the good Samaritan:

And Jesus answering said, A certain man went down from Jerusalem to Jericho, and fell among thieves, which stripped him of his raiment, and wounded him, and departed, leaving him half dead. And by chance there came down a certain priest that way: and when he saw him, he passed by on the other side. And likewise a Levite, when he was at the place, came and looked on him, and passed by on the other side. But a certain Samaritan, as he journeyed, came where he was: and when he saw him, he had compassion on him, And went to him, and bound up his wounds, pouring in oil and wine, and set him on his own beast, and brought him to an inn, and took care of him. And on the morrow when he departed, he took out two pence, and gave them to the host, and said unto him, Take care of him; and whatsoever thou spendest more, when I come again, I will repay thee. Which now of these three, thinkest thou, was neighbour unto him that fell among the thieves? And he said, He that shewed mercy on him. Then said Jesus unto him, Go, and do thou likewise.[42]

There is, perhaps, no verse in the New Testament more often quoted, and assuredly none more pregnant with meaning for human beings in society, than the Golden Rule. "All things whatsoever ye would that men should do to you, do ye even so to them."[43] Here we have the fundamental guiding principle for all human relationships, whether they be between two

---

[40] *Matt.* xvi: 26.   [41] *Ibid.,* iv: 8–10.   [42] *Luke* x: 25–37.   [43] *Matt.* vii: 12.

or more individuals, or between organized groups of individuals. It is an all-inclusive rule, for it demands truth, honesty, fairness, mercy, neighborliness—all the qualities that men and nations would like others to show toward themselves. Thus the Golden Rule is indeed "the law and the prophets."[44] It is the basic precept of our social morality, and the hope of the future is that we may one day accept it as the foundation of our political and legal morality, for without its acceptance there cannot be "on earth peace, good will toward men."

When the Fathers of the newly established Church found themselves under the necessity of considering questions of law and government, they possessed two great sources from which to draw the principles which were to guide them: the New Testament and the philosophy of the ancient world. And they drew from both. In the Gospels and in the writings of St. Paul they found a conception of the brotherhood of man, of the equality of all human beings in the sight of God—a conception which transcended national boundaries and which bore not a little resemblance to doctrines current in the later Greek philosophy and in the Roman adaptation of Stoicism. So, too, they found in the New Testament a justification for civil government and for obedience to that government which, though different in conception and expression, was not unlike the doctrine of the Stoics.[45] The teaching of Christ had been, as we have seen, to "render unto Caesar the things that are Caesar's," and St. Paul, in his Epistle to the Romans, had expounded this doctrine at greater length:

Let every soul be subject unto the higher powers. For there is no power but of God: the powers that be are ordained of God. Whosoever therefore resisteth the power, resisteth the ordinance of God: and they that resist shall receive to themselves damnation. For rulers are not a terror to good works, but to the evil. Wilt thou then not be afraid of the power? do that which is good, and thou shalt have praise of the same: For he is the minister of God to thee for good. But if thou do that which is evil, be afraid; for he beareth not the sword in vain: for he is the minister of God, a revenger to execute wrath upon him that doeth evil. Wherefore ye must needs be subject, not only for wrath, but also for conscience sake. For for this cause pay ye tribute also: for they are God's ministers, attending continually upon this very thing. Render therefore to all their dues: tribute to whom tribute is due; custom to whom custom; fear to whom fear; honour to whom honour.[46]

On this passage Dr. Carlyle[47] comments that it

is of the greatest importance throughout the whole course of mediaeval political thought, being indeed constantly quoted from the second century onwards. . . .

---

[44] *Ibid.* [45] See Chap. vi, *supra.* [46] *Rom.* xiii: 1–7.
[47] *A History of Mediaeval Political Theory in the West* (previously cited), I, 90.

It defines in the profoundest way the Christian theory of the nature of political society.

Again, St. Paul's letter to Titus urges the latter to teach the Christians of Crete "to be subject to principalities and powers," and "to obey magistrates";[48] and his first Epistle to Timothy exhorts Christians to pray "for kings, and for all that are in authority; that we may lead a quiet and peaceable life in all godliness and honesty."[49] In a similar vein the apostle Peter wrote:

> Submit yourselves to every ordinance of man for the Lord's sake: whether it be to the king, as supreme; Or unto governors, as unto them that are sent by him for the punishment of evildoers, and for the praise of them that do well. For so is the will of God, that with well doing ye may put to silence the ignorance of foolish men: As free, and not using your liberty for a cloke of maliciousness, but as the servants of God. Honour all men. Love the brotherhood. Fear God. Honour the king.[50]

In the opinion of Dr. Carlyle,[51] the meaning of St. Paul and St. Peter, from the standpoint of political theory, is that the authority of civil government and of rulers is of divine origin, existing, as they do, for the maintenance of justice, and that therefore obedience to them is a religious as well as a civil obligation. Thus from the beginning it may be said that Christians regarded themselves as members alike of an international community of mankind and of smaller civil communities to which each owed political allegiance.

Turning now to the Christian conception of the natural law, we find that St. Paul had spoken of the law written in the hearts of men;[52] and the Christian theologians identified this with the law of nature which the world had inherited from Greece and Rome.

> It is interesting to notice [says Dr. Carlyle[53]] that the Fathers frequently . . . connect their treatment of the natural law with St. Paul's phrases in Romans. St. Ambrose, for instance, says that it is the Apostle who teaches us that the natural law is in our hearts.[54]

---

[48] *Titus* iii: 1 [49] *I Tim.* ii: 2. [50] *I Pet.* ii: 13–17. [51] *Op. cit.*, I, 90–91.

[52] "For when the Gentiles, which have not the law, do by nature the things contained in the law, these, having not the law, are a law unto themselves: Which shew the work of the law written in their hearts, their conscience also bearing witness" (*Rom.* ii: 14–15).

[53] *Op. cit.*, I, 105–6.

[54] "St. Ambrose, *Ep.* lxxiii. 2: 'Esse autem legem naturalem in cordibus nostris etiam apostolus docet, qui scripsit quia plerumque "et gentes naturaliter ea, quae Legis sunt, faciunt, et cum Legem non legerint, opus tamen Legis scriptum habent in cordibus suis" (Rom. ii. 14, 15). Ea igitur lex non scribitur, sed innascitur: nec aliqua percipitur lectione, sed profluo quodam fonte in singulis exprimitur, et humanis ingeniis hausitur.' Cf. *De Jacob et vita beata* vi."

HEBREW PROPHETS AND CHRISTIANITY 181

Dr. Carlyle also invokes St. Augustine as citing St. Paul's "words in a passage in which he divides law into three species";[55] and, continues the learned author,

> St. Hilary of Poitiers does the same in describing the general scope of the natural law. He defines this as being that a man must not injure his fellow-man, must not take that which belongs to another, must keep himself from fraud and perjury, must not plot against another man's marriage[56]—

faults, it may be added, which are not unknown today. And Dr. Carlyle concludes:

> It is interesting to compare this with the definitions of the natural law by St. Ambrose[57] and by St. Augustine.[58] It is clear that these are derived from Cicero and other ancient writers.

In this respect, therefore, it may be said that the links between the ancient and the Christian worlds are in the nature of a continuous chain.

From Dr. Carlyle's comments on the Christian conception of the natural law one further paragraph must be quoted:

> It is unnecessary to multiply quotations. There seems to be no division of opinion among the Fathers upon the subject. Practically they carry on the same conceptions as those of Cicero and the later philosophers, and while they bring these into connection with the suggestion of St. Paul, they cannot be said either to modify these inherited conceptions or to carry them any farther.[59]

Here we have the chain completed. Indeed Cicero is so relied upon by the great authorities of the Christian Church as almost to be considered a pagan saint.

---

[55] "St. Augustine, *Contra Faustum Manichaeum* xix. 2: 'Sunt autem legum genera tria: unum quidem Hebraeorum, quod peccati et mortis Paulus appellat (Rom. viii. 2). Aliud vero Gentium, quod naturale vocat: "Gentes enim," inquit, "naturaliter quae legis sunt faciunt; et ejusmodi legem non habentes, ipsi sibi sunt lex; qui ostendunt opus legis scriptum in cordibus suis" (Rom. ii. 14, 15). Tertium vero genus legis est veritas, quod perinde significans, apostolus dicit: Lex enim spiritus vitae in Christo Jesu liberavit me a lege peccati et mortis' (Rom. viii. 2)."

[56] "St. Hilary of Poitiers, *Tract. on Ps.* cxviii. 119: 'Lex enim veluti naturalis est, injuriam nemini inferre, nil alienum praeripere, fraude ac perjurio abstinere, alieno conjugio non insidiari. Novit et hanc Apostolus legem, dicens: "Cum enim nationes, quae legem non habent, naturaliter secundum legem faciunt," . . .'"

[57] "St. Ambrose, *De officiis* iii. 3: 'Haec utique lex naturae est, quae nos ad omnem astringit humanitatem, ut alter alteri tanquam unius partes corporis invicem deferamus. Nec detrahendum quidquam putemus, cum contra naturae legem sit non juvare.' St. Ambrose, *De officiis* iii. 24: 'Nihilque judicandum utile, nisi quod in commune prosit. . . . Etenim si una lex naturae omnibus, una utique utilitas universorum, ad consulendum utique omnibus naturae lege constringimur.'"

[58] "St. Augustine, *De diversis questionibus* xxxi: 'Natura jus est quod non opinio genuit, sed, quaedam innata vis inseruit, ut religionem, pietatem, gratiam, vindicationem, observantiam, veritatem.'"

[59] Carlyle, *op. cit.*, I, 105–6.

On the relationship between early Christian thought and pagan philosophy some interesting observations are to be found in a volume on *The Catholic Tradition of the Law of Nations,* by John Eppstein:

> Christianity had now begun to win to itself the best minds of the Empire, the leaders of Roman thought. They did not cease to be Roman in intellectual or in political tradition: all that was consistent with reason and natural law in their philosophy, and therefore consistent with Christianity, they retained so that it became interwoven with Christian thought. The Stoic philosophy which, in its practical consequences, had already led to a beginning of those reforms concerning the treatment of women, slaves and children, for which it is the habit to give Constantine credit, had developed an enlightened notion of private and public duties—and a hierarchy of virtues. The incorporation of these ideas into Christian ethics is an event of no mean importance to our subject.[60]

Mr. Eppstein then reminds us of the connection between Cicero and St. Ambrose (who, it will be remembered, converted St. Augustine to Christianity). Here Mr. Eppstein relies on the authority of Monsignor Batiffol, whom he quotes at length:[61]

> St. Ambrose was a Roman—Roman by race, by culture and even, it must be added, by his career. Bishop and moralist as he was, his ethics were a form of Christianized stoic philosophy. When he wrote his *De Officiis,* the first attempt at a Christian treatise upon Duties, he borrowed from Cicero both the title and the matter of his treatise. Ambrose took from Cicero what he in turn had found in the περὶ καθήκοντος (What is seemly) of the Stoic Panaetius, the Platonic classification of the four cardinal virtues. The Saint introduced this classification into Christian ethics, for which it was certainly an acquisition. Following in the steps of Cicero, Ambrose drew a distinction between the injustice which consists in the active perpetration of it and the injustice which consists in failing to defend someone else who is the victim of an injustice.

Monsignor Batiffol supports his view concerning the relationship between St. Ambrose and Cicero by additional illustrations, of which two may be quoted:

> "There are two sorts of injustice," we read in Cicero; "the one, of those who commit an injury; the other, of those who do not avert the injury from those against whom it is committed, if they have the power to do so" (*De Officiis,* I, 23). We find this distinction reproduced literally in St. Ambrose. . . . Said Cicero: "The foundation of Justice is good faith" (C. *De Officiis,* I, 23). Ambrose exactly repeated these words[62] (A. *De Officiis,* I, 29)—from which it will be seen how great was the Saint's dependence upon that philosopher.[63]

[60] Eppstein, *The Catholic Tradition of the Law of Nations,* p. 57.
[61] *Ibid.*, p. 61, quoting *L'Eglise et le droit de guerre,* pp. 35–37.
[62] But with a different meaning, as Mr. Eppstein points out.   [63] Eppstein, *op. cit.*, p. 62.

HEBREW PROPHETS AND CHRISTIANITY 183

There is another passage from the Monsignor on the writings and methods of St. Ambrose, which is indicative not only of the manner in which the early Fathers ranged far and wide in their search for the enlightened principles which should control human conduct, but also of the way in which they adapted those principles to the ideals of the Christian faith:

> Ambrose, like Cicero himself, was an eclectic: he borrowed, or rejected or corrected as he thought best. He knew that good faith (*fides*) was not always enough, but that it needed to be enlightened. So Ambrose completed the theory of justice with that new feature, which marked the emergence of an authority capable of completing with certitude the uncertainties of the Natural Law, and if need be of acting as the arbiter of conflicts. "*Ecclesia autem quaedam forma justitiae est*" (*De Officiis*, I, 29). The Church is, in a certain sense, the determinant of justice.[64]

In the following pages an examination will be made of the views expressed by the great theologians and laymen of the Middle Ages and the early modern era. And here a word should perhaps be said concerning the choice of certain writers in these two great periods and the exclusion of others. The criterion adopted has been to treat only those authorities through whom the main current of political and legal thought has passed and to omit those who, while their works are of value, do not appreciably add to the views of their predecessors. It is interesting to observe that Mr. Eppstein, confronted by a somewhat similar problem, found it advisable to adopt much the same course:

> A large number of quotations from other mediæval scholastics could be added, from the works of *St. Raymund of Pennafort* [a Spaniard], the great canonist by order of whom, as General of the Dominican Order, St. Thomas wrote his *Summa contra Gentiles,* up to those of *Carletti* and *Joannes Lupus.* . . . We have not, however, found in these writers any new element nor any line of thought which is absent from the works of the Fathers and St. Thomas or which is not developed more clearly by the Neo-scholastics of the sixteenth and seventeenth centuries.[65]

A sentence or two of Professor McIlwain[66] furnishes adequate justification for the plan adopted:

> But we shall miss the main channel if we lose ourselves in an attempt to trace to its source every tributary stream. If, therefore, a writer adequately sums up a great movement of thought, his theory must often suffice here to illustrate the less comprehensive ones made by others.

[64] *Ibid.*
[65] *Ibid.*, p. 68.
[66] *The Growth of Political Thought in the West* (previously cited), p. 319.

Chapter XI

ST. AUGUSTINE (A.D. 354-430)

St. Augustine has appropriately been called "the meeting-place of two worlds."[1] In him are united the best elements of pagan philosophy and the ideals of Christianity. And this union was to be of immense importance to posterity, for St. Augustine, in epitomizing the philosophical conceptions of the Ancient World and harmonizing them with the great principles of his faith, supplied a twofold foundation for our Christian civilization.

He was born a Roman, of Roman parents, although his birthplace was the little town of Tagaste, in the African province of Numidia. At the time of his birth his mother was a Christian, but his father did not embrace Christianity until late in life. He himself was not converted to the faith until he had reached maturity and had come under the influence of Ambrose, the Bishop and statesman of Milan. In the meantime, however, he had acquired an excellent education and had read deeply in Roman literature, especially Cicero.[2] It was chiefly through Latin literature that he became acquainted with the older culture of Greece, for it would seem that his knowledge of Greek was imperfect and indeed that he had small liking for the language of Plato and Aristotle.[3] Nevertheless, he was familiar with Greek conceptions, both of the classic age and of later periods,[4] and his subsequent development was influenced powerfully if indirectly by the current doctrines of Platonism.[5]

Yet, though St. Augustine was in a very real sense the spiritual heir of the ancient world, he was also of his own age and subject to the material influences of a period gravely troubled by war and rumors of war. There were controversies and rebellions within the empire, and on the frontiers the threat of barbarian invasions was becoming year by year more acute. As Augustine grew older, the situation of Rome grew steadily worse. At

---

[1] Figgis, *The Political Aspect of St. Augustine's "City of God,"* p. 7.
[2] On St. Augustine's debt to Cicero, see particularly Combés, *La Doctrine politique de Saint Augustin,* pp. 42–48.
[3] St. Augustine, *Confessions* I. xiii, xiv.   [4] *Ibid.,* IV. xvi; VII. ix, xx.
[5] "C'est à ce fond platonicien que saint Augustin a puisé, non seulement pour donner une armature philosophique à sa théologie, mais pour fournir des assises solides à sa politique. Il le rectifiera, le complétera, l'élargira aux lumières de la foi et de l'Écriture. Mais ce fond sera toujours la trame secrète de sa pensée."—Combés, *op. cit.,* p. 40.

length the barbarian hordes could no longer be held in check, and in 410 Alaric and his Goths poured irresistibly down through Italy and sacked the city of Rome. It is perhaps natural that theories of pacificism should have failed to flourish in such a war-torn world. To the Roman of that day, enlightened though he might be, it would have appeared singularly futile, if not positively wicked, to advocate a doctrine of peace at any price. However terrible war might be, to him it was justified by the urgent necessity of fighting against the invaders for the preservation of everything which he cherished. And St. Augustine, while he wrote eloquently on the subject of peace, was also a Roman who could not ignore the bitter realities which confronted his people. It was therefore inevitable that in the face of these realities he should come, as we shall see, to regard war as permissible and indeed necessary under certain conditions.

St. Augustine was a voluminous writer, and it has been said of him that "even if he be not the greatest of Latin writers, he is assuredly the greatest man that ever wrote Latin."[6] His literary contributions were of a varied nature: letters (often of great length), sermons, numerous tractates, dialogues, and large treatises. Many of them were composed as the result of religious controversies, the history of which is outside the scope of the present chapter. But while St. Augustine's writings are, in large part, *livres de circonstances,* they were destined to become the source books of the theologians and philosophers of the following centuries, exercising a vast influence upon social and political as well as religious thought. His *Confessions* has perhaps been the most widely read of all his works, but it is the *De civitate dei* which has had the greatest effect upon the thought of the Christian world.

In the following pages an examination will be made of St. Augustine's political and legal conceptions, without, however, attempting a detailed analysis of any one of his writings. But since he stands at the gateway, so

---

[6] Souter, *The Earliest Latin Commentaries on the Epistles of St. Paul,* p. 139.

An admirable comment on St. Augustine's style has been made by James Houston Baxter, Regius Professor of Ecclesiastical History in the University of St. Andrews, who says (intro. to his translation of *Select Letters* of St. Augustine, p. xl): "If he be compared with his contemporaries, none has emerged so far from enslavement to rhetoric; no one of them shows less solicitude than he for the frills and flourishes of mere ornament. Of a sober and introspective nature, he is too much in earnest about the truth to be anything but direct, weighty, and unadorned. He made Christian Latin a more pliant and forceful speech than any of his predecessors except that other African, Tertullian. Under stress of his ideas or his emotions it becomes a grave and sonorous vehicle for great and moving thoughts, and only at occasional moments does he condescend to think as much of his method and manner of utterance as of his message. Rhetoric formed indeed the chief staple of contemporary education and Augustine did not escape from the heritage of his age, yet in many respects he is one of the greatest, as well as the last, of the masters of Latin eloquence."

to speak, between the ancient world and the Middle Ages, it may be well to consider for a moment the relationship in philosophical thought between the two periods. The philosophy of the past, as we have seen, was not merely transmitted, more or less imperfectly, to a new age. It was combined with the doctrines of the New Testament; it was given a fresh interpretation in order to make it applicable to new conditions; it entered, in short, upon a new phase of development. In the course of this development it was elaborated and changed from an ancient to a medieval philosophy. Describing this change, a distinguished French authority says:[7]

The Fathers of the Church and the philosophers of the Middle Ages set out from Greek philosophy, from Plato and Aristotle. Now in setting out from a point you move away from it, but you can also take something along with you. While the man Plato and the man Aristotle stand motionless in the historical past, Platonism and Aristotelianism will live with a new life and collaborate in a work all unforeseen by their authors. It was due to them that the Middle Ages was able to achieve a philosophy. They supplied its idea—*perfectum opus rationis*—they pointed out some of its master problems and, along with them, the rational principles that command their solution and even some of the necessary technique. The debt of the Middle Ages to the Greeks was immense, and is fully recognized, but the debt of Hellenism to the Middle Ages is as great, and nothing is less appreciated; for even from mediæval religion Greek philosophy had something to learn. Christianity communicated to it some share in its own vitality and enabled it to enter on a new career.[8]

The beginnings of this process may be discerned very early in the Christian Era, but it was St. Augustine who firmly based medieval philosophy upon the fundamental conceptions of the older world. His structural materials—to employ a figure of speech—were derived from Christianity, but his foundation stones were quarried from ancient philosophy. And his successors throughout the Middle Ages, while they broadened the foundations through an increasing study of the great pagan philosophers, continued the building largely in accordance with St. Augustine's plans.

In view of St. Augustine's familiarity with the political doctrines of the

---

[7] Gilson, *The Spirit of Medieval Philosophy*, pp. 423–24.

[8] Speaking of the philosophies current during the period of the early Church, the Rev. M. C. D'Arcy, S. J., observes that "they descended from the golden age of Greece, but in the passage of time they had become confused and contaminated. The habit of the later age was eclectic, and Stoic and Epicurean ideas were to be found commingled with Platonic and Aristotelian. Pride of place, once enjoyed by Athens, later passed to Alexandria, and in this cockpit of different civilisations a Platonic tradition survived, though it contained many another strain, Jewish, Oriental and Graeco-Roman. Its greatest product was Neo-Platonism. There Plotinus first lived and taught. His philosophy rallied to its support the last defenders of paganism against the conquering religion of Christianity, and later through the influence of St. Augustine it became part of the inheritance of Christian Europe."—*Thomas Aquinas*, pp. 9–10.

older philosophers, it is not surprising that he accepted—and adapted to his purpose—their conceptions of man as a social and political being:

Forasmuch as each man is a part of the human race [he declares],[9] and human nature is something social, and hath for a great and natural good, the power also of friendship; on this account God willed to create all men out of one, in order that they might be held in their society not only by likeness of kind, but also by bond of kindred.

It is the part of wisdom, in short, for man to adapt himself as fully as possible to the requirements of social life.[10] Unfortunately, human beings not only have strong social impulses, but they are also afflicted with what may be called antisocial tendencies—tendencies which result in discord rather than harmony. Were it not for this, human society would be a universal unity instead of a series of units, each separate and distinct from, and frequently in conflict with, other units, and each made up of individuals whose antisocial tendencies are restrained by governments and laws. "The society of mortals spread abroad through the earth everywhere and in the most diverse places, although bound together by a certain fellowship of our common nature, is yet for the most part divided against itself, and the strongest oppress the others, because all follow after their own interests and lusts."[11]

These tendencies, in the conception of St. Augustine, are due to man's sinful nature, and hence laws and government and all the trappings of the state are in the nature of a remedy for human sin. States, it might therefore be said, following St. Augustine's views to their conclusion, constitute society in its imperfect form, the form which it assumed in consequence of the fall of man.

Now if he had not been endowed with human reason, man's antisocial impulses could have led only to indescribable confusion and indeed chaos. The best that might have been hoped for him would have been the social life of the swarm or the pack in which instinct and force are substitutes for law and government. But the state differs from the swarm, from a mere multitude, because of man's powers of reason. Human beings, in a word, are capable not only of association but of organization. The *civitas,* says St. Augustine, "is not made up of any living creatures whatsoever, but is rather a multitude of rational beings, a multitude bound together by the law of one single society."[12] Here we have two fundamental elements of the state. The first, essential to the very existence of the state, consists of the people them-

---

[9] *De bono conjugali* I.
[10] *De civitate dei* XIX. v.
[11] *Ibid.,* XVIII. ii.
[12] *Evangelical Questions,* II. xlvi.

selves. The second element is the quality of reason, which is equally essential to the *civitas* because without it the state—that is, the status of organization—would be impossible. To St. Augustine the state was no superimposed entity, separate and apart from the individuals who were its inhabitants. "Each individual man," he maintains, "like one letter in a language, is as it were the element of a city or kingdom, however far-spreading in its occupation of the earth."[13] Upon this principle, in St. Augustine's opinion, the matter of size has no bearing. It is a principle as applicable in the case of the small city-state as in that of the vast empire. "Do you think a city ends with its walls?" he asks. "A city is in its citizens, not in its walls."[14] Therefore if you reduce the state to its lowest terms, you are confronted neither with the skeleton of some corporate monster nor with a mere body of land enclosed within arbitrary boundaries, but with living men and women dwelling together in an organized group.

As has been observed, St. Augustine, like Cicero, considered the inhabitants of the state to be "bound together" by law. In his exposition of law, first place is given of course to "the eternal law," which St. Augustine defined as "divine order, or the will of God, which requires the preservation of natural order, and forbids the breach of it."[15] This function of the eternal law, the preservation of the natural order, is also the function of the natural law, and hence it is not surprising to find that, in St. Augustine's conception, the law of nature and the law eternal are practically synonymous terms,[16] and are identified with reason. In the dialogue[17] in which his friend, Evodius, Bishop of Uzalis, is represented as an interlocutor, we find the following series of significant rhetorical questions, to which Evodius, of course, returns an affirmative reply:

Augustine: Can it seem to any intelligent person that that law which is called *summa ratio* (highest reason), which we ought ever to obey, and by which the evil merit a miserable, and the good a blessed life, and by which, in short, that law which we call temporal is rightly established and rightly changed, can it seem to any intelligent person that that law is not unchangeable and eternal? Can it ever be unjust that the bad should be miserable and the good happy? or that a virtuous and noble people should set up magistrates for themselves, but a dissolute and wicked people should lack that freedom?

Evodius: I grant that it is an eternal and unchangeable law.

Augustine: I think you also see that in the temporal law there is nothing just and lawful which men have not derived for themselves from that eternal law.

---

[13] *De civitate dei* IV. iii.   [14] *Sermon on the Destruction of the City,* vi.
[15] *Contra Faustum* XXII. 27.
[16] Cf. Kosters, "Le Droit des gens chez St. Augustin," an admirable study, in the *Revue de droit international et de législation comparée*, XIV (1933), especially p. 42.
[17] *On Free Will*, I. vi. 15.

Thus the eternal law is also both the source and the standard for human law. "The author of temporal laws, if he is a good and wise man, consults the eternal law itself, concerning which no soul is permitted to judge, that he may discern for temporal affairs, according to its immutable rules, what ought to be commanded and forbidden."[18]

Now if this procedure were always followed in human lawmaking, legislation everywhere would, in the main, be of a uniform character. But the contrary is so often the case, and the laws and customs of one state so often conflict with those on the same subject in another state, that to some it seemed futile to maintain the existence of a single and universal standard of right and wrong. St. Augustine met this skeptical attitude with a simple but overwhelming example. After stating the opposing view of those who, "distracted by this endless variety of customs . . . have thought that there was no such thing as absolute right, but that every nation took its own custom for right, and that since every nation has a different custom, and right must remain unchangeable, it becomes manifest that there is no such thing as right at all," St. Augustine at once declares:

Such men did not perceive, to take only one example, that the precept, "Whatsoever ye would that men should do to you, do ye even so to them," cannot be altered by any diversity of national customs. And this precept, when it is referred to the love of God, destroys all vices; when to the love of one's neighbour, it puts an end to all crimes.[19]

Nevertheless St. Augustine realized that all peoples had not the same standards. It was inevitable that ideals in less advanced communities should differ from those obtaining in more enlightened states. He was familiar with Cicero's theory that justice is an essential characteristic of the state,[20] but he knew that, judged strictly on that basis, states had been rare indeed, if not wholly nonexistent, throughout history. Yet there had been for many centuries political communities with systems of law and well-established governments. Although they might fail of true justice in many respects, were not these communities really states? It seemed to St. Augustine that they were, and he therefore attempted what doubtless appeared to him a broader definition of the state:

If we discard this [Ciceronian] definition of a people, and, assuming another, say that a people is an assemblage of reasonable beings bound together by a common agreement as to the objects of their love, then, in order to discover the character of any people, we have only to observe what they love. Yet whatever it loves, if only it is an assemblage of reasonable beings and not of beasts, and

---

[18] *On the True Religion*, i. 31.   [19] *De doctrina Christiana* III. xiv.   [20] *Supra*, p. 148.

is bound together by an agreement as to the objects of love, it is reasonably called a people; and it will be a superior people in proportion as it is bound together by higher interests, inferior in proportion as it is bound together by lower. According to this definition of ours, the Roman people is a people, and its weal is without doubt a commonwealth or republic. But what its tastes were in its early and subsequent days, and how it declined into sanguinary seditions and then to social and civil wars, and so burst asunder or rotted off the bond of concord in which the health of a people consists, history shows, and in the preceding books I have related at large. And yet I would not on this account say either that it was not a people, or that its administration was not a republic, so long as there remains an assemblage of reasonable beings bound together by a common agreement as to the objects of their love.[21]

Such a definition seemed to St. Augustine sufficiently elastic to include all nations having a public government.

What I say of this [the Roman] people and of this [Roman] republic I must be understood to say or think of the Athenians or any Greek state, of the Egyptians, of the early Assyrian Babylon, and of every other nation, great or small, which had a public government. For, in general, the city of the ungodly, which did not obey the command of God that it should offer no sacrifice save to Him alone, and which, therefore, could not give to the soul its proper command over the body, nor to the reason its just authority over the vices, is void of true justice.[22]

In a word, St. Augustine was squarely facing the facts of history, and particularly the fact that the states of antiquity, including his own Rome, had not conducted themselves in accordance with the Christian standard of justice. And unfortunately the conduct of nations still continues to fall below that standard. But like St. Augustine we continue to bestow the title of state on delinquent peoples and their governments. We also accept, however, as he did elsewhere, the ideal expressed in the Ciceronian definition. For if they are lacking in justice, "what," St. Augustine demands, "are kingdoms but great robberies?"[23] And the law of the state must always seek to embody justice if it is to be worthy of the name of law. "For," says St. Augustine, "that does not seem to me to be a law which is not just."[24]

Justice, again, must characterize Christian rulers, whose happiness will depend not upon power and material gains but upon whether "they rule justly." They should not be "lifted up amid the praises of those who pay

---

[21] *De civitate dei* XIX. xxi. Cf. also other definitions by St. Augustine: "A community is nothing else than a harmonious collection of individuals."—*Ibid.*, I. xv. "What is a republic but a commonwealth? Therefore its interests are common to all; they are the interests of the State. Now what is a State but a multitude of men bound together by some bond of concord?"—Letter CXXXVIII. ii: *To Marcellinus.*

[22] *De civitate dei* XIX. xxiv.   [23] *Ibid.*, IV. iv.   [24] *On Free Will*, I. v. 11.

them sublime honours, and the obsequiousness of those who salute them with an excessive humility, but remember that they are men." They can be good rulers only "if they are slow to punish, ready to pardon; if they apply that punishment as necessary to government and defence of the republic, and not in order to gratify their own enmity; if they grant pardon, not that iniquity may go unpunished, but with the hope that the transgressor may amend his ways; if they compensate with the lenity of mercy and the liberality of benevolence for whatever severity they may be compelled to decree; if their luxury is as much restrained as it might have been unrestrained; if they prefer to govern depraved desires rather than any nation whatever."[25]

But rulers have seldom indeed measured up to such an ideal. None recognized this more clearly than St. Augustine, and he takes occasion more than once to condemn the sacrifice of subjects to ambitions for power and empire:

Why allege to me the mere names and words of "glory" and "victory"? Tear off the disguise of wild delusion, and look at the naked deeds: weigh them naked, judge them naked.... This vice of restless ambition ... Sallust brands in passing; for when he has spoken with brief but hearty commendation of those primitive times in which life was spent without covetousness, and everyone was sufficiently satisfied with what he had, he goes on: "But after Cyrus in Asia, and the Lacedemonians and Athenians in Greece, began to subdue cities and nations, and to account the lust of sovereignty a sufficient ground for war, and to reckon that the greatest glory consisted in the greatest empire";[26] and so on, as I need not now quote. This lust of sovereignty disturbs and consumes the human race with frightful ills. By this lust Rome was overcome when she triumphed over Alba, and praising her own crime, called it glory. For, as our scriptures say, "the wicked boasteth of his heart's desire, and blesseth the covetous, whom the Lord abhorreth."[27] Away, then, with these deceitful masks, these deluding whitewashes, that things may be truthfully seen and scrutinized. Let no man tell me that this and the other was a "great" man, because he fought and conquered so and so. Gladiators fight and conquer, and this barbarism has its meed of praise; but I think it were better to take the consequences of any sloth, than to seek the glory won by such arms.[28]

Pomp and glory thus acquired were but outward show. In St. Augustine's opinion they added nothing to the spiritual wealth of humanity:

I do not see what it makes for the safety, good morals, and certainly not for the dignity, of men, that some have conquered and others have been conquered, except that it yields them that most insane pomp of human glory, in which

---

[25] *De civitate dei* V. xxiv.
[27] *Ps.* x:3.
[26] Sallust *De coniuratione Catilinae* ii. 2.
[28] *De civitate dei* III. xiv.

"they have received their reward," who burned with excessive desire of it, and carried on most eager wars. For do not their lands pay tribute? Have they any privilege of learning what the others are not privileged to learn? Are there not many Senators in the other countries who do not even know Rome by sight? Take away outward show, and what are all men after all but men?[29]

Of course the nation bent on conquest always attempts to cloak its motives in an altruistic garb, and in this respect Rome, as St. Augustine was well aware, had been no exception:

The imperial city has endeavoured to impose on subject nations not only her yoke, but her language, as a bond of peace. . . . This is true; but how many great wars, how much slaughter and bloodshed, have provided this unity! And though these are past, the end of these miseries has not yet come.[30]

There might, however, in St. Augustine's opinion, be certain occasions in which war was justified. And since his views on this subject were destined to become the accepted doctrine of the future, it will be necessary to consider them at some length.

As we have already seen, during St. Augustine's lifetime Rome was engaged in a desperate and unsuccessful struggle with barbarian invaders. This unhappy condition of affairs could not but influence his views. When the entire Christian world of his day was menaced by non-Christian hordes, the question whether or not war was justified could have only one answer. Nevertheless St. Augustine, as will soon be apparent, rigidly limited his justification of war.

Now the core of his theories on war was the element of justice. And by justice he did not mean merely the outward formalities of warfare to which the Romans had attached so much importance. His keen mind probed to the heart of the question: the cause of the conflict. It was there that justice must exist if war were to be permissible to Christians. And of just causes there were, in St. Augustine's opinion, but two. The first was an injury received for which no adequate reparation was made. Therefore he defined a just war "as one that avenges wrongs, when a nation or state has to be punished, for refusing to make amends for the wrongs inflicted by its subjects, or to restore what it has seized unjustly."[31]

Here we have, in a single sentence, not only a fundamental definition but, by implication, a condemnation of wars of aggression and conquest, which have made so much of history a grim record of death and destruction. To St. Augustine it is clear that the normal condition of human affairs was not war. Rather, he conceived of "the natural order" as being directed to-

---

[29] Augustine *De civ. dei* V. xvii.   [30] *Ibid.*, XIX. vii.   [31] *Questions on Heptateuch*, VI. x.

ward "the peace of mankind."³² He saw the conquering king, lustful for new domains, not as a heroic figure but as an international criminal. "To make war on your neighbours, and thence to proceed to others, and through mere lust of dominion to crush and subdue people who do you no harm, what else is this to be called than great robbery?"³³

The second of the causes which, according to St. Augustine, justified war was a command of God. "That kind of war is undoubtedly just," he maintains, "which God Himself ordains."³⁴ This doctrine is discussed at some length by Mr. John Eppstein.

"A Christian empire," says Mr. Eppstein, "and a Christian army defending the nucleus of the civilized world against heretics and vandals created an atmosphere more favourable to the conception of a holy war waged by a Chosen People than did a pagan empire persecuting a Christian minority."³⁵

St. Augustine, turning to the Bible for guidance, found in the Old Testament ample justification for the belief in wars divinely willed. This is a belief, Mr. Eppstein observes, which "has outlasted the controversies and vicissitudes of Papacy and Empire, the rise and fall of the crusading spirit, the disruption of Christendom and the political development of recent centuries—namely, that war and peace are in the hand of God, that in His grand design He may will or permit war as a scourge to correct the overweening pride of men and punish the violation of His laws."³⁶

In a subsequent paragraph Mr. Eppstein discusses the effects of this belief.

The Old Testament conception of wars willed by God had a powerful effect upon the history of Europe. It is the conception of a holy war; and it was applied to wars enjoined by God's Vice-Regent on earth for the defence of his faithful peoples against the infidels. . . . During the nine intervening centuries the conception of war as the instrument of religion has slowly but definitely disappeared from the Christian philosophy. But, in the interests of historical accuracy, it is necessary to give its proper prominence to St. Augustine's doctrine of wars commanded by God and the powerful effects for good and ill of its ready use and abuse, in an age when the Emperor and, even more, the Pope claimed to be and were universally regarded as Ambassadors of God. It was a time when the threat to the *respublica Christiana* seemed no less terrible or tangible than the threat of the Philistines to the Chosen People of old. It is important to observe how far not only political events but Catholic experience have compelled a change, through many different stages, to a wholly spiritual conception of papal leadership and of the Church militant.³⁷

---

³² *Contra Faustum* XXII. lxxv.   ³³ *De civitate dei* IV. vi.
³⁴ *Questions on Heptateuch,* VI. x.
³⁵ Eppstein, *The Catholic Tradition of the Law of Nations* (previously cited), p. 65.
³⁶ *Ibid.,* p. 66.   ³⁷ *Ibid.,* pp. 66–67.

This change to the present-day conception "is itself a victory for St. Augustine," declares Mr. Eppstein.

The seeming conflict of ideas is a conflict not of principles but of emphasis. And the true emphasis in the Saint's writings as a whole is far less upon righteous battles than upon peace and mercy, forbearance and long suffering. It is by his praise of efforts to compose wars by reason; his exposition of peace as the greatest good of this life, proper outcome of man's natural sociability; his definition of that peace as the tranquillity of order; his linking of human tranquillity as by a mystic ladder to the peace of the Heavenly City—it is by these contributions to the spiritual heritage of men that St. Augustine is now remembered. If his vindication of holy war had a potent influence upon the conduct of nations, still more had his grand conception of the City of God.[38]

This quotation serves as a transition from St. Augustine's doctrine of war to his still more important doctrine of peace. War was, in his view, merely a means to an end, and that end was peace.

Peace should be the object of your desire [he proclaims in a letter to Count Boniface].[39] War should be waged only as a necessity, and waged only that God may by it deliver men from the necessity and preserve them in peace. For peace is not sought in order to the kindling of war, but war is waged in order that peace may be obtained.

We find this doctrine repeated in different form in the treatise *De civitate dei*:

It is obvious that peace is the end sought for by war. For every man seeks peace by waging war, but no man seeks war by making peace.[40]

But peace is more than the goal of war. It is an end in itself because it is essential to the preservation of human society. Therefore the wise man will "lament the necessity" of waging even "just wars."[41] He will realize with St. Augustine that "beyond doubt it is a greater felicity to have a good neighbour at peace, than to conquer a bad one by making war."[42] And when controversies arise—as they inevitably do between states as well as between individuals—St. Augustine would have peaceful settlement by negotiation substituted for an appeal to arms; for whatever glory there may be in war, "it is a higher glory still," he writes to one Darius, who had been sent to Africa to conduct peace negotiations in 429, "to stay war itself with a word, than to slay men with the sword, and to procure or maintain peace by peace, not by war."[43]

But St. Augustine not only advocated peace; he defined it in terms so complete that his definition has never been surpassed:

[38] *The Catholic Tradition* . . . , p. 67. [39] Letter CLXXXIX. 6: *To Boniface*. [40] XIX. xii.
[41] *Ibid.*, vii. [42] *Ibid.*, IV. xv. [43] Letter CCXXIX: *To Darius*.

The peace of the body then consists in the duly proportioned arrangement of its parts. The peace of the irrational soul is the harmonious repose of the appetites, and that of the rational soul the harmony of knowledge and action. The peace of body and soul is the well-ordered and harmonious life and health of the living creature. Peace between man and God is the well-ordered obedience of faith to eternal law. Peace between man and man is well-ordered concord. Domestic peace is the well-ordered concord between those of the family who rule and those who obey. Civil peace is a similar concord among the citizens. The peace of the celestial city is the perfectly ordered and harmonious enjoyment of God, and of one another in God.[44]

And summing up this definition, St. Augustine adds:

The peace of all things is the tranquillity of order. Order is the distribution which allots things equal and unequal, each to its own place.[45]

Peace, in a word, "is a good so great, that even in this earthly and mortal life, there is no word we hear with such pleasure, nothing we desire with such zest, or find to be more thoroughly gratifying."[46]

St. Augustine would have peace exist not only between individuals but between groups of individuals or states. Indeed it may even be said that he conceived of the possibility of an international community in which the member states would be at peace with one another. This all inclusive community, which he termed "the third circle of human society"[47]—the household and the state being the inner circles—was not to be dominated by any single government which would impose peace by force. Though he was a Roman, St. Augustine was not in favor, as we have seen, of a *Pax Romana* brought about and enforced by "many great wars . . . much slaughter and bloodshed."[48] In his international community "all kingdoms would have been small, rejoicing in neighborly concord."[49] Thus the world would be divided into "very many kingdoms of nations," just as "there are very many houses of citizens in a city."[50] Here we have an ideal which, still unrealized, is the hope of the future—an international community in which the many free and independent states of the world shall exist in equality and permanent peace.

The influence of Augustine on the growth of International Law is certain [declares Dr. Figgis[51]]. That he laid down principles which might prove fruitful, if they were needed, cannot be denied. The conception of a world of equal States living in harmony and exchanging mutual services we owe to his mind, expressed in the passage about a world consisting of small States.

[44] *De civitate dei* XIX. xiii. [45] *Ibid.* [46] *Ibid.*, xi. [47] *Ibid.*, vii.
[48] *Ibid.* [49] *Ibid.*, IV. xv. [50] *Ibid.* [51] *Op. cit.*, pp. 103–4.

Chapter XII

ST. ISIDORE OF SEVILLE (c. 560–636) AND GRATIAN'S *DECRETUM*

St. Isidore of Seville (so referred to in order to distinguish him from an Egyptian saint of the same name) was, like Seneca, of Spanish birth. It is generally believed that he was born at Cartagena, although he passed most of his life in Seville, where indeed he was archbishop for nearly forty years, having assumed that office upon the death of his brother Leander, the previous incumbent. He was, it is said, the greatest churchman of his day in Spain, and his works prove him to have been a man of vast learning and remarkable versatility.[1] In the words of Mr. Henry Dwight Sedgwick,

> Isidore is the only man of international reputation that Spain produced during the whole period of Gothic dominion, and also one of the most eminent men of letters—for the author of *El poema del Cid* is unknown—between the Silver Age of Seneca and Quintilian and the *Siglo de Oro* of Cervantes and Lope de Vega. His renown spread all over Europe and remained resplendent until after Dante's time.[2]

In the Spain of St. Isidore's era the culture of the ancient world had been less disrupted by the great barbarian invasions than was the case elsewhere in the empire. Thus it was that the Spaniards, who had become almost wholly Romanized (and indeed had furnished Rome with many men of distinction, among them the Senecas and two emperors, Trajan and Hadrian), played an important part in the conservation of Roman culture and institutions. Bearing this in mind we shall be, perhaps, less surprised at St. Isidore's familiarity—in a period often referred to as the Dark Ages—with the learning of the past.

His best known and—for present purposes—his most important work, *Etymologiarium sive originum libri XX,* is a veritable encyclopedia, dealing

---

[1] Vanderpol, in his authoritative volume *La Doctrine scolastique du droit de guerre,* p. 7, observes of St. Isidore: "Les pères du VIIIe Concile de Tolède lui décernèment publiquement les plus grands éloges, l'appelant 'le plus savant homme qui eût paru pour éclairer les derniers siècles et dont on ne doit prononcer le nom qu'avec respect.'"

[2] *Spain, A Short History of Its Politics, Literature, and Art from Earliest Times to the Present,* p. 24.

concisely and more or less methodically with all of the fields of knowledge of his age.³ To the present-day reader the treatise represents a curious mixture of information and misinformation, of profound learning and equally profound ignorance. Yet to St. Isidore's century and to subsequent centuries the value and usefulness of the *Etymologies* cannot be overestimated. The book was destined long to remain the most accessible medieval repository of classical learning,⁴ and therefore St. Isidore must be counted, with Cicero and St. Augustine, among the important transmitters who preserved and handed on the great social conceptions of the past to their own age and to the future.⁵ And while he was not an educator in the larger sense of that term, it is not too much to say that St. Isidore's *Etymologies* mark a distinct step toward the organization of the medieval universities,⁶ out of which, in turn, have developed our modern institutions of higher learning.

But St. Isidore likewise rendered another important service to posterity in that his *Etymologies* played no small part in the long process of welding the teachings of the Church Fathers and the theories of the classical jurists and philosophers into a single body of doctrine. In this process, according to Dr. Jan Kosters, Vice President of the Supreme Court of the Netherlands and the author of a masterly essay on the origin and development of the law of nations,⁷ St. Isidore of Seville and St. Thomas Aquinas were the chief contributors.

---

³ "Isidore was, as Montalambert calls him, *le dernier savant du monde ancien,* as well as the first Christian encyclopedist."—*An Encyclopedist of the Dark Ages, Isidore of Seville,* by Brehaut, p. 7. The present writer wishes here to acknowledge his indebtedness to Dr. Brehaut's learned study of St. Isidore.

⁴ "In him antiquity reasserted itself," said his contemporary, Braulio, Bishop of Saragossa, "or rather, our time laid in him a picture of the wisdom of antiquity." Quoted from Brehaut, *op. cit.,* p. 23.

A modern evaluation of the *Etymologies* is given by Mr. Sedgwick (*op. cit.,* p. 25): "The immense admiration lavished upon this encyclopaedia during the centuries of ignorance has been paid for by excessive depreciation to-day; it is denounced as stale and unprofitable, mere slender gleanings from the rich harvest of classical learning, with no original thought, no traces of personal experience, no records of observation. This disparagement is unjust. The flood of ignorance was rising fast; books were growing scarcer and scarcer. It was impossible for students in Seville or anywhere else to have access to a good library, so Saint Isidore gathered together, as if he were laying up provisions for an ark, whatever he judged would best suit their need. The book fulfilled its author's intention. 'For centuries,' it is said, 'Saint Isidore was the battle cry of Spanish learning. . . . *Beatus et Lumen, noster Isidorus. . . . Isidorus, noster Varro, Isidorus, noster Plinius.*' "

⁵ In a recent admirable study, *La Guerre comme instrument de secours ou de punition* (pp. 33–34), Beaufort says: "On voit qu'Isidore de Séville reprend pour son propre compte la pensée fondamentale de ses prédécesseurs, à savoir que la vie internationale elle-même est liée à des règles de morale et de droit, que l'arbitraire et l'anarchie ne peuvent y être tolérés."

⁶ Cf. Brehaut, *op. cit.,* chap. iv.

⁷ "Les Fondements du droit des gens," *Bibliotheca Visseriana dissertationum . . .,* IV, 11–12.

Of St. Isidore's various other works—for he was a voluminous writer[8]—only a few can here be mentioned. Many of them were theological, like the *Sententiae,* but others dealt with secular subjects, as in the case of the celebrated *De natura rerum,* a treatise on the phenomena of nature, and the histories, *Historia de regibus Gothorum, Vandalorum et Suevorum.* The latter work was particularly valuable for its record of the Goths, and nearly ten centuries later Mariana, the great Spanish historian, turned to it as the chief source of Gothic history.

Certain parts of the *Etymologies* contain definitions destined to be of fundamental importance in the development of legal theories.[9] For the sake of convenience, several of St. Isidore's basic definitions may be given in a numbered series:

1. All laws are either divine or human;[10]
2. Divine laws depend on nature, human laws on custom; and so the latter differ, since different laws please different peoples;[11]
3. *Ius* is the general term and *lex* is a kind of *ius;*[12]
4. *Ius* is so-called because it is just (*iustum*). All *ius* is made up of laws and customs;[13]
5. *Lex* is a written ordinance;[14]
6. *Mos* is custom approved by its antiquity, or unwritten *lex.*[15]

St. Isidore held that *lex,* the written or statutory law, had its source in the people themselves, deriving its authority from them and remaining valid only with their approval. To be sure he lived in an age when, as has so often been the case throughout history, there was a sharp cleavage between the numerically small aristocratic element and the balance of the population. But, while fully recognizing the existence of this cleavage, he did not

---

[8] "Few writers of any period cover the intellectual interests of their time so completely. To understand Isidore's mental world is nearly to reach the limits of the knowledge of his time."—Brehaut, *op. cit.,* p. 16.

[9] "In addition to the Scriptures," says Brehaut (*op. cit.,* p. 165), speaking of the sources from which St. Isidore drew his conception of law, "and Isidore's authorities on word derivation, he is believed to have drawn on the *Breviarium Alaricianum,* the Theodosian code, the text-books of Gaius and Ulpian and the *Sentences* of Paulus. Although the Justinian code was issued a century before the compilation of the *Etymologies,* it seems improbable that Isidore made any use of it, or had even heard of it."

And in a footnote the same writer adds: "Considering the intellectual stagnation of the time, it seems quite possible that the Justinian code was unheard of wherever it was not actually the law of the land. Vinogradoff gives the conclusion of modern scholarship as to this when he says (*Roman Law in Medieval Europe,* p. 8): 'The *Corpus Juris* of Justinian, which contains the main body of law for later ages, including our own, was accepted and even known only in the East and in those parts of Italy which had been reconquered by Justinian's generals. The rest of the western provinces still clung to the tradition of the preceding period, culminating in the official code of Theodosius II (A. D. 437).'"

[10] *Etymologies* V. ii.   [11] *Ibid.*   [12] *Ibid.,* iii. sec. i.   [13] *Ibid.*   [14] *Ibid.*   [15] *Ibid.*

allow that recognition to blind him to the true nature of law. Thus adapting the older Roman conceptions to his purpose, he declared that "law (*lex*) is an ordinance of the people, which those who are greater by birth, together with the people (*plebibus*), sanction."[16]

Now what, in St. Isidore's opinion were the essential qualities of law? It should be in harmony with reason, for it will then be in harmony also with the moral standard of "religion," with "knowledge," and with the "welfare" of the people.[17] Again, according to St. Isidore, it is necessary that law be "honorable, just, possible of fulfilment, in agreement with nature, in agreement with the usage of the country, appropriate to time and place, necessary, and useful." Law should also be "perfectly clear lest through obscurity it contain anything which might be deceptive." And finally, it should be "written for the common utility of the citizens, no private person having been favored by it."[18] As for equity, it is to be found in both law and custom—and here St. Isidore as we have seen, is careful to note the difference between the written *lex* and the unwritten *mos* derived from long-continued usage.[19]

In dealing with the function of law, St. Isidore is ready with a concise definition: "Every law either permits something," he observes, "or forbids something ... or punishes."[20] This brings us to a consideration of the purpose of law—"why," as St. Isidore puts it, "law is made." His answer is given in two brief sentences.

Laws are made that human temerity may be restrained by fear of them, and that the innocent may be safe among the wicked, and that the capacity of injuring in the wicked themselves may be held in check by dreaded punishment. For human life is regulated by the reward or punishment of the law.[21]

When he discussed the more inclusive term *ius* St. Isidore, writing in Latin, had an advantage over those who express themselves in the English tongue. For *ius,* combining in itself the twofold conception of right and law, has no equivalent in English speech,[22] a fact which is not without significance in relation to the tendency of many expounders of Anglo-Saxon jurisprudence to minimize the relationship between legal and moral conceptions. "*Ius,*" St. Isidore maintains, "is the general term" from which

---

[16] *Ibid.*, II. x. 1. Many of the definitions in Book II, chap. x, are repeated with little or no variation in Book V.

[17] *Ibid.*   [18] *Ibid.*   [19] *Ibid.*   [20] *Ibid.*   [21] *Ibid.*

[22] There are, of course, equivalents in the languages of modern European countries, especially those whose legal development has been deeply influenced by Roman law. Thus we find that today *ius* has become *droit, derecho, diritto, recht, ret,* and so forth.

the corollary follows that *lex* is merely "a kind of *ius*."[23] And, always interested in etymology, he immediately adds, *"ius* is so-called, because it is just."[24] But what is the meaning of the term just, or rather justice? St. Isidore had already dealt with this question in an earlier passage. Justice it is, he explained, which "through right judgment distributes to each his due."[25] Justice, then, is a moral as well as a legal quality. It follows that he who violates the rightful order of things—that is, *ius*—commits injustice. In short, to employ St. Isidore's own concise definition: "Injury is injustice."[26]

Now law in the sense of *ius* was classified by St. Isidore under three headings. For *ius,* in his conception, is "natural, or civil, or international."[27] The first of these classifications he then proceeds to define:

The natural law is the common law of all the nations; in that it is everywhere observed by natural instinct, and not by any ordinance: and such are the union of male with female, the procreation and rearing of children, the possession in common of all things and the common liberty of all; the acquisition of those things which are taken from the heavens or the earth or the sea; in like manner the restoring of property or money given over in trust, and the repelling of violence by force. For this (or whatever is like this) is never held unjust, but natural and equal.[28]

The civil law St. Isidore defines as "that which any people or city establishes as its own law, for human or divine reasons."[29]

The third classification was that of the law of nations, or *ius gentium*. But before taking up St. Isidore's definition of it, it is advisable to examine his conception of society and of the states into which society is divided. Like St. Augustine, he considered the social relations of humankind as being of a threefold nature. There was first the household or family group. Next came the city, or—as was frequently the case both in ancient Greece and in medieval Europe—the city-state, in which the inhabitants are called citizens, according to St. Isidore, "because uniting, they live in one body in order that their life in common may be better provided for and safer."[30] The essential element in such a union is not the territory possessed—important as that might be—nor the protecting walls. "A city," St. Isidore insists, "is a multitude of men, united by the chain of society; it takes its name from the citizens, that is, from the inhabitants of the city themselves."[31] Or, to state this conception in another form, "People," declares St. Isidore, defining the Latin term *populus,* "is the name of the human multitude, bound together by a unanimity of law and harmonious fellowship."[32]

[23] *Etymologies* V. iii.   [24] *Ibid.*   [25] *Ibid.,* II. xxiv.   [26] *Ibid.,* V. xxvi.   [27] *Ibid.,* iv.
[28] *Ibid.*   [29] *Ibid.,* v.   [30] *Ibid.,* IX. iv.   [31] *Ibid.,* XV. ii.   [32] *Ibid.,* IX. iv.

In his conception of society, however, St. Isidore was not preoccupied solely with the family and the state. He glimpsed the larger unity, the "world" which, in his own language, "is the domicile of all mankind."[33] In short, and again to employ his own words, "there are three societies—of families, of cities and of nations."[34] Thus there came to St. Isidore, as to St. Augustine, in a dark period of the Middle Ages, the gleam of prophecy, the vision—dim, perhaps, but destined to be strengthened in his successors— of the society of nations, or the international community.

Three other passages throw light on St. Isidore's social and political doctrines, and particularly his views on the purpose and limitations of government.

He does not rule who does not correct. Therefore, the name of king is held by doing rightly; by sinning, it is lost. Whence indeed, according to the ancients, the proverb thus ran: "You shall be king, if you do rightly; if you do not do rightly you shall not be king." The Royal virtues are especially two: Justice and compassion. But compassion is more to be praised in kings; for justice by itself is harsh.[35]

The second passage (from St. Isidore's *Sententiae*) makes it abundantly clear that he was a firm supporter of the sovereignty of law over ruler as well as subject:

It is just that a Prince obey his own laws. For it will then appear that his laws ought to be kept by all, when he himself shows reverence for them. Princes are bound by their own laws, nor is it fitting in itself that they should be able to reject laws which they set up over their subjects. For the authority of their voice is just, if they do not suffer themselves to do what they forbid their people.[36]

And in the third passage (also from the *Sententiae*) emphasis is laid upon the qualifications and duties of those who are entrusted with the powers of government:

The term *reges* (kings) is derived from *recte agendum* (right action), wherefore the title of King is retained through right conduct, while it is forfeited through sinning. For . . . those persons are rightly called kings who have learned to restrain themselves as well as their subjects by ruling well. . . .

While the kings of this world perceive themselves to be exalted above other men, let them nevertheless acknowledge that they are mortal; and let them not reflect upon the glory of their exaltation in this life, for they should have regard rather for the achievement which they shall bear away with them to the regions beyond death.[37] . . .

He who wields the kingly power aright, must so conduct himself before all,

---

[33] *Etymologies* IX. iv.
[34] *Ibid.*, XV. ii.
[35] *Ibid.*, IX. iii.
[36] *Sententiae* III. li.
[37] *Ibid.*, xlviii.

as to humble himself in his own mind in proportion to the greater honor and exaltation with which he is adorned, setting before himself the example of humility furnished by David (2 *Kings,* vi. 22), who was not puffed up because of his own worth, but rather, humbly abasing himself, declared: Before the Lord, who chose me, I will both abase myself and make myself meaner.

He who wields the kingly power aright sets a pattern of justice in deeds rather than in words. His spirit is not raised up by prosperity, nor is it distressed by adversity. His reliance is not upon his own strength, nor does his heart depart from the Lord. He keeps guard over a humble spirit in the high office of King. Iniquity does not delight him, nor is he inflamed with cupidity. He makes the poor man rich while defrauding none, and what by a just power he could have taken from the people, he frequently concedes out of a compassionate clemency.[38]

St. Isidore's views on society and the state will serve as an introduction to his definition of the scope and content of the *ius gentium*: "The law of nations comprises the seizing, building and fortifying of settlements; wars, captivities, servitudes, postliminies, treaties of peace, truces, the obligation to respect the inviolability of ambassadors, and the prohibition of intermarriage with foreigners."[39]

These examples suggest not so much the older *ius gentium* of the Romans (consisting largely of legal provisions and principles common among all peoples), as the dawning conception of the modern international law of Grotius, "the law of war and peace" applicable to the relations between states. It is called the law of nations, St. Isidore tells us, "because nearly all nations observe it."[40]

The late Professor John Westlake, in his *Chapters on International Law,*[41] offers an illuminating comment on this phase of St. Isidore's views:

Isidore of Seville, writing early in the seventh century of the Christian era, reserves the term *jus gentium* for what we should now describe as international law, so that here for the first time we find that term fairly translatable by "law of nations." All the remaining matter of the old *jus gentium,* namely the law common to all nations, *jus commune omnium nationum,* he includes in *jus naturale.*

What led St. Isidore to make this fundamental distinction, which apparently did not occur to his predecessors, or at least was not adequately stated by them? To this question Professor Westlake supplies an answer:

When Isidore wrote independent kingdoms had been founded by the northern races within the ancient limits of the Roman empire, and it was doubtless owing to that circumstance that the rules prevailing between states acquired importance enough to be treated as a separate branch of legal science with a

---

[38] St. Isidore *Sententiae* III. xlix. [39] *Etymologies,* V. vi. [40] *Ibid.* [41] Page 24.

name of its own. This rapid development of the scientific classification in accordance with the political changes suggests the true cause why in a more enlightened age, and with such excellent principles to start from, the Roman jurists never worked out a system of international law.

To the modern student, after the passage of some thirteen centuries, it seems a "curious phenomenon," as a distinguished Belgian authority[42] on the law of nations has observed, that "in a period when the science of international law had not been formulated," there should have appeared "a definition, or, to employ a more exact term, a description which closely approximates the modern conception." Yet, as it happened, St. Isidore's definitions were not to remain curious but isolated phenomena, forgotten in succeeding centuries. They were destined, as the same author tells us elsewhere,[43] to receive "the highest sanction which they could possibly obtain," in that "they found a place in the *Decretum* of Gratian and thus traversed the second half of the Middle Ages, becoming the subject of endless commentaries."

Now Gratian's object was nothing less than the preparation of "a law book for the Church that should be parallel with the 'Corpus Juris Civilis.'"[44] His *Decretum* was not compiled as an official text, but it soon became the foundation of the classic Church law because it "was so generally used in the universities and courts of the Church."[45] Through its influence on the development of canon law it has also deeply influenced the political and legal philosophy of the modern world.

Of Gratian himself little is known beyond the facts that he was a Benedictine monk of the twelfth century and that, as a master of theology in his monastery at Bologna, he was thoroughly familiar with canon law. It was apparently in the monastery, sometime between the years 1139 and 1159, that he prepared the *Decretum*. For present purposes it will be necessary to indicate but briefly the content of this great collection, which consists of 3,945 canons or chapters, and is divided into three "Parts."[46] The first part "treats of laws of divine and human constitution or, in other words, of ecclesiastical persons and duties"; the second, "of judgments, of criminal and civil causes," with, in addition, a tractate *De penitentia;* and the third "of some of the Sacraments . . . and of Sacramentals."[47] Gratian chose his ma-

[42] Nys, *Le Droit international, les principes, les théories, les faits*, I, 54.
[43] Nys, *Le Droit de la guerre et les précurseurs de Grotius*, p. 13.
[44] Figgis, *The Political Aspect of S. Augustine's City of God* (previously cited), p. 91.
[45] Le Bras, "Canon Law," in *The Legacy of the Middle Ages*, p. 326.
[46] For an account of Gratian and a very authoritative discussion of the *Decretum*, see Archbishop Cicognani, *Canon Law* (previously cited), Part II, chap. xi.   [47] *Ibid.*, p. 277.

terials from many sources, including the Scriptures, ecclesiastical documents, the works of the Fathers of the Church and other ecclesiastical writers, the Roman civil law (i.e., the great compilations of Justinian), the Codes of Theodosius and Alaric, and the Capitularies of the Frankish and German kings. To the texts which he selected, he added commentaries and observations of his own, so that the *Decretum* is in part a treatise as well as a compilation. And though it contained many errors and possessed no actual legal authority because it was "a private, not an authentic collection,"[48] the *Decretum* enjoyed great popularity and "immense authority"[49]—so much so, indeed, that Gratian has been called the "father of canonical science," and his great collection "became the classic text in the study of canon law, just as the 'Sententia' of Peter Lombard did in Theology."[50] Lectures upon it at the University of Bologna were attended by throngs of students from many countries, "sometimes to the number of 10,000,"[51] and in the course of time it gave rise to an extensive literature of summaries, tractates, subsidiary collections, glosses, and commentaries.

As has already been remarked, Gratian included not a few excerpts from St. Isidore. And it is of even greater significance to note that he drew heavily upon St. Augustine, there being in the *Decretum,* according to a trustworthy authority,[52] no less than 530 citations from the latter's writings. Declaring that "the 'Decretum' of Gratian is one of the most important elements in the construction of medieval society," the same authority immediately adds that "the use it makes of Augustine's maxims in all political and semi-political matters is decisive as to his influence."[53]

The interesting history of the canon law during the centuries which followed Gratian's great contribution cannot be pursued here. It must, however, be noted that the canon law as it was gradually developed throughout the Middle Ages profoundly affected the development of secular law and politics, transmitting to the modern world, directly or indirectly, the fundamental moral conceptions of the Church, as well as many of the great principles derived from the ancient world which the Church had assimilated and made her own.

Speaking of the contributions of the classic canon law to modern law, Professor Gabriel Le Bras[54] observes that

the ideas of good faith and equity which underlay the canonist theory of contracts still influence the legislators of to-day, and those shrewd conceptions

---

[48] Cicognani, *Canon Law*, p. 287.   [49] *Ibid.*, p. 289.   [50] *Ibid.*, p. 325.
[51] *Ibid.*, p. 283.   [52] Figgis, *op. cit.*, p. 91.   [53] *Ibid.*, p. 92.
[54] "Canon Law," in *The Legacy of the Middle Ages* (previously cited), p. 361.

of the just price and a just wage are more vital than any system that has been practically applied because they express our permanent ideal. Thus the present is linked to the distant centuries of Innocent III and Gregory VII; and indeed even to those more distant, for many of the ideas which bore fruit in the classic age were the heritage of past civilizations. The care of the poor and the oppressed which was characteristic of Judaism, the Roman love of order and authority, the Greek conceptions of political economy and formal logic, the enthusiasm and scrupulousness of the Celts, which were shown more particularly in their penitential system—all these conquests of the human mind, which seemed to her in accordance with her fundamental principles, went to the enrichment of the Church's law, and were assimilated to her own doctrine after such modification and correction as was required to bring them into harmony with her own point of view.

And Professor Le Bras' conclusion is that "it is indeed the highest moral tradition of the West and of the Mediterranean peoples which has been gathered up and handed down to us in the classic law of the Church."

Chapter XIII

JOHN OF SALISBURY (*c.* 1115–1180)
POLICRATICUS

In the twelfth century, the century of Gratian's *Decretum*, the *Politics* of Aristotle had not yet begun to exert an influence on conceptions of the state. Nevertheless there were current in that century views of the state and its government which were the logical outgrowth of the political doctrines of the early Middle Ages, and these views of the state were embodied by John of Salisbury in a treatise entitled *Policraticus*.

In discussing John of Salisbury, it is well to remember that he was an Englishman, and that he was also a student who became, in the words of Dr. Reginald Lane Poole, "beyond dispute the best-read man of his time."[1] Having studied in the Continental schools under the great doctors of his day, he may be considered as representing the best culture of the age. His knowledge, however, was neither an arid accumulation nor an intellectual burden, but rather a reservoir of the best from scholastic theology mingled with the classical learning of the past, a knowledge reinforced by an early humanism and ripened by friendships and travel. But he was more than a student, for in later life he had an immense and fruitful influence in the administration of the affairs of church and state, holding numerous important offices and becoming eventually Bishop of Chartres.

As an Englishman, John of Salisbury had England in mind when writing the *Policraticus*. Yet it would be incorrect to say that he dealt merely with contemporary matters. That for which he was groping—for it was groping on his part, since materials were not at his disposal for the complete development of his ideas—was the ideal in government and in civil rights. It was, to quote again from Dr. Poole, "the first attempt"—that is to say, in the Middle Ages—"to produce a coherent system which should aspire to the character of a philosophy of politics."[2]

It is important to note that in his *Policraticus* John of Salisbury deals with a society which is fundamentally individualistic. To him common welfare and the common good are, as it were, the sum of the welfare and the good

[1] *Illustrations of the History of Medieval Thought and Learning*, p. 191.
[2] *Ibid.*, p. 204.

of individuals making up society. Nevertheless the individuals in his state were not simply a horde of persons; they were human beings in a status of organization; and John of Salisbury gives us what has become a famous definition of the state, based upon an analogy with the human body:[3]

A commonwealth, according to Plutarch, is a certain body which is endowed with life by the benefit of divine favor, which acts at the prompting of the highest equity, and is ruled by what may be called the moderating power of reason. Those things which establish and implant in us the practice of religion, and transmit to us the worship of God (here I do not follow Plutarch, who says "of the Gods") fill the place of the soul in the body of the commonwealth. And therefore those who preside over the practice of religion should be looked up to and venerated as the soul of the body. For who doubts that the ministers of God's holiness are His representatives? Furthermore, since the soul is, as it were, the prince of the body, and has rulership over the whole thereof, so those whom our author calls the prefects of religion preside over the entire body. Augustus Caesar was to such a degree subject to the priestly power of the pontiffs that in order to set himself free from this subjection and have no one at all over him, he caused himself to be created a pontiff of Vesta, and thereafter had himself promoted to be one of the gods during his own lifetime. The place of the head in the body of the commonwealth is filled by the prince, who is subject only to God and to those who exercise His office and represent Him on earth, even as in the human body the head is quickened and governed by the soul. The place of the heart is filled by the Senate, from which proceeds the initiation of good works and ill. The duties of eyes, ears, and tongue are claimed by the judges and the governors of provinces. Officials and soldiers correspond to the hands. Those who always attend upon the prince are likened to the sides. Financial officers and keepers (I speak now not of those who are in charge of the prisons, but of those who are keepers of the privy chest) may be compared with the stomach and intestines, which, if they become congested through excessive avidity, and retain too tenaciously their accumulations, generate innumerable and incurable diseases, so that through their ailment the whole body is threatened with destruction. The husbandmen correspond to the feet, which always cleave to the soil, and need the more especially the care and foresight of the head, since while they walk upon the earth doing service with their bodies, they meet the more often with stones of stumbling, and therefore deserve aid and protection all the more justly since it is they who raise, sustain, and move forward the weight of the entire body. Take away the support of the feet from the strongest body, and it cannot move forward by its own power, but must creep painfully and shamefully on its hands, or else be moved by means of brute animals.

In the political body, which John of Salisbury thus compares with the human body, the soul is the Church Universal, the guide of the whole body

---

[3] *The Statesman's Book of John of Salisbury*—Being the Fourth, Fifth, and Sixth Books, and Selections from the Seventh and Eighth Books, of the *Policraticus*, pp. 64-65.

and of every member of the body. The head is the prince, who, though he rules in a material domain, is subject to the Church. Here, instead of attempting a separation of the two powers, the purpose is to insure their close coöperation. To summarize the remaining features of the analogy in a few phrases: the heart is the senate; the eyes, ears, and tongues the judges and governors of the provinces; the hands, officials and armed forces; the stomach, the treasury; and the feet the working classes, upon which the state stands. This organic analogy was to appear again and again in the writings of the Middle Ages. It has its dangers, as we know who have seen its perversion of the state into a soulless superbeing. But John of Salisbury's organic state had a soul; it was an affair of individual human beings, not infallible, but wholly dependent upon human nature itself.

There is some difference of opinion as to the source of this organic comparison, John of Salisbury himself having modestly ascribed it to Plutarch, although later scholars have failed to discover the passage to which he refers; but whatever its source, the statement of the comparison, as Professor Dickinson observes in the admirable Introduction to his translation of the *Policraticus,* is "significant as a stage in the transmission of the conception of organic political unity from antiquity to modern times."[4]

The view of the state which John of Salisbury sets forth is largely that of Plato, and in consequence his state has the defects of the Platonic state, in that the relationship of the parts to the whole is static and the entire plan rigidly conceived. Thus the inhabitants are permanently divided into different and exclusive classes, and the bond between them is, as Mr. Dickinson observes,[5] "the passive one of contentment, of willingness on the part of each individual to fulfill the duties of the station allotted to him in the eternal scheme of things." The government of the state was a monarchy—the only form in which John of Salisbury was interested—and there was no provision for what Professor Dickinson calls "any continuous process of reciprocal adaption whereby the relations between the different elements in the body politic shall gradually alter."[6]

John of Salisbury had in mind a limited form of government, limited in the sense that though the prince was in theory subject only to God, he was in fact to be subordinate also to law, and if he proved himself insubordinate he should suffer the consequences. In brief John of Salisbury was committed to the doctrine of tyrannicide if a prince were guilty of misrule. If the prince flouted the law to which he was subordinate, his subjects acquired the right

---

[4] Dickinson, Introduction to *The Statesman's Book of John of Salisbury,* p. xix.
[5] *Ibid.,* p. xxiv.   [6] *Ibid.,* p. xxii.

to enforce the law against him and to punish him not only by deposition but by death.

The author of the *Policraticus,* it may be added, had devoted some attention to the subject of tyrants, and indeed had written a separate tractate on the subject, which he himself describes as "a brief manual" significantly entitled, "Of the Ends of Tyrants." Unfortunately, so far as can be ascertained, no copy of this work, which would be of great interest, is extant.[7]

It would be a mistake, however, to consider the prince of the *Policraticus* as a ruler without power. John of Salisbury depicted him as bearing the burdens of the entire community, that is to say, as being responsible for the good of the community, and in order to cope with this responsibility it was necessary for him to have adequate power. But it was not absolute power; indeed the author quotes with no little unction the opinion of Justinian that it is the glory of the emperor to conform his office to the rule of law— and the law to which the prince must yield was that higher law which is the foundation of justice, equity, and the common good. "Who, indeed, in respect of public matters can properly speak of the will of the prince at all, since therein he may not lawfully have any will of his own apart from that which the law or equity enjoins, or the calculation of the common interest requires?"[8]

The author of the *Policraticus* labored under no delusions as to what tyrannicide meant. He explicitly says that "to kill a tyrant is not merely lawful but right and just" and the authority for this is Scripture itself;

> for whosoever takes up the sword deserves to perish by the sword. And he is understood to take up the sword who usurps it by his own temerity and who does not receive the power of using it from God.[9]

This is interpreted to mean that the prince must make certain that he has divine sanction before he resorts to coercion.

But tyrannicide was not to be based upon a mere dislike of the ruler by his subjects. It was to be based upon the law itself. In the words of John of Salisbury, "the law rightly takes arms against him who disarms the laws," and therefore in his conception tyranny was "not merely a public crime, but, if there could be such a thing, a crime more than public."[10] What this amounts to is the theory that the prince, by scorning the law, becomes himself an outlaw, and therefore, as in the case of any outlaw, he may be lawfully attacked by a private individual. This may be termed the doctrine of

---

[7] *Ibid.,* p. 367, note: "This work of John of Salisbury is not known to be extant."
[8] *Ibid.,* p. 7.   [9] *Ibid.,* p. lxxiii.   [10] *Ibid.,* pp. lxxiii, lxxiv.

tyrannicide in its extreme form. In later centuries it was to be essentially modified: the law might still be enforced against a recalcitrant prince, but only by an agent representing the public and possessing authority from the public. Through this modification tyrannicide was separated from what is now usually called assassination and began to assume certain characteristics of a legal process—characteristics which will be dealt with elsewhere.[11] To John of Salisbury, however, such limitation was unknown simply because he thought of the public power as being exercised only by the prince and therefore, if action were taken against the prince, it could be only on private initiative.

We have seen that the prince was subject to the law. Now John of Salisbury, in common with his predecessors—and indeed with his successors—conceived of a vast reservoir of law existing, independent of any human enactment. To this law individuals, officials, rulers, and governments were alike subject, and they were powerless to change it.

There are [says John of Salisbury] certain precepts of the law which have a perpetual necessity, having the force of law among all nations. . . . And not only do I withdraw from the hands of rulers the power of dispensing with the law, but in my opinion those laws which carry a perpetual injunction or prohibition are not subject at all to their pleasure.[12]

This body of higher law, it may be noted, though independent of human enactments, came to be considered as discoverable in the all-embracing system of Roman law, because, as we have seen, the natural law of Rome had entered the medieval conception of the law of nature.

On the subject of law John of Salisbury's views are in the great tradition which the medieval world inherited from the past, as will be evidenced by the quotation of a few further passages from the *Policraticus*. First a definition of law (based upon Justinian's *Digest*) from the second chapter:[13] "all law is, as it were, a discovery, and a gift from God, a precept of wise men, the corrector of excesses of the will, the bond which knits together the fabric of the state, and the banisher of crime." But apparently the author was not wholly satisfied with this definition, for he expanded it in a later passage, in which, after reiterating that law is a "gift of God," he describes it as "the model of equity, a standard of justice, a likeness of the divine will, the guardian of well-being, a bond of union and solidarity against the vices and the destroyer thereof, a punishment of violence and all wrong-doing."[14]

---

[11] *Infra*, p. 415.   [12] *The Statesman's Book of John of Salisbury*, p. 34.
[13] *Ibid.*, pp. 6–7; *Digest* I. iii. 1–2.
[14] *The Statesmen's Book of John of Salisbury*, p. 335.

If we accept these definitions of law—and it would be difficult to reject them—we can but accept John of Salisbury's conclusion that

> it is therefore fitting that all men should live according to it who lead their lives in a corporate political body. All are accordingly bound by the necessity of keeping the law.[15]

For the foundation of law the author turned to that fundamental precept of Christian conduct, the Golden Rule:[16] "Before the law, under the law, and still under the new covenant of grace, there is one law which is binding upon all men alike: 'What thou wouldst not should be done unto thee, do thou not unto another'; and 'what thou wouldst should be done unto thee, do that unto others.'"

It will have been observed that John of Salisbury's definitions of law included both equity and justice. Therefore, a word as to his conception of these important elements of jurisprudence. Of equity he says,[17] basing his statement on the authority of "the learned jurists," that it

> is a certain fitness of things which compares all things rationally, and seeks to apply like rules of right and wrong to like cases, being impartially disposed toward all persons, and allotting to each that which belongs to him. Of this equity the interpreter is the law, to which the will and intention of equity and justice are known.

Justice being thus linked with equity, it is important to note his explanation of the just and the unjust:[18]

> the principal element of justice is not to do harm, and to prevent, out of a duty of humanity, those who seek to do harm. When you do harm, you fall into injustice. And when you put no obstacle in the way of those who seek to do harm, you then serve and aid injustice.

In one respect it may be said that the unity of the Middle Ages was a unity of law. The idea of a higher and a binding law, of divine origin and unchangeable content, was everywhere accepted. It made possible the simultaneous existence of forms of government which, in the absence of belief in such an all-embracing and all-pervasive law could not but have been in perpetual conflict. In the modern world, this conception of a higher law still exists in the realm of theory, although it has become dimmed by modern notions of law as being exclusively positive, and no longer pervades every phase of the life of individuals and of states. Is it too much to hope that the future may witness a recrudescence of this conception of an ideal law which shall serve as a standard for the individual, the nation, and the international community? Those who hope for an affirmative answer may

[15] *Ibid.*, p. 7.   [16] *Ibid.*, p. 33.   [17] *Ibid.*, p. 6.   [18] *Ibid.*, p. 58.

derive encouragement from the fact that in times of storm and stress humanity's appeal is always to this ideal higher law, rather than to the positive law of the statute books and man-made codes.

There are in the *Policraticus* numerous inconsistencies, and indeed many of the elements which it contains are more or less incompatible; but these defects were inevitable, owing to the fact that the treatise was an expression of political thought in the making, and its value in the history of our present-day theories is enhanced rather than obstructed by these inconsistencies of growth.

The *Policraticus* was, in the language of Dr. Poole,[19] "the first attempt since Augustin to frame an ideal system of government." There was need, however, for a contribution from the classical past before the political doctrines of the Middle Ages could become adequate and acceptable, and this contribution was the *Politics* of Aristotle, which was to be made known to the world in the writings of St. Thomas Aquinas.

[19] *Illustrations of the History of Medieval Thought* (previously cited), p. 190.

Chapter XIV

ST. THOMAS AQUINAS (*c.* 1225–74)

The century or more following the appearance of Gratian's *Decretum* and John of Salisbury's *Policraticus,* may be said to represent the flowering of medieval civilization. To be sure, it was a turbulent era, troubled by wars no less than by clashing opinions. But in spite of these disturbances, the period was one of high ideals, of awakening art, of flourishing universities. In the realm of the mind and spirit the thirteenth century's crowning achievement was the remarkable development of scholasticism. And for this development the greatest of all the schoolmen, the *Doctor Angelicus,* was in large measure responsible.

Born near the town of Aquino in the then Kingdom of Naples, St. Thomas seemed destined, as a member of a noble family related to royalty,[1] to a life of luxury and worldly success. But displaying in early years a complete indifference to rank and position, he chose, while still a youth and in the face of his family's opposition, to join the Dominican Order as a humble friar.[2] He received his early education in his native land, and studied later under the learned Albertus Magnus (canonized by the church on December 16, 1931) in Cologne and Paris, becoming in due course a Master of Theology and a celebrated teacher. Endowed with a profoundly penetrating and logical mind, an extraordinarily retentive memory, and a habit of intense concentration, he was peculiarly well equipped to become a great scholar and teacher and the most illustrious theologian and philosopher of his day.

Time has conclusively proved that the theology of St. Thomas was not of his day only. It survived both his lifetime, and the centuries that followed,[3] and in our own time the Church has not only officially recognized

---

[1] "He was the seventh son, and on both sides his family was illustrious. His mother, Theodora of Theate, was of Norman stock; his father, of the Lombard nobility and nephew of Frederick Barbarossa. In St. Thomas, therefore, North and South met, and their influence is visible both in his personal appearance and in his character and thought."—D'Arcy, *Thomas Aquinas* (previously cited), p. 33.

[2] That he remained throughout life untroubled by ambitions for advancement is indicated by his request to be excused from accepting the archbishopric of Naples, to which Pope Clement IV had appointed him in 1265.

[3] On the influence of St. Thomas and the history of Thomism much has been written in recent years. For an excellent brief account, see D'Arcy, *op. cit.,* chap. x.

his philosophy but has also prescribed its teaching in Catholic institutions of learning throughout the world.[4]

As is true of nearly all of his teachings, his legal and political doctrines have exercised vast influence. In connection with those doctrines it is of the first importance to note that St. Thomas Aquinas introduced the works of Aristotle to the world of his day. It is true that before the advent of St. Thomas, Aristotle was not wholly unknown to medieval Europe; but such of his works as were at the disposal of earlier philosophers of the Middle Ages had come to them more or less indirectly. Thus fragments of them were at first known only through the commentaries of such writers as Boëthius and Cassiodorus. Later, however, they came to the attention of European scholars in the form of Latin translations of Arabic paraphrases

---

[4] "Now above all the Doctors of the Schools towers the figure of Thomas Aquinas, the leader and master of them all, who, as Cajetan observes, 'because he had the utmost reverence for the Doctors of antiquity, seems to have inherited in a way the intellect of all.' [*On II.–II*, qu. 148, art. 4, *in finem*]."—Leo XIII, Encyclical *Aeterni patris*, Aug. 4, 1879; in *Acta sanctae sedis* (Rome, 1879), XII, 97 *et seq*.

"We, for the glory of Almighty God and the honour of the Angelic Doctor, for the increase of the sciences, and for the common benefit of human society, declare by Our Supreme Authority, that St. Thomas Aquinas is Patron of Studies in Universities, Colleges, Lyceums, Catholic Schools; and We desire that he be so held by all."—Leo XIII, Brief of Aug. 4, 1880; *ibid.*, XIII, 56 *et seq*.

The views of Pope Leo XIII were confirmed by his distinguished successors:

". . . the capital theses in the philosophy of St. Thomas are not to be placed in the category of opinions capable of being debated one way or another, but are to be considered as the foundations upon which the whole science of natural and divine things is based."—Pius X, *Motu proprio "Doctoris Angelici,"* June 29, 1914; in *Acta apostolicae sedis, commentarium officiale Annus VI* (Rome, 1909), VI, 336 *et seq*.

"We are happy to recall that the philosophy of Aquinas was revived by the authority and at the instance of Leo XIII; the merit of Our Illustrious Predecessor in so doing is such, as we have said elsewhere, that if he had not been the author of many acts and decrees of surpassing wisdom, this alone would be sufficient to establish his undying glory. Pope Pius X of saintly memory followed shortly afterwards in his footsteps, more particularly in his *Motu Proprio 'Doctoris Angelici.'* . . .

"Let everyone therefore inviolably observe the prescription contained in the Codex of Canon Law that 'the study of philosophy and theology and the teaching of these sciences to their students must be accurately carried out by professors [in seminaries, and similar institutions] according to the arguments, doctrine and principles of St. Thomas which they are inviolately to hold'; and may they conform to this rule so faithfully as to be able to describe him in very truth as their master."—Pius XI, Encyclical *Studiorum ducem*, June 29, 1923; *ibid.*, *Annus XV*, XV, 309 *et seq*.

The provisions of the canons mentioned above are as follows:

"*Canon* 589: Religious who have already studied their humanities should devote themselves for two years at least to philosophy and for four years to theology, following the teaching of St. Thomas (cf. *canon* 1366 sec. 2) in accordance with the instructions of the Holy See."

"*Canon* 1366 sec. 2: The study of philosophy and theology and the teaching of these sciences to their students must be accurately carried out by professors [in seminaries, etc.] according to the arguments, doctrine, and principles of St. Thomas which they are inviolately to hold."—*Codex iuris canonici, Pii X Pont. Max. iussu digestus, Benedicti Papae XV auctoritate promulgatus* (Rome, 1917). *Canon* 589, p. 170; *Canon* 1366 sec. 2, p. 398.

and commentaries, for the Arabs had discovered the Aristotelian tradition in Syria as early as the eighth or ninth century and had prepared versions of Aristotle based, not on the original Greek texts, but on Syriac versions. These somewhat dubious versions, given a Latin garb which separated them still further from Aristotle's original text and meaning, had begun in the later Middle Ages to penetrate into Europe by way of Moorish Spain and the partly Arabic city of Palermo.

But in St. Thomas' day Greek texts of the Aristotelian masterpieces were discovered in the Byzantine Empire, and in consequence of his direct encouragement and collaboration these were translated into Latin by two Dominicans, William of Moerbecke and Henry of Brabant. St. Thomas himself prepared detailed commentaries on various works of Aristotle, and incorporated the best of Aristotelianism into his own philosophy. Thus he became, in the words of one writer, "the Christian Aristotle,"[5] authoritatively interpreting the sage of the ancient world to the Christian world of his day and to the future, and combining as far as possible the thought of both worlds. It has been said, indeed, and rightly, that his system of philosophy depends "on three main authorities—Scripture, Aristotle, and Augustine,"[6] and in consequence he left to posterity a masterly synthesis of Christian and pagan ideals.

The works of St. Thomas are many—more than sixty in number—covering the entire field of theology, then considered an all-embracing science. And while it is not for the layman to attempt an evaluation of his works as a whole, we cannot rightly comprehend the position of St. Thomas and the extent of his contributions to the subject of the present study without examining, however briefly, the fundamental ideas of his legal and political philosophy.

St. Thomas saw the state in terms of human beings who were, in his conception—as in that of Aristotle—social and political animals. This conception he stated more than once in the course of his writings, and particularly in his tractate *De regimine principum*,[7] of which it is generally conceded that the first book and the first four chapters of the second book were composed by him, the subsequent portions being written by one Tholommeo of Lucca.

The human being, as conceived by St. Thomas, having felt the need of society—like the human being of Aristotle—experienced a further need for

---

[5] Kennedy, "St. Thomas Aquinas," in *The Catholic Encyclopedia*, XIV, 671.
[6] Figgis, *The Political Aspect of S. Augustine's City of God* (previously cited), p. 94.
[7] Not to be confused with another work bearing the same title and written in the thirteenth century by Egidius Colonna, who is usually referred to as Egidius Romanus.

organization in society, and this organization is the state. To St. Thomas, as to Aristotle, the state was therefore a natural institution. To both, the state and its laws were a part of the natural order of things rather than, as the later Stoics and their successors held, the result of the fall of man and of his sinful ways.

Now organization implies government, and St. Thomas devoted attention to its establishment and particularly to its purpose, which was, above all, to secure peace and harmony among the people who were to be governed. The government which failed of this purpose, the government which was administered selfishly and for the sake of the ruler, St. Thomas regarded as tyranny, and he would therefore have the power of the king or other chief magistrate so limited that he was unlikely to become a despot. In a word, he held that the people themselves should have a share in their own government. If, in spite of what they considered adequate precautions, people found themselves ruled by a tyrant, St. Thomas frankly stated that they might depose him, even though they had sworn allegiance to him. It is clear that, in the opinion of St. Thomas, they were not bound to regard their prince as possessing a right to rule which had been irrevocably conferred upon him. Their justification for breaking their allegiance with a tyrant was that the relation of ruler and subject is not a one-sided affair, in which duties exist only on the side of the people and rights only on the side of the ruler; it is rather in the nature of a compact, for the ruler chosen, according to St. Thomas, should be approved by the populace, and from this it would logically follow that one who accepted the office of ruler accepted also the duties and conditions attached to it.

As a philosopher and churchman St. Thomas perceived the ultimate futility of temporal glory and the evils that spring from a ruler's thirst for fame and power, and no doubt realized that history would be a record of peace rather than of wars, had it not been for the worldly ambitions of princes and potentates. In his view the purpose of the ruler should be to promote the welfare, spiritual and temporal, of his subjects. Such a purpose implies the duty of the king to serve the people, not to use them for his personal glorification.

St. Thomas held that if the ruler broke faith with the people by abusing his office, the compact between prince and subjects was terminated and the people were free to relieve him of his office.[8] Such action was not sedition

For St. Thomas' views on this subject, see especially his *Summa* I.–II, qu. cv. art. 1; II.–II, qu. xlii, art. 2; and *De regimine principum*, Book I, chap. vi.

(of which St. Thomas did not approve) but rather what we would today term revolution for the sake of righting a rank injustice.

A tyrannical government is not just, because it is directed, not to the common good, but to the private good of the ruler, as the Philosopher states (*Polit*. iii. 5; *Ethic*. viii. 10). Consequently there is no sedition in disturbing a government of this kind, unless indeed the tyrant's rule be disturbed so inordinately that his subjects suffer greater harm from the consequent disturbance than from the tyrant's government. Indeed it is the tyrant rather that is guilty of sedition, since he encourages discord and sedition among his subjects, that he may lord over them more securely; for this is tyranny, being conducive to the private good of the ruler, and to the injury of the multitude.[9]

It is obvious that St. Thomas' conception of kings and princes was far from that of monarchs who considered themselves not only as the very embodiment of the state but as above all criticism. As has been implied, St. Thomas considered that the ruler should be not an ambitious seeker after power and aggrandizement, but a man filled with a sense of the responsibility of his office, whose duty is one of service to his subjects, and who should seek his reward not in material power and wealth, but in the consciousness of heavy duties justly and conscientiously performed. This is a conception of responsibility which has been only too sadly lacking in statesmen of all eras, including our own.

Thus St. Thomas' "state" is in its main outlines that of the Greeks, although its structure is distinctly influenced by the moral conceptions of the great theologian.

Obviously, a people associated in a state must have law, if they are to attain that harmony and peace which St. Thomas conceived of as the common good. And in Part I of the second part of his *Summa Theologica* he dealt at length with the question of law; indeed so fully did he treat of the subject that the sections referred to as Questions 90–108 are appropriately called in the translation a treatise on law. It is essential to examine a few of the fundamental definitions of St. Thomas, in order to grasp the nature and extent of the contribution which he made to law and its philosophy, a contribution upon which the Schoolmen of the ensuing centuries largely based their legal theories.

Two preliminary but fundamental statements are made by St. Thomas. "Law," he says, "is a rule and measure of acts, whereby man is induced to act or is restrained from acting"; and "the rule and measure of human acts is the reason, which is the first principle of human acts."[10] Thus at the

[9] *Summa Theologica* II.–II, qu. 42, art. 2.   [10] *Ibid*., I.–II, qu. 90, art. 1.

very beginning of the "treatise on law" we have law and reason identified. Here St. Thomas is clearly speaking of law as a general conception: not any particular kind of law, but law in the abstract. He felt, no doubt, that the matter was one requiring more thorough elucidation, and he therefore proceeded to supplement these statements: "Although reason is one in itself, yet it directs all things regarding man; so that whatever can be ruled by reason, is contained under the law of reason."[11]

Now the law of reason is closely related to the law of nature, which man becomes aware of through his reason. Thus St. Thomas had previously declared that

just as, in the speculative reason, from naturally known indemonstrable principles, we draw the conclusions of the various sciences, the knowledge of which is not imparted to us by nature, but acquired by the efforts of reason, so too it is from the precepts of the natural law, as from general and indemonstrable principles, that the human reason needs to proceed to the more particular determination of certain matters. These particular determinations, devised by human reason, are called human laws, provided the other essential conditions of law be observed.[12]

The law of nature, which is a divine law—indeed St. Thomas says that it is "promulgated by the very fact that God instilled it into man's mind so as to be known by him naturally"[13]—is applied to man through the medium of reason; or, to put it in another way, man, by using his reason, participates in the eternal or divine law, for St. Thomas declares expressly that "the natural law is nothing else than the rational creature's participation of the eternal law."[14] And in order to make his meaning doubly clear, for the matter was of fundamental importance to his entire theory of law, he restates this conception in somewhat different terms in a later passage. "To the natural law," he says, "belong those things to which a man is inclined naturally: and among these it is proper to man to be inclined to act according to reason."[15]

These passages serve to indicate how St. Thomas linked the natural to the eternal law, and how in turn he linked human law with the natural law through the process of human reason.[16] His further definitions of these several classifications of law must now be considered.

According to St. Thomas the whole universe is "governed by Divine Reason," and that government functions through the eternal law,[17] to which

[11] *Summa* I.–II., qu. 94, art. 2. [12] *Ibid.*, qu. 91, art. 3. [13] *Ibid.*, qu. 90, art. 4.
[14] *Ibid.*, qu. 91, art. 3. [15] *Ibid.*, qu. 94, art. 4.
[16] For an interesting study of the conception of natural law held by St. Thomas Aquinas and his predecessors, see Lottin's *Le Droit naturel chez St. Thomas d'Aquin et ses prédécesseurs*.
[17] St. Thomas *Summa* I.–II, qu. 91, art. 1.

"all actions and movements of the whole of nature are subject."[18] He has demonstrated how man, by the use of reason, is said to participate in the eternal law through the law of nature. Enlarging upon this conception St. Thomas states that "every knowledge of truth is a kind of reflection and participation of the eternal law," and this leads him to another definition of law eternal as "the unchangeable truth."[19] He is now ready to link the natural and the eternal law still more closely. "All men know the truth to a certain extent, at least as to the common principles of the natural law: and as to the others, they partake of the knowledge of truth, some more, some less; and in this respect are more or less cognizant of the eternal law."[20]

After referring to man's ability through reason to apprehend "good" and distinguish it from its opposite, St. Thomas gives us the first principle or primary rule of the natural law:

This is the first precept of law, that *good is to be done and ensued, and evil is to be avoided.* All other precepts of the natural law are based upon this.[21]

The other precepts of the law of nature flow from this primary rule, and therefore while it is true that "the precepts of the natural law are many in themselves," they are nevertheless "based on one common foundation."[22]

To St. Thomas, as will soon be evident, the law of nature was a standard by which to measure or test the laws made by men living in a status of political organization. It was obvious to him that "man cannot live alone in society, paying no heed to others."[23] Human life is made up of human relationships, and these relationships beget not only rights but correlative duties which require definition and enforcement by law. Therefore, as St. Thomas points out, "human law is ordained for the civil community, implying mutual duties of man and his fellows."[24] Now the duties of men toward one another are based upon justice, for "justice properly so-called regards the duty of one man to another."[25] "Wherefore," declares St. Thomas, "human law makes precepts only about acts of justice."[26] To him as to St. Augustine, justice was the essence of law: "As St. Augustine says (*De lib. arb.* i. 5), *that which is not just seems to be no law at all.*"[27] Upon this statement St. Thomas himself comments: "Wherefore the force of law depends on the extent of its justice."[28]

What does St. Thomas mean by justice? He defines it at length, but for present purposes a sentence or two concerning its ultimate moral aim will suffice:

[18] *Ibid.*, qu. 93, art. 5. [19] *Ibid.*, qu. 93, art. 2. [20] *Ibid.*
[21] *Ibid.*, qu. 94, art. 2. [22] *Ibid.* [23] *Ibid.*, qu. 95, art. 3. [24] *Ibid.*, qu. 100, art. 2.
[25] *Ibid.* [26] *Ibid.* [27] *Ibid.*, qu. 95, art. 2. [28] *Ibid.*

Justice has its own special proper object over and above the other virtues, and this object is called the just, which is the same as *right*. Hence it is evident that right is the object of justice.[29]

"Now in human affairs," he explains—and here he shows us why and how the law of nature becomes the standard for all man-made law—"a thing is said to be just, from being right, according to the rule of reason." And, as he had already pointed out, "the first rule of reason is the law of nature."[30] What is the conclusion which follows from these two premises? "Every human law has just so much of the nature of law, as it is derived from the law of nature. But if in any point it deflects from the law of nature, it is no longer a law but a perversion of law."[31]

One further aspect of St. Thomas' philosophy of law must be considered. What was the specific purpose of law so far as the human being is concerned? As to this St. Thomas had definite views: "The law must needs regard principally the relationship to happiness," happiness being the ultimate or "last end of human life."[32] Now rules of conduct which merit the name of law are not intended to confer benefits upon one or two individuals at the expense of others. They are for the benefit of all, or, in the words of St. Thomas: "Every law is ordained to the common good."[33] This is the purpose of law in general. It is the purpose of divine and natural law as applied to human affairs. But what of human law? Here St. Thomas reveals, as he so often does, his dependence upon the "philosopher," as he terms Aristotle, saying that "in order that man might have peace and virtue, it was necessary for laws to be framed: for, as the Philosopher says (*Polit.* i. 2), *as man is the most noble of animals if he be perfect in virtue, so he is the lowest of all, if he be severed from law and righteousness.*"[34]

In his views on the relations between states St. Thomas relies on St. Augustine, adopting the latter's doctrine on the subjects of war and peace. Thus he believed war to be justified only when declared by the supreme and duly constituted authorities of the state, when waged for a just cause—for the avenging of a wrong—and when carried on from beginning to end with "a rightful intention," that is to say, "the advancement of good, or the avoidance of evil."[35] Like St. Augustine also, he maintained that "those who wage war justly aim at peace."[36]

Viewed from another angle—and with his breadth of vision St. Thomas was accustomed to examine questions from all reasonable points of view— war might be considered as a necessary means for the correction of evil and

---

[29] St. Thomas, II.–II, qu. 57, art. 1. [30] I.–II, qu. 95, art. 2. [31] *Ibid.* [32] *Ibid.,* qu. 90, art. 2. [33] *Ibid.* [34] *Ibid.,* qu. 95, art. 1. [35] II.–II, qu. 40, art. 1. [36] *Ibid.*

the preservation of the common good. Although the precepts of the New Testament against resistance and revenge "should always be borne in readiness of mind, so that we be ready to obey them, and, if necessary, to refrain from resistance or self-defence," it might be

necessary sometimes for a man to act otherwise for the common good, or for the good of those with whom he is fighting. Hence Augustine says (*Ep. ad Marcellin.* cxxxviii.): *Those whom we have to punish with a kindly severity, it is necessary to handle in many ways against their will. For when we are stripping a man of the lawlessness of sin, it is good for him to be vanquished, since nothing is more hopeless than the happiness of sinners, whence arises a guilty impunity, and an evil will, like an internal enemy.*[37]

In this sense war was, according to the conception of St. Thomas, in the nature of a charitable action, in that its purpose was the correction of evil and the establishment of lasting peace upon the basis of righteousness.[38] And peace itself was "the work of charity." Thus St. Thomas maintains that while "peace is the *work of justice* indirectly, in so far as justice removes the obstacles to peace," it is on the other hand "the work of charity directly, since charity, according to its very nature, causes peace."[39] How, it may be asked, does peace result from charity? "Charity causes peace," St. Thomas answers, "precisely because it is love of God and of our neighbor."[40] It is clear, therefore, that to St. Thomas charity was the foundation stone of peace between individuals and between states.

Adopting as his definition of peace the conception of St. Augustine, St. Thomas holds, however, that peace is more than concord alone. "Peace includes concord," he observes, "and adds something thereto."[41] What is this "something"? The reply is a commentary on St. Augustine's definition of peace as "well ordered concord."[42]

"Augustine is speaking there of that peace which is between one man and another, and he says that this peace is concord, not indeed any kind of concord, but that which is well ordered, through one man agreeing with another in respect of something befitting to both of them."[43] Such concord, however, must be voluntary. Otherwise, "if one man concord with another, not of his own accord, but through being forced, as it were, by the fear of some evil that besets him, such concord is not really peace, because the order of each concordant is not observed, but is disturbed by some fear-inspiring

---

[37] *Ibid.*
[38] St. Thomas' view of war as an act of charity was destined to exert a profound influence on scholastic thought. To cite but a single important example, Francisco Suárez, as we shall see later (*infra*, chap. xxxiii), treats of war under the caption of charity.
[39] St. Thomas, *op. cit.*, II.–II, qu. 29, art. 3.   [40] *Ibid.*, art. 4.   [41] *Ibid.*, art. 1.
[42] St. Augustine *De civitate dei* XIX. xiii.   [43] St. Thomas, *op. cit.*, II.–II, qu. 29, art. 1.

cause."[44] It is for this reason, we are told, that St. Augustine "premises that *peace is tranquillity of order*."[45]

Granting that peace should be the aim of war, and that, generally speaking, "all wars are waged that men may find a more perfect peace than that which they have had heretofore," St. Thomas points out that in reality the nature of any particular peace depends on the characters of the parties to that peace.

True peace [he insists] is only in good men and about good things. The peace of the wicked is not a true peace but a semblance thereof, wherefore it is written (*Wisdom*, xiv. 22): *Whereas they lived in a great war of ignorance, they call so many and so great evils peace.*[46]

A final passage may be quoted from a work often attributed to St. Thomas.[47] Whether it was written by his hand or by that of his contemporary, Guilelmus Peraldus, we do not know, but certain it is that St. Thomas, if he is not the author of the passage, would willingly have subscribed to the views which it sets forth:

Wise men most frequently avoid war. Thus Solomon, who was exceedingly wise, kept his kingdom in complete peace for nearly forty years. Even though peace is so great a benefit that it is sought through its contrary [i.e., war], nevertheless since peace and war are opposed one to the other, and are in the highest degree incompatible, it is a long road that leads to peace by way of war; therefore another road should be taken. Man will attain to peace more speedily by exercising patience than by waging war, by granting concessions than by making seizures. This being the case, princes ought to be admonished to fear war and to guard against its various consequences.

[44] St. Thomas *Summa* II.–II, qu. 29, art. 1.   [45] *Ibid.*   [46] *Ibid.*, art. 2.
[47] *De eruditione principum* Book VII, chap. viii.

Chapter XV

DANTE ALIGHIERI (1265-1321)

Through the influence of the ancient world, the medieval world was pervaded with—and indeed the political systems of the modern world are based upon—the conception of the political and social nature of man. This was the corner stone, so to speak, of Dante's plea for world peace through world government, in his masterpiece of political prose, *De monarchia*. He considered that human life was directed toward an end—as did no less a philosopher than Aristotle himself—and to discover this end he differentiated man from other animate forms of creation, the peculiar characteristic which set men apart being what he termed "apprehension by means of the potential intellect."[1] Standing alone, this is a somewhat forbidding phrase. What it means is simply that man has a power of understanding and an intellect capable not merely of immediate action but of conceiving ideals for future realization. And since men and women are thus gifted, it is Dante's opinion that "the proper function of the human race, taken in the aggregate, is to actualize continually the entire capacity of the potential intellect."[2]

Now it was clear to Dante—although it may sometimes be doubted whether it is as clear to us—that man can best do this, can attain his end and the ideals which he is capable of formulating, only in a world of peace and law; and peace and law, in Dante's view, meant a unified world. His belief was that such unity could best be achieved by a form of government which included the entire world, and would be able to establish and to maintain peace. The ruler of this world of Dante was to wield power not for his own sake but for the sake of the world united under his sway. Moreover, his government was to be strictly one of law—indeed, he was in a sense to be public universal law personified, for it was Dante's conviction that peace must come through law.

Some years ago—in 1913, to be accurate—Sir William Ramsay, Professor of Latin at the Scottish University of St. Andrews and known to the world at large for his work in biblical archeology, delivered "The Romanes Lec-

[1] *De monarchia* I. iii. 2.   [2] *Ibid.*, I. iv. 1.

ture" at the University of Oxford, under the title of *The Imperial Peace— An Ideal in European History*. The imperial peace to which he referred was that of Dante:[3] "The poet of the Middle Ages, who interpreted with the insight of a prophet the heart of the Mediaeval world, has laid down, as the first principle from which reasoning about the welfare of human society must start, that universal peace is the end for which all our action is and should be ordered."

It is apparent, although Sir William Ramsay does not say so, that Dante had in mind the peace defined by St. Augustine.

When I approach this poet [continues Sir William], I go to him as the seer who could look on the divine truth with the undazzled eye of the prophet; and I quote only from one of his prose works, the Latin treatise on Monarchy. "Of all things," says Dante, "that are ordered to secure blessings to men, peace is the best: by quiet the individual man grows perfect in wisdom; and society as a whole is best fitted in the tranquillity of peace for its proper work, which may be called divine."

Sir William was of the opinion that Dante's use of the term "peace" should be analyzed, lest his great project be misunderstood.

Of all things in the social body, says our prophet, peace is the best. It is necessary to guard against a misapprehension of what is meant here by the word "peace." Dante thinks of peace, not as a negative but as a positive idea. Peace is not the mere absence of war: it is the power that maintains order and makes moral law effective. It is the administrative force of Justice, and it is the necessary condition of freedom.

But justice which produces freedom cannot come of itself.

Now Justice [declares Sir William] implies power: a man cannot act justly to others unless he has the power of giving to all their due. Justice is not the getting of one's due from others: that is a base and unworthy and wholly false conception of the divine power that we call Justice. Justice is the paying of their due to others. It is not a demand for one's own rights; it is the giving to others of their rights. This is a profoundly significant idea; it springs from the insight of a prophet, who has looked deep into the heart of the world. "Justice," says Dante, "is a virtue regulating our conduct towards others," and it cannot be turned into a rule which we can invoke to regulate the conduct of others to us, and to enforce the demands which we make on others.[4]

It is clear from his treatise concerning monarchy that Dante had in mind a world government, but it was not to be a unitary state. It was not his beloved Italy, ruling as a despot over the other nationalities; nor was the source of power to be located in his native city of Florence. It was not to be a monarchy with the powers of a dictator; it was to be the gathering to-

---

[3] *The Imperial Peace*, p. 5.   [4] *Ibid.*, p. 7.

gether of the nations of the world under the aegis of law—a law to be demonstrated and enforced by Dante's monarch for the good of each and every state and not for the mere glorification of his supernational government.

His project looks, in fact, toward an international community, governed by international law, as is pointed out by Sir William Ramsay:[5]

The monarch, according to Dante, is to be the source of international law, and to govern in those matters which are common to all men in all the separate nations with a view to their peace. The cities and nations of the single Empire shall each be ruled by its own separate government or king, because each of these has its own special character and each requires laws adapted to its own conditions.

The member states of the "Empire" were not to lose their independence and Sir William emphasizes this point by adding that Dante

would not merge the separate states in a uniform and homogeneous Monarchy or Empire. These must retain, and ought to retain their own idiosyncracies: such is the law of nature and the character of man.

In a few sentences the learned lecturer then describes the monarch of Dante's universal empire:[6]

The monarch for Dante exists as the best and only means to compass the true end of society. He exists to introduce peace and order a peace that is and that compels order—amid the smaller states governed by their princes and kings. He is as it were the embodiment in human personality of a supreme and absolute international law. He represents the compelling force of right, which makes justice and freedom reign in each separate state of the universal Empire, and enforces equity and order in the mutual relations of these smaller states.

Any consideration of Dante's political theories would be inadequate which did not include the famous passage in Tractate IV of his *Convivio*.[7] This passage is a magnificent plea for peace through the establishment of Dante's universal monarchy.

The root and ground of the imperial majesty is, in truth, the necessity of man's social state, which is ordained for a single end, namely, a life of happiness; to which no one is able to attain by himself without the aid of some one else, inasmuch as man has need of many things for which a single individual cannot suffice. And therefore the Philosopher says that man is by nature a "companionable animal." And just as an individual in order to suffice for himself requires the domestic companionship of the family, so a household to suffice for itself requires a neighbourhood, else it will suffer for many defects which will be hindrances to happiness. And because a single neighbourhood cannot in all respects be self-sufficient, in order to satisfy all its wants there must needs

---

[5] *Ibid.*, p. 8. [6] *Ibid.*, p. 10. [7] *Dante's Convivio.* Trans. by Jackson, pp. 201–2.

be a city. Moreover a city, for the sake of its crafts and for self-defence, must needs have intercourse and brotherly relations with the neighbouring townships, and for this reason kingdoms were constituted. Wherefore, inasmuch as the mind of man does not rest content with a limited possession of land, but always desires to acquire more land, as we perceive by experience, disagreement and wars must needs arise between kingdom and kingdom. Such things are the scourges of townships, and through townships of neighbourhoods, and through neighbourhoods of families, and through families of individuals, and thus happiness is hindered. Wherefore, in order to do away with these wars and their causes, it is necessary that the whole earth, and all that is given to the race of man to possess, should be a monarchy, that is to say, a single princedom; and should have a single prince, who, possessing everything, and having nothing left to desire, should keep kings confined within the borders of their kingdoms, so that peace should reign between them, and townships should rest in peace, and while they so rest neighbourhoods should love each other, and in this mutual love families should satisfy all their wants; and when these are satisfied, a man should live happily, which is the end for which he is born.

The fundamental conception of this passage—of man as a "companionable animal"—is Aristotelian, as Dante himself points out, for the "Philosopher" of the Middle Ages, as well as of the ancient world, was, as we know, Aristotle.

Unfortunately it has been the custom to consider Dante's scheme as primarily an apology for a régime which was dying, if not dead, even in his own day. There seems good ground for arguing, however, that he offered a solution for the problems of the future, the problems magnified by the emergence of the theory of the sovereign, independent, and irresponsible state. We of today are only too sadly aware of the bitter fruits of an uncontrolled and often ruthless nationalism. But it has not invaded our own country, where a federation of the American states has been found possible under a superintending head. Would not a federation of the European states, under a superintending head, tend toward, if it did not actually produce, the tranquillity in Europe which the unity of the American states has produced for Americans?

Perhaps, after needless war following needless war, we shall at last come to the conclusion that a poet may be the best of our prophets.[8] In any event,

[8] "L'idée d'un Saint-Empire n'a pas été seule à provoquer le rêve de Dante. Comme toutes les oeuvres de génie, son traité a de profondes racines, et il en a plusieurs. Avant tout l'idéal politique de l'Antiquité hante l'imagination du grand Gibelin. La conception de Saint Augustin d'une *Civitas Dei*, qui par son organisation assure la paix universelle, 'terrena pax,' l'a profondément influencé. Le traité est peut-être un ouvrage de circonstance, provoqué par l'expédition malheureuse de l'Empereur Henri 7 en Italie (1310–13). Mais c'est là le trait distinctif des grandes oeuvres, qu'elles s'élèvant au-dessus des circonstances extérieures qui les ont provoquées, et Dante développe toute une philosophie politique pour soutenir sa thèse."—Lange, *Histoire de l'internationalisme*, IV, 71.

they are mistaken who consider Dante's dream as merely the product of a dark and dying age.

People talk of the Middle Ages as dark and benighted and barbarous [says Sir William Ramsay]. Yet the ideals and the dreams of that period were often glowing with light. We have not yet realized them; but we have progressed so far that the dreams of a few are now the ideals for which many, both men and women, work and pray and suffer. The dreamers of the Middle Ages were the heralds of the educated peoples of our time.

And commenting upon the ideal of Dante, Sir William observes[9] that

it is an ideal; but the ideal is the power in history. If the ideal could be reproduced in the common man, it ceases to be an ideal and a power. It must remain above us and in front of us; and therein lies its influence on mankind.

And finally, as an estimate of what has been ironically but mistakenly termed Dante's "pretty but idle fancy," Sir William adds:[10]

Modern society, while passing into a new stage of growth, acknowledges and accepts as fundamental all the essential part of Dante's doctrine. An ordered peace, a peace that enforces progress through justice and freedom, is to us, as to Dante, the end and aim of mankind. We are faced by the same problem.

[9] *The Imperial Peace* (previously cited), p. 9.   [10] *Ibid.*, p. 14.

Chapter XVI

THE CHURCH AS AN INSTITUTION
ITS INFLUENCE ON LAW AND POLITICS

Throughout the Middle Ages legal and political developments were profoundly influenced by several distinct yet often closely related factors. Two of these were especially dominant and worked, it might be said, hand in hand during the medieval period: The Christian Church and the Roman law. Two other and lesser factors, seemingly pitted against each other yet eventually reconciled sufficiently to produce an elaborate though somewhat shadowy imperial structure, were the tradition of the Roman Empire, and the customs and institutions of the Teutonic invaders who overran that Empire. Still other factors, operating less obviously yet penetrating deeply into the fabric of medieval thought, were the thin rivulets of ancient learning and philosophy—rivulets destined eventually to swell into the full-bodied streams of the Renaissance, which washed away the barriers between the medieval and the modern worlds. All of these factors, working sometimes independently but more often either in combination or in opposition, produced those theories of law and government of the Middle Ages out of which have grown the legal and political institutions of our day. The less important among such factors have been referred to from time to time in previous pages, and of the two dominant ones, the Roman law has been dealt with at some length. But while the conceptions of the great churchmen, St. Augustine, St. Isidore, St. Thomas Aquinas, and others, have been examined in detail in separate chapters, the influence of the Church as an institution—in certain respects the most powerful of all influences in the development of the theory and practice of law and government, both national and international—has been touched upon but briefly and in passing. The present chapter, therefore, will deal with the Church as an institution, discussing in broad outline its legal and political influence.

In the period of the Church's earlier development, when the ecclesiastical organization was outside the pale of established law, the relation of the temporal government to the Church was characterized by hostility and persecution. All that was changed, however, by the adoption of Christianity as the official religion of the Roman Empire. "The Empire became Christian;

THE CHURCH AS AN INSTITUTION 229

Christianity became imperial."[1] The religious organization and the temporal organization were thus merged, and in due course citizenship came to mean also membership in the Church.[2] Yet the merging of the two organizations was far from being so complete that the one absorbed the other. It would perhaps be more accurate to say that the ecclesiastical and the civil domains overlapped. Now the overlapping of jurisdictions inevitably raises problems: what are the limitations of each and how are conflicts between them to be settled? These questions, at various times and in various forms, were to engage the best minds of the civilized world for more than a thousand years. Upon the dissolution of the Empire the problems were further complicated, for with the coming of the barbarians the Church had not only to redefine its sphere of activities but to preserve that sphere against pagan attack. Even after the conversion of the invaders to Christianity, the position of the Church was difficult, for the new peoples had laws and customs of their own which merged less readily with Christian doctrine than did the institutions of Rome. There were, moreover, internal dissensions resulting in a series of schisms between the Church in the West, firmly established in Rome, and the Church in the East, established in Constantinople—schisms which led at last, in 1059, to the separation of the two bodies.

Confronted by these circumstances, it is not surprising that the Church began at an early date to insist on certain prerogatives which were fundamental to its continued existence in a turbulent world. From the days of its establishment in the Empire, it had asserted its jurisdiction over spiritual matters, with the corollary that in such matters all Christians were subject to that jurisdiction. Again, while maintaining that men must render obedience to the civil ruler in temporal affairs, the Church Fathers pro-

---

[1] Barker, *Church, State and Study—Essays*, p. 134.
[2] The conception of Christianity and Roman citizenship as practically equivalent terms exerted a profound influence on legal and political thought for centuries. An example of this is to be found in Bartolus, of whose views on this subject Professor Francesco Ercole says: "Tutta quanta la Cristianità, ossia l'insieme di tutti gli uomini che professano la religione cristiana, forma il *Populus christianus o romanus*. *Cristianità* e *romanità* sono, nel pensiero di Bartolo, concetti equivalenti: l'una termina, ove termina l'altra. *Romanus* è il popolo *christianus*, perchè, per destinazione divina, Roma è il centro della Cristianità, e la romanità cessa là, ove cessi la Cristianità: per Cristianità ha da intendersi sostanzialmente *cattolicità*: cioè riconoscimento della sovranità religiosa del Papa, o vescovo di Roma, come immediato rappresentante o vicario di Cristo in terra. Chi questa sovranità non riconosca, non soltanto è fuori dalla Cristianità (dal *populus christianus*), ma è anche fuori dalla romanità (dal *populus romanus*). Onde la retta linea di demarcazione segnata da Bartolo tra il *Populus romanus* e i *Populi extranei: extranei* sono quei popoli, che non soltanto non riconoscono la sovranità dell' Imperatore, ma anche, e specialmente, non riconoscono la sovranità del vescovo di Roma: che, anzi, non riconoscono quella, in quanto non riconoscono questa: popolo *extraneus* e popolo *infedele*, o *non cattolico*, sono, di nuovo, termini equipollenti."—*Da Bartolo all' Althusio*, pp. 50–51.

claimed the right of ecclesiastical authorities to discipline the ruler if he violated the laws of the spiritual domain. And in their desire to insure the independence and universality of the Church they also insisted upon the principle that in matters ecclesiastical the temporal courts should have no jurisdiction over the clergy—a principle which was subsequently expanded until in the end it tended to confer practically complete immunity from the authority of civil tribunals upon all ranks of the clergy.[3]

In relation to law and government, what was the effect of these two concurrent and more or less independent jurisdictions under which all medieval Christians lived? This question cannot be answered without considering at some length two elements which characterized Christian society throughout the Middle Ages. The first was a tendency—so often manifested in the course of history, and in so many different ways—toward unity. The Church recognized no national boundaries in spiritual matters. All the inhabitants of Christendom, barring heretics, were alike members of the Church Universal, possessed of equality before the law of God. In that sense the Christian world was a single society[4]—a conception strengthened by the tradition of the Roman Empire and later projected more concretely into temporal affairs when Pope Leo III, on Christmas day of the year 800, placed the imperial crown on the head of Charlemagne.

But here enters the second of the two elements which have been mentioned. For if unity characterized the Middle Ages, it was, so to speak, a divided unity. The theory of a single and universal society was confronted by what Dr. Carlyle[5] calls "the theory of a dualism in the structure of human society," a theory which proceeded upon the principle "that human society is governed by two powers, not by one, by the Temporal and the Spiritual, and that these are embodied in two authorities, the secular and the ecclesiastical, two authorities which are each divine in their origin, and are, each within its own sphere, independent of the other."

This principle had been stated by the early ecclesiastical authorities, and it was "clearly and emphatically restated," continues Dr. Carlyle, "in the

[3] See Lea's article, "The Eve of the Reformation," in *The Cambridge Modern History*, I, 653-92, 660-61.

[4] The conception of a natural universal society dates back, as we have seen in earlier chapters (especially chap. vi), to the Greek and Roman world. But while the natural law of the ancients emphasized unity, it also emphasized the natural rights of the individual. These conceptions in due course were adopted by Christian philosophy. "The Christian Middle Ages," says Dr. Jacob Ter Meulen, "took up these ancient ideas and developed them into a uniform system . . . the highest unit of which covered all the autonomous parts of the social structure like a large cupola arching over the whole."—*Der Gedanke der internationalen Organisation in seiner Entwicklung, 1300-1800*, p. 4.

[5] *A History of Mediaeval Political Theory in the West* (previously cited), IV, 385.

ninth century, and was always present to the minds of men in the eleventh and twelfth."[6] Its importance is obvious, adds the same authority, for it reveals

> the conception that life on its spiritual side is not subject to the temporal authority, but independent of it. It is one aspect, and not the least important, of a new development of the significance of individual personality, of a new conception of liberty.[7]

The theory of this parallel structure of society was a natural and inevitable outcome of the early and successful insistence of the Church, already referred to, that it should have exclusive jurisdiction over spiritual matters. But what of the practical working out of the theory? Without attempting to deal with the numerous difficulties which it encountered, we may turn at once to certain of its consequences. The first, as Dr. Carlyle points out, was that men became accustomed to the conception that the moral and spiritual qualities of humanity are not subject to the domination of the secular authority. Even more fundamental was the acceptance of the idea that, as the spiritual authority was generally if not invariably conceded to possess not only a higher dignity and significance but a universal application, so its teachings must constitute the universal standard for the conduct of temporal affairs. As regards law, the standard which the Church raised aloft for all temporal authorities was the law of nature which was the product of merging or identifying the revealed divine law of the Scriptures with the *ius naturale* of the Stoics and the Romans. And that law of nature was the true sovereign of the medieval world.

> The *lex* which was *rex* to medieval thinkers [says Professor Ernest Barker] was a law which did not proceed from a human legislature. So far as it was revealed, it was the stern daughter of the voice of God; so far as it was natural, it was the inevitable outcome of the reason in man, whereby he discovers the mind of God. From either point of view, it was universal and eternal. It permeated all human society; it knew no end of its validity. It followed that all human actions took place in a pre-existing and all-determining atmosphere of law, and that they were valid when they conformed to its rules and invalid when they did not. "All custom," writes Gratian, "and all written law, which is adverse to natural law, is to be counted null and void." This law is thus the sovereign principle of human society. It limits kings and legislatures internally: it limits states in their relation to states externally. And of this law, because in one of its aspects it is the revelation and commandment of God, the Church is the custodian and exponent.[8]

[6] *Ibid.* [7] *Ibid.*
[8] "Mediaeval Political Thought," introductory chapter to *The Social and Political Ideas of Some Great Mediaeval Thinkers*, ed. by Hearnshaw, p. 19.

What were the consequences of this conception? They have been admirably summarized by Professor Barker.

We can readily see that so long as this idea of a law of nature identical with the law of God continues to be entertained, the Church will continue its attempt to control all human life in its light. We can see that on the strength of this law the Church can supervise Acts of Parliament, control guild ordinances, regulate the keeping of international treaties, inspect the working of royal administration. For all these are under the law; and the Church has the knowledge of the law.[9]

But there was another and, for present purposes, still more important consequence. If law was sovereign, what of the ruler? It should be noted here that the power vested in the medieval king was conceived to be of divine origin, although it was lodged in him through the choice and decision of his subjects who might, for due cause, reverse their choice. Because it was of divine origin, the power of ruling must be exercised by the king in accordance with a divinely inspired standard—the standard of justice and equity raised by the Church. The ruler was thus subject to a threefold limitation. In the words of Professor Barker,[10] "It is a limited kingship which emerges—a kingship limited by the law of nature, limited by the Church, limited by the people."

It is essential here to consider briefly the basis and development of the legal ideals upheld by the Church. As we have seen, they were founded primarily upon the divine law and the ancient law of nature, blended into a single body of principles which were at once natural and of divine origin. In developing these principles into a system the Fathers and the canonists turned for guidance to the Roman jurists and philosophers. Thus throughout the greater part of the Middle Ages legal philosophy—and political philosophy as well—was constructed as a branch of theology. The Roman conceptions of *lex* and *ius,* of *aequitas* and *iustitia,* it may be said, were Christianized in the course of centuries by churchmen who were often men of remarkable spiritual enlightenment. And with these Christianized conceptions, the theologian taught, secular law and government should harmonize. The Church thus became the guardian of the ideals of law and government, as it was of other Christian ideals; and later it assumed the duty of protecting those ideals against the temporal authorities who violated them, and of judging and correcting the violators.

It is not the purpose of the present chapter to describe the evolution of this practice into the doctrine of the full supremacy of the Church in matters

[9] In *The Social and Political Ideas of Some Great Mediaeval Thinkers*, pp. 19–20.
[10] *Ibid.*, p. 22.

THE CHURCH AS AN INSTITUTION 233

temporal as well as spiritual, proclaimed in 1302 by Boniface VIII in the bull *Unam sanctum*. Suffice it to say that the conception of the dualism of society gave way for a time to the sway of universalism; to the conception of the state as subordinated to the Church in both secular and ecclesiastical affairs. During this period the Papal States—founded in the eighth century when Pepin III bestowed the "exarchate of Ravenna . . . with twenty-two towns upon 'St. Peter and his successors' "[11]—expanded until the Holy See itself became a vast territorial state. The prince of the Church became likewise a powerful temporal prince. Now the underlying purpose of this expansion was the further, indeed the complete, unification of Christendom. To quote from Professor Barker's penetrating study of medieval civilization:[12]

Depositary of the truth, and only depositary of the truth, by divine revelation, the Church, under the guidance of the papacy, seeks to realize the truth in every reach of life, and to control, in the light of Christian principle, every play of human activity. Learning and education, trade and commerce, war and peace, are all to be drawn into her orbit. By the application of Christian principle a great synthesis of human life is to be achieved, and the *lex Christi* is to be made a *lex animata in terris*.

Commenting on the vastness and the implications of this purpose, Professor Barker continues:[13]

This was the greatest ambition that has ever been cherished. It meant nothing less than the establishment of a *civitas Dei* on earth. And this kingdom of God was to be very different from that of which St. Augustine had written. His city of God was neither the actual Church nor the actual State, nor a fusion of both. It was a spiritual society of the predestined faithful, and, as such, thoroughly distinct from the State and secular society. The city of God which the great mediaeval popes were seeking to establish was a city of this world, if not of this world only. It was a fusion of the actual Church, reformed by papal direction and governed by papal control, with actual lay society, similarly reformed and similarly governed. Logically this meant a theocracy, and the bull of Boniface VIII, by which he claimed that every human creature was subject to the Roman pontiff, was its necessary outcome. But theocracy was only a means, and a means that was never greatly emphasized in the best days of the papacy. It was the end that mattered; and the end was the moulding of human life into conformity with divine truth.

The attempt to achieve this end, however, was accompanied by a tendency toward increased emphasis on mundane affairs and material ambitions

---

[11] Pullan, *From Justinian to Luther, A. D. 518–1517*, p. 63.
[12] *Church, State and Study—Essays* (previously cited), pp. 44–71, especially 52.
[13] *Ibid.*, pp. 52–53.

in the papal régime. More than one pontiff, busied with the protection and extension of the boundaries of his temporal domain, yielded himself to worldly aspirations, sadly to the prejudice of his spiritual jurisdiction. There were two methods by which this unhappy state of affairs might have been corrected, and it is the opinion of many that the choice of the method advocated by Martin Luther was one of the great misfortunes of history. Of this, and of the other method, reform of the Church from within—as advocated by Erasmus and other great humanists—more will be said in subsequent chapters.[14] For the moment it is enough to state that a solution of the question of the temporal jurisdiction of the papacy was found in the important doctrine of the indirect power of the pope in temporal affairs, so admirably expounded by the Cardinal and Saint, Robert Bellarmine,[15] a doctrine which, with certain modifications, "still holds the field in Catholic theology."[16]

In the meantime, however, the Church's tendency toward secularization, and controversies and abuses which grew out of that tendency, contributed to several results which were of direct or indirect importance to legal and especially to political philosophy. The first was the appearance of social revolts and of anticlerical movements. These in turn, together with certain elements in the "new learning" of the Renaissance, weakened the hold of the Church in various countries, and thus permitted the growth of materialistic views, among them the theory of the unlimited sovereignty of temporal rulers. In consequence of the "exaltation of the State at the expense of the Church,"[17] the conception of a universal human society, coextensive with Christendom, began slowly to fade until eventually, in the heyday of the irresponsible sovereign, it seemed almost to have vanished from the minds of men, to have been blotted out by the spirit of nationalism which has proved to be such a mixed blessing.

Although it had little concrete influence at the time, another phase of the controversies which raged in and about the Church was destined to make an important contribution to political theory. The Great Schism of the fourteenth and fifteenth centuries, which for some forty years divided western Christendom, together with the obvious need for reform, produced the Conciliar Movement, which engrossed the attention of three councils, those of Pisa (1409), Constance (1414-18), and Basel (1431-48). We can

---

[14] See *infra*, chaps. xxix and xxx.   [15] See *infra*, p. 553.
[16] Brodrick, *The Life and Work of Blessed Robert Francis Cardinal Bellarmine, S. J.*, I, 268.
[17] Barker, "Medieval Political Thought," in *The Social and Political Ideas of Some Great Mediaeval Thinkers*, ed. by Hearnshaw (previously cited), p. 32.

THE CHURCH AS AN INSTITUTION

best appreciate the significance of the movement[18] by examining briefly the views of two of its leading figures, Jean Gerson and Nicolas of Cusa.

Gerson, anxious to provide for the healing of the schism, argued that under certain circumstances resistance to the pope was justified by overwhelming necessity.[19] But he distinguished between the office of the pope, which was sacred, and the occupant of the moment who, being human, might fall into errors injurious to the Church and the welfare of its members. Now he was familiar with Aristotle, and in considering the Church as an institution he advocated for it the Aristotelian "mixed" form of government, in which, according to Gerson, the monarchical office of the pope should be supplemented and indeed limited by the council. In this form of government, whether it be established in the spiritual or the temporal domain, the law, and not the ruler, is superior.

Several of Gerson's leading views on the subject of government are set forth in his *Sermo pro justitia ad regem*. Accepting the classical conceptions of society, he held that "man is by nature a civil being," that he requires the aid of his fellows, and for that reason is impelled to join them in common or social activities. Therefore, means for the regulation of such social life become necessary; man must needs establish some form of government. The quality of justice, in Gerson's opinion, "inclines" men to do this, a justice which "is termed civil or political." It is this justice which leads men "to render to each his due" in accordance with the aim and purpose of the society, whether it be temporal or spiritual. The rules of natural justice alone, however, are not sufficient for the establishment of temporal govern-

---

[18] On the political importance of the councils, see Figgis, "The Conciliar Movement and the Papalist Reaction," in *Studies of Political Thought from Gerson to Grotius*, pp. 35–61; the same author's "Politics at the Council of Constance," *Transactions of the Royal Historical Society*, 1899; Cook, "The Conciliar Movement: Church Constitutionalism and the Ideal of Harmony," in *History of Political Philosophy from Plato to Burke*, pp. 254–71; Jacob, "Nicolas of Cusa," in *The Social and Political Ideas of Some Great Thinkers of the Renaissance and the Reformation*, ed. by Hearnshaw, pp. 32–60; and Dunning, *History of Political Theories Ancient and Medieval*, chap. x. For the life and works of Nicolas of Cusa, see Vansteenberghe, *Le Cardinal Nicolas de Cues*. The present discussion of the Conciliar Movement, a subject fraught with some peril for the layman, is based upon all of these writings, but particularly upon those of Dr. Figgis and Professors Cook and Jacob, and upon chap. iii of Dr. Vansteenberghe's exhaustive treatise.

[19] The chief works of Gerson relating to the subject in hand are his *De auferibilitate papae* and his *De potestate ecclesiastica et origine juris*. They were written about the period of the Council of Constance, at which Gerson played an important rôle; but, like his other works, they were not printed until long after his death. Other treatises of interest are his *Sermo pro justitia ad regem* and *Sermo ad regem Franciae nomine universitatis Parisiensis*. The first edition of his many treatises is said to have been published at Cologne in 1483. See *Catholic Encyclopedia*, VI, 533. There were several later editions of Gerson's *Opera*, and certain of his writings were also reproduced in Melchior Goldast's *Monarchiae S. Romani Imperii*. . . .

ment, and therefore they are supplemented by human laws in harmony with the law of nature.

Gerson's views on the origin and nature of authority in a governed society are likewise of interest. In his *Sermo ad regem Franciae nomine universitatis Parisiensis*, he traces the origin of rulers, who are placed in office for "the good of the whole community," with the "common consent of men." Subjects and ruler have mutual obligations toward each other, and to maintain that the sovereign is free from all such obligations is to oppose both "divine law and natural equity." Gerson, it appears, was no supporter of the doctrine of absolute and irresponsible sovereignty. In short, he held that the ruler derived his authority from the people, and that when he abused that authority the people might restrain and correct him, even to the extent of deposing him.[20] It is interesting to note that he deals with this subject in the course of his discussion of the authority of the Church in relation to the pope, and that he supports his contention by citing Aristotle's *Politics*.[21] It is apparent that to Gerson the fundamental principles of government are applicable alike to Church and to State, and therein lies their importance to political philosophy, for limitations to be applied to the ecclesiastical ruler could certainly be applied to the temporal monarch.

In these doctrines we have the conciliar theories in their milder form. They were more comprehensively and forcibly set forth by Nicolas of Cusa in a reasoned statement entitled *De concordantia catholica,* which he presented before the Council of Basel in 1433. The author of this treatise felt the necessity not only of reform within the Church but of reconciling two opposing factions, the one supporting the doctrine of the *plenitudo potestatis* of the pope, the other urging a more democratic form of papal government. In his argument he sought, as one authority tells us, to "bind the present movement to the historical past of the Church,"[22] to emphasize, not uniformity, but the theory of unity in diversity, which harks back to the Platonic doctrine of the one and the many. The Church as a whole was made up of many individual churches in many lands, and unity therefore was to be achieved not only through the pope as head of the Church Universal but through the general councils which were conceived of as being representative bodies. In the conception of Nicolas of Cusa "we derive the authority of the Sacred Councils, not from the Pope, but from the consent of all."[23] The basis of this statement is the doctrine that the authority of

---

[20] See also *infra*, p. 402.

[21] "*Sicut enim tradit Arist. V. Poli. quod ad communitatem totam spectat principis vel correctio, vel totalis destitutio, si irremediabilis perseveret.*"—*De auferibilitate papae.*

[22] Vansteenberghe, *op. cit.,* p. 35.   [23] *De concordantia catholica* II. xiii.

rulers, whatever their domain, is vested in them by the consent of those who are ruled, a consent which may be given by a body representing[24] them—that is, in the present instance, by the General Council as described by Nicolas of Cusa. The Council, representing the Church as a whole, is thus, according to Nicolas, superior in authority to the papal government and it has the power to check that government, in case of necessity, by decree or other appropriate action. He urged, however, that this power should be used with the greatest care and discrimination in the interest of peace and concord and the general good of the Church.

Here was a plan for unity within the Church through a form of federal organization based on the principle of representation. It seemed to Nicolas of Cusa that the same general plan was applicable in the temporal domain —indeed, was essential for the achievement of that unity toward which he aimed. For he believed that while the civil and ecclesiastical governments should be separate and distinct—in accordance with the older medieval theory of dualism—they should nevertheless be parallel in structure. It is necessary here—but without entering into the question of the temporal ruler's relation to the Church councils—to consider briefly the views of Nicolas on civil government.

In discussing the process of lawmaking, Nicolas declares that "what affects all, should have the approval of all."[25] Legislation, in other words, was no royal prerogative; and the law, deriving its authority from the people, should bind all, even the prince. For the best government, in the opinion of Nicolas, is based on the reign of law rather than on the irresponsible rule of a sovereign. Such government, being under the control of the people, will look to the good of all rather than to the advantage of one or a few.

How was government of this nature to be established? Again Nicolas turns to the people as the source, declaring that "every ordered empire or kingdom . . . takes its origin from election."[26] Now the conception of free election by the people "does not originate in the positive law," but is derived "from the natural and divine law."[27] Nicolas, it should be added, subscribed to the ancient doctrine that "all men are by nature free," and therefore he held that government must be by the "agreement and consent" of those who were to be governed.[28]

Naturally, in considering the civil government of Christendom, Nicolas turned to the Holy Roman Empire as the temporal counterpart of the

---

[24] For the views of Nicolas on the subject of representation, see the summary given by Vansteenberghe, *op. cit.*, p. 44.
[25] *De concordantia catholica* III, Preface.
[26] *Ibid.*, III. iv.
[27] *Ibid.*
[28] *Ibid.*, II. xiv.

papacy. And here his aim, in the words of Professor Jacob, was "to reconcile the principle of monarchy with that of federalism."[29] He proposed that to insure order the Empire be divided into twelve districts, with an imperial judicial tribunal in each. There should be a general and more or less representative diet, meeting annually, which was charged with various functions of imperial legislation and reform. The emperor himself was to be chosen by electors, and was to be granted ample power to govern effectively. In these various provisions the principle of representation played a part, although apparently the principle was to operate chiefly through the nobility of the Empire and did not imply much in the way of direct representation of the people as a whole in imperial affairs.[30]

In his own century, and for long centuries thereafter, the plan of Nicolas of Cusa and of other supporters of the Conciliar Movement was destined to fail of realization. The world was not yet ready for the conception of federation. It rejected the theories of the *Catholic Concord,* just as it had rejected Dante's plan for federation[31] more than a century before. Even the doctrines providing for the limitation of the ruling power were ignored until kings and despots, pushing absolutism and the divine-right theory too far, could be checked only by the desperate remedy of tyrannicide.

But constitutional checks have become the accepted order of things in our modern society—except, of course, in those communities afflicted by what may best be described as temporary political aberrations. Today the world is beginning to reconsider its rejection of the federal ideal. It has seen, in the example furnished by the United States of America, that the ideal is no empty dream, that it may be made a reality. To be sure, the international community is full of clashing differences. But is not federation, as Nicolas of Cusa believed, a means for harmonizing those differences, of bringing unity into a world of human beings equal before the law as they are equal before God, of peoples governed by magistrates whom they themselves choose and check by constitutional means?

[29] "Nicolas of Cusa," in *The Social and Political Ideas of Some Great Thinkers of the Renaissance and the Reformation* (previously cited), p. 48.
[30] *De concordantia catholica* III. xxv.   [31] *Supra,* chap. xv.

THE TRANSITION FROM MEDIEVAL
TO MODERN THOUGHT

Chapter XVII

THE SURVIVAL AND INFLUENCE OF ROMAN LAW AND JURISPRUDENCE

Among the contributions to law and politics none is more important to the modern world than the revival of the Roman law during the late Middle Ages.

Great empire builders as the Romans were, they were still greater architects of law. And when their empire crumbled and disappeared, the firmly knit structure of their legal system withstood the barbarian avalanche which threatened to sweep away the civilization of the ancient world. To be sure, Roman jurisprudence was partially buried by the avalanche, but so large a portion of it remained, so to speak, above ground that even the conquerors from the North were unable, as we have seen, to ignore it. And, in the fullness of time, medieval students awakened to the value of the treasure half buried at their feet and, digging away the débris, restored Roman law as a system to the world.

During the dark period following the barbarian invasions, however, the law of Rome survived in practice only in a debased form. In the Eastern Empire, it is true, Justinian's great compilation long endured, to be converted eventually into what is sometimes known as Byzantine or Graeco-Roman law. But its history in the East was destined to be, on the whole, one of steady decline, characterized chiefly by the production of translations, abridgments, abstracts, and epitomes which whittled away much of both the substance and the spirit of the Corpus Juris. Some elements of the original Roman law did survive, however, largely because they were embodied, at the end of the ninth century, in the famous *Basilica* compiled during the reigns of the Emperor Basil I and his son, Leo the Philosopher, and in the so-called *Hexabiblos,* an inferior epitome composed by a fourteenth-century Greek jurist, Harmenopoulos. And indeed certain of these elements may be traced to this day in the modern law of Greece.

It is, however, with the survival of Roman law in Western Europe that we are here chiefly concerned. As was observed elsewhere,[1] the Germanic

---
[1] *Supra,* p. 130.

invaders were faced with the problem of reconciling two systems of law, their own and that of the conquered Roman population. And they met the problem as the Romans themselves had met it long before, i.e., by adopting the principle of the personality of law. Thus the conquered peoples were usually allowed to retain the law of Rome, while the Germanic population lived under its own laws and customs. For the most part, however, the Roman law remained in force not in its original form but in the so-called *leges romanae,* or codes supplied by the Germanic rulers, which for present purposes have a twofold significance in that, in the words of an eminent English authority,[2] while "they represent the decay and barbarization of the law in the West," they likewise "represent the salvage of a part of the ancient legal culture of the Romans in the midst of the vast disturbance and transformation of European society in the early medieval centuries." The most important of these compilations were the *Edict* of Theodoric, which was destined soon to lose its influence owing to Justinian's recovery of Italy and the subsequent invasion of the Lombards; the *Lex Romana Burgundionum* of King Gundobad, which apparently continued in force until the Frankish conquest; and the *Lex Romana Visigothorum*—also referred to as the *Breviarum Alaricionum* because it was compiled by a commission of jurists appointed by Alaric II, King of the Western Goths—which was the most important and influential of the Romano-Barbarian codes. All three, prepared about the beginning of the sixth century, were based upon ante-Justinian law, and at best they preserved classical Roman law and jurisprudence in a decidedly crude and imperfect form. Alaric's *Breviary* was in many respects the most complete of the codes, the most widely known and the longest-lived. Indeed for Western Europe (with the exception of Italy) it was to remain for some centuries the chief source of Roman law. Although it debased and corrupted that law in many respects, it had the advantage of being fairly well adapted to the needs of the time; and the Roman law which thus survived offered, as has already been observed,[3] a common law for the regulation of relationships not only between individuals of different racial groups but between the groups themselves. Moreover, the Germanic conquerors, gradually growing more familiar with the *leges romanae,* and influenced in no small measure by the steadily developing canonical jurisprudence with its foundation of Roman law, began to adopt not only Roman legal terms but also Roman legal conceptions in their own codes of law, often referred to as *leges barbarorum.*

[2] Hazeltine in "Roman and Canon Law in the Middle Ages," published as chap. xxi, *The Cambridge Medieval History,* V, 697-764, 724-25.
[3] *Supra,* p. 131.

INFLUENCE OF ROMAN LAW   243

This slow process of fusion was further promoted and then retarded by two important medieval factors. The first was the rise of the Frankish Empire and the growth both of *formulae* modeled on Roman legal instruments and of imperial legislation in the form of capitularies. Of the capitularies it may be said that they supplanted neither the *leges romanae* nor the *leges barbarorum,* but rather aided in the development of both and

> produced a certain unity of legal evolution throughout Europe. . . . Like the Constitutions of the Roman Emperors, the Capitularies of the Frankish Emperors were a civilizing and unifying force in which Roman and Canon Law played a rôle of high significance.[4]

The second factor was what seems to us today the curious legal phenomenon of feudalism. Essentially, feudalism was "a military system with land as the reward of service."[5] Under its influence law became localized and territorial. Conceptions of legal unity were weakened, and the principle of the personality of law lost ground. Medieval Roman law was not destroyed by feudalism—indeed it contributed not a little to feudal law—but outside of the urban centers the possibility of its further development seemed limited, in a social order consisting of innumerable petty lords and vassals.

Thus in the later medieval period the outlook for Roman law as regards its practical application grew darker. If it were to regain its influence in the world, it could do so only through the reawakening of men to its value not merely as law but as jurisprudence. Such a reawakening—due perhaps in some measure, though indirectly, to the great Crusades—took place in the twelfth century. Its occurrence, however, was so sudden and remarkable as to seem, at first glance, almost inexplicable. But upon examination this reawakening will appear as the logical result of several different though related factors.

In the first place, legal theorizing, rare though it was during the early Middle Ages, had never become wholly nonexistent. It will be helpful here to quote several passages from Sir Paul Vinogradoff's small but masterly volume:[6]

> The life of Roman Law in the barbaric states, as far as we have considered it hitherto, was upheld by the continuance of fragmentary and garbled rules derived more or less directly from the system formed during the prosperous periods of Roman civilization. Can it be said that the barbaric successors of Papinian and Ulpian, of Marcus Aurelius and Constantine, kept also up, to some extent, the threads of theoretical reflection and intelligent teaching, which

---

[4] Hazeltine, *op. cit.,* p. 728.
[5] Jenks, *Law and Politics in the Middle Ages* (previously cited), p. 23.
[6] *Roman Law in Medieval Europe* (previously cited), pp. 36–41.

in former days had served to combine separate details into a reasoned whole? Is there a distinct stream of *jurisprudence* winding its way through the dark ages from the fifth century, when western jurists took part in the codification and interpretation of Imperial Law, to the twelfth century, when a body of learned doctrine sprang up again in Italy and France? These problems have given rise to much controversy among modern scholars.

To the questions which he thus posed, the learned Russian, who became a leading figure of the modern English school of jurisprudence, gives an illuminating answer:

To begin with, it seems clear that even legal learning, as distinguished from legal practice, did not entirely disappear with the downfall of the Empire. It survived to some extent together with other remnants of ancient culture, more especially through the agency of the learned classes of those days—the clerical and monastic orders. . . .

The study of legal books was mainly limited to two narrow grooves. . . . The abstract (*Epitome*) and the gloss are the two channels for the tradition of learning in the course of this barren epoch. . . .

The work of supplying glosses goes on uninterruptedly from classical times right through the Middle Ages. They were the medieval substitutes for translations and commentaries. Short renderings, etymologies, and explanations were inserted over the line to facilitate the interpretation of single terms or words, while longer summaries and notices were jotted down on the margin.[7]

As a result of his extensive investigations, the author reached the following conclusion:

On the strength of these and similar observations we are able to maintain that there was a constant, though thin, stream of legal learning running through the darkest centuries of the Middle Ages, that is, from the fifth to the tenth. The existence of organized law schools is not proved, nor can there be any talk of a very active development of individual thought. But transcripts and abstracts from the fragmentary materials bequeathed by antiquity were made and studied in the *scriptoria* of monasteries or chapters and in the classrooms of teachers of Arts.

The Church's influence on the growth of law, however, extended beyond the preservation of the thread of legal learning. Throughout the Middle

---

[7] The author here adds by way of example: "The gloss to a Turin MS. of the *Institutes* and the gloss to the *Epitome* of the *Codex* in a MS. belonging to the Dean and Chapter of Pistoia (Tuscany), may serve as examples of this type of work. The first was compiled some time before the tenth century, and was based on translations of Byzantine notes to all parts of the *Corpus Juris*. The Pistoia gloss is more original. Its principal elements date also from the ninth century, but it was in use all through the tenth, eleventh, and twelfth centuries, and grew considerably by later additions. Most of the notes have been provided by a person of by no means contemptible intelligence. Though his direct borrowings from the *Corpus Juris* cannot always be traced, he shows in his summaries and in his explanatory remarks an understanding of juridical questions, and is quite able to give the gist of a rule in his own words."

Ages its canon law was rapidly developing. As we have seen, ecclesiastical jurisprudence was based in large part upon Roman jurisprudence, with—of course—certain elements peculiar to the Church and its organization and with, above all, a strong infusion of lofty moral conceptions. And as the canon law became developed and entered more and more into the life of the entire Christian world, men grew accustomed to the idea of law as a part of the moral scheme of things—an idea which is essential to any recrudescence and development of legal philosophy.

In Italy, where the reawakening was to take place, conditions were somewhat different from those in the rest of Western Europe. Justinian's generals had succeeded in recovering the entire peninsula and uniting it for a brief period with the Eastern Empire. More important still from a legal standpoint was the fact that Justinian transmitted to Italy his great compilations, and thus Roman law traced its survival in the Italian peninsula directly to the *Digest* and the *Code,* rather than to the barbarized codifications which were influential elsewhere in Western Christendom. Although the law of Rome passed through a long period of decadence in Italy, it remained sufficiently powerful to compete with the vigorously developed law of the Lombard conquerors, to become partially blended with that law, and eventually to supplant it.

Apparently the teaching of Roman law continued throughout the early Middle Ages in Rome, although the records of this instruction are scanty. Certain it is, however, that the study of the Corpus Juris flourished at Ravenna at the end of the eleventh century. And in Lombardy several of the schools of Lombard law—notably the school at Pavia—had begun to devote no little attention to Roman law.

This brief sketch of the background of the Roman law renascence in Italy, which occurred in Bologna during the twelfth century, can best be supplemented by several passages from Professor Hazeltine's admirable essay on Roman and canon law in the Middle Ages. After referring to the statement of Odofred, a thirteenth-century Italian jurist, that "Ravenna's success as a school was due to the taking of the manuscripts of Justinian's lawbooks from Rome, and that at a later time Bologna's success was equally caused by carrying them there from Ravenna," Professor Hazeltine continues:[8]

Various other causes contributed, however, to the rise of Bologna as the most illustrious of all the Italian law schools of the Middle Ages—the very center of juristic learning and of its diffusion throughout the civilised world.

---

[8] *The Cambridge Medieval History* (previously cited), V, 734.

Bologna's central geographical position and its judicial and commercial importance, the political favour shown to the law school, and the genius of its teachers, were among the leading factors in establishing the fame of the school.

But there were still more important factors which contributed to the high standing enjoyed by the University of Bologna:

... of special importance were the qualities which early distinguished its teaching. The school assimilated and united all of the legal elements derived from the past, and took a broad and independent attitude towards the various divergent tendencies in juridical thought. It adopted and combined the features of legal science already evolved in the schools of Constantinople, Pavia, and Ravenna; and it enjoyed the favouring influences of Pisa and the adjacent Tuscan regions, such as their Renaissance spirit. Byzantine juristic studies formed a background. The method of glosses and parallel passages already applied by Pavese jurists to the texts of Lombard Law was none other than the method chosen by the early Bolognese glossators.

Materials, tradition and political conditions also favored Bologna, as Professor Hazeltine indicates:

Pisa was long in possession of the most complete and most famous of all the manuscript texts of Justinian's *Digest,* the manuscript now in the Laurentian Library at Florence; and distinguished Tuscan jurists, such as Pepo and Gratian, the founder of the new school of Canon Law, taught at Bologna. Finally, owing to the political conditions of the time, Bologna possessed the exceptional advantage of being the one city in Italy where Roman legal study could best establish itself afresh, with every prospect of great success, under its traditional imperial patron.

After observing that "the revival of Roman legal studies at Bologna resulted in a return to the treatment of law as a science which had characterised the work of the classical jurists eight centuries before," Professor Hazeltine adds:[9]

The method adopted by the jurists who established the fame of the Bologna law school was that of the gloss ($\gamma\lambda\hat{\omega}\sigma\sigma\alpha$, equivalent to *verbum, lingua, vox*), or textual interpretation. The jurists themselves thus came to be known as the Glossators; and it was they who gave to the school its earlier tendency and character. Glosses were not a new thing; within the field of law they had already been employed in the study of medieval Lombard and Roman Law. The new feature of the Bolognese school, the one which gives it its unique position, was the application of the glossatorial method for the first time to the texts of the law-books of Justinian.

Among the reasons for the adoption of this method was "the persistent tradition of Justinian's order that his laws should not be altered in sense

---
[9] *The Cambridge Medieval History,* V, 736.

by a liberal as distinct from a literal interpretation." Moreover, as Professor Hazeltine points out, "literal interpretation . . . was particularly needful as a means of arriving at a correct text of the Justinianean codification." And in a few sentences he briefly outlines the development of the gloss:[10]

Although at first, therefore, the gloss was but a short explanation or interpretation of a difficult single word in terms of an equivalent, it soon became also, in the hands of the jurists, an explanation of a passage or of an entire *lex* or even of a legal principle embodied in the text. These two forms of the gloss became known respectively as the "interlinear" and the "marginal." The explanation of a single word was placed above it, between the lines ("interlinear"), while the explanation of a passage was placed beside it on the margin of the text ("marginal"); and to each gloss the glossator affixed his initials or some other mark or indication of his identity. As the work of the school advanced, the gloss became more and more elaborate and lost its original signification. It became, in fact, the means of embodying the results of the master's legal researches. "It included," says Calisse,[11] "critical notes on the variant readings (*variantia*) of different manuscripts. It brought together *loci paralleli,* which helped to elucidate the point. When these passages were in conflict (*antinomia*), it sought to reconcile them or to decide on the preferable one. Thus, finally, we find the gloss developing into a genuine commentary, with all its proper appurtenances—the summary (*summa*), the putting of illustrative cases (*casus*), the deduction of a genuine maxim (*brocardus*), and the discussion of concrete legal problems (*quaestiones*)."

The school of glossators was established at Bologna by Irnerius, and among his disciples and successors were the celebrated "quattuor doctores"

---

[10] *Ibid.,* pp. 736-37. The several stages in this development have also been admirably outlined by a French writer, Pierre de Tourtoulon, "Le Velléien chez les Glossateurs," in *Etudes d'histoire juridique,* prepared in honor of the late Professor Paul Frédéric Girard by his students, I, 432-33.

"Les plus anciennes, les plus modestes et les plus intéressantes gloses sont anonymes. Elles font le plus ardu et le plus savant travail: explication des mots obscurs, leur interprétation juridique et surtout le rapprochement des divers textes qui peuvent avoir entre eux un point de contact. Tant qu'ils n'ont fait que mettre en présence des textes en concordance ou en opposition réelle ou apparente, les vieux glossateurs ne signaient pas leur travail. Ils ne croyaient pas faire oeuvre personnelle ni originale. Mais lorsque deux textes se trouvaient en contradiction et qu'ils croyaient avoir réussi à les concilier, ils ajoutaient leur sigle pour revendiquer le mérite et la responsabilité de cette conciliation. . . .

"Dans une seconde période les gloses sont signées et personnelles, c'est-à-dire qu'un jurisconsulte, qui en marge d'un texte fait une observation quelconque, y mettra toujours son sigle, mais ne le mettra pas s'il reproduit des opinions qui ne sont pas de lui. . . .

"Viennent ensuite les apparatistes, les faiseurs de grandes gloses (*magnarum glosarum*), qui travaillent dans le mêmes sens, sans que leur travail soit identique. Les apparatistes compilent les gloses, donnent l'opinion de leurs adversaires aussi bien que leur propre opinion et signent le tout de telle sorte que dans un manuscrit leur sigle domine lorsqu'il n'est pas le seul. Les faiseurs de grandes gloses fondent ensemble tout ce qui a été dit sur un sujet donné et remplacent beaucoup de petites gloses contradictoires par une seule qui est censée les résumer toutes, mais ne le fait pas toujours très fidèlement."

[11] "See *General Survey of Events, Sources, Persons and Movements in Continental Legal History,* (in Continental Legal History Series Vol. I), p. 137."

(Bulgarus, Martinus, Jacobus, and Hugo), and such distinguished jurists as Vacarius, who introduced the teaching of Roman law into England; Placentinus, who is said to have founded the first Roman law school in France—at Montpelier; Ago, who composed a famous *Summa* of the *Institutes* and the *Codex;* and Accursius, whose "Great Gloss" was the culmination of the glossators' labors and threatened, indeed, to supplant even the texts of Justinian. With Accursius, it may be said that the glossatorial method had passed the limit of its usefulness. The mechanics of the gloss were becoming more important than the basic text—the tail was wagging the dog. Some new method was needed to link the Roman law—which the glossators had so clearly revealed—directly to the life and needs of the time.

This method was supplied by the renowned Italian "post-glossators," or commentators, of the fourteenth century. Among the most outstanding of the commentators were Cino da Pistoia, a friend of Dante and a poet as well as a jurist; the great Bartolus; and his favorite pupil, Baldus, famous both as a Romanist and a canonist. Like the glossators, the influence of the commentators, and especially that of Bartolus, extended far beyond the confines of Italy. Applying the principles of scholasticism to the study of Roman law, they set themselves the task of accommodating the law of Rome, by the power of reason and the force of logic, to the conditions of their own age, of correlating it with the existing statute law and the canon law, in order to evolve a body of law which would be truly a "common" law, universally recognized. That they were successful was due in part to the fact that they undertook their task at a time when the Catholic Church and the Holy Roman Empire were regarded as universal institutions:

> The two supreme social institutions, the Church and the Empire, had welcomed the Roman law. The Church was born under Roman law, and drew therefrom the guarantee of its privileges; except on specific points of conflict of rules, the Church had always recognized the Roman law as valid. The Empire had come to accept it, partly because it furnished that element of universality which the Empire regarded as its own mission, and partly because the Roman law supported the Empire in its justification of absolute supreme power; so that the imperial authority, wherever it extended, favored Roman law. The jurists, in determining the applicability of Roman law in a given region, took as their criterion the fact that the region was subject to the Empire. Wherever Christianity went, moreover, there also the Church took Roman law; so that the influences were reciprocal, and Christianity tended to be coextensive virtually with the imperial authority. Thus the Roman law took on the quality of an international common law, relegating the other systems to the status of local laws for a particular country.[12]

[12] Calisse, "Italy during the Renascence," a translation of part of his *Storia del diritto italiano*, in *The Continental Legal History Series*, I (chap. ii), 117.

INFLUENCE OF ROMAN LAW   249

Yet, however favorable social and political conditions may have been, the commentators could not have achieved the important results with which they are credited without the aid of the scholastic method. They may be—and often are—criticized for their lengthy and at times barren disquisitions on abstract conceptions, for reliance on the quantity rather than the quality of authorities, for finely drawn distinctions and hair-splitting definitions, and for all the defects charged against scholasticism. But the fact remains that by applying the scholastic method to jurisprudence, by painstaking analysis, and the pursuit of abstract conceptions, they were able to reveal many an abstract but universal principle which is fundamental to all law, but which had apparently escaped the notice of their nonscholastic predecessors.

Just as the scholasticism of the Middle Ages [says the late Professor Sohm] was a kind of philosophy, so the doctrines of the Commentators embodied a kind of philosophic jurisprudence. Their jurisprudence was in fact permeated by an idea which dates far back into antiquity, the idea, namely, of a Law of Nature; that is, an eternal, immutable law, equally valid at all times and all places, which can be deduced by an act of reason, by a purely intellectual process, from "the nature of the thing itself." Down to the beginning of the nineteenth century and the advent of Savigny the science of law was entirely dominated by the philosophic point of view represented by the advocates of the law of nature. And in truth the doctrine of the law of nature contains an indestructible element. The human mind is continually urged, as by an instinctive impulse, to get beyond the necessarily imperfect law of the present and to reach out to an ideal type of perfect law. It is hardly surprising, therefore, that the theory of the law of nature should have taken the world by storm, when it presented itself for the first time fortified with all the authority that the jurisprudence of the Commentators could confer upon it.[13]

And summing up the results achieved by the commentators, Professor Sohm adds:[14]

In the main it was the labours of the Commentators that had fitted Roman law for its new career. By working out their scientific conceptions in immediate connexion with the doctrines of Roman law, they were able to present Roman law (in the shape which it assumed under their hands) in the light of a natural law founded on scientific principles, a law, therefore, which claimed to be recognized as a common law valid not only for Italy, but for all countries. In a word, the Commentators raised Roman law for the second time in history to the rank of a universal law.

The glossators and commentators long exercised a dominant influence on legal thought and development in Western Europe. As a result of the

---

[13] *Institutionen* . . . Ledlie trans. (*The Institutes*, previously cited), pp. 149–50.
[14] *Ibid.*, p. 150.

weight and authority which their writings enjoyed (the opinions of Bartolus, indeed, were widely accepted as law[15]), Roman law gained a definite and lasting supremacy over Teutonic law not only in Italy but in France and in Spain and—somewhat later—in Germany.[16]

Other influences subsequently played their part in this process, however, notably the rise of the so-called humanist school of legal thought, which included such eminent jurists as Alciati, Cujas, Dumoulin, Hotman, and the later Pothier, whose eighteenth-century work, *Pandectae Justinianeae in novum ordinem redactae,* paved the way for the preparation of the famous *Code civil* under Napoleon, and for the numerous other codes of civil law adopted in different parts of the world. The one-time dominance of Spain and Portugal in the southern half of the New World led naturally to the adoption of civil law, with its Roman foundation, by the republics of Latin America, while French influence is responsible for the present romanized law of Louisiana and of the Canadian Province of Quebec. Of equal if not greater importance is the fact that Roman law is also "the real foundation," as Professor James Mackintosh observes,[17] "of the municipal law of Holland, France, Germany, and Italy, as well as Scotland"; and that fact, he immediately adds, "opens up an extensive sphere of influence in the dominions and dependencies of these countries beyond the seas."

Thus the "golden law" of Rome, with which the medieval Italian glossators and commentators reëndowed the world, became humanity's greatest

---

[15] Bartolus died in his forty-fourth year; yet in his comparatively short life he achieved remarkable fame as a jurist. To quote a sentence or two from Savigny's monumental *Geschichte des Römischen Rechts im Mittelalter* (VI, 153–54):

"Der Ruhm des Bartolus war so gross, dass kein anderer Rechtslehrer des Mittelalters ihn hierin übertraf, und dieser grosse Ruhm ist um so merwürdiger, als er in einem Alter starb, in welchem manche Andere eben erst anfingen, bekannt zu werden. Die Meisten seiner Zeitgenossen und Nachfolger erwähnen ihn und seine einzelnen Meinungen mit grossem Lobe, ja selbst mit Bewunderung. Noch Alciat behandelt ihn als den Ersten aller Interpreten, so dass er wegen aller Stellen, die er selbst in den Vorlesungen nicht erklärte, lediglich auf Bartolus verweis't. . . .

"Das ungemeine Ansehen des Bartolus beschränkte sich auch nicht auf die Schule und auf das Lob der Schriftsteller, sondern es wurde vorzüglich in Gerichten, ja oft selbst in der Gesetzgebung anerkannt."

For a modern appreciation of Bartolus' work on the conflict of laws, see Beale's Introduction to his translation, *Bartolus on the Conflict of Laws.*

[16] The victory of Roman law in its long struggle with Teutonic law did not mean that the latter was destroyed. To summarize in the briefest form the relationship between the two bodies of law, it may be said that Roman law gained its position of dominance in some part by replacing Teutonic rules, but in larger part by assimilating and blending with itself local customs and laws of Teutonic origin. Thus Lombard law entered into the romanized Italian law; the *droit coutumier* of Northern France became an important element in the development of French law; and early German customs, such as those embodied in the thirteenth century *Sachsenspiegel,* survived to some extent in Germany in spite of the wholesale "reception" of Roman law.

[17] *Roman Law in Modern Practice,* p. 32.

INFLUENCE OF ROMAN LAW

legal heritage. It has often been observed that Roman law holds sway over a domain far more extensive than the greatest empire of the Caesars. In the words of Viscount Bryce, one-time Regius Professor of Civil Law at Oxford and justly ranked among the greatest of English civilians,

> the Roman law is indeed world-wide for it represents the whilom unity of civilized mankind. There is not a problem of jurisprudence which it does not touch: there is scarcely a corner of political science on which its light has not fallen.[18]

Therefore its value lies not only in the fact that—to quote again from Professor Mackintosh—"it is a rich mine for all investigators into the origins of law and civilization," but in the still more important fact that it has, as the same writer points out, a "close affinity with so many modern systems and with the whole structure of international law; its posthumous influence has far exceeded the expectations of its founders."

And on a later page[19] the learned professor paraphrases with approval the remark of Sir Henry Maine "that the reason why every law student should make some study of Roman jurisprudence alongside his own is, not because they *were once* alike, but because they *will be* alike," adding in his own behalf that "it seems to be the destiny of the Civil Law to furnish the ideal type to which all law tends to approximate, as local peculiarities and specialties are laid aside."

And finally, as has been mentioned elsewhere,[20] the *ius gentium*—the most important single element in the legal philosophy of Rome—became the foundation upon which our modern international law developed. For a demonstration of the subsequent contribution of Roman law to international law, we have only to glance over the pages of the leading classic texts on the law of nations—the treatises of Francisco de Vitoria, of Gentili, Suárez, and Grotius—since their pages abound in references to the *Corpus Juris* of Justinian.

> We cannot possibly overstate the value of Roman Jurisprudence as a key to International Law [declared Sir Henry Sumner Maine], and particularly to its most important department. Knowledge of the system and knowledge of the history of the system are equally essential to the comprehension of the Public Law of Nations.[21]

International jurisprudence, in short, is and must always be rooted in the jurisprudence of Rome. To ignore, or to deny, this relationship is to deprive international law of its roots, and without roots it can but wither away.

---

[18] "Valedictory Lecture," *Studies in History and Jurisprudence*, II, 898.
[19] *Roman Law in Modern Practice*, pp. 70–71.   [20] *Supra*, p. 132.
[21] "Roman Law and Legal Education," in *Village Communities in the East and West*, pp. 330–83, 351.

The Roman Law in England

The immense contribution of Roman law to the legal development and institutions of the so-called civil law countries is universally acknowledged. But as regards the question of Roman influence on the legal system which arose in England and which has spread over a very considerable portion of the world, there is a marked diversity of opinion. In view of this lack of agreement, and because the present work is designed primarily for readers in the English-speaking world, it will be advisable to examine the various phases of the question in some detail.

It is a not uncommon view that Anglo-Saxon law has developed largely, if not entirely, without benefit or influence from the great traditions of jurisprudence which arose in the ancient world and which through the centuries to our own day have admittedly been a dominant factor in the formation of Continental legal systems.

Those, however, who have investigated the growth of English law and procedure are of the opinion that the law of Rome has played a rôle—indeed an important rôle—in the development of English legal institutions. To be sure, there is danger of exaggeration either way, but modern legal scholarship is making it evident that both the Roman and the canon law have had a definite and lasting influence on English jurisprudence. It is overlooking historical facts to dismiss the relationship between the Anglo-Saxon and the Continental systems with the broad generalizations that one developed as the law of the courts, the other, from the study of the Roman texts; and that England, being separated physically from the Continent, was also cut off from the Continental legal development.

There is a further general statement to which too much significance can be attached: that the jurisprudence of Great Britain consists chiefly in applying legal principles; the continental, in applying legal texts. It is true that these generalizations are based upon obvious facts, but they relate only to the fundamental differences between the two systems, and leave out of account their points of contact and especially the periods when the historical stream of jurisprudence has, so to speak, overflowed its banks and deeply permeated the English system. The effects of the first great overflow lasted some four centuries, during which time, as Professor Sherman says, "Roman law made rapid strides in Britain."[22] In this period, he adds,

an illustrious galaxy of Roman judges honored Britain with their presence. York was the seat for three years of the highest Roman tribunal with Papinian,

---

[22] Sherman, *Roman Law in the Modern World*, I, 346. Another useful American text, which traces briefly the history of Roman law and deals at length with its influence on the law of the modern world, is Burdick's *Principles of Roman Law and Their Relation to Modern Law*.

the prince of Roman jurisconsults, as chief justice and the famous Ulpian and Paulus as associate justices.

It is, however, an open question whether any definite traces of Roman law actually survived the Teutonic invasions of the fifth century and the numerous subsequent invasions. Yet if the tide of Roman influence receded, it was only for a time; for at the end of the sixth century the second St. Augustine (afterward first Archbishop of Canterbury), a Roman, began the conversion of the Anglo-Saxons to Christianity; and thus the channel of Roman influence was reopened by the Church. It is not without significance that shortly after St. Augustine's sojourn in Britain, Ethelbert, king of Kent, a convert of the same St. Augustine, caused the laws of his kingdom to be written down "according to the Roman mode."[23]

In the following centuries Roman influence seeped into England in various ways. Thus King Alfred had visited Rome in his youth. King Canute had not only visited Rome but had made the acquaintance of the emperor and the pope.[24] Edward the Confessor had lived many years in exile on the Continent, where, it is important to note, Roman legal tradition and learning, though overshadowed by what are called the "dark ages," had survived; for as we have seen, through the early centuries of the medieval period the influence of Roman law persisted on the Continent—albeit in a somewhat attenuated form—and it may well have affected the inhabitants of Britain in so far as they came in touch with Continental learning and institutions—particularly those of the church.

Fundamentally, of course, the medieval law of Britain was Teutonic. We are not here concerned, however, with the Teutonic element in Anglo-Saxon jurisprudence. Suffice it to say that great and lasting changes were wrought in it by the Norman conquerors of the eleventh century, who further opened the way for Continental—and therefore partly Roman—influences on English institutions. Less than a century after the Norman Conquest, Roman law (the study of which had already been revived by the Bologna school of glossators) was being taught at Oxford,[25] and in the thirteenth

---

[23] Sherman, *ibid.*, p. 348, citing Bede, *Historia ecclesiastica*, Vol. II, chap. v, "juxta exempla Romanorum."

[24] *Ibid.*, pp. 348–49.

[25] The Lombard Vacarius, a renowned glossator, accompanied Theobald, Archbishop of Canterbury, to England in 1143, and a few years later began a series of lectures at Oxford similar to those given at the University of Bologna. King Stephen was hostile to the new learning, however, and proscribed the teaching of Roman law. Nevertheless, interest in it continued, and after Stephen's death students turned to its study at Oxford with renewed vigor. Subsequently, in the fourteenth century, interest in the Roman law waned. But the increasing rigidity of the common law in that century provided indirectly for the further entry of Roman law into England, as we shall see (*infra*, p. 257), through the Court of Chancery.

century it was introduced at Cambridge. During this period also there appeared the first important writings of English jurists—Glanvil's *Tractatus de legibus et consuetudinibus regni Angliae tempore regis Henrici secundi compositus,* and Bracton's *De legibus et consuetudinibus Angliae,*[26] both of which, and especially the latter, bear witness to the influence of Roman legal conceptions. Indeed it has been said of Bracton by Sir Paul Vinogradoff (who made a special study of Bracton), that his "use of civilian jurisprudence remains a remarkable monument of the scholarly interest and of the ingenuity of an English lawyer bent on rationalizing the laws and customs of his time and country."[27] And he observes, referring to an article[28] by Professor George E. Woodbine, of Yale University:

I am glad to find that Professor Woodbine sides with me in his general appreciation of Bracton's Romanesque learning. Instead of marking Bracton down on account of his real or supposed blunders and misunderstandings, he points out that in most cases Bracton's peculiarities of rendering and interpretation of Roman doctrines are traceable to the definite plan of using, as it were, Roman bricks for the construction of an English edifice. Like all other leading exponents of customary law in the twelfth and thirteenth centuries, he was dominated by a profound reverence for the wisdom of Roman jurisprudence, and endeavoured to utilize its distinctions and principles for the purpose of arranging and rationalizing the incoherent mass of barbaric and feudal custom.[29]

Another authority on the sources of English law has a comment of interest on this point:

It would be a mistake to gauge the effect of Roman Law by a nice calculation of the especial rules in our law which can be affiliated to it. What men gained by it was not a heap of fresh material for building English Law, but a knowledge of the principles of legal architecture. Bracton's use of it in his *De legibus Angliae* neatly illustrates this.[30]

A French writer has recently joined the group of authorities on English law, M. Lévy-Ullmann, who a few years ago published a volume which

[26] Henricus de Bracton (or Bratton) was an ecclesiastic—Archdeacon of Barnstaple, and later Chancellor of Exeter Cathedral—who wrote, apparently in the years 1256–59, the celebrated work above-mentioned. While authorities differ somewhat as to the nature and extent of the influence exerted upon Bracton by Roman law, the existence of ample evidence of that influence in the treatise *De legibus* is conceded by all. There can be no doubt that Bracton was thoroughly familiar with civil and canon law, much more so than his predecessor Ranulph de Glanvil, who is considered to have been the author of the earliest systematic treatise on the laws of England, written probably during the decade 1180–90.

[27] *The Collected Papers of Paul Vinogradoff,* with a Memoir by The Right Hon. H. A. L. Fisher (previously cited), I, 240.

[28] "The Roman Element in Bracton's De Adquirendo Rerum Dominio," *Yale Law Journal* XXXI, 827.

[29] *The Collected Papers of Paul Vinogradoff,* I, 237.

[30] Winfield, *The Chief Sources of English Legal History,* p. 60.

has been translated from the French,[31] with a foreword by Sir William Holdsworth. In the fifth chapter, under the title "Books of Authority," M. Lévy-Ullmann[32] renders homage to Bracton's services to English law. After a word of appreciation of Professor Woodbine's critical labors, he makes his own the measured opinion of Sir William Holdsworth:

Though it is true that the greater part of the Treatise consists of a body of thoroughly English rules, it can hardly be denied that Bracton used Roman terms, Roman maxims, and Roman doctrines to construct, upon native foundations, a reasonable system of law out of comparatively meagre authorities. Roman law supplied him with the intellectual outlook and the technical language, which enabled him to mould native rules of customary law into a reasonable system.

To which admirable statement of the modern English view concerning the influence of Roman law on Bracton, M. Lévy-Ullmann adds:

It was, therefore, due to the *De Legibus* that English law was framed and shaped into a legal system which made it possible for Bracton's successors, and in particular, for Coke to wage a winning warfare for the supremacy of the Common law.... Moreover, Bracton's work is a manifestation of the increasing importance of institutional books in the development of the Common law.

In this early and formative period there were others who wrote with authority and who reflected to a greater or less degree the Roman influence, as has been pointed out by an eminent English jurist and publicist:[33]

Bracton has incorporated into his book substantial portions of Roman matter, which are reproduced by *Fleta*,[34] and in a less intelligent way by *Britton*.[35]

---

[31] Lévy-Ullmann, *The English Legal Tradition—Its Sources and History*, trans. from the French by Mitchell. In his foreword Sir William Holdsworth observes that English lawyers will find in M. Lévy-Ullmann's treatise "the best of all introductions to the study of the English legal system." In another passage of his foreword the English legal historian says: "it is the best introduction to the study of English law that I know. . . . I know of no book better adapted to the needs of a student, who wishes to get a clear idea of that traditional background of ideas and principles which formed the starting-point of the legislators of the 19th and 20th centuries."

[32] *Ibid.*, pp. 137–38, quoting Holdsworth, *Sources and Literature of the History of English Law* (Oxford, 1925), p. 29.

[33] Scrutton, *The Influence of the Roman Law on the Law of England*, p. 150.

[34] " 'Fleta, seu Commentarius Juris Anglicani,' is so called from its composition in the Fleet Prison, and is believed to have been written about 1292. It is in Latin, and it abridges Bracton carefully, though the arrangement differs, and the work is about half the size of the original. But besides omissions the author adds new matter which is sometimes of a Roman character." Scrutton, *ibid.*, p. 123.

[35] The work known as Britton (perhaps from the fact that it is in the nature of an abbreviation of Bracton) was written in law French between 1290 and 1300. It reproduces some of the Roman material from Bracton, but on the whole its Roman-law content is considerably modified and reduced, as compared with the earlier treatise upon which it is based.

These Roman incorporations are cited without comment by Staunford,[36] and are used by Cowell[37] to show the similarity of the two laws.

And in fact, as Professor Sherman declares, the common law itself "was formed not merely by the influence of legal treatises based on Roman law, such as Bracton's, but more especially by judicial decisions made with the aid of principles derived from the same jurisprudence."[38] Professor Sherman,[39] relying upon the authority of W. A. Hunter,[40] adds that

the English adoption of Roman law was "not an act of legislation, but a long process of custom." It was found necessary to supply the defects of the Common Law, which, having expended its best energies in developing the feudal system, showed no symptoms toward creating an original commercial and movable property law. Use was therefore made of the Roman law, a complete system of law at hand ready for service. But its use and reception were not always acknowledged by English courts.

In the following centuries, however, the effect of Roman upon English law was to be less obvious; for in the course of time there had grown up a decided prejudice against the old civil law. It was held by many to be a "foreign" law, too absolute for the English system. Objections were raised also against the encroachments of the canon law, and these objections tended further to prejudice English men of law against the legal system of Rome. Nevertheless, in spite of this hostility the Roman law (under cover, so to speak) continued century after century its contributions to English legal development. Thus we find that English writs betray more than a trace of Roman ancestry. And in the case of equity, the original purpose of which was to grant a remedy where the common law provided none, the chancel-

---

[36] Sir William Staunford (or Stanford, Stamford, 1509–58), a learned lawyer who became judge of the common pleas in 1554, was the author of a book on the pleas of the crown, posthumously published in 1560—*Les Plees del Coron: divisees in plusieurs titles et common lieux*. Staunford makes much use of Bracton's work.

[37] John Cowell (1554–1611), is best known for his famous work entitled *The Interpreter, a Booke Containing the Signification of Words*. He was a distinguished civilian, and held at Cambridge the posts of regius professor of civil law, master of Trinity Hall, and vice chancellor. For present purposes our interest is in a somewhat less known work, *Institutiones juris anglicani ad methodum et seriem institutionum imperialium compositae et digestae*. Cowell's object in writing this treatise was "to promote the union of Scotland and England by pointing out the resemblances between the common law and the civil law; to give the student of the common law some knowledge of the general principles of law; and to show the students of the civil law that if they would study the common law, they would improve their knowledge of both laws, and cease to be regarded as mere children in legal knowledge. That these ideas were sound is fairly obvious; and at the present day they are, in effect, attained by the training in English law, Roman law and Jurisprudence which students of law at the universities now get. But they were in advance of their time; and the mode in which the book was planned and executed did not altogether recommend them."—Holdsworth, *op. cit.*, V, 21.

[38] Sherman, *op. cit.*, I, 359.   [39] *Ibid.*, p. 360.

[40] *A Systematic and Historical Exposition of Roman Law in the Order of a Code*, p. 112.

lors—most of whom before Sir Thomas More were churchmen[41]—either applied directly the principles of Roman law or framed a remedy based upon Roman precedent to supply the lack of a remedy in the common law.[42] In fact whole passages were lifted from the Roman law, although the chancellors were careful not to have it appear that they were building up a system of law separate and distinct from that of the common law, which system has, of course, not only maintained itself but has greatly influenced jurisprudence in all English-speaking parts of the world.

As might be expected, therefore, the best example of what has just been termed the "under-cover" entrance of Roman law into England is to be found in the development of English equity upon the basis of Roman *aequitas.*

Our system of Equity [says Lord Bryce], built up by the Chancellors, the earlier among them ecclesiastics, takes not only its name but its guiding and formative principles, and many of its positive rules, from the Roman *aequitas,* which was in substance identical with the Law of Nature and the *ius gentium.* For obvious reasons the Chancellors and Masters of the Rolls did not talk much about Nature, and still less would they have talked about the *ius gentium.* They referred rather to the law of God and to Reason. But the ideas were Roman, drawn either from the Canon Law, or directly from the *Digest* and the *Institutes,* and they were applied to English facts in a manner not dissimilar from that of the Roman jurists. The very name, Courts of Conscience [by which the courts of equity were first known], though the conscience may in the immediate sense have been the King's, suggests that moral element on which the Romans insisted so strongly.[43]

---

[41] Tracing the early development of the Court of Chancery, Professor Maitland says, in his *Constitutional History of England,* pp. 221–22: "Ever since the Norman Conquest every king has his chancellor, who has the custody of his great seal, and is at the head of the whole secretarial body of king's clerks. When at the end of Henry III's reign there ceases any longer to be a chief justiciar, the chancellor becomes the king's first minister. Robert Burnell, the chancellor, is Edward I's chief adviser. The chancellor is almost always an ecclesiastic—there are a few instances of lay chancellors in the fourteenth century—generally he is a bishop. In many different ways he has for a long time past been concerned in the administration of law. In the first place it has been his duty, or that of his clerks, to draw up those royal writs (original writs) whereby actions are begun in the king's courts of common law. He has also had some judicial powers of his own—in particular, if it be asserted that the king has made a grant of what does not belong to him, it is for the chancellor to hear the matter, and if need be to advise the king to revoke his grant. Then again he has always been a member of the king's council, and what is more, the specially learned member—that he should be acquainted with canon law and Roman law, as well as with the common law of England, was very desirable. Naturally then if questions of law came before the council, the chancellor's opinion would be taken."

[42] The reliance of the English chancellors on Roman law was so marked that a modern English authority describes the Court of Chancery as being "Roman to the backbone."—Scrutton, *op. cit.,* p. 2.

[43] *Studies in History and Jurisprudence* (previously cited), II, 599.

Sir Henry Maine, in his *Ancient Law*,[44] which marks an epoch in the study of jurisprudence and which is admitted to have founded the historical school, says:

The jurisprudence of the Court of Chancery, which bears the name of Equity in England . . . is extremely complex in its texture, and derives its materials from several heterogeneous sources. The early ecclesiastical chancellors contributed to it, from the Canon Law, many of the principles which lie deepest in its structure. The Roman law, more fertile than the Canon Law in rules applicable to secular disputes, was not seldom resorted to by a later generation of Chancery judges, amid whose recorded dicta we often find entire texts from the *Corpus Juris Civilis* imbedded, with their terms unaltered, though their origin is never acknowledged. Still more recently, and particularly at the middle and during the latter half of the eighteenth century, the mixed systems of jurisprudence and morals constructed by the publicists of the Low Countries appear to have been much studied by English lawyers, and from the chancellorship of Lord Talbot to the commencement of Lord Eldon's chancellorship these works had considerable effect on the rulings of the Court of Chancery.

As for the English ecclesiastical courts they were, of course, neither courts of common law nor of equity, but of the canon law. Now to understand the real influence of Roman law upon English legal development, we must realize that the influence was largely indirect, in that it entered mainly through the canon law rather than directly from the Roman texts; and here it should be remembered that the canon law throughout the centuries remained always in close contact with Rome. As Professor Winfield observes:[45] "It is in the Canon Law which borrowed liberally from Roman Law that we must look for the more abiding influence of Roman Law on our system, rather than in the pure Civil Law."[46]

This is not the place to attempt an examination of the jurisdiction and procedure of the ecclesiastical courts, but it is important to note that they furnished an open channel through which the canon law made itself felt in English institutions.[47]

[44] Page 52.
[45] *The Chief Sources of English Legal History* (previously cited), p. 57.
[46] Sir Frederick Pollock, speaking of English equity, says: "With regard to the contributions made by equity jurisprudence to what is now the common stock, it is well known that they account for most of our Romanist importation. Here it is needful to call to mind the warning given a good many years ago by Langdell. The learning and procedure of the early Chancellors might well enough be called Roman, but not in the classical sense of modern scholars. As between the two rival branches of jurisprudence outside England, they belonged not to the civilian, but to the canonical side; and therefore, when we think we are on the track of Roman influence anywhere between the thirteenth and the seventeenth centuries, it is quite unscientific to jump to a modern edition of the Corpus Juris."—Pollock, *Genius of the Common Law*, pp. 80-81.
[47] "The numerous Ecclesiastical Courts (diocesan, metropolitan, legatine), acquiring after the Norman conquest, in addition to their extensive spiritual jurisdiction, exclusive civil juris-

It must suffice also to refer only briefly to the Court of Chivalry, sometimes termed the Court of the Constable and Marshal, which ceased to exist in 1737 but which during a long period applied Roman law wherever possible in both criminal and civil cases; and to the courts of the universities of Oxford and Cambridge, which were civilian courts in which Roman law was administered in the trials of students for civil suits and minor offenses.

Another interesting development in the history of Roman influence on English law, which must not be overlooked in even a brief résumé, is the organization in 1511, by doctors of law in London practicing before the Ecclesiastical and the Admiralty courts, of the famous "Doctors' Commons" at Gray's Inn. This organization was made up entirely of civilians and canonists and endured for some 350 years,[48] its most outstanding figure having been Sir William Scott (later Lord Stowell),[49] whose brother John (Lord Eldon) was the outstanding figure in the field of equity.

More significant evidence of the influence of the Roman law is to be found in the history of the law merchant. The law merchant (or the *lex mercatoria*) was not only applied by English judges in mercantile disputes from early times but is considered to have been actually embodied in the laws of the realm, and thus came to be recognized as part of the law of England. So general and complete was this recognition of the *lex mercatoria* that Sir Edward Coke described it as "a part of the common law."[50] And Sir William Blackstone, observing that matters of commerce are regulated by their own laws, which all nations agree to take notice of, added[51] that "it is held to be part of the law of England."

---

diction of marriage and testate and intestate succession to personal property, administered the Canon Law—which to things secular is largely Roman law at secondhand. The English Ecclesiastical Courts, always important tribunals, suffered little loss in jurisdiction from the Reformation and retained much of their civil authority until late in the 19th century."— Sherman, *Roman Law in the Modern World* (previously cited), I, 364.

The application of the canon law, it may be added, was not restricted solely to the ecclesiastical courts. Thus, for example, we find its decrees relied upon as "general" law in the Court of Exchequer, as late as 1657, in the case *Stavely v. Ullithorn* (Hardres, 101), wherein it was stated that the decrees of the Council of the Lateran were "General law received in England," that "this council is as forcible as an act of parliament," and finally that "this council, as a general law . . . includes all men's consent."

[48] It closed its doors in 1858, after having numbered among its members some of the most distinguished of the English jurists.

[49] Lord Stowell, it may be remarked, was deeply learned in civil law, and was not averse to citing Roman legal conceptions whenever he found them useful. See, for example, his reference to the Roman *usura maritima* or *foenus nauticum* in connection with bottomry bonds ("The Atlas," 2 Hagg. Ad. 57). See also "The Anna," 5 C. Rob. Ad. 385c; and "The Ville de Varsovie," 2 Dods. Ad. 185-89.

[50] Coke's *Institutes*, II. 58.

[51] *Commentaries on the Laws of England in Four Books Together with a Copious Analysis of the Contents, and Notes* . . . by Cooley (4th ed. by Andrews), Bk. I, 273.

But what was the chief source of the law merchant? Thomas Edward Scrutton,[52] ultimately a lord justice of England, has admirably indicated its source in three brief sentences:

> Now this Law Merchant, thus recognized by the laws of England, drew part of its matter from the Civil law. Being "part of the law of nations," in that it was composed of the customs of merchants of all nations, it included a number of usages which were relics of the Civil law, continuing the practice of the coasts of the Mediterranean. Again, the written laws of the sea, the *Consolato*[53] and the laws of Oleron, which formed part of the Law Merchant, and the latter of which was expressly embodied in the laws of England, were based on the Civil law, with such additions as were necessary to meet the needs of the time.

In the paragraph which follows, after remarking that the *lex mercatoria* had therefore a Roman foundation, the future lord justice adds:[54]

> the importance of this will be seen when we remember that Lord Mansfield, the father of modern Mercantile law, during the 32 years in which he was Lord Chief Justice of the King's Bench, constructed his system of Commercial law by moulding the findings of his special juries as to the usages of merchants (which had often a Roman origin) on principles frequently derived from the Civil law and the law of nations. . . . An example of Lord Mansfield's use of the Civil law will be seen in his exposition of the nature of the equitable action for money had and received, which can be traced, passage by passage, to the *Corpus Juris:* and many of these usages of the merchants, which he thus harmonized, had their origin in the Roman law though their details were of modern growth.[55]

Lord Mansfield may be said to have had a weakness for Roman law because of his birth in Scotland, a Roman law country, and because of his study of Roman law in his early days in the University of Leyden. What

---

[52] *The Influence of the Roman Law on the Laws of England* (previously cited), pp. 179–80.
[53] *Consolato del mare.*   [54] Scrutton, *op. cit.,* pp. 180, 181.
[55] An indication of the prejudice against the open application of Roman-law principles to English cases, is to be seen in the attack of "Junius" (generally admitted to be Sir Philip Francis) against Lord Mansfield: "In contempt or ignorance of the Common law of England, you have made it your study to introduce into the Court where you preside, maxims of jurisprudence unknown to Englishmen. The Roman code, the law of nations, and the opinions of foreign civilians, are your perpetual theme."—*Ibid.,* p. 180.

To this onslaught against the great Scots jurist, Lord Campbell—himself a Scot—replied in the grand manner that for this charge "there is not the slightest colour of pretence. He did not consider the Common law of England . . . a perfect code adapted to the expanded, diversified, and novel requirements of a civilised and commercial nation . . . but in no instance did he ever attempt to substitute Roman rules and maxims for those of the Common law. He made ample use of the compilations of Justinian, but only for a supply of *principles* to guide him upon questions unsettled by prior decisions in England; deriving also similar assistance from the law of nations, and the modern Continental codes."—*Ibid.*

For the measured judgment of enlightened jurists on the services of Lord Mansfield, see also Mr. Justice Buller in *Lickbarrow* v. *Mason* (1787), 2 T. R. 63, 73.

he admired in Roman law was its spirit of justice as distinct from stereotyped legal form; and the service of Lord Mansfield to English law and jurisprudence throughout the world consisted in the introduction and the emphasizing of broad and equitable principles, whenever and wherever the nature of the case would permit. In the United States a distinguished professor of the Harvard Law School has stated Lord Mansfield to be "the greatest magistrate of the English-speaking world."

In connection with the law merchant, the important Court of Admiralty must not be overlooked. Established in the fourteenth century, it necessarily dealt in large part, by reason of its jurisdiction over maritime cases, with the Roman law as embodied in the law merchant, and especially in the laws of Oleron. On the law of the Admiralty Court an admirable passage is contained in Constantin John Colombos' *Treatise on the Law of Prize,* published under the imprint of the Grotius Society:

As to the "course of Admiralty," it should be noted at the outset that Admiralty law has never been considered in England as being strictly municipal law. The venerable Black Book of the Admiralty, in its opening chapter, lays stress on the propriety of the Admiralty judge adhering to the ancient usage and custom of the sea—*la loy marine et anciens coutumes de la mer*—as accepted by all the civilised countries of Europe. A great part of the law and customs is found in codes such as the Rhodian sea law, the laws of Oleron, of Wisbuy, of the Hanse Towns and, principally, in the celebrated *Consolato del Mare,* all of which contain many valuable principles which were used by the English judges in moulding the law and practice of the Admiralty Court. It is noteworthy that Sir Julius Caesar, speaking in the sixteenth century, referred to maritime law as being the "truest and most indifferent judge between all nations," whilst Lord Mansfield, nearly two hundred years afterwards, still held that "all the world were parties to a sentence of a Court of Admiralty." Maritime law was thus considered to be of universal obligation, not because it was prescribed by any single State, but because it rested on the common consent of all civilised communities.[56]

Of the later writers of the sixteenth and seventeenth centuries who were versed in Roman law, several are of outstanding importance. Among these are Arthur Duck, who wrote a treatise on the use and authority of Roman law in modern states;[57] John Selden, thoroughly versed in the common law, as great a lawyer as he was statesman and historian, and in whose memory the Selden Society, which is rendering such immense services to the study

---

[56] Pages 4–5.

[57] *De Usu et Auctoritate Juris Civilis Romanorum in Dominiis Christianorum,* published in 1653. The part relating to England is translated by Beaver (London, 1724).—Sherman, *op. cit.,* I, 377 n.

of the origin and history of English law, has been formed; Richard Zouche, well grounded in the Roman law and indeed a judge of the Admiralty Court and ranked among the classic writers on the law of nations; and Sir Matthew Hale, one of England's great judges, who was deeply learned in the Roman law as well as in the common law, which he administered as Lord Chief Justice of the Court of King's Bench.

Particular mention must be made of Lord Bacon, one of the greatest of English jurists, whether of the seventeenth or any other century, and reputed by some to be the first Englishman who wrote English prose of a classical nature (although the opinion of many is that he shares that honor with Richard Hooker). Bacon was deeply learned in Roman law. He had mastered it and was criticized because he preferred it to the common law, of which his rival Coke was the leading exponent. Indeed one of Bacon's favorite ideas was a codification of the principles of equity embodied in English law, and in proposing this codification, he referred explicitly to the *Digest* of Justinian. As Lord Chancellor he administered a justice which had its basis not merely in Roman law but in the universal conception of the law of nature; for, as he himself had earlier stated in his elaborate and persuasive argument in the leading case of the *Post-Nati*:[58] "Our law"—meaning the law of England—"is grounded upon the law of nature."[59]

[58] Known also as *Calvin's Case* (1609; see 7 Co. Rep. 1). The argument of Bacon, then Solicitor-General, is included in the edition of his *Works* ed. by Spedding, Ellis and Heath, VII, 639, 663.

[59] It is not without interest to note the discussion of the law of nature in Calvin's Case, as recorded by Coke (7 Co. Rep., 12b-13b). In his report of the case, which he regarded as having been "as elaborately, substantially, and judicially argued by the Lord Chancellor, and by my brethren the Judges, as I ever read or heard of any," the reporter wrote: "The law of nature is that which God at the time of creation of the nature of man infused into his heart, for his preservation and direction; and this is *lex aeterna,* the moral law, called also the law of nature. And by this law, written with the finger of God in the heart of man, were the people of God a long time governed, before the law was written by Moses, who was the first reporter or writer of law in the world. The Apostle in the second chapter to the Romans saith, *Cum enim gentes quae legem non habent naturaliter ea quae legis sunt faciunt.* And this is within the command of that moral law, *honora patrem,* which doubtless doth extend to him that is *pater patriae.* And that Apostle saith *Omnis anima potestatibus sublimioribus subdita sit.* And these be the words of the Great Divine, *Hoc Deus in Sacris Scripturis jubet, hoc lex naturae dictari, ut quilibet subditus obediat superio,* and Aristotle, nature's secretary, lib. 5. Aethic. saith, that *jus naturale est, quod apud omnes homines eandem habet potentiam.* And herewith doth agree Bracton, lib. 1. cap. 5. and Fortescue, cap. 8. 12. 13. and 16. Doctor and Student, cap. 2. and 4. And the reason hereof is, for that God and nature is one to all, and therefore the law of God and nature is one to all. . . . And Aristotle 1. Politicorum proveth . . . that magistracy is of nature: for whatsoever is necessary and profitable for the preservation of the society of man is due by the law of nature: but magistracy and government are necessary and profitable for the preservation of the society of man; therefore magistracy and government are of nature. And herewith accordeth Tully, lib. 3. *De legibus, sine imperio nec domus ulla, nec civitas, nec gens, nec hominum universum genus stare, nec ipse denique mundus potest.* This law of nature, which indeed is the eternal

And finally there is Sir William Blackstone,[60] admittedly learned in the common and statute law of England, and held in even higher esteem today than formerly. Acquainted with the Roman law and familiar with Holy Writ, he declared that all human law must be in conformity with the "first principles of the law of nature" as laid down by Justinian, and with "the revealed or divine law of the holy scriptures," the precepts of which are "really a part of the original law of nature." Nor was this all; for he further declared that the law of nature is the basis of the law of nations. Thus in Blackstone we have the doctrine of the New Testament, the law of Justinian, the law of nature, and the law of nations united.

As has been intimated, Roman law had taken root north of the Tweed, and the result has been that in no small measure the law of Scotland today is Roman law, with such changes as are needed to meet changing conditions.[61] Since the union of Scotland and England in 1707 to form the United Kingdom of Great Britain, the Parliament (in which the Scots were long

---

law of the Creator, infused into the heart of the creature at the time of his creation, was two thousand years before any laws written, and before any judicial or municipal laws. And certain it is, that before judicial or municipal laws were made, Kings did decide causes according to natural equity, and were not tied to any rule or formality of law, but did *dare jura*. . . .

"And Pomponius, lib. 2. cap. De Origine Juris, affirmeth that, in Tarquinius Superbus's time there was no civil law written, and that Papirius reduced certain observations into writing, which was called Jus Civile Papirianum. Now the reason wherefore laws were made and published, appeareth in Fortescue, cap. 13. and in Tully, lib. 2. Officiorum: *at cum jus aequabile ab uno viro homines non consequerentur, inventi sunt leges.* . . . albeit judicial or municipal laws have inflicted and imposed in several places, or at several times, divers and several punishments and penalties, for breach or not observance of the law of nature, (for that law only consisted in commanding or prohibiting, without any certain punishment or penalty), yet the very law of nature itself never was nor could be (*a*) altered or changed. And therefore it is certainly true, that (*b*) *jura naturalia sunt immutabilia*. And herewith agreeth Bracton, lib. 1. cap. 5. and Doctor and Student, cap. 5 and 6. And this appeareth plainly and plentifully in our books."

There would seem to be little doubt, from arguments of this character, that the English jurists of Coke's day were familiar with the conception of natural law and its historical background. Nor is it unreasonable to see more than a chance relationship between these arguments on the law of nature and Coke's famous dictum concerning the invalidity of acts of Parliament which were "against common right and reason" (*Bonham's Case*, 8 Co. Rep., 118a).

[60] *Commentaries* (previously cited), Book I, 39-43.

[61] The law of Scotland, unlike the Continental systems, has never been codified. In a way, however, this lack of codification has encouraged Scottish jurists and students to turn directly to the Roman law. "Accordingly, in the absence of a code, direct reference to Roman texts and further adoption of Roman Law in the absence of native authority still remain open in Scotland. The Scottish student may still study Roman Law as Stair regarded it 'not as a law binding by its authority, but as a rule followed for its equity.' This view of Roman Law as a quarry from which may be hewed stones to be joined to native timber in the framing of a Scots Law, is in the spirit of the Bartolists." Muirhead, *An Outline of Roman Law*, p. xxxii.

inadequately represented) has from time to time passed legislation of a general kind applicable alike to both countries. Especially is this so in the case of bills, notes, and such matters, with the result that statutory law for new conditions has become the common law of both countries, whereas in the law affecting primarily Scotland, and not arising from new conditions for which there might not be precedents, the Roman law elements have remained largely undisturbed. Thus an outstanding figure in the sphere of comparative law, M. Lévy-Ullmann, has expressed his belief in no uncertain terms that Scots law is "absolutely Roman in character"—that it is, indeed, more "Romanized" than any other system of law in existence—and furthermore that the law of the future will be, not the common law of England, not the Continental law of European states, but in all likelihood a combination of the two, like the Scots law of today.[62] That is to say, it will, like the Scots law, represent both the Anglo-Saxon and the Continental systems. Thus may be ushered in that unity of law on which, in no small measure, depends the future of our civilization.

APPENDIX

The Law of Nature in the Modern World

THE DISCOVERY OF AMERICA OPENED UP A VAST CONTINENT TO EUROPEAN EXPLOITATION. England was prompt in sending ships westward and in founding settlements. These settlements, which became in the course of time the thirteen American Colonies, were established not under the authority of Parliament but under the authority of the Crown as sovereign of England. Now the colonists

[62] The statement contained in the text is a shortened paraphrase of M. Lévy-Ullmann's prophecy. This prophecy is so arresting that the pertinent passage of the French text of his essay dealing with the law of Scotland is reproduced in full:

"En définitive, le droit écossais, dans son état actuel, nous donne le spectacle de ce que sera un jour (peut-être à la fin de ce siècle), le droit des nations civilisées; une combinaison entre le système anglo-saxon et le système continental. Le droit ainsi unifié—là où il peut l'être—se substituera aux vieux principes gouvernant le conflit des lois, principes qui se sont développés précisément en Grande-Bretagne à la suite des oppositions constantes entre le droit écossais et le droit anglais. Cette unification, sans doute, Messieurs, je ne la conçois guère se réalisant dans le domaine du droit de famille ou celui de la propriété, qui puisent aux diverses sources nationales des traditions parfois inconciliables; mais dans le domaine pratique du droit des affaires, l'esprit à la fois ingénieux et bouillant des Ecossais—*perfervidum ingenium*, écrit l'un d'eux—a déjà jeté un ferment qui fera lever la substance de la législation future: oui, c'est peut-être par l'effort des juristes écossais, qui forment le véritable trait d'union entre le droit du continent et le droit anglo-saxon, que nous verrons apparaître un jour,—ou plutôt, hélas, que nos successeurs verront apparaître—une unité législative qui est, j'en ai le plus ferme espoir, dans l'ordre des choses de l'avenir.—"Le Droit ecossais," *Bulletin de la Société de législation comparée*, LIII (Feb. 16, 1924), pp. 148–49.

considered that they should legislate for themselves through appropriate legislative bodies, just as the inhabitants of England legislated through their Parliament. Years passed; decades passed; the British Colonies from small and isolated settlements grew into colonial commonwealths extending from the Gulf of Mexico north to somewhat indefinite boundaries, which, however, were made definite by the Seven Years' War, in consequence of which France ceded to Great Britain her possessions in North America lying north of the then British Colonies and east of the Mississippi.

The relation of the colonies to their English sovereign, however, had undergone a subtle change. Heretofore, colonial support against France had been important, but now France was no longer an enemy of the north. Therefore, since there was no further danger from Canada, now become a British Colony, it was unnecessary, in the opinion of the sovereign of the day (George III), to conceal the mailed fist in a velvet glove in dealing with the English Colonies to the south of Canada. In other words, the mother country felt able to impose sterner measures upon the English Colonies of North America, there being no longer a fear of French interference in colonial affairs from the north, and no need for friendly colonial support against the French. The result—as we know—was the American Revolution.

There had always been some slight differences of opinion as to the rights and duties of the colonists in their relation to the sovereign. But after the Seven Years' War these differences were greatly magnified when legislation affecting the colonies became the order of the day in England, on the theory that the British Parliament could legislate as freely for the colonies as it did for the United Kingdom. The colonies did not accept that view, having developed, as we have seen, a different conception, according to which they claimed that, while they owed allegiance to the Crown, they had the right to legislate for themselves; and so firmly did they cling to these views that eventually, rather than relinquish them, they declared their independence of the mother country.

So much for the general issue. But upon what specific ground did the colonists differ from the mother country? On the ground that the attempt of the Parliament to interfere with the rights of the colonists was a violation of what James Otis, in his famous speech at Boston in 1764 on writs of assistance, considered the law of nature. His language (and some subsequent passages material to the controversy) are quoted from Professor Ernest Barker's Introduction to his translation of Otto Gierke's *Natural Law and the Theory of Society—1500 to 1800*:[1] "should an Act of Parliament be against any of His"—meaning God's—"natural laws . . . the declaration would be contrary to eternal truth, equity and justice, and consequently void."

Professor Barker prefaces his quotation from the speech of the fiery New England lawyer with a reference to the dictum of a distinguished English judge in 1614 on "the immutable laws of nature," and calls attention to the fact that Otis employed the very expression used by the learned judge, which "becomes

---

[1] Vol. I, xlvii. The subject of "natural rights" has been admirably dealt with by another English authority, Robson, in his recent interesting volume, *Civilisation and the Growth of Law*, Part II, chap. iv.

a battle-cry; it is often used by the great Boston agitator, Samuel Adams; and perhaps at his instigation it is inserted in the Declaration of the first Continental Congress, in 1774, when the deputies declare that the colonies, by the immutable laws of nature, have certain rights, and that certain Acts of Parliament are violations and infringements of these rights." Here it may be remarked that the resistance of the colonies was based both upon violations of natural law and upon the fact that in the colonial conception the British Parliament was devoid of jurisdiction over the colonies. But it was the law of nature which provided the most effective ammunition for colonial arguments. To continue the quotation from Professor Barker:

> In the Puritan atmosphere of North America the secular Law of Nature recovers its theological basis: Samuel Adams claims for his countrymen the indefeasible rights with which "God and Nature have invested" them; and the Declaration of Independence claims for the people of America the station to which they are entitled by "the Laws of Nature and of Nature's God." It was the Law of Nature which, more than any other force, exploded the authority of the British Parliament and the British connection; and it is curious to reflect that Vattel's work on the principles of Natural Law was currently used in the *sodalitas* of the Boston lawyers (a sort of political science club) during the crucial years of the Revolution.

It is perhaps not so curious as Professor Barker suggests that Vattel's work should have been quoted. In the first place, the treatise was the contribution of a distinguished Swiss—and the people of the Western World have always cherished an admiration for Switzerland. In addition, it was then a very recent work, the first edition having been published in 1758. And as it was early translated into English, it is not improbable that copies of the English version were at the disposal of certain American men of affairs, to be read without the need of a French dictionary at their elbows. And finally, Vattel's work was looked upon throughout the world as a standard treatise on international law.

There is another reason of somewhat later date. Mr. C. W. F. Dumas—a Swiss gentleman then living in Amsterdam—who was friendly to the American cause, brought out a new edition of Vattel, to which he prefixed an introduction. Being acquainted with Benjamin Franklin, Mr. Dumas sent three copies to that distinguished American philosopher, statesman, member of the Continental Congress, and of the Committee on Secret [foreign] Correspondence. One copy the recipient was to keep for himself, another was for the Carpenters' Library in Philadelphia, and a third for the College of Massachusetts Bay—known nowadays as Harvard University. Franklin carefully and graciously acknowledged the receipt of the volumes and, keeping his own, saw that the others reached their destinations. In his letter to Mr. Dumas, dated December 19, 1775, he thanked the donor for the volumes and advised him of the use to which the one addressed to him was put by the members of Congress:[2] "It came to us in good season, when the circumstances of a rising State make it necessary frequently to consult the law of nations." It may be remarked that the law of na-

---

[2] *The Revolutionary Diplomatic Correspondence of the United States,* ed. under direction of Congress by Wharton, II, 64.

tions is still frequently consulted in the United States, and that Vattel's statement of that law has been for more than a century looked upon by the Supreme Court of the United States as an authoritative statement. By 1780, five years after the receipt of Mr. Dumas' gift, Vattel's treatise had become a textbook in American colleges—at a time when the United States were still Colonies in the view of the mother country.

But to return to Professor Barker:

Nor was it only in the work of destruction that the theory of Natural Law was employed. It also served the cause of construction. The Virginian "Declaration of Rights" and the Virginian "Constitution or Form of Government" of 1776, and the Pennsylvania Constitution of the same year, which contains both a declaration of rights and "a plan or frame of government," are both founded on the theory of Natural Law.[3]

Now these general notions of natural law were set forth by Vattel. "If we seek to find the general ideas by which these documents were inspired, we shall find them in the first book of Vattel's treatise and particularly in its second and third chapters." Professor Barker leaves it an open question whether or not the framers of these American documents actually used Vattel, it being sufficient from his point of view that "they were using the common stock of ideas on which he had drawn, and which he had presented in lucid French."

The distinguished jurist Mr. Albert de Lapradelle, in his introduction to the edition of Vattel[4] published in the "Classics of International Law" by the Carnegie Institution of Washington, found authority, however, for the conviction that Vattel's *Law of Nations* "was used by the members of the Second Continental Congress, which sat in Philadelphia; by the leading men who directed the policy of the United Colonies until the end of the war; and later, by the men who sat in the Convention of 1787 and drew up the Constitution of the United States."

Professor Barker quotes in support of his views a few words of the Declaration of Independence; but it is material to the present purpose to quote a somewhat longer passage: "When in the Course of human events, it becomes necessary for one people to dissolve the political bands which have connected them with another, and to assume among the powers of the earth, the separate and equal station to which the Laws of Nature and of Nature's God entitle them, a decent respect to the opinions of mankind requires that they should declare the causes which impel them to the separation." Thereupon Jefferson, the framer of the Declaration, proceeded to state the "causes" in philosophical and, it is believed, in universal terms: "We hold these truths to be self-evident, that all men are created equal, that they are endowed by their Creator with certain unalienable Rights, that among these are Life, Liberty and the pursuit of Happiness." A more perfect statement of natural law it would be difficult to find. But these two sentences, important as they may be, are but a preamble to additional clauses

[3] Introduction to Gierke, *Natural Law and the Theory of Society,* p. xlvii.
[4] Vol. III, xxx, note 1, quoting George Maurice Abbott, *A Short History of the Library Company of Philadelphia,* p. 11.

of fundamental importance: "That to secure these rights, Governments are instituted among Men, deriving their just powers from the consent of the governed,—That whenever any Form of Government becomes destructive of these ends, it is the Right of the People to alter or to abolish it, and to institute new Government, laying its foundation on such principles and organizing its powers in such form, as to them shall seem most likely to effect their Safety and Happiness."

The Declaration of Independence was unanimously passed on the second day of July, 1776, by the second of the Continental Congresses, and it was proclaimed two days later, on the fourth of July, which day—rather than the second of July—we Americans look upon as the day of our Independence. The Declaration is also—and appropriately—the first document in which the thirteen states are designated the "united States of America." It has not been repealed. It still is the first statute of the United States of America, and in view of these facts it may be said that the law of nature was, and still is, a fundamental element in the law of the United States.

Here it is advisable to return for a moment to the dictum of the English judge on the immutability of natural law, a dictum which James Otis may have had in mind and which Professor Barker introduces by a sentence of the deepest import—at least to us of the Americas:[5] "The American Revolution, as it ran its course from 1764 to 1776—from the first beginnings of resistance down to the Declaration of Independence and the creation of new colonial constitutions—was inspired by the doctrines of Natural Law." The dictum itself is then quoted by Professor Barker: "An English judge had uttered the *obiter dictum*, in 1614, that 'even an Act of Parliament made against natural equity . . . is void in itself; for *jura naturae sunt immutabilia,* and they are *leges legum.*'" The colonists, as we know, brought with them the law which then existed in England. But apparently they also brought with them the *obiter dictum* of the English judge. In any event, its doctrine was made a permanent part of the American legal and political heritage by the Declaration of Independence of the United States.

But what, it may be asked, is the present attitude of the erstwhile mother country to the law of nature? The evidence on this point is not couched in an *obiter dictum* but in a unanimous opinion of the Chancery Division of the Supreme Court of Judicature in the leading case of *Bradford Corporation* v. *Ferrand*,[6] decided in 1901, which has been neither changed nor overruled. In its essential features the question involved was very simple. What law was to be applied in the matter of rights claimed in connection with a stream of water flowing underground? "The law of nature" is the answer. It will, however, be well to add an extract from the opinion of Mr. Justice (later Lord Justice) Farwell, who delivered his own opinion and that of his colleagues: "The foundation of the right as stated throughout all the cases is jus naturae; . . . Lord Wensleydale"—the earlier Sir James Parke, considered one of the great English judges—

---

[5] Intro. to Gierke, *Natural Law and the Theory of Society* (previously cited), p. xlvi.
[6] L. R. 2 Ch. Div. (1902) 655, 661, 662, 663, 666.

"in *Chasemore* v. *Richards*[7] says: 'It has been now settled that the right to the enjoyment of a natural stream of water on the surface, ex jure naturae, belongs to the proprietor of the adjoining lands, as a natural incident to the right to the soil itself.'" After additional citations, which may be omitted here, Justice Farwell states his conclusion:

I have come to the conclusion, therefore, that jus naturae is used in these cases as expressing that principle in English law which is akin to, if not derived from, the jus naturale of Roman law. English law is, of course, quite independent of Roman law, but the conception of aequum et bonum and the rights flowing therefrom which are included in jus naturale underlie a great part of English common law; although it is not usual to find "the law of nature" or "natural law" referred to in so many words in English cases.[8]

Adverting then to the writers and jurists of earlier days in support of this interpretation, Justice Farwell continued: "I am not, therefore, introducing any novel principle if I regard jus naturae on which the right to running water rests, as meaning that which is aequum et bonum between the upper and lower proprietors." After asking, as was natural for an English judge, "what then is fair and reasonable between the parties?" his lordship, invoking the opinion of Lord Cranworh in *Chasemore* v. *Richards*[9] (from which case he had also quoted, as we have seen, the opinion of Lord Wensleydale), declares that the existence of the right in question "depends on the consideration of what is aequum et bonum between the two parties." Finally, referring to numerous decisions supporting the opinion of the court, including "American decisions," Mr. Justice Farwell concludes that he is confirmed in his "view of what is aequum et bonum by finding that I share it with such eminent persons."

It may be added that in the course of his opinion the learned justice, citing authorities, refers to "'The Law of Nature' by Sir F. Pollock in the *'Journal of Comparative Legislation'* for 1901," an essay which is reproduced in Sir Frederick Pollock's *Essays in the Law*[10] and had already become a classic during the lifetime of its distinguished author. The law natural has long been tacitly or indirectly recognized in English jurisprudence—though usually under the alias of "right reason" or "the law of reason." But in the case of *Bradford Corporation* v. *Ferrand* we have, not indirect, but open and unqualified recognition of the law of nature.

Nor is this all. Since the World War the government of Great Britain has removed any and every doubt, so far as the jurisprudence of Great Britain extends, as to its recognition that the law natural exists and that it is binding upon the British government. How was this accomplished? By Great Britain's signature and ratification of the Statute of the Permanent Court of International Justice, established at The Hague in 1921. Article 38 of the Statute of the court declares that the law which the court shall apply in its decisions shall include "the general principles of law recognized by civilized nations," which clause was proposed by the English member of the committee framing the Statute

---

[7] 7 H. L. C. 382,—on appeal to the House of Lords, the court of ultimate appeal.
[8] See chap. xxi on Christopher St. Germain, *infra*.   [9] 7 H. L. C. 349.   [10] Page 31.

(Lord Phillimore, then member of the Judicial Committee of the Privy Council) as a substitute for the more rhetorical expression, "la conscience juridique du monde civilisé."

Now the "general principles of law recognized by civilized nations" are neither more nor less than the fundamental and universal principles accepted for many centuries by jurists and philosophers on the Continent as constituting the natural law.

But it was not merely Great Britain which recognized the law natural as a law to be applied by the International Court in appropriate cases. The Statute of the court has been signed by some fifty-seven states members of the international community and has been ratified by fifty, so that it can be said that Article 38, recognizing—without naming—the natural law, is binding upon the international community because it has been accepted, in accordance with Francisco de Vitoria's statement,[11] "through a consensus of the greater part of the whole world, especially in behalf of the common good of all."

The law of nature or the law of reason—call it what you will—has had a checkered career throughout the ages, but notwithstanding the storms of skepticism and the thunders of the positive school, it is still the central current in the great stream of jurisprudence. In those countries—on the Continent of Europe and elsewhere—which inherited their civil law from Rome, the natural law as the embodiment of fundamental legal principles and ideals endured many vicissitudes but never completely lost its place in the philosophy of law. And in the common-law countries, over a long period of time it has, as we have seen, been slowly but surely winning recognition.

Its contribution to our modern jurisprudence has been admirably summarized by Dean Pound:

> Our law and the law of Continental Europe were liberalized and modernized in the seventeenth and eighteenth centuries, not by legislation, not by exercise of the will of any sovereign, but by a juristic doctrine that all legal institutions and all legal rules were to be measured by reason and that nothing could stand in law that could not maintain itself in reason. So to-day, while absolute theories of law as a mere expression of the popular will are current in political thinking, a return to juridical idealism is in progress. Once more jurists of Continental Europe are writing elaborate treatises on natural law. In the United States a revival of philosophical jurisprudence has definitely begun and conscious attempt to make the law conform to ideals is once more becoming the creed of jurisprudence.[12]

[11] See chap. xxii, *infra*.   [12] *The Spirit of the Common Law*, pp. 81–82.

Chapter XVIII

MARSIGLIO OF PADUA (c. 1275–1343)

Defensor Pacis

At the end of the thirteenth century and the beginning of the fourteenth, the temporal supremacy of the papacy was asserted by Boniface VIII in what seemed to the temporal sovereigns of that day an exaggerated form. Now it so happened that the assertion in question gave rise to much discussion of the relations between the temporal and the spiritual powers and, in consequence, to attempts to define and describe their respective limits. These efforts caused men to consider anew the problems of political government.

Outstanding among these discussions is the elaborate tractate of Marsiglio of Padua entitled *Defensor pacis*, which dates from the year 1324, a tractate which conceived of lay government as the sole means by which peace was to be brought about in the various states of the world. Marsiglio is usually spoken of as the author, but it is generally conceded that he had an associate—if indeed the associate was not a co-author—John of Jandun. Precisely what contribution each made to the *Defensor pacis* is still an open question, but Mr. C. W. Previté-Orton, who has published a critical edition[1] based upon a collation of all available and relevant manuscripts, is of the opinion that the contributions of John of Jandun were in the nature of advice and suggestions rather than definite parts of the composition.[2] Here, however, the problem of authorship is largely immaterial. The important point is that the *Defensor pacis* shows both Marsiglio of Padua and John of Jandun to have been outspoken Aristotelians. In the case of these collaborators, it was not mere pride of scholarship that caused them to quote Aristotle so freely, and indeed this comment may apply to all—or almost all—of the Aristotelians of the Middle Ages and to scholastic writers in general.

It was, we may be sure [says Dr. Ephraim Emerton], not pride of scholarship, or at least not this alone, that led men of the intellectual quality of Aquinas and

---

[1] *The Defensor Pacis of Marsilius of Padua.*
[2] For a somewhat different view, see Tooley, "The Authorship of the *Defensor Pacis*," in *Transactions of the Royal Historical Society*, 4th Series, IX, 85–106.

Dante to fill their pages so largely with Aristotelian reference and method of demonstration. It was that they desired to give to what were really their own opinions the required sanction of acknowledged authority.[3]

The significance of the *Defensor pacis* was not confined to its own day, for the theories which it advanced were gradually accepted in succeeding centuries. Professor Francis William Coker, of Yale University, in his introduction to the extracts from the *Defensor pacis* included in his invaluable *Readings in Political Philosophy,* says that "it brings forward, early in the fourteenth century, ideas which did not receive wide expression until the time of ecclesiastical reconstruction in the sixteenth century, and the periods of political revolution in the seventeenth and eighteenth centuries."[4] The result has been that the importance of Marsiglio's contribution is frequently overlooked, as Dr. Emerton indicates: "The teaching of Marsiglio entered so subtly but so completely into the doctrine of his successors in the work of national development . . . that it has been overshadowed by their greater fame."[5]

The *Defensor pacis* consists of three *Dictios,* or parts. Only the first, however, deals at length with the organization of the temporal state. As an Aristotelian, Marsiglio of Padua naturally based his conception of the state upon that of Aristotle. Indeed he specifically says that: "According to Aristotle (*Politics* I. 1. [or, *Politics* I. 2])[6] the state is *a perfect community, containing the elements of self-sufficiency . . . ; and thus, while it was created for the sake of life, it continues in existence for the sake of the good life.*"[7] The latter part of this definition is of importance for the thesis of the tractate. In the words of Marsiglio, it "points to the ultimate and perfect purpose" of the state.[8] They who "lead a civil life do not merely live, an activity in which [even] beasts and slaves participate; rather, they live aright —that is to say, with leisure for such noble works as those constituting the practical and theoretical essence of the virtues."[9]

A mere unorganized congregation of human beings is not what Marsiglio had in mind, for in such a group, he says, "contentions and quarrels spring up—which would result, if they were not regulated by the precepts of

---

[3] Emerton, *The Defensor Pacis of Marsiglio of Padua,* p. 10.   [4] Pages 245–46.   [5] *Op. cit.,* p. 1.
[6] It is difficult to check adequately the Aristotelian references given by Marsiglio, owing to the different systems of numbering used in various modern editions of the *Politics;* as well as to the fact that Marsiglio sometimes paraphrases (rather loosely) the trend of an entire passage, when he would seem to be quoting a specific statement. The bracketed numerals represent references supplied by Previté-Orton in his admirable edition of Marsiglio, and correspond to the numbering in Jowett's translation of the *Politics.*
[7] *Dictio* I, chap. iv. sec. 1 (p. 11). This and other passages from the *Defensor pacis* have been translated from Previté-Orton's edition, to which the page citations refer.
[8] *Ibid.* (pp. 11–12).   [9] *Ibid.,* sec. 3 (p. 12).

justice, in battles, in division among human beings, and finally, in a consequent decay of the state."[10] To guard against such strife and confusion, it was "necessary to establish in connection with this intercommunication, a rule of justice, and a guardian or administrator thereof." Furthermore, there was need for the division of the members of the community into various ranks or offices, each of which would aid in providing those things which are "indispensable to persons who live adequately."[11] In other words, the state of Marsiglio was a coöperative state, each member contributing to the "sufficiency" of the whole, which in turn insured the happiness of the individuals.

Now two questions immediately confronted Marsiglio: one, as to the law upon which his "rule of justice" depended; and the other, as to the source of authority in the state. To meet these problems he turned again to Aristotle for guidance, declaring that "we may say truthfully, and in accordance with the conclusion reached by Aristotle (*Politics* III. 6 [or, *Politics* III. 11]), that the 'legislator' (or in other words, the efficient cause of law, in the primary and strict sense) is the people, that is to say, the whole body of citizens, or else the preponderant part thereof."[12] The citizens might act, Marsiglio added, either "through elected representatives," or by means of "an express declaration of will"[13] if they had met as a whole in general assembly. Such action, as we have seen, should be taken only by a "preponderant part" of the people, and lest his reader be in doubt as to the meaning of that term, Marsiglio hastened to offer a word of explanation: "In using the expression 'preponderant part,' I take into consideration both the quantity and the quality of the persons involved, with respect to the community for which a given law is decreed."[14]

Realizing, however, that the citizens, or a "preponderant part" of them, would find difficulty in acting as a whole, he affirmed that they might delegate the duty of lawmaking "to a certain individual or group of individuals"; but he immediately declared that the persons to whom such delegations might be made were not themselves the fundamental legislative authority. They were agents, so to speak, acting under direction. In his own words, they "are not, and cannot be, the legislator in an absolute sense," for they "discharge the legislative function solely for a definite purpose and during a definite period, in accordance with the authority of the primary legislator."[15] In the process of lawmaking, Marsiglio insisted, "this same authority should be the source of additions, eliminations or total alterations,

[10] *Ibid.*, sec. 4 (p. 13). [11] *Ibid.*, secs. 4 and 5 (pp. 13, 14).
[12] *Dictio* I, chap. xii. sec. 3 (p. 49).
[13] *Ibid.* (p. 49). [14] *Ibid.* (p. 49). [15] *Ibid.* (p. 49).

as well as of interpretation and suspension."[16] In other words, Marsiglio seems to have felt that the people themselves should be the ultimate guardians of "the common welfare" and should have the final decision concerning any legislative changes which "the exigencies of time, place, or other circumstances"[17] appeared to require.

After defining "citizen" in the Aristotelian sense as one who "partakes, within the civil community, of either deliberative or judicial authority, in accordance with his station," he reverted to the fundamental tenet of his state: "that human authority to establish laws pertains solely to the whole body of citizens or the preponderant part thereof."[18] This, it may be remarked, he reiterated from time to time, as though it were almost an obsession with him.

But his insistence on this point is to be expected in the light of the political doctrine which he proclaimed:

Men have come together in the civil community for the sake of convenience and in order to live adequately, while avoiding the contrary conditions. Therefore, those matters which relate to the general advantage and disadvantage should be generally known and proclaimed, so that all persons may be enabled to attain that which is advantageous and to repel that which is disadvantageous.[19]

This is still a cardinal doctrine of democracy.

Now it has often been asked, and indeed is asked even to this day: Cannot laws be made better by one than by many? Marsiglio repudiated in advance the ancient and unfortunately still-honored contention which this question implies, employing for that purpose an argument which would not have disgraced the more radical of the schoolmen:

Either the authority to legislate pertains solely to the whole body of citizens, as we have maintained, or else it pertains to a single individual or to a comparatively small number of individuals. [But] it does not pertain exclusively to one individual, for the reasons already set forth . . . ; since such a legislator might enact a bad law, owing to ignorance or malice or both causes—acting, that is to say, with a greater regard for his own personal advantage than for the common advantage—with the result that the law would be tyrannical. Moreover, and for a similar reason, legislative authority does not pertain to a comparatively small number of persons; since they, like that single individual, might commit the fault of enacting a law directed to the advantage of certain (that is, a few) persons rather than to the common advantage; a fault which is seen to occur in oligarchies. Therefore, the aforesaid authority pertains to the whole body of citizens or to the preponderant part thereof.[20]

---

[16] Marsiglio *Defensor pacis*, trans. from Previté-Orton ed. (p. 50). [17] *Ibid.* (p. 50).
[18] *Ibid.*, sec. 4 (p. 50). [19] *Ibid.*, sec. 7 (p. 53). [20] *Ibid.*, sec. 8 (p. 53).

To those who are accustomed to think of the Middle Ages merely as a time of "old, unhappy, far-off things, and battles long ago," it may seem strange to find such "modern" ideas of government expressed more than six centuries before our day. Yet, though Marsiglio was undoubtedly a "radical," he was a man of his age and not, in the real sense of the term, an innovator. "He is not," says Dr. Carlyle, "as appears to be thought by some writers who are not very well acquainted with mediaeval political literature, setting out some new and revolutionary democratic doctrine, but is rather expressing, even if in rather drastic and unqualified terms, the normal judgment and practice of the Middle Ages: he represents not the beginning of some modern and revolutionary doctrine, but the assertion of traditional principles."[21] And the same author adds that Marsiglio "combines the principles of the actual practice of the Middle Ages with conceptions derived, on the one side, from Aristotle, and on the other, to some extent from the Civilians."[22] As for "the normal Mediaeval conception," which he describes as having been "only reinforced by the revived study of the Roman Jurisprudence," Dr. Carlyle declares that conception to have been

> that the community was the source of all political authority, which was indeed derived ultimately from God, but immediately from the community. The community was the source of law, and of the authority of the Ruler, Emperor or King; and it is also clear that, while the Prince was conceived of as having, subject to the law, a large discretion in the exercise of his authority, in fact the Mediaeval Prince normally acted with the counsel and advice of some body of councillors, the chief men of the Community, who were conceived of, however vaguely, as having some kind of representative character.[23]

Without attempting to enlarge upon so admirable a statement, we may cite as examples of representative institutions "in the making" during the Middle Ages, the Cortes of Spain, the States General of France and the Netherlands as well as the Estates of the provinces, the Parliament of England, and the Diet of the Empire.

Marsiglio's own views on the theory and practice of representative government are restated and elaborated in a later chapter of the *Defensor pacis*:

> It becomes necessary to designate . . . the effective cause that establishes and determines the remaining offices or parts of the state. We say, indeed, that this cause, in its primary form, is the legislator; but, that in its secondary form—which is, in a sense, instrumental, or administrative—it is the executive, acting through the legislator's authority as granted by the latter to the executive, and conforming to the pattern laid down for the said [executive] by that same

---

[21] *A History of Mediaeval Political Theory in the West* (previously cited), VI, 9.
[22] *Ibid.*
[23] *Ibid.*, pp. 206-7.

[legislator]; namely, [the pattern of] law, which should invariably be followed [by the executive] in transacting and regulating civil acts to the extent of the latter's ability. . . . For though the legislator, as the primary and proper cause, must determine what persons shall fittingly exercise what kind of functions within the state, nevertheless, the [actual] execution of the said provisions, like that of other legal precepts, is enjoined and (if necessary) restrained by the executive agent. For the execution of legal provisions is more conveniently carried out through the executive[24] than through the whole body of citizens, inasmuch as one individual executive, or a few such persons, suffice for this task, in which the whole community (troubled, moreover, with other and unavoidable labors) would be futilely engaged. Indeed, the community as a whole also performs the task in question when the aforesaid executive agents perform it, since they do so in accordance with the decision (incorporated, that is to say, in law) of the community. Furthermore, these few executives, or one such person, can more readily execute such legal precepts as have already been brought into existence.[25]

It is essential to note that when Marsiglio speaks of an "executive" he has in mind a ruler chosen by election. As to the particular method of selecting or appointing the ruler, he is indifferent, so long as power remains in the people.

The manner of agreeing upon the aforesaid establishment, or election [he says] may perhaps vary with a variety of countries. Nevertheless, whatever these variations may be, the following requirement must be observed in every case, namely, that this election, or establishment, shall always be brought about by the authority of the legislator, that legislator being (as we have repeatedly observed) the whole body of citizens or the preponderant part thereof.[26]

And as we have already seen, Marsiglio's chief executive derives his power, and the very form in which that power is to be exercised, from the legislative power as exercised by the people themselves.

It is thus obvious that the lawmaking body—which is either all or the majority of the people, acting directly or through representatives—is the supreme authority in Marsiglio's state. But he goes even further by declaring in no uncertain terms that the citizens as a whole in their lawmaking capacity have not only "the efficient power to establish, or elect, the executive agent," but also that theirs is the proper function and indeed the right to impose "any diminution of the executive power," and even "deposition therefrom" in the event that "such a step should be expedient for the common welfare."[27] According to Marsiglio the people have power not only

---

[24] *Ipsum;* one would expect *ipsam,* referring grammatically to *pars principans,* but the context leaves little room for doubt as to the logical antecedent, and the Latin of Marsiglio is not Ciceronian.

[25] Marsiglio *Defensor pacis, Dictio* I, chap. xv. sec. 4, trans. from Previté-Orton ed., (pp. 68–69).

[26] *Ibid.,* sec. 2 (p. 67). [27] *Ibid.* (p. 67).

to make but also to unmake their governments. This is the doctrine, as stated in the language of our Declaration of Independence, of government by the "consent of the governed"; and it is also the doctrine, to continue with the Declaration, that "whenever any Form of Government becomes destructive of these ends, it is the Right of the People to alter or to abolish it, and to institute new Government, laying its foundation on such principles and organizing its powers in such form, as to them shall seem most likely to effect their Safety and Happiness."

The consequences of the principles thus advocated by Marsiglio are admirably and succinctly set forth by Dr. Reginald Poole:

Once establish the principle, and the consequences are easy to draw. The king's power is limited in every possible direction. He has the eye of the people or of its delegates on all his actions. He may be restrained or even deposed if he overpass his prescribed bounds; and even though his conduct be not amenable to the letter of the law, he is still subject to the final judgment of the national will. On no side is there any room for despotism; in no point is he absolute.[28]

This is not the place to deal with the religious aspect of Marsiglio's writings, but on their political importance to posterity several additional comments by Dr. Poole must be noted. Speaking in more general terms, he expresses the opinion[29] that the *Defensor pacis* comprises "the whole essence of the political and religious theory which separates modern times from the middle ages." And he adds that "the significance of the later political revolution, even now far from universally realized, lay in the recognition of the people as the source of government, as the sovereign power in the state," which doctrines, Dr. Poole observes, Marsiglio thought out, defined, and stated so clearly that "the modern constitutional statesman . . . has only to develop them and fill in their outline."

"Marsiglio," Dr. Poole concludes, "may be stigmatised as a *doctrinaire,* but he belongs to that rarest class of *doctrinaires* whom future ages may rightly look back upon as prophets."

[28] *Illustrations of the History of Medieval Thought and Learning* (previously cited), p. 235.
[29] *Ibid.,* p. 240.

Chapter XIX

NICCOLÒ MACHIAVELLI (1469–1527)

The Prince

FEW PERSONS WHO FOLLOW THE GRADUAL EVOLUTION OF LEGAL AND POLITICAL ideals through the centuries can escape the conviction that jurisprudence and political science, unlike the exact sciences of the physical world, are permeated with moral conceptions. Justice, equity, right, liberty—these, the very lifeblood of law and government, are ethical concepts. Without them, jurisprudence and political science would be cold and static. There is no need to labor the point, for the pages of history contain ample evidence of the fact that, from the days of Plato onward, legal and political theory has been characterized by life and growth—growth which, viewed in long perspective, has followed a comparatively straight line and has kept pace with the development of man's moral nature.

Yet history also records certain aberrations which have at one time or another threatened to impede this symmetrical growth, and among these is *The Prince* of Machiavelli. For however much in accord with certain usages of his day *The Prince* may have been, and however ably written, it is not in harmony with the normal development of law and political institutions. In the second volume of the present work, therefore, extracts from Machiavelli's *Prince* have not been included.[1] But since his book has unhappily exerted considerable influence on political theory and practice, it must be dealt with here at some length.[2]

Machiavelli's opinions on political matters have been so admirably expressed in *The Prince* as to be literature, and are so clear that he who runs may read. But the character depicted in the book is one whom few enlightened authors today would care to claim as their creation. We have selected this small volume because it is Machiavelli's outstanding contribution to what he would call political science, a contribution which unhappily has done more harm than good because it completely ignores moral values.

---

[1] Extracts from Bodin's *Six Books of the Republic* have also been omitted for reasons of a somewhat similar nature, which reasons will be set forth in a subsequent chapter (chap. xxiii).

[2] For a recent detailed discussion and analysis of *The Prince*, published since this chapter was written, see Gilbert, *Machiavelli's Prince and Its Forerunners*.

Written with great care and circulated in manuscript, *The Prince* was not published until 1532, some four years after its author's death, and curiously enough in the same year in which the "Reading" *On the Indians Recently Discovered* is believed to have been prepared by Francisco de Vitoria, whose ideal in princes was a person of a very different moral and spiritual make-up from the Prince of Machiavelli. Whether Machiavelli planned that *The Prince* should eventually be published or not is a question for scholars to determine. It may be that he intended the world to judge his political ideals only by the treatises which were printed during his lifetime, particularly his *Discourses on the Ten Books of Livy,* in which he set forth his views in more general and more philosophical terms, basing them particularly upon an analysis of those historical precedents which seemed to him of value.

Concerning Machiavelli's views on history, it must suffice here to say that to him history was of interest chiefly because it supplied innumerable instances which he felt that the princes and politicians of his time might advantageously imitate. It is a familiar saying, with the force of a maxim, that a man is known by the company he keeps—company not merely in the restricted sense of those with whom he has friendly intercourse but including the historical personages whom he takes for his guides; and Machiavelli must be judged by his companions, both the quick and the dead. Apparently he did not consider man as a developing creature, slowly but on the whole steadily outgrowing the errors and limitations of his past. "He had," as a recent writer observes, "no faintest conception of the doctrine of evolution; he did not see history as the story of a progressive development."[3] Moreover, it is unfortunate for the world that Machavelli seems to have been interested chiefly in the material profit to be obtained from an imitation of the past. The great moral lessons of history were wholly lost upon him. What he gleaned from the pages of the past as he read them in the light of his own experience and keen but cynical observation, was the harsh doctrine that might makes right; that justice and morality should give way to political expediency; that the strong and unscrupulous man is a law unto himself, unchecked by any higher law; that human beings are in the main foolish pawns in the political game; and that they exist for the state, not the state for human beings, who are possessed of reason and conscience and dignity.

Whether or not Machiavelli's real views are contained—as is frequently insisted—in his *Discourses on Livy,* or whether they are in *The Prince,* or

[3] Muir, *Machiavelli and His Times*, p. 137.

partly in one and partly in the other, the fact remains that it is *The Prince* which has attracted the most attention. It is *The Prince* which people generally think of when Machiavelli's name is mentioned; and it is *The Prince* whose principles have unfortunately entered into the practice of subsequent princes and have been all too often accepted as the guide and the justification of the unscrupulous, with whom success is the sole standard in matters political.

It may be that he did not at the time of writing intend *The Prince* for public consumption and for universal application. But if that be so and it was not the intention of Machiavelli to publish *The Prince* as he had written it, is there not all the greater reason to believe that he was sincere in the expression of views which he hesitated to present to the world at large? It seems but fair to assume that they represented the deeper, inner workings of his mind. And whether or not Machiavelli intended to publish *The Prince,* the important facts are that it was published; that the political maxims advocated by Machiavelli and subsequently foisted upon the world are the basis of Machiavellianism; that they are the very antithesis of the ideals of government which human beings have been painfully and slowly evolving throughout the centuries; and that these "maxims" of Machiavelli have been accepted by many who pride themselves upon what they call their "political realism" but which might more fittingly be termed "political materialism." It will still remain true, when the last word that can be said for *The Prince* has been spoken, that Machiavelli's tractate is a far cry indeed from the moral philosophy of the ancient world and from the Christian ethics expounded by the great theologians of the Middle Ages; that it stands not for progress but for retrogression in the evolution of human government; and that, in a word, it has been not a help but a hindrance to the growth of an enlightened political philosophy.[4]

[4] For a brief but highly stimulating discussion of Machiavelli's views and their influence, see Gooch, "Politics and Morals," in *Day to Day Pamphlets*. Two passages from the lecture are quoted here:

"The enduring vitality of *The Prince* cannot be airily dismissed as a regrettable token of human depravity. Its teaching has been watered down in the course of the centuries, but a sediment of the Florentine gospel is left in numberless thinkers of the last four centuries who bear a better name. In Acton's learned Introduction to Burd's edition of *The Prince,* and in Meinecke's massive treatise *Die Idee der Staatsräson,* we are confronted with a serried array of authorities, some of them of high repute, who, while rejecting the grosser features of the system, argue that public and private morals are not and can never be quite the same; that supreme emergencies call for exceptional methods; that Machiavelli is useful as medicine, though indigestible if consumed as our daily bread. We recall Cavour's revealing cry of distress while he was putting Italy on the map: 'What rascals we should be if we did for ourselves what we do for our country!' However lofty our political ideals, however firm our moral principles, we cannot shirk the rude challenge of *The Prince*. Can rulers, must rulers, invariably attempt to apply the moral law, as the private citizen in civilized communi-

That Machiavelli had a personal motive in composing *The Prince* is shown by the dedicatory Preface, which is a direct appeal to Lorenzo the Magnificent, of Florence. It is indeed a model of the way in which a humble but ambitious suitor would approach a political superior from whom he hoped for place and preferment. As the question of motive is a delicate one and intimately concerns Machiavelli, it is advisable to quote a few continuous passages from the Preface:

> I have found among my possessions none that I so much prize and esteem as a knowledge of the actions of great men, acquired in the course of a long experience of modern affairs and a continual study of antiquity. Which knowledge most carefully and patiently pondered over and sifted by me, and now reduced into this little book, I send to your Magnificence. And though I deem the work unworthy of your greatness, yet am I bold enough to hope that your courtesy will dispose you to accept it, considering that I can offer you no better gift than the means of mastering in a very brief time, all that in the course of so many years, and at the cost of so many hardships and dangers, I have learned, and know.
>
> This work I have not adorned or amplified with rounded periods, swelling and high-flown language, or any other of those extrinsic attractions and allurements wherewith many authors are wont to set off and grace their writings; since it is my desire that it should either pass wholly unhonoured, or that the truth of its matter and the importance of its subject should alone recommend it.

---

ties is rightly expected to do? Or is the art of government, to borrow a phrase of Nietzsche, beyond good and evil?"—*Ibid.*, pp. 13–14.

"The differences in the systems of political philosophy throughout the ages reflect still deeper divergences in our interpretation of man. If we believe, like Machiavelli and Hobbes, that he is nearer to the beasts than to the angels, we shall lean to the doctrines of autocracy and the sovereign state. It is equally natural that those who take a more favourable view should contest the universal supremacy of force, and should preach the gospel of partnership and co-operation on every plane. 'Man,' declared Humboldt, 'is naturally more disposed to beneficent than to selfish actions.' Everyone knows Kant's famous confession of his ever-increasing wonder at the starry heavens above and the moral law within. The conviction that society rests on moral and spiritual foundations was shared by Burke, the greatest of English political thinkers, who described the state as a partnership in all art, in all science, in all perfection. And Mill based the most moving plea for individual liberty ever written on his lofty reading of the character and potentialities of man. Democracy is far more than a type of government, and what is called pacifism is more than a mere theory of international relations. They are both the expression of faith in the ultimate sanity of the common man, in his power to learn from experience, in his capacity for spiritual growth.

"I share this faith. Despite the number and the eminence of his disciples, I believe that Machiavelli is radically unfair to mankind. The professed realist only saw a limited portion of the vast field of reality. The will to power is not the sole key to human nature. History is assuredly a record of strife—the strife of arms and wits; but it is also, as Kropotkin reminded us in an illuminating work, a story of mutual aid. Noble aims in plenty have been formed by men and nations, and many of them have been wholly or partially achieved. With a longer and a wider experience than Machiavelli, we have learned to recognize the solid core of truth in the old adage that honesty is the best policy. The application of the maxims of *The Prince* may achieve a temporary triumph, but they provide no foundation for the enduring happiness, prosperity or security of a state."—*Ibid.*, pp. 18–19.

Nor would I have it thought presumption that a person of mean and humble station should venture to discourse and lay down rules concerning the government of Princes. For as those who make maps of countries place themselves low down in the plains to study the character of mountains and elevated lands, and high up on the mountains to get a better view of the plains, so in like manner to understand the People a man should be a Prince, and to have a clear notion of Princes he should be of the People.

Let your Magnificence, then, accept this little gift in the spirit in which I offer it; wherein, if you diligently read and study it, you will recognize my extreme desire that you should attain to that eminence which Fortune and your own merits promise you. Should you from the height of your greatness some time turn your eyes to these humbler regions, you will know how undeservedly I have to endure the keen and unremitting malignity of Fortune.[5]

Machiavelli's personal motive is thus set forth in language which seems singularly revealing of his personality. But it has been intimated by more than one among those of Machiavelli's commentators, who regard him both as a much-maligned founder of political science and as a model of statecraft, that he had a definite purpose in writing *The Prince* and that therefore it is unjust to judge him as though he had written this tractate for general application. Now it must be admitted that, apart from his hope of personal gain, Machiavelli had a specific purpose in writing *The Prince*. He saw about him an Italy which, besides being subjected to foreign domination, was divided into many factions, each one in a state of hostility toward—or at best in short-lived alliance with—other factions. The quarrel of the papacy and the Holy Roman Empire, the firmly rooted tradition of republicanism in the numerous city-states, the wars of foreign kings (seeking to establish themselves in this or that section of Italy)—all of these factors had brought about in Italy a state of apparently hopeless disunion, amounting to anarchy. The temporal ambitions of Alexander VI, then the unworthy occupant of the papal throne, led to further conflicts at the beginning of the sixteenth century. To the eyes of Machiavelli, Italy seemed, as he himself stated, "more enslaved than the Hebrews, more servile than the Persians, more dispersed than the Athenians, without a head, without order, beaten, despoiled, ravaged, over-run, and enduring every kind of ruin."[6]

Machiavelli, addressing himself direcly to his "magnificent" reader in Florence and referring to the task which he wished Lorenzo to undertake, first assures him that "where the disposition is strong the difficulty cannot

---

[5] Niccolò Machiavelli, *The Prince*. Trans. from the Italian by Thomson, p. vii.

[6] Lodge, "Machiavelli's *Il principe*," in *Transactions of the Royal Historical Society*, Fourth Series, XIII, 7.

be great, provided you follow the methods observed by those whom I have set before you as models,"[7] and he then adds:

This opportunity, then, for Italy at last to look on her deliverer, ought not to be allowed to pass away. With what love he would be received in all those Provinces which have suffered from the foreign inundation, with what thirst for vengeance, with what fixed fidelity, with what devotion, and what tears, no words of mine can declare. What gates would be closed against him? What people would refuse him obedience? What jealousy would stand in his way? What Italian but would yield him homage? This barbarian tyranny stinks in all nostrils.

Decribing the condition of Italy in still more graphic terms, Machiavelli says[8]: "Our country, left almost without life, still waits to know who it is that is to heal her bruises, to put an end to the devastation and plunder of Lombardy, to the exactions and imposts of Naples and Tuscany, and to stanch those wounds of hers which long neglect has changed into running sores."

To Machiavelli, thus surveying a helpless Italy in the light of his own political and diplomatic experience (for he had had great experience, both as diplomatic agent and as head of the foreign department of his own city-state), there may well have come a dream of a united Italy. Now this same dream of union has inspired men in many lands. It is a patriotic dream and one on which posterity has again and again set the seal of its approval. But the dream may be one thing, the plan for its realization quite another. Especially is this true in the case of Machiavelli. Posterity has not condemned his ideal of union, but it does condemn the plan which he evolved in his *Prince* for making that ideal a reality. There is no doubt that he wrote his tractate for a special purpose: that for this purpose he had a special Prince in view—and that he had in mind a special servant of the Prince to carry the purpose into effect. But the fairness of the dream was sullied and obscured by the unworthiness of the means by which it was to be realized. And unfortunately those who have read *The Prince* have too often ignored its special purpose and remembered only the methods which it advocates. The result is, as stated by Sir Richard Lodge[9]—on no less an authority than that of Leopold von Ranke, the father of the modern school of history—"that the commentators have misrepresented Machiavelli by taking as general maxims for all princes and all time what he wrote as

---

[7] *The Prince*, trans. by Thomson, pp. 193, 197.
[8] *Ibid.*, pp. 191–92.   [9] *Ibid.*, p. 3.

advice to a particular prince in peculiar and special circumstances and for his guidance to a definite objective."[10]

But in assessing Machiavelli's contribution to the development of political thought, is this question of misrepresentation by commentators a material one? Are we not more concerned with the simple facts that Machiavelli did write *The Prince;* that he left the manuscript undestroyed at his death, and that it was given to the world in 1532, to exert for centuries an immoral and malign influence?

It may perhaps be contended that Machiavelli's views do no more than reflect many of the political practices of his day. Indeed there is ground for such an opinion when we recall that deceit, treachery, cruelty, the use of poison, and similar practices were then all too prevalent in European courts. But that is in reality no justification of Machiavelli or his teaching. It would seem to signify simply that the author of *The Prince* was afflicted with a sort of moral paralysis which, while it did not prevent him from making the fundamental moral distinction between right and wrong, did prevent him from acting upon that distinction; and in the centuries following he was destined to appeal only to those who were similarly afflicted.[11] Machiavelli acknowledged, in *The Prince,* no moral standard, no universal law, no fundamental conception of right and justice inherent in human nature and applying equally to all human beings. Rather, he translated many a dubious practice of the past and of his own day into political theories and rendered them the more plausible by setting them forth in one of the world's literary masterpieces, *The Prince*.

Among those whom he held up as a model in matters political was Cesare Borgia, "vulgarly spoken of," as Machiavelli says, "as Duke Valentino," who "obtained his Princedom through the favourable fortunes of his father"—Alexander VI, then pope (Cesare Borgia himself being a cardinal)—"and with these lost it, although, so far as in him lay, he used every effort and practised every expedient that a prudent and able man should, who desires to strike root in a State given him by the arms and fortune of another."[12] Machiavelli's comment on this model is interesting:

I know not what lessons I could teach a new Prince more useful than the example of his actions. And if the measures taken by him did not profit him in

---

[10] Ranke's excursus on Machiavelli was appended to his *Zur Kritik neuerer Geschichtschreiber,* pp. 151–74.

[11] "While plain men were shocked by the repudiation not only of Christian ethics but of the ordinary maxims of honourable dealing, the great ones of the earth took the wicked little book to their hearts. It spoke a language they could understand. Here was a breviary for rulers, full of shrewd hints and warnings, compiled by the keenest political brain of the age."—Gooch, *op. cit.,* p. 10.

[12] *The Prince* (previously cited), p. 41.

the end, it was through no fault of his, but from the extraordinary and extreme malignity of Fortune.[13]

After speaking of the father's activity in behalf of his son and the son's unscrupulous maneuvers in his own behalf, Machiavelli attributes to the latter the knowledge that the stern rule of his minister, one Messer Remiro d'Orco, "had generated ill-feeling against himself." Therefore,

> in order to purge the minds of the people and gain their entire good-will, he [Borgia] sought to show them that any cruelty which had been done had not originated with him, but in the harsh disposition of his minister. Availing himself of the pretext this afforded, he one morning caused Remiro to be beheaded and exposed in the market place of Cesena with a block and bloody axe by his side—a savage spectacle which at once astounded and satisfied the populace.[14]

Now what did this model prince do to safeguard his future? He proposed to protect himself,

> First, by exterminating all who were of kin to those Lords whom he had despoiled of their possessions, thereby leaving the new Pope no occasion for interference. Second, by gaining over all the Romans of good birth, so as to be able, as has been said, with their aid, to hold the Pope in check. Third, by bringing the College of Cardinals, so far as possible, under his control. And fourth, by establishing his authority so firmly before his father's death, that he could by himself withstand the shock of a first onset.[15]

Machiavelli then indicates how nearly successful this plan was:

> Of these four objects, at the time when Alexander died,[16] he had already effected three, and had almost carried out the fourth. For of the Lords whose possessions he had usurped, he had put to death all whom he could reach, and very few had escaped. He had gained over the Roman nobility, and had the majority in the College of Cardinals on his side.

Machiavelli's observation on the measures which Cesare Borgia had used and his explanation of their failure should not be omitted:[17]

> And yet such were the fire and courage of the Duke, he knew so well how men must either be conciliated or crushed, and so solid were the foundations he had laid in that brief period, that had these armies [of his enemies] not been upon his back, or had he been in sound health, he must have surmounted every difficulty.
>
> How strong his foundations were may be seen from this, that Romagna waited for him for more than a month. . . . Moreover, since he was able if not to make whom he would Pope, at least to prevent the election of any whom he disliked, had he been in health at the time when Alexander died, all would have been easy for him. But he told me himself at the time when Julius II was created,

---

[13] *Ibid.*, p. 42. [14] *Ibid.*, p. 47. [15] *Ibid.*, p. 49.
[16] Aug. 18, 1503. [17] *The Prince* (previously cited), pp. 51–52.

that he had foreseen and provided for all else that could happen on his father's death, but had never anticipated that when his father died he too should be at death's door.

What now is the conclusion which Machiavelli draws from this example?

Taking all these actions of the Duke together, I can find no fault with him; nay, it seems to me reasonable to put him forward, as I have done, as a pattern for all such as rise to power by good fortune and the help of others. For with his great spirit and high ambition he could not act otherwise than he did, and nothing but the shortness of his father's life and his own illness prevented the success of his designs. Whoever, therefore, on entering a new Princedom, judges it necessary to rid himself of enemies, to conciliate friends, to prevail by force or fraud, to make himself feared yet loved by his subjects, followed and revered by his soldiers, to crush those who can or ought to injure him, to introduce changes in the old order of things, to be at once severe and affable, magnanimous and liberal, to do away with a mutinous army and create a new one, to maintain relations with Kings and Princes on such a footing that they must see it for their interest to aid him, and dangerous to offend, can find no brighter examples than in the actions of this Prince.[18]

Turning now to another and more historical example, that of Agathocles of Sicily, an unworthy man with more than unworthy ambition, Machiavelli asks how he came to survive in spite of his "numberless acts of treachery and cruelty." The answer which he himself supplies is:[19] "I believe that this results from cruelty being well or ill employed." After enlarging upon this theory, as applied by Agathocles, Machiavelli draws a "lesson" from his historical example:[20] "Hence we may learn the lesson that on seizing a State, the usurper should bethink him of all the injuries he must inflict, and inflict them all at a stroke, that he may not have to renew them daily, but be enabled by their discontinuance to reassure men's minds, and win them by benefits."

Subsequent chapters of the book deal with the particular qualities which the Prince should possess. Among these Machiavelli discusses the qualities "of Cruelty and Clemency," posing the question "whether it is better to be Loved or Feared."[21] His answer is:[22] "Since love and fear can hardly exist together, if we must choose between them, it is far safer to be feared than loved." In seeking to justify this doctrine, Machiavelli gives us his conception of humankind:

For of men it may generally be affirmed that they are thankless, fickle, false, studious to avoid danger, greedy of gain, devoted to you while you confer benefits upon them, and ready, as I said before, while the need is remote, to shed

---

[18] *The Prince*, trans. by Thomson, pp. 52–53. [19] *Ibid.*, p. 62. [20] *Ibid.*, p. 63.
[21] *Ibid.*, p. 118. [22] *Ibid.*, p. 120.

their blood, and sacrifice their property, their lives, and their children for you; but when it comes near they turn against you. The Prince, therefore, who without otherwise securing himself builds wholly on their professions is undone.

Nevertheless, in his next sentence he reveals his awareness of human virtues: "For the friendships we buy with a price, and do not gain by greatness and nobility of character, though fairly earned are not made good, but fail us when we need them most."

But for the purpose in hand Machiavelli chose to brush aside the virtues of mankind:

Moreover, men are less careful how they offend him who makes himself loved than him who makes himself feared. For love is held by the tie of obligation, which, because men are a sorry breed, is broken on every prompting of self-interest; but fear is bound by the apprehension of punishment which never loosens its grasp.

Machiavelli was indeed lacking in faith in human nature, for on a later page he adds:[23] "men will always grow rogues on your hands unless they find themselves under a necessity to be honest."

It is perhaps not to be wondered at that, viewing human beings in such a light, Machiavelli favored a tyrannical and unscrupulous government to hold them in check.

To the subject of keeping faith Machiavelli devotes a chapter, in the course of which he shows that for him success was more important than good faith and was, indeed, his sole standard of political policy. Admitting the general view to be that princes should keep faith, Machiavelli immediately adds:[24] "Nevertheless, we see from what has happened in our own days that Princes who have set little store by their word, but have known how to over-reach others by their cunning, have accomplished great things, and in the end had the better of those who trusted to honest dealing."

Machiavelli next refers to the conception that "there are two ways of contending, one in accordance with the laws, the other by force; the first of which is proper to men, the second to beasts." This again was the accepted view, but it was not acceptable to Machiavelli, who says: "But since the first method is often ineffectual, it becomes necessary to resort to the second." Proceeding to develop this theory, he declares:

A Prince should, therefore, understand how to use well both the man and the beast. And this lesson has been covertly taught by the ancient writers, who relate how Achilles and many others of these old Princes were given over to be brought up and trained by Chiron the Centaur; since the only meaning of their

[23] *Ibid.*, pp. 177–78.   [24] *Ibid.*, p. 125.

having for teacher one who was half man and half beast is, that it is necessary for a Prince to know how to use both natures, and that the one without the other has no stability.[25]

The conclusion from this interpretation of Greek mythology would seem to be that if the rule of a prince is to endure, he must be half brute and only half man. Machiavelli immediately gives the prototype of the creature he has in mind:

But since a Prince should know how to use the beast's nature wisely, he ought of beasts to choose both the lion and the fox; for the lion cannot guard himself from the toils, nor the fox from wolves. He must therefore be a fox to discern toils, and a lion to drive off wolves.

But he adds that "to rely wholly on the lion is unwise," meaning thereby that brute force is not enough, there must also be cunning. Therefore, adopting the cunning of the fox, "a prudent Prince neither can nor ought to keep his word when to keep it is hurtful to him and the causes which led him to pledge it are removed," it being apparently for the prince to decide on this moot point. Machiavelli's justification for the views which he had expressed is:[26]

If all men were good, this would not be good advice, but since they are dishonest and do not keep faith with you, you, in return, need not keep faith with them; and no Prince was ever at a loss for plausible reasons to cloak a breach of faith. Of this numberless recent instances could be given, and it might be shown how many solemn treaties and engagements have been rendered inoperative and idle through want of faith in Princes, and that he who has best known to play the fox has had the best success.

For Machiavelli, the example of violation proved merely the failure of the rule of good faith. Today the example of the violation should and does arouse protest, not because the rule has failed but because it has been ignored.

In addition to his favorite model, Cesare Borgia, Machiavelli furnishes a model who had actually succeeded in the employment of the methods prescribed in *The Prince*. It was necessary, he began by way of introduction, "to be skilful in feigning and dissembling. But men are so simple, and governed so absolutely by their present needs, that he who wishes to deceive will never fail in finding willing dupes." In this procedure the model he had in mind had been most successful:

One recent example I will not omit. Pope Alexander VI had no care or thought but how to deceive, and always found material to work on. No man ever had

---

[25] *The Prince*, trans. by Thomson, p. 126.   [26] *Ibid.*, pp. 126–27.

a more effective manner of asseverating, or made promises with more solemn protestations, or observed them less. And yet, because he understood this side of human nature, his frauds always succeeded.[27]

Machiavelli was aware that there were good qualities which the prince might possess, and indeed he mentioned them specifically, though largely for the purpose, it would seem, of indicating when they should not be brought into play. Indeed, for his purpose it was immaterial whether or not the prince, bent on success, actually possessed these good qualities or only simulated them upon occasion.

It is not essential, then, that a Prince should have all the good qualities I have enumerated above, but it is most essential that he should seem to have them. Nay, I will venture to affirm that if he has and invariably practises them all, they are hurtful, whereas the appearance of having them is useful. Thus, it is well to seem merciful, faithful, humane, religious, and upright, and also to be so; but the mind should remain so balanced that were it needful not to be so, you should be able and know how to change to the contrary.[28]

Moreover, Machiavelli insisted that the prince was above ordinary rules:

And you are to understand that a Prince, and most of all a new Prince, cannot observe all those rules of conduct in respect whereof men are accounted good, being often forced, in order to preserve his Princedom, to act in opposition to good faith, charity, humanity, and religion. He must therefore keep his mind ready to shift as the winds and tides of Fortune turn, and, as I have already said, ought not to quit good courses if he can help it, but should know how to follow evil if he must.[29]

In other words, the outward qualities which the Prince was to seem to possess were apparently not unlike the characterizations of an actor, to be put on and cast off as, in his opinion, the requirements of the moment might suggest. As a perfect example of skill in this phase of princely con-

---

[27] *Ibid.*, pp. 127–28.   [28] *Ibid.*, p. 128.
[29] *Ibid.* By way of comment on the "princely" qualities described by Machiavelli, a passage is here quoted from Dr. Gooch's lecture (*op. cit.*, pp. 9–10). "The supreme qualification for the ruler in the eyes of Machiavelli and his disciples is *virtù*, which means not virtue but virility, energy, force of character, remorseless vigour, the head to plan and the arm to strike. The paramount duty of the representative and guardian of the community is to survive and succeed. For this purpose he must circumvent and intimidate his enemies at home and abroad. Half-measures, hesitation, weakness of will and purpose, are the supreme offence. . . . Machiavelli is primarily interested, not in the forms of government, but in the way it is carried on. Governance is a problem of strength and skill, not of ethics and law. A régime must be judged, not by intentions, but by the fruits of its policy. Of such notions as the Respublica Christiana, the unity of civilization, allegiance to humanity, joint responsibility for the welfare of the world, there is not a trace. Virtù, Fortuna, Necessità: here was the new trinity which Machiavelli substituted for the Christian creeds. Each political unit, large or small, must think solely of itself. Thus the morals of the jungle are exalted into a philosophy of life."

duct, Machiavelli refers to a "certain Prince" of his day, "whom it is as well not to name"[30] and who was "always preaching peace and good faith, although the mortal enemy of both; and both," in the opinion of Machiavelli[31] "had he practised as he preaches, would, oftener than once, have lost him his kingdom and authority."

Turning again to the ancient world, Machiavelli refers to Severus of Rome, who cherished imperial ambitions. Having first persuaded the army under his command to march on Rome for the alleged purpose of avenging the death of Pertinax, who had been put to death by the Praetorian guards, Severus was able, without revealing his real purpose, to rush his troops to Italy "before it was known that he had set out."[32] Thus the first part of his deception succeeded. "On his arrival in Rome," Machiavelli continues, "the Senate, through fear, elected him Emperor and put Julianus to death." But how was he to retain the empire of which he was for the moment master? Two obstacles still remained to his complete and final success, "one in Asia, where Niger who commanded the armies of the East had caused himself to be proclaimed Emperor; the other in the West, where Albinus, who also aspired to the Empire, was in command." Deciding that valor should be accompanied by discretion, Severus "resolved to proceed against Niger by arms, against Albinus by artifice." Informing the latter that he desired to share the empire with him, he "sent him the title of Caesar," together with an offer of joint emperorship, which "Albinus accepted as made in good faith." Thereupon Severus, having defeated and slain Niger, "and restored tranquillity in the East," returned to Rome and trumped up charges against Albinus as an excuse for proceeding against him in Gaul, "where he at once deprived him of his dignities and his life."

Machiavelli thus comments on the propriety of Severus' conduct:

Whosoever, therefore, shall examine carefully the actions of this Emperor, will find in him all the fierceness of the lion and all the craft of the fox, and will note how he was feared and respected by the people, yet not hated by the army, and will not be surprised that though a new man, he was able to maintain his hold of so great an Empire. For the splendour of his reputation always shielded him from the odium which the people might otherwise have conceived against him by reason of his cruelty and rapacity.

There should, however, be a certain discretion displayed in the imitation of the past; and indeed Machiavelli expressly says that "a Prince new to

---

[30] Identified as Ferdinand of Aragon. See *Il Principe by Niccolò Machiavelli*, ed. by L. Arthur Burd, p. 307. As we shall see, Ferdinand is soon to be mentioned by name, but in this particular passage it would have been impossible, as Mr. Burd points out, to have referred to him openly without giving offense.

[31] *The Prince* (previously cited), p. 130.   [32] *Ibid.*, p. 144.

the Princedom" need not necessarily imitate all the examples of Severus. He should nevertheless "borrow from Severus those parts of his conduct which are needed to serve as a foundation for his government," and, referring to another example, Machiavelli adds,[33] "and from Marcus those suited to maintain it and render it glorious when once established." The Marcus to whom Machiavelli refers was none other than Marcus Aurelius, of whom he had previously admitted[34] that "being endowed with many virtues which made him revered, he kept, while he lived, both factions within bounds, and was never either hated or despised"—in which respect, Machiavelli would have us believe, he was unique among Roman rulers, all other just and humane emperors having suffered "an unhappy end."

Machiavelli had already referred (but without mentioning his name)[35] to Ferdinand, the husband of the famed Isabella and, when *The Prince* was being written, king of Spain. Now referring openly to him, Machiavelli says that he "may almost be accounted a new Prince, since from a weak King he has become, for fame and glory, the foremost in Christendom."[36] Concerning his achievements, Machiavelli tells his reader that "you will find them all great, and some extraordinary."[37] Inasmuch as the career of Ferdinand is well known, it will suffice here to give, in a final quotation from *The Prince,* Machiavelli's summary of his Spanish model's career:

To enable him to engage in still greater undertakings, always covering himself with the cloak of religion, he had recourse to what may be called *pious cruelty,* in driving out and clearing his Kingdom of the Moors; than which exploit none could be more wonderful or uncommon. Under the same cloak he made war on Africa, invaded Italy, and finally attacked France; and being thus constantly busied in planning and executing vast designs, he held the minds of his subjects in suspense and admiration, and occupied with the results of his actions, which arose one out of another in such close sequence as left neither time nor opportunity to oppose them.

Machiavelli was a man of genius, but unfortunately his was a misdirected genius, and its literary results have survived to the detriment of our common humanity. To counteract his influence, therefore, genius must be matched against genius in the hope that the genius with a moral concept of life will prevail. The genius whose authority is here invoked is that of John Morley, a master of English literature, as Machiavelli was of Italian letters, and deeply versed in state affairs as was Machiavelli. But the voice to which the Englishman listened was not the voice of worldly success

[33] *Ibid.,* p. 152.
[34] *Ibid.,* p. 141.
[35] See p. 290.
[36] *The Prince,* p. 163.
[37] *Ibid.,* p. 164.

which lured the Italian; it was the small voice of conscience, whose warnings are so often drowned by the clamor of ambitions and desires. It was that voice he heeded when confronted by a conflict of the gravest duties of state in the opening days of August, 1914. In those trying days, when the statesmen of the world were being weighed in the balance, he resigned his post in the British ministry that he might not be a party to the declaration of war to which the British government was committing itself, but to which he was unalterably opposed.

Now it happens that John Morley (who accepted a peerage only that he might avoid the bustling of the House of Commons and direct his wisdom in the quiet and reflective atmosphere of the House of Lords) chose Machiavelli as the subject for the Romanes Lecture which he delivered at Oxford in the Sheldonian Theatre, June 2, 1897.[38] On this occasion he viewed the various phases of Machiavelli's career, enumerating him among the half dozen of the world's great geniuses.

However, material greatness was not the standard with my Lord Morley. His was a moral, a spiritual standard. Sitting, as it were, as a judge in the court of conscience and doing justice to Machiavelli the man, and to his literary qualifications, he dispassionately examined and appraised the Italian's contributions to political philosophy as only one could do who, before sitting as a judge in a court, had himself had large experience in political life, but whose conscience was unsullied by its temptations:

If one were to try to put the case for the Machiavellian philosophy in a modern way, it would, I suppose, be something of this kind:—Nature does not work by moral rules. Nature, "red in tooth and claw," does by system all that good men by system avoid. Is not the whole universe of sentient being haunted all day and all night long by the haggard shapes of Hunger, Cruelty, Force, Fear? War again is not conducted by moral rules. To declare war is to suspend not merely *habeas corpus* but the Ten Commandments, and some other good commandments besides. A military manual, by an illustrious hand of our own day, warns us: "As a nation we are brought up to feel it a disgrace even to succeed by falsehood. We keep hammering along with the conviction that honesty is the best policy, and that truth always wins in the long-run. These sentiments do well for a copy-book, but a man who acts upon them had better sheath his sword forever."[39]

Upon which Lord Morley trenchantly commented, in an aside: "This, by the way, may be one reason among others why we should keep the sword sheathed as long as we can."

[38] Morley, *Miscellanies*, Fourth Series, pp. 1-53.   [39] *Ibid.*, pp. 44-45.

Proceeding with his summing up of Machiavelli's "case" Lord Morley continued:

> Why should the ruler of a State be bound by a moral code from which the soldier is free? ... Right and wrong, cause and effect,—are they not two sides of one question? ... In short, means and end are only one transaction. You must regard policy as a whole. The ruler as an individual is, like other men, no more than the generation of leaves, fleeting, a shadow, a dream. But the State lives on after he shall have vanished. He is a trustee for times to come. He is not shaping his own life only; he guides the distant fortunes of a nation. Leaves fall, the tree stands.[40]

It may be assumed that thus far the summary of his "case" would have pleased Machiavelli—although from now on he would, to say the least, have found Lord Morley's observations rather less acceptable.

Such, I take it, is the defence of reason of State, of the worship of nation and empire. Everything that policy requires, justice sanctions. Success is the test. There are no crimes in politics, only blunders. "The man of action is essentially conscienceless" (*Goethe*). "Praised be those," said one, in words much applauded by Machiavelli, "who love their country rather than the safety of their souls." [41]

Having completed his summary, Lord Morley proceeds to approach his judgment by way of a series of searching questions:

> We see now the deep questions that lie behind these sophistries, and all the alarming propositions in which they close. How are we to decide the constant question in national concerns, when and whether one duty overrules another that points the contrary way? It is easy to assert that the authority of moral law is paramount, but who denies that cases may arise of disputable and conflicting moral obligations? Do you condemn Prussia for violating in 1813 the treaties imposed by Napoleon after Jena? Does morality apply only to end and not to means? Is the State means or end? What does it really exist for? For the sake of the individual, his moral and material well-being, or is he mere cog or pinion in the vast thundering machine? How far is it true that citizenship dominates all other relations and duties, and is the most important of them? Are we to test the true civilisation of a State by anything else than the predominance of justice, right, equality, in its laws, its institutions, its relations to neighbours? Is one of the most important aspects of national policy its reaction upon the character itself, and can States enter on courses of duplicity and selfish violence, without paying the penalty in national demoralisation? What are we to think of such sayings as d'Alembert's motto for a virtuous man, "I prefer my family to myself, my country to my family, and humanity to my country"? Is this the true order of honourable attachments for a man of self-respect and conscience? [42]

---

[40] *Ibid.*, p. 145.   [41] *Ibid.*, p. 46.   [42] *Ibid.*, pp. 46–47.

Lord Morley's comment on these questions points the way to his measured judgment of the "case":

To Machiavelli all these questions would have been futile. Yet the world, in spite of a thousand mischances, and a tortoise-pace, has steadily moved away from him and his Romans.

The modern conception of a State has long made it a moral person, capable of right and wrong, just as are the individuals composing it. Civilisation is taken to advance, exactly in proportion as communities leave behind them the violences of external nature, and the unspeakable brutalities of man in a state of war.

Unquestionably improvements have occurred in the standards and character of the state, although it is still true, as Lord Morley points out, that "reason of State has aways been a plea for impeding and resisting them." Such resistance was perhaps especially characteristic of Machiavelli's day and the century which followed:[43]

Las Casas and other churchmen, Machiavelli's contemporaries, fought nobly at the Spanish court against the inhuman treatment of Indians in the New World, and they were defeated by arguments that read like maxims from the *Prince*. Grotius had forerunners in his powerful contribution towards assuaging the abominations of war, but both letter and spirit in Machiavelli made all the other way.

For present purposes three incontrovertible statements will conclude Lord Morley's measured judgment. In the first he declares that "times have come and gone since Machiavelli wrote down his deep truths, but in the great cycles of human change he can have no place among the strong thinkers, the orators, the writers, who have elevated the conception of the State, have humanised the methods and maxims of government, have raised citizenship to be 'a partnership in every virtue and in all perfection.'"

In the second, after referring to Machiavelli's theory that the moral standard had nothing to do with politics, Lord Morley observes: "The effect was fatal even for his own purpose, for what he put aside, whether for the sake of argument or because he thought them in substance irrelevant, were nothing less than the living forces by which societies subsist and governments are strong."[44]

The third statement leaves nothing to be said: "If Machiavelli had been at Jerusalem two thousand years ago, he might have found nobody of any importance in his eyes, save Pontius Pilate and the Roman legionaries. He forgot the potent arms of moral force."[45]

---

[43] *Miscellanies,* Fourth Series, p. 48.   [44] *Ibid.,* p. 50.   [45] *Ibid.,* p. 51.

Chapter XX

BALDASSARE CASTIGLIONE (1478-1529)

The Courtier

It is a curious and a heartening coincidence that the age which produced Machiavelli, with his materialistic outlook, produced also another Italian whose portrait of a cultured, high-minded and noble gentleman was a complete—if unintentional—answer to the delineation of the ignoble Prince of Machiavelli.

Baldassare Castiglione was born in 1478, some nine years after the birth of *The Prince's* author, and he died in 1529, two years after Machiavelli's death. Both were men of the world, active in public affairs, and subject to all the influences—cultural and idealistic, political and material, good, bad, and indifferent—and the temptations of the Italian Renaissance. But where Machiavelli's views were molded, it would seem, by the baser influences, and in his *Prince* the highest good is held to be worldly success, Castiglione's nature responded to the best influences of the Renaissance, and in his *Courtier* he sought to embody the highest ideals which his age had inherited from the past. It is perhaps not too much to say that there has never been portrayed in any book a nobler conception of a gentleman than in Castiglione's *Courtier*.

The book was a labor of love, written slowly and much revised during the leisure hours which could be salvaged from a life devoted in the main to war and diplomacy and other related activities. From time to time Castiglione was entrusted with many an important mission, not only in Italy but abroad—in England, and especially in Spain, where he spent his last years as diplomatic nuncio to the Court of Charles I. But wherever he was, in the field or at court, he sought to—and actually did—put into practice the ideals set forth in his book, and if in the end his career may be called a failure, it was due not to the failure of his ideals but to the dissimulation and lack of good faith prevalent among those whom he served. Yet, though they took advantage of this high-minded and heroic man, they could not but respect him. Even King Charles, who was also the Emperor Charles V, and who deceived the nuncio cruelly with respect to his attitude toward the papacy and left Castiglione a broken man after the sack of Rome, deeply lamented his death and is said to have exclaimed:[1] "I tell you, one of the finest gentlemen in the world is dead."

The Courtier, begun in 1508, was not completed until some eight years later, but for a dozen years thereafter its author postponed publication while he reshaped the revised manuscript and invited criticism from friends. During this period it was passed from hand to hand in manuscript and parts of it were printed without Castiglione's authorization—to his annoyance and regret. At last, in 1528, it was published in Venice and at once embarked on a long career of popularity, both in Italy and abroad.

It was introduced to Spain by the Spanish poet Garcilaso de la Vega (himself the exemplar of the courtier and gentleman in Spain, as Castiglione was in Italy), who persuaded Juan Boscán to translate it into the language of Castile and publish it in 1540.[2]

In France too *The Courtier* soon found translators, and before many years it had become naturalized, so to speak, in England, in consequence of its translation into English by Sir Thomas Hoby, one-time Ambassador to France. Of Hoby's version, it may safely be said that it remains well-nigh a classic to this day, although not a few criticisms can be leveled at it in matters of translation. Yet to quote from Sir Walter Raleigh's scholarly introduction to an edition of Hoby's version in the "Tudor Translations":

When censure has said its last word, *The Courtyer,* as done into English by Thomas Hoby, is still the book of a great age,—the age that made Shakespeare possible. It is rich in fine passages, and even its obscurest recesses are graced by broken and reflected light, thrown back upon it from the torches of those who passed this way and went onward, leading the English speech to a splendid destiny.[3]

Although other English translations were subsequently made, they were inferior to Hoby's and did not, to quote again from Sir Walter Raleigh's introduction,[4] "impair his title to be esteemed the first and last translator of the *Book of the Courtier."*

For many years the influence of Castiglione's masterpiece, both at home and abroad, was immense, and rightly so, for his Courtier not only embodied the best of the Renaissance civilization but also stood preëminently for the high morality and the high ideal of perfection handed down from

---

[1] "Yo vos digo que es muerto uno de los mejores caballeros del mundo."—Raleigh, Intro. to his ed. of *The Book of the Courtier* (Hoby trans.), p. xxiii.

[2] Boscán's translation is considered by not a few to be the best Spanish prose of the reign of Charles V. See Northup's *Introduction to Spanish Literature* (2d ed., 1936), p. 137.

[3] *The Book of the Courtier* (Intro.), previously cited, p. lix.   [4] *Ibid.,* p. lxi.

the ancient world.[5] "This perfection had nowhere been more systematically described and defined," says Sir Walter Raleigh,[6] "than in the works of the ancient philosophers; and it is from Aristotle's *Ethics* that Castiglione borrows the framework of his ideal character." In form, too, *The Courtier* belongs to the great tradition, for the Renaissance revived the dialogue as the most effective form of literary expression.

Although not concerned primarily with legal or political matters, the book does deal with certain important aspects of law and government. Thus, having depicted the courtier who is to serve the prince, the author describes the qualities needed by the prince. Among the most important of these is justice: "Justice [is a] friend to sobermode and goodnesse, queene of all other vertues, because she teacheth to do that, which a man ought to do, and to shon that a man ought to shonn, and therfore is she most perfect, bicause through her the woorkes of the other vertues are brought to passe, and she is a helpe to him that hath her both for him selfe and for others: without the which (as it is commanlye said) Jupiter him selfe coulde not well govern hys kingdome."[7]

The ability to govern was not a common one, in Castiglione's opinion.

That vertue perhappes among all the matters that belong unto man, is the cheeffest and rarest, that is to say, the maner and way to rule and to reigne in

---

[5] Castiglione's Courtier may, indeed, be said upon modern English authority (*Encyclopedia Britannica*, 14th ed., IV, 989) to be, "with but few differences, the type determined on" as "the ideal gentleman of the present day."

It is interesting to note that an English authority of other days, Dr. Samuel Johnson, held *The Courtier* in great esteem, recommending it highly to Boswell: "The best book that ever was written upon good breeding, *Il Corteggiano*, by Castiglione, grew up at the little court of Urbino, and you should read it."—Boswell's *Life of Johnson*, ed. by George Birgbeck Hill (6 vols., Oxford, 1887), V, 276.

On the subject of the qualities of a gentleman a few sentences may be quoted here from the engaging little book by Sedgwick, *In Praise of Gentlemen*, pp. 6–7. After referring to those whom we call gentlemen as being, so to speak, members of a guild, Mr. Sedgwick says: "The outward appointments of a gentleman showed nobility and excellence, but his qualities within were also expected to portray nobility and excellence. His character,—I am speaking of the ideal member of the Guild, for all wool merchants do not always sell fine wool, nor all apothecaries always furnish wholesome drugs, nor all stone-masons always build everlasting walls,—his character was based on the cardinal virtues, Fortitude, Temperance, Prudence, and Justice. And as for accomplishments and characteristics that may be acquired, the Guild prescribed: for the body, quickness, dexterity, control of the limbs, development of the muscles; and for the mind, cultivation of the humanities, of the arts, of knowledge of whatever mankind has done to make our world more beautiful and life pleasanter. And, very much as other guilds were held to justify themselves by what they contributed to society, the Guild of Gentlemen was thought to justify itself, first by public service in war and in government, and secondly by what it did to uphold the higher human values, as by its demonstration of how all human intercourse may be embellished, how conduct may become a fine art, how animal mating may be idealized by courtly love, how speech may be more than purely utilitarian, and so forth. Such, in a general way, were the fruits of civilization, which the Guild of Gentlemen gathered and contributed to the public good."

[6] *The Book of the Courtier* (Intro.), p. lxiv.   [7] *The Book of the Courtier*, p. 310.

the right kinde. Which alone were sufficient to make men happie, and to bring once again into the worlde the golden age, whiche is written to have bine whan Saturnus reigned in the olde time.

The qualities of the good prince will be reflected in his people: "The greatest proofe that the Prince is good, is whan the people are good: because the lief of the Prince is a lawe and ringleader of the Citizins, and upon the condicions of him must needes al others depende." Therefore it is no more fitting for a poorly qualified prince to govern a people than it is "meete for one that is ignorant, to teach: nor for him that is out of order, to give order: nor for him that falleth, to help up an other."[8] He who would rule well, then, must be both wise and reasonable. "Therfore if the Prince will execute these offices aright, it is requisit that he apply all his studie and diligence to get knowleage, afterward to facion within him selfe and observe unchangeablye in everye thinge the lawe of reason."

Having here introduced the law of reason, Castiglione proceeds to describe it in terms which identify it with the familiar conceptions of the law of nature. It is "not written in papers, or in mettall, but graven in his owne [the Prince's] minde that it maye be to him always not onlie familier, but inwarde, and live with him, as a percell of him: to the intent it may night and day, in everye time and place admonish him and speake to him within his hart."

On the same page there is what might easily be taken for a veiled reference to Machiavelli, as though Castiglione had read the Florentine's *Prince* and rejected it. Whether this be true or not, it is certain that he would have rejected it if he had read it.

Corrupt and il disposed mindes discover their vices . . . whan they be filled with authoritie. For then they are not able to carie the heavie burdien of poure, but forsake them selves and scatter on every side greedie desire, pride, wrath, solemnesse and such tirannicall facions as they have within them. Wherupon without regard they persecute the good and wise, and promote the wicked.

The result of such a domination—it cannot be called government—is that[9] of these maners insue infinit damages and the uttre undoinge of the poore people, and often times cruell slaughter or at the least continuall feare to the Tirannes them selves. For good Princis feare not for them selves but for their sakes whom they rule over: and Tyrannes feare verie them whom they rule over. Therfore the more numbre of people they rule over and the mightier they are, the more is their feare and the more enemies they have.

Having thus, whether intentionally or not, condemned Machiavellianism, Castiglione returns to his own prince, saying that it is "also the office of a

[8] *The Book of the Courtier*, p. 315.   [9] *Ibid.*, p. 316.

good Prince so to trade his people and with such lawes and statutes, that they maye lyve in rest and in peace, without daunger and with encrease of welth, and injoye praisablye this ende of their practises and actions, which ought to be quietnesse."[10] By way of contrast Castiglione here refers to the results of a lack of training in the ways and practices of peace:

> there have bine often times manye Commune weales and Princis, that in warr were always most florishinge and mightie, and immediatelye after they have had peace, fell in decaye and lost their puissance and brightnesse, like yron unoccupied. And this came of nothing elles, but bicause they had no good trade of lyving in peace, nor the knowleage to injoie the benefit of ease.

Further repudiating the conduct of princes who continually waged war to gratify their own ambitions, the author of *The Courtier* continues: "And it is not a matter lawfull to be alwayes in warr without seekinge at the ende to come to a peace: although some Princis suppose that their drift ought principally to be, to bringe in subjection their borderers, and therfore traine up their people in a warlyke wyldenesse of spoyle, and murther, and suche matters: they wage them to exercise it, and call it vertue."

It is obvious that although Castiglione had devoted much of his time and talents to war, he was himself in favor of peace. In his opinion, the only reason which justified the prince in arousing a warlike spirit in his people was self-defense against

> whoso woulde attempt to bringe them in bondage, or to do them wrong in any point. Or els to drive out Tirans, and to govern the people well, that were yll handled.[11]

Peace should be the goal of the prince, and to that end, therefore, "ought to be applied the lawes, and al statutes of justice, in punishing the yll, not for malice, but bicause there should be no yll, and least they shoulde be a hinderaunce to the quiet livinge of the good: bicause in very deede it is an uncomelye matter and woorthie blame, that in warr (which of it selfe is nought) men shoulde showe themselves stout and wise, and in peace and rest (which is good) ignoraunt, and so blockishe that they wiste not howe to injoye a benifit."[12] And as in war it was the duty of princes "to bende their people to the profitable and necessarye vertues to come by that ende (which is, peace) so in peace, to come by the end therof also (which is, quietnes) they ought to bend them to honest vertues, which be the end of the profitable."

Of all the duties of the prince, the most important was to insure the administration of justice throughout his realm:

[10] *Ibid.*, p. 318.   [11] *Ibid.*, pp. 318-19.   [12] *Ibid.*, p. 319.

Of cares beelonging to a Prince, the cheeffest is of justice: for maintenance wherof wise and well tryed men shoulde be chosen out for officers, whose wisdome were verie wisdome in deede, accompanied with goodnesse, for elles is it no wisdome, but craft. And where there is a want of this goodnesse, alwayes the art and subtill practise of lawyers is nothing elles, but the uttre decay and destruction of the lawyes and judgementes; and the fault of every offence of theirs is to be layed in him that put them in office.[13]

The prince's duty to see that justice was done carried with it the correlative duty of protecting the liberty of his subjects, and Castiglione defines in a pregnant phrase what he means by liberty:[14] "true liberty ought not to be saide to live as a manne will, but to lyve accordynge to good lawes." The ultimate purpose of the state of Castiglione was the happiness of the citizens, but he had definite ideas as to what constituted happiness. Thus "the best way were, to have the greater part of the Citizins, neyther verye wealthie, nor verye poore: bicause the over wealthy many times were stiff necked and recklesse, the poore, desperate and pikinge."[15] But material wealth, however distributed, would not have first place in Castiglione's state: "I woulde counsell the Prince to do his best to preserve his subjectes in quiet astate, and to give them the gooddes of the mynde, and of the bodye and of fortune: but them of the bodye and fortune, that they maye exercise them of the minde."[16] The true greatness of the ruler should not be measured by the extent nor the populousness of his realm, for "not the multytude of Subjectes, but the woorthynesse of them makes Princis greate."[17] Unfortunately the good prince as described by Castiglione was, as he himself knew, all too uncommon in a "naughty world." Indeed he himself observes regretfully[18] that "the heavens be so scante in bringinge furth excellent Princis, . . . [that] in so manye hundredth yeeres we do scantlye see one." The material rewards of such "excellent Princis" were likely to be much smaller than those awaiting the prince depicted by Machiavelli. But Castiglione would have his prince seek a different reward, the true reward of all good rulers: "perhappes there can not be a greater praise nor more comlye for a Prince, then to call him a good Governour."[19]

[13] *The Book of the Courtier*, p. 322. [14] *Ibid.*, pp. 312–13. [15] *Ibid.*, p. 324.
[16] *Ibid.*, p. 325. [17] *Ibid.*, p. 326. [18] *Ibid.*, p. 332. [19] *Ibid.*, p. 331.

Chapter XXI

CHRISTOPHER ST. GERMAIN (1460–1540)
Doctor and Student

CHRISTOPHER ST. GERMAIN WAS A CONTEMPORARY OF FRANCISCO DE VITORIA, although somewhat older, the span of his life having been the fourscore years from 1460 to 1540; and the complete English edition of both "Dialogues" of his *Doctor and Student* appeared in 1532,[1] the very year that Francisco de Vitoria, then Professor of Theology in the University of Salamanca, began his epoch-making tractate *On the Indians Newly Discovered*, which was to give him the title of founder of the modern law of nations.

Although deeply versed in canon law and keenly interested in the religious controversies of his time, St. Germain was not a churchman but a barrister and a member of the Inner Temple, made up of common-law lawyers. A master of the common law and also of scholastic learning, he was therefore familiar not only with Roman and canon, but also with English law. In addition, he was said to have possessed a library larger than that of any other member of the bar of his day. Apparently he delved to some purpose into the volumes on his shelves, for Sir Paul Vinogradoff (who devoted no little attention to St. Germain), declared that he was "evidently quite at home in the legal learning of the courts, and very well read in the philosophical and jurisprudential writings of his time."[2]

It was to be expected that St. Germain's familiarity with the canon law would make him aware of the fundamental importance of the rôle which equity was playing in the development of English jurisprudence. That there was conflict between the courts of common law and those of equity was well known, but the underlying reason for this conflict—that the structure of the common law was defective (as, for example, in cases involving breach of faith) and that courts administering the canon law sought, in the face of considerable opposition, to provide an equitable cure for those defects—was not so well understood at the beginning of the sixteenth century. St. Germain, having a knowledge both theoretical and practical of the law of his country, and having steeped himself in the canon law, which

[1] For mention of earlier editions, see p. 302.
[2] *Collected Papers* (previously cited), II, 191.

consisted so largely of Roman elements, was in a position to examine critically the rules of the common law and to realize where and to what extent they should have the assistance of Roman equity if they were to be rules of justice, and if the laws of England were to be equitable as well as "legal." This was the purpose to which he addressed himself in writing his famous tractate *Doctor and Student,* the subtitle of which well indicates the general nature and the scope of the work: *Dialogues between a Doctor of Divinity, and a Student in the Laws of England: Containing the Grounds of Those Laws, together with Questions and Cases Concerning the Equity and Conscience Thereof; Also Comparing the Civil, Canon, Common and Statute Laws, And Shewing Wherein They Vary from One Another."*

The first of the two dialogues which make up the book was published in Latin in 1523; the second dialogue appeared in English in 1530. The author then issued an English version of the first dialogue; and in 1532, as mentioned above, an English edition containing both dialogues was printed. In all, some thirty editions of this famous work have been published, the latest having appeared in the United States (Cincinnati) in 1874.

As it happened, the appearance of *Doctor and Student* was extremely opportune, published as it was at the very time when the administration of equity had passed from ecclesiastical hands to those of Sir Thomas More and of professional lawyers, upon the fall of Cardinal Wolsey, former Keeper of the Seals and of the conscience of King Henry VIII—so far as he had any. *Doctor and Student*—showing the connection between canon law and the principles of equity—was thus in the nature of a bridge which enabled English equity to preserve a continuity, in spite of the change in its administration.

It is interesting to note that until the appearance, in the sixties of the eighteenth century, of Blackstone's famous *Commentaries on the Laws of England,* St. Germain's *Doctor and Student* was the recognized text for students of English law in England—and indeed it may still be studied to no little advantage.

There was a broader field, however, in which the treatise of St. Germain exercised an important if much less obvious influence. The dialogues, written at a time when international relations were becoming increasingly important, laid much emphasis upon the law of nature,[3] that body of universally acknowledged rules which were to play so important a part in the development of international law, and which had no little effect on

---

[3] "This dialogue [*Doctor and Student*] is probably the most valuable source of our knowledge concerning the relation of the law of nature to the law of England in the late mediaeval or early modern times."—McIlwain, *The High Court of Parliament and Its Supremacy,* p. 105.

political philosophy and institutions. By familiarizing many with the fundamental conceptions of natural law, by emphasizing the identity of that law with the Anglo-Saxon "right reason," *Doctor and Student* contributed indirectly to the foundations for the betterment of human relations, both as between individuals and between states.

Sir Paul Vinogradoff has justly observed that the English version of the first dialogue is not a translation from the Latin, but rather a "recasting of the text," with the omission of certain "lengthy disquisitions and references," which are, it may be added, of value to the careful student in that they indicate St. Germain's reliance, in his exposition of scholastic philosophy and canon law, on Jean Gerson,[4] a great French theologian of the preceding century and then the leading exponent of the scholastic theories as developed by St. Thomas Aquinas.[5] The Latin version is also valuable—to quote again from Vinogradoff—"in so far as it shows the close dependence of the initial view of conscience and equity entertained by the author on the doctrines of fifteenth-century schoolmen."[6]

The influence of *Doctor and Student* on the development of the English conception of equity is emphasized by the most accredited of modern English legal historians, Sir William S. Holdsworth:[7] "That its importance was great can be seen from the fact that it is cited by practically every writer upon equity down to Blackstone's day."

What was the origin of the conception of equity set forth by St. Germain? In the opinion of Professor Lévy-Ullmann, it may be traced to "a paraphrase of Cicero's *Summum jus, summa injuria*."[8]

---

[4] See *supra*, pp. 235-36.

[5] "St. Germain started in the same way from scholastic philosophy and Canon Law as Bracton started from Roman Law in his time. Both writers wanted scientific distinctions and terms in order to tackle problems of English legal practice, and both began with a kind of reception of general notions which, however, was gradually modified by the treatment of concrete cases and questions. Azo was the interpreter of Civil Law for the thirteenth-century lawyer, John Gerson was the leading exponent of school doctrines for the sixteenth-century jurist. Stray references to the latter may be found even in the revised English text of St. Germain, but a comparison with the Latin *Dialogue* shows that, on nearly all occasions when theories had to be exposed, sentences and quotations were borrowed wholesale from Gerson's writings."—Vinogradoff, *Collected Papers*, II, 191-92.

[6] *Ibid.*, p. 195.   [7] *A History of English Law*, V, 267.

[8] Professor Lévy-Ullmann adds: "This Equity stood by the side of a harsh law, to strengthen it while it was weak, to supply its deficiencies, and to mitigate the rigour of its effects, sometimes unhappy indeed. It could trace a relationship with the αἐπιείκει of the Greeks which Aristotle had defined as 'that which is law, outside the written law,' and 'a just redress of rigorous legal justice.' The *Summum jus* is expressly referred to in the aphorisms on Equity in the decisions of the Chancellors. Aristotle's ἐπιείκεια which Saint-Germain had discovered in the *Regulae Morales* of Gerson, is found again in 'Equity,' not only as the root of the word, but also as the root of the idea."—*The English Legal Tradition* (previously cited), pp. 278-79.

But though the origin of the conception was classical, its immediate derivation was from the canonists and it was, to quote again from Sir William Holdsworth,[9] "St. Germain's popular exposition" which "has made these canonist principles the basis and starting point of English equity."

On this point there is an interesting comment in Vinogradoff's masterly essay on "Reason and Conscience in Sixteenth-Century Jurisprudence":[10] "It seems to me on the whole that a study of St. Germain's *Dialogues* shows conclusively what a stimulating influence was exerted on the English jurisprudence of the fifteenth and sixteenth centuries by the later Schoolmen and Canon lawyers."

No one, therefore, could read *Doctor and Student* without gaining an understanding of the way in which English law has, as Dr. Winfield states,[11] "been influenced by ideas that are brushed aside as irrelevant by modern legislators."[12] And he continues:

It is impossible to read the book without being struck by the amount of fresh air which it pours upon the ill-ventilated technicalities of our mediaeval law. From beginning to end, legal rules are put in the witness-box and cross-examined to credit. Religious and ethical tests are applied to them, and *Doctor and Student* is surprisingly full of the speculative inquiries into the foundation of the Common Law which are almost entirely lacking in the earlier literature.

The subtitle of *Doctor and Student,* previously quoted, indicates the nature and purpose of the book. A sentence in the preface to the English version states more specifically the aim of the author: "The design of this treatise is to inquire into the grounds and reasons of the Common law of England; and to shew how consistent every of its precepts (how surprising soever they may appear at first sight) are with right reason and a good conscience."[13]

Before examining the conception of "right reason" and "good conscience" which St. Germain had in mind, it is advisable to say a word concerning the *dramatis personae* of the dialogues. The Doctor represents of course the

---

[9] *Op. cit.,* v, 268.   [10] *Collected Papers,* II, 204.
[11] *The Chief Sources of English Legal History,* pp. 321, 322.
[12] It is not too much to say that modern legislators, in their feverish anxiety to pass statutes on any and all subjects, have indeed "brushed aside," or at least ignored, the fundamental conceptions of the true nature of law and its development. "There are," observes Messrs. Buckland and McNair (*Roman Law and Common Law, a Comparison in Outline* [previously cited], p. 10), "many legislative bodies in the United States and it is computed that they have produced in the present century more statutes than have been enacted in all the legislatures of the known world in all previous history."
[13] St. Germain, *Doctor and Student,* p. 2 verso.

knowledge of canon law which St. Germain had so thoroughly acquired. He is questioned by the Student, whose field is the laws of England, and their dialogue is meant to throw light on the views of each. Though the subject matter does not readily lend itself to dramatic treatment, the interplay of question and answer does serve to carry the reader easily from topic to topic and adds to the charm of the book.

In his second speech the Doctor, as a true canonist, makes a fourfold division of law in the scholastic manner:

The first is the *law eternal.* The second is the *law of nature* of reasonable creatures. ... The third is the *law of God.* The fourth is the *law of man.*

Of the law of nature of reasonable creatures, the Doctor immediately adds, "the which, as I have heard say, is called by them that be learned in the law of *England,* the *law of reason."*

Again following the schoolmen, the Doctor informs the Student that the eternal law is made known to reasonable creatures in three ways, the first being "by the light of natural reason"; the second, "by heavenly revelation" (this being the divine revealed law of the schoolmen); and the third, through the laws of the state. Turning to the scholastic law of nature, the Doctor declares, as one versed in Roman and canon conceptions, that it may be considered in two ways: in one as referring "to all creatures as well reasonable as unreasonable" (this being the doctrine of Ulpian); and in the other as pertaining "only to creatures reasonable" (which was the generally accepted view of the schoolmen). Again following the scholastic conception, the Doctor adds that this law of nature "is written in the heart of every man, teaching him what is to be done, and what is to be fled," and being so written, it may not be evaded nor may it be changed, so that neither "law, prescription, statute nor custom" may prevail against it.[14] Moreover—and here again the tradition of the schools is evident—"all other laws ... be grounded thereupon."

The law of nature, the Doctor added, was made evident to man by the "natural light of understanding," and therein it differed from the divine law, which was "given by revelation of God."[15]

Now what were the fundamentals of the law of nature? The Doctor represented the views of those who identified the law of nature and the

---

[14] *Ibid.,* pp. 2, 4, 5.
[15] Indeed, there were two differences pointed out by the Doctor: The "law of reason differeth from the law of God in two manners. For the law of God is given by revelation of God; and this law is given by a natural light of understanding. And also the law of God ordereth a man of itself, by a nigh way, to the fecilicity that ever shall endure; and the law of reason ordereth a man to the felicity of this life."—*Ibid.,* p. 6.

New Testament, and he likewise identified the law of nature with the law of reason: "The law of reason teacheth that good is to be loved, and evil is to be fled: also that thou shalt do to another, that thou wouldest another should do unto thee; and that we may do nothing against truth; and that a man must live peacefully with others; that justice is to be done to every man; and also that wrong is not to be done to any man; and that also a trespasser is worthy to be punished; and such other."[16]

From these basic principles there followed—as the scholastic writers were in the habit of saying—certain secondary rules which were in the nature of "necessary conclusions," and of these the Doctor gives an example which should be stated in his own language: from "that commandment, that good is to be beloved; it followeth, that a man should love his benefactor."

Turning now to the relationship between the law of nature (or the law of reason) and human law, the Doctor declares that "the *law of man*"—which is also, as he points out, positive law—"is derived by reason, as a thing which is necessary, and probably following of the law of reason, and of the law of God."[17] And in a later passage, recurring to the relationship between divine and natural law and the law human, the Doctor declares that human law must be judged by a twofold standard:[18] "Where the law of man is in itself directly against the law of reason, or else the law of God," then, says the Doctor, employing the very language of scholasticism, "properly it cannot be called a law, but a corruption."

The Student has apparently listened with great interest to the Doctor's exposition and he now, at the request of his companion, offers in turn to discuss the laws of England in the light of what the Doctor has said. He begins with the important statement that "the first ground of the law of *England* is the *law of reason*." This definition does not wholly content the Doctor, who, being a canonist, is more familiar with the expression "law of nature," and he therefore interrupts by saying: "But I would know what is called the *law of nature* after the laws of *England*." The reply of the Student is famous in the annals of English law:

It is not used among them that be learned in the laws of *England* to reason what thing is commanded or prohibited by the law of nature, and what not, but all the reasoning in that behalf is under this manner. As when any thing is grounded upon the law of nature, they say, that reason will that such a thing be done; and if it be prohibited by the law of nature, they say it is against reason, or that reason will not suffer that to be done.[19]

It is clear that this law of reason was in essence nothing else than the law of nature, a law which furnishes the first principles for all human action.

[16] St. Germain, *op. cit.*, pp. 6-7.   [17] *Ibid.*, p. 10.   [18] *Ibid.*, pp. 146-47.   [19] *Ibid.*, p. 13.

Indeed the Student himself says:[20] "It is to be noted, that all the deriving of reason in the law of *England* proceedeth of the first principles of the law, or of something that is derived of them: and therefore no man may rightwisely judge, ne groundly reason in the laws of *England,* if he be ignorant in the first principles."

The discussion then turns upon custom, and the Student inquires whether, in the Doctor's opinion, custom is held to be a sufficient authority for the formation of law. The answer of the Doctor is of interest. "Doctors hold," he says,[21] "that a law grounded upon a custom is the most surest law: but this thou must always understand therewith, that such a custom is neither contrary to the law of reason, nor the law of God."

A part of the discussion which was of importance in the development of the law of equity deals with the position of conscience in relation to the laws of England. The Doctor is anxious to know how an English litigant may be "holpen by conscience"; but the Student declares that it will be well first to know what conscience is, and he therefore begs the Doctor to take up the tale. We are thereupon favored with a discussion of a term less familiar to readers of our day than to the schoolmen—"sinderesis." The Doctor defines it in various ways, but it will be sufficient here to note the last two definitions, of which one is thus stated: "This *sinderesis* is the beginning of all things that may be learned by speculation or study, and ministreth the general grounds and principles thereof; and also of all things that are to be done by man." As an example of things that are to be done, or not to be done, he says that *"sinderesis* saith no evil is to be done, but that goodness is to be done and followed, and evil to be fled, and such other."

The second definition is: *"Sinderesis* is called by some men the law of reason, for it ministreth the principles of the law of reason, the which be in every man by nature, in that he is a reasonable creature."[22]

Having thus led up to conscience, the Doctor defines it figuratively and in terms which show its relation to the law of reason:

As a light is set in a lantern, that all that is in the house may be seen thereby; so Almighty God hath set conscience in the midst of every reasonable soul, as a light whereby he may discern and know what he ought to do, and what he ought not to do. Therefore forasmuch as it behoveth thee to be occupied in such things as pertain to the law; it is necessary that thou ever hold a pure and clean conscience, specially in such things as concern restitution: for the sin is not forgiven, but if the thing that is wrongfully taken be restored. And I counsel thee also that thou love that is good, and fly that is evil; and that thou do to

---

[20] *Ibid.,* p. 16.   [21] *Ibid.,* pp. 25–26.   [22] *Ibid.,* p. 39.

another, as thou wouldest should be done to thee, and that thou do nothing to other, that thou wouldest not should be done to thee, that thou do nothing against truth, that thou live peaceably with thy neighbour, and that thou do justice to every man as much as in thee is: and also that in every general rule of the law thou do observe and keep equity. And if thou do thus, I trust the light of the lantern, that is, thy conscience, shall never be extincted.[23]

This passage brings up the subject of equity, and here again the Student is anxious for enlightenment from the Doctor, no doubt realizing that the canonist was best qualified to speak on that subject. "Equity," the Doctor obligingly begins, "is a right wiseness that considereth all the particular circumstances of the deed, the which also is tempered with the sweetness of mercy." To this statement he adds the comment: "And such an equity must always be observed in every law of man, and in every general rule thereof: and that knew he well that said thus, *Laws covet to be ruled by equity.*" The wise man treads carefully in claiming his rights under the law, realizing that "If thou take all that the words of the law giveth thee, thou shalt sometime do against the law."[24]

Having thus indicated the broad scope of equity, the Doctor turns now to the "plainer declaration" of "what equity is"; and again it is necessary to quote his language *in extenso*—a language reminiscent of Aristotle's magnificent statement:

sith the deeds and acts of men, for which laws have been ordained, happen in divers manners infinitely, it is not possible to make any general rule of the law, but that it shall fail in some case: and therefore makers of laws take heed to such things as may often come, and not to every particular case, for they could not though they would. And therefore, to follow the words of the law were in some case both against justice and the commonwealth. Wherefore in some cases it is necessary to leave the words of the law, and to follow that reason and justice requireth, and to that intent equity is ordained; that is to say, to temper and mitigate the rigor of the law.

This conception the Doctor knew was that of the ancient world as well as of the medieval world and the world of his day; for he here refers to the fact that equity had been called by some *epieikeia,* which was, of course, originally a Greek conception signifying something in the nature of "an exception," in the Doctor's language, "of the law of God, or of the law of reason, from the general rules of the law of man" in circumstances when those rules "by reason of their generality would in any particular case judge against the law of God, or the law of reason"; that is to say, when the positive human law would violate natural justice. Now this exception, we

[23] St. Germain, *op. cit.,* p. 44. [24] *Ibid.,* pp. 44–45.

are told, "is secretly understood in every general rule of every positive law." It is not a provision against cruel laws or cruelty in the administration of the law; rather, as the Doctor immediately states, "equity followeth the law in all particular cases where right and justice requireth, notwithstanding the general rule of the law be to the contrary." Therefore, if any human law were enacted which by its terms excluded equity, it would be an unreasonable law, and, being unreasonable, would not be law.

The wording of a law might conceivably be open to more than one interpretation, but its aim and purpose, tested by right reason, should always be justice, and the end of equity is the same. Therefore the Doctor defines thus the function of equity at the close of his exposition: "And so it appeareth that equity rather followeth the intent of the law, than the words of the law."[25]

The question of equity was, of course, related to the subject of conscience. In a later passage the Doctor touches upon the relation of law to conscience: "it is holden commonly by all doctors, that the commandments and rules of the law of man, or of a positive law that is lawfully made, bind all that be subjects to the law according to the mind of the maker, and that in the court of conscience."[26]

No wonder *Doctor and Student* was a standard textbook from the time of its publication to, and even after, the appearance of Blackstone's *Commentaries*. It would doubtless benefit our legal ideals if it were read and pondered today; for, as the Doctor implies on more than one occasion, that law which he considered to be the ground of the law of England (the law of reason—or the law of nature) was in conformity with the highest standard of ethics known to the civilized world. In his own words: "Every man is bound by the law of reason to do as he would be done to."[27]

[25] *Ibid.*, p. 46.
[26] *Ibid.*, p. 72.
The "court of conscience" was frequently appealed to by the scholastic writers—especially by the members of the Spanish School. And Grotius, whose debt to Spanish writers is so great that he may fairly be termed a member of the Spanish School, invoked the court of conscience as an international tribunal. See *infra*, p. 528.
[27] St. Germain, *Doctor and Student*, p. 118.

Chapter XXII
FRANCISCO DE VITORIA (c. 1483-1546)

THE DISCOVERY OF AMERICA DEEPLY INFLUENCED MANY FIELDS OF THOUGHT, but nowhere was its influence more profound than upon the development of international law.

A distinguished American novelist—indeed one of the great writers of the English-speaking world—has a charming series of *Twice Told Tales*. Now the repetitions of the story of Columbus and the discovery of America are innumerable; yet it will be necessary here to add one more to the numberless tales of that epoch-making voyage.

Columbus was by birth an Italian. But it was in Portugal and Spain rather than in his native land that he sought the support needed to enable him to sail westward on a voyage of discovery. His request having been refused by the King of Portugal, he determined to lay his project before the Spanish court. It happened that his arrival in Spain coincided with the end of the century-long drive against the Moors within the Spanish Peninsula. Ferdinand and Isabella were on the eve of taking Granada, the last stronghold of the Moors in Spanish territory. On the first day of January in the very memorable year of 1492, Granada fell and Spain found itself at last a united country with a united people.

Before the final defeat of the Moors it seemed doubtful whether the Queen Isabella would agree to finance a westward voyage of discovery, although Columbus had already had the matter laid before Her Catholic Majesty. But after the conquest of Granada an adventurous mood swept over Spain, a mood to which the Queen herself responded.

This is not the place to enter into the details of negotiation and agreement between Columbus and the Spanish sovereigns. Suffice it to say that through the interest of the Queen in the project, three small ships were procured and fitted out, the names of which are famous in the annals of adventure, the "Santa Maria," the "Pinta," and the "Niña," the first a vessel of about 100 tons, the second smaller (50 tons), and the third still smaller (40 tons). Columbus, with a motley crew from many ports, set sail from Palos on the third day of August, 1492, and after a turn to the south he set his course westward and continued westward notwithstanding murmurings

FRANCISCO DE VITORIA

of his crew, until he landed on an unidentified island in the Caribbean Sea on the morning of the twelfth day of October of the year 1492, in which year Spain, as we have seen, had recovered its unity as a kingdom and was about to enter upon the course of empire.

Columbus took possession of the island in the name of Spain, his adopted country, and, proceeding to the South and the West, discovered other and larger islands, among them, on October 27, 1492, the island of Cuba, which over four centuries later was the last of Spain's imperial possessions in the Americas to separate itself from the mother country.

The return of Columbus to Spain, where he recounted in person the news of his astounding adventure, filled Europe with an amazement not unmixed with envy, an amazement which we, in an age when the last frontier is said to have been crossed, may find it difficult to comprehend.

At the news of the discovery of Columbus, Portugal, which had specialized in the Far East, became anxious to increase its possessions in the western and hitherto undiscovered parts of the world. This led to a conflict of interests between the two nations of the Spanish Peninsula. Therefore an agreement was made between Spain and Portugal as to the distribution of the spoils of discovery to the westward.

France was also interested in the New World, and its adventurous seamen crossed the Atlantic, to be followed by a few brave missionaries and numerous colonists.

England was especially interested and through the Cabots—like Columbus of Italian birth—discovered and laid claim to territory which in part remains a British possession to this day and which was, in a sense, the beginning of the empire upon which the sun never sets.

It must be admitted, however, that the interest of countries other than Spain in the Western World was almost wholly material. And indeed there was a large element in Spain, not powerful enough to gain full control but unfortunately strong enough to be highly influential, whose interests were also material. But there was a wholly spiritual element—for there have always been soul-savers as well as money changers and both were to be found in Spain during its Golden Age—which looked upon the aborigines, no matter how backward they might seem to others, as nevertheless possessed of souls which these spiritually minded Spaniards were intent on saving. Therefore many Spanish missionaries, as well as the materially minded adventurers, made their way westward. The leader of the spiritually minded had originally sailed westward as an adventurer and had engaged in material conquests, but, as sometimes happens with the adventurous, he found his better self in the new land. Forsaking his worldly ways, he entered the Dominican Order, an order which at that time and thereafter made a specialty of converting the Indians of the New World. And today Las Casas, the one-time adventurer, is universally known as the "Apostle to the Indies."

As was to be expected, the question soon arose whether God or Mammon should control the destinies of the Western World. The Dominicans were naturally opposed to Mammon and protested against the ill-treatment of the Indians at the hands of the gold-seeking *conquistadores;* and, although the missionaries of the order prevented the enslavement of all the Indians, they were nevertheless unable to protect them against exploitation. However, in so far as the natives were spared, it was because of the efforts of the Dominicans and Spanish missionaries of other orders; and it was because of their anxiety for the souls of their less-advanced brethren of the newly discovered world that the Catholic religion is the prevailing religion in every American republic which once formed part of the vast Spanish empire.

How were the natives to be protected and preserved? Their souls were to be saved by the missionaries. But what of their temporal rights as human beings? What of the administration of justice, and what was that justice to be?

Now it happened that an outstanding advocate of the cause of justice in the newly discovered land was a Dominican, Francisco de Vitoria,[1] *prima* professor of theology at the University of Salamanca from 1526 until his death, twenty years later. Of him it may be said that, as a result of his disquisitions on the subject, he replaced a broken Christendom by the international community and proposed for the backward peoples of the Americas an enlightened justice based upon the New Testament and the Roman law.

In its origin the problem which he treated was theological. A doubt had arisen in the minds of many whether children of non-Christian parents could be baptized without the consent of their parents, who might not be inclined to renounce their native beliefs for the religion of the conquerors. Vitoria, a man of great learning and of a generous outlook upon the world, examined the problem in its various aspects. The question of baptism had often been discussed by the doctors in their commentaries on Peter Lombard's *Sentences* and in the *Summa Theologica* of St. Thomas Aquinas, but naturally without reference to the then-unknown America. In order to deal with this problem arising out of the discoveries of Columbus, Vitoria

---

[1] "Vitoria" is the Spanish form of the name, and has generally been employed in these pages, rather than the Latinized form "Victoria," which is perhaps more familiar to the English-speaking world.

found it necessary to consider not only the rights of the Spaniards, of their sovereigns, and of the church in the New World, but also the rights of the natives. Having decided thus to enlarge the scope of the discussion, making it to all intents and purposes coextensive with the international community, he began with the statement that "The whole of this controversy and discussion was started on account of the aborigines of the New World, commonly called Indians, who came forty years ago"—he was speaking as of 1532—"into the power of the Spaniards, not having been previously known to our world."[2] According to the farsighted Vitoria, the problem as presented could be divided "into three parts."

> In the first part we shall inquire [he declares] by what right these Indian natives came under Spanish sway. In the second part, what rights the Spanish sovereigns obtained over them in temporal and civil matters. In the third part, what rights these sovereigns or the Church obtained over them in matters spiritual and touching religion, in the course of which an answer will be given to the question before us.

It is obvious from this statement that, if Vitoria were to consider these three questions in detail, the fundamental conceptions of the law of nations would necessarily be involved. Fortunately he did consider them in detail; and his broad and enlightened views, set forth in his *Readings on the Indians,* established the foundations of the modern law of nations. This is a fact which has been unanimously recognized by the American republics, the recognition taking the form of the following resolution, adopted December 23, 1933, by the Seventh International Conference of American States at Montevideo:

> The Seventh International Conference of American States,
> RESOLVES, To recommend that a bust of the Spanish theologian, Francisco de Vitoria, be placed in the Headquarters of the Pan American Union, in Washington, as a tribute to the professor of Salamanca who, in the sixteenth century, established the foundations of modern international law.

It may seem strange to present-day readers that a theologian, whose business, so to speak, was soul-saving, should be so deeply interested in what most of us would classify as primarily legal questions. The reason, however, is not far to seek, if we are familiar with the ways of the world in those days. Theology, it is true, was Vitoria's profession, but theology was not regarded in that day (as it too often is in this), as a dry and musty subject.

---

[2] *De Indis,* Sec. I, no. 1; p. 116. These two Readings of Vitoria are published in the "Classics of International Law" series as *De Indis et de iure belli relectiones,* with translation by John Pawley Bate; ed., and with an Introduction, by Ernest Nys. The quotations from *De Indis* and *De iure belli* in the present chapter are taken from Mr. Bate's admirable translation.

Chosen souls like Abraham Lincoln have maintained that "nothing is decided until it is decided right." Vitoria and his fellow theologians would have subscribed to that maxim, for they held that to decide a thing rightly, the rule applied must be moral as well as legal. Hence Vitoria insisted that the jurists, who looked merely at the letter of the law, could not be trusted to discover and to apply the spirit of the law; only theologians could do that. In the present instance, he maintained that only theologians could adequately determine the question which he had set himself to answer:

> I assert [he says] that it is not for jurists to settle this question or at any rate not for jurists only, for since the barbarians in question, as I shall forthwith show, were not in subjection by human law, it is not by human, but by divine law that questions concerning them are to be determined. Now, jurists are not skilled enough in the divine law to be able by themselves to settle questions of this sort.[3]

Hence the American question in its entirety, not merely as a spiritual but as a temporal matter, was to be weighed in the balance of divine law as well as the law of the layman. It is apparent that the theologian's domain was wide and that he must be learned in many subjects. Indeed, in Vitoria's conception the scope of theology was as broad as humanity, for in his previous disquisition *On the Civil Power,* delivered some four years earlier, he had asserted that "the duties and functions of the theologian extend over a field so vast, that no argument, no discussion, no text, seem alien to the practice and purpose of theology."[4]

It is from this large and all-embracing conception of right and wrong that Vitoria proceeded to the discussion of the question which he had put to himself in the first of his *Readings on the Indians,* delivered at Salamanca. Having in the first section of the first "Reading" indicated that the Indians were possessed of their lands in absolute dominion and that the mere fact of their unbelief had nothing to do with their rights of possession and ownership, Vitoria then proceeded to consider certain alleged titles by which the Indians might come under the sway of the Spaniards. The first title rested upon the contention that the Holy Roman Emperor was lord over the world, and the second upon a like contention as regards the head of the Church. Both titles Vitoria categorically denied. It should be said in this connection, as indicating the upright mind and courage of Francisco de Vitoria, that he was not a free agent in either case. As a Spaniard he was

---

[3] *De Indis,* Sec. I; p. 119.
[4] *De potestate civili,* trans. by Gwladys L. Williams, in Appendix C, *The Spanish Origin of International Law,* by J. B. Scott, Part I, p. lxxi.

a subject of Charles I, King of Spain, who, as Charles V, was Holy Roman Emperor, so that a word against the Emperor was a word against his sovereign. At the same time, he was a member of the Dominican Order and subject in every moment of his life to the head of his Church; yet he denied the claim of the pope to exercise sovereignty over the newly discovered world.

But what of other titles which might be invoked? Discussing several of these in turn, Francisco de Vitoria disallowed them in regular order. The third, for example, was title by discovery, which he dismissed in a few words, saying that discovery implied that the land "discovered" was unoccupied, that the Indians had certainly been in occupation when the New World was discovered, and that the Spaniards or other Europeans could no more claim to be discoverers of occupied land than could the aborigines, voyaging eastward to Spain and France, have claimed by discovery the territories of the Spaniards and of the French.

The fourth title alleged was based on the refusal of the aborigines to accept the Christian faith. This title, in the opinion of the Dominican professor at Salamanca, was likewise inadequate, for not only had there been a failure to present the faith to the Indians in a convincing way, but, even if it had been so presented, the rejection of it by them was not sufficient cause for war against them.

As regards the fifth title—that based on the sins of the aborigines—Vitoria denied its adequacy on the ground that, being infidels and not Christians, they were not subject to the jurisdiction of the Church in such matters.

The sixth title was that of voluntary choice. As far as Vitoria could determine—and he had examined the subject very thoroughly—the element of voluntary choice had played very little part in the relations between the Spaniards and the Indians, and he therefore dismissed that title without further ado.

There was a seventh and final title among those rejected by Vitoria. It was based upon the assertion that the Indians and their territory had come into the possession of the Spaniards "by special grant from God." Those who made this assertion Vitoria compared unfavorably with the prophets of the Old Testament, saying:[5]

I am loath to dispute hereon at any length, for it would be hazardous to give credence to one who asserts a prophecy against the common law and against the rules of Scripture, unless his doctrine were confirmed by miracles. Now, no such are adduced by prophets of this type.

[5] *De Indis,* Sec. II, p. 148.

And Vitoria therefore concluded this series of negatives by saying:[6] "Let this suffice about false and inadequate titles to seize the lands of the Indians."

He did not deny, however, that the Spaniards might have titles other than those rejected, and that these titles might lead to lawful Spanish acquisitions in the Americas. The first of the eight possible titles was "that of natural society and fellowship,"[7] which implied the right of the Spaniards to travel to America, to settle in America, to establish themselves there in industry and in commerce and to become naturalized "Americans," if they so desired. Vitoria's discussion of this phase of the subject went far toward laying the foundations of the modern law of nations. Here he bases his discussion upon the *ius gentium* of the Roman law, which in his opinion was identical with or derived from the natural law, and of which the test was the natural reason of man. He therefore begins with the *ius gentium* itself, which, he tells us, "either is natural law or is derived from natural law." The authority which he invokes in support of this statement is the *Institutes* of Justinian,[8] which declare that "what natural reason has established among all nations is called the *jus gentium.*" And here Vitoria puts new wine, so to speak, into old bottles, for he employs the term *ius gentium* —theretofore generally considered as the law common to different peoples rather than as an interstate law—in the sense of the law applicable among nations, as is evident from two important innovations introduced in the passage under consideration. Thus the phrase in the original Latin of the quotation from the *Institutes* just given reads, *"inter omnes homines,"* that is to say, "among all men," but Vitoria paraphrases this expression so that it reads *"inter omnes gentes."* This innovation is fundamental, for the use of *gentes* instead of *homines* converts the old Roman law of nations, governing the relations of men everywhere, into the law of peoples, in the sense of nations or states. And as if to confirm this point Vitoria, in the very next sentence, employs the word *"nationes"* instead of *"gentes,"* thus proving that he considered *gentes* and *nationes* synonymous and that he was dealing with the law and relations of nations.[9] "Congruently herewith," he declares, "it is reckoned among all nations"—and the Latin is *"apud omnes nationes"* —"inhumane to treat visitors and foreigners badly without some special

---

[6] *De Indis*, Sec. II, p. 149.   [7] *Ibid.*, Sec. III, no. 1; p. 151.   [8] I. ii. 1.
[9] The use of the word *nationes* as equivalent to the term *gentes* and the previous substitution of *gentes* for *homines* were pointed out and dwelt upon by the late Ernest Nys as significant stages by which the *ius gentium* of the Romans was finally metamorphosed into the international law of today. See his Introduction to Vitoria, *De Indis et de iure belli relectiones* (previously cited), pp. 42–43.

cause, while, on the other hand, it is humane and correct to treat visitors well."

Vitoria's further arguments on this first justifiable title are likewise of importance in the development of international law. After dealing at some length with the right of citizens of one state to travel within the jurisdiction of another state, and affirming that this is a right conferred by both divine and natural law, he discusses in broad and enlightened terms the rights of trade and settlement in the New World. Here the first foundation of his argument is a passage from the *Digest*[10] of Justinian: "Nature has established a bond of relationship between all men"; from which Vitoria adduces—as Aristotle himself would have done—that "it is contrary to natural law for one man to dissociate himself from another without good reason." Man, declares Vitoria, citing Ovid, "is not a wolf to his fellow man, but a man."

Turning to the rights which the Spaniards might properly enjoy in the material resources of the New World, an important question in Vitoria's day, he begins by stating the principle that what belongs to nobody is "acquired by the first occupant according to the law of nations."[11] This is technically known as the doctrine of *res nullius*. "It follows," continues Vitoria, "that if there be in the earth gold or in the sea pearls or in a river anything else which is not appropriated by the law of nations those will vest in the first occupant, just as the fish in the sea do." This is the concrete expression of an abstract principle of the law of nations.

At this point Vitoria indulges in what might be termed an *obiter dictum* which is of the first importance in the development of his theory of international law: "Indeed, there are many things in this connection which issue from the law of nations, which, because it has a sufficient derivation from natural law, is clearly capable of conferring rights and creating obligations." But it might be maintained that the law of nations contained other elements than those derived from natural law. Vitoria was ready for this contention. "Even if we grant," he goes on to say, "that it is not always derived from natural law, yet there exists clearly enough a consensus of the greater part of the whole world, especially in behalf of the common good of all." Here are two important ideas: first, that international law may be made by agreement, not necessarily of all nations, but of a majority: and secondly, that there must be a standard for international law just as there is for the law of the state, which standard is that it shall be for the common good—the

---
[10] I. i. 3; *De Indis*, Sec. III, no. 3; p. 153.
[11] *Institutes* II. i. 12; *De Indis*, Sec. III, no. 4; p. 153.

good not merely of one or a few but of all. To support this conception, Vitoria introduces in his next statement a series of examples which lead to an unanswerable conclusion: "If after the early days of the creation of the world or its recovery from the flood the majority of mankind decided that ambassadors should everywhere be reckoned inviolable and that the sea should be common and that prisoners of war should be made slaves [instead of being slaughtered, as was the ancient practice] and if this, namely, that strangers should not be driven out, were deemed a desirable principle, it would certainly have the force of law, even though the rest of mankind objected thereto."

Vitoria contemplated that the foreigners repairing to the recently discovered America might wish not merely to reside there and to engage in business but perhaps to become citizens. This citizenship, he considered, could be acquired only upon the basis of domicile; for Vitoria recognized the importance of domicile in matters of nationality as fully as do international lawyers today. He had in mind, however, not only naturalization but also nationality by birth in the Americas: in other words, Vitoria stood for what was to become the American doctrine of *ius soli*. His own language should be given on this important point:

If children of any Spaniard be born there and they wish to acquire citizenship, it seems they can not be barred either from citizenship or from the advantages enjoyed by other citizens. I refer to the case where the parents had their domicile there.[12]

Vitoria had the habit of basing his theories upon a legal foundation, and therefore the present theory was not offered as a personal opinion without authority. "The proof of this," he declares, "is furnished by the rule of the law of nations, that he is to be called and is a citizen who is born within the state."[13] But this was not the only principle which supported his theory; for he immediately adds: "And the confirmation lies in the fact that as man is a civil animal, whoever is born in any one state is not a citizen of another state." Vitoria, it should be observed, was in favor of single nationality and not of dual nationality, and certainly not of the unfortunate condition of those who have no nationality at all, for he says:[14] "If he were not a citizen of the state referred to, he would not be a citizen of any state, to the prejudice of his rights under both natural law and the law of nations."

How successfully this doctrine of nationality may be applied is illustrated by our experience in the United States, for our citizenship is based firmly

---

[12] *De Indis*, Sec. III, no. 5; pp. 153–54.
[13] *Code* X. xxxix. 7; *De Indis*, Sec. III, no. 5; p. 154. [14] *De Indis*, Sec. III, no. 5; p. 154.

on the principle of *ius soli*. It is not too much to say that American citizenship might have been almost nonexistent had nationality by blood been the test, inasmuch as every child born in America of foreigners would, according to the full and strict application of the principle of *ius sanguinis,* have retained its parents' nationality, and—as a result of the practical extermination of the Indians—there might thus have been fewer "Americans" after the settlement of the New World than before.

Having provided for the Americas, as it were, a doctrine of citizenship, Vitoria completed his conception by a pertinent observation on the question of naturalization. With him the matter of acquiring citizenship in a foreign state was not a question of privilege but of right, and he therefore declared that if any foreigner desired to become a citizen in a state of the Indians, through marriage or otherwise, he could not "be impeded," and in consequence he should be free to "enjoy the privileges" of citizenship "just as others do": but with this important proviso, that the naturalized citizen should, as a corollary of his right to naturalization, "submit to the burdens" to which other citizens submitted.

In his discussion of these topics Vitoria recognized the American principalities of the Indians as nations and as possessed of the same rights which the European countries enjoyed. From this recognition it would seem necessarily to follow that the government which the Indians established should be the one which they themselves preferred; and that all inhabitants of their territories—whether natives, naturalized persons, or foreigners—would be obliged to comply with the laws and customs of the country. Therefore the Spaniards should not interfere as of right with the customs of the aborigines, however different those customs might be from their own.

The second of the titles which might justify Spanish acquisitions in the newly discovered lands involved the rights of missionaries. Now the religion of the natives was not to be brushed aside by the Spaniards, although as Christians they would naturally hope to substitute for it the religion of Christ. On the other hand, the right of the Spaniards to their own religion was to be recognized and its observance not prevented by the natives. But while the natives had a right to their own religious beliefs, the Spanish priests, it was held, had likewise the right to lay the Christian religion before the natives "freely and without hindrance," in the hope of converting them to the Church of which they were missionaries. Today these principles propounded by Vitoria are recognized by an enlightened law of nations, and provisions relating to them are to be found in many international treaties.

In the event that missionaries were successful in converting the natives to the new faith, it was the opinion of Vitoria, set forth in his discussion of the third and fourth titles, that these Christian converts should not be interfered with on religious grounds. If they were thus interfered with, the Europeans might properly intervene to protect them. So, too, inhumane treatment meted out to the natives by their government might also constitute a just ground for intervention in native affairs by the Europeans, on the delicate and flexible plea of humanity, and this would be a fifth title. The causes justifying such intervention as enumerated by Vitoria are "the tyranny of those who bear rule among the aborigines of America" and "the tyrannical laws which work wrong to innocent folk there."[15] As examples of such misrule, Vitoria mentions "sacrifice of innocent people or the killing in other ways of uncondemned people for cannibalistic purposes."

The sixth and seventh titles under which the claims of the Spaniards might be justified (the "true and voluntary choice" of Spanish rule by the Indians, and the right to intervene, in wars between the natives, when the Spaniards were allies of one of the parties to the conflict) need not be discussed here. The eighth title, however, is of special importance, for it relates to a theory which has only recently been put into general practice. While Vitoria humanely insisted upon the treatment of the natives as human beings, recognizing them as possessed of the same fundamental rights (and the correlative duties) as citizens of his own country, he nevertheless was aware that the Indians had not reached the European stage of civilization and that in many cases they might be unprepared to organize and to conduct a government in accordance with what the enlightened of his day would consider their best interests. With some hesitation, Vitoria suggested that in such cases it might be appropriate for the Spaniards, in dealing with the natives, "to undertake the administration of their country, providing them with prefects and governors for their towns."[16] In some cases it might even be advisable for the purpose he had in mind to "give them new lords." But all of this was with the highly important proviso: "so long as this was clearly for their benefit." This proviso Vitoria emphasied by a statement in the nature of a warning:

Let this, however, . . . be put forward without dogmatism and subject also to the limitation that any such interposition be for the welfare and in the interests of the Indians and not merely for the profit of the Spaniards. For this is the respect in which all the danger to soul and salvation lies.

In the language of today, certain parts of the New World might, for the good of the native inhabitants, be mandated. But the mandate of Vitoria

---

[15] *De Indis*, Sec. III, no. 15; p. 159.   [16] *Ibid.*, no. 18; p. 161.

was characterized by a quality whose importance cannot be overstressed, particularly with respect to present-day administration of mandates, and that quality was unselfishness on the part of the mandatory.[17]

In his *Readings on the Indians* Vitoria was concerned with international law rather than with political theory. But he had very clear and definite conceptions as to the nature, functions, and government of the state. Certain of his views on the subject may be found in passages scattered throughout his twelve *Relectiones,* but the subject is treated in full, and with the hand of a master, in a "Reading" which, as has been mentioned, he delivered in 1528 at the University of Salamanca some four years before he prepared the *Readings on the Indians.* The state as described by Vitoria was an Aristotelian community of human beings associated because of their social nature and living under a form of government which they themselves should determine, the fundamental purpose of which was to be the administration of justice. "Justice, indeed, cannot be practised," he declared, "except by the multitude."[18] The government might be, according to the wisdom or whim of the people forming it, a monarchy, aristocracy, or a democracy, although Vitoria's preference was for a monarchy. But the form of government was not to be final. It could be changed from time to time by those who made it, namely, the people.

Now power, Vitoria says—as became a theologian—is from God, but its exercise is vested in the political community. "The State, then, possesses this power by divine Disposition; but the material cause in which, by natural and divine law, power of this kind resides, is the State itself, which by its very nature is competent to govern and administer itself, and to order all its powers for the common good."[19] Vitoria defines the power in question as "the faculty, authority, or right to govern the civil State." Since it is of divine origin it cannot be "abrogated by the consent of men," and his argument on this point is interesting and conclusive:

For if man may not renounce the right and the means of defending himself and of using his bodily members for his own advantage, then neither may he renounce power, since these functions pertain to power by natural and divine law. In like manner, the State may in nowise be deprived of this power to protect itself and to guard against injury from its own citizens or from aliens, a function

---

[17] The conception of the international mandate has an interesting background. See, for example, Bentwich, *The Mandates System,* chap. i, especially pp. 7–8. For a more detailed discussion of the Roman-law foundations of the mandates system, see Wright, *Mandates under the League of Nations,* pp. 377–83.
[18] *De potestate civili,* in Appendix C, Scott, *Spanish Origin of International Law* (previously cited), Part I, p. lxxv.
[19] *Ibid.,* p. lxxvii.

which it could not fulfil if there were no public powers; and consequently, if all the citizens should agree to dispense with these powers, in order that they might be bound by no law and that there should be no one to command, the agreement would be null and void, being contrary to natural law.[20]

In this state the laws and not the ruler were supreme, for Vitoria insisted not only that "the laws and constitutions of princess are binding in such a way as to render transgressors guilty in the court of conscience,"[21] but also that "kings and legislators are bound by the laws."[22]

It is possible, perhaps unfortunately, for the human mind to conceive of a particular state as an entity isolated from other states. But such a fanciful conception found no place among Vitoria's political and international doctrines. It was obvious to him that nations, large and small, must have relations one with another, and he therefore thought of them as constituting a society of states, an international community which existed because of the coexistence of the states. And just as a state possessed the power to make laws for the government and well-being of its citizens, so this international commonwealth possessed, in Vitoria's opinion, a right to legislate for the good of society as a whole. His views on this subject, which is as important in our day as it was in his, are expressed with clearness and power:

> International law has not only the force of a pact and agreement among men, but also the force of a law; for the world as a whole, being in a way one single State, has the power to create laws that are just and fitting for all persons, as are the rules of international law. Consequently, it is clear that they who violate these international rules, whether in peace or in war, commit a mortal sin; moreover, in the gravest matters, such as the inviolability of ambassadors, it is not permissible for one country to refuse to be bound by international law, the latter having been established by the authority of the whole world.[23]

This is Vitoria's view of an organized world. It is the view of many today whose ideal may be termed the organic conception of the international community which looks toward a federation of nations.

It should be said in conclusion that Vitoria, a man of peace, admitted and faced squarely the fact of war. With him, however, as with the schoolmen generally, war was permissible only because there was no court of the nations to which resort could be had for the redress of a violation of a rule of international law. St. Augustine's definition of a just cause of war was adopted by Vitoria and thus stated by him: "There is a single and only

---

[20] *De potestate civili*, in J. B. Scott, *op. cit.*, p. lxxxi.   [21] *Ibid.*, p. lxxxiii.
[22] *Ibid.*, p. lxxxix. Some additional comments on Vitoria's political theories will be found in the next chapter, *infra*, pp. 348–50.
[23] *Ibid.*, p. xc. See also *infra*, pp. 559, 560.

just cause for commencing a war, namely, a wrong received."[24] The steps to be taken, in the view of Vitoria, in seeking redress of such an injury were not unlike the steps taken in a national court of justice, up to the point of judgment, at which point the procedure as between states necessarily varied from that between individuals, owing to the nonexistence of an international judge. The plaintiff state proceeded, as it were, *ex parte* in the absence of the defendant state or its representatives, the prince examining the facts and reaching, with the advice of his counselors, a decision as to the rights of his own state. Thus in place of the international judgment there was the decision of the plaintiff state, to be executed by the prince of the plaintiff state.

In the course of time there was established in the New World, following the federation of American states under a superintending head, a court of the states known as the Supreme Court of the United States; and in our day—to be specific, in 1921—there has been established at The Hague the Permanent Court of International Justice, modeled for the most part on the Supreme Court of the federated United States, for the larger but, unfortunately, still embryonic federation of the independent states of the world which Vitoria had in mind.

In the federation of states of the United States there are also federal courts of first instance, sitting in various states of the federation, from whose decisions litigants may appeal to the Supreme Court of the United States; and just as the Permanent Court of International Justice at The Hague is in harmony with Vitoria's conception of a federal community of states, so also would be a series of inferior international courts set up in different regions of the world for the settlement of disputes relating particularly to the regions in question, with the right of appeal from such courts to the Permanent Court of International Justice at The Hague. Then indeed the international community which Vitoria foresaw would be governed by justice and the passionless administration of law.

[24] *De iure belli*, no. 13; trans. by J. P. Bate (previously cited), p. 170.

Chapter XXIII

JEAN BODIN (1530-96)

In 1576 a Frenchman by the name of Jean Bodin, whose eyes were not fixed upon the New World, as Vitoria's had been, but upon the problems of his own country, published *Six livres de la République,* an elaborate tractate which appeared in several editions during his lifetime and was translated by his own hand into Latin, in which language he is said to have been more expert than in his native tongue. It was also rendered into English and published in 1606, having previously been translated into Italian, Spanish, and German. From these bibliographical details it is evident that the book was considered by his contemporaries as one of merit, and posterity has justified the contemporary opinion, for Bodin's *Six Books of the Republic* remains among the classics of political science.

The France of his day—he was born in the city of Angers in 1530 and died sixty-six years later—was a France of turmoil, threatened by dissolution within and attacks from without. It seemed to the author of the *Republic* that the government of his country should be reorganized upon a basis sufficiently stable and conservative to preserve what had proved itself in the past and to protect the development of the future. He had the good fortune to see his dream realized while he was still alive (a good fortune which rarely happens to philosophers), for the accession of Henry of Navarre to the throne of France resulted in a unified France under a strong hand.

But Bodin's fundamental conception of sovereignty soon passed the frontiers of France and became a force with which any student of political science must reckon. In the course of crossing the frontiers, it suffered, to be sure, not a few changes, changes of which it is doubtful if Bodin himself would have approved; but in spite of these changes his treatise stands as the great contribution of France—at least before Montesquieu—to the modern conception of government.

It has been too often the wont of the political scientist to credit Bodin with the doctrine of sovereignty as that doctrine developed after his death. But the fact of the matter is that while the seed of the later flowering of the conception of sovereignty into the theory of the state as the be-all and end-all of human society may be found in Bodin's *Republic,* it remains an open question whether he himself foresaw that his doctrine of sovereignty would subsequently be used to bolster up the divine right of kings.

It was originally intended that selections from Bodin's *Six Books of the Republic* should be included in Volume II of the present work. But investigation and reflection have led to the conclusion that such selections should be omitted for the reason that Bodin's fundamental propositions are not in accord with the long line of development from Plato and Aristotle, culminating (for present purposes) in Hooker's *Ecclesiastical Polity*, the *Freedom of the Seas* by the youthful Grotius, and Francisco Suárez' *De legibus ac Deo legislatore*. The reason is that the outstanding contribution of Bodin was a political theory whose avowed purpose was the welding of communities more or less independent under the domination of a single sovereign monarch whose word was to be law, which theory, when pushed to its ultimate conclusion—as it unfortunately was—was to be succinctly expressed in French in a few short words: "L'état! C'est moi." To Bodin (a man of his age) the conception of an autocratic sovereignty appealed, and he lent it his support for reasons which will presently be described at length. But its acceptance and subsequent exaggeration were destined to be a misfortune to political science and to the world, an obstacle to, rather than a part of, our gradual development of a philosophy of government by the choice and consent of the governed. Nevertheless, since Bodin's theories have exerted a profound influence on many a prince, publicist, and politician, they should not be passed by without an analysis which may serve to justify the opinions here expressed.

The situation of France in the sixteenth century—largely because of the conflicting ambitions of Francis I and Charles V, Holy Roman Emperor and King of Spain, and the resulting disturbances in the period intervening between the death of Francis and the accession of Henry of Navarre—was one of dynastic changes, of rebellion, and well-nigh of disintegration. It was natural, under these circumstances, that enlightened Frenchmen should seek, if not a sign from above, at least a political design that would guide them out of the political forest in which they were lost. That design was sovereignty, and its exponent was Bodin.

It happened that Bodin had an inquisitive and an open mind. He was born a Catholic, but later adopted Protestantism, only to return eventually to the fold, having apparently decided, after investigation, to stand by the faith of his fathers. As one deeply concerned with the public affairs of his country, he saw and appreciated the dangers lurking in the political forest, and he looked at the facts of his time with a clear if not wholly unprejudiced eye. He was interested in political economy, and was indeed an early contributor to that science. By profession he was a lawyer, with something of a philosophical bent and with more than a turn for history. He was not only versed in law; he practiced law, and he lectured on law at the University of Toulouse. Nor was he interested merely in an academic way in public affairs, for he took an active part in them, distinguishing himself as a member of the States-General at Blois and in diplomatic matters.

The salient features of Bodin's career and his services are recounted by an English specialist in political science, who is likewise a clergyman of the Established Church of England, Dr. Robert H. Murray, who begins his discussion of Bodin with the significant statement that "Jean Bodin (1530-96) is a writer second to none in importance during the sixteenth century." Dr. Murray, indicating Bodin's ample qualifications on both the intellectual and the practical side, adds that he was

a jurist, a humanist, and a professor of law at the University of Toulouse. Nor is his equipment on the practical side a whit less satisfactory. The advocate of the king at Laon, the deputy of the Third Estate at the Estates of Blois, the Politique, he was deeply immersed in the affairs of his country.[1]

And he was, to continue the quotation, not only "a man of his own century" but also "a man of all the centuries," in that in his writings "he pleads on behalf of toleration."

Of his qualifications as a political thinker Dr. Murray says:

Bodin touched all aspects of political thought, and on all of them he makes illuminating—if discursive—remarks. He was a scholar, who strove before all to be a thinker; a lawyer, who was as interested in the origin of legal rules as in the rules themselves; a man of the world, who brought all the resources of his shrewd common sense to the investigation of political problems; a sociologist, who neither dealt in names nor played with words.[2]

As Bodin was himself both a student of history and a historian, it will be of interest to examine Dr. Murray's view of his conception of history:

[1] *The History of Political Science from Plato to the Present*, p. 172.
[2] This eulogy would no doubt be appreciated by Bodin's fellow countrymen, who have from time to time called the attention of the world to his claim to universal recognition. See, for example, Professor Chauviré's *Jean Bodin, auteur de la République;* and especially a recent penetrating study of Bodin by M. André Gardot, a specialist well qualified to undertake an authoritative analysis of Bodin's various activities, and particularly of his conceptions which have more or less relation to international law. This analysis was prepared in the form of a series of lectures delivered at the Hague Academy of International Law in 1934, under the title, "Jean Bodin. Sa place parmi les fondateurs du droit international," and was published in *Recueil des cours*, 1934, Vol. 50, pp. 549–747.

History to him—as to Machiavelli—was simply a means of providing intellectual entertainment to the reader, and, above all, practical guidance to the man of affairs. At the same time we acknowledge the wide view he took of its scope, for it included all human "consilia, dicta, facta." He argues that history should be studied in an order proceeding from the general to the particular—from a compendious view of universal history to the thorough investigation of its several portions—in such a manner that the relations of the parts to one another and the whole may be correctly perceived. . . . He anticipates Ranke in holding that it is the office of the historian to record what has happened as it happened. "Historia nihil aliud esse quam veritatis et rerum gestarum veluti tabula."[3]

On Bodin's views concerning the philosophy of law, Dr. Murray makes a brief but interesting comment:

Bodin is philosophic enough in his legal outlook to share the views of Hotman that the enlightened jurist must not confine his attention to the law of Rome. Cujas, learned as he was, Bodin regarded as a mere interpreter of Latin texts. No study of Roman law, he argues, however complete and accurate, can afford more than a partial notion of law. It is absurd to identify Roman law with universal law. There is a universal law, in which all codes of law have their root and rationale, and of which they are but imperfect expressions. In order to reach this law the historians must be consulted as well as the jurists, in order that Persians and Egyptians, Greeks and Hebrews, Spaniards and English, may all find their due place side by side with the Romans. Hotman is a Germanist, but Bodin is a universalist.[4]

Bodin's interests, however, reached a still wider field, for he conceived that the historian and philosopher must also be a geographer.

Dividing nations into northern, middle, and southern, he investigates with amazing fulness of knowledge how climatic and geographical conditions have affected the bodily strength, the courage, the intelligence, the humanity, the chastity, and, in short, the mind, the morals, and manners of their inhabitants. He also indicates—invariably with example after example—what influence mountains and winds, diversities of soil and of situation, have exerted on individuals.[5]

This realization of the importance of geography was not merely a novelty but a contribution of the greatest importance, in that it vastly broadened the outlook of philosopher, historian, and political scientist.

Still we have not reached the end of the catalogue of Bodin's interests. "In the field of political economy," continues Dr. Murray, "Bodin is every whit as original as he is in the field of political philosophy." He here refers to Bodin's controversy with a certain M. Malestroit, master of the mint, who

[3] Murray, op. cit., pp. 173-74.   [4] Ibid., p. 174.   [5] Ibid., p. 175.

had decided views upon currency, his opinion being that the value of gold and silver were invariable and that, if what had formerly sold for four pounds now sold for twelve, this tripling in price occurred because the commodity had become thrice as valuable. Bodin, however, says Dr. Murray, did "not think for a moment that the precious metals in circulation represent the wealth of the community,"[6] and he therefore proceeded to write a devastating reply to the master of the mint.

His views on other economic matters cannot be discussed here, although as an example of their soundness it may be noted that Bodin regarded imports and exports as mutually profitable to the parties concerned and not as a matter in which one party was bound to lose if the other gained.

Dr. Murray has already alluded, as we have seen, to Bodin's views on toleration, and he now adds a brief comment to his previous statement:[7]

A man so enlightened as Bodin was, on some sides of his nature, naturally believed in toleration. . . . The spirit of the wars of religion is as far removed from Bodin as it is from L'Hôpital.[8]

In the preceding passages quoted from Dr. Murray he has done full justice to Bodin's great abilities and merits. He now comments on certain other qualities of the French authority on sovereignty:

The forerunner of Montesquieu, Bodin was also the successor of Aristotle and—little as he liked the idea—also of Machiavelli. The craft and the cunning of the Italian were applied on so grand a scale that it took quite two generations before fundamentally his implications were grasped. Men in some measure were quick enough to perceive that the Italian meant to employ craft and cunning, but they were at least two generations before they perceived that such employment meant a complete break with all mediaeval traditions. In fact, what Machiavelli effected was the divorce of ethics and politics. The rightness or the wrongness of a course was a matter that never crossed the brain of Machiavelli—at least in his public capacity. Even Bodin did not altogether realise the divorce which the *Principe* and the *Discorsi* effected. He never intends to accomplish wrong, yet in order to win he means to succeed wrongly. To Bodin the contrivances of Machiavelli are detestable. Still, for the welfare of the State, one must not be unduly scrupulous over trifles. In his greatest work, his *République*, published in 1577, we receive a quiet reminder that for the success of diplomatic policy the statesman must calculate coldly the chances of the scheme in hand,

---

[6] *The History of Political Science from Plato to the Present*, p. 176.   [7] *Ibid.*, pp. 176–77.

[8] L'Hôpital, the Chancellor of France whose wise and humane views gave rise to the party called *Politique*, which secured a throne for Henry IV and toleration for his people, thus expressed his own views on the subject of toleration: "Tout ainsi que c'est le même soleil qui luit à Paris que celui qui donne sa lumière et sa chaleur à Rome et à Constantinople, ainsi la justice divine et aussi le droit naturel n'est point autre parmi les sauvages de l'Amérique que parmi les chrétiens d'Europe."—Quoted from Gardot, *op. cit.*, p. 560.

and then act promptly to ensure success. He is as certain as Machiavelli that nothing is more to be dreaded than an abortive operation. He holds before us admiringly the example of the Emperor Augustus. Q. Gallius had conspired against the Emperor, who pardoned him publicly, and had him privately killed. . . . In plain English, Bodin is ready to employ any means for the end in view, and he obviously thinks with Machiavelli that the end justifies the means.[9]

To end the quotation here would be unjust to Bodin, and to Dr. Murray's estimate of him. To complete the picture another passage must be quoted:

> To do him justice, however, we by no means think that Bodin saw clearly that ultimately Machiavelli effected as complete a breach between public and private morality as it is possible to effect, and in so effecting destroyed both. *La raison d'État* did not entirely carry the day with the French thinker. Besides, he disliked the Italian on quite different grounds. Modern as his outlook was in some ways, in others it was typically mediaeval. No doubt the State must be strong, but its strength must assist the good life of the nation. He must possess a theory, for he was not a Frenchman for nothing. With all his mind he revolted from the pragmatism of the *Prince*. To him political philosophy was a science as well as an art, and he could not bear the outlook of a man who took a purely practical view of it. Bodin is the last man on earth to see visions and dream dreams. For all that, he must be able to formulate a theory, and one reason of his dislike of the Italian is that he refuses to formulate theories of any kind whatsoever. The contrivances of his crafty and his cunning mind are all he has to offer, and Bodin spurns the offer.[10]

Now Bodin, being a jurist, turned to Rome for most of his legal doctrines, and his legal background greatly influenced his political conceptions. But he was also a man of his time and, while Rome was his foundation, his political structure was medieval in the relationship of the sovereign to his people—which was not that of the Roman emperor but of the medieval king. And while he was familiar with both Plato and Aristotle, he nevertheless claimed and exercised his right to differ from them.

In discarding as a practical man the myth of the prehistoric Golden Age, Bodin also discarded not a few of the ideals of political and social relationships which had become associated with the traditional "age of innocence." His political society was not one aiming to recapture the ideal happiness of the Golden Age, but an organization arising out of social and political expediency and the exigencies of force—a process of involuntary subjection rather than of voluntary consent.

It should be added, however, that Bodin recognized natural law—and also the law of nations—as superior to the law of the state; but his natural law lacked the definiteness of conception of that of the schoolmen, and per-

[9] Murray, *op. cit.*, pp. 177-78. [10] *Ibid.*, p. 178.

haps it is fair to assume that, if Bodin had been more familiar with scholastic doctrines than he was, natural law and natural rights might still further have humanized his conception of the state and of sovereignty.

The *raison d'être* of Bodin's system lies, as has been implied, in the fact that he was living in an age of anarchy. His purpose was to put down anarchy and to secure stable government, and this was to be attained through the installation of a powerful ruler. With his purpose there can be no quarrel. Nor, indeed, will it follow that his goal of a well-organized state is to be repudiated; but the means which he advocated for attaining that goal, and especially the standard by which he judged a well-organized state, were subject to that misinterpretation and distortion which unfortunately resulted—once the saving restraint of the natural law was discarded by his successors—in the irresponsible sovereign.

Now the state, he informs us in the opening chapter of his *Six Books,* "is an association of families and their common affairs, governed by a supreme power and by reason."[11]

This definition—which Bodin says had been "omitted by writers on the state"—he placed at the very beginning of his work, because, as he observes, "it is necessary to consider the final stage of inherited enlightenment and accomplishment, before anything else is said." And completing the thought which he has in mind, he adds:[12] "when the end has been discovered and explored, we may examine the stages through which the goal was reached."

In the several stages of social grouping, the first is the family, and Bodin, after discussing the principles relating to the family or household, concludes that those principles "contain the elements of all political society." The family was subject to its "head," and thus in the family we have the first seed of that sovereignty to which the individual was subjected. The extent of the original subjection to the head of the family is indicated by Bodin's statement that "before any state or commonwealth took form, each *pater familias* had final power of life and death over his children and wives."

But what of the relationship and status of heads of families in larger social groups?

---

[11] Coker, *Readings in Political Philosophy* (rev. ed., 1938), p. 370. With but a few exceptions, all of the passages quoted in the present chapter from the *Six Books of the Republic* are taken from Professor Coker's translation of selections from Bodin, which translation is based upon the Latin text published at Frankfort in 1641, but has been compared by Professor Coker with the earlier French text and with the English version by Richard Knolles, published in London in 1606. The present writer, after examining the Latin text (a copy of the 1641 edition having recently come into his possession) as well as the French and English versions, realized that Professor Coker's selections include all of the essentials of Bodin's political theory, and that his admirable translation could not be bettered.

[12] Coker, *op. cit.*, p. 370.

JEAN BODIN

When, therefore, the head of a house goes forth from the home, where he holds domestic authority, to join with other family heads for the purpose of transacting their common affairs, he then loses the name of master and lord and becomes an associate and a citizen; in a sense, he leaves his home to enter the body politic, and he transacts public instead of domestic business. Indeed a citizen is no other than a free man who is bound by the supreme power of another.

Such a citizen might be free, in the sense that he was not actually a slave, but his subjection to "the supreme power of another" would certainly deprive him of true liberty in the modern sense of that term.

Bodin next traces what he conceives to have been the early development of the state:

Afterwards strength and the desire to rule, as well as avarice and the passion of revenge, armed one against the other, and the issue of war forced the conquered to serve the pleasure of the more powerful. He who showed himself a valiant leader rules then not only over his household but also over his enemies and allies—the latter as conquered friends, to each one of whom was given freedom to live as he pleased, the former (his enemies) as slaves.[13]

At this point Bodin drops his analysis of prehistoric development in order to state its consequences:

Thus that complete liberty which is derived from nature, was taken away, even from the victors, by him whom the latter had chosen as their leader; at least their liberty was diminished; for each, even in his private capacity, had to recognize the supreme authority of another. Thus we see the origin of slaves and subjects, citizens and foreigners, prince and tyrant.[14]

According to this theory the development of states was largely a result of the overgenerous use of the club, resulting in the taking away of the natural rights and liberty of individuals by the force of might. Bodin considers that there was good evidence of this rather brutal process in "reason itself" and in "books." Of "reason" he says, it "teaches us that governments and states were first founded upon force, though we may learn the same thing from history." And of written records Bodin observes: "Books, antiquities and laws are full of testimonies that primitive man held nothing higher than convenience; he would rob, plunder, and kill, or enslave."

As has been noted, Bodin was well grounded in history, and he uses it skillfully for his purposes; but in so doing he finds it necessary to reject certain authorities which the world has long been accustomed to treat with respect. It seemed to him, as he said, that "Aristotle, Demosthenes, and Cicero are wrong; for, following Herodotus (I think) they hold that kings first obtained preferment on account of their reputation for integrity and

[13] *Ibid.*, pp. 371-72.   [14] *Ibid.*, p. 372.

justice." They thus pictured, we are told, "heroic and golden ages," which Bodin elsewhere refutes "by positive arguments and evidence." A few sentences supply what he apparently considers to be adequate evidence for his own theory on the origin and development of government:

Here is proof of my theory: The people of Gao (in Africa) in the preceding generation had heard of neither kingdoms nor the rule of tyrants, until one of them, in his wandering, saw the majestic power of the king of Timbuctu. Thereupon there came upon him the desire to rule over his people; and, being hard pressed by poverty, he began to plunder the merchants and other rich individuals; finally, having thus obtained wealth and having communicated his design to his friends, he gradually acquired control over the entire region. After him his son, calling himself king, found it necessary to preserve with equity and justice the authority which had originated in robbery. This is the origin of the Gaoian kings who in a short time have advanced so rapidly.

No comment on this "proof" seems necessary, other than to observe that Aristotle and Demosthenes, and certainly Cicero, would, it may reasonably be assumed, have treated this theory with even more disdain than Bodin exhibited toward their theories on the origin of government.

In the eighth chapter of the first book of his treatise Bodin comes to grips with what may be considered, for present purposes, the core of his political doctrine: the theory of sovereignty. He proceeds to define sovereignty as "supreme power over citizens and subjects, unrestrained by laws."[15] But what does Bodin mean by "supreme power" (*summa potestas*)? Before quoting his own definition, it is advisable to consider the Roman background of the term *potestas*.

The Roman emperors had been obsessed with the conception of *imperium,* that is, the power to govern conferred by the *lex regia,* which, in the view of the Roman jurists, transferred to the emperor the power which the people had possessed in their republican institutions. This power is designated in the Latin as *imperium* or *potestas,* both being legal and technical, not philosophical, terms, which were employed by Bodin largely with the same significance as that given them by the Romans over a thousand years before.

The conception of the *lex regia* as a voluntary act of the people for the purpose of conferring the power which they themselves possessed upon a person who, through such a delegation of power from the people, became a sovereign (thus resulting in what was, in its essence, a form of compact) was familiar to Bodin, deeply versed as he was in Roman law. But for his purposes it was necessary to ignore the implication of a compact and to

[15] "Maiestas est summa in cives ac subditos legibusque soluta potestas."—Coker, *op. cit.,* p. 374.

conceive of this delegation of power as irrevocable; in short, the people must be considered as having completely and permanently given up all power and authority. Why was such a conception necessary? Because Bodin links the qualification "perpetual" to "supreme," and his reason for this is that unless the supreme power is also "perpetual," it is not "sovereign"; that is to say, if such power is given "to some one or several not perpetually, but for a brief period," they are not sovereigns but rather "custodians of sovereignty,"[16] until the power be withdrawn. Even should supreme power, in the fullest sense of the word, be granted by the people "to some one or few," "unlimited by laws, and without protest or appeal"—still if the grant is subject to revocation, that is not sovereignty; for the people, having granted the power, may take it away. As long as the people have not wholly "divested" themselves of their power, he to whom the exercise of sovereign power is delegated is not possessed of sovereignty in the sense of Bodin, since the people may at their "pleasure" require him to "render account"[17] of his conduct. But what if a ruler is granted supreme power "for life," and such power "is given unlimited by laws," and "not at the pleasure of any one"? Then "certainly," says Bodin, "it must be confessed that sovereign rights have been conceded to such a one." Why? Because "the people in such case have despoiled themselves of their authority, in order to give to another all the privileges of sovereignty, without conditions."[18] For Bodin, therefore, true sovereignty is possessed only by one who, "after God, acknowledges no one greater than himself." Here there is no question of the temporary delegation of power by the people as described above. It is the complete and unqualified relinquishment of the people's sovereignty as long as the prince may live.

Thus a vast gulf separated the sovereign and the citizen. "The prince," declares Bodin, "finds in the commonwealth no one whom he may compare with or prefer to himself; in truth, placed as he has been by Almighty and Immortal God in the degree next His Own, the prince looks down upon all the citizens, beholding them far beneath him; while the private citizen can command no other citizen by any public right, even though he may govern his own household through private and domestic command."[19]

Now what was the relation of this irresponsible prince—that is, irresponsible in the sense that he was bound to give no accounting of his actions to his subjects—to the law? In the first place, as Bodin says, the prince was not bound by the laws of his predecessor. But what of the laws made by

---

[16] *Ibid.*, p. 374. [17] *Ibid.*, p. 375. [18] *Ibid.*
[19] *De republica libri sex* . . . (Latin ed., Frankfort, 1641), Bk. III, chap. iv, p. 447.

himself?—for in Bodin's state the prince is the source of law. The answer is that, "as a prince is bound by no laws of his predecessor, much less is he bound by his own laws." The proof adduced in favor of this statement is the dictum—hardly acceptable to those who hold that man is his own best master—that "One man may receive a command from another, but no man can command himself."[20]

There was a certain customary phrase attached to the laws promulgated in Bodin's day, which he cites with relish in this connection as showing that laws derive their force entirely from "the will of him who makes the law,"[21] the phrase in question being, "because it has so pleased us"—meaning the lawmaking monarch.

In its relation to positive law, public power is separated by Bodin into two divisions, the one being supreme and therefore pertaining to the "sovereign," the other subordinate.

The public power of command exists in two forms: the one is in truth supreme, being above the laws and the magisterial power of command; the other is legal, and subject to the laws. The latter form pertains to magistrates [that is, to officials subordinate to the prince], the former, to sovereignty. Sovereignty in the state knows no superior to itself save only Immortal God, nor even any equal; but the magistrate acknowledges the sovereignty of the prince, and is bound by the prince's laws and commands.

Private citizens, in turn, are bound "first by Immortal God, and subordinately to this obligation, by the laws of the sovereign power and by the commands of magistrates."[22]

Though he thus grants a measure of power to the magistrates, Bodin is careful to protect the supreme power of the sovereign by declaring that the magistrate must obey the royal commands, even though they be contrary to the laws of the land. He may remonstrate, but obey he must in the end, lest the sovereign power be impaired.

Yet there were other laws, as Bodin himself acknowledges. These laws, in the making of which man took no part, were "the laws of God and of nature," and in Bodin's conception both "princes and people are equally bound by them." In a word, his prince was bound—although by no human law—to keep the higher law, and to recognize and obey both the law of God and the law of nature; and the same universal authority Bodin extends to the law of reason and justice, both derived either directly or indirectly from the same divine source.

But suppose the prince has taken oath to observe the laws of his country,

---

[20] Coker, *op. cit.*, p. 375.   [21] *Ibid.*, p. 376.   [22] Bodin, *op. cit.*, Bk. III, chap. v, p. 467.

as has frequently been required of princes throughout history. Such an oath is in effect a compact between the prince and his people and, in the scholastic conception, if violated, such violation releases the people from their obligation of obedience to the prince. Thereupon the right reverts to them to institute another government more responsive to their needs—a right necessarily including the further right to overthrow and completely to abolish the existing government if such action be necessary for their purpose.

In dealing with this topic Bodin makes a threefold distinction. If the prince has simply sworn to himself a formal oath—which is not believed to be a customary procedure—no obligation exists. On the other hand, if a prince swears to another ruler not to abrogate his own laws, Bodin considers the oath binding, provided the prince to whom the promise is made is a party in interest. This also, it may be noted, is a somewhat rare form of royal oath. Finally, there is what may be considered the more usual case, in which the prince has made "sworn promises to his subjects." Is he bound by such promises? Bodin's answer is a well-guarded affirmative, so well-guarded, in fact, that it is almost a negative. In the first place, the promises the prince makes under oath must be reasonable, if they are to put him under obligation, and this reasonableness he himself apparently determines. In the second place, his obligation is not due to his oath but to the promise, it being perhaps considered belittling for the prince to be bound by oath to his inferiors. In the third place, the prince can hold himself to be relieved of his obligation under circumstances so common that it would be hard to conceive of him as remaining long in a state of obligation: "Moreover, as a private person may be relieved of his obligation if he has been circumvented by fraud, deceit, error, or threat, so a prince may be released not only in those cases which tend to impair his sovereignty, but also where his private convenience and domestic affairs are disturbed."[23]

Returning now from the oath to the matter of the prince's relation to the law, Bodin declares that the prince is at liberty to "abrogate, modify, or replace a law made by himself and without the consent of his subjects."[24] There was a condition requisite for such action on his part, namely, that justice "seems to demand it." Here again it would appear that the determination of these demands of justice rests with the prince. Now Bodin maintains that when the prince takes such action, the abrogation, modification, or substitution of the law must be free from obscurity and ambiguity. If he has no "probable reason for abrogating the law, he is acting contrary to the duty of a good prince in seeking such abrogation."[25] But on this

[23] Coker, *op. cit.*, p. 376.   [24] *Ibid.*   [25] *Ibid.*, p. 377.

point it must be observed that sovereigns have seldom had difficulty in discovering "probable" reasons for altering any laws which interfered with what they were pleased to consider their prerogatives.

The oath of the prince to observe the law has been referred to as implying a contract, and obviously this implication occurred to Bodin, for he proceeds to warn us against confusing "laws and contracts." According to him, "law depends upon the will of him who holds supreme power in the state, and who can bind subjects by his law, but cannot bind himself."[26] Under this theory, the law is entirely a unilateral affair. What, however, of contracts between the prince and his subjects? They were mutual and therefore bilateral affairs, and, as Bodin the lawyer well knew, they could not in good faith "be departed from save with the consent of both parties." This might seem a regrettable state of affairs for a "supreme" sovereign, for, as Bodin points out, under these circumstances "the prince seems to have nothing above his subjects." The prince, however, did possess a slight advantage, for Bodin declares that if the purpose of the law, concerning which he was under contract (supported by oath) with the people, ceased to exist, then automatically the prince was released from his obligation under the contract. But the law still existed, and, although it did not bind the prince, it still bound the people because it had not been formally repealed or abrogated. In Bodin's opinion, however, the practice of promising under oath to obey the law was a dangerous one for sovereigns, and he therefore advises the prince not to be bound "by oath to observe the laws,"[27] because by taking the oath he weakens his "supreme authority in the commonwealth."

Bodin next discusses those laws which are the foundation of the supreme power with which he was dealing. Such laws (*imperii leges*) might be termed in effect constitutional laws, for they had to do with the creation and establishment of Bodin's sovereignty. It was his view that the prince cannot "abrogate or modify them" because "they are attached to the very sovereignty with which he is clothed." As an example of the *imperii leges* Bodin cites the Salic law, by virtue whereof only males were eligible to the throne, females being expressly excluded.

There were certain political activities in which the prince's sovereignty was specifically manifested, one of which occurred in the case of a petition presented to the prince by the "estates and orders of the people." Now in

---

[26] Coker, *op. cit.*, p. 377.
[27] "Quanquam Principes benè à doctrina informati, nullo sese iurisiurandi vinculo patiuntur obligari, cum de legib. agitur, aut certè summum Reipublicae imperium non habent."—Bodin, *op. cit.*, Book I, chap. viii, p. 137.

Bodin's opinion the petitioners were not exercising any authority of their own, either by way of commanding, forbidding, or concurring, for such action lay exclusively with the prince, who "by his own judgment and will directs everything," so that "whatever he desires and orders has the force of law." To be sure, there was an opinion rather generally current that "the king is bound by the popular command," but this opinion, Bodin informs us, "must be disregarded," because "such doctrine furnishes seditious men with material for revolutionary plots," with the consequence that there would arise "disturbance in the commonwealth." In the next statement, Bodin separates himself definitely from popular sovereignty and the doctrine which recognizes the source of power as being in the people, and his argument is so important in throwing light upon his views that it should be examined with care: "No reasonable ground," he begins, "can be adduced why subjects should control princes, or why power should be attributed to popular assemblies." The only exception which he would allow to this unequivocal statement would be "in the infancy, madness, or captivity of the prince," under which circumstances "a guardian or deputy may be created by the suffrages of the people." Now the reason for this view was simply that, if power were considered as being lodged in the people or their representatives, its exercise might interfere with, and perhaps nullify, the sovereignty of the Bodinian prince. "If princes," Bodin immediately continues, "were restrained by laws made by these assemblies or by the commands of the people, the power of the prince would be worthless and the royal name a vain thing." This argument points the way to Louis XIV and his absolute power. To the democratic-minded of today Bodin's dictum seems wholly unjustifiable; and indeed its sole justification, in his day, if any existed, could only have been that he was seeking a means of establishing a stable government in the anarchy inherited from feudalism.

What, in Bodin's view, was the function of the people or their representatives in lawmaking? It was merely the registration of the king's laws, so that they "might not be called in question at his death, or before the senate when it acts judicially."[28] But, it may be asked, was the prince yielding any of his sovereign power in convoking "assemblies or estates?" Not at all, says Bodin, although he admits that "a prince grants many things to the assembled people which he would not so readily grant to individuals." This is not, however, because a prince feels greater obligation toward his people as a whole than toward individuals, but merely because "the voices of individuals are not heard so clearly as the voice of the multitude"; or

[28] Coker, *op. cit.*, p. 378.

because the prince, usually relying upon the "eyes and ears of others," stands face to face with the people themselves when he meets the assembly, and as a result of this personal contact, as Bodin puts it, "impelled by shame, religious fear, or his own good disposition, he grants their requests." This would seem almost tantamount to saying that the prince unwillingly recognizes the people in their representative capacity and his responsibility to them in fact, although not in law. Nevertheless Bodin, fearing perhaps that this concession on his part might prejudice the power of his prince, immediately adds: "But the highest privilege of sovereignty consists primarily in giving laws not only to individuals but also to the people as a whole, without their consent."

As we have seen, Bodin did not recommend that the king enter into contracts and promises which would limit his sovereignty; but if contracts had been entered into by his predecessors, they were binding in so far as the "contracts were made for the benefit of the commonwealth." This is an important concession, for it implies that the ultimate purpose of government is "the benefit of the commonwealth." Bodin states a general principle which applies to this entire subject: "But by whatever right a prince obtains his authority, whether by law, testament, popular election, or lot, it is just to fulfil those obligations which were undertaken for the good of the state." This should be a limitation upon the king of the utmost importance—a check flowing directly from natural law itself, which requires the fulfillment of obligations as an act of justice; for, as Bodin declares, to act "otherwise" for selfish purposes would be "contrary to the laws of nature." But here a question arises to which he offers no answer: Who is to determine "the good of the people"? Should the decision be that of the prince, or of the people? In view of the care with which Bodin has safeguarded his prince's sovereignty, it may be assumed that he would have been unwilling to limit that sovereignty by leaving so important a question to the people's decision.

The fact that Bodin iterates and reiterates the importance in the legal hierarchy of the divine law and the law of nature has not infrequently been overlooked. He now adds a third, the law of nations. Here he seems to have in mind more the older *ius gentium* (meaning the law common to all peoples) than the modern law governing the relations among states. This law of nations referred, Bodin informs us, to certain types of compacts and commitments, but not to all types of contracts. Now, if the prince were bound to observe the law of nations, that obligation would constitute another restriction upon his sovereignty, in addition to that imposed by divine and natural law. Bodin here makes an observation of capital importance in that he sets up a standard for the *ius gentium;* for he maintains that this *ius gentium* is binding upon the prince only to the extent that it is "in agreement with the laws of nature and of God." "To these latter laws," he asserts, "all that we have said concerning the obligation of princes must be referred." Therefore, in so far as the *ius gentium* was universal custom in harmony with the law of nature and the divine law, it was binding upon the prince. But if any of the provisions of the *ius gentium* should be unjust, they would then conflict with the divine and natural law. As regards such unjust rules of the *ius gentium,* "the prince may abrogate them and forbid his subjects to follow them." To illustrate this important principle, Bodin refers to the then general practice of slavery (a practice which, to his great credit, he strongly opposed). "This institution," Bodin says, meaning slavery, "was established in many states, by pernicious examples, yet in accord with the law of almost every nation; but through salutary decrees of several princes it has been abolished, in conformity to the laws of nature."[29] Using this single illustration as a basis for the general principle which he wishes to drive home, he at once continues: "What has been said of one thing may be extended to other things of like kind; for a proviso in the whole argumentation is that nothing be sanctioned which is contrary to the laws of God or of nature." This leads Bodin to an important conclusion: "For if justice is the end of the law, and law is the command of the prince, and the prince is the image of the almighty God, then the laws of the prince should bear the stamp of divine laws."

Bodin now takes up another important question, the relationship of custom to law. In the opinion of some, custom did not derive its "power" from the prince, yet it had practically the force of law, from which it might be argued that "the prince is master of law, the people of custom." But such an opinion is not endorsed by Bodin. He first describes the development of custom, stating that, when it is complied with by all, it enters "into the character of men, and acquires force with the lapse of time."[30] On the other hand, the law which Bodin had in mind becomes such at the moment of command on the part of the sovereign; and indeed Bodin concedes that often such law may be in opposition to the desire or approval of those whom the sovereign governs. This clearly and definitely separates the law, as Bodin conceived it, from the custom which he describes as entering into human character. He maintains, therefore, that "the power of law is far greater than that of custom" because, as he points out, custom might "be superseded by laws"; but he denies that the reverse can be true—

[29] Coker, *op. cit.,* p. 379.   [30] *Ibid.*

in which opinion posterity is against him. Indeed, not only posterity but also the weighty authority of his predecessors throughout the Middle Ages are against his views on law and custom.

The general mediaeval conception of law was not that of a command [says Dr. Carlyle], but of custom—a custom enforced no doubt by the community, but which was not, properly speaking, made by the community, but was rather the expression of its life. Bodin thinks of it under the terms of a command, and his statement of this conception is sharp and dogmatic.[31]

Bodin proceeds to make a further distinction between law and custom: the law, he points out, provides rewards and penalties; custom provides neither. Possessing neither penalty nor reward, "custom," he says, summing it all up, "has compelling force only as long as the prince, by adding his endorsement and sanction to the custom, makes it a law."[32] Apparently, Bodin here has in mind express endorsement and not implied consent through silence on the part of the prince.

From all that has been said it appears that Bodin's prince possessed the full sovereign power of the kingdom. But vast as this power may seem, stated in Bodin's terms, nevertheless, there were *temperamenta* and restrictions of various kinds, such as that the prince should not interfere with private property; that he should not alienate his own domain; that he could not wrongfully take the lives of his citizens; that he might neither abrogate nor disobey the fundamental laws of his own principality; and that he must respect good faith. Some of these restrictions, and others as well, were imposed by the divine law and the natural law, and Bodin's prince could not disregard the one or the other—indeed in respect to these laws he was as much under obligation to obey them as the veriest peasant in his realm. In the relation of the sovereign with foreign states, he was bound, as we have seen, by the *ius gentium,* in so far as it was in conformity with the divine law and the law of nature. Thus treaties and conventions entered into by the sovereign would be binding, for the breach of them would be a violation of the good faith demanded by the law of nature, for which the sovereign or his people could be held responsible.[33]

---

[31] *A History of Mediaeval Political Theory* ... (previously cited), VI, 419. In a later passage (*ibid.*, p. 507), the learned author describes somewhat more fully the medieval relationship between law and custom. "To the people of the Middle Ages the positive law was primarily and fundamentally the custom of the community—that is, the expression of the habit of life of the community; it was not properly something deliberately or consciously made. The earlier mediaeval codes, as everyone knows, are not acts of legislation, but records of custom, revised, no doubt, and modified from time to time by the ruler and his wise men, but not, properly speaking, made by them. The feudal laws in the same way were records of custom."

[32] Coker, *op. cit.*, p. 236.   [33] Bodin, *op. cit.*, Book V, chap. vi.

Bodin's invocation of the natural and divine law was not mere rhetoric or adornment of his pages. It should not be forgotten that the *Six Books of the Republic* were written in the third quarter of the sixteenth century, when there was still current throughout the civilized world the conception of natural and divine law as an integral part of the legal systems to which all human beings were subject. These systems were based in their fundamentals upon the Roman law, then in the heyday of its revival, a Roman law developed and Christianized through long centuries by the Fathers of the Church, the canonists and commentators, and generally if not universally accepted throughout the Middle Ages preceding Bodin's century; which law thus developed passed into the legal conceptions of the succeeding centuries and—though the fact is sometimes forgotten—is still an integral part of the jurisprudence of our day.

The influence of Bodin on political science is not to be denied, any more than is the influence of Machiavelli. But the fact remains that the political conceptions of each, either directly or through a process of distortion, have been essentially in the nature of an obstacle to the normal growth of political ideals from their historical bases.

Bodin's plan for ridding his country of the political ills from which it was then suffering consisted in setting up a strong central government, with a monarch subject to so-called fundamental laws, but himself the source of the laws of the realm and not subject to those laws. This plan required that the rights of the people be limited in order that the power of the sovereign might be expanded. Peace and order were to be brought about through emphasis on the supremacy of the personal ruler. To be sure, Bodin's sovereign was limited, as has been shown, by certain categories of law: what we may term the divine law and the law of nature, containing those universal precepts which could not be denied by a ruler without placing himself beyond the pale of enlightened society; the *ius gentium,* likewise obligatory in general, though such of its rules as were in conflict with the preceding category and injurious to the state might be repudiated; and finally, the fundamental law of the realm, of which our modern prototype is constitutional law.

On this third category a comment or two must be made. The constitution of Bodin's day was an unwritten and therefore "customary" constitution. It was a matter of slow, unconscious, and time-out-of-mind growth. And because of the then powerful influence of the element of tradition, it was difficult to amend such a constitution and to extend its application. Therefore the sovereign of Bodin might rest comfortably assured that his wings were not likely to be clipped by constitutional amendments or interpretations. It is not without interest to observe that the development of written constitutions, with vastly more comprehensive provisions than were contained in the "customary" constitutions of Bodin's day, has been tending steadily to narrow the range of the field in which the sovereign remains untrammeled and unchecked by the constitutional law. Indeed the immense sphere covered by Bodin's phrase *"legibus solutus"* has, under the constitutions of modern democratic states, been strictly limited and in some cases reduced almost to the vanishing point.

That Bodin's theory was evolved as a measure of expediency to meet distressing conditions existing at a particular time may be readily admitted. But expediency is seldom the mother of enduring principles. A distinguished authority in the field of political science has observed, for purposes of comparison, that, like Bodin's theory, the theory of Thomas Hobbes grew out of the "disturbed conditions of civil war" in England, and he remarks that such conditions "furnished poor material for a general theory of settled government."[34]

In order to view Bodin's theory in historical perspective and thus assess it at its true value, it will be necessary to consider briefly the ancestry of sovereignty. The more usual conception among the majority of Greeks was that the right to govern should be the prerogative of the select few. This prerogative was based essentially upon power, the power of the few to impose their will and form of government upon the many. For them government was for the most part based rather upon supremacy, their purpose being to have the best government, not the most popular. They believed in a constitution—as anyone at all acquainted with Aristotle is fully aware—but it was a constitution imposed upon the people, not a constitution necessarily accepted by the people as a whole. In other words, the ruler in Greece, be he one or several, made the constitution, whereas in the modern world the constitution makes the ruler.

This view of supremacy received fundamental modification at the hands of the Stoics, who introduced, as we have seen, the epoch-making conception of equality, not merely within a particular state but in every state, and therefore coextensive with mankind. To the Stoics, law was the great bond of political society—law equally applicable to all. In the words of Cicero,

[34] "A Fragment on Sovereignty" by McIlwain, *Political Science Quarterly*, XLVIII (1933), 102–3.

since law is the bond which unites the civic association, and the justice enforced by law is the same for all, by what justice can an association of citizens be held together when there is no equality among the citizens? ... What is a State except an association or partnership in justice?[35]

Thus the beginnings of our modern theory of sovereignty are to be discerned in the Roman state in those phases of its history in which the law is superior to the ruler, not the ruler to the law.

But in the Middle Ages, as has been elsewhere intimated, a different condition of affairs came into being, giving rise to the theory of an undivided Christendom in which law was above the king and in which sovereignty was for the time lost sight of, in the great conception of a universal unity. At the end of the medieval period, however, the decline of feudalism ushered in political conditions which not infrequently closely approximated anarchy and raised again the old questions of government by supremacy or government by law.

Here in justice to Bodin it will be necessary to refer to his predecessors and contemporaries who shared his views on sovereignty. In general, as has been intimated, such views were of little importance during the Middle Ages, for one of the fundamental bases of medieval political theory was the theory that law, and not the ruler, was supreme. Nevertheless, certain isolated writers favored one phase or another of a contrary conception at different times. Thus St. Gregory the Great in the sixth century advanced the doctrine that the power of the temporal ruler is absolute and that, whatever his conduct, he may not be resisted.[36] Another Gregory—called Gregory of Catino—upheld the same doctrine early in the twelfth century.[37] The next writer of importance to deal with the subject was the English reformer Wycliffe, who, in his *De officio regis* (written about 1379) "reasserted the conception of the duty of absolute obedience to the prince, and of the wickedness of resistance."[38] During this period two of the greatest of the civilians, Bartolus and especially his pupil Baldus, expressed the opinion that while the ruler "ought" to comply with the law, he was in reality *legibus solutus*.[39] In the following century Aeneas Sylvius, later to be Pope Pius II, declared in his treatise *De ortu et auctoritate imperii Romani* (written about 1446) that the emperor possessed absolute power and was above the law.[40]

These statements, as has been implied, were exceptional and contrary to the normal medieval theory. But in the sixteenth century the normal theory

---

[35] *De re publica* I. xxxii. 49.
[36] Carlyle, *A History of Mediaeval Political Theory* (previously cited), I, 152 ff.
[37] *Ibid.*, III, 122-23. [38] *Ibid.*, VI, 62. [39] *Ibid.*, pp. 19-20. [40] *Ibid.*, pp. 188-91.

began to lose ground, in the face of more numerous affirmations of the doctrine of royal supremacy. We have already seen[41] how Machiavelli skillfully depicted the absolute and unscrupulous prince. And Martin Luther in his earlier writings was an ardent and unequivocal supporter of the theory of the divine right of kings and of their absolute supremacy over both subjects and law. It is true that he subsequently altered his theories, but unfortunately his early views had already been enthusiastically accepted by not a few ambitious rulers.[42] The English reformer William Tyndale, having been converted to Luther's doctrines of reformation, appears also to have adopted his views on absolutism, for he declared that kings were chosen at God's command and that "when we have anoynted a kyng at his Commandment, he sayth: touch not mine anointed." Warning his readers of the peril of rising against their prince, Tyndale added:

And what jeopardy it is to rise agaynst thy Prince that is anointed over thee, how evill soever he be, see in the story of King David, and throughout all the Bookes of the Kings. The authority of the King is the authority of God; and all the subjects compared to the King are but subjects still (though the King be never so evil).[43]

In Bodin's day one of his most distinguished compatriots, Michel L'Hôpital, for many years Chancellor of France, expressed an opinion somewhat in sympathy with the foregoing views. While believing that the king ought voluntarily to submit to the law, L'Hôpital did not consider him bound by the law. And he declared in no uncertain terms that subjects had no right to rebel against their ruler.[44] It is clear that the great French chancellor, for all his moderation and ability as a statesman, was in favor of an absolute, though preferably benevolent, form of government.

There were also other contemporaries of Bodin who shared his views. Peter Gregory of Toulouse, for example, published his *De republica* in 1596, setting forth in considerable detail the theory of unlimited sovereignty. In general his views on this subject parallel those of Bodin. A few years earlier (in 1581) a Scotsman, Adam Blackwood, published his *Pro regibus apologia,* in which he declared that the authority of the king was unlimited, that the people had no share in the supreme authority, and that no law restrained the royal power.[45]

It is to be expected that the views of Blackwood found favor with James VI of Scotland, who was to become James I of England and who acquired

---

[41] *Supra,* chap. xix.   [42] For a more detailed discussion of Luther, see *infra,* chap. xxix.
[43] *Exposition on Matthew* (1532), cited by Carlyle, *op. cit.,* VI, 290.
[44] Carlyle, *op. cit.,* VI, 415-17.   [45] *Ibid.,* VI, 434-37.

from one source or another exalted opinions on the royal power, particularly as it was to be wielded by himself. At any rate, in the year 1598 James set forth his conception of kingship in *The True Law of Free Monarchies,* in which he expounded the doctrine of absolute royal authority, which was of divine origin and above and beyond the law.

Two other writers with similar views must here be mentioned. The first is William Barclay, who issued in 1600 a treatise, *De regno et regali potestate,* in which, upholding the doctrine of the divine nature of royal authority, he maintained that the king was above all control either by his subjects or by the law. His ruler was, indeed, *legibus solutus,* although he conceded that under certain circumstances an intolerable tyrant might be resisted.[46] And finally Alberico Gentili, whose contributions to international law are discussed in a later chapter,[47] set forth in a tractate, *Regales disputationes tres* (1605), the following opinion,[48] echoing Bodin:

This, then, is the characteristic of sovereignty, that the principate shall never at any time recognize anything as superior to itself, neither man nor law. Therefore this power is both absolute and without limit. "The prince is *legibus solutus*" will be the law, and whatever is pleasing to the prince will be the same as law.

In this passage Gentili is apparently relying upon the well-known statement of Ulpian:[49] "Whatever the Emperor has decreed has the force of law." Others also had supported their theory of supremacy by this statement from the *Corpus Juris,* but they seem to have overlooked the immediately following clause in Ulpian's rule, namely, that "since by the *lex regia* which was passed concerning his sovereignty, the people conferred upon him all their own authority and power." Thus it is clear that Ulpian's conception was that of the people as the actual source of power. What pleased the prince was to have the force of law, but only because the people had transferred to him power which gave him that authority—a power originally vested in themselves. Therefore, if the development of absolutism was influenced by Ulpian's rule, it was largely because certain commentators and theorists seized upon the first half of the rule and neglected or overlooked the second and more fundamental half.

Although the theory of absolute sovereignty must be listed among the abnormal rather than among the normal medieval conceptions, it has thus been briefly summarized in order that Bodin should not, as is sometimes the case, be charged with originating the theory. Yet he was, it is true, its most able and important expounder. And though much may be said in

[46] *Ibid.,* pp. 445–50.   [47] *Infra,* chap. xxv.   [48] *Disputatio prima.*   [49] *Digest* I. iv. 1.

his praise, as regards the theory of sovereignty, the fact of the matter is that, as stated by Dr. Carlyle[50] (whose pages have been the chief source in tracing the development of the theory), Bodin and his sympathizers broke away from the normal conception of "the supremacy of the law over all persons" which "medieval political theory had always maintained." Indeed it is Dr. Carlyle's measured judgment that in the doctrines both of the divine right of kings and their absolute authority, we have conceptions which were "merely intrusive," and which were "wholly alien to the rational and intelligible political tradition of the Middle Ages, that the law was supreme and not the prince."[51] As representative of the normal development from this medieval tradition to which Dr. Carlyle refers, and by way of contrast with the Bodinian doctrine, a passage may be quoted from his analysis of the views of Sir Thomas Smith (1513–77) as set forth in his *De republica Anglorum*.[52] Sir Thomas Smith, it should be added, was not merely a closet commentator; he was a great English statesman and jurist with much practical experience, a renowned classical scholar, and deeply learned in many fields. His treatise was widely read, both the English text which he himself wrote, and the Latin version into which it was translated.

He defines a respublica or commonwealth [Dr. Carlyle observes] as being a multitude of free men united into one, and holding together by mutual wills and contracts, for their protection in peace and war. The fundamental character of the government of the commonwealth of England he describes in sweeping and emphatic words. It belongs to three kinds of men; the king or queen by whose will and authority all things are ruled, the greater and lesser nobles, and the yeomanry, and each of these classes has its part in judgments, in election of officers, in imposing taxation, and in making laws.[53]

Dr. Carlyle then paraphrases Sir Thomas Smith's theories of government as expounded in a later passage.

It is in the Parliament that the whole absolute power resides, for there are present the king, the nobles, the commons, and the clergy are represented by the bishops. It is they who take counsel for the well-being of the kingdom and commonwealth, and when, after long deliberation, a Bill is read three times, discussed in both Houses, approved, and confirmed by the assent of the king, no question can be raised as to what has been decided, for it has the force of law.[54]

Upon this doctrine Dr. Carlyle comments: "There was indeed little or nothing that was new in this, but it is interesting to compare the statement

---

[50] *A History of Mediaeval Political Theory* (previously cited), VI, 517.
[51] *Ibid.*, VI, 519.   [52] First printed in London in 1583.
[53] Carlyle, *op. cit.*, VI, 489.   [54] *Ibid.*, pp. 489–90.

of the 'absolute' authority which resides in Parliament with the conception of Bodin."[55]

To Bodin the ideas of representative government and of law as superior to the chief magistrate were, for his particular purpose, beside the mark. Yet such ideas were far from being unknown in his day. They had, for example, been set forth at length some two centuries before by the Italian Marsiglio of Padua, and in Bodin's own century by Francisco de Vitoria, the Spaniard, some fifty years before the *Six Books of the Republic* was published. Both of these writers are dealt with in other chapters,[56] but this particular phase of their theories must for present purposes be briefly examined here.

Basing his views of government on the principles set forth by Aristotle, Marsiglio of Padua declares that the legislator in the state "is the people, that is to say, the whole body of citizens, or else the preponderant part thereof," and that for purposes of government they may act "either through elected representatives, or by an express declaration of will in the general assembly of the citizens."[57] As a corollary to this theory, Marsiglio held that the entrusting of the function of lawmaking to certain individuals did not make them "the legislator in an absolute sense," but merely signified the delegation of "the legislative function solely for a definite purpose and during a definite period, in accordance with the authority of the primary legislator,"[58] i.e., the people, or a majority of them.

Moreover the chief magistrate or executive (whatever his title might be) was, according to Marsiglio, an agent of the people. He declares that the power "to establish, or elect, the executive agent pertains to the legislator, that is to say, to the whole body of citizens." The citizens likewise have

[55] *Ibid.*, p. 490. Dr. Carlyle thus quotes the language of Sir Thomas Smith in a footnote: "(*De Republica Anglorum*, II. 1) 'The most high and absolute power of the realm of England consisteth in the Parliament. For as in warre where the king himself in person, the nobilitie, the rest of the gentilitie, and the yeomanrie are, is the force and power of England: so in peace and consultation when the Prince is to give . . . the last and highest commandement, the Baronie for the nobilitie and higher, the knights esquiers, gentlemen and commons for the lower part of the commonwealth, the bishoppes for the clergie, bee present to avertise, consult and shew what is good and necessarie for the commonwealth, and to consult together; and upon mature deliberation everie bill or lawe being thrise reade and disputed uppon in either house, the other two partes first each apart, and after the Prince himself in presence of both the parties doeth consent unto and alloweth. That is the Prince's and whole realmes' deede: whereupon justlie no man can complaine, but must accomodate himselfe to finde it good and obey it.' "

[56] *Supra*, chaps. xviii and xxii.

[57] Translated from Previté-Orton, *The Defensor Pacis of Marsilius of Padua* (previously cited), Dictio I, chap. xii. sec. 3 (p. 49).

[58] *Ibid.*

the authority to curb the power of the executive agent, and even to depose him "if such a step should be expedient for the common welfare."[59] Thus in the *Defensor pacis* it is the people who are sovereign and who are the source of power and of control over the government.

In 1528 Vitoria delivered from his chair in the University of Salamanca a public disquisition on the civil power,[60] in which he laid down several important principles. He began with the following general statement:[61] "All power—whether public or private—by which the secular State is governed, is not only just and legitimate, but is so surely ordained of God, that not even by the consent of the whole world can it be destroyed or annulled." This was a doctrine familiar to the schoolmen, but Vitoria supplements it with a theory originally derived from Aristotle, to the effect that "States and commonwealths had not their fount and origin in the invention of man, nor in any artificial manner, but sprang, as it were, from Nature."[62]

The existence of states and commonwealths implied the existence of what Vitoria termed "public powers," which were necessary because "if all were equal"—meaning equal in the sense of freedom from restraint of government—"and subject to no power, each individual would draw away from the others in accordance with his own opinions and will," and the result would be that "the commonwealth would of necessity be torn apart; and the State would be dissolved."[63]

The origin of this power, as Vitoria has said, was divine; but he now reveals his conception of its human exercise:

The State, then, possesses this power by divine Disposition; but the material cause in which, by natural and divine law, power of this kind resides, is the State itself, which by its very nature is competent to govern and administer itself, and to order all its powers for the common good. The proof of this fact is as follows: since by natural and divine law there must be a power for the government of the State, and since—if common, positive, and human laws are laid aside—there is no reason for depositing that power in one person rather than in another; it necessarily follows that the community is self-sufficing and that it has the power to govern itself.[64]

To Vitoria power was of divine origin and its immediate source was in the state. He realized, however, that the exercise of such power by the people as a whole was impracticable. Therefore he considered[65] that "since

---

[59] Marsiglio, *Defensor pacis,* trans. from Previté-Orton ed., chap. xv. sec. 2 (p. 67).
[60] *De potestate civili.*
[61] In J. B. Scott, *The Spanish Origin of International Law* (previously cited), Appendix C, p. lxxii.
[62] *Ibid.,* p. lxxv.   [63] *Ibid.,* p. lxxvi.   [64] *Ibid.,* p. lxxvii.   [65] *Ibid.,* p. lxxviii.

the State possesses power over its own parts, and since this power cannot be exercised by the multitude (which could not conveniently make laws and issue edicts, settle disputes and punish transgressors), it has therefore been necessary that the administration of the State should be entrusted to the care of some person or persons (and it matters not whether this power is entrusted to one or to many)."

Now the popular choice of the officials to whom the exercise of power would be entrusted implied that Vitoria contemplated a government which should represent the people and carry out their wishes. But since the government was theirs to establish, the form should likewise be theirs to choose. Illustrating this corollary, Vitoria cites [66] by way of example "free States such as Venice and Florence," in which "the majority may elect a king even though the rest of the citizens be opposed." To Vitoria the will of the majority was the deciding factor.

This assertion would seem to hold true, not only in view of the fact that such an act is clearly advantageous to the State, but even assuming that an aristocratic or democratic government would be still more expedient. For the State has the power of self-government, and the act of the greater part is the act of the whole; therefore, the State may accept the form of government that it desires, even if this be not the best form.

Because it was fundamental to his theory of government, Vitoria referred more than once to the subject of the majority's will. Thus, after alluding to the doctrine that "the majority of members of a State may set up a king over the whole State," he demonstrates the validity of the principle of majority as opposed to unanimity in expression of the people's will:

For if the State may entrust its power to some one individual, acting thus for its own advantage, it is certain that the dissent of one or of a few could not prevent the rest from caring for the welfare of the State; otherwise—that is, if the consent of all were required—insufficient provision would be made for the good of the State, since unanimous consent is rarely or never found among a multitude. It suffices, then, in order to do anything legitimately, that the majority should agree on the course in question. This point can be satisfactorily demonstrated. For if two parties disagree, it must necessarily result that the sentiment of one party should prevail; and inasmuch as their desires conflict, the sentiment of the party which is in the minority ought not to prevail; therefore it is the sentiment of the majority which should dominate. Moreover, if the consent of all is required in order to create the king, why is it not also required in order that he be not so created? Why is unanimous consent more to be required in an affirmative than in a negative matter? [67]

[66] *Ibid.*, p. lxxxiii. [67] *Ibid.*, p. lxxxii.

Now what of the relation of the government, as thus established, to the laws? Where Bodin's sovereign was to be *legibus solutus,* Vitoria's was not. The question arises, he says,[68] "whether civil laws are binding upon legislators, and in particular, upon kings." Stating first the view later to be defended by Bodin, Vitoria says: "For some persons are of the opinion that these legislators and kings are not so bound, inasmuch as they are over all the State and no one can have an obligation imposed upon him unless it be by a superior."

Having set forth in the correct scholastic manner the opposing theory, Vitoria begins his argument persuasively, to end with a positive denial:

> but it is more probable that kings and legislators are bound by the laws. The proof of this is, first: that a legislator of this sort injures the State, and the other citizens if, being himself a part of the State, he does not bear a part of the burden.

This proof was somewhat "indirect," and therefore Vitoria immediately offered another: "The laws which are made by kings have the same force . . . as if they were made by the whole State; but the laws made by the State are binding upon all; therefore, even those laws which are made by the king, are binding upon the king himself."

But the matter was so important that Vitoria did not consider it sufficiently established even by double proof. Therefore he added[69] a confirmation by analogy, which extends to the whole field of political government: "Under an aristocratic form of government, the decrees of the Senate are binding upon the very senators who issued them; under a popular government the plebiscite is binding upon the whole people; and therefore laws made by the king are in like manner binding upon the king himself." And finally he adds an overwhelming statement of principle which leaves the question of the supremacy of law over the king definitely settled in favor of the law:[70] "Moreover, although the act of creating the law be voluntary on the part of the king; nevertheless, the fact that he is thereby bound or not bound, does not depend upon his own will: just as in the case of pacts; for he who enters into a pact of his own free will, is nevertheless bound thereby."

Whether Bodin was familiar with the works of Marsiglio and Vitoria we do not know. But certain it is that the theories set forth by them had permeated, in one form or another, much of the political thought of Bodin's day, and if he ignored such theories it must have been because he chose to do so rather than because he was unaware of them.

---

[68] Vitoria *De potestate civili,* in Scott, *op. cit.,* App. C, p. lxxxix.   [69] *Ibid.,* pp. lxxxix–xc.
[70] *Ibid.,* p. xc.

JEAN BODIN

In so far as there were limitations of law on the Bodinian sovereign, Bodin contributed a more acceptable theory than that of Hobbes (whose *Leviathan* is beyond the chronological scope of the present work). But on the other hand, in so far as Bodin stood opposed to the people as the source of power, to government as an agency of the people, to representative government by the will of the majority, his doctrine was an obstruction to the development of the long tradition which had been given its fullest medieval expression by Marsiglio of Padua, which had been developed and strengthened in the sixteenth century, especially by Vitoria and other Churchmen, and which was destined to have its most complete application in the governments of the New World.[71]

It should be a source of pleasure to Americans to know that the conceptions of such writers on political science as Marsiglio and Vitoria came into their own in the American conception of the state, as set forth by Mr. Justice Iredell in a masterly opinion of the Supreme Court of the United States, delivered as early as 1793:

A distinction was taken at the bar between a state and the people of a state. It is a distinction I am not capable of comprehending. By a state forming a

---

[71] An interesting comment on Grotius's theory of sovereignty (a subject which does not fall within the scope of the present work) has been made by a learned English writer:
"A jurist may be forgiven for suggesting that, whatever may have been the case in the past, the theory of sovereignty seems, at the present day, to be one of the greatest stumbling-blocks in the path of international progress. Its appearance in the international world is due preeminently to two men, Bodin and Grotius. Bodin's motives may well be suspect. Those of Grotius were entirely honourable, and were at first crowned with brilliant success. Realizing that the religious schism of the sixteenth century had rendered it impossible for Protestant States to accept any longer the shadowy authority of the Pope and Emperor as arbiter in their disputes, and sickened by the horrors of the Thirty Years' War, Grotius set himself to discover a new source of authority, which should supplement the inadequate influence of Divine Law and the conventional rules established by treaties. This new source, the Law of Nature, which he defines as the 'dictate of right reason,' i. e., the natural outcome of the social and rational qualities of mankind, Grotius sought to build up out of the international practices of past ages, especially the practices of that ancient world to which the Renaissance of learning had recently given a greatly enhanced reputation. In order to make his thesis acceptable, he attempted to placate jealousies by releasing all States from any external human authority, that is, in accordance with the accepted views of the day, regarding them as being, so far as their intercourse with one another was concerned, in a 'natural' or pre-political condition. And for that very reason, he urged, they were bound by the only law suitable for such a condition, viz. the Law of Nature, the 'dictate of right reason.'
"Grotius' success was, at first, admittedly, brilliant. His *De Jure Belli ac Pacis* is, judged by its practical influence, one of the world's great books. . . . But the theory on which it was founded was, in fact, a toleration of anarchy; and, in due time, it collapsed, with the results which are painfully obvious. It is hardly too much to say that ever since the Great War, the world has been struggling to escape from the theory of sovereignty in international affairs —from its jealousies, its rivalries, its preposterous pretentions, and its apprehensions—and to build up out of the ruins left by the war, a more wholesome theory of international society."
—Jenks, *The New Jurisprudence*, pp. 82-84.

republic (speaking of it as a moral person), I do not mean the legislature of the state, the executive of the state or the judiciary, but all the citizens which compose that state, and are, if I may so express myself, integral parts of it; all together forming a body politic. . . . in a republic, all the citizens, as such are equal, and no citizen can rightfully exercise any authority over another, but in virtue of a power constitutionally given by the whole community, and such authority, when exercised, is, in effect, an act of the whole community which forms such body politic. In such governments, therefore, the sovereignty resides in the great body of the people, but it resides in them, not as so many distinct individuals, but in their politic capacity only.[72]

As the Supreme Court was sitting in Philadelphia, then the capital of the United States and also of Pennsylvania, it was both natural and gracious that the learned Justice should choose an illustration pertaining to the Commonwealth of Pennsylvania:

Thus A., B., C., and D., [are] citizens of Pennsylvania, and as such, together with all the citizens of Pennsylvania, share in the sovereignty of the state. Suppose, a state to consist exactly of the number of 100,000 citizens, and it were practicable for all of them to assemble at one time and in one place, and that 99,999 did actually assemble: the state would not be, in fact, assembled. Why? Because the state, in fact, is composed of all the citizens, not of a part only, however large that part may be, and one is wanting; in the same manner, as 99 £ is not a hundred, because one pound is wanting to complete the full sum. But as such exactness [i. e., entire unanimity] in human affairs cannot take place, . . . mankind have long practised (except where special exceptions have been solemnly adopted) upon the principle, that the majority shall bind the whole.

A final statement from the same opinion completes what has come to be considered the American conception of sovereignty. Referring to the principles he had just expounded, Justice Iredell said: "The same principles apply as to legislative, executive or judicial acts of the United States, which are acts of the people of the United States, in those respective capacities."

[72] *Penhallow* v. *Doane,* 3 Dallas, 54, 93–94.

Chapter XXIV

BALTHAZAR AYALA (1548–84)

De Jure et Officiis Bellicis et Disciplina Militari

For the most part the preceding chapters have dealt with theorists, men who have discoursed of the law and of the state, and even of international law, from the theoretical and philosophical point of view.

But there is another point of view, that of the practitioner, not a practitioner before the courts as was the distinguished Gentili—to be mentioned later—but a practitioner of international law in its most delicate and at the same time most difficult application: in a word, the international law of the theorist applied to questions arising in the course of war—indeed in the most distressing kind of war, rebellion and insurrection. It was from this point of view that Balthazar Ayala wrote *De jure et officiis bellicis et disciplina militari*.

Ayala was by education and training a jurist and by appointment a legal adviser to the Prince of Parma, Commander-in-Chief of the Armies of Spain in what are now called Belgium and Holland; or, to describe his office in terms of our own day, he was judge advocate general in the Royal Spanish Army in the Low Countries. His father was a Spaniard and his mother a Fleming. One brother was a member of the Council of Brabant; the other, Spanish Ambassador to the court of France. Although he was, like his mother, a native of the Low Countries (having been born in Antwerp), the Low Countries were at that time in the possession of Spain and hence he was of Spanish nationality.

It was but natural that Ayala's views on matters international should be colored by the several important factors which influenced his own life. His legal studies familiarized him with Roman law and its great conceptions of the *ius naturale* and the *ius gentium,* as well as with its civil and military law. And as a well-educated man of his day he was also at home among the classics of the ancient world, the Scriptures, and the leading ecclesiastical authorities. As legal adviser to the Prince of Parma—the Prince being beyond controversy the greatest of the generals serving in the Low Countries, and indeed the greatest soldier of his time—Ayala's views were also influenced by military requirements and by the fact that his duties kept him almost constantly at army headquarters. And finally, as a Spaniard, he was familiar with the writers of the Spanish school, Covarruvias, Soto, Vázquez, and Vitoria. Indeed, it would not be improper to call him a lay, or rather a military, member of the school—although by birth and training he was, it should be added, fundamentally conservative in his outlook.

It appears that Ayala, having prepared notes on the various phases of law bearing upon his profession, including the law of nations, had these notes hurriedly brought together and issued in a volume which he appropriately dedicated to his Prince. From this volume it is evident that Ayala had reached definite conclusions on certain aspects of the law of nations, and, as he was official adviser to the Prince during a rebellion, he also devoted considerable attention to such topics as the relation of subjects to their prince or government, and the treatment of "rebels" in the field. Although the volume was hastily put together, it was, and still is, recognized as a contribution of no mean merit.

Grotius in his *Prolegomena* appears to have been considerably impressed with Ayala, for he refers to him as one of the two writers on the law of nations to whom he ascribed a particular influence. But for some reason—which can perhaps best be explained by the fact that Grotius was a Hollander and therefore sympathized with the rebels whom Ayala condemned—he did not dwell upon the influence of Ayala's contribution as he might have done and as other authorities on international law have done. Referring to certain "special books," as he calls them, on the law of war and the question of their "illumination of history," Grotius adds[1] that such illumination "was attempted on a larger scale, and by referring a great number of examples to some general statements, by Balthazar Ayala; and still more fully, by Alberico Gentili." But the praise which Grotius tenders with the one hand he withdraws with the other:[2] "The causes which determine the characterization of a war as lawful or unlawful"—i. e., just or unjust war, the Latin of Grotius being *bellum justum aut injustum*—"Ayala did not touch upon." A comment on this misstatement by Grotius will appear on a later page.

As would be expected in view of his position and training, Ayala cherished the conservative opinions of his day concerning the state and matters of government. In using the word "state" he[3] means not the soil nor "that

---

[1] *De jure belli ac pacis, libri tres,* Prolegomena, sec. 38 (trans. in "Classics of International Law"), II, 22.
[2] *Ibid.,* II, 23.
[3] *De jure et officiis bellicis et disciplina militari* (trans. in "Classics of International Law"), II, 15.

most sacred concept, fatherland"—which he adds, "would be absurd, for all soil is a brave man's fatherland"—but the state in Cicero's sense of "an assemblage of individuals compacted into a society of identity of law and community of interest." His purpose in this connection was to establish the proper relationship between the prince and his people. In his opinion all authority over the people composing the state was vested in the prince. "There is," Ayala maintains, "such an intimate connection between these two, prince and State, that no one can be an enemy of the former without being also an enemy of the latter, and conversely." The logical implication of this view is that the prince is the state and therefore "disobedience on the part of subjects and rebellion against the prince is treated as a heinous offense." And the further implication is that "no matter how grievous are the burdens which a king imposes on his subjects, they may not rebel, for it is better to bear all ills than to connive at one; and hard as the burden may be which the superior has imposed, borne it must none the less be, and suffered with duteous self-surrender, obedience being a good thing in itself; for it is the general pact of human society that men must obey their kings."[4]

To such an extent is Ayala apparently enamored of royalty that he adds:[5] "kings, therefore, and princes we ought to revere with extreme dutifulness, if they be good, as being sent by God . . . for the punishment of evil-doers and for the praise of them that do well." But what if they be bad?—which, if history is to be believed, is often the case. "We must endure them with patience, for the sins of princes and kings must be borne with and left to the judgment of God, who is pleased at times to visit nations for their sins with iniquitous princes." Here Ayala is speaking of the legitimate prince, the prince whom the law placed upon his throne; now he adds that "a tyrant who forcibly and illegally usurps the throne may be killed by any one if there is no other way of getting rid of his tyranny." But he will not permit any such action against a "prince by right of succession and election." Such a prince he would not allow to "be killed by a private individual, however unjust and cruel his conduct may be, nor may his people put him off the throne or defect from him," the reason being that "a lawful prince, however cruel and unjust, can not be called a usurper." This view Ayala, as a conservative jurist, bolsters up by the *lex regia* and divine ordinance, with the further statement that "all sovereignty and power has been conferred on the prince as against the people." Therefore "the people can not pass in judgment on him."[6] Why? Because the "inferior can not bind the superior by a judgment." In this respect Ayala was indeed a Spaniard,

[4] *Ibid.*, II, 16.   [5] *Ibid.*, II, 17.   [6] *Ibid.*, II, 18.

but of the old school, for Vitoria and Suárez and Vázquez—who were of the newer school of thought—would never have tolerated this doctrine for a moment. Their conception of a king was that of a governor who was clothed by his people with such legal power as they chose to grant him, and if he failed to act in accordance with the grant from the people themselves, those who had made the prince might unmake him.

But in Ayala's conception there were rulers and rulers: one, untouchable as the single and supreme sovereign; the other, open to correction by law, if time permitted, and, if not, to correction by force. "What has been said applies," he informs us,[7] "where the supreme sovereignty is in the hands of a single person; but in cases when it is lodged in the people or in an aristocracy [*optimates*] it is undoubtedly lawful to deal with a tyrant by legal process, if time allows; and, if not, he may be got rid of out of our midst by any means whatsoever." In a word, the king, possessing unlimited sovereignty, was, in Ayala's opinion, above the law and beyond any control by the people. It was only the government possessed of incomplete sovereignty which might be held responsible for its actions.

On the whole question as to whether the people had power to make and unmake kings—as was the conception of Vitoria and Suárez and of the liberal-minded in general—Ayala declares:

to attribute to the people the power to do this (as some would like to do) is not only absurd and improper, but also subversive of the State; a king is not to be forthwith branded tyrant and unjust, because in some little detail of his rule he does not please the people, for on that showing kings would be nobodies. Moreover, we ought not to talk about "monarchy" and "royal power" in cases where a State is governed by a king subject to the approval of the people, since the prosperity of the State is then dependent on the people—than whom nothing could be more foolish and extravagant and, when it blazes out against the good, more insane. For, as Livy says, it is characteristic of the mob to be either humble servants or haughty masters.

It would seem that Ayala in the Netherlands and Bodin in France were contemporaries in more than the mere matter of dates.

What then is the condition of subjects who violate these rules which Ayala conceived to be necessary for the well-being of kingdoms? The subjects who rise against their lawful king (as defined by Ayala) cannot have the rights of war. Why should these rights be denied them? Because only the prince, in Ayala's conception, may declare war, and because the laws of

---

[7] Ayala, *op. cit.*, II, 19.

war apply only when war legally exists—which could not be the case unless it had been declared by the prince.

The charge of Grotius that Ayala did not distinguish between the causes which determine whether a war is lawful or unlawful must now be considered. To meet this criticism by the great Grotius (for he made it, as we have seen, in the Prolegomena to the celebrated *Three Books on the Law of War and Peace*), it is necessary merely to turn to Ayala's Preface for an expression of his views, and there we find lawful and unlawful war clearly distinguished. It seems very strange that Grotius should have made such an unfair criticism, because when he was gathering material to prepare his great treatise, he asked that a copy of Ayala's work, as well as one of the *De jure belli* of Gentili, be sent to him.[8] If he received the Ayala volume, he made but little use of it, citing it indeed but a few times and on minor matters in his treatise *On the Law of War and Peace*.

For the purpose in hand it will be necessary to examine in some detail Ayala's views on the legal aspects of war. In the first place he states the case, as it were, for the opposition, which scoffed at the idea of a law pertaining to war and held that "in war there is no scope at all for justice."[9] Maintaining that "the opinion in question must, however, be unhesitatingly repudiated," Ayala gives, in less than a line of his Preface, a categorical answer to the opinion which he had just stated: "There are laws of war just as much as of peace." Now if war is to be a lawful operation, it must be characterized by justice, for injustice and law are—notwithstanding hair-splitting arguments to the contrary—at opposite poles. Therefore, in an early paragraph of the treatise Ayala specifies the just causes of a war; in other words, the causes which would make war lawful, and these are:[10] "the defense of our own empire, of our persons, of our friends, of our allies, and of our property."

Since war is a very serious matter, it is Ayala's opinion that "a wise man, therefore, will grieve to have to admit that the necessity for a just war has arisen."[11] Nevertheless, the necessity for it having been established, "he will

---

[8] Van Vollenhoven, "On the Genesis of De iure belli ac pacis, Grotius, 1625," *Mededeelingen der Koninklijke Akademie, van Wetenschappen, Afdeeling Letterkunde,* Deel 58, serie B, no. 6, p. 2. The late Professor John Westlake, in his scholarly introduction to the edition of Ayala cited in the present chapter refers (I, 1) thus to Grotius' remarks on his predecessors: "Grotius . . . admits his indebtedness to the industry of Gentilis, though he leaves readers to form their own judgment on the doctrinal use to which Gentilis puts his collections. Of Ayala he only says—and, as we shall see, incorrectly—that he did not touch the causes for which a war is called just or unjust."

[9] *De jure et officiis bellicis* (trans. in "Classics of International Law"), II, vii.
[10] *Ibid.*, II, 10.   [11] *Ibid.*, II, vii–viii.

embark on it, placing the common weal before the interests of individuals lest, unmindful of the well-known dictum of Plato, he should abandon the body of the State as a whole through his wish to protect some given part thereof."

In the Preface, Ayala also adds that the "same principle of justice which lays down rules of war, imposes its laws on soldiers and armies, whereby military discipline is secured."[12] And in support of his view on the impossibility of conducting lawful military operations without regard for that justice which lays down rules, he "borrows" a passage from Livy to the effect that without such rules of war, "the whole course of military service would henceforth be blind, rash, and inconsiderate, after the guise of robbing."[13]

As a second authority, Ayala paraphrases Cicero's *Republic* to the effect that an army's "concerted activities are produced by the coöperation of the most unlike individuals, it being compacted into one by means of reason and discipline out of the intermingled ranks of upper, middle, and lower." To reinforce this view he invokes the ways of musicians, saying that "what musicians style harmony in the case of song is in the case of an army concord, that closest and most efficient bond of military discipline," and he ends his argument with a statement which certainly should exonerate him from any charge, by whomsoever made, of having ignored the rôle of justice, even in war: "Now this"—meaning military order and discipline—"can not exist apart from justice, which is needed for every undertaking and which possesses such power that (in Cicero's words) not even those who batten on wrongdoing and crime can live without some spark of it."

And Ayala thus concludes his Preface: "Let this suffice to explain the motive of this work and to placate those who have ventured to condemn the laws of war (with which the safety of the State is implicated) as being contrary to nature and the peace of the Gospel."

There are, however, some further statements which in justice to Ayala must be quoted.

The second chapter, entitled "Of Just War and Just Causes of War," is a further refutation of those who failed to see in Ayala's treatise a legal standard to test the rightfulness or wrongfulness of war. The whole of Ayala's doctrine on this fundamental point is stated in two paragraphs:

Cicero lays it down that in a well-ordered State the laws of war should be scrupulously observed. Alike in beginning a war and in carrying it on and in ending it, law has a most important position and so has good-faith. . . . For, as

---

[12] *De jure et officiis bellicis*, II, viii.   [13] *Ibid.*, II, ix.

Cicero also says, there are two kinds of strife—one conducted by discussion and the other by force: the one appropriate to men and the other to beasts; and recourse must be had to the latter when the former can not be used . . .; for the use of force against those who will not submit to what is fair nor be restrained by reason is not unjust. Nevertheless, a general, like a surgeon (it was a saying of Scipio's) ought to use steel only in the last resort for effecting his cures.[14]

The second paragraph contains the following important general principle:[15] "War, therefore, is justifiable when its object is to procure peaceful existence and freedom from outrage, and when begun in such a way as that peace may appear to be its sole object."

With these statements it would seem that the defense of Ayala against the charge of Grotius might be rested.

On the general subject of the just causes of war, however, it must be admitted that certain questionable views were subsequently advanced by Ayala.[16] "Our remarks so far about just causes of war deal rather," he informs us, "with considerations of fairness and goodness and propriety, and not with the character of the legal result which is produced." This he follows with a further statement of doctrine, the subsequent adoption of which has had important and unfortunate consequences: "Now, seeing that the right to make war is a prerogative of princes who have no superiors, discussion of the equity of the cause is inappropriate."

Ayala's predecessors among the Spanish schoolmen had insisted that the cause of war should be just in itself and had laid grave emphasis on this factor. On the other hand, Ayala, while conceding the desirability that the cause of war should be just, here emphasized rather the legality of its declaration and of its conduct. "A war," he says, relying upon Roman authorities, "may in one sense be styled just and yet not be waged for just cause; for the word 'just' has varying meanings . . . and does not always indicate justice and equity but sometimes signifies a certain legal completeness." The "legal completeness" which Ayala here has in mind is concerned with the formal declaration of war by the sovereign power of the state and with the requirement that it be "publicly and lawfully waged by those who have the right of waging war."

Whether due to Ayala's dictum or not, the practice of nations from that time onward has unfortunately been in accord with his doctrine of laying emphasis upon the formalities of the declaration instead of upon the cause, which should be the sole justifying factor. Eventually, even the declaration fell into disuse, because it was realized that if the cause itself need not be just, then the declaration was a mere empty formality—a ceremonial

[14] *Ibid.*, II, 7–8.   [15] *Ibid.*, II, 8.   [16] *Ibid.*, II, 22.

hindrance, so to speak, to the immediate waging of war. The Second Hague Peace Conference of 1907 discussed this matter and adopted a convention, on October 18, 1907, which it is believed was complied with by all the parties to the recent World War. The preamble and the first two articles of the convention are quoted:[17]

His Majesty the German Emperor, King of Prussia; [etc.]:

Considering that it is important, in order to ensure the maintenance of pacific relations, that hostilities should not commence without previous warning;

That it is equally important that the existence of a state of war should be notified without delay to neutral Powers;

Being desirous of concluding a Convention to this effect, have appointed the following as their plenipotentiaries:

[Here follow the names of plenipotentiaries.]

Article 1

The contracting Powers recognize that hostilities between themselves must not commence without previous and explicit warning, in the form either of a reasoned declaration of war or of an ultimatum with conditional declaration of war.

Article 2

The existence of a state of war must be notified to the neutral Powers without delay, and shall not take effect in regard to them until after the receipt of a notification, which may, however, be given by telegraph. Neutral Powers, nevertheless, cannot rely on the absence of notification if it is clearly established that they were in fact aware of the existence of a state of war.

This is as far as the convention goes; it did not insist that the declaration should be preceded, in accordance with the doctrine of the schoolmen, by a statement of the just cause which alone might justify war. The view of Ayala, as already remarked, unfortunately prevailed. According to the convention, a declaration—whether or not preceded by an ultimatum—suffices. Such a process does not require an impartial weighing of the justice of a war; it is in effect a justification of war on merely formal grounds, and results in that *bête noir* of the schoolmen, a war proclaimed to be just by both sides.[18]

Rebels are ordinarily regarded by the mother country as not possessed of the rights of war. The mother country may, however, feel itself obliged eventually to admit their possession of war rights, especially if foreign nations recognize the belligerent status of the rebels. If successful to the

---

[17] *The Hague Conventions and Declarations of 1899 and 1907*, ed. by J. B. Scott, p. 96.

[18] In this fourth decade of the twentieth century the provisions of the Hague Convention above quoted are being honored only in their breach, and even Ayala's modest requirements concerning the ceremonial declaration of war have been rejected in favor of "hostilities" which, however extensive and devastating, do not appear to require a declaration.

extent of taking over the government, the rebels, however, frown in their turn upon any further uprising. Grotius, who had a very warm place in his heart for his countrymen in their revolt against Spain, by which they secured their independence after many years of warfare, had no sympathy for those who overturned John of Barneveldt's government—at which time, be it said, Grotius lost the influential position of pensionary of Rotterdam.

Ayala, as an official of the army—which was itself concerned with the suppression of rebellion—was opposed to recognizing the rebels' possession of the rights of belligerents. Harsh doctrine though it seems, it is the way of the world, and indeed is sanctioned by international law.

And we of the United States must not be too hard on Ayala. We have had experiences in both rôles. In the first, we rebelled against the government of Great Britain and His Majesty George III. The American rebellion ceased to be such by becoming a successful revolution, and the Fathers of the American Revolution are enshrined in our history.

In 1861 the southern states of the American Union, dissatisfied with the legitimate government of the United States, sought to withdraw from the Union and set up a government of their own. Their action was, in a sense, the same as the action of their ancestors, but they were branded as rebels by the government which they repudiated, and were declared to be rebels liable to suppression and capture without benefit of the laws of war. It was merely by accident that the so-called rebels of the South were accorded the rights of belligerency under the laws of war, thus affording them the same benefit under that law as the government of the United States was entitled to have.

What was this "accident"? We have it described by Thaddeus Stevens, as quoted by the eminent Scottish jurist and legal philosopher James Lorimer, one time professor at the University of Edinburgh and still held in grateful memory. According to Mr. Stevens (as quoted by Mr. Lorimer), at the beginning of the Civil War it was his opinion that the conflict should be treated as a "simple rebellion,"[19] with the consequence that those implicated in it should be "considered as traitors against the Government of the United States." Mr. Stevens maintained that this was the view of Congress, of which he was then the leading member, and he supposed that it was likewise the view of President Lincoln and of his Cabinet. Apparently this supposition was erroneous, for to his astonishment Mr. Stevens learned shortly afterwards, from the newspapers, of a blockade declared against "the rebel ports." In the light of his views, such a declaration was both a gross mistake and an absurdity, for "if the rebel states were still part of

[19] Lorimer, *Studies National and International*, p. 42.

the Union" and were considered merely as revolting against the established government, then the blockade thus declared by the government was a blockade against itself. "We were," as Mr. Stevens puts it, "blockading the ports of the United States." Much distressed by this state of affairs, Mr. Stevens betook himself at once to Washington "to see the President, ... and to speak to him on the subject."[20] After explaining to the President that in his opinion "the blockade annihilated the position originally taken up by the Government with the rebel States" and that instead of blockading the ports they ought merely "to have been shut" and kept shut by means of a sufficient number of coast guard vessels, Mr. Stevens declared that "by the mere fact of the blockade we recognised in the rebel States the character of independent belligerents." What was the consequence of this? As Mr. Stevens explained it to the President, it was that "we should henceforth be forced to conduct the war not as if we were extinguishing a revolt, but with all the formalities of international law." And a further consequence, not touched upon in the Stevens interview, was that proclamations of neutrality were issued by the outside world.

The result of the interview, we are told, was an admission on the part of President Lincoln that he "knew nothing about international law," and thought that "Seward [then Secretary of State] had been up to all that sort of thing." To this admission Mr. Stevens replied that since the President was a lawyer, he would have expected "the difficulty at once to present itself" to his mind. President Lincoln's answer, as recorded by his interlocutor, should be given in full:

"The reason, don't you see," replied Mr. Lincoln, "is this. I was a pretty fair advocate in one of our Western Courts; but we have very little international law down there. ... It's done now, and we can't help it. We must make the best we can of it."[21]

Upon which Mr. Stevens comments:

In that Mr. Lincoln was right. The mistake was made, and the rebel States from that time were an independent belligerent,—I don't say, mind you, an independent nation,—but certainly an independent belligerent, whom it was necessary to treat according to the rules of international law.

Today, no doubt, such a "mistake" could not occur, for international law is taught in all of the leading universities and colleges of the United States, where, among many other international rules and theories American students may learn, though it is to be hoped they may have no future occasion to apply, Ayala's doctrine on the treatment of rebels.

---

[20] Lorimer, *Studies National and International*, p. 43.   [21] *Ibid.*, p. 43.

Chapter XXV

ALBERICO GENTILI (1552-1608)

ALBERICO GENTILI WAS BORN IN ITALY, WHICH COUNTRY VERY PROPERLY claims him as a distinguished son. He also had the good fortune to be claimed as a distinguished though naturalized son by another country, England, where he became Regius Professor of Civil Law at Oxford, a leading practitioner at the Admiralty Bar, and author of numerous treatises and tractates on law and related subjects. It was in England that he lived his most fruitful years, and it was there that he died in 1608. So highly was he regarded in his adopted country that in 1877 a memorial to him was placed in St. Helen's Church, Bishopsgate, in London.[1] Some thirty years later a statue in honor of Gentili was erected at San Ginesio, his birthplace in Italy.[2]

There are three outstanding contributions of Gentili to international law.[3] They are: *De legationibus libri tres* (London, 1585); *De iure belli libri tres*, originally delivered as a series of lectures at various times in the University of Oxford and revised and issued in permanent form at Hanau in 1598;[4] and *Hispanicae advocationis libri duo*, issued in 1613. Different in content, they are nevertheless alike in origin. Each owed its inception to concrete circumstances. The tractate on *Ambassadors* was suggested, as we shall see, by an incident which took place in the early days of Gentili's residence in England; the *Three Books on War* grew out of the long contemplated invasion of England in 1588 by the Spanish Armada; and the *Two Books of Pleas of a Spanish Advocate*—the advocate being Gentili himself

---

[1] See Introduction by Professor Phillipson to Gentili's masterpiece, *De iure belli libri tres* (published, with trans. by Rolfe, in the "Classics of International Law"), II. 15a.

[2] An increasing interest in Gentili has been displayed by Italian publicists in recent years. See, for example, the group of learned essays, accompanied by an exhaustive bibliography, published by the *Istituto Italiano di Diritto Internazionale*, under the title *Alberico Gentili, scritti e discorsi;* and Bavaj's pamphlet, *Alberico Gentili, fondatore della scienza del diritto internazionale*.

[3] For a recent thoroughgoing study of Gentili and his contributions to international law, see Van der Molen, *Alberico Gentili and the Development of International Law—His Life, Work and Times*.

[4] The first edition was soon followed by a second and third (1604 and 1612). Mention must also be made of the edition of Thomas Erskine Holland (Oxford, 1877). The editions of Gentili's works cited in these pages are those issued by the Carnegie Endowment for International Peace in its series, the "Classics of International Law."

—arose from the fact that he appeared in behalf of Spain in cases which were tried in the English courts of admiralty during the last years of his life. As would therefore be expected, Gentili's contributions to international law are of a practical nature, although he enriched fact with theory and with his very considerable learning.

It will be observed that the impelling cause to the production of these contributions was Spanish; and if Gentili is not to be included with Grotius in the Spanish school, nevertheless he adopted in a very real sense many of the Spanish doctrines, both in theory and in practice.

Professor Thomas Erskine Holland (to be known to posterity as Sir Thomas Holland) devoted much attention in a long lifetime to the works of Gentili and, while it cannot be said that Sir Thomas rediscovered him— for Gentili has long been known to the learned in international law— nevertheless the distinguished English publicist made Gentili better known in our day than he was in his own lifetime. Of his contributions to international law Professor Holland said, in an often-quoted Inaugural Lecture which he delivered at All Souls' College, Oxford, on November 7, 1874:[5]

The first of these [*De legationibus*] treats of a portion of the subject which had been already more thoroughly explored than any other. The last [*Hispanicae advocationis*] is necessarily of a technical nature, dealing mainly with rules of Roman law and with historical precedents; though there is a passage on the pretensions of neutrals expressed with a force and clearness which has never been surpassed: "Ius commerciorum," he says, "aequum est, at hoc aequius, tuendae salutis. Est illud gentium ius, hoc Naturae est. Est illud privatorum, est hoc regnorum. Cedat igitur regno mercatura, homo naturae, pecunia vitae."[6]

The *De Iure Belli* is more original [Sir Thomas continues] than either of these. In it Gentilis combines for the first time the practical discussions of the Catholic theologians with the theory of natural law which had been mainly worked out by the Protestants. His idea of what he calls the "Philosophy of War" is that it belongs to the great commonwealth of mankind: "Non unius est reipublicae sed omnium." . . .

He assumes the existence of Natural Law, as having been already established. . . .

These three books of the *De Iure Belli* of Gentilis supply the model and framework of the first and third books of Grotius; and it may be questioned

---

[5] *Studies in International Law*, pp. 21, 22, 23.

[6] By a slip, doubtless due to a misprint, this passage is quoted by Professor Holland as from the *Hispanicae advocationis*. It is from the *De iure belli*, Book I, chap. xxi. In English translation the passage reads: "The law of trade is just; but that of maintaining one's safety is more so. The former is a law of nations, the latter of nature. The former concerns private citizens, the latter kingdoms. Let trade therefore give way to the kingdom, man to nature, money to life."

ALBERICO GENTILI

whether the matter of Grotius' second book is not too important to be fitly introduced as a mere digression in a treatise on belligerent rights.

I am by no means concerned to place Gentilis on a level with his undeniably greater follower; or to say that his writings do not exhibit, in some degree, the faults with which they have been charged. My object has been merely to call attention to a too much forgotten reputation; and to remind you that the first step taken toward making International Law what it is, was taken, not by Grotius, but by the Perugian refugee, the adopted son of Oxford, Albericus Gentilis.[7]

Gentili arrived in England in 1580. A few years later (in 1584) he was consulted by the English authorities as to what should be done with the charges against Don Bernardino Mendoza, Ambassador of the King of Spain to the Queen of England. Of this incident a brief but authoritative account is given by an early and neutral writer, a Netherlander, Abraham de Wicquefort, who represents the ambassador as constantly engaging in intrigues against the Queen of England (then Elizabeth) and her government. The Spanish ambassador, according to the same authority, was a party to Francis Throckmorton's famous conspiracy against the Queen, and he was also a principal in other similar plots.[8]

Upon the advice, it would appear, of Gentili, the ambassador was not deprived of his life (as was Mary Queen of Scots three years later for taking part in such plots), although there was a strong sentiment in favor of condign punishment of the ambassador; but Gentili was of the opinion— which he firmly stated—that the principle of the inviolability of ambassadors was applicable in the case, and therefore he advised that the matter be referred to the ambassador's royal master, Philip II. This apparently was done, although it may be added that appropriate action was not taken by the Spanish sovereign. Meanwhile, in accordance with the advice of Gentili, the ambassador, instead of being brought to trial, was expelled from the country and deposited in Calais. Of this incident Professor Holland[9] very properly says: "that the opinion given by Gentilis was the right one is now universally admitted."

The case has been thus briefly mentioned because it contributed to the foundation upon which the subsequent reputation of Gentili was to rest. He had been "incorporated" in Oxford three years before—that is to say, upon the strength of the doctor's degree in law which he had received

---

[7] *Studies in International Law*, pp. 22, 23.
[8] *Mémoires touchant les ambassadeurs et les ministres publics*, I, 205, 423.
[9] *Studies in International Law*, p. 10.

in Perugia, he was accorded the degree of doctor of civil law at Oxford and began to lecture at the university. In 1587, upon his return from a brief mission abroad to the Elector of Saxony, he was appointed Regius Professor of Civil Law at Oxford.

In 1584 he chose as a topic of discussion at the university—because of the Mendoza case—the subject of the rights and duties of an ambassador. Some six months later he expanded the lecture which he had delivered and published it under the title, *De legationibus libri tres* (or, in English, *Three Books on Embassies*). The entire volume is somewhat historical in its nature, and especially the first book, which treats of the origin of the various classes or categories of diplomatic agents. The second book is of greater importance than the first and perhaps more interesting, dealing as it does with the privileges and immunities which diplomatic agents should enjoy. The third book is devoted to the qualifications which Gentili felt that every ambassador should have. This last book is of perennial interest; it is at once erudite and readable, and should be mastered by all who take an interest in the use and practice of diplomacy, which has so long been the principal channel for the establishment and conduct of relations among the states of the international community.

After mentioning in general terms, in the first chapter of the third book, the qualifications which an ambassador should have in order to perform the duties of his office, and in the second chapter the requirements in regard to the external circumstances of an ambassador, Gentili indicates by chapter headings[10] the qualities which his ambassador should possess. He should be "a man of good personal appearance" (chapter iii); "a man favored by fortune" (chapter iv)—a requirement still demanded of diplomats, with the result that too often only the wealthy are appointed to such posts; "a man of superior intellectual power" (chapter v)—which quality, as history informs us, is often conspicuous by its absence; "a good speaker" (chapter vi); he should "understand the language of the person with whom he is negotiating" (chapter vii); he should have "a wide knowledge of history" (chapter viii)—for in order to perform his diplomatic duties, the ambassador must know the historical background of the countries in which he is to serve; he should also possess the following qualities: a "knowledge of philosophy" (chapter ix)—not that he need be a philosopher, but he should be of a philosophical mind; "literary attainments" (chapter x)— without being a *littérateur* by profession; "fidelity" (chapter xi), which he should possess in the fullest measure; "courage" (chapter xii); "temperance"

---

[10] *De legationibus libri tres*; trans. by Laing (in "Classics of International Law"), II, 141–85.

(chapter xiii); "prudence and fidelity" (chapters xiv and xv); and finally he should not "deceive his sovereign" (chapter xvi), but should carry out the express instructions of his sovereign without variation (chapter xvii), and with "prudence and courage" (chapter xviii), but if express instructions are lacking, he should confer with his sovereign in order to obtain instructions, although in case of grave need and if time be pressing, he may exercise his own discretion, subject, however, to approval on the part of his sovereign.

These are, in Gentili's opinion, the essential qualifications of an ambassador.

Under the heading of "The Ambassador Should Assert the Dignity of His Embassy" (chapter xix), Gentili deals in a masterly although somewhat lengthy paragraph with a subject which seems still to be a burning one, not merely with ambassadors but also with their suites.[11]

I want ambassadors to have a high and worthy spirit, not only in great affairs but in everything, and to refuse to tolerate the slightest infringement of their dignity. . . . Ambassadors are accustomed (and properly) to insist with the utmost emphasis that no one else, unless some reason makes it imperative, shall have a more honorable place than they; they will not submit to anything of the kind. . . . The prudent ambassador must be well provided with plans by which to extricate himself from all such situations. . . . Sometimes even ambassadorial dignity ought not to be rated so high as to prejudice the consideration of the proper plan (the ambassador will estimate this according to his prudence) for the expeditious accomplishment of the mission. So perhaps the ambassador Theodosius acted shrewdly when he dismounted on meeting the Persian king, for the barbarian, greatly impressed by so signal an honor, granted the ambassador's request. . . . But what if the conduct of the sovereign to whom he is accredited is such as to prevent the ambassador's maintaining his dignity? He ought to consult his own sovereign as to what action is necessary; in the meantime let him restrain himself so as to avoid, as far as possible, every indignity. If he is unable to avoid insult, let him realize first of all that no affront, even the most serious, has any relation whatever to him personally. . . . The same principle holds in the case of every affront. . . . It follows therefore that the manner in which the ambassador should act, either in avenging or suffering an insult, is not a question for him to decide, but for his sovereign.

Under the caption, "The Prudence and Temperance of Ambassadors" (chapter xx), Gentili supports his views with a number of interesting examples, as he also does under the heading, "The Methods of the Prudent Ambassador" (chapter xxi). And he ends with "The Perfect Ambassador" (chapter xxii), who is more often sought than found. Had Gentili lived

[11] *Ibid.*, II, 186–87.

two centuries later, he might well have instanced in this chapter our own Benjamin Franklin as the perfect ambassador, but being of the sixteenth century he naturally chose as an exemplar, as we shall later see, the shining figure of his own age, Sir Philip Sidney. Summing up the qualities of the perfect envoy, Gentili says:

This, as it seems to me, is the sum total of qualities which go to the making of the perfect ambassador. We have discussed them individually, except in the case of certain virtues, which, however, are the ones which lead all the others in their train. The perfect ambassador is one who can accomplish efficiently the business and duties which have been assigned to him or which he himself has recognized the necessity of undertaking. He ought to understand to which class of ambassador he belongs, so as not to assume the wrong rôle. He should himself always comply with the conventionalities and customs of the office which he has assumed, and should insist upon others observing them in their dealings with him. He should know the rights of embassy—their extent and their character—so as to have them ready for immediate application, and it should be his aim to guard their sanctity and sacred associations. His equipment and suite should be marked by a splendor commensurate with the dignity of him who has sent him, and his birth and present position should be of distinction.[12]

As for the essential qualities of "affability" and "dignity," Gentili adds that the ambassador must combine these qualities and must

observe carefully the instructions which the wise have given on the subject. . . . He owes dignity to his principal function, and dignity without affability will tend to isolate him, for he is now no longer among his own people. . . . Graciousness, which adorns all human activities, . . . ought not to be lacking in our ambassador.

But Gentili's ambassador was not to cultivate his dignity at the expense of his "chief function"— that is to say, diplomacy. On this point there was, we are told, no lack of precedents, the one which Gentili cites being taken from Cicero and having to do "with some Spartan ambassadors at Athens." This famous incident is thus recounted: "One day there, when seated in the theater at an entertainment, they stood up and welcomed in their section an old man who had not been given a seat by any of his fellow Athenians, whereupon they were given rounds of applause by the whole audience." This was an exhibition of diplomacy *par excellence*.

Turning now to other ambassadorial qualities, Gentili continues:

The ambassador need not be able to speak on every topic, but he certainly should be able to speak well on those subjects which fall within the departments of politics and civics. Moreover, he must speak in a style that is philosophical rather than rhetorical, and it should be in the native tongue of the person whom

---

[12] *De legationibus*, II, 198–201.

he is addressing. He must pay great attention to history of all kinds. He ought to have also some knowledge of civil [i. e., Roman] law and of sound philosophy. He must feel that the highest kind of loyalty is due from him, and he should manifest this loyalty. Nor should he ever by cavil of any kind swerve from this, for it is the most important part of his office.

Again, when diplomatic negotiations are in progress, the ambassador must be able to expound the views of his government clearly and effectively. In the words of Gentili: "it is the duty of the ambassador not merely to explain his message but to support it by arguments."

Moreover, it was apparently Gentili's conviction that every diplomat must possess in full measure three cardinal virtues to which he had already referred, and which he now mentions again by way of emphasis. "We require in the ambassador," he declares, "conspicuous bravery, notable temperance, and unique prudence."

Having in this masterly manner summed up the qualifications of his ambassador, Gentili says:

Now I think I may appropriately close my discourse. . . . I have endeavored to transmit, so far as lay in my power, a pattern of the excellent ambassador, either specifically described or outlined in discussions of greater sweep, and after that I have made an effort to include my representation within the compass of this smaller picture, not however without the addition of some embellishments.

And Gentili ends both the chapter and the book by referring to the perfect ambassador of his own day, Sir Philip Sidney. It was gracious as well as appropriate to refer to the youthful Sir Philip Sidney as the "living image and example of the perfect ambassador."[13] At the same time Gentili might also have found the qualities which he accredited to Sidney in the person, practice, and writings of Castiglione, who set forth his ideal of the gentleman in *The Courtier*.[14] Unquestionably, however, Sidney embodied all of the qualities of the perfect courtier, and might have been among the greatest of ambassadors but for his heroic and untimely death on the field of battle at Zutphen, in the Netherlands.

Interesting and indeed important in the literature of international law as is Gentili's contribution to the law of ambassadors, it is upon the *Three Books on the Law of War* that his reputation as an internationalist securely rests.

The treatise was written in a stirring period of English history, and of the history of Europe, when the rules governing warfare were of peculiar international importance; when the Spanish ambassador had been sent out

[13] *Ibid.*, II, 201.   [14] See *supra*, chap. xx.

of England for plotting against the life of Her Majesty Queen Elizabeth; when the Virgin Queen and Mary Queen of Scots were approaching the end of a fateful tragedy; when Philip II, King of Spain, was assembling that Armada which might have changed the history of the world, had not England on that occasion—as on many others—displayed its inborn mastery of the seas.

It is no wonder that Gentili, living in an atmosphere of war and rumors of war, of plots and counterplots, of armament and rearmament, should declare that[15] the "philosophy of war belongs to that great community formed by the entire world and the whole human race."

But before dealing at length with the *Three Books on the Law of War,* a word must be said as to their origin. They were the result of a series of what may be called inaugural disputations at the University of Oxford, although it must be said that as finally published they bear little resemblance to occasional addresses or academic exercises. The first part of the treatise was published in 1588, in the very year in which the Spanish Armada came to grief in the English Channel. The second and third parts were published a year later and, as has been stated, the whole, revised and unified, was reissued as a single work in 1598 under the title, *De iure belli libri tres.*

With respect to qualifications for undertaking a treatise on the law of war, Gentili was splendidly equipped. As a master of Roman law he did much, indeed, to rejuvenate its study in England. Moreover, he was at once a classical scholar and a practicing lawyer who dealt with both municipal and international cases. And it is obvious that he was a voracious reader, familiar with much of the literature of the Middle Ages, theological as well as secular. Therefore, he was in a position to base the doctrines which he propounded upon Roman law—and especially upon the law of nature—and in no small part upon the doctrines of the schoolmen, as well as upon the practices of his own day.

However, Gentili shared a weakness which appears to have been characteristic of more than one writer on. the law of nations; for while he readily admitted (in referring to the literature on the law of war) his familiarity with Roman law, he was more chary of confessing his acquaintance with the works of his predecessors from the fall of Rome to his own day. "What, pray," he says,[16] "shall I say of the modern interpreters of Justinian's laws?" In the light of his subsequent voluminous quotations and citations, it must be admitted that his answer is not convincing: "Personally, I have read nothing save a few passages of Lignano's treatise on this subject

---

[15] *De iure belli,* trans. by Rolfe (in "Classics of International Law"), II, 3. [16] *Ibid.,* II, 4.

and some scattered references of others." But even where he admitted a knowledge of them, he declared that he had read them "with no little contempt." His omissions at this point are so obvious that it is unnecessary to dwell upon them, but as a sample—one which has been pointed out by not a few writers of his native land—it may be mentioned that he completely ignores his Italian predecessor, Pierino Belli, with whose work, it is the general consensus of opinion, he must have been familiar. As an illustration of the Italian view of this matter, certain comments by Professor Alessandro De Giorgi, of the University of Parma, may be cited.[17] After subscribing to the view of another eminent Italian, Pasquale Stanislao Mancini, to the effect that Belli's treatise, *De re militari,* had served as a guide for Gentili, Professor De Giorgi further declares that Italy owes its first juridical treatise on the law of nations "not to Alberico Gentili, but to Pierino Belli, who thus occupies the post of precursor of Grotius and Gentili as well." And here Professor De Giorgi adds a parenthetical but very significant phrase, "after Vitoria, of course, who is to be saluted as the father of the science."[18]

On a subsequent page this Italian publicist remarks[19] upon the impropriety of referring to Gentili as "the first expounder of the laws of peace and war and the founder of international law," and the reason which he advances is that, disregarding "the minor writers, he was preceded by the Spaniard, Vitoria, and by the Italian, Belli, both in merit and in time."[20]

Another of Gentili's countrymen, the late Professor Arrigo Cavaglieri, reached a similar conclusion.

Grotius [he observes] mentions the help he derived from the study of Gentili's work, and the latter in turn renders honour to the Spaniard Francisco de Vitoria, to whom it is certain that Pierino Belli also owed much. In the light of such

---

[17] *Della vita e delle opere di Alberico Gentili,* pp. 92–93.   [18] *Ibid.,* p. 80.
[19] *Ibid.,* p. 91.

As revealing Professor De Giorgi's measured judgment on this interesting point, a further passage is quoted from his volume on Gentili:

"We accept the judgment offered by Mancini, that is, that Alberico Gentili is second to Pierino Belli who is in truth the initiator in Italy of the science properly so-called of international law.

"We shall recall here only that both of these writers owe much to the Spaniard, Francis de Vitoria who, as we have said, we believe should be saluted as the true Father of this science. Not that we wish to deny that he made use of materials prepared before him; science is the product of the successive labors of many. Nor do we intend to assert that Vitoria treated the subject fully in every part; but he established in an orderly manner the bases and fixed the cardinal points of the science; he furnished the example of the suitable method; and these contributions are the essentially important ones."—*Ibid.,* p. 82.

[20] For a comparison of the views of these three writers, see the Appendix to the present chapter.

acknowledgements Gentili's absolute silence regarding Belli affords an unpleasant contrast; a contrast which, inasmuch as the similarity in treatment and solution of many questions of the law of war by the two writers cannot be purely accidental, is aggravated by Gentili's lofty affirmation of having been the first to treat of the weighty and difficult subject.[21]

To dwell at greater length upon this Gentilian trait would be to overemphasize a fault which, as has been said, is not uncommon. It was shared to some extent, as will subsequently appear, by Grotius himself, who reveled in authorities without, however, always mentioning them.

Gentili's *De iure belli* was concerned primarily with war. In Book I of the treatise, however, he deals at length with the bases and nature of international law, and the following analysis will therefore be limited to that book. The law of war in his conception was not a separate and distinct set of rules unrelated to other rules of law. He asserts in so many words his "firm belief that questions of war ought to be settled in accordance with the law of nations."[22] This important statement is followed immediately by one even more significant, to the effect that the law of nations "is the law of nature." Here we have evidence of the breadth and depth of Gentili's conception of the law to apply between nations, whether in war or in peace; for that law is not simply—as has been stated by some who have misunderstood him—positive law, but is specifically identified by him with the law of nature itself.

"Although international law," he continues, "is a portion of the divine law, which God left with us after our sin, yet we behold that light amid great darkness; and hence through error, bad habits, obstinacy, and other affections due to darkness we often cannot recognize it."[23] Like the preceding passage, this smacks of the scholastic doctrine, for the international law thus defined is nothing else than the law of nature of the schoolmen, which although of divine origin, is discoverable by human reason, even though that reason be limited by human imperfections. Thus as Gentili himself implies,[24] law is like the truth, which may be discovered "even though it be hidden in a well," if it be diligently sought. "Abundant light," he adds, "is afforded us by the definitions which the authors and founders of our laws are unanimous in giving to this law of nations which we are investigating." What were their definitions? They say, Gentili informs us, "that the law of nations is that which is in use among all the nations of men, which native reason has established among all human beings, and

---

[21] Introduction to the Carnegie Endowment's edition of Belli's *De re militari et bello tractatus* (in "Classics of International Law"), II, 25a.

[22] *De iure belli* (previously cited), II, 5.   [23] *Ibid.,* II, 7–8.   [24] *Ibid.,* II, 8.

which is equally observed by all mankind." This is the great conception which the modern world has inherited from the Greeks, the Romans, and the schoolmen. It is the law of nations made a part of the law of nature,[25] as Gentili himself declares: "Such a law is natural law." And as his authority he quotes a famous line from Cicero: "The agreement of all nations about a matter must be regarded as a law of nature."[26] Upon this fundamental doctrine Gentili makes the important comment that "it must not be understood to mean that all nations actually came together at a given time, and that thus the law of nations was established." The impossibility of such an all-inclusive gathering is obvious, and indeed—as Gentili adds – the writers whom he cites on this subject "do not make any such statement." It was not necessary, in speaking of "all nations" as Cicero did, to consider the term as meaning "absolutely every nation," especially in view of the fact that in Gentili's as well as in Cicero's day not a few nations still remained "unknown." The fundamental truth at the root of the doctrine could be expressed in a single sentence: "that which has successively seemed acceptable to all men should be regarded as representing the intention and purpose of the entire world," a scholastic truism for which Gentili invokes the authority of St. Ambrose and St. Jerome. Law thus universally accepted is not written or statutory law. It is, in the words of Gentili, "like a custom and is established in that same manner."

In dealing with the development of this law Gentili makes use of an interesting analogy: "as the rule of a state and the making of its laws are in the hands of a majority of its citizens, just so is the rule of the world in the hands of the aggregation of the greater part of the world."[27] Here we seem to have a conception of an international community much like that expounded by Francisco de Vitoria in his *Relectio de Indis*.[28]

Apparently Gentili was anxious to establish firmly the fundamental law upon which he proposed to erect his structure of the law of war, and he therefore considers it from various angles and in the light of more than one definition. "There is," he continues,[29] "another and more elegant definition of the law of nations . . . that there are everywhere certain unwritten laws, not enacted by men (since men could not all assemble in one place, nor were they all of one speech), but given to them by God." Of these unwritten laws Gentili gives, in the scholastic manner, two examples: "that one should worship God; . . . that one should honour father and mother." Now these

---

[25] A critical discussion of Gentili's conception of natural law is given by Van der Molen, *op. cit.*, chap. vii, sec. 1.
[26] *Tusculan Disputations*, I. xiii. 30.
[28] Sec. III. 4. See *supra*, p. 322.
[27] *De iure belli*, II, 9.
[29] *De iure belli*, II, 9–10.

precepts are, he tells us, "not written, but inborn." They are concerned, in short, with the inherent duties prescribed by the natural and divine law of the schoolmen. "We have not received them through instruction, but have acquired them at birth; we have gained them, not by training, but by instinct."

Having referred on a previous page to the law of nations as being established by "native reason," Gentili is now confronted with the necessity of an inquiry into the nature of reason. It must be admitted, however, that since he considered himself a man of law rather than of philosophy, he sidestepped the issue, for he says:[30] "To this question the following reply must be made: that natural reason is evident of itself and therefore those who rely upon it are content merely to say: 'This is perfectly clear from nature itself,' 'It is evident from natural reason,' 'He has a knowledge derived from nature,' 'Nature shows'; and there are many remarks of the same kind." Apparently deciding that this treatment of the subject was not wholly adequate, he immediately adds some further examples: "So also 'Just by nature,' 'Nothing is so completely in harmony with natural justice,' 'It is contrary to nature,' 'Nature does not allow,' and hundreds of other phrases." Feeling, perhaps, that a quotation from the philosopher of the Greeks would supply his own lack of philosophy, he ends his quotations with the statement that "Aristotle says: 'By nature all men desire knowledge,' 'All men seem to seek the good,' etc."

Upon these maxims Gentili himself comments: "These things are so well known, that if you should try to prove them, you would render them obscure." Observing that it is futile "to prove what is already manifest," he invokes the authority "of the interpreters of the law," to the effect that "things which are well known ought to be stated, but not demonstrated." This being the case, he considers that "it has been made sufficiently clear that natural law does exist, and that if you should transgress it in any particular, you would desire to conceal the act through very shame"; as in the case of those who violate universally accepted maxims, the transgressor would feel instinctively that his violation "could not be justified."

But even though philosophy was not his proper field, Gentili was enough of a philosopher to realize that his inquiry could not stop here, that he had not settled satisfactorily the relations between the natural law and natural reason. He therefore pushed his inquiry somewhat further, to the conclusion that "natural reason varies constantly according to men's intelligence"—upon which he comments,[31] with perhaps a touch of cynicism, that "many

[30] *De iure belli*, II, 10.   [31] *Ibid.*, II, 11.

are led not so much by that reason as by fantasy." Nevertheless, he is firmly convinced that "the laws which were laid down by the philosophers and approved by the judgment of every age undoubtedly possess natural reason."

There was another and more specific source from which Gentili derived the foundations for his law of nations, and that source was the Roman law. Here he could speak as a specialist and as one who was the heir of a thousand years not only of precedents based upon the Roman law, but of experience in its use and adaptation to the changing conditions of the world which succeeded Rome. "The law," he says,[32] "which is written in those books of Justinian is not merely that of the state, but also that of the nations and of nature." The Roman state as such, however, had long since vanished. To be sure, there was a Holy Roman Empire, and the mere fact of the survival of the form of empire might and did account in some measure for the survival of the Roman law itself. But the empire, as it existed in Gentili's day, was no longer that of Justinian except in outer form, and there were not a few even then who foresaw its doom. Did that mean the end of the Roman law? No, says Gentili, and the reason is that the law of Rome was so "in accord" with the law of nations and of nature that, "if the empire were destroyed, the law itself, although long buried, would yet rise again and diffuse itself among all the nations of mankind." Now this is both a prophecy and a fact, for the Roman law has survived the ravages of time, and, although the Holy Roman Empire vanished in form as well as in fact more than a century ago, the Roman law lives on and, to employ the phrase of Gentili, is diffusing itself "among all the nations of mankind." Or as D'Aguesseau puts it, "The grand destinies of Rome are not yet accomplished; she reigns throughout the world by her reason, after having ceased to reign by her authority."[33] This magnificent statement of D'Aguesseau is as true as it is eloquent. Roman law came to be looked upon, especially in the later Middle Ages, as the embodiment of reason and, because it was thus identified with reason, it was regarded as the law of nature and the law of every country; and from century to century, because of its universality, it was slowly and unconsciously but none the less surely becoming accepted as the basis for the "reasonable" law of nations which Vitoria,[34] at the beginning of our modern era, was to proclaim at Salamanca. Thus we see the great threefold influence which Roman law has had—as the immutable law of nature, as the law of reason, and as the law of states composed of reasoning people.

[32] *Ibid.*, II, 17.
[33] Quoted from Kent's *Commentaries* (Boston, 1896), I, 517.
[34] See *supra*, p. 313.

Now Gentili had in mind a very definite purpose, because of which he felt it necessary to establish his law of nations on an impregnable basis. That purpose was to emphasize the legal aspect of war, so that international conflicts might, so far as possible, be brought under the control of international law. The matter was of great moment and therefore he at once invoked authorities which could not be impugned by the Christian world—the authority "of Augustine and of the other theologians"—to demonstrate a fundamental proposition, consisting of two distinct but related assertions: first,[35] "reason shows that war has its origin in necessity"; and secondly, "this necessity arises because there cannot be judicial processes between supreme sovereigns or free peoples unless they themselves consent, since they acknowledge no judge or superior." This is the scholastic conception of war as a suit conducted by force between princes, in the absence of a superior tribunal, a procedure to be permitted, however, only in the case of necessity. Gentili, it is apparent, did not foresee that the establishment of a permanent international court of justice might eventually dispense with the "necessity" of war.

In this view there was implicit the idea of a community of states and a law to govern their relations, and, in order that there might be no mistake as to his thesis (i. e., that the rules of war should be definitely conceived as a part of the law of nations) Gentili drives his point home by a reference to the status of pirates and robbers, who, he declares,[36] "do not come under the law of war," the reason being that the law of war "is derived from the law of nations, and malefactors do not enjoy the privileges of a law to which they are foes." This conclusion leads to a further conclusion—in the form of a rhetorical question—which is even more essential to the Gentilian system: "How can the law, which is nothing but an agreement and a compact, extend to those who have withdrawn from the agreement and broken the treaty of the human race?"

There was another reason for insisting that war must be "necessary" if it is to be lawful, and that reason Gentili finds[37] in the principle that "whereas there are two modes of contention, one by argument and the other by force, one should not resort to the latter if it is possible to use the former." But what is implied by the term "argument" as a means which must be tried and exhausted before the employment of force is permissible? It does not imply merely heated discussion, for that procedure can but aggravate rather than settle the dispute. What Gentili has in mind is "argument and process of law, without recourse to arms"; in a word, to

---

[35] Gentili, *De iure belli* (previously cited), II, 15.   [36] *Ibid.*, II, 22.   [37] *Ibid.*, II, 15.

use his own term, "arbitration." And it being the duty of the parties in dispute to submit to arbitration, the party which does not submit is declared by Gentili, on the authority of Thucydides (who is cited in the margin of the text), to be an aggressor. This declaration Gentili enforces by a wealth of historical examples, at the conclusion of which he clinches his point by another rhetorical question, followed by an answer which is even more acceptable in our day than it was in his:[38] "But why do I multiply examples, as if any one could not call to mind a great number of such occurrences in every age?" Gentili thus answers his own question: "Why, to be sure, in order that those who avoid this kind of contest by arbitration and resort at once to the other, that is, to force, may understand that they are setting their faces against justice, humanity, and good precedent, and that they are rushing to arms of their own free will, because they are unwilling to submit to any one's verdict." If controversies within the state could be and were settled peaceably, why should justice not be administered between the states by arbitral tribunals? "For why," he adds, "should the disputes of private individuals be settled by arbitration and those of sovereigns not be thus decided, when the former are often greater than these public ones, or at any rate much less clear." A citizen who insisted on enforcing his own rights instead of appealing to the court was punishable. Why should a belligerent sovereign be permitted to spurn a judicial settlement?

It is better and more worthy of a citizen, says the law, not to use the compulsion of force. In the disputes of sovereigns more experienced judges can be secured and those who are less corruptible, who will hear and decide the cases with the whole world, as it were, for witnesses and spectators.

As a practical man Gentili recognized, however, that it was the unfortunate wont of sovereigns to reject arbitration as a means of settling disputes between them. Such rejection justified the other party to the dispute in taking up arms, "even for a doubtful matter," Gentili held,[39] although he felt that in such doubtful circumstances the sovereign in question should act "with greater hesitation." Nevertheless the onus rested upon him who had refused the offer of arbitration. "Naturally, a man's cause is proved to be bad," says Gentili, "when he will not submit it to examination" —a principle leading to the further comment that "we ought never to shrink from an investigation of our claims."

War, then, Gentili regarded as the exceptional remedy—we of today are beginning to doubt whether it should ever be a remedy at all—but in his

[38] *Ibid.*, II, 16.   [39] *Ibid.*, II, 93.

conception it could be considered as a remedial action only when it was waged for a just cause, for in international as in domestic law the purpose of a remedy is to bring about justice. Therefore, justice there must be in the cause of a war if it were to be lawfully prosecuted, and the fact that many wars were unjustly waged for inadequate and unjust causes was, in Gentili's opinion, no refutation of this principle. As would be expected, he deals at length with this phase of his subject, prefacing his discussion with the general assertion that the reasons for war must be just, "for an unjust cause is no cause at all."[40]

In his own century, as in preceding centuries, the question of religion had unfortunately loomed large among the causes of war. Gentili had very definite views on the injustice of such cause, and he based these on what he considered the best of authorities, including the *Relectiones theologicae* of Francisco de Vitoria of the University of Salamanca, of whom he says:[41] "the learned Vitoria declares that this principle of not making war from religious motives is approved by all without exception, and that religion was not a just reason for the war of his Spanish countrymen against the Indians." And lest it be thought that he had found but one among the Spanish schoolmen to support his view, Gentili immediately adds: "Diego de Covarruvias, also a Spaniard and a learned jurist, names several canonists and theologians who preach this same doctrine." This, however was not all, for he could and did invoke an authority of his native land. "And Baldus," he continues, "also declared with reference to Innocent that war is not lawful against infidels who live at peace with us and do us no harm."

Gentili had himself suffered as a result of differences of opinion regarding religious matters; indeed that had been the primary cause of his leaving Italy and settling in England. It need not surprise us, therefore, that he expressed himself somewhat emphatically upon this point. "Since the laws of religion," he says,[42] "do not properly exist between man and man, therefore no man's rights are violated by a difference in religion, nor is it lawful to make war because of religion." His assertion is buttressed by the liberal and logical argument that

religion is a relationship with God. Its laws are divine, that is between God and man; they are not human, namely, between man and man. Therefore a man cannot complain of being wronged because others differ from him in religion.

This syllogism presents an unanswerable argument in favor of the right to freedom of religion and of conscience.

[40] *De iure belli*, II, 35. [41] *Ibid.*, II, 39. [42] *Ibid.*, II, 41.

But what if the state religion, that is to say, the religion of the ruler, is different from that of certain of his subjects? Again Gentili felt a personal interest in the question which he raises. As an answer he adopts the view of Bodin: "I accept the argument of Bodin, that violence should not be employed against subjects who have embraced another religion than that of their ruler."[43] Unfortunately this broad and humanitarian view was not generally accepted in Gentili's day, for religious wars—the greatest in the world—were to break out within the next century, plunging the most civilized states of Europe into years of misery.

But there are also economic causes of war—as we of today know only too well—and among these was one with which the Spanish schoolmen, particularly Vitoria, had dealt in some detail and with which Grotius was to concern himself at greater length at the opening of the following century: the question of the right of travel and of trade with foreign countries. Now commerce, in Gentili's opinion, was "in accordance with the law of nations."[44] He was somewhat familiar with the great controversies of his day and with the solutions propounded by the internationalists of Spain, the country which was most interested in them. Not unnaturally, therefore, he referred both to these controversies, which had arisen out of the discovery of the New World, and to their solution, declaring that one reason why the war of the Spaniards in "the remote Indies . . . seems to be justified" was that "the inhabitants prohibited other men from commerce with them" —on which his marginal authority is again the *Relectiones* of Vitoria. His own conclusion on the subject is that the Spaniards had a just cause of war if the Indians actually prevented them from exercising the right of commerce in the New World.

But closely connected with this important subject was the question of the freedom of the seas, a question disposed of by Gentili in a manner which must have appealed to Grotius (for the young as well as the older Grotius was familiar with Gentili's writings on the law of nations).[45] Of the sea Gentili says:[46] "This is by nature open to all men and its use is common to all, like that of the air." Upon this premise his unanswerable conclusion is that it "cannot therefore be shut off by any one." Wishing to make the doctrine more concrete, he introduces a number of interesting examples, among them the attempt of the Venetians to extend their jurisdiction over

[43] *Ibid.*, II, 44.
[44] *Ibid.*, II, 89.
[45] Gentili is mentioned at some length in the Prolegomena of Grotius's *On The Law of War and Peace*, and is cited several times in the treatise *De iure praedae*, composed in Grotius's youth but never published by him. For further details concerning the latter treatise, see *infra*, chap. xxxi.
[46] *De iure belli*, II, 90.

the sea, on the ground that they had become possessors of a portion of it. Gentili declares[47] that he could not "admit that view, which by vain circumlocution violates the law of nature," and his reason is that "if the sea had been opened to all by nature, it ought to be closed to no one."

But economic matters, important as they are, were not to be exalted above the claims of humanity; and here Gentili reveals himself after all as something of a philosopher as well as lawyer:

The law of trade is just [he says], but that of maintaining one's safety is more so. The former is a law of nations, the latter of nature. The former concerns private citizens, the latter kingdoms. Let trade therefore give way to the kingdom, man to nature, money to life.[48]

These dicta lead up to certain principles which must control not only individuals but also nations, if they and their inhabitants are to survive economic and other crises.

Those are the principles on which legal contests are settled, namely, that one should yield to the worthier, more expedient, and more just law; that the profane should yield to the sacred, the things of the body to those of the spirit, the interests of fortune to those of the person, the law which includes both equity and the natural law to the natural law, that which enjoins the protection of strangers to one which enjoins the protection of our own, that which involves the individual advantage to that which involves the public welfare, the strict law to the just one, cases which are not necessary to those which are, that which permits to that which commands and forbids, the new to the old.[49]

On previous pages, Gentili had referred in passing to the treatment of pirates, but he now deals with them more at length, in terms which have both merited and met with acceptance and which indicate again his conviction that the union of mankind is at once a natural and a juridical phenomenon. Repeating his earlier statement that pirates are considered to have "violated the common law of nations," he continues,

And if a war against pirates justly calls all men to arms because of love for our neighbour and the desire to live in peace, so also do the general violation of the common law of humanity and a wrong done to mankind. Piracy is contrary to the law of nations and the league of human society.[50]

This statement might be termed an anticipation as well as a prophecy of an international community unified by the bonds of law. "War should be made against pirates by all men," Gentili concludes, "because in the violation of that law we are all injured, and individuals in turn can find their personal rights violated."

[47] *De iure belli*, II, 91. [48] *Ibid.*, II, 101. [49] *Ibid.*, II, 101–2. [50] *Ibid.*, II, 124.

The world, as Gentili saw it, was united, indeed, by a threefold bond. "Not only is the civil law," he declares "an agreement and a bond of union among citizens, but the same is true of the law of nations as regards nations, and the law of nature as regards mankind." It is in these conceptions that Gentili made his great contribution to the philosophy of international law. Though he wrote of war, he looked beyond war toward peace, as is clearly evidenced by the final paragraph of the first of his *Three Books*.

These are the things which may furnish a just cause for war. And yet it behoves just men to cut off the causes of wars at their source, as our lawgiver Justinian said. Do Thou, O God, Father of Justice, remove from us even these causes. Do away with all war. Grant, O Lord, peace in our days, give us peace. "Come to us, kindly peace." [51]

The third of the works dealing with international law which made Gentili's reputation in his day—a reputation which has grown and is still growing—is the *Hispanicae advocationis libri duo*,[52] or in our English tongue, *The Pleas of a Spanish Advocate*.

It was not inappropriate that Gentili should have been chosen to represent the Spaniards. Although a staunch supporter of the rights of England, his adopted country, he had nevertheless rendered a service to Spain, as we have seen, in advising that a Spanish ambassador in London, because of the immunity conferred on his office by the law of nations, should not be tried and executed under the laws of the land, in consequence of his conspiracy against the life of Queen Eliazbeth. The wisdom of his advice must also have impressed the English, for the proposal of a subsequent Spanish ambassador that Gentili should be retained as counsel for the defense of the interests of Spain appears to have been agreeable to Elizabeth's successor, James I of England and VI of Scotland.

But Gentili's appointment was not due merely to the good will of authorities of the two countries. The chief reasons for selecting him as advocate were his experience and marked ability as a practitioner, and his exceptional knowledge of the legal rules and principles applicable to the numerous cases before the Court of Admiralty in which Spanish as well as English interests were involved.

Of the two books of the *Spanish Pleas,* the first deals with questions of international law, including those affecting neutrality, while the second is concerned principally with private law. Perhaps the most effective way to

[51] *Ibid.,* II, 127.
[52] Published, with intro. and Trans. by Abbott, in the "Classics of International Law."

show Gentili in action is to examine one of his arguments in the first book —this time in behalf of the English—with the aid of the admirable analysis supplied by Professor Frank Frost Abbott in an introduction to his translation of the Pleas.[53]

Professor Abbott thus introduces the twentieth plea of the first book, which he considers one of the most interesting of Gentili's cases:[54]

An English ship while *en route* to Constantinople with a cargo of general merchandise and powder, "pulvis tormentarius," as Gentili calls it, was seized by the Sardinians and Maltese and the cargo confiscated. Gentili appeared for the English owners to contest the right of confiscation. Let us present his conclusions in the same systematic way in which he sets them forth in his plea in court.

At the beginning of his plea Gentili marshaled the arguments, Professor Abbott explains, "firstly, secondly, and so forth, from the standpoint of the Sardinians and Maltese":

(1) The civil law, as it stands in the Code of Justinian, prescribes capital punishment for anyone who shall furnish the barbarians with munitions of war.

(2) The canon law imposes excommunication upon Christians who send arms to the Saracens, and the Saracens are amalgamated with the Turks.

(3) The precedent of the Hanseatic cities which were forbidden to furnish munitions of war to the Spaniards, when Spain and England were at war, shows that it is contrary to the Law of Nations for a neutral people to send arms to belligerent nations with whom they are at peace, and in this connection he coins the apothegm: "Do not unto others what ye would not that they should do unto you."

(4) The treaty between England and Spain forbids either people to furnish aid to the enemy of the other, and Spain is the ally of the Emperor who is at war with the Turks.

Gentili then proceeds, Professor Abbott says, to reply to his opponents' arguments:[55]

(1) Part of the cargo was made up of lawful merchandise, and that at least is exempt from confiscation, unless it can be shown that the owners of the lawful merchandise were cognizant of the unlawful goods.

(2) The English were *en route*. They might have turned back before reaching Constantinople. The offense had not been committed until the act was complete.

(3) The powder may have been intended for the ship's defense. Even in those States where the exportation of grain is forbidden, a man going abroad may take enough with him for his journey, and if the English had any powder left over it would have been lawful for them to sell it at their journey's end.

(4) The carriage of powder would not be unlawful *per se*. The powder might have been used by one faction of the Turks against another.

---

[53] *Hispanicae advocationis*, Vol. I.   [54] *Ibid.*, I, 16a.   [55] *Ibid.*, I, 17a.

(5) The English owners made out manifests before the proper English officials and, under the Orders in Council of Queen Elizabeth, may carry their goods anywhere. The English have therefore observed the English statutes and they can not be held amenable to the laws of any other sovereign.

(6) The treaty between England and Spain does not apply in this case, because Spain is not at war with Turkey, and the naming of the King of Spain among the allies of the Emperor is a formality without meaning. Accordingly Gentili concludes that the Maltese may obstruct the trade of England with the Turks, but may not punish English ship-owners in person or in property.

This résumé is an admirable demonstration of Gentili's method. His practice was to set forth, in the strongest terms at his disposal, the views of his opponent which he was shortly to contest. "Indeed the early part of most of his arguments," observes Professor Abbott,[56] "consists of a categorical statement of the case of the opposite side, supported by the laws and text-writers who could be cited in its defense." Thus it may be said that Gentili adopted the scholastic method of argument.

His professorship at Oxford is a sufficient guaranty of his legal learning. The logical trend of his mind is evidenced here as in his other works, and is no doubt due in part to the fact that Gentili was a Latin by birth and education. That he was a learned man in more than one field of knowledge is evident to anyone who opens his books, and it is not surprising that he seems occasionally to be borne down by the weight of his learning. But what may seem to us now to be a parade of knowledge was but the customary literary practice of his day—a practice of many of the schoolmen as well as of lay writers.

If at times we are wearied by the authorities he cites in support of a principle which to us seems self-evident, we should remember that he was writing in a day when the number of examples, rather than their intrinsic value, weighed not only in the decision of the judges but in the general acceptance of opinions set forth in learned works. And if Gentili is criticized on this score, what should be said of Grotius, whose accumulation of authorities—a quotation in approximately every third line of his *De jure belli ac pacis*—is even more imposing and overpowering than that of his Italian predecessor? There were, in fact, few writers of the fifteenth and sixteenth centuries, and of earlier centuries, who did not feel it necessary for their purpose to sprinkle their pages freely with the wit and wisdom of the ages, so freely, indeed, that the citations often tended to interfere with, if not to obscure, the argument. An outstanding exception to this almost universal practice is to be found in the *Relectiones* of Francisco de

[56] *Ibid.*, p. 16a.

Vitoria, Professor of Theology at the University of Salamanca, who possessed what was in his day the almost unique gift of saying much in little, and who used authorities sparingly, in comparison with the literary practice of the time, but with the utmost effect.[57]

Gentili, however, was a man of his age in this, as in other ways, and his style and his method must be judged by the standards of his century. But while the general method of presentation in our day may differ from that of Gentili's day, it must in fairness be said that he presented his arguments logically and convincingly, and that many a sententious passage in his *Spanish Pleas,* when removed from its context will stand alone as an apothegm. It will be interesting to examine a few of these apothegms (chiefly from the first book of the *Spanish Pleas*) as quoted or paraphrased under the heading "Obiter Dicta,"[58] by Professor Abbott.

1. War is not a hunt. Political territory is something more than a private domain.

Apparently Gentili was not in sympathy with hunting down human beings and with the practice of certain monarchs of identifying their kingdoms with their own personal property.

2. Whatever stands in the original is implied in full in the citation.

The conclusion to which this dictum leads is that whenever an author cites a passage without qualification, he does so with approval of all that is contained in the passage.

3. The dicta of learned men should be interpreted in accordance with the laws and the authorities which they have cited.

This may be considered as a corollary of the preceding statement.

4. The last statement of a writer is to be preferred to an earlier one.

Such indeed is the general rule, although occasionally nature seems to reverse her process and an author's youthful works are preferred by posterity to his later productions.

5. An edict of a monarch affecting the subjects of another monarch must be interpreted in accordance with the treaty between the monarchs.

In stating this principle Gentili had in mind the treaty between Great Britain and Spain,[59] the purpose of which was to protect the rights of the

---

[57] See *supra,* chap. xxii, for a discussion of Vitoria's writings.
[58] Gentili, *Hispanicae advocationis,* I, 41a–43a.
[59] Treaty of "perpetual peace and alliance," concluded in 1604.

subjects of each sovereign within the territory or the jurisdiction of the other. Such protection is now so generally granted that, though provisions regarding it are still included in treaties, the principle involved is almost universally recognized, even without treaties.

6. A skipper sailing under letters of marque is rather committing piracy than carrying on war. He does not follow the laws of war and he directs his efforts against non-combatants.

Such in principle was the conclusion of the parties to the Declaration of Paris of 1856, which is today the common law of nations.

7. Ownership can not hang in the air.

Perhaps the best comment on this is that it should not hang and would not for any length of time, if the action of courts, national and international, were reasonably expedited.

8. The law, which is based on natural reason, both teaches that justice should be rendered to everybody, . . . and holds everywhere.

Here natural law appears, as it usually did in England, in the guise of natural reason.

9. The Englishman follows the law of his native land, not the canon or civil law.

This is still a popular view, but the fact remains that many a principle of the Roman and canon law is so deeply imbedded in the law of England that its origin has long since been overlooked or forgotten.[60] It may be remarked in passing that Gentili's statement might be reversed with more truth—that the law of England has also followed the Englishman.

10. The kinship of princes does not determine public policy.

This was a statement of principle rather than of fact; for in times past the ties of kinship have led many a sovereign to contract unfortunate alliances which have led to war.

11. The civil law, especially in maritime cases, is a sort of Law of Nations.

The law of Rome, as applied in maritime cases, has more than once been codified in a form accepted by the majority of nations, as in the case of the great maritime codes of the Middle Ages. And its principles are also to be found embodied in many civil-law codes of the present day.

---

[60] See *supra*, pp. 252 ff.

12. The law governing pirates and wild beasts is not applicable to enemies, i.e., there are laws of war.

The remaining dicta (some of which are from Professor Abbott's selections from the first book of the *Pleas of a Spanish Advocate,* while others have been culled from the second book) may be quoted without comment:

13. The Law of Nations allows trade in times of peace with any nation, even with the Turks.
14. Between a prince and the subject of another nation ... the Law of Nations should apply.
15. Contracts with princes ... imply good faith.
16. ... just as the right of defense ought not to be denied to those who have been injured, so the way ought not to be opened to bad faith.[61]
17. Reason is the rule. Cases are cases, and do not restrict reason or the rule which comes from reason.[62]
18. Commonly accepted opinions today have the same authority as the responses of wise men had in olden times, and from these it was not lawful for a judge to depart. They are regarded as law, and they come under the head of law.[63]
19. In judicial proceedings the party who keeps silent is always regarded as the consenting party, and this case expounders of the law everywhere accept.[64]
20. Nothing is so natural and in consonance with equity as giving effect to the intention of the man who wishes to make a transfer to another.[65]
21. Philosophers teach that a fair price is not a fixed point, but may vary somewhat. Do I say "the philosophers"? All the jurists and all theologians hold the same view. The theologians give this further warning that one should not look back or wait in the hope of securing more than a fair gain in the future.[66]

The philosophical and scholastic elements in Gentili's three treatises constitute his permanent contribution to international law and international relations. Thus his treatment of the rules of warfare is of his day; their day is past, because the methods of warfare have altered (for the worse, in the opinion of those who support the cause of peace) and the rules of warfare have changed. Therefore Gentili's treatment of these matters is primarily of historical interest.

His great contributions were his conceptions of a community of nations governed by a law of nations, of the inevitableness of justice in human relations, of the sanctity of good faith, and his contention that peaceful settlement by arbitration should be substituted for war. These are enduring things.

---

[61] *Hispanicae advocationis,* II, 162.   [62] *Ibid.,* p. 173.   [63] *Ibid.,* p. 175.
[64] *Ibid.,* p. 177.   [65] *Ibid.,* II, 213.   [66] *Ibid.,* pp. 221–22.

Appendix

Pierino Belli (1502–75): His Relation to Vitoria and Gentili

On a preceding page mention has been made of Alberico Gentili's unacknowledged debt to Pierino Belli, and the latter's indebtedness to Francisco de Vitoria. As a demonstration of this relationship it will suffice to point out certain striking similarities between Belli's doctrines and those of Vitoria and Gentili.

A few words of comment, however, should precede the comparison. Vitoria's *De Indis et de iure belli Relectiones*,[1] prepared in 1532, were first published in 1557. It was apparently not until after the latter date that Belli began work on his treatise *De re militari et bello*, which appeared in 1563. Gentili's *De iure belli* was issued in preliminary form in the years 1588 and 1589, and in definitive form in 1598. Belli had served for many years in the armies both of Charles V, Holy Roman Emperor, who was also Charles I of Spain, and of the latter's son, Philip II of Spain. It is not unreasonable to assume, therefore, that the author of *De re militari et bello* was acquainted with the Spanish literature on the law of war and of nations, including Vitoria's *Relectiones*. As for Gentili, we know that he was familiar with the *Relectiones*, and that he was also acquainted with Belli's treatise because he specifically cited it in his *Hispanicae advocationis libri duo*.

The views of all three writers on the necessity for a just cause of war are strikingly similar. To Belli the righteous war was that waged because of an injury received or threatened.[2] This is the Augustinian doctrine stated by Vitoria,[3] that "there is a single and only just cause for commencing a war, namely, a wrong received," a conception which is echoed by Gentili.[4]

Vitoria,[5] as we know, insisted that the prince should be certain of the justice of his cause before undertaking war. Belli, too, entertained definite views on this point. Thus he asks, "with justice absent, what is warfare other than open brigandage?"[6] As for Gentili,[7] his opinion on the subject in hand is expressed with the brevity of a maxim: "an unjust cause is no cause at all."

Who was to declare and wage war? In the opinion of Vitoria[8] this should be done by the "perfect" state, through its representatives or chief magistrate, and by "perfect" state Vitoria meant a state "complete in itself" with "its own laws and its own council, and its own magistrates." The statement of Belli[9] is almost a paraphrase of Vitoria: "any people or nation living under its own laws and at its own charges, and any king or other ruler who is fully independent, may

---

[1] For a discussion of Vitoria, see *supra*, chap. xxii.

[2] *De re militari*, p. 61. This and the following citations are taken from Volume II of the Carnegie Endowment's edition in its "Classics of International Law." The first volume contains a reproduction of the edition of 1563, and the second an English translation by the late Herbert C. Nutting.

[3] *De Indis et de iure belli*, "Classics of International Law" (previously cited), p. 170.

[4] *De iure belli*, "Classics of International Law" (previously cited), II, 83.

[5] *De Indis*, pp. 173–74.   [6] *De re militari*, II, dedication to Philip II.

[7] *De iure belli*, II, 35.   [8] *De Indis*, pp. 168–69.   [9] *De re militari*, II, 7.

declare war at will and when occasion arises." Gentili[10] likewise devoted a chapter to this topic under the title "war is waged by sovereigns."

The sovereign, however, would be justified in declaring war only if no other adequate means for settlement of the controversy between the parties were available. Thus in the conception of Vitoria,[11] "if one party wants to settle and make a division or compromise as to part of the claim, the other is bound to accept his proposal, even if that other be the stronger and able to seize the whole by armed force; nor would he have a just cause of war." In harmony with this view is the pertinent query of Belli:[12] "Inasmuch as wars are waged to secure restitution, or to avert or even to avenge injury, what need is there to fight, if justice and satisfaction are offered?" This query he himself answered on a later page: "If war is declared against a person who shows himself ready to abide by the law and the award of referees touching the matter of complaint, warlike proceedings should be stopped; for war ought to be a court of last resort."[13] Gentili also expressed his conviction on this point in the form of a rhetorical question and an answer:

Why should the disputes of private individuals be settled by arbitration and those of sovereigns not be thus decided, when the former are often greater than these public ones, or at any rate much less clear? It is better and more worthy of a citizen, says the law, not to use the compulsion of force. In the disputes of sovereigns more experienced judges can be secured and those who are less corruptible, who will hear and decide the cases with the whole world, as it were, for witnesses and spectators.[14]

We have seen[15] that Vitoria sought to extend the law of the nations of Christendom to the world at large. It is interesting to find that Belli, touching upon the international status of the "Saracens and barbarians and other foreign nations which acknowledge neither Emperor nor Pope," subscribed to Vitoria's doctrine. "I do not see," observes Belli,[16] "what is to prevent these nations—being free—from taking advantage of the law of nations, which is always operative and belongs to every age." And Gentili,[17] who identified the law of nations with the law of nature, conceived of both as applying to all mankind.

Each of the three writers was convinced that war should be undertaken only under the spur of urgent necessity. Vitoria[18] advocated the most earnest examination of the causes of war by both the prince and his advisers, in order to ascertain whether hostilities were justified by the facts. Belli[19] insisted, on the unanimous authority of "all good men," that "wars are to be undertaken only for reasons that are at once serious and cogent and just." In his opinion, for which he vouched the authority of Baldus, "unjust wars are sheer brigandage."[20] Gentili,[21] also relying on Baldus, referred to unjust and needless aggression as "practising brigandage" and maintains that "unless it is necessary, war cannot be just, since a just war is said to be declared as the result of necessity."[22]

[10] *De iure belli* (Book I, chap. iii), II, 15.   [11] *De Indis*, p. 175.
[12] *De re militari*, II, 8.   [13] *Ibid.*, p. 11.   [14] *De iure belli*, II, 16.
[15] *Supra*, p. 312.   [16] *De re militari*, II, 10.   [17] *De iure belli*, II, 7–8, 9–10, 67, 124.
[18] *De Indis et de iure belli*, pp. 173–74.   [19] *De re militari*, II, p. 59.   [20] *Ibid.*
[21] *De iure belli*, II, 31–32.   [22] *Ibid.*, II, 20.

Vitoria's conception of war was that the conflict was in the nature of a "force suit," and that force was justifiable only because there was no competent judge with jurisdiction over the parties. Therefore the victor should consider himself as "sitting as judge between two States," [23] that is to say, between the plaintiff state and the defendant state. Even before victory is won, the prince who is carrying on a just war should consider himself as acting in the place of a judge.

If there were any competent judge over the two belligerents, he would have to condemn the unjust aggressors and authors of wrong, not only to make restitution of what they have carried off, but also to make good the expenses of the war to the other side, and also all damages. But a prince who is carrying on a just war is as it were his own judge in matters touching the war.[24]

Naturally Vitoria felt that the royal judge should limit his sentence to a reasonable assessment of damages for the wrong done by the defendant state. Therefore he declared that "if necessity and the principle of war require the seizure of the larger part of the enemy's land, and the capture of numerous cities, they ought to be restored when the strife is adjusted and the war is over, only so much being retained as is just, in way of compensation for damages caused and expenses incurred and of vengeance for wrongs done, and with due regard for equity and humanity, seeing that punishment ought to be proportionate to the fault." [25]

Belli shared this view, although he did not develop it so fully. Nevertheless the conception of the prince as a judge is implicit in his statement—upon which, however, he did not "insist"—that Christian rulers "should understand that, even when they have undertaken war for just cause, as soon as they have realized enough from the war fully to indemnify themselves for the occasion that gave rise to hostilities, they should terminate the war."[26] Gentili's statement on this subject, while less lofty in sentiment than that of Vitoria, is explicit and unmistakable:

It is the victor who has the power to decide which is the just cause, and also his own reason for entering the contest. Accordingly, he can hardly pronounce the cause of the vanquished just, without pronouncing his own victorious cause unjust; and therefore he will not do it. Moreover, although a war may be undertaken justly by both sides, it cannot, however, appear so to both parties. Yet since the victor in this case assumes the character of a just judge and is not merely a partisan, he ought, so far as is possible, to have regard to the principles of justice and along with his own rights to maintain those of the other party. In the judgment, too, which he passes as to the punishment to be inflicted upon the vanquished, he ought to show the moderation appropriate to his twofold character.[27]

Vitoria strongly condemned the ancient theory that all strangers were to be considered enemies. In his view a foreigner was not to be looked upon with suspicion merely because he was a foreigner. "It is reckoned among all nations inhumane," he declares, "to treat visitors and foreigners badly without some special cause."[28] Vitoria was here dealing with the relations of the Spaniards

---

[23] Vitoria, *De Indis et de iure belli*, p. 187.   [24] *Ibid.*, p. 171.
[25] *Ibid.*, p. 185.   [26] Belli, *De re militari*, II, 60.
[27] Gentili, *De iure belli*, II, 299.   [28] Vitoria, *De Indis et de iure belli*, p. 151.

with those "strangers" of the New World, the Indians. Apparently Belli was not unfamiliar with the question of the Indians' status. Distinguishing between the actual enemy and the stranger, he pointed out that "strangers are those who never at any time have been associated in friendship or by any treaty, being unknown either through war or peace, such as were those far away nations to the Portuguese and Spaniards, separated by the long voyage across the Ocean."[29] Gentili, in turn, refused to accept the old dictum that it is the nature of man to regard all foreigners with hostility. In his imperfect state man only too often substitutes enmity for friendship. Yet it was Gentili's opinion that all men are much more like than they are unlike. "We are by nature all akin," he maintains, and he therefore concludes that "there is no natural repugnance between man and man."[30] It was only when men reverted to their more barbarous attitude that the foreigner was considered an enemy, merely because his ways were strange and alien.

We have seen that the sovereign was under obligation to be certain of the justice of his cause before declaring war. But what of his subjects? According to Vitoria,[31] the latter might accept the decision of the prince and serve in the war unless that decision was so manifestly wrong as to convince the subjects that the war was unjustified. As a military man, Belli felt that the soldier should render unquestioning obedience, this being in accordance with "the rule of service" and the requirements of military discipline. Belli,[32] however, quotes with approval an important proviso to this rule, "unless the king orders something that is contrary to the law of God." The subject should act under this proviso, however, only when the issue of right and wrong was clearly defined. In doubtful matters, he should obey orders without question. Belli cited St. Augustine as his authority, and we find that Gentili also relies upon the doctor and saint in expressing a similar view. He adds, however, that "it is not for subjects to inquire too curiously which side took up arms with the better right."[33]

On the treatment of prisoners, Vitoria held that, even though the old rule of making them slaves still obtained in wars with pagans,

inasmuch as, by the law of nations, it is a received rule of Christendom that Christians do not become slaves in right of war, this enslaving is not lawful in a war between Christians; but if it is necessary having regard to the end and aim of war, it would be lawful to carry away even innocent captives, such as children and women, not indeed into slavery, but so that we may receive a money-ransom for them. This, however, must not be pushed beyond what the necessity of the war may demand and what the custom of lawful belligerents has allowed.[34]

The statement of Belli is to the same effect.

For Christians [he says], no less than Romans, are brothers and fellow-citizens to one another. . . . Being brothers, therefore, and not enemies, even though they go to war, Christians do not become slaves of the captors.[35]

[29] *De re militari*, II, 286.
[30] Gentili, *De iure belli*, II, 54.
[31] *De Indis et de iure belli*, pp. 173-74.
[32] *De re militari*, II, 63.
[33] Gentili, *De iure belli*, II, 125-26.
[34] *De Indis et de iure belli*, p. 181.
[35] *De re militari*, II, 116.

Both Vitoria and Belli insisted that captives should be spared whenever possible.[36] Gentili was less outspoken on this phase of the subject of war. In general his views were not unlike those of Belli, although he permitted cruelty to prisoners in certain cases.[37]

When these three authorities composed their writings on the law of war, the doctrine of neutrality was in its infancy. Nevertheless we find traces of it in the works of each writer. According to Vitoria,[38] "the spoliation of foreigners and travelers on enemy soil, unless they are obviously at fault, is in no wise lawful, they not being enemies." Belli expressed his theory on this subject in somewhat different terms. Dealing with the right of innocent passage through neutral territory, he insisted that the neutral would be justified in resisting attempts on the part of the soldiers to plunder neutral property along their route. He also declared that enemies could not be taken prisoners in neutral territory; and adopting the view of Joannes of Imola, an Italian canonist, he added that the neutral in enemy territory should not be molested as long as he observed his neutrality.[39] Gentili's attitude[40] toward neutrals, it may be added, was substantially the same as that of Belli.

On the manner of conducting war, Vitoria[41] laid down numerous *temperamenta* designed to minimize the cruelty and suffering inflicted by belligerents. Among other things he proclaimed that "it is undoubtedly unjust in the extreme to deliver up a city, especially a Christian city, to be sacked, without the greatest necessity and weightiest reason." In the opinion of Belli,[42] the "sacking of cities is in large measure unwarranted." He maintained that "cities ought not to be plundered except for some great wrong and crime in which the whole population (or at any rate the greater part) has shared." It cannot be said that Gentili[43] felt so strongly upon this subject; nevertheless he would not have cities given over to destruction except for what he considered adequate cause.

For present purposes the foregoing comparison must suffice. As a final step—by way of contrast, however, rather than of comparison—a passage will be quoted from each of the three writers, which embodied, it may be assumed, his philosophical views on war. The first passage (to reverse the chronological order) is from Gentili:

Now may the Great and Good God lead princes to put an end once for all to war and piously keep the terms of peace and of treaties. "Peace is a work full of virtue, peace is the end of labours, peace is the reward for a completed war, and the price of peril endured. In peace the stars are strong and earth's creatures are at rest. Nothing without peace is dear to God." Again and again I beseech thee, O God, put an end to wars; do Thou give us peace, pardoning our sins, and made propitious to us through thy Son our Saviour Jesus Christ.[44]

The passage from Belli is considerably less rhetorical in style, but more impressive in content:

---

[36] Vitoria, *op. cit.*, p. 183; Belli, *op. cit.*, II, 85–86, 317.
[37] *De iure belli*, II, 208–40.
[38] *De Indis et de iure belli*, p. 181.
[39] Belli, *op. cit.*, II, 98–99.
[40] *De iure belli*, II, 263.
[41] *De Indis et de iure belli*, p. 185.
[42] *De re militari*, II, 131.
[43] *De iure belli*, II, 319.
[44] *Ibid.*, II, 433.

Sovereigns, therefore, should be wary of undertaking war on insufficient or unjust grounds. For though they may be secure in point of law, they are, however, not free from responsibility in the sight of God. And though they often have at their side evil advisers, ecclesiastical as well as lay (who, either to curry favour or through fear, frame all their speeches to suit them, and manufacture and seek out justifications for their party, so that it may appear that their cause is righteous—of whom it may truly be said "seeking excuses for sins"), good kings and sovereigns should bring their insight and wisdom to bear, examining their own hearts. For therein they will discover right counsels and truth and just judgment as to war.[45]

And finally, there are the three canons of Vitoria, in which he summed up the whole of his philosophy on war:

First canon: Assuming that a prince has authority to make war, he should first of all not go seeking occasions and causes of war, but should, if possible, live in peace with all men, as St. Paul enjoins on us (*Romans,* ch. 12). Moreover, he should reflect that others are his neighbors, whom we are bound to love as ourselves, and that we all have one common Lord, before whose tribunal we shall have to render our account. For it is the extreme of savagery to seek for and rejoice in grounds for killing and destroying men whom God has created and for whom Christ died. But only under compulsion and reluctantly should he come to the necessity of war.

Second canon: When war for a just cause has broken out, it must not be waged so as to ruin the people against whom it is directed, but only so as to obtain one's rights and the defense of one's country and in order that from that war peace and security may in time result.

Third canon: When victory has been won and the war is over, the victory should be utilized with moderation and Christian humility, and the victor ought to deem that he is sitting as judge between two States, the one which has been wronged and the one which has done the wrong, so that it will be as judge and not as accuser that he will deliver the judgment whereby the injured state can obtain satisfaction, and this, so far as possible should involve the offending state in the least degree of calamity and misfortune, the offending individuals being chastised within lawful limits; and an especial reason for this is that in general among Christians all the fault is to be laid at the door of their princes, for subjects when fighting for their princes act in good faith and it is thoroughly unjust, in the words of the poet, that—

Quidquid delirant reges, plectantur Achivi.

(For every folly their Kings commit the punishment should fall upon the Greeks.)[46]

---

[45] Belli, *De re militari,* II, 297–98.   [46] Vitoria, *De Indis et de iure belli,* p. 187.

CHAPTER XXVI

TYRANNY VERSUS LIBERTY

The Doctrine of Tyrannicide and Its Development

From time immemorial clans, tribes, and peoples have enjoyed the sometimes dubious advantage of living under heads or leaders who acquired their positions by inheritance, by election, or by force. And the ambitious of all races have cherished the immemorial desire to obtain such leading position by one or the other of these methods. It has likewise been the immemorial desire of the clans, tribes, or peoples to rid themselves of those who had usurped the headship, as well as of those who, legally in power, had illegally abused it.

Thus from the earliest days of recorded history there have been tyrants—usurpers, despots, dictators, claiming supreme and irresponsible power. For the evils of tyranny many cures have been advocated and tried, culminating in that ultimate remedy not infrequently administered by oppressed and desperate peoples—tyrannicide. This subject is one so intimately connected with political government and with certain phases of law that some account must be given of the methods of dealing with tyrants in the Hellenic world, in the Roman world, and in the Middle Ages, and of the metamorphosis of those methods into a constitutional practice in the modern era.[1]

One of the most famous of the early examples of tyrannicide is to be found in ancient Athens. The tyrant Pisistratus, in the sixth century before Christ, was succeeded by his two sons, one of whom—Hipparchus—was assassinated by the youthful Harmodius and his friend Aristogiton. The actual motive of the assassination was less political than personal, but its ultimate effect was to free the city from the tyrannical rule of the Pisistradae. And this incident, it may be said, marks the adoption of tyrannicide by the Greeks as a recognized, though not constitutional, method of ridding them-

---

[1] For a learned discussion of the historical development of legal and political conceptions of tyranny and tyrannicide, with particular reference to their expression by Italian publicists, see the essay "Il 'Tractatus de Tyranno' di Coluccio Salutati," and especially chap. iv, by Professor Francesco Ercole. This essay was first published in German as an introduction to the edition of Salutati's *Tractatus* issued in Berlin (1914), and was subsequently included, in an Italian version, in Professor Ercole's volume *Da Bartolo all'Althusio* (previously cited), pp. 219-389.

selves of rulers whom for various reasons they did not like. The tyrannicides Harmodius and Aristogiton forefeited their lives for their deed, but they were looked upon by the Greeks as martyrs to liberty. The Athenians soon immortalized them in verse and prose, as well as in marble, and on festival days, as Duruy relates in his *History of Greece,* they chanted: "I will carry the sword under the myrtle-branch, as did Harmodius and Aristogiton when they slew the tyrant, and established equality in Athens."[2]

Plato, the mouthpiece of Socrates, defined tyranny as the "worst disorder of a state."[3] And his conclusion is that the tyrant "has run away from the region of law and reason,"[4] that of all men he is the most miserable, and that the value and true pleasure of the tyrant's days are almost as nothing compared with those of the legitimate sovereign—a comparison which might be mathematically expressed in terms of time by the ratio of twelve hours to twelve months.[5]

But in the domain of tyrannicide, as with so many phases of political science, the philosopher Aristotle supplied a definition upon which posterity has never improved. Having referred to tyranny as the opposite, indeed "the perversion" or "counterpart of the perfect monarchy,"[6] he continues: "this tyranny is just that arbitrary power of an individual which is responsible to no one, and governs all alike, whether equals or betters, with a view to its own advantage, not to that of its subjects, and therefore against their will."[7] The aim of tyrannical government, indeed, is that the subject shall be but pawns in the great political game, in which the only standard is the tyrant's profit and advantage. But what of the "pawns"? "No freeman," Aristotle declares roundly, "if he can escape from it, will endure such a government."[8]

Demosthenes—a contemporary of Aristotle—fearful of future tyranny, held similar views,[9] views shared likewise by his rival Aeschines.[10] But political scientists and orators were not the only ones to give expression to the Greek hatred of tyranny. The great dramatist and philosopher-poet, Euripides, friend of Pericles and Socrates, depicts Theseus as proclaiming:

> No worse foe than the despot hath a state,
> Under whom, first, can be no common laws,
> But one rules, keeping in his private hands
> The law: so is equality no more.

---

[2] Quoted by Allison in his ed. of Milton's *The Tenure of Kings and Magistrates,* p. 157.
[3] *Republic,* VIII. 544.　　　[4] *Ibid.,* IX. 587.　　　[5] *Ibid.,* 587–88.
[6] *Politics,* III. vii. 5; IV. x. 3; *Nicomachean Ethics,* viii. 10.　　　[7] *Politics,* IV. x. 4.
[8] *Ibid.*　　　[9] *Against Leptines,* secs. 160–61.
[10] Speech, *Against Timarchus,* secs. 4–6; *Against Ctesiphon,* secs. 6–7.

> ... the land's best, whose wisdom he discerns,
> He slayeth, fearing lest they shake his throne.
> How can a state be established then in strength,
> When, even as sweeps the scythe o'er springtide mead,
> One lops the brave young hearts like flower-blooms?
> What boots it to win wealth and store for sons,
> When all one's toil but swells a despot's hoard?[11]

It is true that the Greeks did not invariably condemn all forms of despotic government. There were those who favored the benevolent autocrat—so long as he remained benevolent. Indeed Plato's philosopher king would have possessed vast, not to say dictatorial, powers. The kindly despot and the philosopher king, however, were to have ruled unselfishly, seeking always to promote the good of the state. But the selfish tyrant, using the state and its people for his own ends, was anathema to the Greeks, and for such an evil they turned to the doctrine of tyrannicide as the ultimate and only certain cure. It was a doctrine not to be appealed to except as a last resort; nevertheless, when put into practice, that practice was justified as a means of protecting and preserving the fundamental rights of the people, as an extra-legal remedy to be applied in the absence or failure of legal remedies.

Like many another Greek doctrine, that of tyrannicide made its way to Rome, where it was sanctioned by Polybius who, though born in Greece, spent many years of his life in the imperial city. Now Polybius would have been one of the world's great historians if he had possessed a style equal to his vast knowledge, critical judgment, and love of truth. But in spite of his deficiencies in style, and in spite of the fact that only part of his *Histories* has survived, his work ranks among the great source books of ancient history, and was valued highly by the Romans as well as the Greeks. He may therefore be considered as speaking for both peoples when he declares that "the slayer of a traitor or a tyrant everywhere meets with honor and distinction,"[12] and that "the very word 'tyrant' alone conveys to us the height of impiety and comprises in itself the sum of all human defiance of law and justice."[13] Later, referring to the origin of the practice of tyrannicide, he adds that the first conspiracies against tyrants "were not the work of the worst men, but of the noblest, most high-spirited, and most courageous, because such men are least able to brook the insolence of princes."[14]

The doctrine of tyrannicide, however, had made its appearance in Rome earlier than the time of Polybius—although in its application it resulted in

[11] *Suppliants*, lines 430–49. [12] *Histories*, II. 56. [13] *Ibid.*, II. 59. [14] *Ibid.*, VI. 7.

expelling rather than assassinating the incumbent of the throne. Every schoolboy knows that upon the expulsion of Tarquin the Proud, the kingship was abolished and the monarch succeeded by consuls, two in number, both of whom were elected for a year and, possessing equal powers and exchanging duties at frequent intervals, serve each as a check upon the other.

The Romans, like the Greeks, gave literary expression to the doctrine of tyrannicide. A few examples must suffice here, the first being from Cicero, who indicates his familiarity with Greek conceptions:

> The Greeks accord divine honours to those men who have slain despots. What sights have I seen in Athens and in other cities of Greece! What religious rights ordained in their honour! What magnificent musical compositions and odes! Their worship reaches almost to the observance and commemoration proper to immortal beings.[15]

The Roman conception of tyrannicide, as Cicero reveals it, was similar to that of the Greeks:

> What more atrocious crime can there be than to kill a fellow-man, and especially an intimate friend? But if anyone kills a tyrant—be he never so intimate a friend—he has not laden his soul with guilt, has he? The Roman People, at all events, are not of that opinion; for of all glorious deeds they hold such an one to be the most noble.[16]

In another passage Cicero, who himself died a martyr to the cause of liberty, refers to a certain Phalaris, "the cruel and inhuman tyrant" of Agrigentum, and asserts in behalf of the Romans:

> we have no ties of fellowship with a tyrant, but rather the bitterest feud; and it is not opposed to nature to rob, if one can, a man whom it is morally right to kill;—nay, all that pestilent and abominable race should be exterminated from human society. . . . As certain members are amputated, if they show signs themselves of being bloodless and virtually lifeless and thus jeopardize the health of the other parts of the body, so those fierce and savage monsters in human form should be cut off from what may be called the common body of humanity.[17]

The younger Seneca, too, had pronounced views on the subject of tyranny. Contrasting the mercy of good rulers with the cruelty of tyrants, he asks the significant question:[18] "Why is it that kings have grown old and have handed on their thrones to children and grandchildren, while a tyrant's sway is accursed and short?" Again, referring to the sorry state of the Athenians under the Thirty Tyrants, he asks:

[15] *Pro Milone* xxix.   [16] *De officiis* III. iv.   [17] *Ibid.*, III. vi.   [18] *De clementia* I. xi. 4.

Can you find any city more wretched than was that of the Athenians when it was being torn to pieces by the Thirty Tyrants? . . . Could that city ever find peace in which there were as many tyrants as there might be satellites?[19]

The difficulty of coping with such a multiheaded tyranny, Seneca points out, was that there were not sufficient patriotic spirits bold enough to attempt, in the accepted Greek tradition, to put an end to the whole group of despots. "Where," he asks, "could the wretched state find enough Harmodiuses?" In one of his tragedies, too, Seneca wrote lines which leave no doubt of his views. "May savage and cruel tyrants rule no more" is the prayer of Hercules in *Hercules furens*.[20] And the same character expresses the view that "no greater, richer victim can be sacrificed to Jove than an unrighteous king"[21]—a sentiment reëchoed and indeed paraphrased centuries later by the sometimes whimsical but always learned and philosophical English divine, Robert Burton: "A tyrant is the best sacrifice to Jupiter, as the ancients held."[22]

The present brief survey must omit many other resounding passages on tyrants and their end which enliven the pages of classical literature. But enough have been quoted to indicate that tyrannicide was well established among the tenets of political philosophy in ancient Greece and Rome.

In the Middle Ages "it was the normal principle," says Dr. Carlyle, "that resistance to unlawful authority, and even the deposition of tyrannical princes, was legitimate."[23] The development and application of this principle were investigated by a distinguished French philosopher, Charles Bréchillet Jourdain, whose learned essays on the medieval period were published, some two years after his death in 1886, in a remarkable work entitled *Excursions historiques et philosophiques à travers le moyen âge*. For present purposes we may accompany him on only one of the "excursions" in this volume, that on "La royauté française et le droit populaire."

Jourdain began with St. Isidore of Seville, quoting a passage from the third book of his *Sententiae*,[24] which is a *eulogium* of the good ruler and a condemnation of the bad one. The good king is one who, according to St. Isidore, "governs with wisdom," and the title of king should be bestowed only "upon good Princes," but "should not be applied to bad ones." The bad prince is to be designated as a "tyrant," and in St. Isidore's time the usage "prevailed of calling bad kings who crush the people beneath the weight of their ambition and their cruelty 'tyrants.'" Indeed, it was St.

---

[19] *De tranquillitate animi* v. 1.   [20] Lines 936–37.   [21] Lines 922–24.
[22] *Anatomy of Melancholy*, Part II, sec. iii, mem. 1, subsec. 1.
[23] Carlyle, *A History of Mediaeval Political Theory* (previously cited), VI, 131.
[24] Chap. xlviii, quoted by Jourdain, *op. cit.*, p. 517.

Isidore's opinion that *rex,* the Latin word for king, was derived from *recte,* signifying right-doing, and therefore that the royal ruler deserved his name only if he measured up to the prevailing standard of right conduct.

According to Jourdain, one Jonas—not he of the Old Testament but a Bishop of Orléans of that name—developed the text of Isidore, observing[25] "that the king is so called because it is his mission to rule his people with piety, justice and clemency." If he fails in that mission, as not infrequently happens in the case of princes, he does not merit the name of king but that of "tyrant."

Turning next to the Abbot of St. Mihiel (a town and a battlefield made familiar to Americans by the World War), Jourdain[26] thus summarizes the duties of the prince, as set forth in the abbot's treatise, *Via regia:* "To love God and his neighbor, to show himself just, merciful, clement, pacific; to place his glory not in riches, but in virtue; to distrust arrogance and envy, to surround himself with good counsel, and to act with prudence; to repress his anger, to drive away flatterers, and not to permit money to be falsified." If kings had lived up to the abbot's high standard, democracy would doubtless have been much less successful than it has been in supplanting monarchical government.

In a subsequent passage Jourdain observes that John of Salisbury[27] apparently subscribed to the doctrine of St. Isidore that the king should obey the law, even though it be made by himself; but the Englishman expressed his views with "more energy."[28] The more energetic statement of John of Salisbury, as quoted by Jourdain, is that

All men are subject to the obligation to keep the law. . . . Accordingly when one says that the prince is freed from the fetters of the law, it does not mean that the prince is permitted to do wrong; it is because the love of justice alone, and not fear of punishment, is the motive which ought to urge the prince to show himself equitable, procure the weal of the State, and prefer in all things the utility of the citizens before his personal caprice. When it is a question of the public business, who would put the will of the prince first? He is permitted to desire only the things which are desired by the law, conformable to equity, or indeed those which are commanded by the general interest.[29]

This twelfth-century churchman clearly distinguishes his "king" from the "tyrant." Between them, he says,[30] "there is this sole difference: that the king obeys the law, governs his people according to the law, considers

---

[25] Jourdain, *Excursions historiques et philosophiques à travers le moyen âge,* p. 518.
[26] *Ibid.,* p. 519.
[27] For a discussion of John of Salisbury's *Policraticus,* see chap. xiii, *supra.*
[28] Jourdain, *op. cit.,* p. 523.
[29] *Policraticus,* Book IV, chap. i, quoted from Jourdain, *ibid.*
[30] Jourdain, *op. cit.,* pp. 523–24.

himself as the minister of the law, lays claim, for himself, in virtue of the law, to the first part in duties and public cares, and finally has no other title of superiority, save that in the State particular persons have each his own charge, while all the cares together weigh upon the prince."

In view of his insistence in these passages on the possession and exercise of royal virtues, it is not surprising that John of Salisbury indulged, as Jourdain says, in "bitter eloquence" when he proceeded to compare the tyrant with the ideal king.

The tyrant according to the picture which the philosophers have left us of one, is he who oppresses the people with a violent domination, while the true king governs by the laws. But the law is even the gift of God; it is the form of equity, the rule of justice, the work of the divine will, the guaranty of safety, a principle of force and of union for the people, the reason of duties, the destruction and death of vices, the chastisement of violence and crime. . . . The prince defends the law and the liberty of the people; the tyrant fancies that he has done nothing, in so far as he has not annihilated the laws and reduced the people into slavery. The prince is, in a way, the image of divinity: the tyrant is the image of violence which rebels against God, and of perversity, daughter of Hell. Image of divinity, the prince ought to be loved, venerated, obeyed; image of diabolic perversity, the tyrant ought, in most cases, to be put to death.[31]

It is thus, comments Jourdain, that "John of Salisbury arouses passion for the reign of laws, and aversion to tyranny so far as to permit, or rather to counsel, the killing of tyrants."[32] That this counsel is not a slip of the pen, in the warmth of composition, is indicated, in the opinion of Jourdain, by the fact that John of Salisbury "wrote an entire chapter in order to show that every tyrant is a public enemy, that it is not only lawful, but even just and equitable to put them to death."[33]

The ideal prince described by John of Salisbury was shortly to be realized in the person of Louis IX. "The son of Blanche of Castile on the throne," declares Jourdain, "was indeed the king of whom the first age of Scholasticism had dreamed."[34] Louis IX might be reproached

with political faults, but never with anything which the most austere morality could censure. To the qualities of the spirit and the heart which a Prince ought to possess, he joined virtues which elevated the Christian to saintliness. He knew his rights, and he knew how to have them respected—but he was still more deeply penetrated with the realization of his duties. No one was bound by the law to the same degree as he. If he would not allow the laws to be violated by anyone, he was himself the first to observe them. His decisions, whatever

---

[31] *Policraticus*, Book VIII, chap. xvii, quoted from Jourdain, *op. cit.*, p. 524.
[32] Jourdain, *op. cit.*, pp. 524–25.   [33] *Ibid.*, p. 525.   [34] *Ibid.*, pp. 528–29.

they were, were not the arbitrary acts of authority; he was moved not by caprice, but by virtue. Equality was his constant rule, even with regard to his enemies. As he would rather die than commit a mortal sin, he scrupulously avoided causing the slightest injustice to another. He kept the great obedient, and at the same time he was compassionate towards the lowly and the weak. He loved to hear their plaints in person, and to judge their differences. The judgments which he rendered beneath the oak of Vincennes are, in some measure, examples of the vigilant protection which he extended to all his people. . . . The government of Louis IX brings into relief the character of high morality and paternal justice, of gentleness without weakness, of firmness without arrogance, with which the royal power could be invested in the hands of a capable and enlightened Prince, . . .

Here Jourdain offers an interesting comparison and comment. Referring first to Bossuet, he more than intimates that the distinguished churchman, in his book, *La Politique tirée de l'Ecriture Sainte,* "had before his eyes the monarchy of Louis XIV" and that "he was seeking to find in this model most of the traits which he announced had been borrowed from the Bible." And Jourdain adds:

It would not be absolutely exact to pretend that the reign of Louis IX had in the same way furnished the Doctors of that age with the great number of political ideas sown throughout their works. Nevertheless, the opinions which they express, the rules they lay down; the counsels they give are in many respects as a commentary on the acts of the holy King.[35]

Certainly St. Louis, in the opinion of Jourdain, would have approved numerous passages in the writings of St. Thomas Aquinas because they were so much in harmony with the principles which the saintly ruler himself practiced.[36] The passages which the author has in mind[37] are those in which "the Angel of the Schools teaches that the purpose of all government is the weal of the community; that governments are not established for the personal satisfaction of those who are at their head, but for the public usefulness; that Kings are the shepherds of nations, and that the good shepherd considers, before all else, the interest of his flock." And Jourdain further affirms[38] that St. Louis would have recognized his own ideals, could he

---

[35] Jourdain, *op. cit.*, pp. 529–30.

[36] An English historian in a recent comment on Louis IX has stated that "in his own person he was the ideal of the medieval knight and king. For the first time in the Middle Ages a king in active secular life was an indubitable saint. St. Louis was neither weak nor a recluse, but he ruled his kingdom as a religious duty. His justice, his love of peace, and his goodness made him enforce equally the rights of the vassals and the Crown, so that opposition to him seemed mere selfishness and unrighteousness."—Previté-Orton, *A History of Europe from 1198 to 1378* (being Vol. III in Methuen's "History of Medieval and Modern Europe"), p. 114.

[37] Jourdain, *op. cit.*, p. 530.   [38] *Ibid.*

have read the teachings of St. Thomas Aquinas "that a Prince truly worthy of the name of King ought to seek neither riches, nor power, nor glory—so often bought at the price of the blood and fortunes of the people; that the only goods worthy of him are the Eternal goods; that it is towards them that he ought to bend the design of his efforts and his hopes; that his first duty towards his subjects is to inspire them with the love of virtue, and thus to open to them the way towards final happiness."[39]

St. Thomas himself, as Jourdain points out, had pronounced views on the subject of tyranny:

Where is the security, the holy Doctor asks, where law is a vain rule, and where the will—or rather, the caprice—of a single man takes its place? The tyrant, in accordance with the passion which possesses him, gives himself over to all kinds of oppression. If he is covetous, he seizes the goods of the people; if he is violent, he spills blood on the least pretext; he kills by caprice, not by justice. He persecutes the good still more than the wicked, frightened by their virtue, which he regards as a menace to his unjust domination. He is the enemy of concord and peace; he sows new divisions and distrusts between the citizens, or adds fuel to old ones; he impedes what might help to reconcile the different wills; he dishonors souls by terror, he renders them incapable of every virile and courageous effort. Unhappy are the nations bowed under such a yoke! It is no more cruel to be prey to a wild beast than to fall into the hands of a tyrant.[40]

In the century following that of St. Thomas Aquinas, Marsiglio of Padua,[41] intent on developing the theory that the source both of law and of the executive power is in the people, was led by the force of logic ("so respected in the Schools," observes Jourdain) "to recognize in the legislator, that is to say, in the people, the right of correcting the prince, or to put it more clearly, of deposing him, if he transgresses the laws."[42] Marsiglio's theory of sovereignty, as stated by Jourdain, is that "The people are the first sovereign."[43]

The spirit of Marsiglio's theories is to be found in a treatise by Nicholas Oresme *On the Invention of Money*. Although not concerned primarily with political matters, the entire treatise, Jourdain says, "breathes the love of a wise liberty," and "the hatred of tyranny," and predicts the "immediate downfall" of "those monarchies which oppress their subjects beneath a

---

[39] For a conception of the prince completely antagonistic to the practice of Louis IX and the ideals of St. Thomas, see Machiavelli's portrait of what he conceived to be a perfect prince, as delineated in his tractate, *Il principe*, written over two centuries later. This tractate is discussed *supra*, chap. xix.
[40] Jourdain, *op. cit.*, pp. 531–32.
[41] For a discussion of Marsiglio's *Defensor pacis*, see chap. xviii, *supra*.
[42] *Ibid.*, p. 540. [43] *Ibid.*

hated yoke." The best way for kings to retain their thrones and to pass them on to their children was, Nicholas Oresme declared, the way pointed out by Aristotle—not to abuse their power. And, referring again to Aristotle, he added that it would be better for both people and monarchy if the minimum of "arbitrary decision" were left to the king. Let the king, therefore, to quote Jourdain's paraphrase of Oresme, "guard against disturbing them" —the people—"in the exercise of their liberty; let him not lay claim to absolute power; let him be content with what law and custom grant him."[44]

Two other authorities should not be overlooked here, although they are but a confirmation of St. Thomas. One of these was Gerson, an eminent French divine and for many years chancellor of the University of Paris. Although in later years he was to oppose strongly the theory of tyrannicide as practiced by assassins, he did not hesitate in an earlier period to indulge in what Jourdain calls "austere counsels for royalty, energetic revindications of the right of the people, hatred of tyranny."[45] It was, the chancellor of the university said,[46] "an error to believe that kings can, at their pleasure, use the persons and goods of their subjects, and arbitrarily burden them with taxes unless such actions are essential for the public good." To behave thus "is not to act like a King, but like a tyrant." As Jourdain points out, this was not the only erroneous belief attacked by Gerson. "It is another error to believe that Kings are freed from every obligation towards their subjects; on the contrary, indeed: according to the natural law and the divine law they owe them fidelity and protection. If they fail in this duty, if they conduct themselves unjustly, above all if they persevere in their wrong-doing, then the following rule is applicable: that it is permitted to repel force by force." And Gerson here recalled a passage from Seneca which has been mentioned on a previous page: "Does not Seneca say that there is no sacrifice more agreeable to God than a tyrant?" Upon which Jourdain, alluding to Gerson's subsequent opposition to tyrannicide on the eve of and during the Council of Constance, offers the comment that this was a "strange citation in the mouth of a writer" who was to oppose "with such indefatigable ardor the libel of Jean Petit in favor of tyrannicide."[47] But in the earlier period of his chancellorship, Gerson—speaking this time, we are told, before Charles VI—did not mince matters.[48] "Rarely does a tyrant," he proclaimed, "die a natural death; he is hated of God and of the world; and there is scarcely so small a man who wisheth to hazard his own life to attempt the life of a tyrant but can find some manner and way to kill him and deliver the country."

[44] Jourdain, op. cit., p. 541.
[46] Quoted from Jourdain, ibid.
[47] Ibid.
[45] Ibid., p. 550.
[48] Ibid., pp. 551–52.

The present examination of Jourdain's essay may be concluded by reproducing his quotation from the famous address of Philippe Pot, seigneur de la Roche, who near the close of the fifteenth century summed up the enlightened conceptions of the Middle Ages on the subject of kings and tyrants:

As history tells us, and as I learned from my fathers, in the beginning the sovereign people created Kings by their vote, and they preferred particularly men who surpassed the others in virtue and ability. In effect, each people elected a King for its utility. Yes, Princes were not made in order to make a profit out of the people and enrich themselves at their expense, but, forgetting their own interests, to enrich the people, and conduct them from good to better. If they sometimes do the opposite, certainly they are tyrants and bad shepherds who, themselves eating their flock, acquire the manners and name of wolves, rather than the manners and name of shepherds. . . . Have you not often read that the State is the thing of the people? But, if it is their thing, how is it that they will neglect it, or will not have a care for it? How is it that flatterers attribute sovereignty to the Prince who exists only by [sufferance of] the people? Among the Romans, was not each magistrate named by election? Was a law promulgated there before it had been first reported to the people and approved by them? In many countries still, following the ancient custom, they elect the King. . . . I want you to agree that the State is the thing of the people, that they confided it to the Kings, and that those who have held it by force or otherwise without any consent from the people are deemed tyrants, and usurpers of the property of another.[49]

Unhappily, because of the turmoil of the Reformation, this doctrine of popular sovereignty was to be replaced by that of the divine right of kings. Yet before long Catholic publicists (especially the Jesuits), and Protestants as well, were to espouse the conceptions summarized by Philippe Pot, and they succeeded in making the older doctrine the inheritance of the modern world.

At the beginning of the modern era there were four Catholic contributions to this doctrine, three of them by Jesuits and one by a lay publicist, which are still considered outstanding: Robert Parsons' *Conference about the Next Succession to the Crown of England;* Juan Mariana's *De rege et regis institutione;* Francisco Suárez' *Defensio fidei catholicae adversus Anglicanae sectae errores;* and Etienne de la Boétie's *Discours de la servitude volontaire.* But the doctrine which the Catholics professed in terms which are truly classic was also stated in the same period by Protestant publicists: by François Hotman, by Theodore Beza, by the author of the *Vindiciae contra tyrannos,* and by George Buchanan.

[49] *Ibid.*, pp. 556–57.

La Boétie, an intimate friend of Montaigne, was the first of the Catholic group to take the field. His essay, *Discours de la servitude volontaire*,[50] generally known as *Contr'un*, seems to have been a youthful exercise but, like not a few other youthful exercises, it has stood the test of time. Small in compass, it nevertheless dealt with the subject of tyranny on broad and historical lines, its arguments being based largely upon Greek and Roman examples. Holding that liberty is a natural heritage of mankind, La Boétie considers that man unhappily has only too often forgotten this heritage and allowed himself to become the prey of tyrants. Such servitude may originally have been involuntary, in that it was imposed by force. But if it is supinely accepted—if the tyrant is not overthrown by a people anxious to regain the freedom which is theirs by nature—then through its acceptance the servitude becomes voluntary and, as the result of evil custom, may seem at last to be the natural order of things. That it is not a part of the natural order La Boétie demonstrates beyond all question and argument. And his conclusion is apparently that tyrants, if they escape punishment in this life, will not escape it hereafter: "For my part, I hold—and rightly hold, since in the eyes of God the all bounteous and supremely gentle, there is nothing else so inacceptable as tyranny—that in the lower world He has in store for tyrants and their accomplices a special punishment."[51]

Some years later the English Jesuit Parsons found time during a somewhat turbulent career to prepare a work whose purpose was to secure a Catholic successor to the throne of the Virgin Queen, Elizabeth. As we have seen, its title was, appropriately enough, *A Conference about the Next Succession to the Crown of England*.[52] The *Conference* is composed in the traditional dialogue form, and its setting, like that of More's *Utopia*, is a city of the Low Countries.[53] The little book aroused both dismay and indignation in Elizabeth's day—it was, indeed, banned throughout her domain —and was regarded by James I as extremely dangerous to his cause.[54]

---

[50] The date of La Boétie's composition is uncertain. It was apparently first printed in 1574, in Simon Goulart's *Mémoires de l'estat de France sous Charles IX*, although before that time it had passed through various hands and its influence had already been felt.

[51] For a more elaborate discussion of the contribution of La Boétie, as well as of the treatises of Suárez and Mariana, the *Vindiciae contra tyrannos*, and the treatise of Buchanan, and the practical consequences of these theories, see J. B. Scott, *The Catholic Conception of International Law*, V–XI, 261–436. Because of the detailed treatment already supplied in those chapters, a somewhat summary discussion of these writers is given here.

[52] First published in France, under the pseudonym R. Doleman, in 1594.

[53] The dialogue of the *Utopia* takes place at Antwerp; that of the *Conference* at Amsterdam. Like More, Parsons was a master of the English tongue, and his clear, vigorous prose was commended by no less an authority than Swift. For a discussion of More, see chap. xxvii, *infra*.

[54] For interesting and enlightening comments on the *Conference*, see McIlwain's *The Political Works of James I*, Introd., pp. l–li, xcii–xciv.

Of chief interest here is the first part of the work, which consists in the main of the "Discourse of a Civil Lawyer," one of the two principal characters of the dialogue. In his discourse the Civil Lawyer early reaches the conclusion that the commonwealth has "authority to chuse and change her Government," and "also to limit the same with what laws and conditions she pleaseth." The possession of such authority by the commonwealth would appear to provide ample safeguard against tyranny. But the Civil Lawyer considers it necessary to go into further detail, and he therefore specifies certain "helps" with which a thoughtful people should provide their ruler. The first of these "helps" is law; the second "Counsels," such as the "Parliaments of England and France"; and the third "Counsellors," meaning bodies of advisers—somewhat analogous, we might say, to modern cabinets—whose duty was not alone to give advice but also to act as a check upon the sovereign. But what if the ruler, becoming intoxicated with power, attempts to disregard these aids to good government? The Civil Lawyer's answer is unequivocal. Kings, he declares, may be dispossessed of their office "if they fulfil not the Laws and Conditions by which, and for which, their Dignity was given them."

Developing this thought with convincing and elaborate arguments—too elaborate, indeed, to be followed here in detail—the Civil Lawyer establishes the important thesis that the relationship between governor and governed is contractual in its nature. Therefore, if the prince violates his contract with the people, if he evades the "Equity, Oath, Conscience, Justice, and Law prescribed unto him," and "becometh a tyrant," the people as a whole are not only released from their duty of obedience and allegiance, but are entitled—indeed, bound, in order to save the commonwealth from destruction—"to Resist, Chasten, and Remove" the erring prince from the office which he has abused.

After noting how tyrannicide was thus justified by an Englishman, it will be interesting to turn next to his Spanish contemporary, Mariana. Theologian, economist, and still the greatest of Spain's historians,[55] he was also deeply versed in matters of government, and in the first book of his treatise *De rege et regis institutione* (published in 1599) he set forth certain views which are in full harmony with those propounded by the enemies of tyranny throughout the ages.

Adopting the classical conception of man as a sociable animal impelled

[55] His *Historiae de rebus Hispaniae* was published in 1592. According to Fitzmaurice-Kelly, *A New History of Spanish Literature* (Oxford, 1926), p. 345, "Great historians are rare everywhere. The combination of learning, critical judgment and literary accomplishment which goes to make up their equipment is very infrequent. But it is found in Juan de Mariana."

to fellowship and association by his desires and needs, Mariana first traces the development of the various forms of government and law, in accordance with the accepted doctrines of the schoolmen. He then proceeds, by way of contrast, to discuss in detail and with telling effect the virtues of the good ruler and the vices of the tyrant. The one receives his power from the people and employs it solely for the promotion of happiness, well-being and good will among the people. The other may come into power legitimately, but more often he seizes it by violence or intrigue; and however he may acquire power, he uses it for his own selfish ends. If he appears to have some temporary consideration for the general welfare, it is only for the purpose of strengthening his own position and the pretense is soon discarded. The good king is the guide and protector of his subjects, and is loved by all. The tyrant is the enemy of all upright men, whom he distrusts and fears and whom—because of his fear—he constantly persecutes.

What, then, in Mariana's conception, is the cure for tyranny? He reviews the arguments for and against tyrannicide and comes to the conclusion that the usurper, seizing and exercising power by violent and illegal means and without the consent of the people, may be killed by any individual whatsoever. The situation, however, with respect to the prince who acquires his power legally but who exercises it tyrannically and therefore illegally, seems at first to present certain difficulties. Since he is legally in office, can anything be done? In Mariana's opinion something could and should be done to deliver the country from such a prince. If the tyranny has not developed to the point where public assemblies have been abolished, then legal steps, determined upon by common agreement in the assembly, should be taken against the erring prince. He should first be warned to mend his ways. If such action fails of result, he should be deprived of his power by a legal sentence. And if he resists the sentence, he should be declared an enemy of the state. Thus the public assembly might, by the "right of defense and, moreover, by the state's own superior authority," to quote Mariana's words, decree "the slaying of the prince by the sword, as a declared public enemy."[56] If, on the other hand, the tyranny has progressed so far that no public assembly is permitted, but the people are nevertheless united in their desire to rid themselves of their oppressive ruler, then any individual is justified, according to Mariana's thesis, in attempting to destroy the tyrant, since such action is in accordance with the public will. In short, Mariana advocated the employment, if possible, of constitutional means in coping with tyrants; but where such means were no longer available he did not hesitate to approve of out-and-out tyrannicide.

[56] *De rege et regis institutione*, Book I, chap. vi.

A few years after the publication of Mariana's *De rege et regis institutione*, another outstanding Spanish Jesuit, Francisco Suárez, found occasion to discuss the measures which might properly be taken against a monarch who ignored his duties and violated the rights of the people. Suárez' views on the state and on the people as the source of civil power will be mentioned elsewhere,[57] and hence it will suffice here to consider certain passages in his famous *Defensio fidei catholicae adversus Anglicanae sectae errores*,[58] which contain his views on tyrannicide. The principal circumstance which gave rise to this treatise (first published in 1613) was the attempt on the part of James I of England and VI of Scotland to exact from his Catholic subjects an oath of allegiance, which, among other things, denied the right of the people to rid themselves of a prince who had been excommunicated for his misdeeds by the pope. In dealing with this question, Suárez maintains, as did his predecessors, that a tyrant who had acquired his power illegally, by usurpation, might be killed by a private person acting, not for personal vengeance, but for the good of the state.

On the lawful sovereign who had become a tyrant through abuse of his power, however, Suárez is less willing to approve the infliction of the death penalty by a private individual. In spite of the king's misrule, an attempt on his life by one of his subjects would, Suárez holds, be unjustifiable save in extreme instances, as when the tyrant, waging aggressive war on the state, threatens its destruction and the slaughter of its citizens. The distinction between the two cases would seem to be that the usurper is wholly ouside the law, and therefore may properly be regarded and treated as an enemy by each and every citizen with the good of his country at heart; while an attack on a lawful king, even though he were more or less disposed toward tyranny, would constitute an act of lèse majesté and could be justified only by the direst necessity. But there was another remedy to be applied in the case of the lawful monarch who, though he might not be a menace to the very existence of the state, nevertheless showed a tendency to abuse the authority granted to him. Under the natural law, Suárez maintained, the state had the power to depose such a ruler, and to punish him—even with death if his misdeeds are of a nature to warrant such punishment. Both the deposition and the punishment, however, must result from legal sentences imposed by the citizens, or—we may assume—by their representatives in solemn conclave. Here we have due process of law; in other words, the beginning of our modern impeachment, which must be considered on a later page.[59]

Of the several Protestant writers who dealt with the subject of tyranny

[57] *Infra*, chap. xxxiii.   [58] Book VI, especially chap. iv.   [59] *Infra*, p. 415.

and its cure one of the most interesting was François Hotman, author of the *Franco-Gallia,* a treatise first published in 1573, and some years later reissued in enlarged form. Although marred by numerous inaccuracies, it remains an example of extraordinary historical learning. Hotman was, indeed, one of the most eminent scholars and jurists of his day. Though born a Catholic, he became a Huguenot early in his career, and his *Franco-Gallia* may be considered as setting forth the views on monarchy held by the more moderate Huguenot leaders. Hotman's treatise, as the late Professor Ernest Nys observed,[60] embodied the aristocratic aspirations of the Protestant party, and hence it did not go so far as to counsel tyrannicide.

Basing his arguments on a wealth of historical illustrations, Hotman proves that, as far as France is concerned, the king obtains his office through the approval of the people. Such approval might be direct, as in the case of the formal election of the monarch; or indirect, when the people exercised their right of choice by giving tacit consent to dynastic succession. In this conception is clearly implied government by consent of the governed, with the king as a chief magistrate whose duty it is to execute the laws for the benefit of the people.

Hotman found, moreover, in his examination of French history, that the people or their representatives had from early times exercised the power lodged in them of overthrowing for good cause the kings whom they had installed in office. This should preferably be done, he maintained, by means of a public trial; that is to say, the deposition of the king should be a legal process. It is apparent, therefore, that there was nothing sacrosanct about Hotman's king. He was but a "mortal man," and if he ventured to flout the law of the land or the will of the people, he might be brought to trial. And the conclusion to which Hotman's historical research led him was that "we may easily perceive that our *Commonwealth,* which at first was *founded* and *establish'd* upon the *Principles of Liberty,* maintained it self in the same free and sacred State (even by Force and Arms) against all the Power of Tyrants for more than Eleven Hundred Years."[61]

Another French Protestant, Theodore de Beza, writing at about the same time as Hotman, made a contribution of some importance to the subject under discussion. His tractate, *Du droit des magistrats sur les sujets,* although apparently written originally in Latin, was first published in French in 1573-74. Beza was an ardent supporter of Calvinism—indeed, he was perhaps the ablest of all Calvin's disciples—but the terrible massacre of St.

---

[60] *Les Théories politiques et le droit international en France jusqu'au* XVIIIe *siècle,* p. 90.
[61] Quoted from the English trans. of the *Franco-Gallia,* p. 122.

Bartholomew's Day in 1572 caused him to reconsider and in part to reject his master's sweeping dictum on submission to the ruler. Granting that unfailing obedience would be due to princes if they were always and invariably mouthpieces for divine commands, Beza observes that only too often the opposite is the case. What, then, may the subject do when his ruler resorts to tyranny? In dealing with this question Beza first considers the origin of magistracies—that is to say, of government by a chief magistrate. Now such a magistrate does not create the people, but on the contrary is created *by* the people, their purpose being to set up a government which will protect and promote their well-being. And if the magistrate acts in violation of this purpose, he is clearly on the way to becoming a tyrant.

Dealing first with the usurping tyrant, Beza concludes that he should, where possible, be disposed of by legal means—i. e., by action on the part of the authorities of the state; but if such means fail, then private individuals may proceed against the usurper in order to save their state.

The case of the sovereign lawfully in office but guilty of tyrannical misconduct seems to Beza to call for more detailed consideration. Arguing in part from historical examples, he advances the opinion that a tyrant of that type should be dealt with by ministers of state and other representatives of the people who possess authority under the laws of the land to resist and even to punish the erring sovereign. Such conduct on their part is not to be termed sedition, but is merely the performance of their duty to their country. Next, discussing the question from the legal standpoint, Beza points out that a contractual relation exists between the sovereign and his subjects, the submission of the latter to the former being on the condition, tacit or expressed, that the sovereign will govern justly and equitably. Since those who enter voluntarily into contracts may annul them on sufficient grounds, it would seem to follow that those who set up a king under certain conditions, have a right to depose him if he violates those conditions. In Beza's opinion, however, the deposition must be undertaken, not by private individuals, but by the duly constituted authorities of the state, who are specially charged with the protection of the common welfare.

The third among the Protestant writings on the subject is the *Vindiciae contra tyrannos,* composed probably in 1574–76 and published in 1579. The identity of the writer was concealed under the pseudonym "Stephanus Junius Brutus Celta," and to this day the authorship of the book has not been settled to the satisfaction of scholars.[62] Some investigators would award

---

[62] On the background and authorship of *Vindiciae contra tyrannos,* see Laski's "Historical Introduction" to the English trans. of 1689, as reprinted under the title, *A Defence of Liberty*

the honor—for it is an honor—of having written the *Vindiciae* to Hubert Languet, while others favor Duplessis-Mornay. For many years Languet was more generally considered the author, later the pendulum swung to Mornay, and at present it seems to be swinging again to Languet.

But whoever the author may have been, the book itself was of great importance, not because of its originality but because it stated in systematic and complete form the views of the Huguenots on the doctrine of tyrannicide. However, while its influence in sixteenth-century France—and in Holland as well—was considerable, the *Vindiciae* was more influential still in seventeenth-century England, where the theory of tyrannicide was put into practice in order to rid the country of the theory of the divine right of kings as embraced by the royal house of Stewart and particularly as personified in King Charles I.

For present purposes the third part of the *Vindiciae* is of special interest, for it is there that the author treats of such matters as the superiority of the people over the prince and their right to resist him should he become tyrannical. Stating the general thesis that the sovereign is established by the people themselves, that he derives his powers as well as his position from them, and that his duty as sovereign is to devote himself wholly to promoting the common welfare, the author adds the corollary that the sovereign must also acknowledge the law as his superior. There is, however, a further and equally important corollary, which we have encountered in previous tractates: that the making of kings by the people results in a pact or contract between ruler and subjects. According to the *Vindiciae,* the people stipulate that the king shall rule justly and in conformity with the law, and the king promises to do so—upon which, in turn, the people promise obedience as long as the king keeps his promise to them. If he fails in this respect, he not only forfeits the right to exact obedience but becomes subject to punishment by the people as a whole or by their representatives. In other words, the faithless king is a tyrant and may be treated accordingly.

Resistance to the usurper-tyrant by any and every individual is justified in the *Vindiciae* on the same grounds as in the preceding tractates which have been examined, although in even more logical and incontrovertible

---

against Tyrants—a Translation of the Vindiciae contra tyrannos by Junius Brutus, pp. 1–60, especially pp. 57–60.

Another excellent discussion of the *Vindiciae,* dealing with both its authorship and influence, is to be found in Professor Barker's *Church, State and Study—Essays* (previously cited), under the title "A Huguenot Theory of Politics," pp. 72–108. On the question of the authorship of the treatise, see further the same learned writer's conclusions in "The Authorship of the *Vindiciae contra tyrannos,*" *Cambridge Historical Journal* (1930), pp. 164–81.

terms. As for the legal sovereign, if he begins to show symptoms of tyranny, he should be warned to mend his ways by the people's representatives. Should he disregard warnings and persist in his misdeeds, breaking his contract with his subjects, he may be considered as being "guilty of rebellion against the majesty of the people," and they may therefore, under the leadership of the appropriate officers of state, take up arms against him, "as against the enemy of the commonwealth." It is the people as a whole, however, who may take such action, and not private persons as such.

Of his views on tyrannicide it may be said that the author of the *Vindiciae* himself supplies the best summary:[63]

Princes are chosen by God, and established by the people. As all particulars [individuals] considered one by one, are inferior to the prince; so the whole body of the people and officers of state, who represent that body, are the princes' superiors. In the receiving and inauguration of a prince, there are covenants and contracts passed between him and the people, which are tacit and expressed, natural or civil; to wit, to obey him faithfully whilst he commands justly, that he serving the commonwealth, all men shall serve him, that whilst he governs according to law, all shall be submitted to his government, etc. The officers of the kingdom are the guardians and protectors of these covenants and contracts. He who maliciously or wilfully violates these conditions, is questionless a tyrant by practice. And therefore the officers of state may judge him according to the laws. And if he support his tyranny by strong hands, their duty binds them, when by no other means it can be effected by force of arms to suppress him.

As the *Vindiciae* is supposed to have been written by a Frenchman—for both Languet and Duplessis-Mornay were French—it is reasonable to assume that French conditions were in the mind of the author. But it may well be that, as he wrote, his mind dwelt also on conditions in neighboring lands—especially in the Low Countries, whence there might be danger of a Spanish attack on France if the sovereign of Spain were successful in bending his rebellious Flemish subjects to his will. Such a surmise is not wholly without foundation, for we know that both Languet and Mornay were friends of William the Silent, the head and front of the revolt in the Low Countries. Especially Languet was his friend; and it is fair to say that if the situation in France justified the *Vindiciae,* the situation in the Low Countries would have been an additional and almost equally cogent justification.

In any event it may be interesting to consider certain developments in

[63] *Vindiciae contra tyrannos*—reprint of English trans. of 1689 (previously cited), p. 212. This passage occurs at the end of "The Third Question," dealing at length with the problem "Whether it be lawful to resist a prince who doth oppress or ruin a public state, and how far such resistance may be extended: by whom, how, and by what right or law it is permitted."

the Low Countries, since they led to the practical application of the doctrine set forth in the *Vindiciae*. It will be sufficient for present purposes to say that the vast domain of Charles the Bold, Duke of Burgundy, including Franche-Comté and the seventeen provinces of the Low Countries, passed upon his death in 1477 to his daughter, Mary of Burgundy. Through her marriage to Maximilian I and the marriage of their son Philip the Handsome to the daughter of Ferdinand and Isabella, the Low Country provinces passed to Mary's grandson, Charles I of Spain and the fifth of the Holy Roman Emperors. Now Charles was himself a Lowlander, having been born in Ghent, and though he taxed the provinces heavily, they submitted to that and to other burdens because he had been born and reared among them and was therefore one of their own.

But in 1555 an important and impressive ceremony occurred at Brussels which was destined to alter materially the attitude of the seventeen provinces toward their ruling house. On the twenty-fifth of October of that year, Charles entered the great Hall of the Golden Fleece, leaning upon the arm of William, the young Prince of Orange, and, in the presence of many notables and representatives of the people convoked for the occasion, solemnly and formally renounced his sovereignty over the Netherland Provinces in favor of his son Philip. In the course of a moving address to the assembled Lowlanders, delivered in their own language, he asked them to give to his son the same loyalty and support they had never failed to accord the father. Naturally on such an occasion the newly invested sovereign would be expected to make a gracious address to his new subjects. Unfortunately the only language at his command was Spanish. He did not know Flemish, as did his father, nor did he speak French with any fluency. After a few halting words in the latter tongue he found it necessary to call upon an obliging bishop in the assembly to complete his remarks for him. Thus, as far as the Netherlanders were concerned, he began his reign as a foreigner. And time and experience but confirmed their feeling toward him. Even during his few years in the Low Countries, they must have found his solemn visage and sedentary habits unsympathetic. It was almost inevitable that they should come to look upon his government with suspicion, as that of a foreign despot. This suspicion was heightened when, four years after his accession, he withdrew to his Spanish domain, never again to set foot upon Flemish soil. Thereafter he ruled the Low Countries as an absentee monarch, his authority being exercised by persons of his appointment.

Philip had sworn, the day following the proclamation of his sovereignty, and after receiving the promise of allegiance from the deputies of the provinces, to observe faithfully the ancient rights, privileges and customs of the Low Countries. This was in effect a contract between ruler and subjects. And here it is worth pausing for a moment to observe that this conception of a contract between the prince and his people, expressed in the ceremony of coronation, is not the least important of medieval political contributions. To quote a few sentences from a profound student of the Middle Ages:

> The principle of the contract between the ruler and the ruled was, on the other hand, the general assumption of all mediaeval political theory, and it was upon this that there were built up the principles of the nature and limitations of the authority of the prince. . . . In these mutual oaths the prince swore to maintain not only abstract justice, but the concrete law, and the people swore to obey the prince. This was indeed an intelligible and practical conception of the relations of ruler and ruled; indeed it was only another form of the principle that the law was supreme. The contractual conception then goes back to the earlier Middle Ages, but it continued to find expression throughout them in the importance attached to the coronation oaths.[64]

Philip violated the oath he had sworn to his subjects in the Low Countries, and the violations, together with various other factors, led eventually to the revolt of his Netherland subjects. At first, however, they went no farther than to call Philip's attention to his violations of their rights and customs. But their pleas had little effect and, after more than a quarter of a century of misrule and misunderstanding on the part of their sovereign, the Northern Provinces, under the leadership of William of Orange, upon whose arm Charles V had leaned in relinquishing the Low Countries, passed an Act of Abjuration in which, as of July 26, 1581, they formally terminated the contract and ended their allegiance to Philip by declaring him deposed from all sovereignty over them because of his tyranny.

As was to be expected, considering his character and political ambitions, Philip did not accept his deposition with good grace. Indeed, he stubbornly persisted in his attempts to reduce the provinces to his will. But hard as he tried, he never succeeded in regaining the sovereignty from which he had been formally deposed by the representatives of the people in the Northern Provinces.

After a long-drawn conflict, an armistice was concluded in 1609 between Philip's son, Philip III, and the United Provinces, as they were then called. And later still, as a consequence of the Thirty Years' War, his grandson,

[64] Carlyle, *A History of Mediaeval Political Theory* (previously cited), VI, 520-21.

Philip IV of Spain, recognized in a formal treaty the complete independence of the United Provinces of the Netherlands.

In the incidents thus briefly related, we have an example of the theory of tyrannicide in action, not in its oldest and simplest form of regicide, but in the more moderate and constitutional form of deposition. And in the following centuries the theory in its moderated form was to be put into practice again and again, not only in Europe but in the New World, where colonies, in groups or singly, proceeded to declare their independence of European sovereigns and thus, as far as they were concerned, dethroned those whom they considered tyrants.

The *Vindiciae contra tyrannos* played no small part in this process of dethroning tyrants in both the Old and the New Worlds. But a rôle equally if not more important was played by another work, the *De jure regni apud Scotos* by George Buchanan, published in the same year, 1579, at Edinburgh —which city, curiously enough, likewise appears as the place of publication on the title-page of the *Vindiciae,* although the latter is supposed to have been secretly printed on the Continent, probably in Basel.[65]

Now Buchanan, who spent many years abroad, was a profoundly learned man and a humanist—indeed, he has been called "the prince of Humanists"[66]—and as such he was welcomed everywhere by scholars, among whom were Beza and Languet. He was no doubt as conversant with the political theories of his day as he was with history and classical learning. The *De jure regni apud Scotos* immediately aroused great interest, so much so that three editions of it were called for within three years' time. Its influence was not merely of Buchanan's day. Milton turned to it as his chief source, in preparing his *Tenure of Kings and Magistrates,*[67] as a justification of the beheading of Charles I. Subsequently, too, English translations of the *De jure regni* were published, one having been printed in 1766—ten years before the signing of the American Declaration of Independence—in Philadelphia by Andrew Stewart, a Scotsman by birth. And Thomas Jefferson, the author of the Declaration, possessed a complete edition of Buchanan's works and must therefore have been familiar with the latter's theories on the subject of tyranny.

In publishing the *De jure regni* Buchanan had in view the enlightenment of James VI of Scotland, whom he had formerly tutored. It is a pity that the young king did not take his tutor's precepts more to heart, for they

---

[65] Barker, "The Authorship of the *Vindiciae contra tyrannos*" (previously cited), *Cambridge Historical Review* (1930), p. 165.
[66] Gooch, *Political Thought in England from Bacon to Halifax,* p. 10.
[67] Allison ed. (previously cited), pp. xxxviii–xxxix.

might then have prevented him, as James I of England, from becoming obsessed with the theory of the divine right of kings, and thus have saved the royal head of his son, Charles I. In any event, Buchanan, as we shall see, had very definite ideas on the subject of kingship.

It was his view, as set forth in the form of a Socratic dialogue between himself and one Thomas Maitland, that kingship originated in more or less formal election by the people, who, drawn together by natural desires and needs, chose one among them as a "leader," "prince," or "governor" to rule for the common good. But the king was not to rule arbitrarily, for Buchanan would not only have him bound by a pact with the people but equally bound by laws—laws not imposed by himself but made and interpreted by the representatives of the people.

If the king is dominated by selfish motives and seeks to override the laws, he is then no longer a king in the proper sense of that term, but a tyrant. Such a ruler, by his actions, places himself beyond the pale and is to be accounted the enemy of God and man. After examining at length both the Scriptures and secular authorities, Buchanan comes to certain conclusions on the proper methods of dealing with the tyrant. If possible he should be condemned and punished by judicial process, since, like any subject of his realm, he is amenable to law—which, we are reminded, is no respecter of persons. But, it may be objected (and indeed was objected by Buchanan's interlocutor) that tyrants are seldom willing to submit to judgment. In that event, Buchanan replies, resort must be had to force, as in the case of any other malefactor. The king who has become a tyrant has violated his covenant with the people and has become a menace to the very society for whose preservation and advancement he was created king. In so doing he has not only forfeited all authority over his people but has become their enemy, against whom they may declare lawful war. And once war is justly undertaken for a just cause, adds Buchanan, applying the law of war to the matter in hand, it becomes lawful for the people as a whole, or for any one of them, to kill the enemy.

The essential purpose of tyrannicide as a political doctrine is the protection of the inherent rights of the governed against governors who, for selfish motives, seek by one means or another to repress or destroy those rights. Gradually the emphasis in this doctrine has shifted from the indiscriminate killing of tyrants to a procedure in which law and judicial condemnation and penalties are the means for restraining, punishing or removing tyrannical rulers. With the development of constitutions, in other words, there has been evolved a well-defined legal process for the removal of unconstitutional magistrates. Today a provision for this process, under the name of "impeachment," exists in the Constitution of the United States and in the constitutions of many of the civilized nations of the world.

Such provisions are not yet universal. And it is conceivable that the constitutional remedy for tyranny may be eluded by the craft of an unscrupulous ruler. But in either event the ancient remedy still remains, and it is not likely to be long overlooked by an oppressed and desperate people. It should not be forgotten that within the memory of living generations many a throne and chief magistrate's office has been deprived of its one-time occupant by a populace which found no remedy available but force for the protection of rights and the preservation of that political liberty which is the birthright of human beings.[68]

The Development of Liberty

Long and slow and checkered has been the development of the right of peoples to govern themselves through laws of their own making or acceptance, whereby their welfare and their happiness may be achieved. Throughout history there have been favored classes and the favored classes have sought, often successfully, to determine the nature and form of government.

After many centuries, it would seem that the people as a whole are coming into their own. The great democratic ideals cherished in the past only by a few have begun in the last century or so to bear fruit. The philosophic conception that every human being, simply because he is a human being instead of an animal, has the rights of a human being, has emerged from the philosopher's closet and is being realized in the field and the market place.

Now the fundamental right of the individual from the legal standpoint is equality before the law, and from the social and political standpoint, an equal opportunity to provide for his welfare and to achieve happiness, both of which are the admitted ends of society under any proper form of government. The status of equality, legal, social, and economic, with its accompanying rights, is dependent upon that most precious of human possessions,

---

[68] For an interesting discussion of the doctrine of tyrannicide and its influence on the development of political liberty, see Lecky, *History of the Rise and Influence of the Spirit of Rationalism in Europe*, II, 149–207.

The American doctrine on this subject was stated in classic terms by Abraham Lincoln in his first inaugural address: "This country, with its institutions, belongs to the people who inhabit it. Whenever they shall grow weary of the existing government, they can exercise their constitutional right of amending it, or their revolutionary right to dismember or overthrow it."

liberty, for without liberty there can be no universal equality in law and opportunity.

Liberty and slavery are inevitably in opposition, for they are mutually exclusive. Slavery is a relic of the rule of force and, like the rule of force, it dies hard. For centuries, mankind—including the philosophers, who should have known better—sought to justify slavery and to give it legal status. It was long ago recognized that all men are "born free"—indeed we find that expression in the Roman law itself[69]—and that such freedom by birth was a principle of the natural law. Yet the institution of slavery was so firmly established that one after another, the jurists, the philosophers, and the legislators, sought to evade the natural law by arguing that, while it conferred liberty upon all human beings, it did not prohibit taking that liberty away.

But in spite of this reasoning and in spite of the weight of the authorities who gave it their sanction, the world came at last to the realization that if liberty is right, then slavery must be wrong. The achievement of this realization was a gradual and a painful process, and the victory of liberty, resulting in the condemnation of the pernicious doctrine of the legality of slavery, has caused from beginning to end untold suffering and bloodshed, as we in the United States know only too well. Yet even today the long struggle continues.

Lord Acton spent a lifetime [it is said], collecting material for a History of Liberty. He never wrote it: but, if he had, it would have been a History of Mankind.[70]

Slavery as an accepted institution no longer exists in the civilized world, but unfortunately it still persists here and there in more or less disguised form. Wherever liberty is incomplete; wherever there is exploitation of human beings; wherever there is oppression; and wherever human rights are denied or ignored—there liberty has not yet conquered slavery. In the past, liberty was acquired at a terrific cost. Today the struggle is less bloody, but it is still a struggle. And in the future? It may be that "This liberty will look easy by and by when nobody dies to get it."[71]

Just what is the nature and meaning of this liberty which has been so precious to humanity? To begin with, a distinction must be made. Liberty, as far as human beings in society are concerned, is not merely untrammelled

[69] *Digest* I. i. 4.
[70] Zimmern, "Progress in Government," an essay published in *Progress and History*, pp. 151–88, 152.
[71] Maxwell Anderson, *Valley Forge,* A Play in Three Acts (Anderson House, Washington, 1934), p. 166.

freedom of action: the right of each to do as he pleases at all times and in all places, without respect to others. Such freedom would be simply license. Liberty is a reasonable concept. Indeed, according to Milton,[72]

> . . . true liberty . . . always with right reason dwells
> Twined, and from her hath no divisible being.

Liberty is also a social concept and a thing of law. Now the primary aim of law is the establishment and maintenance of order in society, and liberty therefore means the exercise of rights without the disturbance of that order. "Liberty under the law" is a well-worn phrase, but it embodies a fundamental truth, for it implies that each individual may legally enjoy his liberty only in so far as he does not infringe the liberty of others.

It will be useful here to turn for a moment to the conception of liberty propounded by a seventeenth-century philosopher, Spinoza, who is today ranked among the few great lights of philosophical thought throughout the ages. "Spinoza," said the late Sir Frederick Pollock, "was a firm and consistent supporter of political liberty."[73] And Ernest Renan, whose enlightened views on the state have been quoted elsewhere,[74] hails Spinoza as one of the great advocates of liberty.[75]

On the purpose of government Spinoza laid down the following broad and liberal concept: "The ultimate aim of government is not to rule, or restrain, by fear, nor to exact obedience, but contrariwise, to free every man from fear, that he may live in all possible security, in other words, to strengthen his natural right to exist and work without injury to himself or others."[76]

Upon this premise Spinoza made a statement of fundamental importance:

No, the object of government is not to change men from rational beings into beasts or puppets, but to enable them to develop their minds and bodies in security, and to employ their reason unshackled; neither showing hatred, anger, or deceit, nor watched with the eyes of jealousy and injustice. In fact, the true aim of government is liberty.[77]

Liberty, however, is often restricted, and is at times so nearly obliterated that it seems to have ceased to exist. But under these circumstances liberty is rather dormant than dead.

---

[72] *Paradise Lost*, Book XII, lines 83–85.   [73] *Spinoza, His Life and Philosophy*, p. 315.
[74] *Supra*, pp. 28 ff.
[75] Essay on Spinoza, in *Nouvelles études d'histoire religieuse*, pp. 499–533, especially pp. 511–14.
[76] *Tractatus Theologico-Politicus*, trans. by Elwes, "The Chief Works of Benedict de Spinoza," I, 258–59.
[77] *Ibid.*, p. 259.

TYRANNY VERSUS LIBERTY

"Let it be granted that freedom may be crushed, and men be so bound down, that they do not dare to utter a whisper, save at the bidding of their rulers; nevertheless this can never be carried to the pitch of making them think according to authority, so that the necessary consequences would be that men would daily be thinking one thing and saying another, to the corruption of good faith, that mainstay of government, and to the fostering of hateful flattery and perfidy, whence spring stratagems, and the corruption of every good art."[78]

Nor does Spinoza believe that freedom of speech can be eradicated:

"It is far from possible to impose uniformity of speech, for the more rulers strive to curtail freedom of speech, the more obstinately are they resisted; not indeed by the avaricious, the flatterers, and other numskulls, who think supreme salvation consists in filling their stomachs and gloating over their money-bags, but by those whom good education, sound morality, and virtue have rendered more free."[79] People will cling tenaciously to their opinions, as he points out, when they are convinced that those opinions are right:

Men, as generally constituted, are most prone to resent the branding as criminal of opinions which they believe to be true, and the proscription as wicked of that which inspires them with piety towards God and man; hence they are ready to forswear the laws and conspire against the authorities, thinking it not shameful but honourable to stir up seditions and perpetuate any sort of crime with this end in view. Such being the constitution of human nature, we see that laws directed against opinions affect the generous-minded rather than the wicked, and are adapted less for coercing criminals than for irritating the upright; so that they cannot be maintained without great peril to the state.[80]

Commenting on the effects of such laws, Spinoza adds: "Such laws are almost always useless, for those who hold that the opinions proscribed are sound, cannot possibly obey the law; whereas those who already reject them as false, accept the law as a kind of privilege, and make such boast of it, that authority is powerless to repeal it, even if such a course be subsequently desired."[81]

But these are not the only effects of laws and government which deprive men of liberty.

What greater misfortune for a state can be conceived than that honourable men should be sent like criminals into exile, because they hold diverse opinions which they cannot disguise? What, I say, can be more hurtful than that men who have committed no crime or wickedness should, simply because they are enlightened, be treated as enemies and put to death, and that the scaffold, the terror of evildoers, should become the arena where the highest examples of tolerance and

---

[78] *Ibid.*, p. 261.   [79] *Ibid.*, pp. 261–62.   [80] *Ibid.*, p. 262.   [81] *Ibid.*

virtue are displayed to the people with all the marks of ignominy that authority can devise? [82]

The government which denies true liberty to citizens is likely to have but a precarious existence. In Spinoza's opinion,

> if governments are to retain a firm hold of authority and not be compelled to yield to agitators, it is imperative that freedom of judgment should be granted, so that men may live together in harmony, however diverse, or even openly contradictory their opinions may be. We cannot doubt that such is the best system of government and open to the fewest objections, since it is the one most in harmony with human nature.[83]

Liberty as thus conceived means on the one hand, the unrestricted enjoyment of fundamental human rights. But on the other hand, it means that liberty depends upon the recognition and performance of equally fundamental human duties. It is obvious that an ordered society cannot exist without a conception of duties as well as of rights. In every human community the individual's liberty of action is linked, firmly and inextricably, with the obligation to respect the equal liberty of action of other persons in the society of which he is a member. Therefore, every right which the possession of liberty confers upon the individual is accompanied by a correlative duty not to interfere with the proper exercise of rights by others, and the function of law and government is to maintain that condition of order which assures the protection, for each member of society, of his liberty and of the rights which flow therefrom, within the necessary limitation which imposes upon him a due respect for the liberty and rights of others. When a government ignores this primary function, it is oppressive, not to say tyrannical. The more it permits the liberty of the members of society to be curtailed, the less worthy is it of being dignified by the name of government and the greater its danger of being overthrown by a justly incensed people. And when it is overthrown, woe betide those who were responsible for the oppression and tyranny. "Freedom suppressed and again regained," warns Cicero, "bites with keener fangs than freedom never endangered."[84]

If man is fully to understand his duties toward his fellows and the meaning and purpose of the government under which he lives, he must first comprehend the nature and extent of his inherent rights as a human being. There is perhaps no better statement of those rights, and of the obligation of governments to see that they are recognized and protected, than that in the Declaration of the International Rights of Man, adopted by the *Institut*

---

[82] Spinoza, *op. cit.*, p. 263.   [83] *Ibid.*   [84] *De officiis* II. vii. 24.

de Droit International at its session at Briarcliff, in the state of New York, on Columbus Day, October 12, 1929. The preamble to this document supplies the doctrinal foundation upon which the provisions of its several articles rest:

Considering:
That the juridical conscience of the civilized world demands the recognition for the individual of rights preserved from all infringement on the part of the State;

That the declarations of rights, written into a large number of constitutions and especially into the American and French Constitutions of the end of the 18th century, are ordained not only for the citizen, but for man;

That the 14th Amendment of the Constitution of the United States prescribes as follows: ". . . nor shall any State deprive any person of life, liberty, or property, without due process of law; nor deny to any person within its jurisdiction the equal protection of the laws";

That the Supreme Court of the United States has unanimously decided that by the terms of this amendment it is applicable within the jurisdiction of the United States "to every person without distinction of race, color or nationality, and that the equal protection of the laws is a guarantee of the protection of equal laws";

That it is important to extend to the entire world international recognition of the rights of man.

Following the preamble are six articles dealing with the fundamental rights of human beings, including that of equality without distinctions based upon sex or other factors:

Article 1

It is the duty of every State to recognize the equal right of every individual to life, liberty and property, and to accord to all within its territory the full and entire protection of this right, without distinction as to nationality, sex, race, language, or religion.

Article 2

It is the duty of every State to recognize the right of every individual to the free practice, both public and private, of every faith, religion, or belief, provided that the said practice shall not be incompatible with public order and good morals.

Article 3

It is the duty of every State to recognize the right of every individual both to the free use of the language of his choice and to the teaching of such language.

Article 4

No motive based, directly or indirectly, on distinctions of sex, race, language, or religion empowers States to refuse to any of their nationals private and public rights, especially admission to establishments of public instruction, and the exercise of the different economic activities and of professions and industries.

Article 5

The equality herein contemplated is not to be nominal, but effective. It excludes all discrimination, direct or indirect.

Article 6

Except for motives based upon its general legislation, no State shall have the right to withdraw its nationality from those whom it should not, for reasons of sex, race, language, or religion, deprive of the guarantees contemplated in the preceding articles.

When this conception of human rights has been completely woven into the fabric of society, tyranny and slavery will have vanished from the face of the earth.

THE ERA OF REFORM

Chapter XXVII

ST. THOMAS MORE (1478-1535)

In the long and varied development of human ideals, certain great figures tower high above all others. They are not dimmed by time and change. From age to age they stand out serene and clear against the stormy background of history. To countless generations these figures have symbolized what is noblest in human aspirations, not alone because of what they wrote or said, but because their own lives were as a pattern and a demonstration of the ideals which they professed. They are few in number, and to their ranks posterity may not lightly add. Of this small and lonely company is St. Thomas More, lawyer, statesman and diplomat, theologian, reformer and saint of the Church, and withal a dreamer of great dreams for the betterment of mankind.

If one were to seek a single key to the character of the many-sided More, it might well be found in the fact that he was and always remained a sincere Christian in practice as well as in theory. From his youth onward his entire life was profoundly influenced by his religious convictions—convictions so firm and enduring that eventually, rather than violate them, he suffered imprisonment and a martyr's death. To the influence of his religious beliefs must be credited in large part his strong sense of right, of justice and fairness, his power of discerning the ills of the society in which he lived,[1] and his passion for practical reform.

There were, however, other keys which are necessary to a full comprehension of his character. Among these the most important were his education and his friendships. Of More's education it may be said at once that he ranks high among the great humanists of his age, and indeed of all time. And it was in the world of the humanities that he found his truest friends, both of the classical past and of his own day. At an early age he became well grounded in Latin, and though his formal schooling was interrupted by some years of service in the home of John Morton—already Archbishop of Canterbury and Lord Chancellor, and later to become Cardinal—his experiences in the Morton household were in themselves the

---

[1] For a recent interesting discussion of the "Social Theories of St. Thomas More," see the article under that title by Richard O'Sullivan, *The Dublin Review*, CIC (July, 1936), 46-62.

best of introductions to a knowledge of manners and men, of history and law, and of the whole sweep of Renaissance culture. It was at the recommendation of the Archbishop, who prophesied a "marvellous" future for the young page, that More was sent to Oxford—probably in the very year of Columbus' discovery of America. There he perfected his knowledge of Latin and became an ardent student of Greek. There, too, he came under the influence of two eminent scholars and humanists, Grocyn and Linacre; and it is not unlikely that he also met John Colet, one of the most important members of that small group often termed "The Oxford Reformers."[2] But whether or not More was in touch with Colet during his stay at Oxford, it is certain that he became intimately associated with the latter a few years afterwards in London, when Colet became Dean of St. Paul's Cathedral. More not only followed the Dean's sermons assiduously, but also selected him as a father confessor.

Because of his influence on both More and Erasmus, it is advisable to consider briefly certain of Colet's views. Though his scholarship was less profound than that of his most learned contemporaries, he possessed a clear and vigorous mind, well tempered by humanistic culture. Studying for some years in France and Italy, he absorbed much of the new learning; but instead of pursuing that learning as an end in itself, he used it as a lamp to guide him in the pursuit of his favorite subject, theology. The theology, however, which he proceeded to expound upon his return to England differed in certain respects from the conventional conceptions of that science. It seemed to Colet that the Christian religion was in some danger of straying from its true course. Its foundation, in his opinion, should be the text of the New Testament, together with the fundamental writings of the Fathers of the Early Church. But in the centuries that had followed the work of the Early Church Fathers, a host of commentaries, expositions, and finespun interpretations had been composed by innumerable writers, and the result was, Colet felt, that the original message of the New Testament had been obscured. Theologians seemed to rely more upon what had been written about the Scriptures than upon the Scriptures themselves. To Colet the New Testament, apart from the parables, meant just what it said and needed no elaborate paraphernalia of interpretation. Thus he did not regard the Epistles of St. Paul, for example, as being written in the form of riddles, to be painfully deciphered. To him they were real letters, with a genuine and profound meaning for all who would study them with open and recep-

---

[2] The classical treatise on this group is Frederic Seebohm's volume, *The Oxford Reformers*, first published in 1867, and reissued in revised and enlarged form two years later.

tive minds. In brief, Colet advocated a return to the foundations of Christian doctrine, a process which required the sweeping aside of some of the more cumbersome trappings of medieval theology. He sought a simplification of religion through what may be called theological reform—a goal toward which Erasmus also aimed, although, as we shall see,[3] with a clearer perception of the obstacles to be overcome.

Now Colet, as More's spiritual adviser, imbued him with the passion for reform. But as More eventually chose a secular rather than a monastic career, it was natural that his plans for reform, as they ultimately developed, should be aimed largely at the correction of material wrongs. The choice of career, however, was one of great difficulty for the young man. Deeply religious though he was, he was also aware that, given the passionate temperament with which he was endowed, a hasty and ill-considered decision would be worse than folly.

His father, Sir John More—himself a lawyer of distinction, who late in life became successively judge of the Common Pleas and of the King's Bench—was anxious that his son should follow his own profession. The young More therefore left Oxford to study law, first at New Inn and later at Lincoln's Inn, becoming in due course a full-fledged barrister. But still he had reached no decision as to the path which he should follow. For some years he gave much serious thought to the question of entering the Carthusian Order or becoming a Franciscan friar, and he tested his capacity for such a career by living a rigorously monastic life.

Eventually, however, two influences led him to choose a secular career. The first was that of Colet, who, knowing so well the nature and temperament of his young protégé, advised him to give up the plan of entering a religious order. The second influence More encountered in the works of a gifted Italian scholar, Pico della Mirandola, who, though he died in his thirty-second year, had already established a reputation for extraordinary brilliance and learning. Pico, too, had felt drawn toward a religious life and, had it not been for his early death, might well have carried out his expressed intention of entering the Dominican Order. More was attracted by his writings, and particularly by Pico's life, written by the latter's nephew. In this biography, which More translated into English, he found the record of one who had been more than a little successful in reconciling in himself absorbing interests in the various fields of scholarship, theology, philosophy, and literature. Here was a layman whose range of interests had been even wider than his own. To More, becoming increasingly aware that

[3] *Infra*, p. 488.

he was not really fitted by nature for a career in orders, the thought came that the next best thing—perhaps, after all, the best thing—would be for him to pattern his life as a layman upon that of Pico. Thus, at long last, his decision was reached, and in the year 1505 he married and gave himself up to a secular career—or rather, to a series of careers, for, as has been indicated, he was a man of great and varied abilities.

Though he was successful in many fields of activity, his chief profession was the law. To More that profession was far from being merely a means of gaining a livelihood. His colleagues, indeed, must have regarded some of his views on the functions of the lawyer as decidedly unconventional. He seems to have conceived that the first and foremost duty of the man of law was to see that justice was done. This meant, not dragging as many cases as possible into the courts, but adjusting them in the simplest and most direct manner. Therefore More advised his clients to settle their controversies amicably, either by direct negotiations or by some form of arbitration. In the event that this advice could not, for one reason or another, be accepted and suit had to be brought in court, More's efforts as counsel were directed towards seeing that justice prevailed. We are told, too, that he

> would never undertake to defend a case unless he could first satisfy himself of its justice; if it seemed to him that his clients were in the wrong, he would tell them so plainly, and beg them to give up the case, saying that it was not right either for him or for them to go on with it. If they still persisted, he would resign the case and refer them to other lawyers.[4]

And though he charged but moderate—and often merely nominal—fees, his practice grew so rapidly that it provided him with an ample income. Later, when he become Lord Chancellor (and succeeded in clearing the docket, for the first time on record, of all pending cases), he remained as firm and incorruptible a friend of justice as ever. His son-in-law, William Roper,[5] has transmitted to us a statement made by More during his chancellorship which indicates the standard of strict impartiality to which he adhered: "I assure thee on my faith, that if the parties will at my handes call for iustice, then, al were it my father stood on the one side, and the Divill on the tother, his cause being good, the Divill should haue right."

Although it was the custom of the day for litigants to make gifts to the Chancellor, More declined to retain any of the numerous valuable presents offered to him. Yet his refusals were so gracious in words and action that the would-be donors could have suffered no injury to their feelings. Roper

---

[4] Routh, *Sir Thomas More and His Friends, 1477-1535*, pp. 32-33.
[5] *The Lyfe of Sir Thomas Moore, Knighte*, ed. by Hitchcock, p. 42.

recounts a famous instance in which Lord Wiltshire, the father of Anne Boleyn, raised against More the charge of accepting a bribe in the form of "a faire greate gilte Cuppe" from one Parnell, a litigant in the Court of Chancery. The accusation fails completely in the face of the facts related by Roper.[6] As soon as More had received the cup from the lady, who delivered it in behalf of her husband,

immediately thereuppon he caused his butler to fill it with wyne, *and* of that cupp drancke to her; *and* that when [he had soe donne, and] she pleadged him, then as freely as her husband had geuen it to him, Euen so freely gave he the same vnto her agayne, to geeue vnto her husband for his neweyeares gifte; w*hi*ch, at his instant requeste, thoughe muche against her will, at length yeat she was [fayne] to receave, as her self, *and* certayne other there, presently before them deposed. Thus was the greate mountayne turned scant to a litle molehill.

There is another charming anecdote of a gift in the holiday season which met much the same reception. Upon New Year's Day, according to Roper,[7] there came to More

one m*istr*es Crocker, a Rich widowe, for whom, w*i*th no small paine, he had made a decree in the Chauncery against the Lord of Arondell, to present him with a ,payr*e* of gloves, *and* fourty pound*es* in Angels in them, for a newe year*es* gifte. Of whom he thancfully re*ce*yning the gloues, but refucing the money, said vnto her: "Mistres, since it were againste good manner[s] to forsake a gentle womans newe yeares gifte, I am content to take your gloues, but as for y*o*ur money I vtterley refuse." So, muche against her mynde, inforced he her to take her gold againe.

Of all the contemporary sketches of More the most felicitous and sympathetic is that written by his intimate friend Erasmus, in a letter to Ulrich von Hutten, dated at Antwerp the twenty-third of July, 1519.[8] Hutten, it appeared, was an admirer of More's writings, and they had inspired in him a desire to know as much as possible about their author—a desire which he had made known to Erasmus.

To begin [wrote Erasmus in reply] where you know least of More, in build and stature he is not what would be described as tall, but he is not noticeably short; and there is such proportion in all his limbs that it never occurs to one to wish him in any way different. His skin is bright and clear, and so, too, his face, which is neither pale nor ruddy, except for a faint glow which shines over

---

[6] *Ibid.*, pp. 62-63.   [7] *Ibid.*, p. 63.
[8] This letter is published in Latin in the collection *Opus epistolarum Des. Erasmi Roterodami*, ed. by P. S. and H. M. Allen, IV, 13-23. It has also been rendered into English by Mr. Allen, with the exception of a few irrelevant sentences, and published in the little volume, *Sir Thomas More, Selections from His English Works and from the Lives by Erasmus and Roper*, ed. by P. S. and H. M. Allen, pp. 1-9.

it all. His hair is auburn, tinged with black, or, if you like, black tinged with auburn; his beard thin, his eyes blue-grey, but with spots of different colour—a kind which is thought to show a very happy temperament, and is much liked in England, though our countrymen prefer black. No eyes, they say, are more free from blemish.[9]

And Erasmus' comment on this description of More's physical appearance is: "His nature may be read in his face, always pleasant and friendly and cheerful, with a readiness to smile: indeed its inclination is towards merriment rather than to grave dignity, though very far removed from silly buffoonery."[10]

"How charming he must have looked when a lad," continues Erasmus, "one can see even now in his riper age." And referring to his own long friendship with More, he immediately adds, "I knew him first when he was not more than 23, now he is a little over 40."[11]

After commenting on the simplicity of More's personal habits, his "singularly clear and articulate" speech, his disregard of needless formalities, Erasmus depicts the character of the man whose outward appearance and habits he has thus described.

He has always liked equality and hated despotism, and so at one time he shunned intimacy with princes; for round the quietest throne is bustle and rivalry and luxury and sham, with marks of mastery and servitude. Even into Henry VIII's court he was only drawn with great reluctance. . . . Of freedom and leisure he can never have enough: but while he thankfully enjoys his leisure when he can get it, no one is more alert or more ready to take trouble when need arises.[12]

It was Erasmus' opinion that by reason of "his straight-forward loyal nature" More was "naturally endowed for friendship."[13] His circle of friends was large, and indeed he derived his chief enjoyment from "the company and conversation of men sincere and like-minded with himself,"[14] games and other amusements having no attraction for him. And though he might be and often was "careless of his own affairs," he was always so ready to help others that, in Erasmus' opinion, one could not do better than to consider More as "a pattern of true friendship."[15]

Among the characteristics which drew friends were his cheerful nature and his sense of humor.

To live with he is singularly sweet and conversible; cheering the low-spirited and in times of distress relieving the general gloom. From his boyhood he has

---

[9] Allen, *Sir Thomas More, Selections*, p. 2.   [10] *Ibid.*   [11] *Ibid.*
[12] *Ibid.*, p. 3.   [13] *Ibid.*, p. 4.   [14] *Ibid.*   [15] *Ibid.*

had a natural delight in jokes: but always avoiding vulgarity and taking care not to wound. As a young man he wrote and acted some little plays. He rejoices in brilliant sallies, seasoned with real wit, and a clever retort delights him, even when against himself.[16]

It was these characteristics, according to Erasmus, which led him to amuse himself with epigrams and in translating Lucian. "And," he adds, "it was he who made me write the *Praise of Folly*, like setting a camel to dance."[17]

More found much in life to amuse him, but his sense of humor was of the kind which enabled him to see through popular fallacies at a glance. "No one," observed Erasmus, "is less swayed by public opinion," and "no one shows more common sense in his judgments."[18]

As we have already seen, More was a humanist.

From his earliest years [the letter continues], he followed after good learning. As a young man he took up Greek literature and philosophy.[19]

This interest in classical learning, according to Erasmus, was disturbing to More's father, who, anxious that his son should enter his own profession, adopted somewhat stern measures to persuade the young man to the study of law. It was a hard profession to master, and apparently More dreaded devoting himself to the study of a subject which, in the opinion of Erasmus, had "little in common with true learning."[20] Yielding, however, as we have seen, to his father's wishes, More "turned his strong and quick wits to the law with such success that no one's counsel was in greater demand, and no professional lawyer had a better practice."[21]

But he found time, too, for the study of theology. And however busy he was in later life, he always had time to devote not only to learning but to the wise upbringing and education of his children. On this topic Erasmus' account may be supplemented by a few statements from a modern writer:[22]

More's deep interest in the new learning found practical expression in the education of his children. He not only chose for them the best available teachers in divinity, classics, astronomy, and music, but himself supervised and shared their studies, using for their benefit his inimitable gift for turning the driest subjects into a delightful pastime. . . .

Even his frequent absence from home was turned to account in his plan of education, and Latin composition was practised and improved by correspondence. His letters to his family, composed in careful Latin, were full of good advice, and never without some amusing pleasantry. They were eagerly read, and read again, till they almost fell to pieces. He demanded replies from each one of the children, and these were closely criticized, but always with loving appreciation and encouragement.

---

[16] *Ibid.*   [17] *Ibid.*   [18] *Ibid.*   [19] *Ibid.*, p. 5.
[20] *Ibid.*   [21] *Ibid.*   [22] Routh, *op. cit.*, pp. 123, 124.

And the same author observes that

it was a fortunate occurrence for More's countrywomen that his three elder children were daughters, and girls of a high level of intelligence. In his own household Utopian principles of equal instruction for the sexes were put into practice, and in this way More did as much to advance the education of girls in England as Colet did for boys at his school of St. Paul's.[23]

More's home life was indeed a happy one, and Erasmus speaks feelingly of the "charm" with which his friend

rules his whole household, so that strife and quarrels are unknown. Should any arise, he composes them at once; never feeling anger with any one, nor leaving him sore. Indeed, fate seems to have made this home for special happiness; every one who lives in it prospers, and none has ever fallen into disgrace.[24]

In following his profession More, as has already been stated, was more interested in aiding his clients than in collecting fees.

Money [declared Erasmus] has no charms for him. He has set aside from his property a sum which he considers sufficient for his children; and what is left he spends freely. When he was still dependent on his practice, he thought more of his clients' advantage than of his own, and gave disinterested counsel to all: in most cases urging litigants to make up their quarrels and so avoid expense. If they would not hear him—for some people seem to enjoy lawsuits—he showed them how to keep their expenses down.[25]

After commenting on More's reluctance to enter the service of Henry VIII, and his subsequent yielding to royal insistence, Erasmus refers to More's marked ability and success in dealing with his duties at court. But success and high office did not change him nor cause him to forget his friends. Declaring that "with all this honour, there has come no touch of pride," Erasmus continues:

Amid so much business he has time to remember his old friends and to return now and then to the studies he loves. All his dignity, all his influence with his royal master, he uses to serve the state and to help his friends. His aim has always been to be helpful and sympathetic; and now more than ever, when he has the more power to help. Some he relieves with money, others he protects by his authority, others with a word of commendation he brings on the road to promotion. When he can do nothing else, he will always advise those who consult him; and no one ever goes away disappointed. Indeed you might say that he is the public patron of all who are in want. He thinks it great gain to deliver the oppressed, to extricate the harassed from their troubles, and to reconcile those who have quarrelled. No one is more ready to do a service or less ready

---

[23] Routh, *op. cit.*, p. 127. On More's views concerning education, see also the chapter "The School of Sir Thomas More," in Clayton, *Sir Thomas More, a Short Study*, pp. 35-44.
[24] Allen, *Sir Thomas More, Selections*, p. 6.   [25] *Ibid.*, pp. 6-7.

to expect one. With so many titles to happiness, he is yet singularly free from the headiness which often accompanies good fortune.[26]

A final quotation from Erasmus' sketch reveals More as at once a genius and a Christian gentleman:

> Scarcely any one is happier at impromptu speaking, for he has a pretty wit and a ready tongue. His thoughts are quick to fly on ever in advance. His memory is wide awake: and having, so to speak, all its cash ready, produces without hesitation anything that may be required. In argument no one could be more acute: indeed he often puzzles the most learned theologians on their own ground. John Colet, a man of correct and penetrating judgment, sometimes says that in all Britain there is only one genius: though that island is so rich in men of ability.
>
> More is a man of true piety, which he practises with regularity, yet without a trace of superstition. At definite hours he addresses his prayers to God, not in set phrases but with words which come straight from his heart. When he talks with his friends about the world to come, you can see that he is speaking in all sincerity and with good hope. Such is More the courtier: and then people think that Christians are only to be found in monasteries![27]

As has already been intimated, More's interest turned more toward reform in secular than in theological matters. He was a keen observer, and as he viewed conditions then existing, especially in his own country, he saw much that cried out for change and improvement. The great mass of the population was wholly without education and lived in wretched, unsanitary homes. The majority of them were in a state of desperate and seemingly hopeless poverty, and were held in check by harsh laws and the power of the small ruling class.

Much distressed by these conditions, More apparently probed deeply, seeking the causes. He found not only that wages were being reduced, but that unemployment existed on a large scale. Multitudes of soldiers, disbanded after the great wars which had dissipated the wealth of the country, were unable to find work. Confronted by the alternatives of stealing or starving, they chose the former. Many of them gathered into ragged bands and roamed the countryside, seizing whatever they could lay their hands upon.

But there was another reason for so much unemployment and misery. Wool-raising had become increasingly profitable. The Continental markets at Bruges and elsewhere offered prices which aroused the cupidity of the great landowners who raised sheep. If they were to produce more wool, however, they must have more grazing land. To provide such land many

---

[26] *Ibid.*, pp. 7–8.   [27] *Ibid.*, pp. 8–9.

small farmers were ejected from their acres, and thus immense fields of formerly tillable land were converted into pasturage. The large landowners contrived also to enclose within their increasing domains large areas of the public lands, thus destroying the ancient communal type of agriculture. Whole country hamlets and villages were depopulated. Those farmers not required for sheep tending were turned adrift to become beggars or worse. The results were deplorable: a great decrease in food products, with resultant higher prices; an ever-growing horde of jobless men with their miserable and underfed families; and—always a danger sign if governments will but heed it—a widening chasm between the poverty-stricken many and the wealthy few.

To these conditions must be added another factor, the infliction of heavy penalties for minor offenses. Under the then-existing system of law and justice, petty crimes were punishable by death, and in consequence there were wholesale executions of poor wretches, many of whom were guilty of no greater crime than pilfering to avoid starvation. The result of this iniquitous system was an increase in more serious crimes. Knowing that the death penalty awaited them even for small offenses, those who were driven to lawbreaking not unnaturally decided that they risked no more for a grave than for a petty crime.

These various evils of society could not but arouse to action one who was at heart an ardent reformer. But More was too practical a man to believe that there was any possibility of successfully attacking the problem directly and openly. Such tactics would, to state it mildly, have met with the coolest reception from the reigning monarch, Henry VIII, and they would have aroused the bitter opposition of the nobility. How, then, could the needed reforms be effectively advocated? After much reflection More hit upon the plan of clothing his ideas in a fictional dress, of presenting them to the world in the guise of a description of an ideal commonwealth.

Such a method was not, of course, an original one. More was well acquainted with the details of Plato's ideal commonwealth and with his mythical Atlantis. He was also familiar with St. Augustine's great conception of a spiritual commonwealth, for he had not only studied deeply the *De civitate Dei* but had delivered a series of lectures upon it. More was likewise indebted to a famous tractate of his own day, Amerigo Vespucci's account of his four voyages, published in Latin in 1507 as an appendix to the *Cosmographiae introductio*. Indeed Hythlodaye, the chief character of the *Utopia,* is not only represented as having accompanied Vespucci on three of his voyages, but describes in his narrative not a few of the details which are mentioned by the navigator, especially in the latter's account of his second voyage. Thus the New World as well as the ancient world contributed to the *Utopia*.

Yet however much he owed to his predecessors and to travelers' tales, More produced in the *Utopia* a wholly original work, destined to be one of the few books of the ages.[28] In his own day it was a revolutionary book, yet so skillfully composed that it incited men, not to hasty and thoughtless action, but to the sane thinking upon which all sound and progressive action is based. It was written with the evils of sixteenth-century England in mind, but its conceptions are set forth in such universal terms that it still appeals to men of various creeds, to reformers and radicals, socialists and communists—and indeed to all who believe that the world we live in can be made happier and better. Today More is the hero, as Professor R. W. Chambers points out, to both Catholic and communist.

Four hundred and two years before it came into existence, he sketched out the pattern of the Communist state. Those eyes which Holbein drew, anxiously but fearlessly peering into the future, had seen far indeed. And More's political disciples are found far outside the ranks of Communists and Socialists. More's description of the commonwealth of his day as "a conspiracy of rich men, procuring their own commodities under the name of the commonwealth" has roused the conscience of social reformers from his day to ours.

More is the hero of the Catholic, because he gave his life "in and for the faith of the Holy Catholic Church." He should be the hero of all men of good will, because he died for unity; died that the prayer of his Master at his first Eucharist might be fulfilled, "That they all may be one."[29]

Though he must have long had his ideal commonwealth in mind, it was not until 1515 that he found time to undertake the writing of the *Utopia*. In that year he was appointed member of a diplomatic mission to Flanders, going first to Bruges and later to Antwerp. There, with greater leisure at his disposal, he found time not only for conversations with many scholars and men of affairs, but also to begin the *Utopia*. Apparently he wrote the whole of the second part of the book in Antwerp, and upon his return to England set himself the task of writing a first part. It is this first part which reveals the evils for which reforms were so badly needed; the second part, describing the ideal commonwealth of Utopia, suggests, often seriously but at times whimsically, remedies for the world's ills. It is as

---

[28] "Not Hobbes nor Hume in fact has dived so deep into the pools of political philosophy; not Burke nor Mill has kept so well abreast of the swift undercurrent of our time."—Cecil, *A Portrait of Thomas More, Scholar, Statesman, Saint*, p. 3.

[29] *Thomas More*, p. 395.

though More invited the reader to "look here, upon this picture, and on this."

Nevertheless the division of the *Utopia* into two parts or "Books," as an English authority has pointed out, "is really an arbitrary one."[30] And the same writer adds in justification of such a statement:

> The object of both is the same, though the end is obtained in one case by the direct reprobation of evils, and in the other generally by inference from the perfect State the constitution of which is described. To all appearance, More, after he had written the second book, saw that the nature of the fiction would prevent it containing much that he wished to declare; he therefore wrote an introductory book in which he expressed his meaning more fully. The first book, then, is so plainly the necessary complement of the second, that the evils of which More complained may be gathered indifferently from each.[31]

For present purposes it will be interesting to choose a few passages from the first book (indicating the evils which More discerned in the world of his day) and to compare them with passages in the second book which prescribe methods for curing these ills of society.

The first passage is the statement of Raphaell Hythlodaye—who, as the narrator of experiences in the far-off land of Utopia, is the chief speaker of the dialogue—that

> the moste parte of all princes haue more delyte in warlike matters and feates of cheualrie (the knowlege whereof I nother haue nor desire), than in the good feates of peace; and employe muche more study howe by right or by wrong to enlarge their dominions, than howe well and peaceablie to rule and gouerne that they haue all redie.[32]

Moreover, as Hythlodaye adds, the advisers of princes were for the most part sycophants, or else so sure of the rightness of their own views that they condemned all others—especially if the latter contained any "taint" of new ideas. Thus, we are told, they would argue against proposed changes in some such manner as the following:

> "Thies thinges" (say they) "pleased oure forefathers and auncetours: wolde god wee coulde be so wise as they were." And as though they had wittely concluded the matter, and with this answere stoppid euery mans mouthe, they sitt downe agayn. As who should saye it were a very daungerous matter, if a man in any pointe should be founde wiser then his forefathers were.[33]

How differently things were managed in Utopia! After referring to the local officials, the "Syphoagrauntes" (of which there was one elected by

---

[30] Hutton, *Sir Thomas More*, p. 116.   [31] *Ibid.*
[32] *Sir Thomas More's Utopia*, ed., with an intro. and notes, by Collins, p. 9. The text of this edition is the famous translation by Robynson, first published in 1551.
[33] *Ibid.*, p. 10.

every 30 families or farms) and the "Tranibores" (one elected by each 300 families), Hythlodaye thus describes the election of the prince:

> As concerninge the electyon of the prynce, all the Syphoagrauntes, which be in number 200, first be sworne to chewse him whome they thynke moste mete and expedyente. Then by a secrete electyon they name prynce one of those .iiii. whome the people before named vnto them. For owte of the .iiii. quarters of the citie there be .iiii. chosen, owte of euerye quarter one, to stande for the election, whiche be put vp to the counsell. The princes office contineweth all his liffe time, onles he be deposed or put downe for suspition of tirannye.[34]

Hythlodaye refers next to the duties of the prince's counsellors:

> The Tranibores euerye thyrde daye, and sumtymes, if neade be, oftener, come into the councell howse with the prynce. Theire councell is concernynge the common wealth. Yf there be annye controuersyes amonge the commoners, whyche be very fewe, they dyspatche and ende them by and by. They take euer ii. Siphograntes to them in cowncell, and euerye daye a newe coupel. And that ys prouydede that no thynge towchynge the common wealthe shalbe confyrmed and ratifyed, on les yt haue bene reasonede of an debatede iii. dayes in the cowncell, before yt be decreed. It is deathe to haue annye consultatyon for the common wealthe owte of the cownsell, or the place of the common electyon.[35]

There was a specific reason for such a provision, as Hythlodaye immediately explained:

> Thys statute, they saye, was made to thentente, that the prynce and Tranibores myghte not easely conspire together to oppresse the people by tyrannye, and to chaunge the state of the weale publique. Therefore matters of greate weyghte and importaunce be brought to the electyon house of the syphograuntes, whyche open the matter to their familyes; and afterwarde, when they haue consulted among them selfes, they shewe their deuyse to the cowncell. Sumtyme the matter is brought before the cowncell of the hole Ilande.[36]

It is clear that the Utopian council was a deliberative body in the fullest sense of the term, and that its sole purpose was to promote the common welfare. Provision was therefore made to avoid rash decisions by the councilors:

> Furthermore thys custome also the cowncell vseth, to dyspute or reason of no matter the same daye that it ys fyrste proposed or putt furthe, but to dyfferre it to the nexte syttynge of the cownsell. Bycause that no man when he hathe rasshelye there spoken that cummeth fyrste to hys tonges ende, shalt then afterwarde rather studye for reasons wherewyth to defende and confyrme hys fyrste folyshe sentence, than for the commodytye of the common wealthe; as one rather wyllynge the harme or hynderaunce of the weale publyque, then annye losse or dymynutyon of hys owne existymatyon; and as one that wolde not for

---

[34] *Ibid.*, p. 57.   [35] *Ibid.*, pp. 57–58.   [36] *Ibid.*, p. 58.

shame (which is a verye folyshe shame) be cowntede annye thynge ouerseen in the matter at the fyrste; who at the fyrste owghte to haue spoken rather wysely then hastely or rashelye.[37]

What, however, of war, which, according to the statement of Hythlodaye already quoted from the first book, was the chief sport and occupation of the European princes of that day? In the second book he informs us that, although the Utopians might on rare occasions undertake warfare, they did so only

in the defence of their owne cowntreye, or to dryue owte of theyr frendes lande the enemyes that be comen in, or by their powre to deliuer from the yocke and bondage of tyrannye some people that be oppressed wyth tyranny. Whyche thynge they doo of meere pytye and compassion.[38]

But their real feelings on the subject were summed up by Hythlodaye in a single sentence: "Warre or battel as a thinge very beastelye, and yet to no kynde of beastes in so muche vse as it is to man, they do detest and abhorre; and, contrarye to the custome almost of all other natyons, they cownte nothinge so much against glorie, as glory gotten in warre."[39] They might occasionally, upon request, support the cause of a friendly people unjustly treated in commercial affairs, although they never considered controversies over their own commercial relations sufficient to justify war. Unlike European princes, they apparently had no desire whatever to expand their domain by force and conquest. The sole exception is to be found in Hythlodaye's statement that, if they were troubled by over-population, the Utopians sent colonies to unoccupied land in neighboring countries, and would if necessary defend with arms what they considered their right to make use of empty and therefore wasted land. In their view, the employment of force was justified when a people held needed land "voyde and vacaunt to no good nor profitable vse, kepyng other from the vse and possession of it, whiche notwithstandyng by the lawe of nature ought thereof to be nowryshed and relieued."[40]

It would seem that Hythlodaye—and therefore More—had no very high opinion of international relations as they were conducted in Europe. To illustrate, he imagines in the first book[41] the plottings and plannings of the French king against his neighbors—a truce on the one hand, bribery on the other, the conclusion of a treaty here, a league there—all of which agreements were designed simply to disguise the real purposes of the king. In the second book we find that the Utopians would have none of such inter-

---

[37] *Sir Thomas More's Utopia*, Collins ed., p. 58.   [38] *Ibid.*, p. 110.
[39] *Ibid.*   [40] *Ibid.*, p. 67.   [41] *Ibid.*, pp. 31–32.

national relations. Wherever possible they manifested an unselfish friendship toward neighboring countries. But as for leagues, Hythlodaye declares,

> which in other places betwene countrey and countrey be so ofte concluded, broken, and made agayne, they neuer make none with anye nacion. For to what purpose serue leagues? saye they; as though nature had not set sufficient loue betwene man and man. And who so regardeth not nature, thynke yowe that he wyll passe for wordes? They be brought into thys opinion chiefely bicause that in thoes parties of the worlde leagues betwene princes be wont to be kept and obserued very slenderly.[42]

Of course, "here in Europa," adds Hythlodaye with biting sarcasm,

> and especiallye in thies partes, where the faythe and religion of Christe reygneth, the maiestie of leagues is euerye where estemed holly and inuiolable; partlye through the iustice and goodnes of princes, and partelye through the reuerence of great byshoppes. Whyche, lyke as they make no promysse themselfes, but they doo verye religiouslye perfourme the same, so they exhorte all prynces in any wyse to abyde by theyre promisses; and them that refuse or denye so to do, by theire pontificall powre and aucthorytie they compell therto. And surely they thynke well that it myght seme a verye reprochefull thynge, yf in the leagues of them, whyche by a peculiare name be called faythfull, faythe shoulde haue no place.[43]

But the Utopians, although—fortunately for them—they had enjoyed no experience in the international affairs of Europe, were sufficiently aware of the shortcomings of human nature, and especially the nature of rulers, to repose no confidence in leagues. In the words of Hythlodaye,

> in that newefonnde parte of the worlde, whiche is scaselye so farre from vs beyonde the lyne equinoctiall, as owre lyfe and manners be dissidente from theirs, no truste nor confydence is in leagues. But the mo and holyer cerymonies the league is knytte vp with, the soner it is broken, by some cauillation founde in the woordes; whyche manye tymes of purpose be so craftelye put in and placed, that the bandes can neuer be so sure nor so stronge, but they wyll fynde some hole open to crepe owte at, and to breake bothe league and trewthe.[44]

The trouble, as Hythlodaye saw it, was that there were two standards of justice, one for the state and one for the individual.

> The whiche crafty dealynge [he exclaims], yea, the whiche fraude and deceyte, yf they shoulde knowe it to bee practysed amonge pryuate men in theire bargaynes and contractes, they woulde incontinent crye owte at it with a sower countenaunce, as an offence most detestable, and worthie to be punyshed with a shamefull death; yea, euen verye they that auaunce themselfes authours of like councel geuen to princes.[45]

[42] Ibid., p. 107.   [43] Ibid., pp. 107–8.   [44] Ibid., p. 108.   [45] Ibid.

The result apparently was that not a few thought either

that all iustice is but a basse and a lowe vertue, and whiche aualeth it self farre vnder the hyghe dignitie of kynges; or, at the least wyse, that there be two iustices; the one mete for the inferioure sorte of the people, goinge a fote and crepynge by lowe on the grounde, and bounde downe on euery side with many bandes, because it shall not run at rouers: the other a pryncely vertue, whiche lyke as it is of muche hygher maiestie then the other poore iustice, so also it is of muche more lybertie, as to the whiche nothinge is vnlawful that it lusteth after.[46]

But the Utopians had another and still more fundamental reason for disapproving of leagues. In their opinion the custom of entering into such agreements

causeth men (as though nations which be separate a sondre by the space of a lytle hyl or a ryuer, were coupled together by no societe or bonde of nature), to thynke them selfes borne aduersaryes and enemyes one to an other; and that it is lawfull for the one to seke the death and destruction of the other, if leagues were not; yea, and that, after the leagues be accorded, fryndeshyppe dothe not growe and encrease; but the lycence of robbynge and stealynge doth styll remayne, as farfurthe as, for lacke of forsight and aduisement in writinge the woordes of the league, anny sentence or clause to the contrary is not therin suffycyentlye comprehended.[47]

The Utopians utterly rejected such a view. Their conception looked toward an international fellowship,

that is, that no man ought to be counted an enemy, whyche hath done no iniury; and that the felowshyppe of nature is a stronge league; and that men be better and more surely knitte togethers by loue and beneuolence, then by couenauntes of leagues; by hartie affection of minde, then by woordes.[48]

It will be interesting also to contrast certain passages on the administration of law and justice in the two books of the *Utopia*. In the first book Hythlodaye reports the comments of a certain English lawyer on the harsh so-called justice, which, under the then-existing laws, inflicted the death penalty for minor crimes. More, speaking of course through Hythlodaye, reveals the evil effects of such a system, to which reference has been made on a previous page. But this was not the only indictment which Hythlodaye brought against the law. Using an imaginative instance—which unfortunately bore a close resemblance to actual facts—he "supposes" a ruler to be busy with his advisers devising schemes for the raising of money. One adviser

putteth the kyng in remembraunce of certeyn olde and moughte-eaten lawes, that of long tyme haue not bene put in execution; whiche, because no man can

---

[46] *More's Utopia*, Collins ed., pp. 108–9.   [47] *Ibid.*, p. 109.   [48] *Ibid.*

remembre that they were made, euerie man hath transgressed. The fynes of thies lawes he counselleth the kynge to require: for there is no waye so proffytable, nor more honorable; as the whiche hath a shewe and coloure of iustice.[49]

Another adviser suggests that the king

forbidde manye thynges vnder great penalties and fines, especially suche thynges as is for the peoples profit not be vsed; and afterward to dispence for money with them, which by this prohibicion susteyne losse and dammage. For by this meanes the fauour of the people is wonne, and proffite riseth two wayes: first by takyng forfaytes of them whom couetousnes of gaynes hath brought in daunger of thys statute; and also by sellynge preuyleges and licences; whiche the better that the prynce is forsothe, the deerer he selleth them; as one that is lothe to graunte to any pryuate persone any thyng that is agaynste the proffyt of hys people; and therfore maye sell none but at an exceding dere pryce.[50]

Still another adviser "giueth the kynge counsell to endaunger vnto hys grace the iudges of the Reyalme, that he maye haue them euer on hys syde; whyche muste in euerye matter despute and reason for the kynges rygth."[51] In short, the king's "yes men" (to employ a phrase of our own day), having unanimously agreed that "no abundance of gold can be sufficient for a prince," are likewise in agreement that

a kynge, thoughe he would, can do nothynge uniustly; for all that all men haue, yea also the men them selfes, be all his; and that euery man hath so much of his owne as the kynges gentilnes hath not taken from hym; and that it shalbe moste for the kynges aduauntage that his subiectes haue very lytle or nothing in their possession; as whose sauegarde dothe herein consiste, that his people do not waxe wanton and wealthie through riches and libertie; because, where thies thinges be, there men be not wonte patientlye to obeye harde, vniuste, and vnlawfull commaundementes; where as, on the other part, neade and pouertie doth holde downe and kepe vnder stowte courages, and maketh them patient perforce, takyng from them bolde and rebellynge stomakes.[52]

Turning now to justice and law in Utopia, we find that the death penalty was but rarely imposed in that country. For most misdeeds, in fact, there was "no prescript punyshment appoynted by anye lawe." The proper authorities, therefore, were free to use their good judgment in dealing with each case. Thus, "accordinge to the heynousenes of the offence, or contrarye, so the punyshemente is moderated by the discretion of the councell."[53] The Utopians apparently took a common-sense view of punishment, feeling that it should operate both to restrain malefactors and to benefit the state. Therefore

moste commenlye the moste heynous faultes be punyshed with the incommoditie of bondage. For that they suppose to be to the offenders no lesse griefe, and to

---
[49] *Ibid.*, p. 35.   [50] *Ibid.*   [51] *Ibid.*   [52] *Ibid.*, p. 36.   [53] *Ibid.*, p. 103.

the common wealth more profitable, then if they should hastely put them to death, and make them out of the waye. For there cummeth more profite of theire laboure, then of theire deathe; and by theire example they feare other the lenger from lyke offences.[54]

If certain criminals, however, turned out to be incorrigible, "if they, beinge thus vsed, doo rebell and kicke agayne, then forsothe they be slayne as desperate and wilde beastes, whom nother pryson nor chayne could restraine and kepe vnder."[55] On the other hand, if they accepted their punishment and regretted their misdeeds, they might again become normal members of society.

But they whiche take theire bondage patientlye be not left all hopeles. For after they haue bene broken and tamed with longe myseries, yf then they shewe suche repentaunce, wherebye it maye be perceaued that they be soryer for theire offence then for theire punyshemente, sumtymes by the Pryncres prerogatyue, and sumtymes by the voyce and consent of the people, theire bondage other is mitigated, or els cleane remytted and forgeuen.[56]

The contrast between those abuses of law and government which More observed around him, and conditions in Utopia, is still further developed in Hythlodaye's account. The Utopians, he declared, lived in harmony, and

no magistrate is other hawte or ferefull. Fathers they be called, and lyke fathers they vse themselfes. The citizens (as it is their dewtie) do willingly exhibite vnto them dewe honoure, without any compulsion. Nor the prince hymselfe is not knowen from the other by his apparel, nor by a crown or diademe or cappe of maintenaunce, but by a littell sheffe of corne caried before hym.[57]

The Utopians, it appears, had little use for legal restrictions.

Thei haue [continues Hythlodaye] but few lawes. For to people so instructe and institute very fewe do suffice. Yea this thynge they chieflye reproue amonge other nations, that innumerable bokes of lawes and expositions vpon the same be not sufficient. But they thinke it against al right and iustice, that men shuld be bound to thoes lawes, whiche other be in numbre mo then be able to be readde, or els blinder and darker, then that any man can well vnderstande them.[58]

Having so few laws, the Utopians had little need for lawyers. Therefore

they vtterly exclude and bannyshe all proctours and sergeauntes at the lawe, which craftely handell matters, and subtelly dispute of the lawes. For they thinke it most mete, that euery man shuld pleade his owne matter, and tell the same tale before the iudge, that he would tel to his man of lawe. So shall there be lesse circumstaunce of wordes, and the trwth shal soner cum to light.[59]

But what of the judge? Hythlodaye outlines the judicial function in a few phrases: "the iudge with a discrete iudgement doth waye the wordes

---

[54] *More's Utopia*, Collins ed., pp. 103–4.   [55] *Ibid.*, p. 104.   [56] *Ibid.*
[57] *Ibid.*, p. 105.   [58] *Ibid.*, pp. 105–6.   [59] *Ibid.*, p. 106.

of hym whom no lawier hath instruct with deceit; and whiles he helpeth and beareth out simple wittes agaynst the false and malicious circumuertions of craftie chyldren."[60]

Such a straightforward, efficient system of justice as that of the Utopians was not to be found in other countries, Hythlodaye observed, and the reason was simply that those countries had such a vast number of "blynd and intricate lawes." But in Utopia, he points out, everyone could be skilled in the law.

For, as I sayde, they haue verye fewe lawes; and the playnner and grosser that anye interpretation is, that they allowe as most iuste. For all lawes (saye they) bee made and publysshed onelye to thenthente, that by them euerye man shoulde be put in remembraunce of hys dewtye. But the craftye and subtyll interpretation of them can put verye fewe in that remembraunce (for they be but fewe that do perceaue them); where as the simple, the plaine, and grosse meaning of the lawes is open to euerye man.[61]

Some mention has already been made of social and economic evils prevailing in England in the early part of the sixteenth century. In the first book of the *Utopia* More furnishes, in the language of Hythlodaye, a detailed description of those unfortunate conditions: of ignorance and widespread unemployment, the prevalence of poverty and crime, the dislocation of agriculture through overemphasis on wool production, the resultant high prices, and the concentration of wealth in the hands of a few who often wasted it in riotous living. And in the second book More suggests, often seriously but sometimes fancifully, remedies for the ills of society.

Thus, in depicting Utopian institutions, Hythlodaye describes for us a system of communism in which there is employment for everybody, poverty is unknown, agriculture produces more than plenty for all, money is not used, crime is reduced to a minimum, and both overwork and idle or harmful amusements are replaced by ample leisure pleasantly and profitably employed. In Utopia, training in useful activities, and education for the true enjoyment of leisure, were available to all. Since wealth belonged to all, no Utopian was either rich or poor. Each was required to contribute labor for the common welfare, yet because all shared in useful labor, the hours of work were but six each day.

Of each twenty-four hours, Hythlodaye explains, the Utopians

appoynte and assygne only vi. of those houres to woorke; iii. before none, vpon the whyche they goo streyghte to dyner; and after dyner, when they haue rested ii houres, then they woorke iii.; and vpon that they goo to supper. About viii. of the clocke in the euenynge (cowntynge one of the clocke at the fyrste houre after

---

[60] *Ibid*. [61] *Ibid*.

none) they go to bedde. viii. houres they giue to sleape. All the voide time, that is betwene the houres of woorke, slepe, and meate, that they be suffered to bestowe, euerye man as he lyketh beste hym selfe: not to thyntente they shoulde myspende thys tyme in ryote, or sloughfullenes; but, beynge then lycensed from the laboure of theyr owne occupacyons, to bestowe the time wel and thriftely vpon some other good science, as shall please them.[62]

In the early morning they might attend the various public lectures given daily, or follow other pursuits which interested them; or again, "yf any man had rather bestowe thys tyme vpon hys owne occupatyon (as yt chaunceth in manye, whose myndes ryse not in the contemplatyon of annye scyence lyberal), he is not letted nor prohibited, but is also praysed and commended, as profitable to the common wealthe."[63] In the evenings "after supper," the Utopians gave one hour over to play,

in somer in their gardeynes, in winter in their commen halles, where they dyne and suppe. There they exercise them selfes in musyke, or els in honeste and holsome communicacion. Diceplaye, and suche other folish and pernicious games, they knowe not.[64]

To the skeptic of More's age, as to the skeptic of our own, the theory of a six-hour working day seemed an economic fallacy. Aware of this skepticism More meets it by providing Hythlodaye with an answer to the scoffers:

But here, lease you be deceaued, one thinge you muste looke more narrowly vpon. For seinge they bestowe but vi. houres in woork, perchaunce you maye thinke that the lacke of some necessarye thinges hereof may ensewe. But this is nothinge so. For that small time is not only inough, but also to muche, for the stoore and abundaunce of all thinges that be requisite, other for the necessitie or commoditie of liffe.[65]

Realizing that this statement alone will not convince the skeptic with conventional ideas about the working day, Hythlodaye immediately continues:

The whiche thing yow also shall perceaue, if you weye and consider with your selfes how great a parte of the people in other contreis lyueth ydle. First, almoost all women, which be the halfe of the hole numbre; or els, if the women be annye where occupied, their most comonlye in their steade the men be ydle. Besydes thys, how great, and howe ydle a companye ys theyr of prystes, and relygyous men, as they call them? Put there to all ryche men, specyallye all landed men, whyche comonly be called gentylmen, and noble men. Take into this numbre also their seruauntes; I meane, all that flocke of stout, bragging, russhe bucklers. Ioyne to them also sturdy and valiaunt beggers, clokinge their idle leffe

---

[62] *More's Utopia*, Collins ed., pp. 60–61.   [63] *Ibid.*, p. 61.   [64] *Ibid.*   [65] *Ibid.*, pp. 61–62.

vnder the colour of some disease or sickenes. And truely you shall find them much fewer then you thought, by whose labour all these thynges be gotten, that men vse and lyue bye.[66]

This, however, was but part of Hythlodaye's demonstration.

> Nowe consyder wyth youre selfe [he adds], of thies fewe that do woorke, how few be occupied in necessary woorkes. For where money beareth all the swing, ther many vayne and superfluous occupations must nedys be vsed, to serue only for ryotous superfluyte and vnhonest pleasure. For the same multytude that now is occupied in woorke, if they were deuided into so few occupations as the necessary vse of nature requyreth, in so greate plentye of thinges, as then of necessity wolde ensue, doubtles the prices wolde be to lytle for the artifycers to maynteyne theyre lyuynges. But yf all thyes, that be nowe bisiede about vnprofitable occupations, with all the hole flocke of them that lyue ydellye and slouthfullye, whyche consume and waste euerye one of them more of thies thinges that come by other mens laboure, then ii. of the work men themselfes doo; yf all thyes (I saye) were sette to profytable occupatyons, yowe easelye perceaue howe lytle tyme wolde be enoughe, yea and to muche, to stoore vs wyth all thynges that maye be requysyte other for necessytye, or for commodytye; yea, or for pleasure, so that the same pleasure be trewe and naturall.[67]

As regards material things the Utopians, it is clear, had a standard of value quite different from that of the rest of the world. Indeed, their views and practice on this point were so unconventional that Hythlodaye was prepared to have his description of them greeted with incredulity. Gold and silver, for example, the Utopians considered of no worth except for occasional dealings with foreigners. To emphasize their lack of value, they employed these metals only for ignominious purposes. Thus, we are told, "of gold and siluer they make commonlye chamber pottes and other like vesselles that serue for most vile vses," and they fashioned chains of gold and silver to bind prisoners. Again, "who so euer for any offence be infamed, by their eares hange ringes of golde; vpon their fingers they were ringes of golde, and about their neckes chaynes of gold; and in conclusion their heades be tiede about with golde."[68] In short, "by all meanes that may be, they procure to haue gold and siluer emong them in reproche and infamy."[69] The result was that gold and silver, "which other nations do as greuously and sorroufully forgo, as in a maner from their owne liues: if they should all togethers at ones be taken from the vtopians, no man there wold thinke that he had lost the worth of one farthing."[70]

Precious stones, too, the Utopians considered of no real value. If they chanced to find pearls or other jewels, they gave them as playthings to their children. The latter, while

[66] *Ibid.*, p. 62.   [67] *Ibid.*, pp. 62–63.   [68] *Ibid.*, p. 77.   [69] *Ibid.*   [70] *Ibid.*, pp. 77–78.

in the first yeares of their childhod they make much and be fond and proud of such ornamentes, so when they be a little more growen in yeares and discretion, perceiuing that none but children do were such toies and trifeles, they lay them awaye euen of theyre owne shamefastenes, wythowte annye biddyng of there parentes: euen as oure chyldren, when they waxe bygge, doo caste awaye nuttes, brouches, and puppettes.[71]

It is apparent that the Utopians set little store by the vanities of life. They dressed simply, as they lived simply, and had no desire for useless luxuries, vain honors, and "counterfeit" pleasures. Here More takes a sly dig at gaming and hunting, two of the chief "pleasures" of the wealthy in his own country. The Utopians, we are told, could find no pleasure in the foolish game of "castynge the dice upon a table."[72] And

what delite can there be [they wondered], and not rather dyspleasure, in hearynge the barkynge and howlynge of dogges? Or what greater pleasure is there to be felte, when a dogge followeth an hare, then when a dogge followeth a dogge? for one thynge is done in both; that is to saye, runninge; if thou haste pleasure therein. But if the hope of slaughter, and the expectation of tearynge in pieces the beaste dothe please the, thou shouldest rather be moued with pitie to see a seely innocent hare murdered of a dogge; the weake of the stronger; the fearefull of the fearce; the innocente of the cruell and vnmercyfull.[73]

The people of Utopia, in short, would have none of the "noble sport" of the huntsman.

Therefore all thys exercyse of huntynge, as a thynge vnworthye to be vsed of free men, the Vtopians haue reiected to their bochers; to the whiche crafte (as wee sayde before) they appointe ther bondmen. For they counte huntyng the loweste, vyleste, and moste abiecte parte of bocherye; and the other partes of it more profytable and more honeste, as whiche do brynge muche more commoditie; and doo kyll beastes onlye for necessytie. Where as the hunter seketh nothynge but pleasure of the seely and wofull beastes slaughter and murder. The whiche pleasure in beholdyng death they thynke dothe ryse in the very beastes, other of a cruell affection of mynde, or els to be chaunged in continuaunce of time into crueltie, by longe vse of so cruell a pleasure.[74]

And finally, by way of completing the contrast between Utopia and the contemporary world of More, a passage may be quoted from the end of the *Utopia's* second book, in which Hythlodaye sums up his indictment of the evils of society. Having pictured the happy state of affairs in Utopia, Hythlodaye turns to conditions existing in European nations, "among whom," he exclaims with some bitterness, "I forsake God, if I can fynde any signe or token of equitie and iustice."[75] As the succeeding indictment is of some length, it is here divided into a series of numbered paragraphs.

[71] *More's Utopia,* Collins ed., p. 78.   [72] *Ibid.,* p. 89.   [73] *Ibid.*   [74] *Ibid.*   [75] *Ibid.,* p. 139.

1. For what iustice is this, that a ryche goldsmythe or an vsurer, or, to be shorte, any of them, whyche other doo nothyng at all; or els that whiche they do is suche, that it is not very necessary to the commen wealthe; should haue a pleasaunt and a welthy lyuynge, other by Idilnes, or by vnnecessary busynes? when in the meane tyme poore labourers, carters, yronsmythes, carpenters, and plowmen, by so great and continual toyle, as drawyng and bearyng beastes be skant able to susteine; and agayn so necessary toyle that with out it no commen wealth were able to continewe and endure one yere; do yet get so harde and poore a lyuing, and lyue so wretched and miserable a lyfe, that the state and condition of the labouring beastes maye seme muche better and welthier. For they be not put to so contynuall laboure, nor theire lyuynge is not muche worse; yea, to them much pleasaunter; takynge no thowghte in the meane season for the tyme to come.[76]

2. But thies seilie poore wretches be presently tormented with barreyne and vnfrutefull labour. And the remembraunce of theire poore indigent and begerlye olde age kylleth them vp. For theire dayly wages is so lytle that it will not suffice for the same daye; muche lesse it yeldeth any ouerplus, that may dayly be layde vp for the relyefe of olde age.[77]

3. Is not thys an vniust and an vnkynd publyque weale, whyche gyueth great fees and rewardes to gentelmen, as they call them, and to goldsmythes, and to suche other, whiche be other ydell persones or els onlye flatterers, and deuysers of vayne pleasures; and, of the contrary parte, maketh no gentle prouision for poore plowmen, coliars, laborers, carters, yronsmythes, and carpenters; without whome no commen wealth can continewe?[78]

4. But when it hath abused the laboures of theire lusty and flowringe age, at the laste, when they be oppressed with olde age and syckenes, being nedye, poore, and indigent of all thynges; then, forgettynge theire so many paynfull watchynges, not remembrynge theire so many and so great benefytes; recompenseth and acquyteth them moste vnkyndly with myserable death.[79]

5. And yet besides this the riche men not only by priuate fraud, but also by commen lawes, do euery day plucke and snatche away from the poore some parte of their daily liuing. So, where as it semed before uniuste to recompense with vnkindnes their paynes that haue bene beneficiall to the publique weale, nowe they haue to this their wrong and vniuste dealinge (whiche is yet a muche worse pointe), geuen the name of iustice, yea, and that by force of a law.[80]

6. Therfore when I consider and way in my mind all thies commen wealthes which now a dayes any where do florish, so god helpe me, I can perceaue nothing but a certein conspiracy of riche men, procuringe theire owne commodities vnder the name and title of the commen wealth.[81]

7. They inuent and deuise all meanes and craftes, first how to kipe safely without feare of lesing that they haue vniustly gathered together; and next how to hire and abuse the woorke and labour of the poore for as litle money as may be.[82]

---

[76] Ibid.
[77] Ibid., pp. 139-40.
[78] Ibid., p. 140.
[79] Ibid.
[80] Ibid.
[81] Ibid.
[82] Ibid., pp. 140-41.

8. Thies deuyses when the riche men haue decreed to be kept and obserued for the commen wealthes sake, that is to saye, for the wealth also of the poore people, then they be made lawes.[83]

9. But thies most wicked and vicious men, when they haue by their vnsatiable couetousnes deuided emong themselfes all those thinges which wold haue suffised all men, yet howe farre be they from the wealth and felicity of the vtopian commen wealth? owt of the which in that all the desire of moneye with the vse therof is vtterly secluded and bannisshed, howe great a heape of cares is cut away? How greate an occasion of wickednes and mischiefe is plucked vp by the rotes?[84]

10. For who knoweth not that fraud, theft, rauine, brauling, quarrelling, brabling, striffe, chiding, contention, murder, treason, poisoning; which by dayly punishmentes are rather reuenged then refrained; do dye when money dieth? And also that feare, griefe, care, laboures, and watchinges, do perishe, euen the very same moment that money perissheth? Yea, pouerty it selfe, which only semed to lacke money, if money were gone, it also wold decrease and vanishe away.[85]

11. And that you may perceaue this more plainly, consider with your selfes some barrein and vnfrutefull yeare, wherin many thousandes of people haue starued for honger. I dare be bolde to say, that in the end of that penury so much corne or grain might haue bene found in the riche mens barnes, if they had bene searched, as being deuided emong them, whome famine and pestilence hath killed, no man at all should haue felt that plage and penury.[86]

12. So easely might men gett their liuinge, if that same worthye princesse, lady money, did not alon stoppe vp the way betwene vs and our liuing; whiche a goddes name was very excellently deuised and inuented, that by her the way therto should be opened.[87]

13. I am sewer the ryche men perceaue thys, nor they be not ignoraunte how much better yt werre to lacke noo necessarye thynge then to abunde with ouermuch superfluyte; to be rydde owte of innumerable cares and trowbles, then to be beseiged wyth greate ryches. And I dowte not that other the respecte of euery mans priuate commoditie, or els the aucthority of oure sauioure Christe (which for his great wisdom could not but know what were best, and for his inestimable goodnes cold not but counsell to that which he knew to be best) wold haue brought all the worlde long agoo into the lawes of this weale publique, if it were not that one only beast, the princesse and mother of all mischiefe, pride, doth withstonde and let it.[88]

14. She measureth not wealth and prosperity by here own commodities, but by the miseriies and incommodities of other. She wold not by her good will be made a goddes, if there were no wretches left, whom she might be lady ouer to mocke and scorne; ouer whose miseries her felicity might shine, whose pouerty she might vexe, torment, and encrease by gorgiously setting furthe her riches. This hell hound crepeth in to mens hartes, and plucketh them backe from

---

[83] *More's Utopia*, Collins ed., p. 141.   [84] *Ibid.*   [85] *Ibid.*
[86] *Ibid.*   [87] *Ibid.*, pp. 141–42.   [88] *Ibid.*, p. 142.

entering the right pathe of liffe; and is so depely roted in mens brestes, that she can not be plucked out.[89]

Here we may imagine that, having completed his indictment, Hythlodaye paused for a moment. Then, harking back to the ideal conditions of Utopia, and speaking doubtless in a quieter tone, he made, as More tells us, "an ende of his tale:"[90]

This forme and fassion of a weale publique, which I wold gladly wisshe vnto all nations, I am glad yet that it hath chaunced to the Vtopians; which haue followed those institutions of liffe, wherby they haue laid such fondations of their common wealth, as shall continew and last, not only wealthely, but also, as farre as mans wit maye iudge and coniecture, shall endure for euer. For seinge the chiefe causes of ambition and sedition with other vices be plucked vp by the rootes and abandoned at home, there can be no ieopardye of domesticall dissention; which alone hathe caste vnder fote and broughte to noughte the well fortefied and strongly defenced wealth and riches of many cities. But for asmuch as perfect concord remaineth, and holsome lawes be executed at home, the enuy of all forrein princes be not able to shake or moue the empire, though they haue many tymes long ago gone about to do it, beinge euermore dreuen backe.[91]

Although the *Utopia* is throughout imaginative, says Professor Hugh Goitein,[92] the imagination employed in its writing is that of practical wisdom.

And that [he continues] is the secret of the *Utopia's* success. There are books in plenty that give free rein to the imagination, and by their flight from reality cheat the illusions of life. But no such work has ever enjoyed a tithe of the influence the *Utopia* has wielded. From whatever point of view we look at it its success has been remarkable. No one standard can measure it, and critics find it hard to select anything like a representative indication.[93]

The truth is that the appeal of the *Utopia* is universal.

It struck a responsive chord in the hearts of thoughtful men and women everywhere in Europe, and Utopia became the day-dream of the Renaissance. The history of modern Europe is the story of the development of the Renaissance forces, and as each in turn has helped to mould the frame of its social life, it has realised one or other aspect of that wonderful dream.[94]

The gradual adoption of More's "Utopian" ideas is thus described by Professor Goitein:

Slowly, but inevitably, the stuff of Utopia has replaced the outworn fabric of European society. So thoroughly has this process worked itself out that at the

---

[89] *Ibid.* [90] *Ibid.*, p. 143. [91] *Ibid.*, pp. 142-43.
[92] In the Introduction to his edition of the *Utopia* published in the volume, *Sir Thomas More, The Utopia . . . Francis, Lord Bacon, The New Atlantis.*
[93] *Ibid.*, pp. 20-21. [94] *Ibid.*, p. 21.

beginning of the last century there were only two of its cardinal ideas still unrealised, and of these the abolition of chattel slavery was fast becoming the most urgent public question of the day. It was this that kindled for the last time the embers of the Renaissance fires.[95]

The occasion for this revival of the fire of the Renaissance was, we are told, "a ghastly comedy" which

had been enacting in Europe. The Congress of Vienna had staged a masque of the chief political vices with the crowning of virtue for an interlude. With stately phrase and solemn gesture the world was declared rid of chattel slavery. But the humour of Utopia was not to be baulked. The spirit of More walked the earth once more.[96]

But how was this spirit to manifest itself?

It touched the minds of a small band of Englishmen, who learnt that true religion is not to retire from the world when evil triumphs, but to make the world its home and mould social life after the pattern it divines. It touched them with its pristine courage, its undaunted patience, its sacramental handling of all common things. Theirs was the fire of his imagination, theirs, too, his passionate humanism. And they set themselves to do what the Treaty had pretended to do, nowise daunted by its gigantic cheat.[97]

There is, however, still another great dream to be realized, Professor Goitein reminds us in a concluding passage:

And thus it comes about that, with chattel slavery banished, there is but one thing left to realise of the day-dream of the Renaissance—to rid the world of organised war. All too recently an even ghastlier comedy has been enacting in Europe with a varied masque but a similar interlude. With stately phrase and solemn gesture the world was declared rid of organized war. But the humour of Utopia. . . . But that is a theme for other pens. Our concern is but with day-dreams, the daydreams of an artist who, despite the gloom, can see the sun on the wall, and when the sun goes down and the stars appear can feel the calm of an all pervading peace slowly steal over a careworn world.[98]

In considering More's place in history, many have thought of him chiefly as embodying the great principle of freedom of conscience. Did he not himself tell the judges who unjustly condemned him to death that the claims of conscience come before all else in this world? And because he refused to violate his conscience by taking the oath which his sovereign demanded, he was executed—on perjured evidence. Yet the issues involved were more fundamental even than freedom of conscience. Henry VIII sought to make himself arbiter not only of human law but of that higher law which for long, long centuries men have regarded as of divine origin.

---

[95] Introduction of Goitein to his ed. of *Sir Thomas More, The Utopia* . . . , p. 21.
[96] *Ibid.* [97] *Ibid.*, pp. 21-22. [98] *Ibid.*, p. 22.

More was loyal to his king, but with him loyalty to the temporal authorities should and must come after loyalty to God. The oath which Henry demanded of him conflicted with his conception of his duty under the higher law, and he therefore declined to take it. The essential cause of More's stand was his belief, as Professor R. W. Chambers tells us, "that there is a Divine and a Natural Law, which cannot be set aside to provide a shortcut for the despotism of the omni-competent state."[99]

The importance of this belief not only in More's age but in our age and in ages to come cannot be overstressed. It is largely because many have rejected it, or have accepted it but half-heartedly, that the theory of the omnipotent state has long been with us. The question of acceptance or rejection still confronts us with all its implications, and upon our answer, "upon . . . whether or no we place Divine Law in the last resort above the Law of the State—depends the whole future of the world."[100]

The courage of St. Thomas More is at once a challenge and a guide to posterity.

More's death was one of those mighty events [declares Professor Chambers in language appropriate to the thought], for their own sakes infinitely valuable, in which a great man has given proof of "man's unconquerable mind," by facing death rather than say what he believes to be untrue. *Upon the fact that there are men and women willing to do this, depends the value of all human life, which otherwise can be only what it was to poor Macbeth*

a tale
Told by an idiot, full of sound and fury,
Signifying nothing.[101]

---

[99] *The Place of Sir Thomas More in English Literature and History*, p. 113.
[100] *Ibid.*, p. 118.   [101] *Ibid.*, pp. 87–88.

Chapter XXVIII

CALVINISM

THE CONCEPTIONS OF JOHN CALVIN (1509–64) PRESENT A STRIKING CONTRAST to those of St. Thomas More. They were destined, however, to exert a powerful influence on the development of modern political thought, though their actual effect was to be singularly different from anything anticipated by the great leader of the Geneva Reform.

Born of a Catholic family at Noyon, in Picardy, Calvin received an excellent education which his father at first intended as preparation for the Church. Later, however, the law was thought to be his calling, and Calvin therefore left the University of Paris for Orleans, where he studied and subsequently taught and practiced law. But while still in his early twenties he became deeply interested in the religious controversies of the day. Apparently he was particularly influenced at this period by the clear thinking of Erasmus on the one hand, and on the other by certain of Luther's religious views. The result was that he renounced the Catholic faith and gave the rest of his life to the cause of reform.

It soon became manifest that he was developing very definite views of his own on that subject. It was impossible, however, for him to put these views into effect in France, and he therefore withdrew to Basel, later repairing to Geneva where—except for a brief three-year period—he passed the rest of his life, and where he found conditions suitable for translating his doctrines into practice.

No attempt can be made here to deal with Calvin's theological views as such, but it will be necessary to examine certain aspects of the system which he developed and expounded in successive editions of his *Institutes of the Christian Religion*.[1] In his conception, emphasis in the attainment of Chris-

---

[1] First published, in brief and summary form, in 1536, this small work, was greatly enlarged, and reissued in 1539. The first two editions were in Latin, but were followed by a French version in 1541. Other Latin editions prepared by Calvin, in enlarged and revised form, were published in 1543, 1550, and 1559, French versions of these new editions appearing in 1545, 1551, and 1560. In this process of revision the *Institutes* grew from a small tractate of only six chapters into a treatise of eighty chapters. Calvin was an accomplished Latinist, but it was when he wrote in his native tongue that the full power, eloquence, and lucidity of his style became apparent. His place in the literature of France is secure, for he demonstrated that French prose could be effectively used for the clear, vigorous, and logical expression of ideas, however abstract they might be.

tian ideals should be placed on an active and strenuous rather than a contemplative life. But while the activities of such a life were to be subject to the supervision of the secular authorities, they were likewise subject to the constant scrutiny of the authorities of the Protestant Church. And since the officials of the state must themselves be members of the Church, and could thus be called to account by the appropriate organs of the Church, it becomes clear that to Calvin, in the last analysis, the supreme authority in the temporal as well as the spiritual field is the Church. In this view of things the true sovereign of the state is God, the magistrate, as well as the pastor, being the "vicar" of God. And the ultimate purpose of government is to maintain the true religion in doctrine and worship. The state exists, in short, for the glory of God. Hence all proper human activities, however secular in nature, are directed toward that end, with the result that the workaday virtues, industry, thrift and saving, are sanctified, as it were, and raised toward the level of the moral virtues. Worldly activities are thus given a spiritual status, and it is but a step further to place a religious stamp of approval upon worldly success—a step which some who followed Calvin did not hesitate to take.

The state, then, according to the *Institutes,* is of divine origin and not a product of human reason. Indeed Calvin appears to have entertained no very flattering opinion of man as a reasoning creature. Human beings were prone to evil, and therefore a wise and merciful God had provided the state, with a government having the power to coerce men to good behavior. The *corpus juris* of Calvin's state was the Bible, and the authority of its ruler was of divine origin. This being the case, subjects owed full and complete obedience to their superiors. To disobey the ruler would be to defy one who is ordained of God. But what if princes are cruel and tyrannical? It is not for subjects to question their actions, Calvin maintains. They must yield both obedience and reverence to the prince (however erring he may be), and should regard his misconduct as a punishment for their own sins. Their only remedy lies in flight, or in prayer that they may be delivered from tyranny.

There were two exceptions to this doctrine, upon which Calvin did not dwell at length, but which appealed to many of his successors. If the ruler

---

"Rapporté à la date de sa publication, le grand ouvrage de Calvin est d'une originalité littéraire qu'il convient de souligner. En 1541, un livre de théologie en langue vulgaire est une innovation. Depuis la restitution des bonnes lettres, la prose française n'avait été illustrée que par des vers, des romans et des contes. Dans l'*Institution de la religion chrétienne,* notre 'vulgaire' parlait pour la première fois,—avec quelle éloquence!—de philosophie, de théologie, de morale, de spiritualité. Calvin est une des gloires les plus originales de nos lettres du XVIe siècle."—Bédier and Hazard, *Histoire de la littérature française,* I, 151.

required of his subjects actions which entailed disobedience to God, his command should not be obeyed. This, it may be said, was the view almost universally accepted and it was therefore accepted by Calvin. In such circumstances, he held, passive disobedience was justified. But were there no circumstances which would justify something more than a mere passive refusal to obey on the part of subjects? As far as the individual subject was concerned, Calvin's answer to this question was in the negative. He did grant, however, that under certain forms of government there might exist a constitutional right—or rather, duty—to resist tyranny. But any such function of restraining the ruler must needs be vested by law in duly constituted organs or officials of the state.[2] It is not a matter which concerns the private person. The most that the latter might do under this system would be to report any irregularities of government to the authorities constitutionally empowered to deal with those matters—if any such authorities existed.

Even for one of the Presbyterian persuasion, it is sometimes difficult to deal altogether calmly with Calvin's political theories. As set forth in the *Institutes,* they cannot but arouse a degree of impatience in the enlightened reader of the present day. The fact of the matter is that, in his preoccupation with the task of imposing his conception of religious salvation upon the people, Calvin had little time to consider their rights as human beings.[3] Fortunately those who adopted his doctrines found it possible—and indeed necessary—to apply them in such manner that they became, so to speak, tools for the forging of liberal principles of government. "It is perhaps one of the minor ironies of history," comments a learned English scholar,[4] "that one whose explicit teaching was almost wholly on the side of established authority should have given a powerful impulse to movements toward freedom and democracy." In France, Calvinists promoted the Huguenot cause of resistance to tyranny with pen and sword; in Scotland, John Knox and his followers interpreted Calvinism as imposing upon them the duty of overthrowing princes who opposed the doctrines of Geneva; in Holland, the Dutch conception of Calvinism was a leading factor in the

---

[2] Calvin mentions in this connection two "popular magistrates" whose office is "to curb the tyranny of kings" (Book IV, chap. xx, sec. 31), and by way of illustration he refers to the "ephori" of the Spartans, the "tribunes of the people" in Rome, and the "demarchs" in Athens.

[3] This is not the place to deal with Calvin's personal characteristics, but it may be said in passing that many have been repelled by his austerity and the harshness (as in the case of the execution of Servetus) of which he was capable in his religious zeal.

[4] Rev. W. R. Matthews in his essay "John Calvin," published in *The Social and Political Ideas of Some Great Thinkers of the Renaissance and the Reformation,* ed. by Hearnshaw, p. 215.

long struggle of the United Provinces for independence; even in Germany, the followers of Calvin, though not so numerous as those of Luther, made their views felt in matters political; and in England, Calvinists played an important rôle in the development of the Puritan theories of government which were to be put into effect in the New World.

Among the immediate followers of Calvin it was Johannes Althusius (c. 1557–1638) who made the most complete exposition of the Calvinistic political theory. Of this German writer and thinker a modern scholar has said: "Calvinist by faith, humanist through his studies at Basel, lawyer in his profession of teacher and city attorney, theorist by temperament and inclination, he is the most profound political thinker between Bodin and Hobbes."[5] "Althusius," adds the same writer, "is the political theorist of Calvinism *par excellence*."[6] The chief work of Althusius, and the one which is of interest here, is his elaborate treatise *Politica methodice digesta*, first published in 1603, of which two revised editions and several reprints appeared during the succeeding half century. For over two centuries thereafter, however, the treatise was but little read, and it was not until 1880 that it was rescued from oblivion by Otto von Gierke in his learned volume, *Johannes Althusius und die Entwicklung der naturrechtlichen Staatstheorien*. Althusius' influence on the subsequent development of political theory was therefore of a limited nature, but in view of his position among the early expounders of certain conceptions of government and the state as these were developed or modified by Calvinist doctrines, it will be well to consider briefly the theories set forth in his *Politica*.

As a devout Calvinist, Althusius vouched the Bible as his chief authority in matters of government, and indeed he cites the Scriptures several thousand times in the course of his long treatise. But he was also well acquainted with ancient literature, with the Roman law, and with political theories and institutions of his day, especially those in the German city-states. He became legal adviser to the City of Emden, and for many years took a lively interest in its political life, his view as a Calvinist being that an active career is preferable to a contemplative life. As would be expected, in the light of his religious convictions, he was also active in the Church, serving as a member of the council of elders; and his religious views naturally colored his political views, with the result that in his treatise government and religion have many points of contact. He maintains in the

---

[5] Carl Joachim Friedrich, in the intro. to his ed. of Althusius' *Politica methodice digesta*, p. xv.

[6] *Ibid.*, p. xvii.

Politica that authority and government are divinely instituted,[7] that the ruler is a servant of God.[8] The state is thus endowed with an aura of sanctity; it is a part of the divine order of things in which church and state are interdependent.

But the actual establishment of Althusius' state was the result of human decision and action. The power to form the state, in other words, belonged to the people. Not, however, to the people *en masse,* as a single large group of separate and distinct individuals. Here we come to the central thesis of the *Politica*—that the units which form the state are groups, rather than individuals.[9] In Althusius' view, human beings were driven by necessity into group formations in an ascending series, beginning with the family and ending with the state.[10] Each larger group is made up of smaller groups, with the result that since he is a unit only of the smallest group, the individual as such tends to disappear from view by the time we reach the state. Within the small groups the individuals coöperate for the common good, and the aim of the central government is to coördinate the group activities. To this conception Althusius found it necessary to add the further conception of a group-personality. Each association of individuals is conceived to be a group-person, with rights growing out of its formation and pertaining to its sphere of activities. These rights affect its members because of their membership status, but they are not the "natural rights" of the individual which we have encountered elsewhere. Indeed, in such a complex form of association, which proceeds, as it were, from the bottom upward, any natural rights with which the individual may have started tend to become submerged in the conception of an all-inclusive state which, in

---

[7] Althusius *Politica,* chap. i. 12.   [8] *Ibid.,* chap. ix. 21.

[9] It should be noted that Althusius is not wholly consistent on this point, for he does refer at times to the people as a whole.

[10] See especially chaps. i–v of the *Politica*.

A concise analysis of this phase of Althusius' doctrine is given by Lewis: "So there resulted for him a pure natural-law social structure in which family, vocational association, *Gemeinde,* and province stood as necessary and organic members (*Gliederungen*) between the individual and the state; in which the wider association was always constructed from the corporate union of narrower associations and through them first received its members; in which each narrower association, as a true and spontaneous (*originäres*) community, created of itself a special community life and its own sphere of rights, and of these surrendered to the higher association only as many as this higher association required for fulfilling its specific purpose; in which, finally, the state, in all else, is generically similar to its member associations and differs from them only in its exclusive sovereignty, which, as the highest earthly legal power, acquires a multitude of new and peculiar attributes and functions, but finds an impassable barrier in the original right of the narrower association, with the passing of which barrier it becomes void, since, through the breach of the compact of union, the members recover their right to full sovereignty."—*The Genossenschaft-Theory of Otto von Gierke,* p. 128.

swallowing up the various categories of group persons, has also in the same process swallowed up the individual.

This is not to deny a large element of truth in Althusius' theory of the state. There *are* many associations of individuals, and most of them—though not all—exist within the state. In law, such groups are treated as persons, in order that they may be endowed with legal rights and duties. Yet there is, and doubtless will long remain, a conflict of views as to their actual status. Is their personality real, or is it wholly fictitious? Can the group properly be considered a person, or is its so-called personality simply a mask concealing the real, the "natural" persons who have formed it?[11] Is the state merely an association of groups which, in turn, are made up of further groups, with the individual hidden away at the bottom of the scale?[12] Such questions open up vast fields of speculation and argument—far too vast to be explored here. A few observations may, however, be offered regarding these problems.

The first is that the Althusian conception of the state tends to minimize the importance of the human being as a factor of political life. To be sure, that state could not exist without inhabitants, but the individual inhabitants as such are absorbed into—one might almost say devoured by—the group-persons with which the government of the state, as so conceived, is primarily concerned.[13] Now the group-person, whatever other attributes it

[11] "The group at its highest, when it almost seems to merge plurality into unity, is still to me so many individual human beings. What raises it to its highest is not the emergence of a real new personality, over and above the personalities of its members; it is simply the height or quality of the common purpose which individual persons agree in holding and willing—the width, the depth, and the permanence of that purpose. Purposes all; and it is by their purposes that I should judge, range, classify, and also criticize groups."—Barker, *The Citizen's Choice,* pp. 177-78.

[12] It may well have been such a conception that Swift was satirizing when he wrote (On Poetry: a Rhapsody):

    So, naturalists observe, a flea
    Hath smaller fleas that on him prey;
    And these have smaller still to bite 'em;
    And so proceed *ad infinitum.*

See also the verse in similar strain by Augustus De Morgan (*A Budget of Paradoxes,* p. 377):

    Great fleas have little fleas upon their backs to bite 'em,
    And little fleas have lesser fleas, and so *ad infinitum.*
    And the great fleas themselves, in turn, have greater fleas to go on;
    While these again have greater still, and greater still, and so on.

[13] This absorption of the individual is a conception which has had many opponents among the advocates of democracy. The opposing view was stated in classic terms by Emilio Castelar, a great Spanish patriot, orator, and publicist of the last century: "The ideal of a perfect society consists in this, that neither the nation nor humanity shall absorb the individual, but rather that both shall be based upon the capacities and rights of the individual."—*La civilización en los cinco primeros siglos del Christianismo,* I, 13.

may have, does not possess a soul. Nor has it conscience, imagination, power of reason of its own, or sense of its own innate dignity. We do not speak of the group-person as having the right to life, liberty, and the pursuit of happiness. And the government of that state which is conceived as being established by and made up of group-persons is likely to manifest only a remote interest in the essential qualities and rights of the human being.

There is another phase of this subject so important that it may not be passed over without comment. Althusius himself was not in favor of tyranny.[14] The fact remains, however, that the formation of any group tends to concentrate power in the hands of the few who manage the affairs of the group, and that when the lower groups are included in higher groups, and the latter in still higher ones, there is danger that power will become increasingly concentrated until, at the top of the series, we are confronted by absolutism. That this is a very real danger has been demonstrated in our own day.

It is perhaps worth noting [a leading student of Althusius observed a few years ago], that to-day the two most intense embodiments of the idea of state absolutism, namely Italy and Russia, have both developed systems which exactly correspond to what Althusius sets forth. In Italy the system is a hierarchy of corporations, whereas in Russia it is a hierarchy of Soviets or councils.[15]

Let us admit without argument that there are groups or associations which play an important rôle in the life of the state. But let us also remember that the fundamental definition of democracy is government *by the people*—people who exercise the functions of government directly in their assemblies, or indirectly through agents whom they themselves choose and who are responsible to the principals who have chosen them. The democracy may include groups, large and small, but these groups do not hide the individuals from the state and from its government. Cutting across all groups and associations in the democratic state is the immediate and direct interest of the people themselves in a government of their own creation, a government responsible not to groups but to the people as individuals, a government which they may modify or change if it fails to meet their needs. The group theory, carried to its full conclusion, subordinates the individual to the small group, to the larger groups, to the all-inclusive state. The group-personality with which each association is credited tends to become increasingly dominant as larger and larger groups are superimposed one on top of the other. If we push the theory too far we find ourselves in the end

---

[14] *Politica*, chap. xxviii.   [15] Friedrich, *op. cit.*, p. lxxxviii.

confronted by a state which has become a super-personality overriding all other personalities, whether group or individual.

Such a conception is a far cry indeed from the ideals of democracy. It is a conception in which the people are expected to justify their existence by devoting their labor and their lives to the advancement of the state. In a democracy, the state can justify its existence only by promoting the welfare of the people as individuals. Do the people exist for the state, or does the state exist for the people? Is the state to be worshiped as a political idol,[16] or is it to be regarded simply as a means to an end—the happiness of men and women? These are not new questions. In centuries past they have troubled many peoples. And the answers given to them today will affect not only the present but the near and the distant future.

There were certain other effects of Calvinism on political theory which should not be overlooked, particularly as they have influenced the development of political institutions in the Western World. An American historian, the late Professor Herbert D. Foster, has dealt very adequately with this phase of the subject, and a few passages will therefore be quoted from his interesting essay, "International Calvinism through Locks and the Revolution of 1688."[17]

There were, according to Professor Foster, five concepts of political doctrine which were espoused by Calvinists and transmitted by John Locke to the then English colonies of North America. The first of the five concepts was that of a fundamental law of divine origin, which Calvinist writers soon identified with the law of nature. "Calvinists made no pretense," says Professor Foster, "of originating the idea of a law of nature, but constantly cited in its support not only Scripture but also Roman law and classical writers."[18] In the course of time, the followers of Calvin adopted the practice of embodying this law in written documents of a constitutional nature.

Scores of such fundamental written laws—the "Lawes and Statutes of Geneva," Dutch Declaration of Independence and Union of Utrecht, Edict of Nantes, Puritan constitutional documents in Scotland, Old and New England (of nation, colony, town, and church), and the Bill of Rights of 1689—illustrate the Calvinistic habit of embodying convictions in written form and working institutions. Locke himself not only believed in a fundamental "law of nature," "contained

---

[16] For a vigorous denunciation of the state as a political idol, see Joad, *Guide to the Philosophy of Morals and Politics*, p. 768.

[17] Published in *The American Historical Review*, XXXII (April, 1927), 475-99.

[18] *Ibid.*, p. 489.

in the book of the law of Moses," but also drew up a written constitution for a church of the Independent, Huguenot type, and for the colony of Carolina, with its remarkable provisions for tolerance. The idea of fundamental law was put into successful practice in the Revolution of 1688, and was combined by Locke and other Calvinists with the other points in political Calvinism into a working system.[19]

The second concept was that of natural rights. The earlier Calvinist writers soon adopted the theory of these rights in connection with their conception of the natural law.

Before Locke [declares Professor Foster], practically all his natural rights of equality, liberty, life, property, conscience, and reason had been taught by Calvinists as corollaries of the fundamental law of God and nature which created man free, equal, and rational. Locke was familiar with a dozen of these writers, and also with the revolutions on Calvinistic principles in Scotland, France, Holland, and England, which had fought for these rights, culminating in the Revolution of 1688.[20]

The third concept was of a twofold nature, including both the theory of contract and the theory of consent of the people. Just as there was a mutual relation between God and man, the Calvinists maintained, so also there was a mutual relation between ruler and people, and this relation was in the nature of a contract. The theory of the political contract was widely accepted by Calvin's followers. According to Professor Foster, "this doctrine of a mutual contract, for violation of which the people or their representatives should resist the ruler, had been taught by over sixty Calvinists, and successfully practised by Calvinists in six countries before Locke popularized it in his *Government*."[21]

Now contracts are matters of consent, and the contract theory therefore led to the doctrine that magistrates may rule only with the consent of the people—a doctrine which was derived from Calvin's church and transferred to the political arena. And in this transfer "Locke," we are told, "followed the footsteps of a dozen Calvinists."[22]

Again, the adoption of the theories of contract and consent opened the way to a fourth concept.

Believing that rulers received their power by consent of the people, and could govern only when they observed their contract, the logically minded Calvinist was bound in time to "take the next step" and recognize the sovereignty of the people. Calvin foresaw that this question would arise, "when rulers break faith with the people," but he felt it to be untimely, with the danger of civil war and commotions toward the close of his life especially in France, to discuss the

---

[19] Foster, *op. cit.*, pp. 489–90.   [20] *Ibid.*, p. 491.   [21] *Ibid.*, p. 492.   [22] *Ibid.*, p. 493.

question. "Calvin looks asquint that way," as Filmer justly remarked, and went so far as to teach that magistrates were "responsible to God and the people."[23]

But though Calvin merely looked "asquint that way," many of his followers did not hesitate to face the issue squarely and to adopt and profess without reservation the concept of popular sovereignty. By the time of Locke this concept was widely accepted, we are told, and he merely "repeats this teaching of over thirty international Calvinists, with the majority of whom he was familiar."[24]

Finally, many Calvinist writers accepted and taught the theory of resistance to tyranny.[25] Indeed, on more than one occasion they linked theory with practice, as in the case of Locke. "The Revolution of 1688 which Locke aided and justified, and his own teaching of resistance to tyranny through responsible representatives, which he based upon fundamental law, contract, natural rights, and sovereignty of the people, were in the main historical outgrowths of international Calvinism."[26]

Two additional passages should be quoted from Professor Foster's essay, as a summary of this phase of the subject. The first indicates in general terms the political contributions of the Calvinists:

Calvinists did not claim to be original. They built upon the past; but they "took the next step," possibly the most distinguishing contribution of Calvinism. Ancient and medieval writers had taught fundamental law, natural rights, contract, sovereignty of the people, obedience to God rather than man. Each of these teachings Calvinists carried a step further, notably in changing passive refusal to obey into active resistance through lay representatives following a "calling," ordained of God, and responsible, not to "God and the Church," but to "God and the people." With a possible exception on this point, the contribution of Calvinism was not in originating, but in (1) carrying theories to logical conclusions; (2) tying them all together into a workable system; (3) developing the type of people capable of putting them into practice; (4) demonstrating that their principles worked successfully in practice.[27]

The second passage deals with the Calvinism both of Locke and of the American colonists:

Locke himself typifies the Calvinism productive of civil and religious liberty that filtered from international sources through this calm thinker and man of affairs. The Calvinism assimilated and carried over by Locke possessed the liberal, international character of the Calvinistic commonwealths founded or expanded by thousands of exiles for conscience' sake—shrewd Genevan traders, prosperous

---

[23] *Ibid.*, p. 494.
[24] *Ibid.*, p. 496.
[25] For a discussion of this doctrine and its historical development, see *supra*, chap. xxvi.
[26] Foster, *op. cit.*, p. 497.
[27] *Ibid.*, p. 498.

Huguenot artisans and bankers, indomitable Dutch merchants, canny Scots, thrifty Scotch-Irish, and resourceful Puritans, and the Calvinists from all these lands who made up the majority of the seventeenth-century colonists in America.[28]

There was still another feature of Calvinism, not directly referred to by Professor Foster, which was destined to influence political thought. Calvin did not, of course, originate the doctrine of representative government. Indeed, the government which he established at Geneva was in practice more autocratic than democratic. In his provisions for the government of the church, however, he provided for the election of the various officers and representative governing bodies by the members of the congregation. And as a result of the spread of Calvinism, this provision for government in matters spiritual by representatives became a familiar and accepted principle in many lands—a principle which was soon seen to be applicable in temporal affairs and was in due course accepted by Calvinists as a full-fledged political doctrine.

An illustration of the development of this doctrine is to be found in the history of the Scottish Church. In contrast with the Church of England, which owed its establishment and growth largely to monarchs and statesmen, the Church of Scotland was the work of courageous—if sometimes, by our present standards, narrow-minded—divines, enthusiastically supported by the people. Adopting Calvin's tenet that the consent of the congregation was required in the appointment of each minister, and establishing a General Assembly of the Kirk which was more representative in fact than the Scottish Parliament, the Church leaders north of the Tweed founded a Kirk of Scotland characterized by strongly popular elements.

Their successors, however, had to struggle for the preservation of those popular elements, and for the very existence of the kirk itself. It is not necessary here to enter into the sorry tale of intervention and mismanagement in religious affairs in Scotland by the Stewart monarchs, nor into the long controversy over the patronage system by which ministers came to be appointed without the consent of their congregations. Suffice it to say that for centuries the Scottish Church contended both for the right to manage its own affairs without intervention from the state, and for the right of free choice and consent on the part of congregations in selecting their pastors.

There were certain principles which were in part a cause and in part a product of the controversy. These principles were cogently set forth in a famous letter written by the eminent Scottish geologist and man of letters,

---

[28] Foster, *op. cit.*, p. 498.

Hugh Miller, to Lord Brougham in the year 1839. The letter was a reply to a speech by his lordship relating to a patronage case, in which the decision of the court of session, adverse to the Church, was confirmed by the House of Lords.[29]

Referring to Lord Brougham's previously expressed views in favor of liberal reforms in representative government, Hugh Miller wrote:

You had declared, whether wisely or otherwise, that men possessed of no property qualification, and as humble and as little taught as the individual who now addresses you, should be admitted, on the strength of their moral and intellectual qualities alone, to exercise a voice in the legislature of the country. Could I suppose for a moment that you deemed that portion of these very men which falls to the share of Scotland unfitted to exercise a voice in the election of a parish minister? or, rather,—for I understate the case,—that you held them unworthy of being emancipated from the thraldom of a degrading law, the remnant of a barbarous code, which conveys them over by thousands and miles square to the charge of patronage-courting clergymen, practically unacquainted with the religion they profess to teach?[30]

With more than a touch of satire the letter continues:

Surely the people of Scotland are not so changed but that they know at least as much of the doctrines of the New Testament as of the principles of civil government, and of the requisites of a gospel minister as of the qualifications of a member of Parliament![31]

Could his lordship, in deciding against the cause of the Church, have been unaware that democratic theories were the result of the long search for arguments in behalf of religious freedom—that, indeed, "our discovery of the principles of civil liberty was merely a sort of chance-consequence of the search"?[32]

"I am a plain, untaught man," Hugh Miller declared, "but the opinions which I hold regarding the law of patronage are those entertained by the great bulk of my countrymen, and entitled on that account to some little respect."[33] As a preface to his statement of those opinions, he referred to the early account, drawn up by John Knox, of the origin of Scottish Presbyterianism and the practice not only of electing Church leaders and officials, but also of holding representative assemblies to which the various churches of Scotland sent "their best and wisest to deliberate in council" and to draw up for the Church as a whole "wise laws," "books of order and of discipline," and "Catechisms and Confessions of Faith."[34]

[29] *Presbytery of Auchterarder* v. *the Earl of Kinnoul and Rev. Robert Young*, Macl. & R. [1839]; 9 H. L. 220; 6 Cl. & F. 646.
[30] *The Life and Works of Hugh Miller*, VI (part 2), 21.
[31] *Ibid.* [32] *Ibid.*, p. 22. [33] *Ibid.*, p. 23. [34] *Ibid.*, p. 25.

These practices had entered into the foundation of ecclesiastical government in Scotland; they were based on the principle that the Church consists of human beings who possess rights of self-government in the spiritual domain.

Where is the flaw in our logic [demands Hugh Miller], when we infer that the members of our Church constitute our Church, and that it is the part and right of these members in their collective capacity to elect their ministers? I, my lord, am an integral part of the Church of Scotland, and of such integral parts, and of nothing else, is the body of this Church composed.[35]

Referring specifically to the decision confirmed by the House of Lords (a case involving the appointment of a minister by Lord Kinnoul without the assent of the congregation), the writer continues with a touch of indignation:

The Earl of Kinnoul is not the Church, nor any of the other patrons of Scotland. Why, then, are these men suffered to exercise, and that so exclusively, one of the Church's most sacred privileges? You tell us of "existing institutions, vested rights, positive interests." Do we not know that the slaveholders, who have so long and so stubbornly withstood your lordship's truly noble appeals in behalf of the African bondsmen, have been employing an exactly similar language for the last fifty years; and that the onward progress of man to the high place which God has willed him to occupy has been impeded at every step by "existing institutions, vested rights, positive interests"?[36]

There were other examples equally pertinent to the argument:

My grandfather was a grown man at a period when the neighboring proprietor could have dragged him from his cottage, and hung him up on the gallows-hill of the barony. It is not yet a century since the colliers of our southern districts were serfs bound to the soil. The mischievous and intolerant law of patronage still presses its dead weight on our consciences. But what of all that, my lord? Is it not in accordance with the high destiny of the species that the fit and the right should triumph over the established?[37]

The Christian religion, proclaimed Hugh Miller, is a religion of the people. It is no "artificial" religion, no mere abstract creed appealing to the intellect rather than to the heart. Here the argument must be one of fact rather than of principle.

Question the principle as you please, but look, I beseech you, to the fact. Who was that most popular of all preachers, whom the immense multitudes of Judea followed into waste and solitary places, and of whom it is so expressly told that the "common people heard him gladly"? And what the religion taught by the twelve unlettered men, whose labors revolutionized the morals of the world?

---

[35] *The Life and Works of Hugh Miller*, p. 26.   [36] *Ibid.*   [37] *Ibid.*, pp. 26–27.

CALVINISM

Christianity, in its primitive integrity, is essentially a popular religion; and what we complain of in the Churchmen opposed to the popular voice is, that they have divested it of this vital principle.[38]

Lord Brougham, it appears, had detected signs of rebellion in the refusal of the General Assembly of the Church to accept the pastor appointed by the Earl of Kinnoul. But was it rebellion to refuse obedience to an unjust law? "Take your seat, my lord," invited Hugh Miller ironically, "and try the members of this refractory court"—the General Assembly—"for their new and unheard-of offence."[39] These members were admittedly "wise and large-minded men—men admired for their genius, and revered for their piety, wherever the light of learning or religion has yet found its way."[40]

But what was the offense with which this assembly had been charged? In the language of the letter addressed to Lord Brougham,

a certain law of the country, which was passed rather more than a hundred and twenty years ago, through the influence of very bad men, and for a very bad purpose, has demanded that this assembly proceed forthwith to impose on a resisting people a singularly unpopular clergyman. And the assembly have refused; courteously and humbly, 'tis true, but still most firmly.[41]

This action had been taken because it was the judgment of the assembly that

we must not force this unpopular clergyman on the people: our consciences will not suffer us to do it; and as the laws which control our consciences cannot be altered, whereas those which govern the country are in a state of continual change, suffer us, we beseech you, to confer with the makers of those changing laws, that this bad law may be made so much better as to agree with the fixed law of our consciences.[42]

Upon this "offence" Hugh Miller comments with increasing irony:

Now, such, my lord, is the heinous offence committed by these men. You could not believe they were so wicked; you could imagine the crime itself, but not in connection with them; you said it was indecorous, preposterous, monstrous, to believe that *they could* be so wicked. But you did ill to speak of Christ on the occasion. It is against Bolingbroke's law, not the law of Christ, that these men have offended.[43]

His lordship had been born in Edinburgh and was, at least on his mother's side, of Scottish descent. With this in mind, perhaps, Hugh Miller strikes a note of reproach.

Nay, my lord, you should have known the Church of Scotland better. Consult her history, and see whether she has not as determinedly opposed herself to wicked laws as to wicked men. The very act which first indicated her existence

---

[38] *Ibid.*, p. 31.   [39] *Ibid.*, p. 36.   [40] *Ibid.*, p. 37.   [41] *Ibid.*   [42] *Ibid.*   [43] *Ibid.*

as a Church was her opposition to the law. And fearfully did she suffer for it. . . . But there was a law to which she was not opposed—a fixed and immutable law; and God fought for her, and she waxed mighty in the midst of her great suffering; and at length, when her fierce and cruel persecutors had gone to their place, the unjust and intolerant law against which she had so long struggled in sorrow and great weakness was expunged from the statute-book.[44]

According to history, the letter continues,

in all her after conflicts, it was not the Church that yielded to the law, but the law that yielded to the Church. Need I remind your lordship of her struggles in the days of Mary, of James, of Charles? Need I say that, subsequent to the Restoration, she opposed herself to the law for twenty-eight years together; and that the graves which lie solitary among our hills, and the tombs which occupy the malefactors' corner in our public burying-grounds, remain to testify of the heavy penalty which she paid?[45]

But in the fullness of time the descendants of the "ancient monarchs" who had sought to annul the rights and liberties of the Scottish Church

became fugitive and vagabond on the face of the earth. The law to which our Church would not yield, yielded to her; and that better law which your lordship so pointedly condemns as unworthy of the Revolution, but which thousands among the wise and good of my countrymen, and many, many thousands of humble individuals like myself, have been accustomed to regard as so entirely in its purest spirit, was made to occupy their place.[46]

When man-made law opposed the higher law, the Church stood firm against the law of man, even though that stand were termed rebellion.

We do not think the worse of our Church, my lord, for her many contests with the law; not a whit the better of her opposers for their having had the law on their side. The public prosecutor in the time of Charles II. was perhaps as able a lawyer as even your lordship, but we have been accustomed to execrate his memory as "the bloody Mackenzie."[47]

The hands of the rich, the highborn, the conservative, are ever against such "rebellion." But their disapproval is of no real importance to those who struggle for fundamental principles.

The Church has offended many of her noblest and wealthiest, it is said, and they are flying from her in crowds. Well, what matters it?—let the chaff fly! We care not though she shake off, in her wholesome exercise, some of the indolent humors which have hung about her so long. The vital principle will act with all the more vigor when they are gone. She may yet have to pour forth her life's blood through some incurable and deadly wound; for do we not know that though *the Church* be eternal, churches are born and die? But the blow will

---

[44] *The Life and Works of Hugh Miller*, pp. 37-38.   [45] *Ibid.*, p. 38.   [46] *Ibid.*
[47] *Ibid.*

be dealt in a different quarrel, and on other and lower ground,—not when her ministers, for the sake of the spiritual, lessen their hold of the secular; not when, convinced of the justice of the old quarrel, they take up their position on the well-trodden battle-field of her saints and her martyrs; not when they stand side by side with her people, to contend for their common rights, in accordance with the dictates of their consciences, and agreeably to the law of their God.[48]

Such was the spirit, such were the principles which animated the followers of Calvin in Scotland. Not a few of them brought the same spirit and the same principles to the New World and wove them into their conceptions of civil as well as of religious freedom.

Thus it came to pass, by one of those curious ironies of history, that, notwithstanding the dubious doctrine of predestination, the teachings of a man who ruled the people of Geneva with an iron hand eventually led his followers in later centuries to espouse conceptions which in the fullness of time were to be summarized in the noble phrases of Abraham Lincoln, "Government of the people, by the people and for the people." It was, indeed, to borrow a phrase or two from a distinguished English essayist,[49] a "strange paradox, that in the suppression of the liberties of Geneva was sown the seed of liberty in Europe"—and, it might well be added, in the English colonies of North America—and "that by the demoralizing tenet of fatalism was evoked a moral energy which Christianity had not felt since the era of persecution."

[48] *Ibid.*, p. 39.
[49] Pattison, "Calvin at Geneva," first published in the *Westminster Review*, 1858, and included in *Essays by the Late Mark Pattison*, collected by Professor Nettleship, II, 7.

Chapter XXIX
MARTIN LUTHER (1483-1546)

At the end of the fifteenth century the bonds of a united Christendom had become sadly weakened. Ambitions for increasing temporal power and fuller independence were stirring in the restless minds of many a king and princeling. The sovereign pontiffs themselves had yielded to the lure of worldly ambitions until, by the reign of Alexander VI, the pontifical office had become little more than a means "for the accomplishment of political ends."[1] On a smaller scale many a prince-bishop, too, ruled his domain as a wealthy temporal sovereign. Between independent and semi-independent rulers tortuous political scheming was the order of the day. Thus much of Europe became involved in a web of plots and counter-plots, of treaties made only to be broken, of wars in which mercenary troops were increasingly used. The Holy Roman Empire was more of a fiction than a fact, a fiction to which only the shrewd ability of Charles V was to give a semblance of reality for a few brief decades.

Upon this state of affairs, earnest Christians looked with more than a little sadness and misgiving. Their Church had become a strange combination of true piety and material corruption. Many felt that the evils which had grown up should be corrected, but how could this be done without bringing about still greater evils? Could the Church itself be reformed, or was it necessary to break away and start afresh? These and similar questions came to disturb thoughtful people. Religious doubts and fears preyed upon minds already troubled by material anxieties—fear of the Turkish hordes threatening Europe, dread of the plague which came like a periodic scourge.

Into such a world Martin Luther was born, at Eisleben in Prussian Saxony, in the year 1483. He was of peasant stock, but his father had prospered in the mines and was able to see that his son obtained an excellent education. He hoped that the youth would become a lawyer, and with that in view sent him to the University of Erfurt, then the most famous of German universities and a center of both scholasticism and humanism

[1] Clayton, *Luther and His Work*, p. 7.

But Luther, though he studied the classics and delved deeply into philosophy, apparently felt little enthusiasm for humanism itself. He was uneasy in mind, troubled by fits of depression, by doubts, by fears for the salvation of his own soul. He completed his preliminary studies with marked success, however, and to please his father took up the study of law. But at the same time his religious doubts led him to give much time to the study of theology and the Scriptures, in search for the assurance of salvation. His search was apparently unsuccessful, for in 1505 he turned suddenly to the cloister, in the hope that there he might discover the assurance which he craved.

Yet in the Order of the Augustinian Eremites, which he joined, he seems to have found no real solace for what we can only regard as his morbid fears. Other members of the order, though not fully comprehending his difficulties, gave him some help, and he continued his theological studies with enthusiasm. Within a few years he was appointed an instructor at the newly opened University of Wittenberg, and seemed well on his way to a successful ecclesiastical career. He was sent to Rome to lay certain matters relating to his order before the Curia. Not long after his return to Germany he became professor of theology at Wittenberg. To his associates Luther was clearly a man with a future. And so he was, but it was to be a different future from any that they—or he—anticipated.

He was still preoccupied with his own religious problem, still groping after something, he knew not what, which would assure him that his soul was safe and would thus release him from those attacks of dreadful terror to which he was subject. Gradually, through study, teaching, and preaching, he developed certain conceptions which brought him a sense of comfort and security. What were these conceptions? With no attempt at theological analysis of them, they may be briefly paraphrased as a general proposition accompanied by several corollaries:

1. It is faith alone which justifies and leads Christians to salvation.

2. Hence they will be judged only by their faith, and not by their works. In other words, works alone will never win salvation, although the faithful will naturally do good works because of their faith.

3. Freedom of will is denied—a doctrine to which Erasmus felt called upon to take prompt exception.[2]

---

[2] Erasmus published a tractate (*De libero arbitrio*) on the subject in 1524. Luther attempted to meet the great humanist's attack with his *De servo arbitrio* (1525), but Erasmus, retorting the following year with his *Hyperaspistes,* was counted the victor, and Luther dropped the controversy. For a brief but spirited account of the relations between Erasmus and Luther, see Funck-Brentano, *Luther,* trans. from the French by Buckley, chap. xvi. See also chap. xxx in the present volume, "Desiderius Erasmus."

4. "Original sin is born in us by nature";[3] and "although it is forgiven, nevertheless it lives and works and raves and assails us until the body dies."[4]

These conceptions did not emerge distinctly until Luther had taught and pondered for several years. But eventually he became aware that his ideas differed profoundly from those set forth in scholastic theology. Yet his views must be right, he felt, for they had brought him peace and security of mind. Therefore, scholastic theology must be wrong. On this point his conviction grew steadily with the years, until at last he could tolerate no opposition, either from the Catholic Church or from those who had accepted but sought to modify his doctrines. From that conviction it was but a short step to the further conviction that he was an inspired prophet, and Luther took that step.[5]

Yet, though fundamentally his religious conceptions were based on personal experience, and were the product of his struggle against personal fears, he was also deeply influenced by external factors. In Rome he had visited all of the shrines and churches with a deep feeling of reverence. But he had also seen or heard much of pomp and vanity, ambition which would not stop at sacrilege, depravity, and vice. These things did not at the time arouse in him the fever for reform, but they remained graven in his memory, to become, when subsequently he rebelled against the Church, the target of many a blast which he launched at Rome.

The immediate cause which brought him into open conflict with the papal régime, however, was a matter which directly concerned his own country—the sale of indulgences in Germany by one John Tetzel, a Dominican of marked rhetorical gifts, who had been appointed for that purpose. No attempt need be made here to discuss the practice of selling indulgences as it had developed in Luther's day. Suffice it to say that the true doctrine of indulgences had been distorted into a method of raising revenues for the papal coffers. By the beginning of the sixteenth century the sale of pardons in Germany "had become," as a learned Catholic biographer of Luther states, "a public scandal."[6] Luther, aroused to action by Tetzel's campaign,

---

[3] *Treatise on Good Works* (1520), published in *Works of Martin Luther*, a selection of treatises trans. and ed. by a group of Lutheran pastors, I, 285.

[4] *Argument in Defense of Articles of Martin Luther* (1521), *Works*, III, 34.

[5] Denying the accusations that his teachings caused dissension and revolt and insisting that he had ever been a peace maker, Luther exclaimed bitterly of his accusers: "This is the thanks I deserve! To be sure I desire no other, for so it went with all the prophets and apostles, and with Christ Himself."—*Exhortation to the Clergy Assembled at the Diet of Augsburg* (1530), *Works*, IV, 335.

[6] Clayton, *Luther and His Work* (previously cited), p. 42.

protested vigorously against what he and many others in Germany considered a grave abuse. He not only preached sermons on the subject but also, following the custom of the day, prepared a lengthy series of ninety-five articles or theses, in which he set forth his views on the current methods of preaching and selling indulgences. On November 1, 1517, he posted a copy of the theses on the door of the chapel at Wittenberg, which served as a bulletin board for university notices. Other copies he transmitted to theologians at various German universities. The document aroused immediate interest and support as a criticism of an unjustifiable practice.

Had Luther carried the matter no farther, the controversy which his theses had aroused might well have died down. But he soon found it impossible to be content with a mere protest at practices which needed reform. As his religious conceptions developed, he felt called upon to attack tenets of the Catholic faith, and eventually to question the authority of the pope. By the year 1520 he was definitely in revolt against the papacy. In the following year he was formally excommunicated as a heretic, and having firmly rejected all attempts to make him recant at the Imperial Diet of Worms, was declared an outlaw by edict of the diet.

Thus condemned by both papacy and empire, he became subject to seizure and trial. But having attended the diet under a safe-conduct, he was allowed to depart unmolested. And the edict was never executed. For a time he went into hiding in the Wartburg, a feudal castle of the Elector Frederick of Saxony. But within a year he was back at Wittenberg, in defiance of the imperial authorities. Meanwhile his doctrines had been preached by his disciples, and were being widely accepted. The unity of Christendom was no longer merely threatened, it was broken: what is called the Reformation had already begun.

The spreading and influence of Luther's doctrines were due in part to his remarkable ability as a preacher, for unquestionably he must be ranked among the world's great orators. He could at will thunder coarse invective, reason acutely, or argue persuasively. His literary skill was even more marked and, though most of his innumerable writings were of a sharply controversial nature, they bear witness to his extraordinary command of homely but forceful German. But his supreme contribution to literature was his translation of the Bible (the New Testament from the Greek, the Old from the Hebrew), a contribution which made the Scriptures available in the everyday language of his people[7] and thus unified and forged the German dialects into a national tongue.[8]

The influence wielded by him, however, was not always easy to control. The rebellion which he had started soon threatened to get out of hand, for extremists pushed his doctrines far beyond what Luther, himself essentially a conservative, actually intended. Even at Wittenberg only his prompt return from hiding prevented the intrusion of revolutionary theories of reform by forceful means. Elsewhere, more or less radical doctrines were eventually engrafted on Lutheran theology, with the result that various sects arose, against which Luther waged a continual warfare of words. It was one thing for him to have taken issue with the Catholic Church; it was quite another thing, apparently, for other Protestants to take issue with his doctrines. The tolerance which characterized his earlier teachings gradually waned, and in the course of time we find him advocating the theory he had once rejected —"the maintenance of pure religion by force."[9]

Another question which seemed easy of solution at first, but which later returned to vex him, was that of marriage. As early as 1522 he had issued a pamphlet against celibacy among the clergy. Many of his fellow clergymen proceeded to put this doctrine into immediate practice, and in 1525, after a period of hesitation and doubt, Luther himself married, choosing as a wife Catherine von Bora, a former nun. The marriage problem seemed thus happily settled, but some fifteen years later it cropped up in another and uglier form. The Landgrave Philip of Hesse, a supporter of the Protestant cause, conceived a violent passion for a young woman of noble birth, Margaret von der Saal. But he already had a wife and seven children, and his father-in-law, Duke George of Saxony, would not have tolerated divorce proceedings. Philip thereupon bethought him of a scheme whereby he might have two wives. It would, he argued, be necessary only to have religious

---

[7] To his translation of the Bible Luther devoted much labor and endless pains to searching for simple and familiar words. The German text "must," he insisted, "be adorned with simplicity."—Letter to Spalatin, March 30, 1522, printed in Preserved Smith's two-volume ed. of *Luther's Correspondence and Other Contemporary Letters*, II, 119. And later, "sweating" over the Old Testament, he exclaims, "How. hard it is to make these Hebrew writers talk German!"—Letter to Wenzel Link, June 14, 1528, Preserved Smith, *op. cit.*, p. 445.

[8] The only translation into the English tongue comparable to Luther's German version of the Bible is William Tyndale's translation (first published in 1526), which "judged by its influence, was the greatest work of English prose ever achieved by a single individual. Following, like Luther, the Greek text of Erasmus, he also made good use of Luther's own translation, and rivaled the great German in a style which so successfully combined dignity, brevity, and familiarity that it worked a revolution in English prose. Tyndale's New Testament was substantially the New Testament of the King James version."—Bates, *Biography of the Bible* (previously cited), pp. 109-10.

[9] Allen, *A History of Political Thought in the Sixteenth Century* (previously cited), p. 26.

sanction in the form of an approval of the second marriage from the leaders of the Protestant Church. Accordingly, he requested such approval from Luther and his associates, implying, by way of persuasion, that if it were not forthcoming he might find it impossible to continue his support of the reformers. To Luther the request was not without precedent, for he had already, in 1531, advised Henry VIII of England that it would be better for him to take Anne Boleyn as a second wife than to divorce Catharine of Aragon.[10] Nevertheless, he appears to have given his approval to Philip's proposed bigamy with no little reluctance. He could justify it only on the dubious grounds of expediency, as necessary to retain Philip's support. Melanchthon, Luther's chief lieutenant in reform, was persuaded to add his signature to the document of consent, it being stipulated that both the document and the marriage should be kept secret. But secrecy in the matter proved to be impossible. The facts soon became public property, and the Lutheran cause suffered as a result. Melanchthon felt deep shame at the part he had played in the incident, but Luther, apparently less sensitive in such things, brazened the matter out with the argument that secret consent was not public consent, and demanded that Philip deny the marriage.[11] For all his specious arguments, however, the damage had been done, and there was no repairing the moral injury to the Lutheran cause.

In the year of Luther's marriage another incident—or rather, a series of incidents—occurred which profoundly affected both his views and his influence. For many years there had been signs of unrest and discontent among the peasants of Germany. They were still heavily burdened with feudal services, with increased taxes and other intolerable exactions. There was in consequence a feeling of hostility among them against the nobility and against officials of the Church, especially those who controlled large temporal domains. Now Luther was himself of peasant origin, as we have seen, and he felt some sympathy for the peasants' hard lot. But his was not the pro-

---

[10] For an interesting account of Luther's relations with Henry VIII, see Preserved Smith's article, "Luther and Henry VIII," in *The English Historical Review*, XXV (Oct., 1910), 656-69. The Wittenberg reformer's advice to the English monarch has been Englished as follows:

"I do not now question (he writes) the worth of a papal dispensation in such matters, but I say that even if the king sinned in marrying his brother's widow it would be a much more atrocious sin cruelly to put her away now. . . . Rather let him take another queen, following the example of the patriarchs, who had many wives even before the law of Moses sanctioned the practice, but let him not thrust his present spouse from her royal position."—*Ibid.*, pp. 665-66.

[11] Boehmer, *Luther and the Reformation in the Light of Modern Research*, English trans. by Potter, p. 221. This work, by one of Germany's leading Protestant ecclesiastical historians, was first published in 1904 under the title *Luther im Lichte der neueren Forschung*, but was much enlarged in later editions.

found sympathy which leads men to espouse the cause of the oppressed. One of his finest tractates is on the liberty of the Christian man, but it is concerned with spiritual liberty, with "liberty of faith,"[12] not with political or economic freedom. The truth is that Luther's abiding interest was in theological, not in political or economic, reform. It was not his purpose to induce the peasants of his country to rebel against their masters. Nevertheless he who incites to revolt in one field must bear some measure of responsibility if the revolt spreads to other fields. And there can be no doubt that Luther's rebellion in matters theological did play a part in the development of the Peasant Revolt of 1525. Moreover, in his writings he had not only denounced princes of the Church but had declared princes generally to be "the greatest fools or the worst knaves on earth."[13] "God Almighty," he maintained, "has made our rulers mad."[14] He had asserted that men would not continue to suffer the tyranny of princes,[15] that clergy and laity should be equal before the law,[16] and that "a Christian man is a perfectly free lord of all, subject to none."[17] To be sure, these and similar statements were not intended to stand by themselves. Read in their full context they can hardly be taken as an incitement to revolution, for Luther, as we shall see, was a firm believer in submission to temporal government. But his followers were not always careful to read the whole of his tractates. Not a few of the extremists were inclined rather to seize on a phrase here and a phrase there which suited their purpose, and to make those phrases a text in haranguing the peasants. Popular unrest developed apace and the danger of a violent outbreak grew more acute. Serious reformers sought to explain to the peasants that they misunderstood the Lutheran doctrines. But their voices were unheeded in the increasing stress and excitement.

Luther himself was angry with the peasants. The strength of his cause, he felt, lay in the support of princes, and he feared for German Protestantism if these royal supporters were overthrown. He did not wish his doctrines to become identified with rebellions and revolutions. It was true that he himself had rebelled against the Church, but that was a different matter. Let the peasants keep to their allotted station in life. They had certain grievances, he admitted in his reply to the Twelve Articles of the Swabian Peasants, and the princes were not wholly in the right. But rebellion was wholly wrong.

---

[12] *A Treatise on Christian Liberty* (1520), *Works*, II, 343.
[13] *Secular Authority: To What Extent It Should Be Obeyed* (1523), *Works*, III, 258.
[14] *Ibid.*, p. 230.   [15] *Ibid.*, p. 261.
[16] *An Open Letter to the Christian Nobility* (1520), *Works*, II, 71–72.
[17] *A Treatise on Christian Liberty, ibid.*, p. 312.

Things were moving too fast, however, for such a circumspect answer to have any effect. The revolt broke out in earnest and spread from the countryside into the towns. Luther's anger at the peasants turned into a fury which produced his terrible tractates "Against the Robbing and Murdering Hordes of Peasants," and "An Open Letter Concerning the Hard Book against the Peasants."[18] He exhorted the princes to put the rebels to the sword, to slay them without mercy, and the princes did so. It is estimated that in suppressing the rebellion, 100,000 peasants were executed. The two tractates make extremely unpleasant reading, and no purpose will be served in analyzing them here.

It is advisable to consider for a moment, however, what justification, if any, Luther had in writing them. On this question, an English historian has offered a number of highly pertinent comments.

It is almost a commonplace with Lutheran writers [says Professor A. F. Pollard][19] to justify Luther's action on the ground that the Peasants' Revolt was revolutionary, unlawful, immoral, while the religious movement was reforming, lawful, and moral; but the hard and fast line which is thus drawn vanishes on a closer investigation. The peasants had no constitutional means wherewith to attain their ends, and there is no reason to suppose that they would have resorted to force unless force had been prepared to resist them; if, as Luther maintained, it was the Christian's duty to tolerate worldly ills, it was incumbent on Christian Princes as well as on Christian peasants; and if, as he said, the Peasants' Revolt was a punishment divinely ordained for the Princes, what right had they to resist?[20]

Moreover, Luther and his followers were themselves no strangers to rebellion. They "were only content with constitutional means," as Professor Pollard observes, "so long as they proved successful"; when such means failed

Lutherans also resorted to arms against their lawful Emperor. Nor was there anything in the peasants' demands more essentially revolutionary than the repudiation of the Pope's authority and the wholesale appropriation of ecclesiastical property. The distinction between the two movements has for its basis the fact that the one was successful, the other was not; while the Peasants' Revolt failed, the Reformation triumphed, and then discarded its revolutionary guise and assumed the respectable garb of law and order.[21]

The fact of the matter is, the same writer maintains, that Luther

saved the Reformation by cutting it adrift from the failing cause of the peasants and tying it to the chariot wheels of the triumphant Princes. If he had not been

---

[18] *Works*, Vol. IV.
[19] "Social Revolution and Catholic Reaction in Germany," *The Cambridge Modern History*, II, chap. vi.   [20] *Ibid.*, pp. 193–94.   [21] *Ibid.*, p. 194.

the apostle of revolution, he had at least commanded the army in which all the revolutionaries fought. He had now repudiated his left wing and was forced to depend on his right.[22]

What were the consequences of this repudiation?

The movement from 1521 to 1525 had been national, and Luther had been its hero; from the position of national hero he now sank to be the prophet of a sect, and a sect which depended for existence upon the support of political powers . . .; it was to punish the ungodly, he said, that the sword had been placed in the hands of authority, and it was in vain that the Elector Frederick reminded him of his previous teaching, that men should let only the Word fight for them. Separated from the Western Church and alienated from the bulk of the German people, Lutheran divines leant upon territorial Princes, and repaid their support with undue servility.[23]

Henry VIII himself, according to Professor Pollard,

extorted from his bishops no more degrading compliance than the condoning by Melanchthon and others of Philip of Hesse's bigamy. Melanchthon came to regard the commands of princes as the ordinances of God, while Luther looked upon them as Bishops of the Church, and has been classed by Treitschke with Machiavelli as a champion of the indefeasible rights of the State.[24]

These comments bring us to a consideration of Luther's political conceptions. An eminent authority on the history of political thought has observed that "Luther was not a systematic political thinker, that indeed he can hardly be described as a political thinker at all."[25] He was concerned with problems of government and the state only in so far as he was obliged to consider those problems in connection with the realization of his theological program. Had it been possible for him to expound his religious theories without reference to the state, he would doubtless have ignored political matters entirely. But it seemed essential to him to have political support, and he therefore devoted some attention to temporal government. Yet however much a reformer he was in the religious field, he was in matters political fundamentally conservative, and even reactionary.

Luther shared the familiar view that government was a punishment and a remedy for sin, and thus that temporal power would find no place among a sinless people. "If all the world," he says, "were composed of real Christians, that is, true believers, no prince, king, lord, sword, or law would be needed."[26] But true Christians were few in number. "Since, however, no

---

[22] Pollard in *Cambridge Modern History*, II, 194.   [23] *Ibid.*   [24] *Ibid.*

[25] Carlyle, *op. cit.*, VI, 273. "Martin Luther," adds another authority (Preserved Smith, "Luther and Henry VIII," *The English Historical Review* XXV [Oct., 1910], 656), "was the least politically-minded of all the reformers."

[26] *Secular Authority: To What Extent It Should Be Obeyed*, in *Works*, III, 234.

one is by nature Christian or pious, but every one sinful and evil, God places the restraints of the law upon them all, so that they may not dare give rein to their desires and commit outward, wicked deeds."[27] It is clear that Luther had no very high opinion of humanity at large. Men must be held severely in check, they must be subjected "to the sword." By way of illustration we have the following statement: "Even so, a wild, savage beast is fastened with chains and bands, so that it cannot bite and tear as is its wont, although it gladly would do so."[28] And applying his illustration more specifically Luther adds: "If it were not so, seeing that the whole world is evil and that among thousands there is scarcely one true Christian, men would devour one another, and no one could preserve wife and child, support himself and serve God; and thus the world would be reduced to chaos."[29]

This temporal power restraining men from, and penalizing them for, an innate wickedness was, in Luther's conception, of divine ordination. "God Himself appoints and preserves all rulership."[30] Therefore, Luther describes "wordly government" as "a creation and an ordinance of God,"[31] and "the State" as "God's servant and workman to punish the evil and protect the good."[32]

In keeping with his belief that human beings were, on the whole, a wicked lot, Luther advocated a strict and indeed a harsh government. He preached freedom and equality in the spiritual domain, but the temporal régime, he insisted, could not endure if it were founded on those qualities. "A worldly kingdom cannot stand unless there is in it an inequality of persons, so that some are free, some imprisoned, some lords, some subjects."[33] It was Luther's opinion that

> the world needs a strict, hard temporal government that will compel and constrain the wicked not to steal and rob and to return what they borrow, even though a Christian ought not demand it, or even hope to get it back. This is necessary in order that the world may not become a desert, peace may not perish, and trade and society may not be utterly destroyed.[34]

The rule of the Gospel was ideal, but Luther as a practical man did not believe that the application of that rule alone would have much effect in a

---

[27] *Ibid.*, p. 235.   [28] *Ibid.*, p. 236.   [29] *Ibid.*

[30] *An Exposition of the Eighty-second Psalm* (1530), *Works*, IV, 290.

[31] *A Sermon on Keeping Children in School* (1530), *Works*, IV, 158–59. *Cf.* also *Secular Authority* . . ., *ibid.*, III, 231.

[32] *Secular Authority* . . ., in *Works*, III, 245.

[33] *Admonition to Peace: A Reply to the Twelve Articles of the Swabian Peasants* (1525), *Works*, IV, 240.

[34] *On Trading and Usury* (1524), *Works*, IV, 22.

sinful world. Laws backed by force were necessary in human affairs, and we must therefore "let the sword hew briskly and boldly against the transgressors." No one ought to think, he announced, "that the world can be ruled without blood; the sword of the ruler must be red and bloody; for the world will and must be evil, and the sword is God's rod and vengeance upon it."[35]

Still, Luther—though apparently not very hopefully—advocated good government by a wise prince, a prince who had learned, both from sacred writings and history, skill and discretion in ruling his people.[36] "Temporal government," he considered, "next to the preaching-office, is the highest service of God and the most useful office on earth."[37] The virtues of the good prince were not merely "royal" but "divine."[38] But what were these virtues? Luther names three, and the first indicates clearly how much he had come to rely upon the secular power for support of his religious cause. Thus the prince is to "secure justice" for those who are truly Christian—according, of course, to Lutheran standards—and to "repress those who are godless."[39] He should not waste his time and treasure on showy buildings, nor even on imposing churches, but should rather (is it permissible to assume that Luther was here thinking of himself?) "support or protect a poor, pious pastor."[40]

The second royal virtue is the administration of justice in a general sense, but with particular attention to "the poor, the orphans, and the widows."[41] This virtue requires of the ruler that he make and preserve just laws, and that he suppress worldly desires for "honor, power, luxury, selfish profit, and self-will."[42]

The third of the trio of virtues Luther concisely designates as "peacemaking." That is to say, the prince should keep order in his realm, and avoid war, when possible, with other peoples. For this purpose he needs to be "equipped" with laws and, as we would expect from Luther's frequent references to the sword, with arms.

It is not without interest to note that as a corollary to the princely virtues Luther imposes the princely duty of suppressing heresy of various kinds and of settling religious disputes.[43] Here, as in various other doctrines, Luther's views had changed with the years. As a younger man he had written in favor of toleration on the part of the secular authorities, urging that since "belief or unbelief is a matter of every one's conscience, and since this is no lessening of the secular power, the latter should be content and

---

[35] *On Trading and Usury,* in *Works,* IV, 23.
[36] *Treatise on Good Works* (1520), *Works,* I, 265–66.
[37] *An Exposition of the Eighty-second Psalm* (1530), *Works,* IV, 298.   [38] *Ibid.*
[39] *Ibid.,* p. 299.   [40] *Ibid.*   [41] *Ibid.,* p. 300.   [42] *Ibid.,* p. 302.   [43] *Ibid.,* pp. 309–13.

attend to its own affairs and permit men to believe one thing or another, as they are able and willing, and constrain no one by force."[44] But his experience in the Peasant Revolt, and with other Protestant sects which declined to follow the path he had marked out, inclined him more and more toward intolerance and the use of force in imposing his own views.

Other duties also the prince had. Indeed, his duties were "fourfold: First, that toward God consists in true confidence and in sincere prayer; second, that toward his subjects consists in love and Christian service; third, that toward his counselors and rulers consists in an open mind and unfettered judgment; fourth, that toward evil doers consists in proper zeal and firmness."[45] If he fulfills these duties, his state will be

right, outwardly and inwardly, pleasing to God and to the people. But he must expect much envy and sorrow,—the cross will soon rest on the shoulders of such a ruler.[46]

As for the duty of subjects, it may be summed up in two words—submission and obedience. Luther was at some pains to make clear "how high and how glorious God will have rulers held," and how men ought therefore "to obey them, as His officers, and be subject to them with all fear and reverence, as to God Himself."[47] The ruler, being divinely ordained, was as a god among men, and was in Luther's conception responsible to God but not to the people. Subjects were therefore not to judge nor restrain their princes, even if they suffered from misgovernment. God would punish or discipline the erring rulers; the rôle of the people was to "be quiet, keep the peace, be obedient, and suffer."[48] The true Christian (in Luther's opinion, as we have seen, there were not many of these) needed "no law or sword" himself, but for the sake of others he should nevertheless submit to temporal government. "Because the sword is a very great benefit and necessary to the whole world, to preserve peace, to punish sin and to prevent evil, he submits most willingly to the rule of the sword, pays tax, honors those in authority, serves, helps, and does all he can to further the government, that it may be sustained and held in honor and fear."[49]

But what if rulers were tyrants, cruelly oppressing their subjects? Still it was the people's duty to submit and suffer in silence, considering tyranny as a punishment for their sins. "The world is far too wicked to be worthy of good and pious lords,"[50] Luther holds. Therefore, "As humbly as I conduct myself when God sends me a sickness, so humbly should I conduct

---

[44] *Secular Authority* . . ., in *Works*, III, 253. [45] *Ibid.*, p. 271. [46] *Ibid.*
[47] *Exposition of the Eighty-second Psalm*, in *Works*, IV, 290.
[48] *Ibid.*, p. 291. [49] *Secular Authority* . . ., in *Works*, III, 239.
[50] *Treatise Concerning the Ban* (1520), *Works*, II, 51.

'myself toward the evil government, which the same God also sends me."[51] Insurrection, to Luther, was among the unpardonable sins.[52] "My sympathies are and always will be with those against whom insurrection is made, however wrong the cause they stand for, and opposed to those who make insurrection, however much they may be in the right."[53] Thus Luther wrote in 1522, proclaiming that "God has forbidden insurrection."[54] And three years later, as we have seen, he poured the vials of his wrath upon the German peasants for having dared to rebel against the harsh rule of their princes. The weight of ancient authority and the precedents of history were against him here, and he knew it.

The heathens, because they knew nothing of God, did not know that temporal government is God's ordinance, for they held it as the good fortune and the deed of men and therefore they jumped right in here and thought that it was not only right, but also praiseworthy to depose, kill and drive out worthless and wicked rulers. Therefore, the Greeks, in public laws, promised jewels and presents to tyrannicides, that is, to those who stab or otherwise destroy a tyrant. The Romans in the days of their empire followed mightily after this example and themselves killed almost the majority of their emperors, so that in that great empire, almost no emperor was ever slain by his enemies and yet few of them died in their beds a natural death. The people of Israel and Judah also slew and destroyed some of their kings.[55]

In his obsession, however, with the idea that rulers must be inviolable, Luther flouted both authority and precedents.

But these examples are not enough for us, for we are not asking here what the heathen or the Jews have done, but what is the right and the just thing to do, not only before God in the spirit, but also in the divine external ordinance of temporal government. For if today or tomorrow a people rises up and deposes their lord or slays him,—well, that will happen, and the lords must expect it, if it is God's decree;—but it does not follow that for that reason it is a right and just act. I have never known a case of this kind that was just, and even now I cannot imagine one. The peasants in their rebellion alleged that the lords would not allow the Gospel to be preached and robbed the poor people, and, therefore that they must be overthrown; but I have answered this by saying that although the lords did wrong in this, it would not therefore be just or right to do wrong in return, that is, to be disobedient and destroy God's ordinance, which is not

---

[51] *Treatise Concerning the Ban,* in *Works,* II, 51.

[52] "My opinion," he wrote to a devoted follower (Nicholas von Amsdorf, in a letter of May 30, 1525, printed in Preserved Smith, *Luther's Correspondence,* II, 319–20), "is that it is better all the peasants be killed than that the magistrates and princes perish, because the peasants took the sword without divine authority."

[53] *An Earnest Exhortation for All Christians, Warning Them against Insurrection and Rebellion* (1522), *Works,* III, 212.

[54] *Ibid.* [55] *Whether Soldiers, too, Can Be Saved* (1526), *Works,* V, 43–44.

ours. On the contrary, we ought to suffer wrong and if prince or lord will not tolerate the Gospel, then we ought to go into another princedom where the Gospel is preached, as Christ says in *Matthew*, x, "If they persecute you in one city flee into another."[56]

But what if the ruler's tyranny were due to madness? This question halted Luther's blast against tyrannicide, but only for a moment.

It is just, to be sure, that if a prince, king, or lord goes crazy, he should be deposed and put under restraint, for he is not to be considered a man since his reason is gone. Yes, you say a raving tyrant is crazy, too, or is to be considered even worse than a madman, for he does much more harm. That answer puts me in a tight place, for such a statement makes a great appearance and seems to be in accord with justice. Nevertheless, it is my opinion that the cases of madmen and tyrants are not the same; for a madman can neither do nor tolerate anything reasonable, nor is there any hope for him because the light of reason has gone out. But a tyrant, however much of this kind of thing he does, knows that he does wrong. He has his conscience and his knowledge, and there is hope that he may do better, allow himself to be instructed, and learn, and follow advice, none of which things can be hoped for in a crazy man, who is like a clod or a stone. Moreover, such conduct has a bad result or sets a bad example. If it is called right to murder or drive out tyrants, the thing grows and it becomes a common sign of self-will to call men tyrants who are not tyrants, and even to kill them if the mob takes a notion to do so.[57]

Here Luther found it advantageous to accept the support of history, which he had so positively rejected in a preceding paragraph.

This [he declares] the Roman histories show us. They killed many a fine emperor only because they did not like him or he did not do what they wanted, and did not let them be lords, and held them for their servants and monkeys as happened to Galba, Pertinax, Gordian, Alexander and others.[58]

And his conclusion is that

we cannot pipe much to the mob. It goes mad too quickly, and it is better to take ten ells from it than to allow to it a hand-breadth, nay a finger's-breadth in such a case, and it is better that the tyrants do the wrong a hundred times than that they once do wrong to the tyrants.[59]

But what if the tyrant had broken constitutional restraints, had violated, let us say, "an oath to his subjects to rule according to prescribed articles"?[60] Luther was aware that such restraints existed in more than one country, for he specifically cites those in effect in France and Denmark. But he cited them only to brush them aside.

I answer: It is fine and just that rulers govern according to laws and administer them and do not rule according to their self-will. Nevertheless, I add this,—

---

[56] *Ibid.*, p. 44.   [57] *Ibid.*, pp. 44–45.   [58] *Ibid.*, p. 45.   [59] *Ibid.*   [60] *Ibid.*, p. 51.

not only does a king promise to keep the law of his land or the articles of election, but God Himself commands him to be righteous, and he promises to do so. Well, then, if this king keeps neither God's law nor the law of the land, ought you to attack him, judge him, and take vengeance on him? Who has committed that to you?[61]

It was not man's right, but God's, to judge and punish the royal offender.

There were, of course, limits to the temporal power. Princes had complete authority in worldly matters, but they were not to interfere in spiritual affairs—a rule which Luther early qualified, however, as we have seen, by making it the prince's duty to deal with heretics and support the true religion. But apart from that considerable qualification, the ruler should not dictate in the domain of religion. Thus, if he ordered his subjects to disregard "the Commandments of God," the subjects should not obey him.[62] Apparently, however, as in the case of royal interference with preaching of the gospel, disobedience of royal orders of that nature was to be merely passive.[63] Indeed, we are told that if a temporal lord insists on this or that religious belief, or on the relinquishment of certain religious books, the proper reply would be:

Dear Lord, I owe you obedience with life and goods; command me within the limits of your power on earth, and I will obey. But if you command me to believe, and to put away books, I will not obey; for in this case you are a tyrant and overreach yourself, and command where you have neither right nor power, etc. Should he take your property for this, and punish such disobedience, blessed are you. Thank God that you are worthy to suffer for the sake of the divine Word, and let him rave, fool that he is.[64]

Was Luther, then, so firmly convinced of the divine ordination of kings and princes that under no circumstances would be permit any resistance to the temporal powers? Before dealing with this question it must be noted that his interest in it, as in all political matters, was "practical" rather than theoretical. His religious doctrines needed the support, he believed, of secular authorities, and hence he conceived of them as a bulwark of defense against his enemies. He was sincerely convinced, moreover, that violence was always an evil and should be sternly repressed. This was the function of princes, who had been divinely instituted for that purpose. In the course of time, however, the Lutheran cause appeared to be threatened by the empire. And Luther, reviewing the whole matter in the light of practical considerations, found it necessary to revise somewhat his earlier views. He came to the conclusion that resistance to the emperor was justified under

[61] *Whether Soldiers, too, Can Be Saved*, in *Works*, V, 51.
[62] *Treatise on Good Works*, in *Works*, I, 271.   [63] *Ibid.*
[64] *Secular Authority . . .*, in *Works*, III, 257.

certain conditions, and that such justification was based upon the law of the empire, which sanctioned resistance in the face of real injustice.[65]

Unfortunately for posterity, it was Luther's earlier views which were more fully expressed and much more widely known. Kings and princes who read in his tractates passages about the divine ordination of rulers no doubt found his theology more acceptable because of those passages. And is it improbable that many a prince who felt no sympathy whatever for Luther's religious views, took to his heart the doctrine of divine right and non-resistance? At any rate the doctrine entered the political thought of Europe, there to remain for many a day. "It was," says Dr. Figgis, "by transferring the notion of non-resistance from the Imperial to the princely, and from the ecclesiastical to the lay power, that Luther gave to the doctrine of the Divine Right of Kings such universal and enduring prevalence."[66]

[65] In the sixth volume (pp. 280–84) of his *History of Medieval Political Theory*, Dr. Carlyle has discussed this phase of Luther's development with his usual insight and lucidity, citing in that connection various passages in the Reformer's later correspondence.

[66] *From Gerson to Grotius*, p. 80.

Chapter XXX

DESIDERIUS ERASMUS (*c.* 1466-1536)

Desiderius Erasmus was born in an age of change, of new learning and old doubts, of ancient and mellowed institutions yielding to another and different order, of retreating horizons alike in the physical and the spiritual domains. Feudalism was already doomed, the age of chivalry was passing into history. A contemporary of Columbus and Copernicus, of Luther and Machiavelli, of Francisco de Vitoria and St. Thomas More, Erasmus witnessed the advent of the modren world heralded by new knowledge of the earth and of the heavens, by new ideas and customs replacing the old. In the words of a distinguished English historian,

A new continent had risen up beyond the western sea. The floor of heaven, inlaid with stars, had sunk back into an infinite abyss of immeasurable space: and the firm earth itself, unfixed from its foundations, was seen to be but a small atom in the awful vastness of the universe. In the fabric of habit in which they had so laboriously built for themselves mankind were to remain no longer.[1]

But the modern era was not based solely upon the discovery of things new and strange to the peoples of Europe. It was founded also upon the intellectual contributions of the past, often inappropriately described as the "new learning." "Next to the discovery of the New World, the recovery of the ancient world is," Lord Acton observes,[2] "the second landmark that divides us from the Middle Ages and marks the transition to modern life." In this process of recovery Erasmus played an important and, indeed, the leading rôle. Disregarding the prejudices and narrowing systems of thought prevalent among so many of his contemporaries, he gave himself wholeheartedly to the task of transmitting the learning of the past to his own day and to the future. He was not an innovator, a promoter of new and radical ideas. "No discoveries are associated with him," says the late P. S. Allen, the leading authority of our day on Erasmus' life and letters,[3] "he led no new movement of thought." His great purpose, like that of Cicero, was to transmit to his contemporaries and to posterity treasures of the mind and of the spirit from the distant past. "He devoted himself on equal terms,"

---

[1] Froude, *History of England*, I, 65-66. [2] *Lectures on Modern History*, p. 71.
[3] P. S. Allen, *Erasmus, Lectures and Wayfaring Sketches*, p. 1.

to quote again from Lord Acton, "to classical and to Christian antiquity, and drew from both alike the same lessons of morality and wisdom."[4]

In his own age Erasmus exerted a potent influence in many lands, and today his influence is still a factor to be reckoned with in more than one fair field of human ideals. When the writings of most of his contemporaries are forgotten except by the few interested in incunabula, Erasmus' best-known works are still being printed and read, four hundred years after his death. There are many reasons for this, and Allen has summarized most of them in a few happily phrased and penetrating lines:

> He [Erasmus] has many sides, to win sympathy; and whatever subject he touches, he illuminates. The scholar, the theologian, the grammarian, all recognize the importance of his work, even though it may now be out of date, or where they may not agree with it; the historian turns over his pages with delight, never knowing what he may not find; for the student of education or of morals there is much that is directly important; the peacemakers reprint his exhortations in that great cause from generation to generation; lovers of literature find his lighter works ever new. And for those who are interested in human nature—and who is not?—there is a gallery of characters, almost as rich as in Theophrastus or in Earle: the bright schoolboy, the reluctant canon, the poor student, the brilliant friend, the horseman, the gay courtier, the anxious traveller, the matchless scholar, courted and besought of kings, yet holding them all at arm's length; finally the Master lapped in the devotion of his followers, toiling daily with them in his "mill," now exacting and imperious, laying on them burdens heavy as his own, now charming them with natural, unforced merriment. It is this wonderful combination which has placed him where he stands. His intensely human temperament kept him from the pedestal of Bernard; his wide sympathies from the stern convictions of Zwingli or Calvin. His sense of humour preserved him from domineering with Luther; his delicacy from rollicking in the mud with Rabelais; his sincerity saved him from the withering bitterness of Voltaire. Above all he could not be dull.[5]

"Wit, brilliance, charm," says Allen elsewhere,[6] cataloging Erasmus' social qualities, "quick thought and ready tongue, and that open confidence which disarms—all these were his; and he smiled his way into men's hearts long before they realized his wonderful powers."

Yet for all his great gifts, the early life of Erasmus was not an easy one. Apparently, he was of illegitimate birth, although we have but meager facts concerning his parentage and early childhood. We do know, however, that he was born at Rotterdam, that his schooling began at Gouda when he was very young, that he served as a choir boy in Utrecht, and that his education was continued in the famous school for boys at Deventer. After

[4] Acton, *op. cit.*, p. 87.   [5] Allen, *op. cit.*, pp. 26–27.   [6] *Ibid.*, p. 2.

the death of his parents he attended still another school, kept by the order known as the Brethren of the Common Life. Much of this schooling, as we may judge from Allen's essay on the schools of the period,[7] was by our standards of an arid and wearisome nature. Erasmus, it would seem, made no very rapid progress in these early studies.[8] This was no doubt due to the fact that he found prevailing methods of teaching uncongenial, for in later life he looked back on his instruction at Deventer as "barbarous."[9] And indeed his schoolboy experiences left so deep an impression on him that in later years, as we shall see, he became greatly interested in educational reforms.

Nevertheless because of—or perhaps in spite of—this "barbarous education," Erasmus' hunger for knowledge, and especially for classical learning, had been aroused and he was anxious to proceed to a university. But his guardians looked with little favor on the ancient classics, and persuaded Erasmus, somewhat against his will, to enter an Augustinian monastery at Steyn where, in due course, he became a member of the order. It may be— and so Erasmus himself sometimes felt in later years—that it was a mistake for him to have taken the canonical vows. He was beyond all doubt a religious man, but throughout his life he struggled to remain independent of mind and free of spirit, and life in the cloister under the rules of the order did not permit him the freedom he felt to be essential if he were to work effectively in his own way. Therefore, though he made some progress in his studies at Steyn, we can understand his pleasure in leaving the cloister, at the age of twenty-five, to become secretary to the Bishop of Cambray and, a few years later, to study at the University of Paris, where the older scholasticism and the newer humanism were already at odds. Needless to say, Erasmus enthusiastically embraced the cause of humanism.

But his life at the university was not an easy one. The funds at his disposal were inadequate and his health suffered. To make ends meet he found it necessary to give up time to informal teaching or tutoring, among his

---

[7] *The Age of Erasmus*, pp. 33-65.

[8] Nathan Bailey, an English lexicographer of the eighteenth century, makes the following pertinent observation on this point in his translation of Erasmus' *Colloquies*: "They have in Holland, an ill-grounded Tradition; that Erasmus, when he was young, was a dull Boy, and slow at Learning; but Monsieur Bayle has sufficiently refuted that Error, tho' were it true, it were no more Dishonour to him, than it was to Thomas Aquinas, Suárez, and others."— *The Colloquies of Desiderius Erasmus Concerning Men, Manners and Things*, trans. by Bailey and ed., with notes, by the Rev. E. Johnson, I, 10.

[9] See Erasmus' *Compendium vitae*, in *The Epistles of Erasmus from His Earliest Letters to His Fifty-first Year*, trans. by Nichols, I, 7. For a discussion of the authenticity of the *Compendium vitae*, see Allen, *Opus epistolarum Des. Erasmi Roterodami*, I (Appendix I), 575-78.

later pupils being the young Lord Mountjoy. The latter, returning to England in the early summer of 1499, invited his mentor to accompany him, and thus Erasmus came into contact with Thomas More and John Colet. Now it is a truism that a man is known by his friends. A person whose affections go out to those with a spiritual outlook is himself a man of spirit. The intimate association of Erasmus with Colet and More is in itself the best evidence of the Dutch humanist's character and qualities.

More was then in his early twenties, Erasmus a decade older, but each immediately recognized in the other a kindred spirit and they entered into an intimate and lifelong friendship. An amusing anecdote is told of their first meeting. They chanced to be seated at the dinner table of a mutual friend, but though More had heard of the learned Erasmus and Erasmus had been told that the young More was a genius, they had for some reason not been introduced and neither was aware of the other's identity.

After the fashion of the day [we are told] a discussion arose between the two, when Erasmus, himself brilliant in debate, was so much impressed by the wit and readiness of his unknown young opponent, that at last he exclaimed: "You are no one if not More!" To this More instantly retorted: "And *you* are Erasmus —or the Devil!" ("Aut tu es Morus, aut nullus." "Aut tu es Erasmus, aut diabolus.")[10]—

a remark, it should be added, which Erasmus rightly accepted as a merry compliment to his "skill and subtlety in argument."[11]

The friendship thus begun deepened with the years. The two humanists were more often apart than together, as a result of Erasmus' restless travels hither and yon across Europe, but correspondence between them was frequent and often lengthy. Erasmus on his trips to England stayed at his friend's home, and, as we have seen,[12] wrote a sketch of him for which More's biographers must be eternally grateful. And More, though apparently he did not attempt to portray Erasmus, encouraged him in his work, congratulated him upon his triumphs, and defended him against detractors.[13]

Equally important in the direction and development of Erasmus' work was his meeting with Colet, then lecturing at Oxford on the New Testament. The two found a common ground at once in their interest in the Scriptures. As has been stated elsewhere,[14] Colet believed that Christians

---

[10] Routh, *Sir Thomas More and His Friends* (previously cited), pp. 15–16.
[11] *Ibid.*, p. 16.   [12] *Supra*, pp. 429 ff.
[13] An interesting example of More's "passionate and indignant defence" is given by Froude in his *Life and Letters of Erasmus*, lectures delivered at Oxford, 1893–94, pp. 143–49.
[14] *Supra*, p. 426.

should turn to the Bible as the source of their religion, and he communicated his enthusiasm on this subejct to his new friend from the Continent. Erasmus at once shared his views on the fundamental importance of the biblical texts, but as a scholar he also realized that their goal could never be reached with the faulty Latin texts of the Scriptures and the Church Fathers then available. Therefore to Colet's invitation to begin lecturing at once in Oxford,

Erasmus, more clear-sighted and not too old to surmount a new fence [says Allen], replied that he must first go and learn Greek: "without which," as Colet afterwards admitted, "we are nothing." He went and in five years came back, ready for his lifework. Colet, who had meanwhile become Dean of St. Paul's, supplied him with manuscripts from the Chapter Library, and led him on to attack the very centre of the position, to throw new light on the foundation of their religion, by a new translation of the New Testament.[15]

The results of this great undertaking will be examined in more detail a little later. For the moment it will suffice to add a further comment by Allen on the career of Erasmus.

From this time onwards, from 1506, Erasmus' career was settled. He was destined to be the leader of a new school of scientific study; bringing to bear upon sacred learning the critical scholarship which in the preceding century the Italians had applied almost exclusively to the classics.[16]

For some years he worked busily not only upon the Scriptures but upon numerous works of a different nature, moral exhortations, witty satires and colloquies, tracts and collections of homilies on education, peace, government, marriage, and countless other subjects. His fame grew steadily until he had correspondents in every important court and seat of learning in Europe. Kings and nobles, churchmen and scholars, statesmen and reformers, bombarded him with letters. And he replied to most of them, if not to all, for the Latin which he had so perfectly mastered flowed freely and rapidly from his pen. The financial aid from patrons which he had at one time so badly needed, and had obtained with difficulty, now came to him almost unasked.

The year 1516 marked his complete conquest of the learned world, for it was in that year that he published two books "which," Allen assures us, "mark an epoch in the study of divinity, the New Testament in Greek with a Latin translation and notes by Erasmus, and Jerome in nine folio volumes."[17]

But neither fame nor illness (never robust, he suffered increasingly from ill health to the end of his life) prevented him from continuing his work.

[15] *Erasmus, Lectures and Wayfaring Sketches* (previously cited), pp. 82–83.
[16] *Ibid.*, p. 83. [17] *Ibid.*

Year after year he wrote, edited, published, and republished. With the aid of the printing press he made his age familiar with the pagan and Christian classics. Of the Church Fathers alone, the famous Swiss printer Froben published for him what Allen describes as "a whole gallery of the Fathers, about thirty folio volumes of them."[18] And at frequent intervals editions or translations of Greek and Roman authors appeared, textbooks for students, essays (singly and in collections which doubled and trebled in size from printing to printing), as well as selections from the letters—themselves often complete essays—to his innumerable correspondents.

In connection with Erasmus' enormous literary output it is necessary to consider briefly his relation to learning and the purpose which he had in mind. He was admittedly the prince of humanists, but what does that well-deserved appellation mean? In the case of Erasmus it meant first of all that he sensed the continuity of history. The present is linked to—indeed, grows out of—the past and can be understood only through study of the great contributions of the past. "Erasmus," says Dr. Murray, "has a reverential attitude to the past: it has handed down truth to the present."[19] Others might conceive of a hopeless contradiction between pagan antiquity and Christianity. Not so Erasmus. To him the pagan wisdom of the ancient world was as a precursor of Christianity. In the light of history he saw a long process of development, with the religion of Christ as at once the unification and the loftiest expression of man's spiritual conceptions, and with truth as the everlasting goal. This does not mean that Erasmus indiscriminately worshiped the ancients. He was first of all a Christian, then a humanist. "From Antiquity," as one of his countrymen points out,[20] "he only chooses those elements which in ethical tendency are in conformity with his Christian ideal." He recognized at their full value the great cultural contributions of the ancient world and he labored long and hard to transmit them to the modern world. The successful result of his labors has been summed up in a single brief sentence by the Dutch historian whom we have just quoted: "Erasmus made current the classic spirit."[21]

"To politics, to religion and to education," declares Professor Preserved Smith, "he applied the lessons he had learned from the great poets and philosophers of antiquity."[22] And the same writer adds:
if the political and religious purposes of Erasmus looked back to the ages of Pericles, Cicero, and St. Paul, still more did his ideal of personal culture and of

---

[18] *Ibid.*, p. 84.
[19] Robert H. Murray, *Erasmus and Luther: Their Attitude to Toleration,* p. 30.
[20] Huizinga, *Erasmus,* in the "Great Hollanders" series ed. by Bok, p. 130.
[21] *Ibid.*, p. 50.
[22] "Erasmus, Enemy of Pedantry," in *The American Scholar,* VI (winter issue, 1937), 89.

the good private life rest on the firm basis of the classics. Few men have ever known and still fewer ever enjoyed and assimilated the classics as did he. Next to the *"philosophia Christi," "bonae literae"* were nearest to his heart.[23]

Defining humanists as "the men who sought and who found culture in the writers of Athens and of Rome and who could then have found it nowhere else," Professor Smith proceeds to summarize Erasmus' contribution to humanism:

> The true humanist must not only passively absorb culture; he must add to it, create it, and diffuse it himself. Of all men who have written in Latin since the death of Augustine Erasmus contributed most to the stock of the world's literature. In his commentaries and paraphrases one gets, not indeed the best scientific exegesis, but the best interpretation of the ancient thought in modern terms. In his numerous essays on pedagogy and on style one gets the best apology for a classical education and the best advice on how to attain it. In his *Handbook of a Christian Knight* and in his *Discussion of Free Will* one gets the best program for an ethical, undogmatic, practical, and happy piety. Outstanding among all his works are the *Praise of Folly* and the *Colloquies*.[24]

Of the *Praise of Folly* Professor Smith says that it

> is the gentlest satire ever penned. The whip in the hand of Juvenal, of Swift, and of a Sinclair Lewis has turned into a feather with which to tickle mankind and make it laugh at its own foibles. Folly is no longer a vice to be scourged but an amiable weakness to be indulged and ever so gently turned to good account.[25]

As for the famous *Colloquies* (which became the accepted school reader of the sixteenth century, and in succeeding centuries were reprinted many times), they are described as

> little stories told with such consummate art that many famous dramatists and novelists—Rabelais, Ben Jonson, Sardou, Margaret of Navarre, Walter Scott and Charles Reade, for example—have borrowed plots and incident from them. Each has a little moral lesson, not obtruded but insinuated with such art as to make it imperceptible, like those drugs administered in sugar pills. Almost all the stories tell of real incidents in the life of the author or of his friends.[26]

Professor Smith, after rightly including Erasmus' letters in "the list of his major writings"[27]—for they must take rank with the few great epistolary collections of the ages, both as literature and for their value in revealing Erasmus and his age to posterity—gives his measured judgment on the literary style of the Erasmian contributions:

> That Erasmus was one of the great stylists of the world will be admitted by all who can read him freely in the original. Few men have ever worked more conscientiously and more intelligently for a style; and still fewer have achieved it in so large a measure. Erasmus told his pupils how to write well; and then,

---

[23] P. Smith in *The American Scholar*, VI, 90.
[24] *Ibid.*, p. 91.   [25] *Ibid.*   [26] *Ibid.*   [27] *Ibid.*, pp. 91–92.

unlike many other teachers, did it himself. The senence structure is the clearest possible; the choice of vocabulary is exquisite; the use of antithesis, idiom, meiosis, emphasis and metaphor is perfect. The taste and quality of the Latinity eludes description. It is so delicately flavored with classic reminiscence, and yet so individual. It is at times so epigrammatic and so witty, and at other times so soft and so subtle. If Addison had had the wit of Voltaire and the subtlety of Henry James he might have written like Erasmus. The combination of such irreconcilables is impossible? Yes; but Erasmus achieved it.[28]

But Erasmus was more than a humanist. He was a scholar who, as we have already seen, devoted himself heart and soul to the science of divinity. In the conventional sense of the term he was not a theologian, and the fine points of doctrine interested him not at all. The true development of Christianity required, he felt (as did Colet), a more direct study of the Scriptures. He realized at once, however, that this was not a simple matter. The Bible was divinely inspired, but at the same time it was a historical document; and the direct study of it in the fullest sense of the term would be possible only if the Scriptures were available in their original form. Here was a task for the critical scholar: The Old Testament must be examined and translated from the Hebrew, the New Testament from the Greek. Erasmus determined to concentrate his attention on the New Testament, and with this in view he gave much time over a period of years to the study of Greek. Having become proficient in it, he then devoted himself to the preparation of a Latin translation and the editing of a Greek text. Both, as we have seen, were published in 1516. Thus he gave to the world its first printed edition of the New Testament in Greek. It was not a definitive text, for the critical standards of Erasmus, high as they were in his own day, cannot compare with those of a later age.[29] Indeed, he himself was never wholly satisfied with the work, for he reëdited it four times, the last edition appearing only a year before his death. Nevertheless, though "as an achievement of scholarship," in Allen's words, "it has long been superseded," it has remained "the foundation of the learning of today."[30]

[28] *Ibid.*, p. 92.
[29] Erasmus' outstanding achievement in scholarship is his edition of the Church Fathers, especially Jerome. In the language of Professor Preserved Smith (*op. cit.*, p. 88), "his very best work was in the field of patristics. His familiarity with the subject matter and his command of the language used by the great fathers have never been excelled. Probably no one editor, not even Migne, has done as much as he did to establish the correct texts of these authors."
[30] *Erasmus, Lectures and Wayfaring Sketches* (previously cited), p. 74. Also of interest here is the recent comment of a Belgian writer, Professor Henri de Vocht, of the University of Louvain: "C'est ainsi qu'Erasme, en remplaçant l'imitation traditionnelle par l'investigation scientifique, en écartant la réception passive d'un enseignement pour introduire la recherche active et l'interprétation critique, fit progresser la culture intellectuelle et la civilisation humaine à pas de géant."—*Erasme, sa vie et son oeuvre*, p. 40.

Erasmus' aim, it should be added, was not scholarship as an end in itself. He indicated plainly the broader purpose he had in view in preparing the *Novum instrumentum,* as he called his edition of the New Testament. Mr. Seebohm, in his justly famous volume on *The Oxford Reformers,*[31] has supplied a slightly abridged but splendidly Englished version of a passage from the "Paraclesis" which Erasmus prefixed to his *Novum instrumentum,* and which explains clearly the great objective toward which he was working.

Speaking of the "philosophy of Christ," Erasmus calls attention to the ease with which it may be learned by those with open hearts. It is not difficult and complicated like other philosophies, and is excluded from "no age, no sex, no condition of life," provided only that texts of the Scriptures are made available to all.

I utterly dissent from those who are unwilling that the sacred Scriptures should be read by the unlearned translated into their vulgar tongue, as though Christ had taught such subtleties that they can scarcely be understood even by a few theologians, or as though the strength of the Christian religion consisted in men's ignorance of it. The mysteries of kings it may be safer to conceal, but Christ wished his mysteries to be published as openly as possible.

And there follows a passage in which Erasmus lifts prose to the plane of poetry:

I wish that even the weakest woman should read the Gospel—should read the epistles of Paul. And I wish these were translated into all languages, so that they might be read and understood, not only by Scots and Irishmen, but also by Turks and Saracens. To make them understood is surely the first step. It may be that they might be ridiculed by many, but some would take them to heart. I long that the husbandman should sing portions of them to himself as he follows the plough, that the weaver should hum them to the tune of his shuttle, that the traveller should beguile with their stories the tedium of his journey.

Erasmus was, indeed, the apostle of enlightenment—an enlightenment which included both knowledge and a lofty moral standard. It was his conviction that the advancement of learning was the most fundamental of all steps in the progress of civilization, and to that advancement he devoted his life. In a day when travel meant hardships in the face of which the learned of our day would falter and shrink, he undertook many a long and wearisome journey in pursuit of his great quest. As his fame grew he was welcomed royally wherever he went. Princes endeavored to attach him to their courts; the learned of many lands begged him to remain with

---

[31] Pages 202-4.

them.[32] His work was interrupted by innumerable visitors, among them Ferdinand Columbus, son of the discoverer of the New World. The great and the near-great sought his counsel, aid, and influence. Had he wished, he might have held high office in both state and Church, but again and again he refused positions which, he felt, would restrict his precious freedom. A cardinal's hat awaited his acceptance, but he would have none of it. Determined to preserve his intellectual independence, he accepted in his early years only such aid from patrons as he felt to be necessary for his purposes, and in later years when his reputation had brought him ample wealth for his needs he was "inexorable in refusing honours and places that would have hindered him from his work."[33] Nothing but the hand of death itself could bring to an end his long fight for the advancement of learning.

It was a fight on more than one front, as we have seen. For in addition to his great contributions in the fields of scholarship, religion, and classical knowledge, Erasmus' genius made itself felt in other fields—in religious reform, in education, in politics, peace, and internationalism.

Erasmus had no liking for controversy. Arrogance of mind, dogmatism, the partisan spirit, were foreign to his nature. Reason was the governor of his mind, and true reason, seeing both sides of a controversy, discerns the right in each and seeks to harmonize them. If driven to it, Erasmus could descend to take up the cudgels of dispute, but his heart was not in the controversy for he much preferred the quiet and lonelier height, lighted by knowledge and reason.

He saw that there were abuses in the Church, and he unhesitatingly pointed them out, with a satire now delicate and gentle, now keen as a surgeon's knife. The orthodox theologians suspected him of heretical tendencies, yet the truth was that Erasmus remained all his life essentially a conservative reformer. He saw clearly the necessity of reform, but he wanted no revolution, no destruction of the great religious organization of which he was a member, and which was the one institution in existence which embodied the ideal of unity in a very human world of dissension and strife. It was his conviction—so strong that we may almost call it an obsession—that the evils of the Church, like those of the temporal domain, were caused by ignorance, and that they could and would be banished by the gradual conquest of knowledge.

---

[32] "Chaque foyer de culture est son asile, chaque université sa demeure, chaque cour princière son hôtel. Partout on le recherche et on l'accueille avec joie."—Th. Quoniam, *Erasme*, p. 10.

[33] Allen, *The Age of Erasmus* (previously cited), p. 133.

To others who pointed out current abuses he was often helpful so long as they did not advocate destructive cures. Thus in the early days of Luther's campaign he was not without sympathy for the German reformer's efforts, until he realized that Luther would brook no restraints, that he was becoming a menace to the unity which Erasmus so deeply cherished. He had no wish, however, to become embroiled in the rising controversy. Rather, he sought some means of settling the differences peaceably. Professor Smith[34] has sketched his attitude during this early period in a few sentences. Referring to the hostile reception of Luther's works in England, he quotes a letter from Erasmus to one John Oecolampadius[35] stating that they would have been burned but for the intervention "of a certain humble though vigilant friend.[36] Not that I undertake to judge Luther's works," he adds with characteristic caution, "but this tyranny by no means pleased me." A year earlier Erasmus had written "to Wolsey, gently excusing Luther, but at the same time deprecating the idea that he (Erasmus) was in any way a supporter of the new movement." And during the ensuing two years he did all in his power to heal the schism and to secure a fair hearing for the reformer. By personal interview, by a number of pamphlets, mostly anonymous, and by letters he urged on the public, and especially on men in power, the advisability of using argument rather than force in crushing the suspected heretic.[37]

Erasmus' way was the way of reasonable argument, of counsel, of composing differences, of emphasizing points of agreement instead of stressing points of dispute. It would have been easy for one in his position to join the leaders of reform or reaction, and to become himself a leader, if it had been his nature or his desire to assume an aggressive rôle. But Erasmus well knew that all movement is not improvement; that every so-called "advance" is not progress. He saw both sides, and not wholly approving either, it was his fate to disappoint both. What we sometimes forget is that it is not easy to be moderate when one lives in a world of extremes, and that there is a degree of heroism in hewing firmly to a middle course in the face of criticism from both sides. But time has justified Erasmus, though it has

---

[34] "Luther and Henry VIII," in *The English Historical Review* (previously cited), pp. 656–57.

[35] Dated May 15, 1520; printed in Allen, *Opus epistolarum Des. Erasmi Roterodami*, IV, 260, No. 1102.

[36] The "friend" in question was Erasmus himself.

[37] A letter from Erasmus to Luther dated Aug. 1, 1520, further illustrates the attitude of the great humanist toward the reformer and his dogmatic convictions (Allen, *Opus epistolarum*, Vol. VIII, letter no. 1127a, inserted among preliminary pages): "It is not for me, my Luther, to give you advice; nevertheless, if you entirely condemn all philosophy, you will find yourself confronted not only with all the Academics, but with all the ancients, too, and even your own Augustine, to whom you lend a willing adherence."

dealt less kindly with the extremists. "In the long run," maintains Dr. Murray,[38] "progress is more real and more secure when it is built on the Erasmian than when it is built on the Lutheran plan."

The voice of God is not alone in the storm-wind or the earthquake [continues the same writer], or the fire of a Luther; it is in the still, quiet utterance of an Erasmus. He understood, he appreciated the mediaeval Church as no one except perhaps Dante had understood and appreciated her. His understanding and his appreciation revealed her innermost principle. His insight proved that he, and men like him, had outgrown the forms of this principle, and that it was ready to enter into fresh forms of life and thought.[39]

Dr. Murray offers, in various chapters of his thoughtful study of Erasmus and Luther, a series of striking contrasts between the two great figures of the Reformation, and these passages are here brought together, by way of concluding this phase of the subject, in numbered paragraphs.

1. Evolution was the way of Erasmus: revolution proved the way of Luther. The binding tie with the past inspires the one: it makes no appeal to the other. To Erasmus there was no weapon equal to persuasion. . . . His breadth was his weakness at the time, but his strength with the generations to come. The narrowness of Luther was his strength at the time, but his weakness with the generations to come. He possessed that robust dogmatism, that strong conviction, which is utterly alien to the temperament of the scholar. Erasmus doubtless wished he were as sure of some things as Luther was of everything. It was emphatically by faith that Luther obtained a good report: it was no less emphatically by works that Erasmus trusted to obtain a good report.[40]

2. The moderation of the attitude of Erasmus, the candour of soul combined with the reserves of his mind left him without controlling power over the crowd. Leadership in his case was not forthcoming. The one employed the popularity of the pulpit, the other the seclusion of the study. Erasmus had studied the world of books, but had he studied the book of the world? The history of Erasmus is the history of a mind: the history of Luther is the history of a man. Religious progress is for the one clearness: for the other it is enrichment. The one believes in a revelation perfect and complete: the other believes in a revelation slow and gradual. The light Luther derived from the sacred record must be absolutely pellucid. The summer haze that surrounds all great thought was not for him.[41]

3. To the end Erasmus entirely used Latin, while Luther largely used German. Luther was too national in his outlook to influence men of other lands. Erasmus was the exact type to move them, but his appeal was to the cultivated. Luther saw his native land as clearly as Zwingli saw his beloved Switzerland. Erasmus saw neither Germany, nor France, nor Spain, nor Italy, nor England, but the whole of Europe. The one is German, the other universal.[42]

---

[38] *Erasmus and Luther* (previously cited), p. 379. [39] *Ibid.*, p. 383.
[40] *Ibid.*, p. 85.   [41] *Ibid.*   [42] *Ibid.*, p. 92.

4. According to Luther natural reason, apart from the Holy Spirit, is without knowledge: in divine matters man is in complete darkness. The essence of man's condition is sin, and man is only sin. Belief meant to Luther the losing of individuality in God, the submission of man's liberty to His absolute will, thereby creating in spite of himself a dualism. To Erasmus it meant the realization of all man's ideals in God, the union of faith and action, the essential oneness of all our intellectual and moral forces. Long before Pascal, Erasmus held with him that there are *deux excès: exalter la nature ou la condamner*. The humanists tended so much to make reason dictator in religion that Luther desired to banish it entirely from religion. As a Christian Erasmus did not believe in the natural goodness of man, though as a humanist he equally did not believe in his utter corruption. Experience, he thought, is decisively against the view that man's nature is totally depraved. Erasmus strove towards some better unity of all the facts given by nature, revelation and history. The faith which seizes cannot, he saw, be set in permanent opposition to the reason which verifies: all truth is one, and he endeavoured so to grasp it. There was a passing want of harmony between the conceptions of the past and the knowledge—the knowledge achieved by the Erasmian method—but that was all. The theology of Luther had been formed by a blending of mysticism and Austinianism; that of Erasmus is a blending of Churchmanship and humanity. Luther is a disciple of Jesus. Erasmus is a disciple of Jesus and also of Plato. He does not—nay, he cannot—separate his faith from a general theory of the universe. The mind of Luther embraces God and the justification of man. The mind of Erasmus embraces this and an intellectual system as well. The reformer requires the certainty of his salvation, the humanist the certainty of truth. Luther, like so many reformers, e. g. John Calvin and Calvin's precursor, Guillaume Farel, attributed his conversion to a sudden revelation. Erasmus believed in progressive, not sudden, revelations.[43]

5. Luther raised a storm in order to tear away the fading leaves from the tree, whereas Erasmus imitated nature in a tamer mood, pushing off the old leaf by the action of the bud which contains the leaf of next year. The time was out of joint, and Erasmus was only too pleased to have been born to straighten it—could it be done in a philosophical manner. His desire to obtain peace and unity for the Church—and his desire was most genuine—and at the same time procure a serene atmosphere during the process, constitutes a poignant element in the history of the time. He had many admirers: he had no devotees. *Credo in Newmannum* was once a watchword which inspired a movement. *Credo in Lutherum* was once a watchword which inspired a movement of another age. For the German reformer had a genius for action. He united two qualities, and these were religious enthusiasm and that power for action which imposed his views on those with whom he came into contact. His ardent and inflexible soul, inspired by enthusiastic mysticism, gave him an incomparable driving force, whose relentlessness crushed all opposition. Impassioned in his faith, he appeals to the passion of others. Is he not a master of the irony of insult? Did any one ever say *Credo in Erasmum?*[44]

---

[43] Robert H. Murray, *Erasmus and Luther*, p. 86.   [44] *Ibid.*, pp. 93-94.

6. All causes require a formula. What had the humanist to offer? He had a system, a scholarly system, which insisted on the necessity of always consulting the sources in the best available text. What appeal could it make to the peasant? Erasmus had the freest of minds, the broadest of outlooks. On the other hand Luther possessed the power of an "idée fixe." Erasmus, moreover, had a horror of dogmatism, and dogmatic a leader must be. He had no convenient catchword, no cohesion in doctrine, or precision in formula like "faith without works" or "justification by faith." He had no gifts for an appeal to *hoi polloi*. He was as incapable of moving the masses as the Scots humanist, Buchanan. Luther was as capable of moving them as Knox himself. Luther is as much the man of the brochure as Erasmus is the man of the book. Erasmus appealed to Reuchlin, Copernicus, Vives, Sir Thomas More and Rabelais. For, in spite of his limitations, he was one of the greatest of the sons of men, greater for succeeding generations than for his own. His many-sided mind diffused seminal ideas which brought forth fruit abundantly. Montaigne consulted his *Adages,* and who can measure the influence of Montaigne on the cause of freedom of thought? From the *Colloquies* the *politiques* of sixteenth-century France learnt those lessons of toleration they put into practice. Even in his own day his work remained in closer contact with Luther than the reformer ever dreamt. The reformer's friend was Melanchthon, and on Philip Melanchthon there rested the very spirit of Erasmus, making him the most broad-minded of the German reformers. Like Oliver Cromwell, Erasmus's direct plans for reform, the reform of the Church, failed; his indirect, that is his system, succeeded. What keeps his memory green is the permanent stimulus he gave to life and thought.[45]

7. The main question with Luther, as with Newman, is the salvation of his soul. The main question with Erasmus is the certainty of truth. To Luther the Law reveals the beginnings of the knowledge of all things, human as well as divine. The truth is that Luther as little requires a general theory as an average Englishman, whereas Erasmus cannot live without such a theory. The humanist resists the natural tendency of the Hellenic mind to dualism. There is a unity which excludes all difference: that is Luther's. There is also a unity which includes all difference: that is Erasmus's.[46]

8. The tragedy was that Erasmus possessed no gifts for practical leadership. The action of Luther at the moment attained more than was accomplished by his rival's balance of acumen and learning. All causes require a champion, a martyr, and a seer. Luther was a champion and he possessed the spirit of martyrdom: the quality of seership was largely denied him. Erasmus was a champion without a trace of the heroic spirit. He, however, possessed in no mean degree the gifts of seership. He had sceptical acumen, he had military loyalty to his method, and this combination was one that left him a puzzle at the moment, but a permanent force of the future. For any great cause there is needed the champion of the past—and the past is the seed-plot of the present and the future: there is also needed the martyr to the exigencies of the present, often in conflict with the past; and there is also needed the prophetic soul. Erasmus possessed two of these great

---

[45] *Ibid.,* pp. 94-95.   [46] *Ibid.,* p. 233.

gifts, and it is by virtue of their possession that his is an influence which grows from more to more. He brought from heaven to earth a fresh sense of the relation of man to the unseen.[47]

Erasmus was deeply interested in the promotion and improvement of education. Many of his works were intended to serve mainly as schoolbooks, and their vast influence has led one writer on Erasmus to call him "the Schoolmaster of Europe."[48] Reference has already been made to the *Colloquies* which so long served as a school reader; in order to demonstrate that Erasmus concerned himself not merely with general conceptions of enlightenment but with specific problems and methods of instruction, it will suffice here to give the titles of several of his more important tractates on the subject of education: his *De ratione studii* (1512), *De duplici copia verborum ac rerum commentarii duo* (1512), *Libellus de conscribendis epistolis* (1521), *Christiani matrimonii institutio* (1526), *De civitate morum puerilium* (1526), and *Libellus novus et elegans de pueris statim ac liberaliter instituendis* (1529).

What does Erasmus stand for in the field of education? In dealing with this question it is necessary to consider certain of his convictions which were fundamental to the principles lying at the root of his theory of education. The most fundamental of all was his conviction that culture was universal, that it was limited by no temporal boundaries, that the great republic of letters knew no frontiers except the frontiers of civilization itself. Therefore, his system of education dealt not with national elements but with elements common to all of Christendom—the Bible, the Church Fathers, and classical literature. And it was doubtless for this reason, in part at least, that Erasmus stressed the use of Latin, the one common language of Europe amid a babbling multitude of diverse tongues and dialects. A universal religion, a universal culture, a universal language—these constituted the threefold foundation of Erasmus' conception of a system of education which should promote a brotherhood of religion, of knowledge, and of speech. To be sure, the Erasmian republic of letters was not all-embracing in the sense that it included both high and low, rich and poor. In his day popular education was still a far-off dream; learning was a luxury which, for the most part, could be afforded only by the prosperous and well-to-do. No doubt he would have welcomed a system which offered education to all, irrespective of birth or property. But it was to be many and many a long year before such a system began to be even partially realized in the modern

---

[47] Robert H. Murray, *Erasmus and Luther*, pp. 383–84.
[48] Mangan, *Life, Character and Influence of Desiderius Erasmus of Rotterdam*, II, 395.

world. In the sixteenth century Erasmus had to face sixteenth-century conditions, and the best he could hope for poorer people was that they might be able to familiarize themselves with the New Testament—which, after all, is the best possible introduction to education if thoroughly mastered and, even though never supplemented by further learning, contains that which is requisite for the making of a high-minded Christian.

It should not be forgotten that with Erasmus the moral element in education was always paramount. Throughout his writings on the instruction of the young is to be found an ever-recurring emphasis on the moral virtues, on sincere piety, and the elements of Christian practice. He had no great interest in education for specialized purposes, for professions or careers in particular fields. These might be important in themselves, but what he had in mind was the development of ideals and character, the groundwork, as it were, of liberal education without which professions and other specialized careers lead to narrow or one-sided lives. Before he specialized, in other words, a student must imbibe the moral precepts, the broad culture, and the amenities which would prepare him for living in the best sense. Wisdom and spiritual well-being, according to Erasmus, must go hand in hand. "The highest gifts of all no man can give to another, even to his child," he declares, "but we can store his"—meaning the child's—"mind with that sound wisdom and learning whereby he may attain to the best."[49]

Erasmus has himself stated his conception of the nature and purpose of education in clear and simple terms:

To dumb creatures Mother Nature has given an innate power or instinct, whereby they may in great part attain to their right capacities. But Providence in granting to man alone the privilege of reason has thrown the burden of development of the human being upon training. Well, therefore, has it been said that the first means, the second, and the third means to happiness is right training or education. Sound education is the condition of real wisdom. And if an education which is soundly planned and carefully carried out is the very fount of all human excellence, so, on the other hand, careless and unworthy training is the true source of folly and vice. This *capacity for training* is, indeed, the chief aptitude which has been bestowed upon humanity. Unto the animals nature has given swiftness of foot or of wing, keenness of sight, strength or size of frame, and various weapons of defence. To Man, instead of physical powers, is given a mind apt for training; in this single gift all others are comprised, for him, at least, who turns it to due profit. We see that where native instinct is strong—as in squirrels or bees—capacity for being taught is wanting. Man, lack-

---

[49] *Libellus novus et elegans de pueris statim ac liberaliter instituendis,* trans. in Woodward, *Desiderius Erasmus Concerning the Aim and Method of Education,* pp. 180–222, especially 185. The present writer is much indebted to this little volume on Erasmus' views concerning education, a subject in which he has long been deeply interested.

ing instinct, can do little or nothing of innate power; scarce can he eat, or walk, or speak, unless he be guided thereto. How then can we expect that he should become competent to the duties of life unless straightway and with much diligence he be brought under the discipline of a worthy education?[50]

As for methods of education, Erasmus abounded in suggestions and precepts. He had seen—and had been deeply impressed by—More's arrangements for the education of his family. It was, indeed, in the More household that he became converted to the view that women should be properly educated—a view which he more than once strenuously defended, at the same time attacking the frivolous instruction which was so often meted out to girls. Erasmus had also discussed the subject of education with Colet, and he took great interest in Colet's foundation of St. Paul's School, to which the English divine devoted much of his time and fortune. So keenly was Erasmus' interest stimulated by the school (one of the landmarks in the history of English education) that he prepared several of his educational tractates for use in connection with the new institution.

Of the many educational precepts which Erasmus laid down, only a few may be referred to here, and those largely in Erasmus' own words. While he stressed the importance of beginning education in the home, he was naturally more interested in the school. Now a school, to be a success, must have good teachers, and Erasmus therefore devoted some attention to the teacher's qualifications. He must be the kind of person who will be admired by his students and will win them to knowledge, not drive them by fear.

A poor master [observes Erasmus] relies almost wholly upon fear of punishment as the motive to work. To frighten an entire class is easier than to teach one boy properly.[51]

And to emphasize his point Erasmus draws an illustration from the political field. "It is equally true of States: the rule which carries the respect and consent of the citizens demands higher qualities in the Prince than does the tyranny of force."[52] Moreover, the teacher must be "competent to recognize the best in the mass of erudition open to him, which in turn signifies that he has read far more widely than the range of authors to be taught by him."[53] He must not merely think but must be certain that he knows whereof he teaches. The actual practice of teaching soon reveals deficiencies. Indeed, "in no other way can we so certainly learn the difference between what we *know,* and what we *think we know.*"[54] To Erasmus the teacher rightly equipped "ranks," as one authority observes, "with

---

[50] *De pueris instituendis,* trans. in Woodward, *op. cit.,* pp. 183–84.   [51] *Ibid.,* p. 205.
[52] *Ibid.*   [53] *De ratione studii,* trans. in Woodward, *op. cit.,* p. 166.   [54] *Ibid.*

wise kingship, upright officials and a devoted clergy, as one of the four pillars of national well-being."[55] Teaching seemed to him "amongst the highest of Christian duties, and the noblest of intellectual careers."[56]

And finally, as an illustration of the methods of teaching which Erasmus advocated, two charming passages must be quoted on the teaching of languages (which could never be mastered, Erasmus believed, by mere drill in grammatical rules):

First of all, I give the leading place to practice in spoken language, which it is so great a task for adults to accomplish. As I have already said, this is an exercise of the child's powers of imitation, which it shares with certain birds. As an aid to this study can anything be better adapted to the youthful capacity than the reading of ancient Fables? For they appeal by their romance, they are good for moral lessons, they help vocabulary. There is nothing a boy more readily listens to than an apologue of Aesop, who under cover of pleasant story teaches the youth the very essence of philosophy. You relate, again, how Circe transforms the comrades of Ulysses into swine and other animals. It is a story to rouse interest and, perhaps, amusement; but the lesson is therein driven home that men who will not yield to the guidance of reason, but follow the enticements of the senses, are no more than brute beasts. Could a stoic philosopher preach a graver truth? The poetry styled Bucolic is easy to understand; Comedy is intelligible to boys, and teaches them many deep truths of life in its lighter vein. Then it is time to teach the names of objects—a subject in which even learned men are apt to be uncertain. Lastly, short sentences containing quaint conceits, proverbs, pithy sayings, such as in ancient times were the current coin of philosophy.[57]

But there were other methods for the teaching of languages, and Erasmus expounds them wisely and well:

Progress in learning a language is much furthered if the child be brought up amongst people who are gifted talkers. Descriptions and stories are impressed the better if to good narrative power the teacher or parent can add the help of pictorial illustration. The same method can be more particularly applied to the teaching of natural objects. Names and characteristics of trees, flowers, and animals can be thus learnt: specially is this plan needful where the creature described is wholly unfamiliar to the child. . . . A picture is shown, containing an elephant, in combat with a dragon. At once the class shows curiosity. How shall the master proceed? He states the Greek and Latin names for elephant, giving the Latin genitive case as well. He then points to the trunk, giving the Greek and Latin for it, and the purpose of the organ: he will explain that the elephant breathes as well as feeds by its means. The tusks are next dealt with, the uses and rarity of ivory; if possible he will produce something made of it. The dragon is shown to be of the large Indian species. He states the Greek and Latin equivalents for "dragon," their similarity in form, and their feminines. . . . Boys, too, will

---

[55] Woodward, *op. cit.*, p. 95.
[56] *Ibid.*, pp. 99–100.   [57] *De pueris instituendis*, trans. in Woodward, *op. cit.*, p. 212.

generally be attracted by pictures of hunting scenes, through which a wealth of information about trees, plants, birds, and animals may be imparted in a most delightful and yet instructive manner. In choosing subject-matter of this kind it is desirable to take some pains to discuss what is naturally attractive to the youthful mind, and discard what is of too advanced a kind. . . . Brightness, attractiveness, these make the only appeals to a boy in the field of learning. Is not this why the ancients fabled the Muses to be comely maidens, given to the song and the dance, and companions to the Graces? It was their doctrine also that excellence in true learning was only to be attained by those who find pleasure in its pursuit; and for this cause the liberal arts were by them called "Humanitas."[58]

The foregoing summary of Erasmus' general theories of education will serve as an introduction to his views on the particular subject of education for political purposes. His conception of society was a moral conception, and he believed that the education of those entrusted with the government of society should have a firm moral foundation. It is therefore but natural that his ideas on politics, as was recently stated by one who has given no little attention to Erasmus' political theories,[59] should be "intimately involved in his theories of ethics."

Now it has long been an accepted doctrine among political thinkers that those to whom the conduct of government is entrusted should have the best possible training for their task, both in moral theory and in practical principals. Plato held up the ideal of the philosopher-king; Aristole maintained that the ruler must be both good and wise; Cicero echoed and restated the views of both; and Seneca, St. Augustine, St. Thomas Aquinas, and many others accepted and elaborated the same doctrine. Erasmus, therefore, had the best of precedents and the weightiest of authorities when he decided to prepare his tractate on the education of a Christian prince (*Institutio principis christiani*),[60] first published in the year 1516. But before examining this famous work (some forty editions of it have appeared,[61] of which at least eighteen were printed before Erasmus' death), it is well to note that he alluded to political matters in many other works. His interests ranged nimbly over the whole field of humanistic thought, and he was perhaps at his best in the type of loose commentary where his mind could roam freely from subject to subject, unrestricted by narrow limitations. In these com-

---

[58] *De pueris instituendis,* trans. in Woodward, *op. cit.,* pp. 213, 214.
[59] This remark and subsequent quotations from Erasmus' *Prince* are reprinted from Born, *The Education of a Christian Prince, by Desiderius Erasmus,* translated with an introduction on Erasmus and on Ancient and Medieval Political Thought, p. 4.
[60] For an extended examination of the predecessors of Erasmus' *Prince* in political literature, see Born, *ibid.,* Introduction, chaps. iii–vi.
[61] Born, *op. cit.,* pp. 27–28.

mentaries references to political subjects crop up frequently, and sometimes unexpectedly.

In a tractate of 1530, cast in the form of a letter to one John Rinck, a jurist, Erasmus dealt with the subject of *War against the Turks,* and incidentally revealed his clear perception of the faults of rulers:

All monarchs are cut from the same cloth. Some are busied with collecting the sinews of war; some, with leaders and machines; but hardly any are planning for the betterment of human life, which is the [ultimate] source of everything else and pertains with equal importance to all alike.[62]

This was no new thought with Erasmus, for he had already expressed it in different form in his *Colloquies.* In a dialogue between George and Livinus (abbreviated to Ge. and Li.) on "Courtesy in Saluting," we find the following passage:[63]

Ge. Whence come all these tumultuary Wars?
Li. Whence should they come but from the Ambition of Monarchs?
Ge. But it would be more their Prudence to appease these Storms of human Affairs.
Li. Appease 'em! Ay, so they do, as the South Wind does the Sea. They fancy themselves to be Gods, and that the World was made for their Sakes.
Ge. Nay, rather a Prince was made for the Good of the Commonwealth, and not the Commonwealth for the Sake of the Prince.

Another work offers numerous counsels of perfection for monarchs:

Let kings then grow wise [was Erasmus' advice], wise for the people, not for themselves only; and let them be truly wise, in the proper sense of the word, not merely cunning, but really wise, so as to place their Majesty, their felicity, their wealth, and their splendour, in such things, and such only, as render them personally great, personally superior to those whom the fortune of birth has ranked, in a civil sense, below them. Let them acquire those amiable dispositions towards the commonwealth, the great body of the people, which a father feels for his family.[64]

Supplying a standard by which the monarch might judge himself, Erasmus continues:

Let a king think himself great in proportion as his people are good; let him estimate his own happiness by the happiness of those whom he governs; let him deem himself glorious in proportion as his subjects are free; rich, if the public are rich; and flourishing, if he can but keep the community flourishing in consequence of uninterrupted peace.[65]

---

[62] Quoted by Born, *op. cit.,* pp. 8–9. The same author furnishes in a few pages (4–20) an admirable guide to the many passages in Erasmus' writings on political doctrines, both national and international.
[63] *The Colloquies,* trans. by Bailey, I, 38.
[64] *The Complaint of Peace,* pp. 50–51.
[65] *Ibid.,* p. 51.

Erasmus' third piece of advice to the ruler is equally pertinent.

Let him exercise his power as far as he pleases, within those bounds which he will always see clearly, when he remembers, that he is a man governing men, a free man at the head of freemen, a christian presiding over a nation of christians. In return for his good behaviour, let the people pay him just so much reverence, and yield him just so many privileges and prerogatives as are for the public good, and no more. A good king will require no more; and as to the unreasonable desires of a bad king, the people should unite to check and repel them.[66]

Summing up his conception of kingship in a phrase or two, Erasmus supplies us with a compact definition of the true king:[67] "He is really a King who aims at the Good of his People, and not his own; governing them by Law and Justice."

And finally a few passages should be quoted from what was—and still remains—the most popular of all Erasmus' books, his *Praise of Folly*. Folly, he revealed, was no respecter of high rank or royal blood. Too many rulers, he asserts "believe they have discharg'd all the duty of a Prince if they Hunt every day, keep a Stable of fine Horses, sell Dignities and Commanderies, and invent new wayes of draining the Citizens' Purses and bringing it into their own Exchequer; but under such dainty new-found names, that though the thing be most injust in it self, it carries yet some face of equity."[68]

With biting satire Erasmus proceeds to expose the common vices of rulers which they sought to conceal behind royal trappings. For this purpose he would have us "suppose" or picture to ourselves the type of ruler all too frequently encountered, "a man ignorant of Laws, little less than an enemy to the publique good, and minding nothing but his own, given up to Pleasure, a hater of Learning, Liberty, and Justice, studying nothing less than the publique safety, but measuring every thing by his own will and profit."[69] Yet such an individual—unless his unworthiness be revealed by satire and ridicule—may masquerade before the world with "a golden Chain, that declares the accord of all Vertues linkt one to another; a Crown set with Diamonds, that should put him in mind how he ought to excell all others in Heroick Vertues; besides a Scepter, the Emblem of Justice and an untainted heart; and lastly, a Purple Robe, a Badge of that Charity he owes the Common-wealth."[70]

---

[66] *The Complaint of Peace*, p. 51. [67] *Colloquies*, III, 38.
[68] *The Praise of Folly*, trans. by Wilson, 1668; ed. with an Introduction by Mrs. P. S. Allen, p. 140.
[69] *Ibid.* [70] *Ibid.*, p. 141.

Men plotted and struggled for thrones large and small, yet as Erasmus' wise Folly (a descendant, apparently of those keen-witted court "fools" who so often outshone their royal masters in wit and wisdom) pertinently asks, "if they had the least proportion of sound judgment, what life were more unpleasant than theirs, or so much to be avoided?"[71]

And Folly—stating, we may be sure, Erasmus' own views—answers the question just propounded in a passage which should be quoted in full:

> For who ever did but truly weigh with himself how great a burthen lies upon his shoulders that would truly discharge the duty of a Prince, he would not think it worth his while to make his way to a Crown by Perjury and Parricide. He would consider that he that takes a Scepter in his hand should manage the Publick, not his Private Interest; study nothing but the common good; and not in the least go contrary to those Laws whereof himself is both the Author and Exactor: that he is to take an account of the good or evil administration of all his magistrates and subordinate Officers; that, though he is but one, all men's Eyes are upon him, and in his power it is, either like a good Planet to give life and safety to mankind by his harmless influence, or like a fatal Comet to send mischief and destruction: that the vices of other men are not alike felt, nor so generally communicated; and that a Prince stands in that place that his least deviation from the Rule of Honesty and Honour reaches farther than himself, and opens a gap to many men's ruine. Besides, that the fortune of Princes has many things attending it that are but too apt to train 'em out of the way, as Pleasure, Liberty, Flattery, Excess; for which cause he should the more diligently endeavour and set a watch o're himself, lest perhaps he be led aside and fail in his duty. Lastly, to say nothing of Treasons, ill will and such other Mischiefs he's in jeopardy of, that that True King is over his head, who in a short time will cal him to account for every the least trespass, and that so much the more severely, by how much more mighty was the Empire committed to his charge. These and the like if a Prince should duly weigh, and weigh it he would if he were wise, he would neither be able to sleep nor take any hearty repast.[72]

In his tractate, *The Education of a Christian Prince*,[73] Erasmus set himself the task of dealing systematically with the problem of educating those who were to wield political power. It was his conviction that those who trained rulers to follow the straight and narrow path of good government must be numbered among society's greatest benefactors. A nation might owe much to a good prince, but the good prince himself it owed "to the man who made him such by his moral principles."[74]

---

[71] *Ibid.*, p. 138.   [72] *Ibid.*, pp. 138–40.

[73] For present purposes only the first two chapters of Erasmus' *Prince* will be examined. A more detailed analysis of the tractate, especially chaps. iii–xi, will be found in J. B. Scott, *The Spanish Origin of International Law*, Part I, pp. 34–47.

[74] *The Education of a Christian Prince*, in Born, *op. cit.*, p. 141.

What, in general terms, should be the aim and purpose of the young prince's education? First of all, it should build his character, both by strengthening it where signs of weakness are discernible and by inculcating the positive virtues so that he will not merely refrain from vices [75] but will form the habit of acting with "wisdom, magnanimity, temperance and integrity."[76] It is of equal importance that the prince be thoroughly grounded in the soundest principles of government. The trial-and-error method of acquiring wisdom may suffice for the individual, but if relied on by the prince it is more than likely to bring disaster upon his country. "That sort of wisdom is too expensive for the state," declares Erasmus. Therefore he insisted that "the instruction of the prince in accordance with established principles and ideas must take precedence over all else so that he may gain his knowledge from theory and not experience."[77] Again, taking a leaf from Plato's *Republic,* Erasmus held that the tutor of the prince should seek to make a philosopher of his royal pupil. The ruler must have a philosophical mind if he is to avoid falling into tyranny. "Do not think," Erasmus exclaims, "that Plato rashly advanced the idea, which was lauded by the most praiseworthy men, that the blessed state will be that in which the princes are philosophers, or in which the philosophers seize the principate."[78] But just what, it may be asked, did Erasmus mean by the term "philosopher"? Apparently foreseeing this question, he supplies us immediately with an answer:

I do not mean by philosopher, one who is learned in the ways of dialectic or physics, but one who casts aside the false pseudo-realities and with open mind seeks and follows the truth. To be a philosopher and to be a Christian is synonymous in fact. The only difference is in the nomenclature.[79]

Above all, the prince's education must supply him with standards. He must learn that "there can be no good prince who is not also a good man";[80] that "it is the province of a prince to surpass all in stainless character and wisdom";[81] that "you cannot rule over others until you yourself have obeyed the course of honor";[82] that to judge a prince to be great because of "his ability to dance gracefully, dice expertly, drink with a gusto, swell with pride, plunder the people with kingly grandeur,"[83] and similarly misconduct himself, is to judge by false standards; that the true standard of the prince should be the moral standard of the New Testament; and finally that he must therefore be his own "severest critic"[84] and must "measure everything by the Christian standard."[85]

---

[75] Erasmus, *The Education of a Christian Prince,* in Born, *op. cit.,* p. 144.
[76] *Ibid.,* p. 151. [77] *Ibid.,* p. 156. [78] *Ibid.,* p. 150.
[79] *Ibid.* [80] *Ibid.,* p. 189. [81] *Ibid.,* p. 153.
[82] *Ibid.,* p. 189. [83] *Ibid.,* p. 150. [84] *Ibid.,* p. 156. [85] *Ibid.,* p. 199.

Consequently it is the duty of the prince's tutor to first see that his pupil loves and honors virtue as the finest quality of all, the most felicitous, the most fitting a prince; and that he loathes and shuns moral turpitude as the foulest and most terrible of things. Lest the young prince be accustomed to regard riches as an indispensable necessity, to be gained by right or wrong, he should learn that those are not true honors which are commonly acclaimed as such.[86]

The tutor must make it very clear to "the young prince that nobility, statues, wax masks, family-trees, all the pomp of heralds, over which the great mass of people stupidly swell with pride, are only empty terms unless supported by deeds worth while,"[87] and that "the prestige of a prince, his greatness, his majesty, must not be developed and preserved by fortune's wild display, but by wisdom, solidarity, and good deeds."[88] The royal pupil should be taught that "only those who govern the state not for themselves but for the good of the state itself, deserve the title 'prince.'"[89]

How is all this wisdom to be impressed upon the prince? In his childhood, the teacher may follow much the same methods as those advocated by Erasmus for educating children of humbler station—the use of stories, fables, myths, and analogies. But "before all else the story of Christ" and "of His teachings"[90] should be made part of the daily lesson, for the future ruler must early "be taught that the teachings of Christ apply to no one more than to the prince."[91]

As the prince grows older, more advanced methods of instruction should be employed. The tutor should introduce him to books, being careful, however, to select wisely the literature to be read. Erasmus, as we know, advocated the reading of the Scriptures by people in all walks of life, and it need not surprise us, therefore, that he advised the tutor to place first upon the royal reading program selected books from the Old Testament and the Gospels of the New Testament.[92] Later the prince should read the best of the classical authors. Of these Erasmus names several, apparently in the order in which he would have them read: Plutarch, Seneca, Aristotle, Cicero, and Plato. History, Erasmus admits, contains "a great fund of wisdom," but here the prince must be taught to "read with discretion."[93] For the historians' pages are crowded with evil as well as with good characters, and the prince must not be misled into admiring ancient despots and tyrants. Erasmus therefore earnestly warns the prince:

When you hear about Achilles, Xerxes, Cyrus, Darius, and Julius Caesar, do not be carried away and deluded by the great names. You are hearing about great raging robbers, for that is what Seneca has called them on various occasions.[94]

[86] *Ibid.*, p. 148.   [87] *Ibid.*, pp. 148-49.   [88] *Ibid.*, p. 149.   [89] *Ibid.*, pp. 160-61.
[90] *Ibid.*, p. 148.   [91] *Ibid.*   [92] *Ibid.*, p. 200.   [93] *Ibid.*, p. 201.   [94] *Ibid.*

The prince should also be taught that the outer appurtenances of his office are not merely the adornments of power, but are rather symbols of the qualities he should possess. Erasmus dwells upon this point in a passage which must be quoted at length:

> What does the anointing mean if not greatness, leniency, and clemency on the part of the prince, since cruelty is almost always the companion of great power? What does the gold mean except outstanding wisdom? What significance has the sparkle of the gems, except extraordinary virtues as different as possible from the common run? What does the warm rich purple mean, if not the essence of love for the state? And why the scepter, unless as a mark of a spirit clinging strongly to justice, turned aside by none of life's diversions? But if the prince has none of these qualities, these symbols are not ornaments to him, but stand as accusations against him. If a necklace, a scepter, royal purple robes, a train of attendants are all that make a king, what is to prevent the actors who come on the stage decked with all the pomp of state from being called king? What is it that distinguishes a real king from the actor? It is the spirit befitting a prince. I mean he must be like a father to the state. It is on this basis that the people swore allegiance to him. The crown, the scepter, the royal robes, the collar, the sword belt are all marks or symbols of good qualities in the good prince; in a bad one, they are accusations of vice.[95]

Every page of Erasmus' *Prince* is so packed with wisdom and sound political sense that it is difficult to refrain from quoting at greater length. Here, however, it must suffice to include but two more passages in which he sets forth in concise and pungent sentences the royal duties for which the prince's education should prepare him:

> Follow the right, do violence to no one, plunder no one, sell no public office, be corrupted by no bribes. To be sure, your treasury will have far less in it than otherwise, but take no thought for that loss, if only you have acquired the interest from justice. While you are using every means and interest to benefit the state, your life is fraught with care; you rob your youth and genius of their pleasures; you wear yourself down with long hours of toil. Forget that and enjoy yourself in the consciousness of right. As you would rather stand for an injury than avenge it at great loss to the state, perchance you will lose a little something of your empire. Bear that; consider that you have gained a great deal because you have brought hurt to fewer than you would otherwise have done. Do your private emotions as a man—reproachful anger, love for your wife, hatred of an enemy, shame—urge you to do what is not right and what is not to the welfare of the state? Let the thought of honor win. Let the concern for the state completely cover your personal ambitions. If you cannot defend your realm without violating justice, without wanton loss of human life, without great loss to religion, give up and yield to the importunities of the age! If you cannot look out for the possessions of your subjects without danger to your own life, set the

---

[95] *The Education of a Christian Prince*, in Born, *op. cit.*, p. 152.

safety of the people before your very life! But while you are conducting yourself in this fashion, which befits a true Christian prince, there will be plenty to call you a dolt, and no prince at all! Hold fast to your cause. It is far better to be a just man than an unjust prince. It is clear now, I think, that even the greatest kings are not without their crosses, if they want to follow the course of right at all times, as they should.[96]

The second passage is an admonition on the proper use of the ruler's power:

Power without goodness is unmitigated tyranny; without wisdom it brings chaos, not domain. In the first place, then, in so much as fortune gave you power, make it your duty to gain for yourself the best store of wisdom possible, so you may clearly see the objectives to be striven for and the courses to avoid. In the next place, try to fill as many needs as possible for everyone, for that is the province of goodness. Make your power serve you to this end, that you can be of as much assistance as you want to be. But no, your desire in this respect should always exceed your means! On the other hand, always cause less hurt than you could have caused.[97]

Erasmus, it should be said, devoted so much attention to the education of princes because, in his age as in previous ages, the monarchical form of government was the commonest form and the one most generally approved by statesmen and philosophers.[98] In many countries the people as a whole were eventually to control the government, but in Erasmus' day democracy was still a dream of the future. Confronted by these facts, he felt that the only means of insuring good government was to provide the best education possible for those who were destined to wield political power. Whether he dimly foresaw a day when government would be of the people and by the people as well as for the people, we do not know. But we do know, from his own words, that he accepted the ancient principle, "Nature created all men equal";[99] and we may fairly assume that, had he lived in a later age, he would not have been content with educating princes to perform their royal duties, but would have insisted on education of the people at large in the rights and duties of self-government and enlightened citizenship.

For all his interest in good government within the state, however, Erasmus held no brief for the state as an end in itself. While Luther was developing into a patriotic German, Erasmus remained a citizen of Europe and of the international commonwealth of letters. Fanaticism, national passions, racial antipathies—all these were really foreign to his nature. In the face of factions and the threat of disruption, he steadfastly advocated the principles of compromise and unity, which, had they prevailed, might well have substituted

[96] *Ibid.*, pp. 154–55.   [97] *Ibid.*, p. 158.   [98] *Ibid.*, p. 173.   [99] *Ibid.*, p. 177.

an international community of Christendom for the international anarchy of the succeeding centuries. How could the threat of disruption have been met? Erasmus supplied an answer to that question in his *Liber de sarcienda ecclesiae concordia,* in which he states in a sentence the essence of his views: "First we must all do our duty—popes and princes, monks and magistrates, priests and laymen, we must all do what lies before us, without ambition or quarrelling, in that spirit of accommodation which makes for concord: only taking care not to compromise away the great foundations of life."[100] Allen has summarized in a paragraph the advice which Erasmus offered in this treatise—advice which, unhappily, the world failed to accept:

What then is the counsel that Erasmus gives? Agree with one another quickly, and dwell upon the points of your agreement. Define as little as possible, for that way lies division. Make concessions, especially about what may be only matters of individual taste—remembering that things which seem quite intolerable in those we do not like, we can learn to put up with in our friends. His words were useful to the age for which he wrote them: they seem to me just as useful to-day.[101]

What Erasmus really longed for, what he hoped might eventually develop, was a vast but peaceful community of peoples firmly bound together by ties of the mind and the spirit. Intellectual coöperation and spiritual harmony, not treaties founded on suspicion and distrust, were to be the bases of his internationalism. This dream of Erasmus was far in advance of his day; and it is still in advance of our day. Yet we may derive no little hope from the fact that it is no longer the dream of one man or of a few men; it is slowly but surely becoming the dream of humanity. And the more universal such a dream becomes, the nearer it approaches fulfillment.

It has sometimes been said that Erasmus dwelt in a world apart, that he was bookish and impractical. Perhaps he was, if it be considered impractical to hitch one's wagon to a star, to look beyond grim and forbidding obstacles, with eyes fixed on a far-off goal. The trouble with most "practical" people is that they lose sight of the goal—or fail altogether to see it—in worrying over the obstacles.

It would be a mistake, however, to assume that Erasmus was unaware of obstacles. If he was a man of books, he was also a man of the world. No mere impractical dreamer could have satirized as he did the follies and vices of his day. To take but a single instance, the matter of racial prejudices, which is perhaps the greatest of all obstacles to true internationalism. Far from being blind to such prejudices, Erasmus was keenly aware of them

---

[100] Trans. by Allen, *Erasmus, Lectures and Wayfaring Sketches,* pp. 89-90.
[101] *Ibid.,* p. 98.

and assailed them with the full force of his eloquence. It was commonly said, he writes, that an Englishman

is the natural enemy of a Frenchman, because he is a Frenchman. A man born on this side the river Tweed must hate a Scotchman, because he is a Scotchman. A German naturally disagees with a Frank; a Spaniard with both.[102]

What is Erasmus' comment on these prejudices?

O, villanous depravity! The name of a place or region, in itself a circumstance of indifference, shall be enough to dissever your hearts more widely than the distance of place, your persons! A name is nothing; but there are many circumstances, very important realities, which ought to endear and unite men of different nations. As an Englishman, you bear ill-will to a Frenchman, Why not rather, as a man to a man, do you not bear him good will? Why not as a christian to a christian? How happens it, that such a frivolous thing as a name, avails more with you than the tender ties of nature, the strong bonds of christianity?[103]

Erasmus' own conception of the true unity of mankind is revealed in two other passages in his famous *Complaint of Peace:*

Place, local distance, separates the persons of men, but not their minds. Hearts can gravitate to each other through intervening seas and mountains. The river Rhine once separated the Frenchman from the German, but it was beyond its power to separate the christian from the christian. The Pyrenean mountains divide the Spaniards from the French, but they break not that invisible bond which holds them together in defiance of all partition, the communion of the Church. A little gut of a sea divides the English from the French; but if the whole Atlantic ocean rolled between them, it could not disjoin them as men united by nature; and while they mutually retain the christian religion, still more [are they] indissolubly cemented by grace.[104]

Let the lovers of discord, and the promoters of bloodshed between nations, divided only by a name and a channel, rather reflect that this world, the whole of the planet called earth, is the common country of all who live and breathe upon it, if the title of one's country is allowed to be a sufficient reason for unity among fellow-countrymen; and let them also remember, that all men, however distinguished by political or accidental causes, are sprung from the same parents, if consanguinity and affinity are allowed to be available to concord and peace. If the Church also is a subdivision of this one great universal family, a family of itself consisting of all who belong to that Church, and if the being of the same family necessarily connects all the members in a common interest and a common regard for each other, then the opposers must be ingenious in their malice, if they can deny, that all who are of the same Church, the grand catholic Church of all christendom, must also have a common interest, a common regard for each other, and, therefore, be united in love.[105]

[102] *The Complaint of Peace* (previously cited), p. 61.
[103] Ibid., pp. 61–62.   [104] Ibid., p. 62.   [105] Ibid., pp. 63–64.

Lack of unity in the world meant not only confusion, but war. And war seemed to Erasmus the very antithesis of Christianity, in which alone he saw the hope of a spiritual union of mankind. There had been many attempts to reconcile war with the Christian doctrine, but to Erasmus such reconciliation was impossible.

Every page of the christian scriptures [he tells us], whether you read those parts of the Old Testament which have a reference to christianity, or the New, speaks of little else but peace and concord; and yet the whole life of the greater portion of christians, is employed in nothing so much as the concerns of war. It is, really, more than brutal ferocity which can neither be broken in, nor mitigated in its violence, by so many concurrent circumstances. It were best to lay aside the name of christian at once, or else to give proof of the doctrine of Christ, by its only criterion, brotherly love.[106]

And Erasmus proceeds to ask certain penetrating questions which could not easily be answered by belligerent Christians:

Now, what possible agreement can there be between camps and a church? A church implies union and association; camps, disunion and discord. If you say you belong to the Church, what can you have to do with the operations of war? If you say you do not belong to the Church, what have you to do with Christ?[107]

Yet in his day, as in ours, the support of God was invoked on both sides in wars between Christian nations. And "divine service is also performed to the same Christ in both armies at the same time." To Erasmus this was "a shocking sight."[108] As for the placing of Christian symbols on battle flags, especially those borne by mercenary soldiers, such a practice aroused Erasmus' ire.

What [he demands] hast thou to do with the cross of Christ on thy banners, thou bloodstained soldier? With such a disposition as thine, with deeds like thine, of robbery and murder, thy proper standard would be a dragon, a tiger, or a wolf![109]

All the doctrines of Christ were doctrines of peace, but especially (and here Erasmus was not fully in accord with the teachings of theologians who sought a justification of war) the doctrine of charity.

There is one special precept, which Christ called his, that is, Charity. And what thing is so repugnant to charity as War? Christ saluted his disciples with the blessed luck of peace. Unto his disciples he gave nothing save peace, saving peace he left them nothing.[110]

---

[106] *The Complaint of Peace*, pp. 31–32.   [107] *Ibid.*, p. 33.   [108] *Ibid.*, p. 45.   [109] *Ibid.* p. 44.

[110] *Dulce bellum inexpertis*. The version here quoted is a reprint of the first (1533–34) English translation, published under the title *Erasmus against War*, with an Introduction by Mackail, p. 34. This small work is an expansion of Erasmus' letter of March 14, 1514, to Antony of Bergen, abbot of St. Bertin (printed in Allen, *Opus epistolarum*, I, 551, No. 288). In enlarged form it was also published again and again as a separate tractate.

Man's true destiny was not warfare, Erasmus taught. Nature had dedicated him rather to "kindness, benevolence, and amity."[111] She had endowed him with a love of society, with feelings of friendship and affection, with the powers of reason and speech, with laughter and tears. Yet in spite of these endowments men wasted their blood and their lives in endless warfare, not only against strangers but even against their own countrymen, so that in Erasmus' words, "it chanceth oftentimes, that the brother fighteth with the brother, one kinsman with another, friend against friend."[112]

Indeed, it sometimes seemed to Erasmus that the more "civilized" men became, the more terrible grew their warfare. For in earlier times they had at least followed certain rules of war, observed certain forms and ceremonies, used simple weapons. But in his day—and his statement applies, unfortunately, with even greater force in our own day—men ignored the old rules and devised with "ingenious craft"[113] new and more terrible weapons of destruction, until Erasmus felt constrained to ask: "War, what other thing else is it than a common manslaughter of many men together?"[114] In the fever of warfare men ignored law, the guardian of the state and indeed of society. "If there cannot be a greater misfortune to the commonwealth, than a general neglect and disobedience of the laws, let it be considered as a certain truth, that the voice of law, divine or human, is never heard amid the clangor of arms, and the din of battle."[115]

Of course those who declare war always parade a host of reasons to justify their action. Erasmus, however, swept them all aside and revealed the real causes of war.

> I am well aware of the excuse which men, ever ingenious in devising mischief to themselves as well as others, offer in extenuation of their conduct in going to war. They allege, that they are compelled to it; that they are dragged against their will to war. I answer them, deal fairly; pull off the mask, throw away all false colours, consult your own heart, and you will find that anger, ambition, and folly, are the compulsory force that has dragged you to war, and not any necessity; unless, indeed, you call the insatiable cravings of a covetous mind, necessity. Reserve your outside pretences to deceive the thoughtless vulgar. God is not mocked with paint and varnish.[116]

It is infinitely better, in Erasmus' opinion—for he was a pacifist in the best sense of the term—to incur a loss for the sake of peace than to win a war at an infinitely greater loss. "Yet methinks," he adds, "a royal objector says, 'I would very willingly give up such and such points if I were a private man, and the things in question were my own property; but I am a

---

[111] *Ibid.*, p. 7.   [112] *Ibid.*, p. 10.   [113] *Ibid.*, p. 21.
[114] *Ibid.*, p. 23.   [115] *The Complaint of Peace*, p. 67.   [116] *Ibid.*, pp. 47–48.

king, and whether I like it or not, am under the necessity of acting as I do, for the public.'"[117]

What is Erasmus' answer to such an argument?

For the public, says your Majesty? Let me tell you, "that the king will not easily be induced to enter on a war, who has no regard but for the public." On the contrary, we see that almost all the real causes of wars, are things which have no reference at all to the welfare of the public. Is your object to claim and gain possession of this or that part of another's territory, what is that to the welfare of the people? Do you desire to take royal revenge on a crowned head in your vicinity, who has presumed to refuse your daughter in marriage, or repudiated her after marriage; what is that to the welfare of the people? How is it, in the smallest degree, a business of the State, the community at large? If you mean really to support your august Majesty and royal dignity, the only way is to support the character of a good, just, and wise man, by taking all these things into your most serious consideration, and acting accordingly.[118]

Then there is national pride in the guise of "national honor," which is not only a stumblingblock to peace but, in the form of reservations, has contributed to the futility of many a high-sounding treaty. Let us see what Erasmus has to say on this subject:

Men must not be too zealous about a phantom called national glory, often inconsistent with individual happiness. Gentle behaviour on one side, will tend to secure it on the other; but the insolence of a haughty minister may give unpardonable offence, and be dearly paid for by the sufferings of the nation over which he domineers.[119]

To the haughty minister and the arrogant ruler Erasmus more than once spoke blunt and wholesome truths. As regards war he insisted that, since the people themselves must bear the heavy burden of fighting and hardships, they should be consulted before war was declared—a doctrine which, it may be noted in passing, has many adherents in our own day. "A measure the most dangerous to the existence of a State as a war must be," he declares, "should not be entered into by a king, by a minister, by a junto of ambitious, avaricious, or revengeful men, but by the full and unanimous consent of the whole people."[120]

Unfortunately this was not the conception of the reigning monarchs, who appeared to consider the "whole christian people as a swinish multitude, as

---

[117] *The Complaint of Peace*, p. 72.

[118] *Ibid*. A like answer, briefer but in the same vein, is given in the tractate *Dulce bellum inexpertis* (in *Erasmus against War*, p. 60): "Ye say ye make war for the safeguard of the commonweal, yea, but noway sooner nor more unthriftily may the commonweal perish than by war. For before ye enter into the field, ye have already hurt more your country than ye can do good getting the victory. Ye waste the citizens' goods, ye fill the houses with lamentation, ye fill all the country with thieves, robbers, and ravishers. For these are the relics of war."

[119] *The Complaint of Peace*, p. 55.   [120] *Ibid.*, p. 55.

so little worthy of their regard, that they would set the world on fire, without consulting the people, to revenge the disappointment of their own selfish desires, or to secure their full gratification."[121] Such rulers might argue that they were obliged to govern despotically to protect "their own august Majesty" from "ill-designing men,"[122] but Erasmus met that argument by referring to "the Roman emperors, Antoninus Pius and Antoninus the philosopher"—the latter better known to modern readers as Marcus Aurelius —who were "the only ones that were never attacked."[123]

From these two instances [he continues] it appears, that no kings sit more firmly on their thrones, than they who shew that they are ready at any time to quit them, when their resignation appears likely to benefit the public; and that their power is a trust resumable at will, reposed in them by the people for the good of the people, and not to gratify their own pride or avarice, by lavishing away other men's blood and money.[124]

In another passage Erasmus speaks even more plainly:

The power and authority over men, which be free by Nature, and over brute beasts, is not all one. What power and sovereignty soever you have, you have it by the consent of the people. And if I be not deceived, he that hath authority to give, hath authority to take away again.[125]

Erasmus did more, however, than merely argue against war. He made various specific proposals for the preservation of peace—proposals which are decidedly pertinent at the present time. First it is advisable to note his warning against the wrong foundations for peace.

Firm and permanent peace is not to be secured by marrying one royal family to another, nor by treaties and alliances made between such deceitful and imperfect creatures as men; for from these very family connexions, treaties, and alliances, we see wars chiefly originate. No; the fountains from which the streams of this evil flow must be cleansed. It is from the corrupt passions of the human heart, that the tumults of war arise.[126]

If there is to be peace, he goes on, the government must be headed by wise and good men rather than by corrupt and ambitious despots. Instead of dreaming of conquests they should devote themselves to developing their own domains and to the furtherance of international amity and good will. They must seek prudent counsel, hearken to the voice of the people, and above all really desire peace.

Upon the whole it must be said, that the first and most important step towards peace, is sincerely to desire it. They who once love peace in their hearts, will eagerly seize every opportunity of establishing or recovering it. All obstacles to

---

[121] *Ibid.*, p. 73.   [122] *Ibid.*   [123] *Ibid.*   [124] *Ibid.*, pp. 73-74.
[125] *Erasmus against War*, pp. 50-51.   [126] *The Complaint of Peace*, p. 50.

it they will despise or remove, all hardships and difficulties they will bear with patience, so long as they keep this one great blessing, including as it does so many others, whole and entire. On the contrary, men in our times go out of their way to seek occasions of war; and whatever makes for peace, they run down in their sophistical speeches, or even basely conceal from the public; but whatever tends to promote their favourite war system, they industriously exaggerate and enflame, not scrupling to propagate lies of the most mischievous kind, false or garbled intelligence, and the grossest misrepresentation of the enemy.[127]

But Erasmus had a still more concrete proposal which was nothing less than international arbitration. Why should princes rush to war over their differences, he asks, when they might reach a settlement by legal means?

Suppose some differences, like those of conjugal life, to happen between neighbouring princes, why should they immediately draw the sword, and proceed to the last sad extremities? There are laws, there are sagacious men, there are worthy clergymen, there are right reverend bishops, by whose salutary advice all disagreements might be reconciled, and all disturbance checked at its origin. Why do kings not make these, instead of the sword, their umpires? Even if the arbitrators were unjust, which is not likely when removed from all undue influence, the disagreeing parties would come off with less injury than if they had recourse to arms, to the irrational and doubtful decision of war. There is scarcely any peace so unjust, but it is preferable, upon the whole, to the justest war.[128]

Ultimately, however, the cause of peace, Erasmus believed, rests with the people themselves. Therefore, after calling upon the kings, the clergy, and the nobles to abolish war, he turned to the people:

I appeal to all who call themselves christians, I urge them, as they would manifest their sincerity and preserve their consistency, to unite with one heart and one soul, in the abolition of war, and the establishment of perpetual and universal peace.

Here, and in this instance shew the world, how much can be effected by the union of the multitude, the mass of the people, against the despotism of the few and the powerful.[129]

Erasmus brought a new concept, says an Austrian writer, Stefan Zweig, "to freshen European thought."[130] And Mr. Zweig summarizes this concept in a passage of some length, but so admirably that it must be quoted in full:

Languages, which had hitherto formed an impenetrable wall between nation and nation, must no longer separate the peoples. A bridge would be built by means

---

[127] Erasmus, *The Complaint of Peace*, p. 60.
[128] *Ibid.*, pp. 48-49. This plea for arbitration was no new idea to Erasmus. He had earlier outlined it in his letter to Antony of Bergen, above referred to, and in the *Dulce bellum inexpertis*.
[129] *Ibid.*, p. 79.   [130] *Erasmus of Rotterdam*, English trans. by Eden and Cedar Paul, p. 107.

of a universal tongue, the Latin of the humanists. At the same time the concept of a fatherland for each nation would have to be proved untenable because it formed too narrow an ideal. It should be replaced by the European, the supranational ideal. "The entire world is one common fatherland," declared Erasmus in his *Querela pacis* (Complaint of Peace), and from this commanding position he looked down upon the senseless quarrels between the nations, the hatred between English, Germans, and French, to exclaim: "Why do such foolish names still exist to keep us sundered, since we are united in the name of Christ?" Disputes between Europeans seemed to the humanists to be the outcome of misunderstandings arising from too narrowminded an outlook, too faulty an education; the duty of coming generations of Europeans would be to replace the vainglorious claims of petty princelings, of fanatical sectarians, and of national egoists by sympathetic cooperation, by emphasizing that which could lead to harmony, by raising the European spirit to preside over the national spirit, to change Christianity as a simple religious congregation into a universal and all-embracing Christliness, where love of mankind and a desire to serve meekly and devotedly should prevail. Erasmus, we see, aimed higher than merely achieving a cosmopolitan community. What he showed was a resolute will to create a new spiritual form of unity in the West. Before his day there had been men to promote the notion of a united Europe, the Roman Caesars, for example, with their idea of the "pax Romana," Charlemagne, and, at a later date, Napoleon. But these autocrats worked with fire and sword, endeavoured to compel the nations to unite under the threat of violence and the fist of the conqueror, which weighed heavily on the weaker in order to bind them the tighter to the strong. The great difference between their idea and that of Erasmus was that to him European unity seemed to be a moral idea, utterly unselfish, a spiritual demand. With him began to be postulated the concept (which many are still advocating today) of a United States of Europe·under the aegis of a common culture and a common civilization.[131]

The greatest message of Erasmus to posterity was the message of internationalism, a spiritual, a cultural internationalism transcending national and racial barriers. More than four centuries have passed since his death in Basel, but this message is still fresh and stimulating to the humanists of our day. Indeed, the enlightened in many lands and in growing numbers are coming to believe that the salvation of humanity lies in the realization of Erasmus' hopes and ideals.

[131] *Ibid.*, pp. 107-9.

THE BEGINNING OF THE MODERN AGE

Chapter XXXI

HUGO GROTIUS AND THE *MARE LIBERUM*

Huig de Groot, whose name is more familiar in its latinized form of Hugo Grotius, was a native Hollander, born in Delft on the tenth of April, 1583. But he belongs to the world as well as to the Netherlands, for he contributed greatly to the law of the international community which is now regarded (in harmony with the doctrines proclaimed long ago by Francisco de Vitoria) as being coextensive with humanity.

Grotius browsed in many a field of learning and his contributions in each were important. If he did not look upon the world from the heights of Parnassus, he was nevertheless an excellent poet. His Latin verse—when Latin verse was the test of culture and literary polish—was regarded by competent critics as the best of his day and generation. Even at nine years of age his ability in versification was recognized.

He was deeply interested in history and had barely turned twenty when he was appointed historiographer of Holland. His *Annales et historiae de rebus belgicis*[1]—the most important of his several historical works—places him among the three great historians of the Netherlands, the others being Hooft, his contemporary, and—two centuries or more later—Fruin, whose comparatively recent death was a loss to the science of history.

Grotius was also deeply interested in religious questions; indeed it may be said that he was born a theologian.

He was likewise a man of affairs, for he held successively, while still a young man, the distinguished positions of advocate-fiscal of Holland, and of pensionary of the city of Rotterdam. And before the famous trial in 1619, which resulted in his imprisonment and subsequent exile from his native land, he was looked upon as the successor of the great John of Barneveldt, who had for many years held the high office of grand pensionary of Holland.

But it would be wearisome to continue the list of Grotius' attainments. Suffice it to say for present purposes that he was a lawyer by profession, a jurist by inclination, and a master of international law as regards both its theory and its practical application. His *Three Books on the Law of War*

---

[1] Written by Grotius in 1612, but first published in 1657, twelve years after his death in 1645.

and Peace (De jure belli ac pacis libri tres) of 1625 were the greatest landmark of his century in the literature of international law; and they are appreciated today to such a degree that many look upon him as the founder of international law, although it would be more accurate to say that in Grotius international law found a master compiler and expounder. At any rate, the universal consensus of opinion is that the publication of the treatise *De jure belli ac pacis* marked an epoch in international relations and in the modern conception of international law. But this masterpiece of Grotius is of such importance that it cannot be adequately considered or discussed in a work of the present scope and limitations. Therefore it is reserved for subsequent detailed treatment in another volume.[2]

Fortunately, there is a shorter work by Grotius which sets forth in brief compass a good many of the fundamental principles of international law later expounded by him at length in *De jure belli ac pacis*. It will be necessary to examine somewhat in detail this smaller and earlier masterpiece, the *Mare liberum,* which contains the essence of Grotius' early views as set forth in his youthful treatise, the *Commentary on the Law of Prize (De jure praedae commentarius)*.

But, it may be asked, why not discuss the *Commentary* itself rather than a part of it? Of the two reasons for deciding to limit the present chapter to the *Mare liberum,* the first is that while the *De jure praedae* seems short in comparison with the long treatise *On the Law of War and Peace,* it is, nevertheless, far too large for present purposes. At best only a fragment of the *Commentary* could be examined here. Now it so happens that Grotius himself selected a fragment of it to stand by itself as a separate tractate— the twelfth chapter. This chapter he published anonymously early in 1609, under the title *Mare liberum,* in order to influence the negotiations then in full swing between Spain and the United Netherlands, which materialized in the twelve-year armistice of that year.

The second reason is that for more than two centuries the *Commentary* was unknown to the public and therefore could not influence the negotiations of its day nor affect the development of international law as did the *Mare liberum.* Even the manuscript of the *Commentary,* which Grotius had never published, was not discovered until 1864, when it came to light among papers found in the house of one of Grotius' descendants. These papers of the great man, as often happens, were sold under the hammer and the

---

[2] The third and concluding part of *The Spanish Origin of International Law*. The first part of this series, entitled, *Francisco de Vitoria and His Law of Nations,* has already been published by the Clarendon Press, for the Carnegie Endowment for International Peace.

manuscript of the *Commentary on the Law of Prize,* in Grotius' own handwriting, was purchased by the University of Leyden (of which he was an alumnus) and there carefully examined by Professor Fruin of the university, who advised its publication, considering it to be in the nature of a first draft of Grotius' *De jure belli ac pacis.* The learned historian, however, was not content with a mere oral statement to that effect. He wrote an essay, or rather a monograph, entitled *Een onuitgegeven werk van Hugo de Groot* (1868),[3] in which he discussed in detail the origin of the *Commentary,* its relationship to the *Mare liberum,* and above and beyond all its position as what might be called "a draft" or a "first sketch" of the "masterpiece of the author's riper age."[4]

Professor Fruin, from his careful examination of the manuscript of the *Commentary,* felt himself justified in stating that the claim of Grotius' admirers that he was the founder of international law could be based upon the *Commentary* quite as soundly as upon the later and more elaborate treatment of 1625.[5] And an English writer of our day goes even further in expressing the opinion that if Grotius is to be considered the founder of international law, his claim to that honor should be based less upon *De jure belli ac pacis* than upon the twelfth chapter of the *Commentary,* the *Mare liberum.*[6]

Now the *Mare liberum* is what our French friends would call an *essai de circonstance.* It was an assertion, during a period of controversy, of the freedom of the seas, a doctrine founded upon Spanish precedent and upon the principles and theories of the schoolmen, as stated in Francisco de Vitoria's *De Indis* and in the writings of Vázquez de Menchaca. But even apart from references to these authorities, the entire text is, in both spirit and substance, in complete harmony with the contributions of the Spanish school of international law.

Until comparatively recently our antiquarian knowledge, so to speak, of the text of the *Mare liberum* had been derived from the early Elzevir editions, some of which are so small that they may be carried in the waistcoat

---

[3] Translated as *An Unpublished Work of Hugo Grotius,* in the "Bibliotheca Visseriana" series, Vol. V.

[4] *Ibid.,* p. 3.

[5] Fruin, *op. cit.,* pp. 59, 67.

[6] Knight, *The Life and Works of Hugo Grotius,* "The Grotius Society Publications," No. 4, p. 112.

Sir Thomas Wemyss Fulton in his standard treatise, *The Sovereignty of the Seas* (p. 338), says that "the little book of Grotius was at once a reasoned appeal for the freedom of the seas in the general interest of mankind, and the source from which the principles of the Law of Nations have come."

pocket.[7] The discovery of the *Commentary*, however, and its publication in 1868[8] have made it possible to examine the original text of the tractate and to consider its relation to the other chapters of *De jure praedae*.

It is supposed that the *Commentary on the Law of Prize* was written in or about the year 1604, in consequence of the capture off the Malaccas, by a Netherland merchant vessel in the employ of the Dutch East India Company, of a Portuguese galleon, the "Catharina," returning from the Indian seas with an exceptionally rich cargo. With no little difficulty this cargo was conveyed halfway around the world to the Dutch port of Amsterdam and there condemned as lawful prize and sold, distribution of the proceeds being ultimately made to the company, to the captors, and to other interested parties.

The case was an extraordinary one in that the Portuguese vessel had been captured by a Dutch merchant ship at a time when the Netherlands, although at war with Spain, was not technically at war with Portugal. To be sure, there was no little hostility in the East Indies between the Portuguese traders, who had an established and lucrative commerce with the natives, and the Dutch, who were bent on obtaining a share of that trade. That the Netherlands, however, long preferred to avoid open warfare is evident from the fact that the masters of Dutch vessels trading in the East Indies were for some years ordered to use their armament only for self-defense. But in the face of increasing Portuguese hostility they not infrequently ignored these orders, as in the case now being considered. Under ordinary circumstances, the capture of the "Catharina" would have been considered illegal, even if it were not held to smack of piracy. But the circumstances

---

[7] The Carnegie Endowment for International Peace issued, at the time when the "freedom of the seas" was a catchword, during the World War, an English version of the famous *Mare liberum* as *The Freedom of the Seas*, translated with a revision of the Latin text of 1633 by Magoffin. The same organization has in press, in its "Classics of International Law," a new edition of the *Commentary on the Law of Prize*, an edition comprising a collotype reproduction of the manuscript in Grotius' own handwriting, with all of his corrections and emendations and additional inserted passages; this edition will include a printed Latin text scrupulously following the manuscript and containing not only the body of the manuscript but also the additions and the deleted passages (which have been painstakingly deciphered), and an English translation. As a companion volume a new and revised edition of the *Mare liberum* is also being prepared, which will include a reproduction of the printed Latin text of the Elzevir edition, and a collotype reproduction of chap. xii of the *Commentary* (the original of the *Mare liberum*) and a revised English translation. Grotius' great treatise *On the Law of War and Peace* was published in the "Classics" series a few years ago, both in the original Latin and in English translation.

[8] Hugonis Grotii, *De jure praedae commentarius*, ed. by Hamaker.

In 1934 a Dutch translation of Grotius' *Commentary* was published in Leyden, with an Introduction by Dr. Mulhuysen. The translation, prepared by Dr. Onno Danisté, was issued under the title Huigh de Groot, *Verhandeling over het Recht op Buit*.

were not ordinary, at least in the opinion of the Dutch. The novelty of the situation as well as the richness of the cargo aroused deep interest among all who were directly or indirectly concerned in the matter. Indeed, the case attracted no little attention in the outside world. And it was destined to become, because of Grotius' *Commentary,* one of the outstanding historical cases of international law.

Grotius appears to have been profoundly interested in the legal phases of the matter. Although barely twenty-one when the "Catharina" reached the Netherlands, he was nevertheless already well established at the bar and was known among the members of his profession as deeply learned in Roman law. He appears to have been appointed by the Dutch East India Company to prepare an extended argument or brief in defense of the capture, and he therefore mastered the case in all its details, as is evident from the most casual examination of his brief, the *Commentary,* or even of its twelfth chapter which was to become the *Mare liberum.*

Now it happened that a certain Jacob Boreel was an influential member of the Dutch East India Company and that his son, Jan Boreel, was an intimate and confidential friend of Grotius. The young Boreel naturally had knowledge of the *Commentary* and as a friend he thought highly of Grotius' work. In the year 1608 he apparently called a portion of the *Commentary* to the attention of his father and other members of the company—the twelfth chapter, to be explicit—in the hope that they would be interested in having it printed, since it might well be of service to the Dutch in the negotiations between Spain and the Netherlands which were then at a deadlock over the question of the Dutch right to trade in the East Indies. These facts, long surmised, were substantiated by Fruin, as may be seen from the Appendix to his monograph.[9] The result of Jan Boreel's action was that Grotius was requested late in the year to detach the twelfth chapter from the *Commentary* and to issue it in printed form. It is possible that he had already toyed with the thought of such action; if so he had doubtless forgotten the project, for in the preceding months his mind had been full of another and more personal project (one of the utmost importance to himself as it turned out)—his marriage with Maria van Reigersberg, to whom Grotius was indebted the rest of his life as few men in history have been indebted to their wives. However, upon receiving the company's communication some months after his marriage, Grotius acted without delay. He removed the twelfth chapter from the *Commentary,* slightly revising it for

---

[9] *An Unpublished Work of Hugo Grotius* in the *Bibliotheca Visseriana* (previously cited), V, 72 *et seq.*

independent publication, and in the early days of 1609 gave it anonymously to the world under the title of *Mare liberum*. To the tractate thus published Grotius prefixed an appeal "To the rulers and to the Free and Independent Nations of Christendom,"[10] in the nature of a prologue, which would have done him honor at any period of his career. It represents Grotius in action: the young man, full of vivacity and with his future before him; not the disillusioned Grotius of later years, escaping from an unjust imprisonment and subsisting in Paris on a precarious income largely derived from his wife's properties.

The address to the Christian rulers is couched in the grand style. The young and spirited Grotius took the bull by the horns and roundly informed the rulers of Christendom that there is a "delusion . . . as old as it is detestable with which many men, especially those who by their wealth and power exercise the greatest influence, persuade themselves"—or, as he himself believed, tried to persuade themselves—"that justice and injustice are distinguished the one from the other not by their own nature, but in some fashion merely by the opinion and the custom of mankind." Declaring that such men consider laws and equity as having been invented simply to repress disputes and rebellions of persons of subordinate birth while they themselves, perched in "high position," were allowed "to dispense all justice in accordance with their own good pleasure," a pleasure "to be bounded only by their own view of what is expedient," he emphatically condemns this opinion as "absurd and unnatural"; and while admitting that it has "gained considerable currency," he attributes this unfortunate fact to "the common frailty of the human race."

But there were others of a more enlightened opinion, "independent and wise and devout men." Such men looked upon God as "the founder and ruler of the universe" and as "the Father of all mankind," and demonstrated that

He had not separated human beings, as He had the rest of living things, into different species and various divisions, but had willed them to be of one race and to be known by one name. . . . Furthermore He had given them the same origin, the same structural organism, the ability to look each other in the face, language too, and other means of communication, in order that they all might recognize their natural social bond and kinship.[11]

But these "wise and devout men" insisted upon a further truth—that human organization of the family, of the household, and of the state were of divine origin and that God "had drawn up certain laws not graven on

---

[10] *The Freedom of the Seas*, trans. by Magoffin (previously cited), p. 1. [11] *Ibid.*, pp. 1-2.

tablets of bronze or stone but written in the minds and on the hearts of every individual, where even the unwilling and the refractory must read them." Moreover, these "wise and devout men"—it need hardly be added that Grotius had the theologians in mind—held that "these laws were binding on great and small alike." In this passage Grotius confesses his belief in the scholastic conception of the eternal and divine and natural law.

Turning next to the subject of property, he declares that there are two kinds: one kind is held and enjoyed "in common with all other men," and the other belongs to each individual and "to no one else." Thus by nature certain things are for the common use of all and others "through the industry and labour of each man become his own." There are adequate laws covering both types of property, Grotius maintains. Now as the knowledge of "these facts" is inherent in the very nature of man, and their force is universally "recognized," Grotius pertinently asks: "What, O Christian Kings and Nations, ought you to think, and what ought you to do?"[12] Since princes insisted that the trade and property rights of their subjects should be respected, should they not be willing to apply the same principles in international relations?

This, it may be said, is a question which has seldom been satisfactorily answered by a prince. The answer, according to Grotius,[13] is that "every one can know what his own duty is from the very demands he makes of others," a reply which would seem to be in strict accord with the morality of the New Testament and which is tantamount to a statement that right and duty are correlative.

As examples of rights and their correlative duties, there were certain fundamental matters to which Grotius called the attention of his royal audience: the right of "every man . . . to manage and dispose of his own property"; the "equal and indiscriminate right" of all citizens "to use rivers and public places"; and the right of "freedom of travel and of trade."

Now in the opinion of Grotius—and it is an opinion which has stood the test of time—the fundamental principles upon which these rights were based, were not only essential to the existence of that "small society which we call a state" but were necessary also "to uphold the social structure of the whole human race and to maintain the harmony thereof."

Grotius here reminds the princes that they are responsible for the punishment of their subjects who violate these fundamental principles. But what of the princes themselves, if they should yield to the temptation to infringe these sacred and inherent rights in their relations with other states? In

[12] *Ibid.* [13] *Ibid.*, p. 3.

Grotius' day it was the common opinion that the prince was supreme within his own jurisdiction and responsible to no human agency for his conduct, whatever its nature. He was, however, responsible to his Creator, to whom punishment for his trespasses was reserved. Having stated this view, the young Grotius continues, in a purple passage which has but few parallels in the annals of international law:

> But although He reserves to himself the final punishment, slow and unseen but none the less inevitable, yet He appoints to intervene in human affairs two judges whom the luckiest of sinners does not escape, namely, Conscience, or the innate estimation of oneself, and Public Opinion, or the estimation of others. These tribunals are open to those who are debarred from all others; to these the powerless appeal; in them are defeated those who are wont to win by might, those who put no bounds to their presumption, those who consider cheap anything bought at the price of human blood, those who defend injustice by injustice, men whose wickedness is so manifest that they must needs be condemned by the unanimous judgment of the good, and cannot be cleared before the bar of their own souls.[14]

We have here a supreme tribunal of two chambers. The first is the court of conscience, to which the schoolmen had appealed through the centuries and to which every nation or people in distress appeals when all other recourse has failed. The second chamber of this double and final court is public opinion, a court to which even the most powerful of individuals feels constrained to appeal. He who ignores it, in matters great or small, does so at his peril.

Grotius now proceeds to state the nature and the origin of the case to which his previous observations have been as an introduction and which he proposes to lay before the "double tribunal." It was not a petty case of the kind that "private citizens" might "bring against their neighbors about dripping eaves or party walls," nor was it a trifling dispute about "boundary lines or the possession of a river or an island." What then was the nature of the case? "It is a case which concerns practically the entire expanse of the high seas, the right of navigation, the freedom of trade!"[15]

For the sake of emphasis Grotius' statement of the points at issue is here given in numbered paragraphs:

1. Can the vast, the boundless sea be the appanage of one kingdom alone, and it not the greatest?

2. Can any one nation have the right to prevent other nations which so desire, from selling to one another, from bartering with one another, actually from communicating with one another?

---

[14] *The Freedom of the Seas,* trans. by Magoffin, pp. 3–4.   [15] *Ibid.,* p. 4.

3. Can any nation give away what it never owned, or discover what already belonged to some one else?

4. Does a manifest injustice of long standing create a specific right?

In this statement Grotius reveals himself as a master of his profession, for he has skillfully phrased the points at issue in the form of questions which make any other reply than a negative practically impossible, and such a reply would in effect condemn the speaker for the opposition out of his own mouth.

The appeal to the rulers of Christendom is a small document but one of considerable importance. It not only states the relationship of the princes to international law, their duty to refrain from violating that law and to provide for its execution, but also indicates, in the following paragraph, the source of the law which Grotius invoked in behalf of his countrymen. "In this controversy," he says, "we appeal to those jurists among the Spanish themselves"—as we shall see later, particularly Vitoria and Vázquez de Menchaca—"who are especially skilled both in divine and human law." And in the next he adds, "we actually invoke the very laws of Spain itself." It may here be observed that the international law of Grotius' Spanish authorities was the international law of his day and was destined to be that of the future. Those authorities, however, based their law of nations largely upon the law of nature, and therefore Grotius also appealed to that law.

"The law," he continues,[16] "by which our case must be decided is not difficult to find, seeing that it is the same among all nations; and it is easy to understand, seeing that it is innate in every individual and implanted in his mind." In this statement the young Grotius subscribes, as did the older Grotius, to the scholastic conception of the law natural.[17] Enlarging

---

[16] *Ibid.*, p. 5.

[17] This conception, as we have seen, was founded upon the Stoic theory of the *ius naturale*: and it is interesting to note the observation of an American writer that Grotius, in developing his own conception of natural law upon "a purely rational foundation," "reverted substantially to the Stoic philosophy." This will be evident to all who take the pains to note in *De jure belli ac pacis* the hundreds of references to such leading expounders of Stoicism as Cicero and Seneca. "Grotius' method, however," comments the same writer, "differed somewhat from that of the Stoics in that he did not individualize his natural law but, leaning perceptibly toward the Aristotelian principle of the social impulse that eventually expressed itself in law, he was able to establish a legal system that existed irrespective of the reason of any single individual." A further statement by the writer in question is of considerable interest:

"In his division of positive and natural law Grotius also adhered to the Stoic view. For him natural law was characterized by its immutability and the agreement of peoples in its prescriptions because of their rational convictions. Positive law, on the other hand, he conceived to be purely volitional. It originated in the will of the civil authority; it was the expression of will that proceeded from the consensus of various persons. All law that had a sanction beyond the confines of natural law was accordingly consensual. The relationship of the two systems of natural and positive law was to be found in the fact that the binding force of the agreement implied in this consensual law rested eventually upon the natural law."—Goebel, *The Equality of States, a Study in the History of Law*, p. 78.

upon that conception, and emphasizing the universality of the law of nature, he adds:

> Moreover the law to which we appeal is one such as no king ought to deny to his subjects, and one no Christian ought to refuse to a non-Christian. For it is a law derived from nature, the common mother of us all, whose bounty falls on all, and whose sway extends over those who rule nations, and which is held most sacred by those who are most scrupulously just.

As an internationally minded man—for at an early age Grotius was already an internationalist and thoroughly grounded in the rules and practice of international law—he looked to an international settlement if national agencies and diplomatic procedure should fail in the adjustment of controversies between states. Invoking the practices of the past in support of this view, he declares:

> In ancient times among the more civilized peoples it was held to be the greatest of all crimes to make war upon those who were willing to submit to arbitration the settlement of their difficulties; but against those who declined so fair an offer all others turned, and with their combined resources overwhelmed them, not as enemies of any one nation, but as enemies of them all alike. So for this very object we see that treaties are made and arbiters appointed.[18]

Here Grotius reveals to us his conception of the neighborly standard which should prevail between nations, and of the sanction to be applied against aggressors.

His appeal to the rulers of the Christian world was a novel and masterly introduction and in itself no mean contribution to the law of nations. With this introduction Grotius has cleared the deck for action—to use a maritime figure of speech not inappropriate in a prize case. In the opening paragraph of Chapter I he immediately comes to grips with two principles fundamental to his thesis: first, the freedom of the seas as a right of navigation; second, the freedom of the seas as a means of trading with the nations of the world.

"My intention," he declares,[19] "is to demonstrate briefly and clearly that the Dutch—that is to say, the subjects of the United Netherlands—have the right to sail to the East Indies, as they are now doing, and to engage in trade with the people there." This is his thesis, and he next indicates the firm foundation for the argument by which he intends to sustain it: "I shall base my argument on the following most specific and unimpeachable axiom of the Law of Nations, called a primary rule or first principle, the spirit of which is self-evident and immutable, to wit: Every nation is free to travel to every other nation, and to trade with it."

[18] Grotius, *The Freedom of the Seas* (previously cited), p. 6.   [19] *Ibid.*, p. 7.

It is worth emphasizing here that this "principle" of the law of nations was fundamental to his purpose, and that he was therefore at some pains to describe it as both "axiomatic" and "unimpeachable," and as a "primary rule" which was in spirit not only "self-evident" but also "immutable."

Now where did Grotius find this principle which he described in such broad and positive terms? He found it, as is apparent from his own words, and from the accompanying reference, in the *Relectiones* of the Spanish theologian Francisco de Vitoria. "Victoria holds that the Spaniards could have shown just reasons for making war upon the Aztecs and the Indians in America, more plausible reasons certainly than were alleged, if they really were prevented from traveling or sojourning among those peoples, and were denied the right to share in those things which by the Law of Nations or by Custom are common to all, and finally if they were debarred from trade."[20] Here Grotius refers specifically to seven propositions in Vitoria's *Relectio de Indis*,[21] and for good measure he cites in addition the authority of Covarruvias, Spanish canonist, statesman, and jurist.

Now Vitoria's seven propositions to which Grotius refers are:

1. The Spaniards have a right to travel into the lands in question and to sojourn there, provided they do no harm to the natives, and the natives may not prevent them.[22]

This right was based on the primordial principle "of natural society and fellowship," a principle Grotius himself had already accepted,[23] stating that those "who deny this law, destroy this most praiseworthy bond of human fellowship, remove the opportunities for doing mutual service, in a word do violence to Nature herself."

Let us now complete Vitoria's first proposition and continue with the remaining six:[24]

... Proof of this may in the first place be derived from the law of nations (*jus gentium*), which either is natural law or is derived from natural law (*Inst.*,

---

[20] *Ibid.*, p. 9.
[21] "Grotius's citation is actually of Section II, which deals with different matters, but there can be no doubt that his reference is to the *third* section. The great Hollander frequently quoted from a memory which rarely betrayed him—although it would seem to have done so in the present instance. Curiously enough the Simon (1696) edition of Victoria, reproduced photographically in the Carnegie Institution edition, ... has, as the result of a typographical slip in the running head above the passage in question, the very error into which Grotius had fallen—that is, the running head reads Section II when it should be Section III."—J. B. Scott, *The Spanish Origin of International Law* (previously cited), p. 160, n. 1.
[22] Vitoria, *De Indis* (previously cited), Sec. III, no. 2, p. 151, in "Classics of International Law." For a discussion of Vitoria, see chap. xxii, *supra*.
[23] Grotius, *The Freedom of the Seas*, p. 8.
[24] Vitoria, *op. cit.*, Sec. III, nos. 2–8; pp. 151, 152, 153–54, 155.

I. ii. 1): "What natural reason has established among all nations is called the *jus gentium.*" . . .

2. The Spaniards may lawfully carry on trade among the native Indians, so long as they do no harm to their country, as, for instance, by importing thither wares which the natives lack and by exporting thence either gold or silver or other wares of which the natives have abundance. . . .

3. If there are among the Indians any things which are treated as common both to citizens and to strangers, the Indians may not prevent the Spaniards from a communication and participation in them. . . .[25]

4. If children of any Spaniard be born there and they wish to acquire citizenship, it seems they can not be barred either from citizenship or from the advantages enjoyed by other citizens—I refer to the case where the parents had their domicile there. The proof of this is furnished by the rule of the law of nations, that he is to be called and is a citizen who is born within the state (*Code,* VII. lxii. 11 [*Code,* X. xxxix. 7]). . . .

5. If the Indian natives wish to prevent the Spaniards from enjoying any of their above-named rights under the law of nations, for instance, trade or other above-named matter, the Spaniards ought in the first place to use reason and persuasion in order to remove scandal and ought to show in all possible methods that they do not come to the hurt of the natives, but wish to sojourn as peaceful guests and to travel without doing the natives any harm; and they ought to show this not only by word, but also by reason, according to the saying, "It behoveth the prudent to make trial of everything by words first." . . . But when the Indians deny the Spaniards their rights under the law of nations they do them a wrong. Therefore, if it be necessary, in order to preserve their right, that they should go to war, they may lawfully do so. . . .

6. If after recourse to all other measures, the Spaniards are unable to obtain safety as regards the native Indians, save by seizing their cities and reducing them to subjection, they may lawfully proceed to these extremities. . . .

7. If, after the Spaniards have used all diligence, both in deed and in word, to show that nothing will come from them to interfere with the peace and

---

[25] It is in connection with this third proposition that Vitoria (*op. cit.,* Sec. III, no. 4; p. 153) states his important definition of international law, with which Grotius was no doubt familiar: "Inasmuch as things that belong to nobody are acquired by the first occupant according to the law of nations (*Inst.,* II. i. 12), it follows that if there be in the earth gold or in the sea pearls or in a river anything else which is not appropriated by the law of nations those will vest in the first occupant, just as the fish in the sea do. And, indeed, there are many things in this connection which issue from the law of nations, which, because it has a sufficient derivation from natural law, is clearly capable of conferring rights and creating obligations. And even if we grant that it is not always derived from natural law, yet there exists clearly enough a consensus of the greater part of the whole world, especially in behalf of the common good of all. For if after the early days of the creation of the world or its recovery from the flood the majority of mankind decided that ambassadors should everywhere be reckoned inviolable and that the sea should be common and that prisoners of war should be made slaves [a practice ameliorating the ancient practice of killing prisoners], and if this, namely, that strangers should not be driven out, were deemed a desirable principle, it would certainly have the force of law, even though the rest of mankind objected thereto."

This is not merely Vitoria's law of nations; it is essentially Grotius' law of nations as well—evident alike in the longer treatise of 1625 and in the earlier masterpiece.

well-being of the aborigines, the latter nevertheless persist in their hostility and do their best to destroy the Spaniards, then they can make war on the Indians, no longer as on innocent folk, but as against forsworn enemies, and may enforce against them all the rights of war.

It will be possible here to consider only the more important passages in the *Mare liberum*. These, however, contain the essence of Grotius' argument, and incidentally serve to establish him as a member of the Spanish school. Thus, in discussing the question of discovery in relation to the controversy which is the subject of *The Freedom of the Seas,* Grotius lays down the doctrine that

discovery *per se* gives no legal rights over things unless before the alleged discovery they were *res nullius*. Now these Indians of the East, on the arrival of the Portuguese, although some of them were idolators, and some Mohammedans, and therefore sunk in grievous sin, had none the less perfect public and private ownership of their goods and possessions, from which they could not be dispossessed without just cause.[26]

This question Vitoria[27] had treated with a master hand in the first section of his *Relectio de Indis,* where he declared, as regards the Spanish claims to the lands of the Indians, that neither mortal sin nor unbelief on the part of the inhabitants of the New World would deprive them of dominion and ownership. Hence we should not need to speculate as to the source from which Grotius derived this doctrine, even if he had not himself immediately added, using terms which denote the care with which he had read Vitoria's disquisitions and the completeness with which he had mastered the principles which they expounded: "The Spanish writer Victoria, following other writers of the highest authority, has the most certain warrant for his conclusion that Christians, whether of the laity or of the clergy, cannot deprive infidels of their civil power and sovereignty merely on the ground that they are infidels, unless some other wrong has been done by them."[28] Vitoria's opinion of this subject is stated in more than one of his *Readings*— and indeed in this particular instance Grotius cited not *De Indis,* but the earlier *Relectio, De potestate civili,* of 1528.

Involved in the question which Grotius was considering, as it had been also involved in the questions dealt with by Vitoria, was the extent of the power of the pope. Here again Grotius relies heavily upon the schoolmen of Spain as well as upon other theologians. A brief passage at the end of his third chapter will serve to indicate his method of treating the subject: "It follows . . . according to the opinions of Cajetan and Victoria and the

---

[26] *The Freedom of the Seas,* p. 13.   [27] *De Indis,* Sec. I, nos. 4-7, 19; pp. 120-22, 125.
[28] Grotius, *The Freedom of the Seas,* p. 13.

more authoritative of the Theologians and writers on Canon Law, that there is no clear title against the East Indians, based either on the ground that the Pope made an absolute grant of those provinces as if he were their sovereign, or on the pretext that the East Indians do not recognize his sovereignty."[29]

These, however, were not the only instances in which Grotius relied upon the doctrines of Vitoria. As has been noted in a previous chapter, Vitoria considered certain grounds which might have justified the Spaniards in making war on the Indians of the Western World. Grotius likewise considers the right of the Portuguese to make war on the natives of the East Indies. As might be expected, he invokes the doctrine of the Spanish schoolmen on this question and particularly on the question of the right to convert individuals by force. "I have often heard that it has been decreed by the Council of Spain, and by the Churchmen, especially the Dominicans, that the Americans (Aztecs and Indians) should be converted to the Faith by the preaching of the Word alone, and not by war, and even that their liberty of which they had been robbed in the name of religion should be restored."[30] Maintaining that the Portuguese were not in fact interested in the "extension of the faith," Grotius adds[31] (paraphrasing Vitoria, although without mentioning his name): "Nay, the very thing that is true of them, is the very thing which has been written of the Spaniards in America by a Spaniard, namely, that nothing is heard of miracles or wonders or examples of devout and religious life such as might convert others to the same faith, but on the other hand no end of scandals, of crimes, of impious deeds."[32]

In concluding this phase of his argument and maintaining that the peoples of the newly discovered lands were not "chattels" but "free men and *sui juris*," Grotius (specifically citing Vitoria's *De Indis*) adds as his final proof: "This is not denied even by the Spanish jurists themselves."

After stating in his own words the broad-minded view of St. Thomas Aquinas to the effect that religious belief does not "do away with either natural or human law from which sovereignty is derived," Grotius again turns to Vitoria, referring to him by name this time and citing his *Relectio de Indis*:[33] "Victoria then is right in saying that the Spaniards have no more

---

[29] Grotius, *The Freedom of the Seas*, pp. 16–17. [30] *Ibid.*, p. 20. [31] *Ibid.*, p. 21.
[32] The passage from Vitoria which Grotius here paraphrases is the fifth proposition of the second section in the *Relectio de Indis* (p. 144): "It is not sufficiently clear to me that the Christian faith has yet been so put before the aborigines and announced to them that they are bound to believe it or commit fresh sin. I say this because (as appears from my second proposition) they are not bound to believe unless the faith be put before them with persuasive demonstration. Now, I hear of no miracles or signs or religious patterns of life; nay, on the other hand, I hear of many scandals and cruel crimes and acts of impiety."
[33] *The Freedom of the Seas*, p. 13.

legal right over the Indians because of their religion, than the Indians would have had over the Spaniards if they had happened to be the first foreigners to come to Spain." Grotius' next statement is likewise based upon Vitoria's views, although in this instance he apparently did not feel it necessary to give an additional reference: "Nor are the East Indians stupid and unthinking; on the contrary they are intelligent and shrewd, so that a pretext for subduing them on the ground of their character could not be sustained."

In the opening lines of the first chapter of the *Mare liberum*, Grotius had stated, as we have seen, that he would "demonstrate" the right of the Dutch to travel and trade in the East Indies, and that his argument was to be based upon the law of nations, particularly the specific rule of the law of nations that "every nation is free to travel to every other nation, and to trade with it."[34] This subject had been dealt with by Vitoria[35]—briefly, it is true, but none the less convincingly and in a manner adequate to his purpose in writing *De Indis*. Grotius, however, felt the need for more exhaustive treatment for his special purpose. Therefore in later pages he discussed the subject in detail, adopting as his general text the brief but classical statement:[36] "it is a universal law that the sea and its use are common to all." The question at issue was large indeed and of the utmost importance, and Grotius must have experienced some worry at first over both his argument and his authorities. But he had the good fortune to solve both problems at once by finding an authority (again a Spaniard) whose demonstration was so full, so clear, and so convincing, that he renounced the attempt to improve upon it and incorporated it in the very language of its author. Grotius explains with enthusiasm that this authority is Vázquez, "that glory of Spain, who leaves nothing ever to be desired when it comes to subtle examination of the law or to the exposition of the principles of liberty," and who treated the "entire question" which confronted Grotius "most thoroughly."

In view of the youthful Grotius' marked admiration for this Spanish jurist, it will be advisable here to consider briefly the latter's contribution to the Spanish school. Fernando Vázquez de Menchaca (for such was his full name) was a younger contemporary of Vitoria. He was born in 1512 at Valladolid, of a family active in legal, political, and administrative affairs, his father and one of his brothers having been prominent members of the Council of Castile, while another brother became a member of the Council of the Indies. Although Vázquez was not actually a disciple of Vitoria, he

---

[34] *Ibid.*, p. 7.
[35] *De Indis*, Sec. III, nos. 1–3; pp. 151–53.
[36] *The Freedom of the Seas*, p. 52.

studied law at Salamanca shortly after the great theologian's death in 1546, and subsequently taught Roman law there. Profoundly learned in the law, he became one of the chief legal authorities of his day, holding numerous important offices and being chosen by Philip II to serve as a jurist at the Council of Trent.

His great prestige, however, was due chiefly to his writings. Of these the most important for posterity was his large treatise *Illustrium controversiarum aliarumque usu frequentium,* in which he discussed at length and with great learning many political and legal problems. He was deeply interested, as Grotius had intimated, in "the principles of liberty", and the problems of government.[37]

Now Vázquez de Menchaca might well be called a schoolman, for he was bred in the tradition of the schools, and was imbued with their thought. Therefore, although he dedicated his treatise to Philip II, he freely and courageously propounded a conception of the royal power quite different from that of his sovereign.[38] "The kingdom," he maintained, citing a wealth of authorities from Plato to Erasmus, "is not to be subordinated to the king, but rather the king to the kingdom and to the good of the state or of the citizens."[39] This was a logical consequence of the doctrine (to which Vázquez subscribed) of man's equality under the natural law,[40] and of the essential sovereignty of the people.[41] He was unequivocally opposed to the Aristotelian dictum that some men are slaves by nature, which he considered

[37] For a more extended and highly informative analysis of Vázquez' theories, see the monograph, *Fernando Vázquez de Menchaca* (1512–69), by Adolfo Miaja de la Muela. This publication was issued by the Sección de Estudios Americanistas of the University of Valladolid in the series "Internacionalistas españoles del siglo XVI," and contains an interesting preface by Camilo Barcia Trelles. See also the following papers printed in the *Anuario de la Asociación Francisco de Vitoria* (Vol. IV, Madrid, 1933): "Vázquez de Menchaca y el Derecho de gentes," by Villanova (pp. 17–36); and "La sumisión del Soberano a la ley en Vitoria, Vázquez de Menchaca y Suárez," by Torres (pp. 129–54).

[38] Referring to Vázquez' "love of freedom and frankness," Professor Fruin (*An Unpublished Work of Hugo Grotius,* in *Bibliotheca Visseriana* . . ., V, 62) observes that in this respect the Spanish jurist "surpasses" Grotius. When reading Vázquez' *Controversiarum,* Professor Fruin continues, admirably summarizing the Spaniard's views on government, "one cannot understand how such a book was dedicated to Philip II; it looks like irony to inscribe to a king by the grace of God, who detests the idea of his subjects having any share of the government, a book in which it is openly taught that the divine right of magistrates does not exist; that the prince is for the sake of the people, not the people for the sake of the prince, and that, therefore, the prince must have the weal of his people at heart exclusively, and not his private interests; that the power entrusted to princes exclusively in the interest of the subjects, may . . . if their interest demands it, be limited and even completely revoked."

[39] *Controversiarum,* Preface, Sec. 104. Of this work, first published in 1563 (Barcelona), a new edition, with a Spanish translation, is being prepared at the University of Valladolid by Professor Fidel Rodríguez Alcalde. Three volumes of this edition have already been published.

[40] *Ibid.,* chap. xx, secs. 24–26.   [41] *Ibid.,* Preface, sec. 86.

to have been uttered as a sop to the vanity—and an excuse for the tyranny—of Alexander the Great, Aristotle's one-time pupil.[42] In the opinion of the Spanish jurist, such flattery and adulation of rulers were in truth grave injuries to mankind, encouraging as they do the misdeeds of princes.

Rulers there must be, of course, or there could not be that government which is essential to man in society. For if in the golden age—with the legend of which Vázquez was familiar[43]—the artificial restraints of political organization and law had not been necessary, that age was no more, and men living in groups had need of government with a sovereign at its head. And though he apparently thought of government as being in one sense an artificial creation, he was familiar enough with Aristotle not only to disagree with him at times but also to understand fully and to accept the Aristotelian view of society as a natural phenomenon. Indeed we find him voicing with approval the familiar truism that "man is a sociable being,"[44] that instinctively he seeks union and fellowship with his kind. But discord arises in social life, and hence the need for civil power and a duly constituted authority to exercise it. Such authority was of divine origin, but the vesting of it in any particular person or persons, by election or otherwise, was according to Vázquez a function of the people, who should be free to choose the form of political government which they considered best—even to the extent of changing the government if necessary, or of reserving the powers of government in whole or in part to themselves.[45]

Now the prince or other sovereign ruler, whatever his title, having been granted authority which is of divine origin, is in this sense *Dei vicarius et minister ac substitutus in terris*.[46] But this is not to say that Vázquez claimed for Philip II or any other ruler that "divine right" which was to become an obsession with James I of England. The author of the *Controversiarum* was no advocate of irresponsible government nor tyranny. In his conception all types of sovereignty should look to the good of the state and its citizens.[47] Moreover, those entrusted with the powers of government should, he insisted, be subject to the laws of the land.[48] It is clear, therefore, that Vázquez' conception of sovereignty was in the final analysis a conception of the sovereignty of law.[49]

Human law, the civil law of the state, he viewed as being in the nature of a contract on the part of the citizens of the state with one another, and

[42] *Ibid.*, secs. 4–12.
[44] *Ibid.*, Preface, sec. 122; chap. i, sec. 25.
[46] *Ibid.*, Preface, sec. 139.
[48] *Ibid.*, chap. i, sec. 25.
[43] *Ibid.*, chap. xli, secs. 33–34.
[45] *Ibid.*, Preface, sec. 125.
[47] *Ibid.*, chap. xxx, sec. 3.
[49] *Ibid.*, chap. xlv.

hence (as in the case of all contracts) the validity and binding force of the law must depend upon the consent of the parties—i. e., of the citizens.[50] Moreover, man-made law must pass a threefold test: it must be made for the common good, and it must be in accord with both the divine and the natural law.[51]

As for Vázquez' conception of the divine and the natural law, it is sufficient here to observe that his views on these two classifications of the "higher" law were similar to those of the schoolmen generally. But a word or two should be said of his theories regarding the law of nations, before returning to Grotius' thoroughgoing examination—and indeed appropriation—of the Spaniard's leading doctrines bearing upon the question of the freedom of the seas. In general the law of nations was for Vázquez so closely bound up with natural law that he frequently refers to them as being practically identical. It should be noted, however, that he divides the *ius gentium* into two categories: the primary or natural, and the secondary law of nations. The first is, to all intents and purposes, simply that part of natural law which is recognized by the majority of peoples. The secondary law of nations consists of the body of rules and customs which has been generally accepted and is therefore a more or less universal but positive law applicable between states. This body of law is not immutable, being susceptible of alteration and modification like the civil law.[52] But the primary law of nations, consisting as it does of rules of the natural law—which Vázquez defines as "right reason" implanted by God in the human being[53]—cannot be changed or altered in any way.[54]

Although it may be said that Vázquez' star went down with the loss of Spain's preëminence in the international world, it is today in the ascendant and his *Controversiarum* is now regaining some part of the authority which it enjoyed in Grotius' day. The best evidence which can be given of its acceptance at that time as unimpeachable authority is that the young Grotius, full of ambition as he was, made no attempt to improve upon the statement of the Spanish jurist as regards the freedom of the seas, but based his entire argument upon Vázquez' thesis, which he quoted word for word.

It is evident that Grotius had carefully read and pondered the work of this jurisconsult of Spain, for he refers to the fact that Vázquez had supported his own thesis by many authorities, of which Grotius in turn availed

---

[50] Vázquez, *Controversiarum*, chap. lii, sec. 9–10; chap. lv, sec. 3.
[51] *Ibid.*, chap. xxix, sec. 21; chap. xxx, sec. 1; chap. xlvi, sec. 2.
[52] *Ibid.*, chap. lxxxix, secs. 25–26.
[53] *Ibid.*, chap. xxvii, sec. 11. [54] *Ibid.*, chap. lxxxix, sec. 28.

himself. Now, as is the case of all great theses, certain objections might be raised against the Spaniard's views, but, in Grotius' opinion, Vázquez had dealt effectively with them. The young Hollander precedes his quotation of passages from Vázquez by the statement that, before meeting certain objections, the Spanish jurist made "the just and reasonable statement that the truth of all these matters depends upon a true conception both of the law of nature and the law of nations."[55] To this view Grotius likewise subscribes.

If there were customs incompatible with the law of nations, they were (to paraphrase Grotius, who in turn is paraphrasing Vázquez) not worthy of the name of law and hence, however long they had endured, were not justified and could not obtain legal effect and force, even though they were apparently approved "by the consent, the protection, or the practice . . . of many nations." Now these statements, Grotius continues, "he [Vázquez] confirms by a number of examples, and particularly by the testimony of Alfonso de Castro the Spanish theologian"[56] (whom Vázquez was here citing, it should be added, not on the question of the freedom of the seas, but upon the fundamental principles which he was expounding).

Having laid his foundations—or rather those of Vázquez—Grotius now proceeds to appropriate the Spaniard's superstructure.

"It is evident therefore" [Grotius says, quoting Vázquez, word for word] "how much to be suspected is the opinion of those persons mentioned above, who think that the Genoese or the Venetians can without injustice prohibit other nations from navigating the gulfs or bays of their respective seas, as if they had a prescriptive right to the very water itself. Such an act is not only contrary to the laws, but is contrary also to natural law or the primary law of nations, which we have said is immutable. And this is seen to be true because by that same law not only the seas or waters, but also all other immovables were *res communes*. And although in later times there was a partial abandonment of that law, in so far as concerns sovereignty and ownership of lands—which by natual law at first were held in common, then distinguished and divided, and thus finally separated from the primitive community of use;—nevertheless it was different as regards sovereignty [*dominium*] over the sea, which from the beginning of the world down to this very day is and always has been a *res communis*, and which, as is well known, has in no wise changed from that status.[57]

"And although," he continues, "I have often heard that a great many Portuguese believe that their king has a prescriptive right over the navigation of the vast seas of the West Indies (probably the vast East Indies too) such that other

---

[55] Grotius, *The Freedom of the Seas* (previously cited), p. 52.

[56] Alfonso de Castro (1495-1558) was the author of an authoritative work, *De potestate legis poenalis*.

[57] *The Freedom of the Seas*, pp. 53-54.

nations are not allowed to traverse those waters; and although the common people among our own Spaniards seem to be of the same opinion, namely, that absolutely no one in the world except us Spaniards ourselves has the least right to navigate the great and immense sea which stretches to the regions of the Indies once subdued by our most powerful kings, as if that right has been ours alone by prescription; although, I repeat, I have heard both these things, nevertheless the belief of all those people is no less extravagantly foolish than that of those who are always cherishing the same delusions with respect to the Genoese and Venetians. Indeed the opinions of them all appear the more manifestly absurd, because no one of those nations can erect a prescription against itself; that is to say, not the Venetian republic, nor the Genoese republic, nor the kingdom of Spain nor of Portugal can raise prescriptions against rights they already possess by nature. For the one who claims a prescriptive right and the one who suffers by the establishment of such a claim must not be one and the same person.

"Against other nations they are even much less competent to raise a prescription, because the right of prescription is only a municipal right, as we have shown above at some length. Therefore such a right ceases to have any effect as between rulers or nations who do not recognize a superior in the temporal domain. For so far as the merely municipal laws of any place are concerned, they do not affect foreign peoples, nations, or even individuals, any more than if they did not exist or never had existed. Therefore it was necessary to have a recourse to the common law of nations, primary as well as secondary, and to use a law which clearly had not admitted any such prescription and usurpation of the sea. For today the use of the waters is common, exactly as it has been since the creation of the world. Therefore no man has a right nor can acquire a right over the seas and waters which would be prejudicial to their common use. Besides, there is both in natural and divine law that famous rule: 'Whatsoever ye would that men should not do to you, do not ye even so to them.' Hence it follows, since navigation cannot harm any one except the navigator himself, it is only just that no one either can or ought to be interdicted therefrom, lest nature, free in her own realm, and least hurtful to herself, be found impeding the liberty of navigation, and thus offending against the accepted precept and rule that all things are supposed to be permitted which are not found expressly forbidden. Besides, not only would it be contrary to natural law to wish to prevent such free navigation, but we are even bound to do the opposite, that is, bound to assist such navigation in whatever way we can, when it can be done without any prejudice to ourselves."[58]

Grotius here adds a connecting line between paragraphs of his generous quotation:[59]

After Vázquez had established his point by the help of many authorities both human and divine, he added: "It appears then, from what has gone before that the opinion held by Johannes Faber, Angeli, Baldus, and Franciscus Balbus, whom we have cited above, is not to be trusted, because they think that places

---

[58] Grotius, *The Freedom of the Seas*, pp. 54–55.   [59] *Ibid.*, pp. 55–56.

common by the law of nations, even if not open to acquisition by prescription, can nevertheless be acquired by custom; but this is entirely false, and is a teaching [*traditio*] which is both obscure and vague, which lacks the faintest glimmer of reasonableness, and which sets up a law in word but not in fact. For it is well established from the examples taken from the seas of the Spaniards, Portuguese, Venetians, Genoese, and others, that an exclusive right of navigation and a right of prohibiting others from navigation is no more to be acquired by custom than by prescription. And it is apparent that the reason is the same in both cases. And since according to the laws and reasons adduced above this would be contrary to natural equity and would not bring benefit but only injury, therefore as it could not be introduced by an express law, neither could it be introduced by a tacit or implied law, and that is what custom is. And far from justifying itself by any lapse of time, it rather becomes worse, and every day more injurious."

Grotius himself interrupts the quotation from Vázquez, but only to paraphrase, in preparation for a further quotation:

Vázquez next shows that from the time of the earliest occupation of the earth every people possessed the right of hunting in its own territory, and of fishing in its own rivers. After those rights were once separated from the ancient community of rights in such a way that they admitted of particular attachments, they could be acquired by prescription based upon such an efflux of time that "the memory of its beginning does not exist," as if by the tacit permission of a nation.[60]

After appropriating further passages from his Spanish mentor Grotius adds a final quotation: "A little farther on Vázquez says: 'Things which are imprescriptible by the disposition of the law, may not become objects of prescription even after the lapse of a thousand years.'" This passage ends Grotius' elaborate borrowing from Vázquez on the freedom of the seas, and upon it he makes a final comment: "This statement he supports by countless citations from the jurists."[61]

The argument of Grotius is continued for a number of pages, but the fact of the matter is that he could have rested his case without further argument upon the firm basis laid by the Spanish authority to which he appealed. For present purposes it will suffice to turn at once to his general conclusion:[62] "Therefore freedom of trade is based on a primitive right of nations which has a natural and permanent cause; and so that right cannot be destroyed, or at all events it may not be destroyed except by the consent of all nations." Having thus established his own thesis, Grotius is ready to hurl defiance at the Portuguese.

[60] *Ibid.*, p. 56.   [61] *Ibid.*, p. 58.   [62] *Ibid.*, pp. 63-64.

Therefore [he exclaims], the Portuguese may cry as loud and as long as they shall please: "You are cutting down our profits"! The Dutch will answer: "Nay! we are but looking out for our own interests! Are you angry because we share with you in the winds and the sea? Pray, who had promised that you would always have those advantages? You are secure in the possession of that with which we are quite content."[63]

Now Grotius was a citizen of the world and, in the domain of doctrine, of morality, and of international law, an associate of the Spanish schoolmen. Yet he is likewise so distinctly a Hollander that it is only his own countrymen who can fittingly and with full authority express a measured and definitive opinion of his services to the law of nations.

No one of his countrymen of recent times can be considered as more familiar with the Holland of Grotius' day and with Grotius' contributions than Robert Fruin, one-time Professor of National History in the University of Leyden. And no jurist of our day could be considered more competent to pass upon Grotius' works than the late Willem Van der Vlugt, Dean of the Law Faculty of the University of Leyden, the university in which the young Grotius studied and of which he is still the outstanding ornament.

Professor Fruin, as we have already seen, passed upon the manuscript of the *Commentary on the Law of Prize* and recommended its publication. He was deeply interested in the *Commentary,* for in his opinion it was in some respects to be preferred to the elaborate masterpiece, *On the Law of War and Peace,* of 1625. He expressed the opinion that the later work was but an amplification of the youthful tractate, composed with the deliberation of a man of mature years. Indeed the treatise *On the Law of War and Peace,* although written at greater length and in more circumspect language, contained the same principles and doctrines, very often the same authorities, and not infrequently the same phraseology, as the *Commentary* which Grotius had enthusiastically composed in his youth.

On the basis of his examination of the *Commentary,* Professor Fruin reached several interesting and important conclusions. In the first of these, referring to a point he had made on a previous page, he says: "If, then, it be true that De Groot's merit with regard to the law of nations consists, not in revealing a new law, different from what hitherto had been considered justice, but in pointing out the source whence the acknowledged law proceeded and all rights have to be deduced, I make bold to assert that this merit is still more clearly revealed by the work of his youth, now published for the first time, than by the world-famous book of his manhood."[64]

---

[63] Grotius, *The Freedom of the Seas,* p. 71.
[64] *An Unpublished Work of Hugo Grotius,* in *Bibliotheca Visseriana,* V, 67.

In speaking of Grotius' indebtedness to the Spanish authors for his "natural right," Professor Fruin says:[65] "I need not remind the reader that, according to the usual representation, he is the founder of natural right as much as of the law of nations." But this "natural right," or law of nature, was, in Fruin's opinion, derived from the doctrines of the Spanish authors, for he continues, stating a second conclusion:

And Vasquius and Covarruvia especially have been his masters in this matter. It is only because those authors are no longer read, because De Groot eclipsed them by his glory and doomed them to oblivion, that their merit in this respect has not been appreciated.

Now for a third extract from Professor Fruin. After referring to Albericus Gentilis as a precursor of Grotius and stating that the Italian jurist "is inferior to the great Spanish lawyers and theologians of Charles V's and Philip II's time," Professor Fruin adds a third conclusion:[66]

Of the theologians I will only mention Franciscus Victoria, though besides him Dominicus Sotus also occupies a place of honour. Between 1530 and 1540 Victoria wrote amongst others two *relationes* "De Indis noviter inventis" and "De jure belli" and these two treatises more than any other book provided our author with the subject matter which he worked up into his system. . . . De Groot could often refer to his [Vitoria's] authority, especially to oppose the claims of Spaniards and Portuguese to the exclusive right of exploiting the two Indies; the readers of *Mare liberum* will remember this.[67]

In 1925, on the three-hundredth anniversary of the publication of *De jure belli ac pacis*, Professor Van der Vlugt delivered an admirable series of lectures before the Hague Academy of International Law. This learned Netherlander—whose recent death was a blow to the science of law—dealt at length with the debt of Grotius to the Spanish publicists, basing his views on the evidence furnished by the *Commentary on the Law of Prize* and especially by the *Mare liberum*. The present chapter may best be completed by translating without comment Professor Van der Vlugt's conclusion as to the relationship of Grotius to Vitoria and through him to the Spanish school:

We have already stated repeatedly, that beginning with the passage cited from St. Thomas[68] all the literature dealing with rights and duties in international affairs, in so far as it exercised a profound influence upon contem-

---

[65] *Ibid.*, p. 63.   [66] *Ibid.*, p. 61.

[67] Referring to Grotius' mention of Vitoria in his treatise on the *Law of War and Peace*, Professor Fruin adds: "In the prolegomena of the *Jus belli ac pacis* De Groot mentions him and praises him as he deserves, but with less gratefulness than I should have expected. . . . Of the Spanish jurists he there praises Covarruvia and Vasquius especially, to whom he is indeed greatly indebted."

[68] *Summa Theologica*, II.-II, qu. 40, art. 1.

poraries and the generations following, was inspired by the manual of the confession. The part of the *Summa* of St. Thomas Aquinas treating of morality is a manual of the confessor; manuals of a like character are the works of the "summists" who followed and imitated "the Angelic Doctor"; and manuals of the same tendency are the *Relectiones* of Vitoria and the writings of those who copied his views with more or less originality—works with which Grotius, young as he was, was already acquainted in some measure. What was the occasion, however, which at the beginning of his career first caused him to study a problem pertaining to the law of nations with a view to submitting the result of his labor to the public? It is said to have been a sensational incident which occurred in the year 1604 in the Straits of Malacca. The East India Company, from the beginning exposed to the hostility of the Portuguese, was obliged to defend itself by capturing enemy ships. The first prize seized in this connection by Jacob van Heemskerk gave rise to the incident in question. This incident was concerned with the formal refusal on the part of certain share-holders, partisans of peace at any price, to a division of the profits which had been received from the sale of the prize. There was a violent tumult among the partisans and their adversaries. Whether from patriotic feeling or from an earnest desire to serve friends who sought his aid, our precocious young man took his pen in hand in order to reassure the disturbed consciences. Thus was born the special pleading *De Iure Praedae,* a book which can, without a shadow of paradox, be characterized as "the counsel given by a lay-confessor upon a matter of conscience which divided his fellow-Protestants." The voluminous manuscript was to remain unpublished. It was not until two hundred and sixty years later that a fortunate chance brought it to the attention of the public. But in any case the habit of the confessional had taken possession of the mind of the author. Moreover, during the long period of time above mentioned, the special pleading of Grotius did not remain completely unknown. When, in 1608, negotiations were opened with Spain which led in the following year to the famous armistice, the Government of Spain, exercising the real and alleged rights which had formerly been those of Portugal, strove with all the means in its power to make Holland renounce its trade in the Indies. Threatened again in its vitally important commerce, the Company charged Grotius with the refutation of the arguments which served as a basis for the Spanish claim. Grotius again set to work, separating from his unpublished manuscript the fragment which dealt particularly with the subject in controversy. But again the success of his labor was to be a thing of the future. A suspension of hostilities having been suddenly decided upon, the work (which was moreover anonymous) made its appearance too late. The fame of the author was eventually to make that of the book; the fame of the book did nothing for that of the author. . . . Grotius' tractate had only the value of a study made at second hand, a study based upon the wisdom of the Spaniards. In its first half it is a development of the leading doctrine of Vitoria: that every people has the right to visit other peoples and to trade with them. The second half is an amplification of the theme which had been restated by Vázquez, according to which an exclusive right of navigating the seas in whole or in part should not be admitted to the profit of any nation whatsoever. Such were the contents of the tractate. In short, this first essay, in its foundation as in its form, succeeded in making Grotius familiar with the method of the guides of conscience, his contemporaries, in matters of international morality.[69]

[69] "L'Oeuvre de Grotius et son influence sur le développement du droit international," published in *Recueil des cours, 1925*, of the Hague Academy of International Law, Vol. 7, pp. 399, 418–20.

CHAPTER XXXII

ST. ROBERT BELLARMINE (1542-1621)

THERE ARE THREE MEN OF DIFFERENT COUNTRIES, WITH WIDELY DIFFERENT backgrounds, who might have been, both from their lives and the legal and political doctrines which they professed, members of the same family. They are: Francisco Suárez,[1] a Spaniard, born in 1548; Richard Hooker,[2] an Englishman, born in 1553 (an eventful year in English history); and St. Robert Bellarmine, an Italian, born in 1542.

If the three did not grow up together, nevertheless, in spite of geographical distances, they discussed the same questions; and their views on the origin of government, its nature and extent, were similar, if not identical. Each is representative of the most enlightened views of his countrymen in this domain, and the three were writing on kindred subjects, if not together, at least at the same time. Suárez was the greatest of the political and legal philosophers of his century (indeed many consider him the greatest of modern times); Hooker was the outstanding exponent of that conception of law and government which has prevailed in the English-speaking world, for his doctrine was the doctrine of the Englishmen settling in new lands, and today lies at the foundation of the government of all English-speaking peoples, whether in the homeland, in the continental countries of Australasia, or in America; and Bellarmine, strange as it may seem, has perhaps the greatest claim to the gratitude of the people of the United States, because he stated and defended in advance those principles of government which the United States have made their own and upon which their government firmly rests. If we of the United States were to have a patron—and in our case a political—saint (Protestant in large part though we be), we might indeed do well to choose the Cardinal and sainted Bellarmine.

Bellarmine was born in Monte Pulciano, Tuscany, on October 4, 1542. His mother—a noble woman whose fine traits the saint inherited—was the sister of Pope Marcellus II (whose only fault, it might be said, was his short tenure of his exalted office, for he died within a few weeks after

[1] See chap. xxxiii, *infra*.   [2] See chap. xxxiv, *infra*.

ascending the throne of St. Peter). Thus in a sense Bellarmine's vocation had been marked out for him, although it was his own choice.³

Carefully educated in Italy, Bellarmine entered the order of the Society of Jesus (of which he, like Suárez, is one of the outstanding figures), later completing his studies at the famed University of Louvain.

Now Bellarmine, as his whole life shows, had a powerful and discriminating mind. Able to see both sides of a question, his own views were nevertheless definite and clear, and his exceptional abilities enabled him to present those views in a manner at once persuasive and convincing. It was because of these qualities that he was chosen as defender of the faith which he professed. His masterpiece, *De controversiis,* dealing with the religious controversies of his time, is still a standard work, notwithstanding the changes which have taken place in the life and thought of the world in the past two centuries. It is upon one section of this masterpiece, entitled *De laicis* (or the *Treatise on Civil Government*) that his reputation as a political scientist would securely rest, irrespective of his many other claims.

That he was outstanding in the domain of political science, we have on the unimpeachable if unwilling authority of a Protestant. This authority is none other than Sir Robert Filmer, whose *Patriarcha*—a defense of the theory of the divine right of kings, as exemplified in the Stewart dynasty—was left among his manuscripts at his death in 1653 and first published in 1680. Its opening paragraph reads:

Since the time that school divinity began to flourish there hath been a common opinion maintained, as well by divines as by divers other learned men, which affirms,—

"Mankind is naturally endowed and born with freedom from all subjection, and at liberty to choose what form of government it please, and that the power which any one man hath over others was at first bestowed according to the discretion of the multitude."⁴

Whence, in Filmer's opinion, did this doctrine come which he had set himself to controvert? "This tenet was first hatched in the schools, and hath been fostered by all succeeding Papists for good divinity." To a man of his convictions its source was bad enough, but the extent of its acceptance was still worse: "The divines, also, of the Reformed Churches have entertained it, and the common people everywhere tenderly embrace it as being

---

³ For full details concerning Bellarmine's life and work, the reader is referred to the excellent two-volume study by Brodrick, *The Life and Work of Blessed Robert Francis Cardinal Bellarmine, S.J.*

⁴ *Two Treatises on Civil Government by John Locke, Preceded by Sir Robert Filmer's "Patriarcha,"* with an Introduction by Morley, p. 11.

most plausible to flesh and blood, for that it prodigally distributes a portion of liberty to the meanest of the multitude."

After asserting that this doctrine which the "Papists" held "for good divinity" was contrary to Holy Writ, Filmer adds:[5] "Yet upon the ground of this doctrine, both Jesuits and some other zealous favourers of the Geneva discipline have built a perilous conclusion"—that is to say, "perilous" to the doctrine (the divine right of kings) of which Filmer was an acknowledged defender—"which is, that the people or multitude have power to punish or deprive the prince if he transgress the laws of the kingdom." As examples of those who had "built" this conclusion, Filmer cited certain authors:

witness Parsons and Buchanan; the first, under the name of Dolman,[6] in the third chapter of his first book [entitled *A Conference about the Next Succession* —which was to bear fruit in the deposition of James II and the election of William of Orange] labours to prove that kings have been lawfully chastised by their commonwealths. The latter [Buchanan], in his book "De jure regni apud Scotos," maintains a liberty of the people to depose their prince.

But Parsons, a Jesuit, and Buchanan, a Presbyterian, were not the only authors to whom Filmer referred. It appeared to him that Cardinal Bellarmine and Calvin both looked "asquint this way." Although it has been questioned that Calvin "squinted" that way, there can be no doubt about Bellarmine's views.

Now Sir Robert Filmer was an honest and upright man and, desiring to be fair, he laid down "cautions"[7] which he doubtless thought would make his discussion of the question more impartial. The first caution was that he had "nothing to do to meddle with mysteries of state, such as *arcana imperii*, or cabinet councils, [which] the vulgar may not pry into." The second caution was "not to question or quarrel at the rights or liberties of this or any other nation." "My task," he continues, "is chiefly to inquire from whom these first came, not to dispute what or how many these are, but whether they were derived from the laws of natural liberty or from the grace and bounty of princes." The third caution was a warning that he "must not detract from the worth of all those learned men who are of a contrary opinion in the point of natural liberty." He justifies his examination of those whom he pronounces his betters, however, by a statement in the nature of a proverb: "A dwarf sometimes may see that which a giant looks over."

After this series of cautions, he begins a direct attack upon his opponents: Late writers have taken up too much upon trust from the subtile schoolmen, who to be sure to thrust down the king below the pope, thought it the safest

---

[5] Filmer, *op. cit.*, pp. 11–12.
[6] Robert Parsons, S.J. (1546–1610) wrote under the pseudonym of Dolman (or Doleman).
[7] *Op. cit.*, pp. 12–13.

course to advance the people above the king, that so the papal power might take place of the regal. Thus many an ignorant subject hath been fooled into this faith, that a man may become a martyr for his country by being a traitor to his prince; whereas the new coined distinction of subjects into royalists and patriots is most unnatural, since the relation between king and people is so great that their well-being is so reciprocal.[8]

Sir Robert was certainly right in his apprehension that if this doctrine, which he rightly attributed to the schoolmen, should prevail, the people as the source of power would indeed be superior to the king. On another point it is also possible to agree with Filmer, albeit not with the thought he had in mind: that men who opposed their prince in the cause of liberty have often become martyrs to such a noble cause, inasmuch as liberty has usually been bought at the price of many a life which the world could ill spare.

Turning to the subject of liberty and the man who in his opinion was largely responsible for the doctrine which he sought to refute, Filmer continues: "To make evident the grounds of this question, about the natural liberty of mankind, I will lay down some passages of Cardinal Bellarmine that may best unfold the state of this controversy." Here he proceeds to give an almost literal translation of Bellarmine's statement on the civil power.

Secular or civil power (saith he) is instituted by men; it is in the people, unless they bestow it on a prince. This power is immediately in the whole multitude, as in the subject of it; for this power is in the divine law, but the divine law hath given this power to no particular man—if the positive law be taken away, there is left no reason why amongst a multitude (who are equal) one rather than another should bear rule over the rest. Power is given by the multitude to one man, or to more by the same law of nature; for the commonwealth cannot exercise this power, therefore it is bound to bestow it upon some one man, or some few. It depends upon the consent of the multitude to ordain over themselves a king, or consul, or other magistrates; and if there be a lawful cause, the multitude may change the kingdom into an aristocracy or democracy.[9]

On this passage Filmer's comment is: "Thus far Bellarmine, in which passages are comprised the strength of all that ever I have read or heard produced for the natural liberty of the subject."

Such, indeed, is an accurate statement of the views of Filmer's antagonist which, if Filmer were living today, he would find in both thought and substance in the Declaration of Independence of the United States of America.

Now Thomas Jefferson was the draftsman of the Declaration of Independence, to which he wisely prefixed some general observations on the right of the people to choose the government which they preferred and to which he added an enumeration of the causes which in his opinion, as well

---

[8] *Ibid.*, p. 14.   [9] *Ibid.*

as in the opinion of his fellow countrymen, forced the American colonies to separate from Great Britain, the mother country.

The problem which confronted the colonial representatives was not merely that the colonies had grown up and therefore were of a mind to set up for themselves and be no longer subject to the leading-strings of the once necessary mother. The issues involved were far more fundamental than that, and Jefferson very properly thought it becoming, therefore, to say in behalf of his fellow countrymen that "a decent respect to the opinions of mankind requires that they should declare the causes which impel them to the separation." The foundations upon which in the opening sentence he based the inherent rights of the colonists are none other than "the Laws of Nature and of Nature's God"—a conception which has run almost like a refrain through so many chapters of the present volume. Then follows in the Declaration an enumeration of these rights: "We hold these truths to be self-evident, that all men are created equal, that they are endowed by their Creator with certain unalienable Rights, that among these are Life, Liberty and the pursuit of Happiness."

But Jefferson recognized—as did those for whom he spoke—that something more than an enumeration of rights was required; for those rights, while they might be self-evident to him and to his countrymen, were not so self-evident to the mother country that they would be accorded upon request. Therefore Jefferson's Declaration proceeds to set forth in brief but perfect form a complete philosophy of government: "That to secure these rights, Governments are instituted among Men, deriving their just powers"—mark the word "just"—"from the consent of the governed." This is the purpose of the institution of government. But the instituted government may cease to accomplish its purpose. What is the remedy? "Whenever any Form of Government becomes destructive of these ends, it is the right of the People to alter or to abolish it, and to institute new Government, laying its foundation on such principles and organizing its powers in such form, as to them shall seem most likely to effect their Safety and Happiness." Such were the great principles of the Declaration of Independence, which was in fact a solemn profession of political faith, for those who signed the document pledged in its support their lives, their fortunes, and their sacred honor. It embodies the conception of government in the Western World. To carry that conception into effect the Constitution of the United States was drafted and ratified. It is still on the statute books, the oldest written constitution of any existing nation.

Now Jefferson knew and said that the ideas to which he was giving definite form and shape for the benefit of his countrymen were not his own.[10] Nevertheless, his statement of these ideas was so correct in substance and so literary in form that the Declaration of Independence is and will always remain a classic of the English tongue. These ideas were to no small extent the doctrines of the Middle Ages, although their ultimate ancestry reached far back into antiquity. In the modern era they were stated not only by Bellarmine, but also, as we shall see,[11] by John Locke. Undoubtedly Jefferson knew precisely where in political literature these ideas could be found and if he were in doubt as to chapter and verse, so to speak, he could have refreshed his memory by consulting a volume in his possession (which today is placed upon the list of reserved books in the Library of Congress, to be looked at and admired but not withdrawn). It is none other than a copy of the original edition, dated 1680, of Filmer's *Patriarcha,* the title-page of which reads: "*Patriarcha;* or the *Natural Power of Kings. By the Learned Sir Robert Filmer Baronet* . . . London, Printed for Ric. Chiswell in St. Paul's Church-Yard, Matthew Gillyflower and William Henchman in Westminster Hall, 1680."

There is something in Jefferson's copy of the original edition which was obviously added subsequent to its publication. The addition is in the margin, opposite the very passage in which Filmer analyzes Bellarmine's views, as quoted on a previous page. It is a line made in lead pencil, apparently to call special attention to the doctrines of Bellarmine. Now lead pencils were in use before the Declaration of Independence was drafted and signed and, lacking evidence to prove that Jefferson did not himself make the mark in question, we may well incline to the belief that it is Jefferson's mark until the contrary is proved. In any event, the political philosophy of Jefferson was the political philosophy of Bellarmine as set forth by Filmer.

But however great is Bellarmine's contribution to political science and the theory of the state, he was fully as successful in dealing with a highly important international problem as he was in treating the problems of govern-

---

[10] See, for example, Jefferson's letter to James Madison, dated Aug. 30, 1823, and also his letter to Henry Lee of May 8, 1825, both reproduced in Paul Leicester Ford's *The Works of Thomas Jefferson* (12 vols., New York and London, 1905), XII, 306–9 and 408–9. See also *The State and the Church* by Ryan and Millar, p. 118, and the chapter "Our Medieval Inheritance of Liberty," pp. 166–94; also Millar's *Unpopular Essays in the Philosophy of History,* pp. 75–76, 116. For an interesting comparison between the doctrines of Bellarmine and the principles proclaimed by Jefferson, see Hunt's article entitled "The Virginia Declaration of Rights and Cardinal Bellarmine," *Catholic Historical Review,* III (1917), 276–89. Reference may also be made to an address by J. B. Scott, entitled "St. Robert Bellarmine and Our Political Heritage," delivered at the Law School of Georgetown University, Washington, D. C., May 13, 1931, and printed in the *Georgetown College Journal,* LX (November, 1931), 19–31.

[11] *Infra,* pp. 597 ff.

ment. In order to appreciate the importance of his international contribution, it will be necessary to consider briefly certain facts and developments relating to the question which confronted him.

In his day the patrimony of St. Peter was a state, a kingdom, it might even be said. The official title of His Holiness was then *"Re e Papa"*—and such, indeed, his title remains today, although his temporal domain has shrunk in size as the subjects of his spiritual jurisdiction have increased in numbers. Now the independence of the Papal States was long recognized by the world at large, but in 1870 they were invaded and annexed by United Italy. The pope nevertheless maintained his claim for more than half a century to sovereignty over the kingdom of which he had been deprived, until, on February 11, 1929, a treaty was concluded between His Holiness Pius XI, on the one hand, and Victor Emmanuel III, King of Italy, on the other, for the settlement of boundaries and other questions. The result was that, small as is the present Vatican State (a little over one hundred acres),[12] the treaty restored in fact as well as in theory the titles of the pope as a temporal sovereign, by virtue of which he has the right to confer, in temporal matters, on a footing of legal equality with the representatives of all the nations of the world.

But His Holiness had never lost his spiritual jurisdiction over his Christian subjects in any and every part of the world, a jurisdiction for which the temporal kingdom was intended to supply the material background. It may be said, therefore, that both the spiritual sovereignty and the temporal sovereignty of the pope exist today as they have throughout the centuries, although the outward extent of the material domain is greatly diminished. But it should be borne in mind that the spiritual jurisdiction does not depend upon this temporal sovereignty. It arises from the generally acknowledged right of His Holiness to secure, through appropriate channels, adequate protection in matters spiritual for the members of the Holy Roman Catholic Church in every foreign state. The securing of such protection is, in fact, both a right and a duty. In the case of the temporal state, the duty of protection may be called a temporal duty; on the part of the papal state, it is a spiritual duty. The right and the duty to extend protection are acknowledged and exercised in each sphere. Thus a temporal state may intervene diplomatically in behalf of the rights of its subjects just as His Holiness intervenes as a spiritual sovereign in behalf of the members of his Church. In the case of temporal sovereigns, the agreement which grows out of the

---

[12] Forty-four hectares in the metric system of measurement, less than one-third the size of the territory (149 hectares) of the diminutive Principality of Monaco.

diplomatic intervention is called a treaty or convention; in the case of His Holiness, the agreement made both with reference to the protection of his spiritual subjects—those professing the Catholic faith—and with reference to other ecclesiastical matters is termed a concordat.

Now the temporal and the spiritual realms were for centuries not clearly distinguished, the unity of Christendom having been regarded as both religious and temporal, under which conception the need for compacts or agreements between the two domains was less obvious than it later became. However, with the advent of distinct, separate, and independent nations—independent not only of each other but asserting in the course of time independence of papal supremacy—the demarcation between the spiritual and the temporal realms became a recognized fact. What then was to be the relation between the two realms? For relations they must have. We have seen that Vitoria and Suárez alike denied the world-wide temporal supremacy of both pope and emperor. But each insisted on the right of the pope to intervene in temporal affairs whenever necessary for the accomplishment of spiritual ends. It is to the eternal credit of Cardinal Bellarmine that he propounded so clearly this doctrine of the indirect power of the pope in temporal matters that he was and still is its most accredited advocate. His doctrine provided a *modus vivendi* during a period in which the secular states were so intoxicated with their new conception of independence and nationality that the papal right of intervention in temporal affairs for spiritual purposes was not infrequently disputed even when it was tolerated, and in fact was on occasion squarely denied by temporal sovereigns, jealous of their own interests. But Bellarmine's doctrine was destined to receive its full international application through the increasing use of the concordat, which thus became the legal channel for the relationships between the spiritual and temporal domains and therefore an integral part of international law. In Professor McIlwain's language,

Cardinal Bellarmine's sixteenth-century doctrine of the indirect power of the Pope in secular matters was not new in principle, but it had a new "international" application for which there had been less occasion before the late medieval period. The concordats made the theory of the indirect power a logical necessity.[13]

It is not without interest to note that the temporal state may also intervene in behalf of the non-material interests of its citizens. In so intervening, the secular sovereign necessarily exercises directly temporal power in furtherance of a spiritual purpose. This procedure is essentially the same as that followed

---

[13] *The Growth of Political Power in the West* (previously cited), p. 352.

by the papal sovereign. Now the recognition of the concordat as a legal instrument in international law carries with it an important and indeed fundamental corollary: the recognition of the sovereign pontiff's right to protect by diplomatic process and agreement the rights of his spiritual subjects, wherever they may dwell. Thus, although the distinction between a concordat and a treaty may seem at first sight to be a distinction between an instrument used for spiritual purposes and one which is used for material purposes, such distinction is nevertheless misleading, in that a treaty or convention may also be used by the temporal power in behalf of a spiritual cause.[14]

[14] An example of the exercise of this temporal power by the United States for a spiritual purpose is to be found in the treaty with the Netherlands of Oct. 8, 1782, Article 4:

"There shall be an entire and perfect liberty of Conscience allowed to the Subjects and Inhabitants of each Party, and to their Families: and no one shall be molested in regard to his worship, provided he submits, as to the public demonstration of it, to the Laws of the Country."

Another example, in which the United States sought to exercise the protection of the spiritual rights of its citizens in China (whether Catholic or Protestant), is the Treaty between the United States and China, June 18, 1858, Article XXIX:

"The principles of the Christian religion as professed by the Protestant and Roman Catholic churches, are recognized as teaching men to do good, and to do to others as they would have others do to them. Hereafter, those who quietly profess and teach these doctrines shall not be harassed or persecuted on account of their faith. Any person, whether citizen of the United States or Chinese convert, who according to these tenets, peaceably teach and practice [sic] the principles of Christianity, shall in no case be interfered with or molested."

See also the treaty between the same countries dated July 28, 1868, Article IV:

"The 29th Article of the treaty of the 18th of June, 1858, having stipulated for the exemption of Christian citizens of the United States and Chinese converts, from persecution in China on account of their faith, it is further agreed that citizens of the United States in China of every religious persuasion, and Chinese subjects in the United States, shall enjoy entire liberty of conscience, and shall be exempt from all disability or persecution on account of their religious faith or worship in either country."

Also the treaty of Oct. 8, 1903, between the same countries, Article XIV:

"The principles of the Christian religion, as professed by the Protestant and Roman Catholic Churches, are recognized as teaching men to do good and to do to others as they would have others do to them. Those who quietly profess and teach these doctrines shall not be harassed or persecuted on account of their faith. Any person, whether citizen of the United States or Chinese convert, who, according to these tenets, peaceably teaches and practices the principles of Christianity shall in no case be interfered with or molested therefor. No restrictions shall be placed on Chinese joining Christian churches. Converts and non-converts, being Chinese subjects, shall alike conform to the laws of China; and shall pay due respect to those in authority, living together in peace and amity; and the fact of being converts shall not protect them from the consequences of any offense they may have committed before or may commit after their admission into the church, or exempt them from paying legal taxes levied on Chinese subjects generally, except taxes levied and contributions for the support of religious customs and practices contrary to their faith. Missionaries shall not interfere with the exercise by the native authorities of their jurisdiction over Chinese subjects; nor shall the native authorities make any distinction between converts and non-converts, but shall administer the laws without partiality so that both classes can live together in peace.

"Missionary societies of the United States shall be permitted to rent and to lease in perpetuity, as the property of such societies, buildings or lands in all parts of the Empire for missionary purposes and, after the title deeds have been found in order and duly stamped by the local authorities, to erect such suitable buildings as may be required for carrying on their good work."

No discussion of this subject would be complete without an examination of certain articles in the epoch-making Treaty of St. John Lateran (as the convention between His Holiness and the King of Italy is known).

Just as the papal sovereign may conclude agreements concerning the protection of the spiritual rights of his subjects, so also he may conclude agreements—which are in fact as well as in form treaties or conventions—dealing with temporal matters, in so far as these relate to the Vatican State as a temporal community. Thus the present treaty-making power of the Vatican may, like that of any sovereign state, be exerted for a twofold purpose; and the perfect example of this is to be found in the Treaty of February 11, 1929, already referred to, consisting of three separate agreements, the three, however, forming a whole. The first and second deal with temporal matters; the first, recognition of the Vatican State as a temporal state, entitled to all the rights and subject to all the duties of such a state; and the second, financial arrangements. The third, dealing at length with matters pertaining to the Church and the spiritual jurisdiction, is the great modern example of the concordat. From the first agreement (the treaty of sovereign Italy with the equally sovereign Vatican State) we quote a few passages, in order that there may be no doubt as to the international standing of His Holiness and the Vatican State.

The preamble of the first agreement states the ends and purposes of the negotiation and the equality of the contracting parties:

Whereas, the Holy See and Italy have both recognized the desirability of eliminating every cause of disagreement existing between them by coming to a definite understanding of their mutual relations which shall be in accordance with justice and compatible with the dignity of the two High Contracting Parties and which, by assuring permanently to the Holy See a status of fact and of right guaranteeing to it absolute independence in the exercise of its mission in the world, the said Holy See may acknowledge as definitively and irrevocably settled the "Roman Question" which arose in 1870 with the annexation of Rome to the Kingdom of Italy under the dynasty of the House of Savoy;

And whereas, for the purpose of assuring to the Holy See absolute and visible independence and of guaranteeing to it indisputable sovereignty also in the field of international relations, it has been deemed necessary to establish the State of the Vatican, and to recognize so far as the latter is concerned, complete ownership, exclusive and absolute power and sovereign jurisdiction on the part of the Holy See.[15]

---

[15] The official Italian text of the preamble reads.
"*Premesso:*

"Che la Santa Sede e l'Italia hanno riconosciuto la convenienza di eliminare ogni ragione di dissidio fra loro esistente con l'addivenire ad una sistemazione definitiva dei reciproci rapporti, che sia conforme a giustizia ed alla dignità delle due Alte Parti e che, assicurando alla Santa Sede in modo stabile una condizione di fatto e di diritto la quale Le garantisca

For present purposes the quotation from the body of the agreement may begin with Article 2:

Art. 2.

Italy recognizes the sovereignty of the Holy See in the field of international relations as an attribute that pertains to the very nature of the Holy See, in conformity with its traditions and with the demands of its mission in the world.

Art. 3.

Italy recognizes full possession and exclusive and absolute power and sovereign jurisdiction of the Holy See over the Vatican, as at present constituted, with all its appurtenances and endowments. . . .

Art. 4.

The sovereignty and exclusive jurisdiction which Italy recognizes on the part of the Holy See with regard to the State of the Vatican implies that there can be no interference on the part of the Italian Government therein, nor any other authority than that of the Holy See.[16]

In the ninth article international law is introduced:

Art. 9.

In conformity with the provisions of international law, all persons having a fixed residence within the State of the Vatican are subject to the sovereignty of the Holy See. . . .[17]

The right of the Holy See to send and receive diplomatic representatives is also specifically recognized:

---

l'assoluta indipendenza per l'adempimento della Sua alta missione nel mondo, consenta alla Santa Sede stessa di riconoscere composta in modo definitivo ed irrevocabile la 'Questione Romana,' sorta nel 1870 con l'annessione di Roma al Regno d'Italia sotto la dinastia di Casa Savoia;

"Che dovendosi, per assicurare alla Santa Sede l'assoluta evisibile indipendenza, garentirLe una sovranità indiscutibile pur nel campo internazionale, si è ravvisata la necessità di costituire, con particolari modalità, la Città del Vaticano, riconoscendo sulla medesima alla Santa Sede la piena proprietà e l'esclusiva ed assoluta potestà e giurisdizione sovrana."

[16] "Art. 2.

"L'Italia riconosce la sovranità della Santa Sede nel campo internazionale come attributo inerente alla sua natura, in conformità alla sua tradizione ed alle esigenze della sua missione nel mondo.

"Art. 3.

"L'Italia riconosce alla Santa Sede la piena proprietà e la esclusiva ed assoluta potestà e giurisdizione sovrana sul Vaticano, com'è attualmente costituito, con tutte le sue pertinenze e dotazioni. . . .

"Art. 4.

"La sovranità e la giurisdizione esclusiva, che l'Italia riconosce alla Santa Sede sulla Città del Vaticano, importa che nella medesima non possa esplicarsi alcuna ingerenza da parte del Governo Italiano e che non vi sia altra autorità che quella della Santa Sede.

[17] "In conformità alle norme del diritto internazionale sono soggette alla sovranità della Santa Sede tutte le persone aventi stabile residenza nella Città del Vaticano. . . .

Art. 12.

Italy recognizes the right of the Holy See to send and to receive diplomatic representatives according to the general provisions of international law. . . .[18]

And finally, there is a declaration concerning the use which the Holy See will make of its sovereignty in relation to international affairs:

Art. 24.

With regard to the sovereignty pertaining to it in the field of international relations, the Holy See declares that it wishes to remain and will remain extraneous to all temporal disputes between nations, and to international congresses convoked for the settlement of such disputes, unless the contending parties make a joint appeal to its mission of peace; nevertheless, it reserves the right in every case to exercise its moral and spiritual power.

In consequence of this declaration, the State of the Vatican will always and in every case be considered neutral and inviolable territory.[19]

The name of Cardinal Bellarmine, Saint and Doctor of the Holy Roman Catholic Church, is destined to live because of his distinguished ecclesiastical career. But he is also gratefully remembered for his contributions to political theory and international law. These have had profound and far-reaching consequences which, as is not infrequently the case with those who build for the future, he could hardly have foreseen. His theories of government for secular states contained the seeds of the American conception of the state, which, it is believed, will in the course of time bear generous fruit in the four corners of the world. And his theory of the indirect power was the connecting bridge, as it were, between the medieval conception of the relationship of the spiritual with the temporal power and the accepted modern doctrine whereby the Holy See has become recognized as a sovereign temporal power in the fullest sense of international law, while keeping intact its right "to exercise its moral and spiritual power"[20] throughout the world. In both domains, temporal and spiritual, Bellarmine's reputation grows with the centuries.

---

[18] "L'Italia riconosce alla Santa Sede il diritto di legazione attivo e passivo secondo le regole generali del diritto internazionale. . . .

[19] "La Santa Sede, in relazione alla sovranità che le compete anche nel campo internazionale, dichiara che Essa vuole rimanere e rimarrà estranea alle competizioni temporali fra gli altri Stati ed ai Congressi internazionali indetti per tale oggetto, a meno che le parti contendenti facciano concorde appello alla sua missione di pace, riservandosi in ogni caso di far valere la sua potestà morale e spirituale.

"In conseguenza di ciò la Città del Vaticano sarà sempre ed in ogni caso considerata territorio neutrale ed inviolabile.

[20] See Art. 24, *supra*.

Chapter XXXIII

FRANCISCO SUÁREZ (1548-1617)

It is often considered that scholasticism enjoyed its golden age during the medieval period, and that thereafter it lapsed into a permanent decline. Yet in certain countries scholasticism continued to flourish (and indeed took on new life) during the fifteenth and sixteenth centuries. The truth is that much of the philosophy of scholasticism, including its legal and political philosophy, is of perennial interest. And today the best elements of scholasticism are winning their way in many quarters. An instance of this is to be seen in the action of the Seventh Pan-American Conference,[1] which recognized Francisco de Vitoria, a Spanish schoolman, as having laid the foundations of modern international law.

Another Spanish theologian, Francisco Suárez (sometimes known as "the last of the great schoolmen"),[2] is also coming into his own, although it may be said that his name has long been familiar to the comparatively few who have dealt with the philosophy of law. Today the esteem of these few for Suárez' work is shared by an increasing number whose opinion has been put into words by a leading American authority in the statement that Suárez is the "prince of modern jurists." Suárez produced three large tomes which contain an exhaustive treatment of legal, political, and international philosophy. The first of these masterpieces is the *Tractatus de legibus ac Deo legislatore,* a large volume of ten books, published at Coimbra in the year 1612, Suárez being then *prima* professor of theology at the University of Coimbra. The second is the *Defensio fidei Catholicae adversus Anglicanae sectae errores,* published in 1613, also at Coimbra, the occasion for which was the oath of allegiance which James I of England and VI of Scotland had exacted from his Catholic subjects, unjustly in their opinion, in

---

[1] The text of the resolution adopted by the Seventh Conference is given *supra,* p. 313.
[2] Sherwood, "Francisco Suárez," in *Transactions of the Grotius Society,* XII, 19-28, 21.
The verdict of an eminent French philosopher and publicist, Paul Janet, should also be noted here: "Enfin Suárez est incontestablement l'écrivain le plus considérable de l'ordre des Jésuites. Ses principes sont élevés et profonds. Il ne paraît pas se servir de la science comme d'un instrument de domination. C'est un homme d'école et non de parti; il représente la grande tradition du moyen âge. Il en a la droiture, la sincérité, la passion logique; c'est le digne élève de saint Thomas d'Aquin: c'est le dernier des scholastiques."—*Histoire de la science politique dans ses rapports avec la morale,* II, 55-56.

the opinion of their Church, and in the opinion of posterity. The third treatise, which contains a disquisition on the law of war, was the *Opus de triplici virtute theologica,* left in manuscript at Suárez' death in 1617 and published four years later.

Vitoria gave their modern expression to fundamental principles of international law which had been slowly maturing through the centuries. But that expression lacked a complete philosophic background. The great contribution of Suárez was to endow the modern world with an adequate philosophic basis for law in general, for the state, and for the law of nations.

The international conceptions of the two Spanish schoolmen, as will soon appear, were similar in many respects, but not identical. They differed chiefly in their conceptions of the international community. Vitoria conceived of it as an organic community which would aim toward a federation of the states of the world. The international community of Suárez, on the other hand, was more in the nature of a loose confederation of states.

Approximately a century and a half ago the thirteen erstwhile British colonies in the Western World were confronted by the necessity of choosing between these two types of union. Having first tried the confederation and found it inadequate for their purposes, the thirteen American states decided in favor of federation. Today the international community is confronted by a somewhat similar problem, to which confederation or federation appear to be the ultimate answers. Only experience can tell whether the world's choice will be the international community of Vitoria, or that of Suárez.

On a previous page[3] a passage was quoted from Vitoria illustrating his conception of an organized international community. The international community of Suárez—an inorganic rather than an organic community—is developed at somewhat greater length:[4]

The rational basis ... of this phase of law [the law of nations] consists in the fact that the human race, into howsoever many different peoples and kingdoms it may be divided, always preserves a certain unity, not only as a species, but also a moral and political unity (as it were) enjoined by the natural precept of mutual love and mercy; a precept which applies to all, even to strangers of every nation.

Therefore, although a given sovereign state, commonwealth, or kingdom may constitute a perfect community in itself, consisting of its own members, nevertheless each one of these states is also in a certain sense, and viewed in relation to the human race, a member of this universal society; for these states when

---

[3] *Supra,* p. 322.
[4] *De legibus ac Deo legislatore,* Book II, chap. xix, sec. 9. The translation is from *Francisco Suárez, Selections,* which is to appear in the "Classics of International Law" and is now in press.

standing alone are never so self-sufficient that they do not require some mutual assistance, association, and intercourse, at times for their own greater welfare and advantage, but at other times because also of some moral necessity or need. This fact is made manifest by actual usage.

Consequently such communities have need of some system of law whereby they may be directed and properly ordered with regard to this kind of intercourse and association; and although that guidance is in large measure provided by natural reason, it is not provided in sufficient measure and in a direct manner with respect to all matters; therefore it was possible for certain special rules of law to be introduced through the practice of these same nations. For just as in one state or province law is introduced by custom, so among the human race as a whole it was possible for laws to be introduced by the habitual conduct of nations. This was the more feasible because the matters comprised within the law in question are few, very closely related to natural law and most easily deduced therefrom in a manner so advantageous and so in harmony with nature itself that, while this derivation [of the law of nations from the natural law] may not be self-evident—that is, not essentially and absolutely required for moral rectitude—it is nevertheless quite in accord with nature, and universally acceptable for its own sake.

In an earlier volume a comparison was made of the views of the two great Spaniards on international organization, and for present purposes that comparison may be reproduced here:[5]

There was, however, an essential difference between the international community of Suárez and that of Victoria. To the former, the community of states was inorganic. It existed because the states existed and had need of relations, one with the other, of "mutual assistance, association and intercourse." But the community which he [Suárez] had in mind was not an organized community with law-making and law-enforcing powers. The laws of the international community of Victoria were created because the community had "the power to create" them, just as it had the power, backed by the authority of the world, to enforce them. The international community of Suárez was governed by laws introduced slowly, unconsciously, by custom, in his own words, "by the habitual conduct of nations."

We of today are not infrequently pleased to consider ourselves as originators, especially in matters international; but in point of fact the two great modern conceptions of the international community are the conceptions of Victoria and of Suárez. The one—an organized community—the statesmen of the world had in mind when they developed the vast and complicated machinery of Geneva. The other—that of an inorganic community, a gradual development growing out of the mere coexistence of states—has found expression in the international machinery set up at The Hague. The choice of the future lies between the two.

In both a sanction is contemplated. In the one, it is a legal and a physical sanction, the authority of the world supported by law and expressed through

---

[5] *The Catholic Conception of International Law,* by J. B. Scott, p. 484.

physical means. In the other, the sanction is a moral and spiritual force which, also supported by law, is based fundamentally, however, not upon physical action but upon the moral principle which underlies all human relationships, good faith.

In developing his legal and political philosophy, Suárez set forth at length his conceptions of law and of the state, including certain general observations on the law of nations.

It will shorten matters here to say that in general the views of Suárez concerning the state are those of Vitoria. The views of both are based upon Aristotle: Men and women are sociable animals; they neither can, nor do they, live alone; they dwell together in a regulated society, in which the regulating power—of divine origin—resides in all the people who form the social group. Now a regulated society, as Suárez conceives it, is a political community organized for the common welfare of its members, and such a community requires government; not government imposed from above, however, but government as the agency of the community. But no analysis of Suárez' views on this point can equal the force and logic of his own words:

It is impossible to conceive of a unified political body without political government or disposition thereto; since, in the first place, this unity arises, in a large measure, from subjection to one and the same rule and to some common superior power; while furthermore, if there were no such government, this body could not be directed towards one [common] end, and the general welfare. It is, then, repugnant to natural reason to assume the existence of a group of human beings united in the form of a single political body, without postulating the existence of some common power which the individual members of the community are bound to obey; and therefore, if this power does not reside in any specific individual, it must necessarily exist in the community as a whole.[6]

But the entire community cannot conveniently exercise such power. Therefore the people delegate its exercise to an agency consisting of one or more persons. And although this agency governs the community, its power and authority come from the people. "Civil power," says Suárez,[7] "whenever it resides—in the right and ordinary course of law—in the person of one individual, or prince, has flowed from the people as a community, either directly or indirectly; nor could it otherwise be justly held." The "reason" which Suárez offers in support of this view is the doctrine of government by consent of the governed:[8] "A reason for this view, supplied by what we have said above, is the fact that such power, in the very nature of things, resides immediately in the community; and therefore, in order that it may

---

[6] *De legibus,* Book III, chap. ii, sec. 4.   [7] *Ibid.,* Book III, chap. iv, sec. 2.   [8] *Ibid.*

justly come to reside in a given individual as in a sovereign prince, it must necessarily be bestowed upon him by the consent of the community."

It is interesting to notice that Suárez contemplated rule by the majority, and in that majority he held that the woman of the same age as the man should possess the same right to vote. Speaking of the exclusion from suffrage of women and of men below the age of twenty-five, he declares:

> Some would also entirely exclude women on the ground that they can exercise no legislative authority. Among men, they exclude all below the age of twenty-five years. However, I cannot find any basis in law or any justification in reason for the exclusion of the last two groups.[9]

In discussing the subject of law, Suárez begins with a general definition of the term "law," basing it upon the definition of St. Thomas Aquinas, which, as we have already seen,[10] is "a rule and measure of acts whereby man is induced to act or is restrained from acting." After considering this definition in detail, Suárez expands it for his purposes to read:[11] "strictly and absolutely speaking, only that which is a measure of rectitude, viewed absolutely, and consequently, only that which is a right and virtuous rule, can be called law." To this definition he adds another (for law, as all jurists know, may be defined in more ways than one), based this time not only upon the authority of St. Thomas but also upon that of the Roman jurist Papinian "law is a common, just, and stable precept, which has been sufficiently promulgated"[12]—a statement which might well be printed on the title-page of every book on the nature, theory, and application of law.

Justice, as would be expected, is a fundamental element in Suárez' definition. It pertains—or should pertain—alike to the individual, to the group, and to the international community. A rule which is unjust is not law in the Suarezian sense. There is, in other words, something above and beyond the legislature, an eternal and all-pervasive justice, which, not made by a legislature, cannot be modified or revoked by it. It is, as it were, the primary element of all law, customary, constitutional, or legislative.

But to Suárez law must possess stability as well as universality of application and justice, because an unstable law is likely to be neither universal nor just in its application. And of course the law, whatever its origin, must be made known, because if it is not promulgated, we cannot expect that it will be observed.

There are many kinds of law, but in the conception of Suárez there are three, eternal law, divine law, and natural law, which have existed at all

---

[9] *De legibus,* Book VII, chap. ix, sec. 14.
[11] *De legibus,* Book I, chap. i, sec. 6.
[10] *Supra,* p. 217.
[12] *Ibid.,* Book I, chap. xii, sec. 5.

times and in all places. First among these three branches of law he places the eternal law, which he describes as the "source and origin of all laws"[13]—an emanation from the Creator of the world. The second, or divine, law likewise emanates from the Creator, who has mercifully revealed its precepts that they may become not only the possession but the guide of all human beings, this revelation being, in the terms of Suárez, a "species of promulgation."[14] The third kind of law is termed natural—meaning that it is in accordance with nature, that is to say, the nature which God himself has created. Therefore the law natural is said to be eternal. It is also divine because of its origin. And finally it is natural to man as one of God's creatures, and its existence is discoverable by the eye of human reason. To drive this point home, Suárez describes the law of nature as being "the natural light of the intellect—which is itself at hand, in readiness to prescribe what must be done— ... since men retain that law in their hearts, although they may be engaged in no [specific] act of reflection or judgment."[15]

Further revealing the relationship between the eternal and the natural law in the human being, Suárez shows how man is linked to the eternal by natural law discovered through right reason: "All men necessarily behold within themselves some sort of participation in the eternal law, since there is no rational person who does not in some manner judge that the virtuous course of action must be followed and the base avoided; and in this sense, it is said that men have some knowledge of the eternal law."[16]

Like the divine law, the natural law may not be changed by man because both are the law of the Creator. The natural law, moreover, is the form of the eternal law directed especially to God's creatures in their lives and in their intercourse one with another. And while it is unchangeable, human conditions, as we know, change from time to time; and reasonable beings, such as Suárez and the members of the scholastic school generously considered their fellow creatures to be, would therefore bring into being human laws—in harmony with and based upon the natural law—to meet the changing conditions. Thus as human reason develops, the application of natural law through human law likewise develops and changes, although the natural law itself remains eternally the same, being, as we have seen, eternal in its nature.

This conception is so fundamental to the schoolmen that it warrants elaboration, even at the risk of some repetition. The natural law of Suárez comprised those everlasting principles which are sometimes described as

[13] *Ibid.*, Book II, Introduction.
[14] *Ibid.*, Book II, chap. iv, sec. 7.
[15] *Ibid*, Book II, chap. v, sec. 14.
[16] *Ibid.*, Book II, chap. iv, sec. 9.

the eternal verities and which the Greeks with a clearer vision termed "design in nature." All men are more like one another than they are different from one another, and the natural law is a law common to all human beings sharing a common nature, a law consisting of those fundamentals of rational human nature without which man would be but a four-footed beast.

Now if natural law is "design in nature," if it consists of the eternal verities, it is obvious that in that sense it is completely and absolutely immutable; but the extent to which the great "design"—to employ the Greek term—is discoverable by man depends upon human progress and development, and therefore the application of the natural law to human affairs through the light of reason must—and indeed does—vary in the onward and upward march of man. It is not, however, the natural law which changes; it is man who changes, and therefore the application of the natural law to man. The fundamental law of nature, being derived from the eternal law, remains unaltered. As human reason develops, so the natural law in its relation to human beings also develops through discovery by "the natural light of the intellect," to employ the phrase of Suárez.

By way of illustration mention may here be made of three basic rights under the natural law: the right to life (which may be called the most basic of all rights); the right to liberty (without which man is a slave, shut off from the world which he was born to inherit); and the right to the pursuit of happiness (without which there is no reason for living, or for liberty). So thought Thomas Jefferson, author of the immortal Declaration of Independence of the United States of America, and so thought his nameless predecessors through whose martyrdom these rights had been defended in the older world.

A good example is quickly followed, and the American example has made its way around the world. The principles for which it stands were adopted a few years later by Republican France in the ringing phrase, Liberté, Egalité, Fraternité; and a decade ago these principles received their newest and most international expression in a Declaration issued by the *Institut de Droit International,* appropriately meeting in the United States in 1929.[17]

It is impossible within the compass of a single chapter to deal in any detail with Suárez' legal philosophy, and hence it must suffice here to consider only a few more of his fundamental conceptions.

Now the *ius gentium* is the link, as it were, between the natural law and

[17] For the text of this declaration, see *supra,* p. 421.

human law, Suárez, declaring that "the *ius gentium* is the most closely related to the natural law."[18] Indeed the law of nations, as has already been observed,[19] was not infrequently identified with the law of nature, and the relationship was, as Suárez has pointed out, extremely intimate. Thus while the *ius gentium* originally consisted of the laws or practices of the different peoples, the Romans, finding that the practices of non-Romans who settled in Rome or who dwelt elsewhere in the ever-conquering Roman Empire, were based upon the same fundamental principles, eventually came to regard the *ius gentium* (or the law of the peoples) as being practically the same as the universal law of nature, believing it to be derived from universal principles inherent in human nature. The actual rules of the *ius gentium* as they came subsequently to be formulated by the later Roman jurists were therefore largely based upon fundamental principles of the *ius naturale* (natural law).[20]

There was, however, as Suárez pointed out, a real distinction between the *ius naturale* and the *ius gentium,* in that the latter was essentially man-made law, embodying, to be sure, the rules derived from the natural law but nevertheless depending both for its formation and its application upon the human will. Again, the same distinction between the *ius gentium* and the natural law was evidenced by the fact that the *ius gentium* evolved largely through human custom among various peoples, during a long period of time, and this custom has its origin directly or indirectly in the human will.

Now Suárez as a Romanist—and few men were more familiar than he with the jurisprudence of Rome—realized that the *ius gentium* (as thus defined) was not applied in the days of ancient Rome to states in their relations with one another but rather to the non-Roman individuals of different localities in their relations with non-Romans of other localities or with Roman citizens. Such an application among persons of different nationality was possible because the fundamentals of this law were universal, in that they were based upon principles of law common to many communities within their respective jurisdictions. Thus these principles were derived from what Suárez terms "a body of laws which individual states or kingdoms observe within their own borders."[21] But Suárez, following in the footsteps of Vitoria, had in mind also the *ius gentium* as it began to develop in what we may call the post-Roman period, after the dissolution of the Empire, a *ius gentium* which was eventually to become our modern inter-

---

[18] *De legibus,* Book II, Introduction.   [19] *Supra,* chap. vii, *passim.*
[20] For a detailed discussion of the *ius gentium* and the natural law in Rome, see *supra,* pp. 111, 125-27, 134-36.
[21] *De legibus,* Book II, chap. xix, sec. 8.

national law[22]—"the law which," Suárez tells us, "all the various peoples and nations ought to observe in their relations with each other."[23]

One of the most important elements in Suárez' system of jurisprudence is that of good faith. Now good faith, as Suárez himself says, pertains "most decidedly to the province of the natural law."[24] To this conception he returns again and again in the course of his treatise on law. Thus he maintains that human laws requiring the observance of agreements and promises are simply declaratory of the natural law:

> It should be further noted that, among the precepts of the natural law, there are certain precepts—dealing with pacts, agreements, obligations—which are introduced through the will of men: for example, the laws relating to the observance of vows and of human promises, whether these be made in simple form or confirmed by oath; and the same is true of other contracts, according to the particular characteristics of each; and true, also, of rights, natural and legal, arising therefrom.[25]

Moreover, while man-made law regulates the form and procedure of entering into agreements, Suárez insists that "in the case of any contract or commercial agreement . . . the observance of the contract after it has been made . . . pertains to the natural law."[26] And he applies the same doctrine in the international field, for as regards compacts on such matters as "peace, truces and ambassadors" he declares that "all the rules on these points have their foundation in some human agreement, in which both the power to contract a treaty or convention and the obligation arising from that treaty or convention and demanding good faith and justice have regard to the law of nature."[27]

Good faith was to Suárez a natural principle, a principle which stood behind every obligation pertaining to the individual, to the state, or to the international community. The obligation itself might arise in many ways, depending upon the varieties of relations among human beings, whether individuals or groups, but the immediate consequence of the obligation, when it was contracted, was the inevitable, unchanging requirement that it be carried out; that good faith be observed; that, in the words of a maxim long familiar to those learned in the law, *pacta sunt servanda*. Therefore this universal principle of good faith attaches to any and every agreement the moment it is formed. And without good faith, anything which man makes in the nature of an agreement (from the smallest contract to a uni-

---

[22] On this development of the Roman *ius gentium*, see *supra*, pp. 131–32.
[23] *De legibus*, Book II, chap. xix, sec. 8.
[24] *Ibid.*, chap. xvii, sec. 6, at end.
[25] *Ibid.*, chap. xiv, sec. 7.
[26] *Ibid.*, chap. xix, sec. 7.
[27] *Ibid.*, chap. xviii, sec. 7.

versal treaty) is, as Hamlet would say, but "words, words, words"—and empty words at that.

Natural law, then, plants every human agreement upon the foundation of good faith; and the obligation arising from every such agreement must of course be executed, if good faith is not to be violated. The specific method of execution is a matter for human regulation, to be determined by human will, but the requirement that the obligation shall be carried out is not a matter of human law or of human will but of the immutable law of nature. In view of that requirement, the law of nature may be said also to enjoin upon every lawmaking body the duty to provide the machinery for the execution of obligations entered into in whatever manner. And by imposing this duty the natural law provides, so to speak, a natural sanction of good faith to stand as a bulwark and protector of every human obligation.

An interesting comment on Suárez' contribution to political science and jurisprudence, of which only the main outlines have been traced here, is given in an essay by A. L. Lilley, a distinguished churchman of the Established Church of England.[28] A few passages from this admirable essay will serve to complete the present chapter. "What, then," asks Dr. Lilley in concluding his essay, "was most significant and of most permanent value in this elaborate treatment of the nature of law and political power which we owe to Suárez?" In replying to this query the author says:

> First of all I would say his clear reaffirmation, as against all the doubts and hesitations of the later mediaeval writers and also as against the practical denial of the new school of rational jurists, of the Natural Law, *i.e.,* of certain general principles of right inherent in the universal human reason, and having therefore the true character of law as directly willed by the Author of reason, as sufficiently promulgated in virtue of their rational character, and as therefore universally binding upon free rational beings.

This fundamental "reaffirmation" by Suárez was accompanied, Dr. Lilley points out, by several affirmations which are almost equally important:

> That these fundamental principles of justice universally known to men as men represented the actual nature of God and not merely His arbitrary will; that they

---

[28] "Francisco Suárez," in *The Social and Political Ideas of Some Great Thinkers of the Sixteenth and Seventeenth Centuries*, ed. by Hearnshaw, pp. 102-4.

The reader interested in a full account of Suárez and his voluminous writings, theological, philosophical, legal, and political, will find extremely interesting the two-volume work by his most recent and most accredited biographer, Scorraille, *François Suárez, de la Compagnie de Jésus.*

A Spanish version of Scorraille's book has been published under the title *El P. Francisco Suárez de la Compañía de Jesús.*

or immediate inferences from them appeared in the mass of customary right which had become accepted by all nations; that the will of the human legislator, whether ecclesiastical or civil, might indeed add to but could not annul or violate them; that the obligation to obey them could not be dispensed by any earthly authority; finally, that they were prior to every particular Divine Revelation—these were affirmations which made law the sovereign and accepted arbiter of human destiny and not the chance product of human convenience or, on the other hand, the arbitrary decrees of a power whose will man had no means of understanding and yet must under penalty obey.

There were other outstanding contributions by Suárez, especially in the political field, according to the learned English divine:

Suárez did political theory a service in establishing on grounds of right and reason the complete independence of the secular state, its right as a *societas perfecta,* unhindered by the interference of any alien authority, to determine the requirements and conditions of its own continued existence. Here, indeed, exception may be taken to the use of the term "secular state." For Suárez, like Bellarmine, while denying absolutely the right of the Pope as supreme ecclesiastical ruler to interfere in the secular affairs of the civil state, yet reserved such a right where the interests of religion were concerned.

Finally still another service which Suárez rendered to political philosophy and indeed to political practice is described in a preceding passage of Dr. Lilley's text:

Suárez, it seems to me, rendered an inestimable service by reaffirming in a more modern form the mediaeval doctrine of popular sovereignty. . . . If the ecclesiastical society was of Divine origin and ordering, so also must the civil society be if its independence were to be sufficiently guaranteed. The secular publicists for the most part met the difficulty by claiming an immediate Divine appointment for the civil ruler. Suárez scouted the notion as a fantastic perversion of history.

As Dr. Lilley points out, Suárez, whose views he here paraphrases, met and routed the arguments advanced by his opponents on this question:

The Divine appointment of the Kings of Israel to which the theorists of Divine Right triumphantly pointed was a special instance which it was merely absurd in the face of history as a whole to invoke. No, the Divine mandate of the temporal ruler was a mediated mandate. And it was mediated exactly through the delegation of his power from the political community, whose very existence was a consequence of the Natural Law and therefore of Divine ordering and origin.

And the eminent English churchman makes a comment which goes to the heart of the democratic conception of government:

Whatever judgment may be formed of the correspondence of either of these theories with historic fact, there is no doubt as to which of them has proved to have the greater measure of pragmatic truth. The total community whose well-being the State exists to preserve is the natural judge of what its well-being is, and, at least on Suárez' assumption of the existence and character of Natural Law, it is a competent judge. And to its judgment the temporary trustee of its sovereign power is always in the last resort responsible.

CHAPTER XXXIV

RICHARD HOOKER (c. 1553-1600)

Of the Laws of Ecclesiastical Polity

THE POLITICAL DOCTRINES OF THE GREAT SCHOOLMEN WERE DESTINED TO FIND a welcome in many lands. In England they were adopted wholeheartedly by Richard Hooker (a Protestant contemporary of Suárez) whose *Ecclesiastical Polity* was an important contribution both to political philosophy and to English literature.[1] It is not too much to say that Hooker's theories, expressed in his own tongue, if not superior in substance were nevertheless superior in literary form to those of any of the schoolmen. Concerning his place in literature it will suffice to cite the reply of Alfred Lord Tennyson as to the six authors who had written the most majestic English prose. Of the six mentioned by the English bard the first two were Richard Hooker and Lord Bacon.[2] This tribute, it should be remembered, was from a poet whose ear was attuned to the melody and splendor of the English tongue.

It is interesting in certain respects to contrast the first book of the *Ecclesiastical Polity* with the *Mare liberum* of Grotius.[3] The one was concerned primarily with philosophic conceptions; the other was more factual in its nature, dealing as it did with concrete problems in the relations of states.

---

[1] "This eminent work [*Laws of Ecclesiastical Polity*] may justly be reckoned to mark an era in our literature; for if passages of much good sense and even of a vigorous eloquence are scattered in several earlier writers in prose, yet none of these, except perhaps Latimer and Ascham, and Sir Philip Sidney in his Arcadia, can be said to have acquired enough reputation to be generally known even by name, much less are read in the present day; and it is indeed not a little remarkable that England, until near the end of the sixteenth century, had given few proofs in literature of that intellectual power which was about to develop itself with such unmatchable energy in Shakespeare and Bacon. We cannot indeed place Hooker (but whom dare we to place?) by the side of these master-spirits; yet he has abundant claims to be counted among the luminaries of English literature. He not only opened the mine, but explored the depths, of our native eloquence. So stately and graceful is the march of his periods, so various the fall of his musical cadences upon the ear, so rich in images, so condensed in sentences, so grave and noble his diction, so little is there of vulgarity in his racy idiom, of pedantry in his learned phrase, that I know not whether any later writer has more admirably displayed the capacities of our language, or produced passages more worthy of comparison with the splendid monuments of antiquity."—Hallam, *The Constitutional History of England*, I, 214-15.

[2] E. T. Cook in the article on Ruskin, *Dictionary of National Biography*, Supplement, III (New York and London, 1901), 315.

[3] For a discussion of the *Mare liberum*, see chap. xxxi, *supra*.

The first book of the *Ecclesiastical Polity* is concerned with political and legal theories; the *Mare liberum* is an essay on international law, small in size but large in content. Each work is a masterpiece. The first is still the best summary in the English language of the political and legal doctrines set forth by the scholastic writers in Spain; and the second is the most effective and concrete, as well as the handiest, statement in Latin by a non-Spanish writer, of certain leading doctrines of the Spanish schoolmen on international law.

In the domain of political science, Hooker is rated "not merely as a controversialist but as a political thinker," who "was incomparably the greatest Englishman of the sixteenth century and on the Continent had few compeers."[4]

According to Izaak Walton,[5] Richard Hooker was born about 1553 (the exact year being uncertain) and died some forty-seven years later. Hooker was a very learned man, deeply versed in the classics and in Hebrew. He had taken orders in the Church of England and was appointed in early life to the distinguished post of Master of the Temple. There he found himself in congenial company as regards the lawyers but very much less so with the afternoon lecturer at the Temple,[6] who belonged to the Presbyterian sect, so that it was said of the twain that the services were of Canterbury in the morning, and of Geneva in the afternoon. Out of this difference of views grew the *Ecclesiastical Polity*.

Modest and retiring, Hooker found the atmosphere of controversy most uncongenial. After a few years in London he left the Temple for a quiet parish in the country, having decided after much reflection to lay his side of the controversy before the public, together with a full examination of the subject of church laws and government. There he was able to devote much time to study and to the preparation of his manuscript.

The *Ecclesiastical Polity* consists of eight books, four being published about the year 1593 or 1594, and the fifth in 1597. The five books therefore appeared before Hooker's death in 1600, so that the text as published can be looked upon as having met with the author's approval. Years later Books VI, VII, and VIII (to complete the work) were issued, but assuredly not as Hooker would have published them—if, indeed, he can be said to have written them. Of these three, the sixth, in its published form, seems indeed to be more or less a travesty of Hooker's views, whereas the seventh and

[4] John William Allen, *A History of Political Thought in the Sixteenth Century*, p. 184.
[5] *The Lives of John Donne, Sir Henry Wotton, Richard Hooker. George Herbert & Robert Sanderson*, in "The World's Classics," p. 162.
[6] Walter Travers (1548?–1635).

eighth are in accordance with the doctrines which he had professed in the parts published during his lifetime. It is in the earlier books and especially in the first, however, that Hooker is seen at his best as one of the glories of English literature and as an outstanding philosopher.

The "judicious Hallam," who himself, following Locke,[7] spoke of Hooker as the "judicious Hooker," expressly says of him that he was the first of English writers who was sufficiently educated to read Greek literature in the original. And in comparing the qualities of the *Ecclesiastical Polity* with those of other masterpieces, Mr. Hallam selects Cicero's *De legibus* as more nearly resembling it:

> If we compare the first book of the Ecclesiastical Polity with what bears perhaps most resemblance to it of anything extant, the treatise of Cicero de Legibus, it will appear somewhat perhaps inferior, through the imperfection of our language, which, with all its force and dignity, does not equal the Latin in either of these qualities, and certainly more tedious and diffuse in some of its reasonings, but by no means less high-toned in sentiment, or less bright in fancy, and far more comprehensive and profound in the foundations of its philosophy.[8]

The part of the *Ecclesiastical Polity* to be considered here is the first book, dealing with law and government, with a definition of the law of nations—a term which, as Sir Frederick Pollock says, Hooker was "the very first writer to use ... in English in the specialised sense now so familiar to us as to be the only one generally understood."[9]

Now Hooker's first book is in the nature of an introduction to the *Ecclesiastical Polity*, and there he laid the foundation both deep and firm upon which to erect his spiritual edifice. To the student of political science, however, the first book is not merely an introduction; it is a treatise on the whole theory of government, which is clearly the product of a vigorous and independent mind, but which is also based on the fundamental theories of human relationships as they had evolved through the centuries from the Greeks to the schoolmen, to which theories Hooker gave definite expression in the English tongue. On this point Dr. Carlyle,[10] after observing of Hooker that probably no "political thinker of the sixteenth century is equal to him in breadth and justice of thought," thus continues:

> Hooker was a great and independent thinker, but his independence consisted not in ignoring the past and the great political writers of the past, but in gather-

---

[7] It is of interest to note that Locke, in the second of his *Two Treatises on Civil Government*, cited as his leading authority the *Ecclesiastical Polity*, whose author he referred to as "the judicious Hooker," an adjective so appropriate that posterity may be said to have coupled it permanently with the name of the great English philosopher and churchman.

[8] *Introduction to the Literature of Europe*, I, 215.   [9] *Cambridge Modern History*, XII, 709.

[10] *A History of Mediaeval Political Theory in the West* (previously cited), VI, 350, 351.

ing together and putting into clear and intelligibly ordered form the principles and implications of the past, not as one who was bound and restricted by its authority, but as one who thought out again for himself the great principles and traditions of mediaeval society. For it is indeed perhaps the most interesting aspect of his work that he repeated, restated, and enlarged the normal conceptions of the political civilization of mediaeval Europe and handed them down to the modern world.

In preparation for his discussion of the theory of government, Hooker first devotes attention to the philosophy of law. He begins this phase of the subject with a broad and general definition: "That which doth assign unto each thing the kind, that which doth moderate the force and power, that which doth appoint the form and measure of working, the same we term a *Law*."[11] Law in this sense is universal, in that "All things therefore do work after a sort according to law." In the manner of the schoolmen Hooker then takes up the various kinds of law, beginning, of course, with the eternal law:

The law whereby he [God] worketh is eternal, and therefore can have no shew or colour of mutability. . . . This law . . . we may name eternal, being *that order which God before all ages hath set down with himself, for himself to do all things by.*[12]

In his comment on this definition Hooker discusses the theory of the eternal law and its relation to other forms of law:

I am not ignorant that by law eternal the learned for the most part do understand the order, not which God hath eternally purposed himself in all his works to observe, but rather that which with himself he hath set down as expedient to be kept by all his creatures, according to the several condition wherewith he hath endued them. They who thus are accustomed to speak apply the name of *Law* unto that only rule of working which superior authority imposeth; whereas we somewhat more enlarging the sense thereof term any kind of rule or canon, whereby actions are framed, a law. Now that law which, as it is laid up in the bosom of God, they call *eternal,* receiveth according unto the different kinds of things which are subject unto it different and sundry kinds of names. That part of it which ordereth natural agents we call usually nature's law; that which Angels do clearly behold and without any swerving observe is a law *celestial* and heavenly; the law of *reason,* that which bindeth creatures reasonable in this world, and with which by reason they may most plainly perceive themselves bound; that which bindeth them, and is not known but by special revelation from God, *Divine* law; *human* law, that which out of the law either of reason or of God men probably gathering to be expedient, they make it a law. All things therefore, which are as they ought to be, are conformed unto *this second law eternal;* and even those things which to this eternal law are not conformable,

---

[11] Hooker, *Of the Laws of Ecclesiastical Polity,* I, 5.   [12] *Ibid.,* p. 10.

are notwithstanding in some sort ordered by *the first eternal law*. For what good or evil is there under the sun, what action correspondent or repugnant unto the law which God hath imposed upon his creatures, but in or upon it God doth work according to the law which himself hath eternally purposed to keep; that is to say, the *first law eternal*. So that a twofold law eternal being thus made, it is not hard to conceive how they both take place in all things.[13]

The authorities relied upon by Hooker in this passage, it should be noted, are the *Summa theologica* of St. Thomas Aquinas and St. Augustine's *De civitate Dei* and *Confessions*.[14]

Having thus discussed the eternal law, he turns to a second type of law which is fundamental in his philosophy, and with which, as one versed in the writings of the schoolmen, he was thoroughly familiar:[15]

To come to the law of nature . . . thereby we sometimes mean that manner of working which God hath set for each created thing to keep; yet forasmuch as those things are termed most properly natural agents, which keep the law of their kind unwittingly, as the heaven and elements of the world, which can do no otherwise than they do; and forasmuch as we give unto intellectual natures the name of *voluntary* agents, that so we may distinguish them from the other; expedient it will be, that we sever the law of nature observed by the one from that which the other is tied unto.

This is an important distinction, for it draws the line between that law which applies to all nature, animate and inanimate (and which is obeyed involuntarily), and the other law of nature, narrower in scope, to which obedience is rendered wittingly and voluntarily by those subject to it. In his discussion of the first type of natural law Hooker says:[16]

Touching the former, their strict keeping of one tenure, statute, and law, is spoken of by all, but hath in it more than men have as yet attained to know, or perhaps ever shall attain, seeing the travail of wading herein is given of God to the sons of men, that perceiving how much the least thing in the world hath in it more than the wisest are able to reach unto, they may by this means learn humility.

Scientists are still learning how much there is to be discovered of the laws which regulate the universe, and the most learned of them would be more than ready to agree with Hooker—as no doubt Hamlet, too, would have agreed—that this body of natural laws "hath in it more than men have as yet attained to know, or perhaps ever shall attain."

On the universal natural law applying to all things created in the universe, Hooker adds a comment in which the richness and cadence of his style are, as always, fitted to the beauty and dignity of his thought:[17]

---

[13] Hooker, *op. cit.*, I, 10–11.
[14] *Ibid.*, p. 11, note t.   [15] *Ibid.*, p. 12.   [16] *Ibid.*   [17] *Ibid.*, p. 13.

This world's first creation, and the preservation since of things created, what is it but only so far forth a manifestation by execution, what the eternal law of God is concerning things natural? And as it cometh to pass in a kingdom rightly ordered, that after a law is once published, it presently takes effect far and wide, all states framing themselves thereunto; even so let us think it fareth in the natural course of the world: since the time that God did first proclaim the edicts of his law upon it, heaven and earth have hearkened unto his voice, and their labour hath been to do his will.

The second type of natural law to which Hooker has referred was customarily termed in England the law of reason. He proceeds to approach this law by way of another distinction which enables him (though he does not specifically refer to it) to avoid the trouble-making definition of Ulpian, who extended the natural law to all creatures. Inanimate objects, Hooker points out, are devoid of all intelligence, whereas animate creatures possess "understanding" in greater or less degree; but one group of animate creatures is said to possess this attribute to such a degree that they are as a class set apart, and in them the enhanced quality of understanding becomes the power of reason. Consequently it was but natural that the law of nature applicable to this "reasonable" group should be described as the law of reason.

Now the chief function of reason, in the view of Hooker, is to distinguish between right and wrong. In other words, reason is the source of those rules which require that man do good instead of evil. He has given us a perfect statement of this conception in less than a dozen words:[18] "the laws of well-doing are the dictates of right reason."

In the eighth part of the first book Hooker further develops this conception: "A law," he informs us,[19] "generally taken, is a directive rule unto goodness of operation"; and this concept is then linked with the rule of reason:[20] "The rule of voluntary agents on earth is the sentence that reason giveth concerning the goodness of those things which they are to do."

Enlarging upon this theory, Hooker introduces the principles of equality and reciprocity which enjoin duties in order to protect fundamental human rights:

My desire to be loved of my equals in nature as much as possible may be, imposeth upon me a natural duty of bearing to them-ward fully the like affection. From which relation of equality between ourselves and them that are as ourselves, what several rules and canons natural reason hath drawn for direction of life no man is ignorant; as namely, *That because we would take no harm, we must therefore do none; That sith we would not be in any thing extremely dealt with,*

---

[18] *Ibid.*, pp. 29–30.   [19] *Ibid.*, p. 36.   [20] *Ibid.*, p. 37.

we must ouselves avoid all extremity in our dealings; That from all violence and wrong we are utterly to abstain; with such like.[21]

In view of Hooker's familiarity with the New Testament it might be assumed that this formulation of our natural duties was derived solely from biblical sources, were it not that he himself furnishes as his first authorities Justinian's *Code* and *Digest*.[22] But as the second authority he does cite the New Testament.[23]

The relationship between reason and law was so fundamental to his philosophy that Hooker here restated his conception:

A law is properly that which reason in such sort defineth to be good that it must be done. And the law of reason or human nature is that which men by discourse of natural reason have rightly found out themselves to be all for ever bound unto in their actions.

But how are men to become acquainted with these laws of reason?

Laws of reason . . . are investigable by reason, without the help of revelation supernatural and divine. . . . In such sort they are investigable, that the knowledge of them is general, the world hath always been acquainted with them; according to that which one in Sophocles observeth concerning a branch of this law, *It is no child of to-day's or yesterday's birth, but hath been no man knoweth how long sithence.* It is not agreed upon by one, or two, or few, but by all: which we may not so understand, as if every particular man in the whole world did know and confess whatsoever the law of reason doth contain; but this law is such that being proposed no man can reject it as being unreasonable and unjust. Again, there is nothing in it but any man (having natural perfection of wit and ripeness of judgment) may by labour and travail find out.[24]

Here Hooker rounds out his thought by an additional statement on the nature of the law of reason:

And to conclude, the general principles thereof are such, as it is not easy to find men ignorant of them. Law rational therefore, which men commonly use to call the law of nature, meaning thereby the law which human nature knoweth itself in reason universally bound unto, which also for that cause may be termed most fitly the law of reason; this law, I say, comprehendeth all those things which men by the light of their natural understanding evidently know, or at leastwise may know, to be beseeming or unbeseeming, virtuous or vicious, good or evil for them to do.

[21] Hooker, *Of the Laws of Ecclesiastical Polity,* I, 41.
[22] "Quod quis in se approbat, in alio reprobare non posse." L. *in arenam,* C. de inof. test. [*Cod. Just.* p. 254. ed. Lugd. 1553.] "Quod quisque juris in alium statueret, ipsum quoque eodem uti debere." L. *quod quisque.* [*Digest.* lib. ii. tit. 2, tom. 1. p. 60. Lugd. 1552.] "Ab omni penitus injuria atque vi abstinendum." L. i. sect. I. *Quod vi, aut clam.* [*Ibid.* lib. xliii. tit. 23, tom. 3. p. 335.]—Hooker, *ibid.*
[23] *Matt.* 22: 40. On these two commandments hangeth the whole law.—Hooker, *ibid.*
[24] Hooker, *op. cit.,* pp. 42–43.

But there is a limit to all things, even to the law of reason, as Hooker indicates in introducing an elaborate quotation from St. Augustine:

> Yet do we not therefore so far extend the law of reason, as to contain in it all manner laws whereunto reasonable creatures are bound, but (as hath been showed), we restrain it to those only duties, which all men by force of natural wit either do or might understand to be such duties as concern all men. Certain *half-waking men there are* (as Saint Augustine noteth),[25] *who neither altogether asleep in folly, nor yet thoroughly awake in the light of true understanding, have thought that there is not at all any thing just and righteous in itself; but look, wherewith nations are inured, the same they take to be right and just. Whereupon their conclusion is, that seeing each sort of people hath a different kind of right from other, and that which is right of its own nature must be everywhere one and the same, therefore in itself there is nothing right. These good folk,* saith he (*that I may not trouble their wits with rehearsal of too many things*), *have not looked so far into the world as to perceive that* "*Do as thou wouldest be done unto,*" *is a sentence which all nations under heaven are agreed upon. Refer this sentence to the love of God, and it extinguisheth all heinous crimes; refer it to the love of thy neighbour, and all grievous wrongs it banisheth out of the world.*[26]

Hooker's quotation has here been given in full as evidence of his familiarity with the writings of St. Augustine, for whose authority he obviously cherished a profound respect. Those who read the *Ecclesiastical Polity* will find that Hooker was likewise familiar with St. Augustine's successors, and that he possessed a first-hand knowledge of Greek authorities—especially Aristotle—and of the Roman law as set forth in Justinian's compilations.

Having quoted St. Augustine, he then interprets the quotation: "Wherefore as touching the law of reason, this was (it seemeth) Saint Augustine's judgment: namely, that there are in it some things which stand as principles universally agreed upon; and that out of those principles, which are in themselves evident, the greatest moral duties we owe towards God or man may without any great difficulty be concluded."[27] Now these "principles universally agreed upon" Hooker considered as the standard or norm of the moral duties inherent in human relationships. Therefore they should be the test of the custom growing out of such relationships. But this test was not always applied:[28] "If then it be here demanded, by what means it should come to pass (the greatest part of the law moral being so easy for all men to know) that so many thousands of men notwithstanding have been ignorant even of principal moral duties, not imagining the breach of

---

[25] *De doctrina Christiana,* Book III, chap. xiv.
[26] Hooker, *Of the Laws of Ecclesiastical Polity,* I, 44.
[27] Hooker, *op. cit.,* p. 45.
[28] *Ibid.*

them to be sin: I deny not but lewd and wicked custom, beginning perhaps at the first amongst few, afterwards spreading into greater multitudes, and so continuing from time to time, may be of force even in plain things to smother the light of natural understanding; because men will not bend their wits to examine whether things wherewith they have been accustomed be good or evil." The implication of this answer is that there is in man not only reason but the instinct to follow whomsoever he considers the leader (as the sheep follow the bellwether of the flock), and that in blindly following the leader he closes his eyes, as it were, to the light of natural understanding.

Hooker next indicates the general content of the "laws of reason" and distinguishes them from man-made laws:

> Within the compass of . . . laws [of reason], we do not only comprehend whatsoever may be easily known to belong to the duty of all men, but even whatsoever may possibly be known to be of that quality, so that the same be by *necessary* consequence deduced out of clear and manifest principles. For if once we descend unto probable collections what is convenient for men, we are then in the territory where free and arbitrary determinations, the territory where human laws take place.[29]

Here Hooker has applied to the laws of reason the scholastic division of natural law into a primary law consisting of first principles, and a secondary law consisting of deductions from those principles, this law, both in its relative and its absolute sense, being clearly distinguished from the purely human law which flows from the will and decision of human beings as such. As a free agent man may, if he chooses, flout the law of nature, but only at his peril. Pointing out by way of analogy that the sun, the moon and the stars, moving in their courses by the universal law of nature, would violate that law to their own destruction if they left those courses, Hooker asks: "Is it possible that, man being not only the noblest creature in the world, but even a very world in himself, his transgressing the law of his nature should draw no manner of harm after it?"[30]

The choice between obedience and transgression lies with each individual, for the law of reason is a voluntary law.

> Amongst creatures in this world [Hooker declares in the ninth section of his first book], only man's observation of the law of nature is *Righteousness,* only man's transgression *Sin.* And the reason of this is the difference in his manner of observing or transgressing the law of his nature. He doth not otherwise than voluntarily the one or the other.

[29] Hooker, *Of the Laws of Ecclesiastical Polity*, I, 47.   [30] *Ibid.*, p. 48.

The natural law of the physical universe is involuntary in that the things subject to it have no will of their own, whereas man is a creature of reason and discretion.

In the tenth section of the first book reason is the bridge by which Hooker passes from legal to political philosophy, as may be seen by the marginal note or heading of the section: "How reason doth lead men unto the making of human laws whereby politic societies are governed; and to agreement about laws whereby the fellowship or communion of independent societies standeth."[31]

Hooker's purpose was to consider human beings, not in isolation, but in society, for he accepted the Aristotelian theory that men in general are not fitted for a solitary life:

> forasmuch as we are not by ourselves sufficient to furnish ourselves with competent store of things needful for such a life as our nature doth desire, a life fit for the dignity of man; therefore to supply those defects and imperfections which are in us living single and solely by ourselves, we are naturally induced to seek communion and fellowship with others.[32]

But this tendency toward communion and fellowship, and the primary needs from which it arises, lead to further developments of a political nature: "This was the cause of men's uniting themselves at the first in politic societies; which societies could not be without government, nor government without a distinct kind of law."[33]

There are two "foundations" for such a union of men—foundations "which bear up public societies." The first is "a natural inclination whereby all men desire sociable life and fellowship." The second is the agreement of the members, or, in Hooker's words, "an order expressly or secretly agreed upon touching the manner of their union in living together." Such an agreement is the fundamental law of the social group; it is "that which we call the law of a commonweal, the very soul of a politic body, the parts whereof are by law animated, held together, and set on work in such actions as the common good requireth."[34]

Thus Hooker supplies a twofold basis for human associations: the first is the natural social tendency which is innate or instinctive, rather than the result of deliberate choice on the part of the individual members; the second is a compact on the form of association in which human beings voluntarily participate. This form of association may be expressly determined or secretly agreed upon. The term "expressly" denotes an express contract between the participants. The phrase "secretly agreed upon" can only mean "not

---

[31] *Ibid.*, p. 50.   [32] *Ibid.*, pp. 50–51.   [33] *Ibid.*, p. 51.   [34] *Ibid.*

expressly," and therefore does not imply a formal contract. But the phrase does imply an informal agreement which may be likened to the quasi-contract of Roman law. Therefore, whether the agreement be "express" or "secret," it is productive of legal consequences, as Hooker well knew because of his familiarity with Justinian's *Digest*.

Now if human beings were perfect, they would have no need for laws. Of course the primary purpose of law is to promote the common good of men and women in society, but it does this negatively, so to speak, by restraining them from wrongdoing. Therefore it may be said that while the underlying purpose of the law is the promotion of the general welfare, its immediate concern is with man the transgressor, rather than with man as the embodiment of rectitude and virtue.

Laws politic [observes Hooker], ordained for external order and regiment amongst men, are never framed as they should be, unless presuming the will of man to be inwardly obstinate, rebellious, and averse from all obedience unto the sacred laws of his nature; in a word, unless presuming man to be in regard of his depraved mind little better than a wild beast, they do accordingly provide notwithstanding so to frame his outward actions, that they do no hindrance unto the common good for which societies are instituted: unless they do this, they are not perfect.

That common good, however, which is the goal of society, and which laws promote and protect, should not be something separate and distinct from the goal of the individual members. What is this goal toward which the individual aims? To this question Hooker supplies the answer in a pithy sentence: "All men desire to lead in this world a happy life." In his conception the end and purpose of the state or commonwealth (or of any other form of political organization) is the protection of man in his pursuit of happiness. Happiness, if we take the world as it is—at least in our day—apparently is often thought of in terms of riches. Hooker, however, while admitting that "riches be a thing which every man wisheth," immediately expresses his own opinion that

no man of judgment can esteem it better to be rich, than wise, virtuous, and religious. If we be both or either of these, it is not because we are so born. For unto the world we come as empty of the one as of the other, as naked in mind as we are in body.[35]

In a brief passage Hooker now supplies what might be called a thumbnail sketch of the purpose and nature of government:

To take away ... mutual grievances, injuries, and wrongs [among men], there was no way but only by growing unto composition and agreement amongst

---
[35] Hooker, *Of the Laws of Ecclesiastical Polity*, I, 52–53.

themselves, by ordaining some kind of government public, and by yielding themselves subject thereunto; that unto whom they granted authority to rule and govern, by them the peace, tranquillity, and happy estate of the rest might be procured.[36]

Following this sketch is a series of statements supplying a philosophical justification of government, and because of their importance they are here set out in numerical sequence:

  1. Men always knew that when force and injury was offered they might be defenders of themselves.

  2. They knew that howsoever men may seek their own commodity, yet if this were done with injury unto others it was not to be suffered, but by all men and by all good means to be withstood.

  3. ... they knew that no man might in reason take upon him to determine his own right, and according to his own determination proceed in maintenance thereof, inasmuch as every man is towards himself and them whom he greatly affecteth partial; and therefore that strifes and troubles would be endless, except they gave their common consent all to be ordered by some whom they should agree upon.

  4. Without ... consent there was no reason that one man should take upon him to be lord or judge over another; because, although there be according to the opinion of some very great and judicious men a kind of natural right in the noble, wise, and virtuous, to govern them which are of servile disposition; nevertheless for manifestation of this their right, and men's more peaceable contentment on both sides, the assent of them who are to be governed seemeth necessary.[37]

This theory of government by the consent of the governed may well have been considered by most of Hooker's contemporaries as the height of radicalism; but today many of the peoples of the world—especially Americans familiar with the Declaration of Independence—look upon it as a fundamental doctrine of government. And it may be added that in his own day Hooker's theory of government was already established as sound scholastic doctrine. Indeed, Dr. Carlyle in commenting on the passage just quoted declares that "Hooker here represents the normal conception of the Middle Ages, which had been only reinforced by the revived study of the Roman Law, that all political authority is in some sense derived from the community."[38]

Now the government which Hooker had in mind was not a chance phenomenon; it was the result of "deliberate advice, consultation, and composition between men." There was no absolute dictum of the law of nature requiring that men live under what Hooker describes as a "public regi-

[36] *Ibid.*, p. 54.   [37] *Ibid.*
[38] *A History of Mediaeval Political Theory in the West* (previously cited), VI, 354.

ment," but since men were supposed to have fallen from an original, higher estate, they could not exist in what had become a naughty world without some form of government. In other words, "the corruption of our nature being presupposed . . . some kind of regiment the law of nature doth require," although, as Hooker says, its form may be "a thing arbitrary,"[39] meaning that the nature and kind of government depend upon the choice of the governed. Men being what they are, it was obvious to Hooker that government there must be, for without it there would be anarchy; in his own terse statement, "utterly to take away all kind of public government in the world, were apparently to overturn the whole world."

The choice of government should be with the governed; but the choice should be based on experience and guided by intelligence. Otherwise, there was danger of the governing power becoming concentrated in the hands of a single ruler; and experience had demonstrated to those who would learn from it "that to live by one man's will became the cause of all men's misery"—a classic description of the results of despotism and dictatorship.

It is evident that Hooker knew human nature, and he therefore knew that uncontrolled dictation by one human being of the actions to be performed by others would eventually lead to rebellion against the dictator. Even the just dictator meets with opposition, however wise his commands may be; but on the other hand when men are "told the same by a law," they "think very well and reasonably of it." Why, Hooker himself asks, should men prefer law to the command of the dictator? To this question he replies:[40] "They presume that the law doth speak with all indifferency; that the law hath no side-respect to their persons; that the law is as it were an oracle proceeded from wisdom and understanding." Reasonable men therefore chose a government of law rather than of men. In other words, the governed, exercising their right to choose their form of government, turned from the despot "unto laws, wherein all men might see their duties beforehand, and know the penalties of transgressing them."[41]

Now the aim of law whether it "bindeth universally," as does natural law, or only locally, as in the case of positive law, is not only to point out what is "good" but to "enjoin it," and to do that the law must have "a certain constraining force." Since laws were to possess these highly important functions, it was evident to Hooker that they should be framed not only with the utmost care but by those best qualified by wisdom and experience. "Laws are matters of principal consequence; men of common capacity and but ordinary judgment are not able (for how should they?)

---

[39] Hooker, *op. cit.*, pp. 55–56.   [40] *Ibid.*, p. 58.   [41] *Ibid.*, p. 56.

to discern what things are fittest for each kind and state of regiment."[42] Moreover, laws wisely made are much more likely to be obeyed, as Hooker points out: "we cannot be ignorant how much our obedience unto laws dependeth upon this point."

It is apparent that to Hooker the whole subject of law in the political community is a matter of supreme importance, for he deals with it at length, and his views are so fundamental to the philosophy of government that, as on a previous page, they are stated in a series of paragraphs:[43]

1. Laws do not take their constraining force from the quality of such as devise them, but from that power which doth give them the strength of laws.

2. By the natural law . . . the lawful power of making laws to command whole politic societies of men belongeth so properly unto the same entire societies, that for any prince or potentate of what kind soever upon earth to exercise the same of himself, and not either by express commission immediately and personally received from God, or else by authority derived at the first from their consent upon whose persons they impose laws, it is no better than mere tyranny.

3. Laws they are not therefore which public approbation hath not made so.

4. But approbation not only they give who personally declare their assent by voice, sign, or act, but also when others do it in their names by right originally at the least derived from them.

5. As in parliaments, councils, and the like assemblies, although we be not personally ourselves present, notwithstanding our assent is, by reason of others, agents there in our behalf. And what we do by others, no reason but that it should stand as our deed, no less effectually to bind us than if ourselves had done it in person.

6. Sith men naturally have no full and perfect power to command whole politic multitudes of men, therefore utterly without our consent we could in such sort be at no man's commandment living. And to be commanded we do consent, when that society whereof we are part hath at any time before consented, without revoking the same after by the like universal agreement.

7. Wherefore as any man's deed past is as good as long as himself continueth; so the act of a public society of men done five hundred years sithence standeth as theirs who presently are of the same societies, because corporations are immortal; we were then alive in our predecessors, and they in their successors do live still.

The law of the state as here conceived is no command of an irresponsible king or prince, for the power to make such law rests with the inhabitants of the state and may be exercised only by them or by their duly appointed representatives. Law thus properly made and publicly approved is no temporary affair, for its duration, like the duration of the state itself, is not dependent upon the lives of the individuals who constitute the state.

[42] *Ibid.*, p. 58.   [43] *Ibid.*, pp. 58-59.

In Hooker's conception every law should be appropriate and suitable to the special circumstances and customs of the people whom the law is to affect, and he therefore admonished lawmakers to "have an eye to the place where, and to the men amongst whom"[44] the law is to be made, promulgated, and obeyed.

But Hooker was an Englishman, and on the general question of the subject matter of law he naturally refers to the doctrines accepted in his own country. He himself was deeply read in the law both of England and of Rome, tradition having it that he was much given to discussing legal questions. Alluding in the present instance to Staunford's Preface to the *Pleas of the Crown* he says:[45]

Now as the learned in the law of this land observe, that our statutes sometimes are only the affirmation or ratification of that which by common law was held before; so here it is not to be omitted that generally all laws human, which are made for the ordering of politic societies, be either such as establish some duty whereunto all men by the law of reason did before stand bound; or else such as make that a duty now which before was none.

In his division of man-made law into that which is declaratory of the law of nature (or the law of reason) and that which deals not with the law of reason as such, although it must pass the test of reason, but with what the theologians called "indifferent" matters, which became, as the result of human law, a matter of statutory duty where before no duty was involved, Hooker is following closely the scholastic legal tradition. By way of illustration of the first of these divisions of human law mention may be made of the insistence of the early parliaments on the enactment, in the form of statutes, of various concessions which from time to time had been wrung from the English sovereigns. These concessions the legislators thought it advisable to transform from charters, which might conceivably be revoked and were not infrequently violated, into obligatory statutes. The inducement by which the crown was led (not always with good grace) to agree to such action was usually a financial one, the early parliaments having often insisted upon the redress of grievances by the enactment of statutes before they proceeded to vote the subsidies which for the most part were the matters of greatest interest in that day, and for many a day, to the royal mind. The concessions thus transferred from charter to statute were in many instances concerned with what we of today call "natural rights," and having once made their way into statutes they became permanently embodied in the English constitution.

[44] Hooker, *Of the Laws of Ecclesiastical Polity*, I, 61.   [45] *Ibid.*, p. 62.

In continuing his discussion of human legislation which is declaratory of the law of reason Hooker adds:

> That which plain or necessary reason bindeth men unto may be in sundry considerations expedient to be ratified by human law. . . . Whereas men before stood bound in conscience to do as the law of reason teacheth, they are now by virtue of human law become constrainable, and if they outwardly transgress, punishable.[46]

Thus human law, in addition to being declaratory of the law of reason, also provides that law with a sanction.

Of the second type of human law, which does not pretend to embody the law of reason, Hooker says:[47] "As for laws which are *merely* human, the matter of them is any thing which reason doth but probably teach to be fit and convenient; so that till such time as law hath passed amongst men about it, of itself it bindeth no man." In other words, these laws constitute the great body of human legislation which deals, not with fundamental principles (although it should be in harmony with those principles), but with the many and shifting circumstances of social and political life. Such laws may be more or less permanent, but often they are passed to meet some temporary situation or need.

Hooker now turns to another body of law which he regarded as being of the utmost importance to human society, the law applicable to the relations of state with state:

> Now besides that law which simply concerneth men as men, and that which belongeth unto them as they are men linked with others in some form of politic society, there is a third kind of law which toucheth all such several bodies politic, so far forth as one of them hath public commerce with another. And this third is the *law of nations*.[48]

As an Aristotelian, Hooker considered that human beings had an inclination to society, and that political organization was a natural means of satisfying this inclination. But he was also aware that the social aspirations of human beings—at least in their saner moments—extended far beyond state frontiers. "We covet (if it might be)," he declares, "to have a kind of society and fellowship even with all mankind." This larger fellowship, which in his day was somewhat misunderstood, and in which we of the present day are not overenlightened, he illustrates by references to Socrates and to the ancient land of Israel:

> Which thing Socrates intending to signify professed himself a citizen, not of this or that commonwealth, but of the world. And an effect of that very natural

---

[46] *Ibid.*, pp. 62–63.   [47] *Ibid.*, p. 63.   [48] *Ibid.*, p. 64.

desire in us, (a manifest token that we wish after a sort an universal fellowship with all men,) appeareth by the wonderful delight men have, some to visit foreign countries, some to discover nations not heard of in former ages, we all to know the affairs and dealings of other people, yea to be in league of amity with them: and this not only for traffic's sake, or to the end that when many are confederated each may make other the more strong, but for such cause also as moved the Queen of Saba to visit Salomon; and in a word, because nature doth presume that how many men there are in the world, so many Gods as it were there are, or at leastwise such they should be towards men.[49]

Now in Hooker's law of nations there were primary and secondary laws, and of these he gives us illustrations:

Primary laws of nations are such as concern embassage, such as belong to the courteous entertainment of foreigners and strangers, such as serve for commodious traffic, and the like.
Secondary laws in the same kind are such as this present unquiet world is most familiarly acquainted with; I mean laws of arms, which yet are much better known than kept.[50]

To Hooker the law of nations which dealt with peace was obviously more important than the so-called law of nations which dealt with war.

It is probable that comparatively few people of his time either understood or would have dared to uphold the superiority of the law of nations over the law of a single nation. But to Hooker this law of nations was a universal law, which abrogated the law of any and every nation (even though that nation be his beloved England) inconsistent with its terms. His view on this most important point is given within the compass of a single paragraph, and that a short one:

The strength and virtue of that law is such that no particular nation can lawfully prejudice the same by any their several laws and ordinances, more than a man by his private resolutions the law of the whole commonwealth or state wherein he liveth. For as civil law, being the act of the whole body politic, doth therefore overrule each several part of the same body; so there is no reason that any one commonwealth of itself should to the prejudice of another annihilate that whereupon the whole world hath agreed.

In the final section of his first book on *Ecclesiastical Polity* Hooker supplies an epitome of his conceptions of the function of law in society, and what is recognized as the most magnificent eulogy of law in English legal literature.

[49] Hooker, *Of the Laws of Ecclesiastical Polity*, I, 65.   [50] *Ibid.*, p. 66.

The epitome consists of but half a dozen sentences:

... in moral actions, divine law helpeth exceedingly the law of reason to guide man's life; but in supernatural it alone guideth.

Proceed we further; let us place man in some public society with others, whether civil or spiritual; and in this case there is no remedy but we must add yet a further law. For although even here likewise the laws of nature and reason be of necessary use, yet somewhat over and besides them is necessary, namely, human and positive law, together with that law which is of commerce between grand societies, the law of nations, and of nations Christian. ... The public power of all societies is above every soul contained in the same societies. And the principal use of that power is to give laws unto all that are under it; which laws in such case we must obey, unless there be reason shewed which may necessarily enforce that the law of reason or of God doth enjoin the contrary. Because except our own private and but probable resolutions be by the law of public determinations overruled, we take away all possibility of sociable life in the world.[51]

And the eulogy, in the final paragraph of the first book, brings his discussion of government and law to a close on a note of majestic and lofty eloquence:

Wherefore that here we may briefly end: of Law there can be no less acknowledged, than that her seat is the bosom of God, her voice the harmony of the world; all things in heaven and earth do her homage, the very least as feeling her care, and the greatest as not exempted from her power; both Angels and men and creatures of what condition soever, though each in different sort and manner, yet all with uniform consent, admiring her as the mother of their peace and joy.[52]

It is not to be wondered at that in Hooker's lifetime his stately prose caught the eye of the reader, just as the grandeur and cadence of his sentences charm the ear of every man and woman who is privileged to hear them read today. But the dignity of his prose is equaled by the dignity of his conception of the individual in his varied relationships. His definitions of law in its several phases, and of government by consent of the governed are deeply and firmly embedded in the law and government of modern England. The early Pilgrims carried these conceptions across a stormy ocean and planted them in the New World, their theories and form of government as they subsequently developed being destined to become, as they still are, the hope of the future.

Henry Hallam, distinguished English historian, not merely of the constitutional development of his country but of the literature of Europe, has accounts of both Hooker and Suárez; indeed in one passage he specifically

[51] *Ibid.*, pp. 102–3.   [52] *Ibid.*, p. 106.

compares the fundamental definition of Suárez with the equally fundamental closing sentence of Hooker's first book of the *Ecclesiastical Polity.* Referring to Suárez' definition of "eternal law," Mr. Hallam declares that it is nothing else in substance, than the celebrated sentence on law, which concludes the first book of Hooker's *Ecclesiastical Polity.* Whoever takes the pains to understand Suárez, will perceive that he asserts exactly that which is unrolled in the majestic eloquence of our countryman.[53]

Certain interesting observations by Dean Church, whose views carry the weight of authority because of his familiarity with Hooker's writings, may here be quoted by way of comment on Mr. Hallam's comparison:

Of Hooker's work, the First Book . . . is a treatise on the idea and grounds of government generally: and though it is meant to provide a basis for his conclusions in the following Books, both on the larger and the more detailed questions of the moment about "Ecclesiastical Polity," its theory is applicable, and he himself applies it, in a wider range. The outlines of the theory are to be found in the great work of Thomas Aquinas, the *Summa Theologiae,* in which he systematized the philosophy which S. Augustine had derived from Greece: but, as Mr. Hallam observes, Hooker "was perhaps the first of our writers who had any considerable acquaintance with the philosophers of Greece," and he brings out this knowledge not merely in quotation, but in a "spirit of reflection and comprehensiveness, which the study of antiquity alone could have infused," and which fills out the precise and severe outlines of the schools with a life and richness of meaning which belong to the works and the times in which philosophy began. The Book "On the Nature of Law in General" falls into three main divisions: (1) On law, conceived as governing all intelligent working, and therefore the working of God himself; and as imposed by Him on creation, whether on unconscious nature, or on moral beings beyond our sphere (ch. i-iv.); (2) on the *law natural,* the law of action for men, as shewn by nature, that is, by reason, as it guides individuals, societies, and the relations of societies among themselves, and is the foundation of human law (ch. v-x.); (3) On the *law supernatural,* of which the record and exponent is Scripture, and which, presupposing and embodying the law natural or rational, adds knowledge and guidance beyond it, and makes up for its defaults and completes it: on the true domain and purpose of the law of Scripture, and on the conditions on which is grounded the distinction between laws immutable and mutable (ch. xi-xvi). With this comprehensive survey as given in the headings of Hooker's chapters we may compare the abstract given by Mr. Hallam of a nearly contemporary work, the *Tractatus de Legibus ac Deo legislatore* of Suarez, "by far the greatest man in the department of moral philosophy which the order of Loyola produced, in this age, or perhaps in any other." Suarez was probably writing at the same time as Hooker; but his book was not, I believe, published till the beginning of the next century. "Suarez," says Mr. Hallam, "begins by laying down the

---

[53] *Introduction to the Literature of Europe* (previously cited), II, 505-6.

position, that all legislative as well as all paternal power is derived from God, and that the authority of every law resolves itself into his. For either the law proceeds immediately from God, or, if it be human, it proceeds from man, as his vicar and minister. . . ."

Differences there were, as Dean Church properly points out after reproducing at length Mr. Hallam's summary of the *De legibus,* yet in fundamentals Hooker and Suárez were as one:[54]

The similarity in the general conception of the two writers and their ways of laying out the grounds is obvious.[55]

But great as is Hallam's authority and great as is that of Dean Church (who, had it not been for ill health, would doubtless have been raised to the See of Canterbury), there is a still more striking appreciation—by one whose authority was even greater—of the views contained in the first book of the *Ecclesiastical Polity.* In his *Life of Richard Hooker,* Izaak Walton has left us this precious record:[56]

. . . I have been told more than forty years past, that either Cardinal *Allen,* or learned Doctor *Stapleton* (both English men, and in *Italy* about the time when *Hookers* four Books were first printed:) meeting with this general fame of them, were desirous to read an Author that both the Reformed and the learned of their own *Romish* Church did so much magnifie, and therefore caused them to be sent for to *Rome;* and after reading them, boasted to the Pope (which then

---

[54] As further evidence, if any were needed, of Hooker's familiarity with, and appreciation of, the great historical and scholastic doctrines, a passage may be quoted from the Rev. Norman Sykes' essay on Hooker in the series edited by Professor Hearnshaw (*The Social and Political Ideas of Some Great Thinkers of the Sixteenth and Seventeenth Centuries,* pp. 71, 78): "In his endeavour to elucidate the several kinds of law by which the universe is governed Hooker followed with deliberate fidelity the system expounded by the mediaeval scholastics." Later he adds: "It is unnecessary to emphasize the detailed correspondence between Hooker's exposition of the universal province of law and that of the Thomist philosophy. In reaction against the Puritan narrowness he had deliberately turned back to the traditional scholastic doctrine."

A final comment from this writer concerning a point not touched on in the present chapter—Hooker's appreciation of the unity of history—must be added (*ibid.,* pp. 85, 88):

"Upon a general reading of the *Ecclesiastical Polity* perhaps the most striking characteristic which impresses itself upon the student is the author's gift of historical thinking. Few have had a finer sense of the value of historical tradition than Hooker. To him the unity and continuity of history was neither a phrase nor a fallacy, but a practical truth as well as an inspiration. . . . The very keynote of his writings is the wisdom of the scribe who 'brought out of his treasure-store things old and new.'

". . . Yet the most powerful impression produced upon one reader is that of the reverence for the historic past which characterised Hooker. . . . His return to the scholastic philosophy was not a mere controversial *ruse de guerre;* rather it was the expression of his deep conviction of the value of historical tradition and of the continuity of corporate life. The wisdom of Hooker is the principle of true conservatism, and he realised the abiding significance of this principle as an essential constituent of human nature. 'For no man having drunk of old wine, straightway desireth new; for he saith, "The old is better." ' "

[55] In his Introduction to the edition of Hooker's text cited in the present chapter, pp. xxiii–xxv.

[56] *The Lives of John Donne, Sir Henry Wotton, Richard Hooker* . . ., pp. 211–12.

was *Clement* the eighth) *that though he had lately said he never met with an English Book whose Writer deserved the name of Author; yet there now appear'd a wonder to them, and it would be so to his Holiness, if it were in Latin, for a poore obscure English Priest had writ four such Books of Laws, and Church Polity, and in a Style that exprest such a Grave, and so Humble Majesty, with such clear demonstration of Reason, that in all their readings they had not met with any that exceeded him;* and this begot in the Pope an earnest desire that Doctor *Stapleton* should bring the said four Books, and looking on the English read a part of them to him in Latin; which Doctor *Stapleton* did, to the end of the first Book; at the conclusion of which, the Pope spake to this purpose; *There is no Learning that this man hath not searcht into; nothing too hard for his understanding; this man indeed deserves the name of an Author; his Books will get reverence by Age, for there is in them such seeds of Eternity, that if the rest be like this, they shall last till the last fire shall consume all learning.*[57]

[57] There is an interesting reference to this incident in a letter from Henry King, Lord Bishop of Chichester, to Walton under date of Nov. 17, 1664 (Walton, *op. cit.*, p. 18): "I am glad you mention how much value *Thomas Stapleton,* Pope *Clement* the VIII and other Eminent men of the Romish Perswasion, have put upon his [Hooker's] Books; having been told the same in my Youth by Persons of worth that have travelled *Italy.*"

EPILOGUE

Chapter XXXV
EPILOGUE

THE PURPOSE OF THE PRECEDING CHAPTERS HAS BEEN TO DISCUSS IN MORE OR less chronological order what are believed to be the principal contributions to legal, political, and international ideals. If we are to appreciate the significance and subsequent trend of those contributions, however, and something of their relationships to other phases of human activity, it will be well to look back for a moment over the long course of their development—to attempt, in other words, to see them in perspective, to view the past as though it were a panorama spread before us.

Far distant in time, yet strangely near to us in mind and spirit, is ancient Greece, whose philosophers, poets, and artists endowed posterity with a sense of the value of truth and beauty, of human dignity and unity. And though the Greeks long held themselves aloof from the "barbarians" in other lands, they came eventually to the realization, through the philosophy of the Stoics and their contacts with the outer world, that the bond of humanity is more important than geography and proud distinctions of race and culture.

Less distant in the measure of centuries is the vast and magnificent empire built by the Romans. Like all things of material splendor, the empire was doomed to crumble and vanish; but the Romans also built an empire of law which has weathered the ravages of time and remains today as an eternal monument to their strong sense of order and justice. The Romans left more than their law as a heritage, however. They preserved and handed on (largely through the efforts of Cicero) the philosophy of the Greeks, adding to it something of their own practical qualities. They left, too, as did the Greeks, splendid fragments of their literature and the tradition of their civilization.

Then, nearer at hand in the panorama, lies a vast area of darker hue. Yet what we discern is not darkness but rather a temporary shadow on the scene. And that shadow—to continue the figure—was already pierced as it fell by a light from the East, for the darkest period of the so-called Dark Ages was illuminated by Christianity, whose spread was not halted by invading hordes nor the crash of empire. The great churchmen of the Middle

Ages, building new conceptions and a new philosophy for the future, merged with the Christian doctrine the best contributions from the classical past, from Plato, Aristotle, and the Stoics, from Cicero and the treasure house of Roman jurisprudence. St. Augustine laid foundations which still stand firm; St. Isidore of Seville labored in a period of transition and confusion to preserve knowledge from threatened destruction; and Gratian, the learned monk of Bologna, gave to the Church a unified body of jurisprudence based on the law of Rome. Christianity conquered Europe and brought with it a new sense of unity, a deeper unity than that of Roman citizenship, deeper even than the unity of the Stoics—the unity of a single religion and a Church Universal.

Gradually the shadow lifted. Toward the end of the Middle Ages, indeed, it vanished like a thin fog under the rays of a rising sun. It would be nearer the truth, however, to speak of the reflected rays of a sun long set, for it was the learning of the ancient world which drove away the mists of medievalism. The "new learning," which was in fact the old learning discovered anew, awakened the minds of men and stimulated them to activity in many fields. Manuscripts of the texts of Justinian aroused an abiding interest in jurisprudence, and St. Thomas Aquinas reintroduced and restated the philosophy of Aristotle. The study of the literature and philosophy of the past gave rise to humanism, with its conception of human beings as creatures of reason, of worth and dignity, capable of infinite development through education based on the accumulated wisdom of the past.

Though Dante and Petrarch may be said to have opened the door to the development of humanism, neither the one nor the other followed classical models. Rather, they found in ancient literature a stimulus to the development of their own genius. Many there were, of course, who did imitate the masterpieces of the past, or who studied them for their own sake, since enthusiasm for the "new learning" often led scholars to an indiscriminate worship of antiquity. Yet their labor, however uncritical it may have been, was of vast importance in that it insured for their own age and for posterity the preservation of the great contributions of Greece and Rome. And in due course these contributions ceased to be the mold and pattern of literary expression and became the inspiration for new and original literature, as they had been for the masterpieces of Dante.

In the fine arts that inspiration operated less directly because but little of ancient art had been recovered. The painting, sculpture, and architecture of the Renaissance therefore owed comparatively little to antique models, but derived a powerful stimulus from the classical revival in general. Some imitation there was, especially in architecture, but the great masters of Italy's golden age of art—Cimabue, Giotto, Leonardo da Vinci, Donatello, Raphael, Michelangelo, and Titian, to mention but a few—produced works of true originality. Their great genius was their own, though it was warmed and lighted by the glow of genius from the past; their art drew largely from classical mythology and from religion for its subject matter, but it remained natural, unpedantic, and, above all, human.

Indeed, the Renaissance in its various phases might be summarized as an awakening to the dignity of the human being. That many-sided genius, Leonardo da Vinci, and others of a scientific turn, began to study both man and man's environment. Methods for human control over nature were devised, discoveries were the order of the time. A New World was revealed to peoples ready for the conquest of new domains. And from his chair at the University of Salamanca, Francisco de Vitoria proclaimed that the inhabitants of that New World were human beings whose rights were the same as those possessed by the inhabitants of the Old World.

As a part of this great awakening there arose in the minds of many an increasingly disturbing realization that all was not well in society, that men and women were being deprived of their rights as human beings by social evils. The vast organization of the Church, too, had become so gravely warped that it failed to respond to human needs. Here and there, clearsighted people saw the need for reform, among them St. Thomas More, who gave to humanity a program of social betterment which is still the guide of those who labor for a better world. Erasmus, the greatest of the humanists, would have reformed both Church and society through education and enlightenment, but unfortunately for his own age and for posterity his wise counsels were drowned in the clamor which arose over the reformation of the Church. Increasing confusion and passion and eventually warfare distracted the attention of Europe from other than religious problems.

Further complications were added by dynastic ambitions, by the rising tide of nationalism and by commercial rivalries. Soon the slowly emerging conceptions of human rights were stifled not only by religious persecutions but by a series of conflicts which burst into destructive flame in the Thirty Years' War (1618-48). Thenceforth, there was but little intermission between wars, for hardly had one ceased than another began in a different region. The Peace of Westphalia, which closed the Thirty Years' War in 1648, brought no permanent peace. France continued her struggle with Spain until 1659, but the Peace of the Pyrenees between the two countries lasted less than a decade. Other nations were drawn into new controversies which carried the devastating wars of Europe—despite occasional so-called peace treaties—into the eighteenth century, and they continued, in one area or another, throughout most of that century. The war of the Spanish Succession (1701-14), the long struggle between Russia and Sweden, the War of the Polish Succession (1733-35), the War of the Austrian Succession (1741-48), the great conflicts between France and England in different parts of the world from the middle of the century onward—to list only a few of the eighteenth-century wars—kept Europe in almost constant turmoil. Campaigns extended into the New World, and indeed the English colonists were called upon to take an active part in the war against France. A few years later the colonists began a war of their own against the mother country (1775-83), and although their struggle for independence was not, as regards the size of military and naval forces involved, a great war, it was destined, as we know, to have important consequences.

Before the close of the eighteenth century the Napoleonic wars had begun, from which Europe was to have no real peace until 1815, when the Battle of Waterloo put an end to Napoleon's career. The later nineteenth century was marked by many wars in various parts of the world, among them the American Civil War (1861-65) and the various Prussian conquests which were the result of Bismarck's policy and which culminated in the Franco-Prussian War (1870-71) and the establishment of the German Empire under the domination of Prussia. For some years thereafter European nations enjoyed a measure of peace from brutalizing warfare, though there were wars elsewhere and occasional brief conflicts in one corner or another of Europe. But this period of comparative quiet, hailed by many as the beginning of a more peaceful era, was apparently but a lull before the great conflagration of 1914-18, the World War which threatened to end our civilization.

This very brief summary of the sanguinary history of the past three centuries will serve to indicate why the survey in the preceding chapters ends prior to the Thirty Years' War. Legal and political ideals do not flourish amid the clash of arms. Rather, they are pushed into the background by philosophies stemming from the maxim that might makes right, and by various political doctrines of absolutism, such as those proclaimed by Sir Robert Filmer and Thomas Hobbes, by Bishop Bossuet and the German philosopher Hegel.

But the spirit of reform, however much relegated to the background, did survive. In the minds of the enlightened few the dream of human betterment, based on the recognition and protection of the natural rights of

EPILOGUE

human beings, slowly took shape. During the early part of the stormy period of religious controversy forward-looking churchmen—chief among them Francisco de Vitoria, St. Robert Bellarmine, Francisco Suárez, and the Protestant Richard Hooker—laid foundations whereon later generations were to build not only a moral conception of the international community, but the structure of democracy, in which the people are acknowledged as the source of power, and government is their agency, not their master. In an epilogue no attempt can be made to trace the gradual development of modern democratic theories, with their international implications and their stimulus toward social reforms. At most only a few outstanding figures of the English-speaking world can be briefly discussed, in order to indicate the nature of that development.

The first is John Locke, whose *Two Treatises on Civil Government* were originally published in 1690. In these two treatises, and particularly in the second, Locke set forth a political philosophy which was destined to exercise a vast influence in the New as well as in the Old World.[1]

It was his conception that by nature all men were in a state of "perfect freedom" and "equality."[2] This natural state of mankind was in accordance with the law of nature, which was synonymous with reason. Unfortunately, this law was not clearly revealed to all men, owing to their deficiencies in the power of reasoning, and therefore the individual man in his natural condition ran the risk of an invasion of his freedom and equality and his natural right to "life, health, liberty or possessions."[3] To guard against these dangers, so Locke held, man was "willing to quit this condition which, however free, is full of fears and continual dangers; and it is not without reason that he seeks out and is willing to join in society with others who are already united, or have a mind to unite for the mutual preservation of

---

[1] As an example of a present-day appreciation of Locke's contribution to political philosophy, a few sentences are quoted from an editorial printed in the *London Times* of Aug. 29, 1932: "It was the political theory of Locke which affected the nation at large most deeply. Nor did it only affect England. It penetrated into France, and passed through Rousseau into the French Revolution; it penetrated into the North American Colonies, and passed through Samuel Adams and Thomas Jefferson into the American Declaration of Independence. We are generally prone to think of Locke as the exponent of the Social Contract. It would be more just to think of him as the exponent of the sovereignty of Natural Law. He put into plain English, and he dressed in an English dress of sober grey cloth, doctrines which ultimately go back to the Porch and the Stoic teachers of antiquity. There is, he taught, a Natural Law rooted and grounded in the reasonable nature of man; there are Natural Rights, existing in virtue of such law, among which the right of property in things with which men have mixed their labour is cardinal; and finally there is a natural system of government, under which all political power is a trust for the benefit of the people (to ensure their living by natural law, and in the enjoyment of natural rights), and the people themselves are at once the creators and the beneficiaries of that trust."

[2] Locke, *Two Treatises on Civil Government*, p. 192.   [3] *Ibid.*, p. 194.

their lives, liberties and estates, which I call by the general name—property."[4] This union did not deprive man of his liberty, but rather changed it:

> The natural liberty of man is to be free from any superior power on earth, and not to be under the will or legislative authority of man, but to have only the law of Nature for his rule. The liberty of man in society is to be under no other legislative power but that established by consent in the commonwealth, nor under the dominion of any will, or restraint of any law, but what that legislative shall enact according to the trust put in it.[5]

Having united in a political society for the enjoyment of their natural rights in peace and safety, the individuals thus joining themselves together had need of law for the peaceable conduct of their affairs, and they therefore set up a legislature, or, as Locke terms it "the legislative," which should be their supreme organ of government. Yet, however powerful it might be, it was not to be "absolutely arbitrary over the lives and fortunes of the people."[6] The legislature was, or should be, according to Locke's argument, the agent of the people; in other words, to quote his own language, "the people submitted themselves to legislators of their own making."[7] Therefore they could and did entrust to the legislature certain powers only, beyond which that body could not lawfully proceed. As Locke himself pertinently observes:

> Nobody can transfer to another more power than he has in himself, and nobody has an absolute arbitrary power over himself, or over any other, to destroy his own life, or take away the life or property of another. A man ... cannot subject himself to the arbitrary power of another; and having, in the state of Nature, no arbitrary power over the life, liberty, or possession of another, but only so much as the law of Nature gave him for the preservation of himself and the rest of mankind, this is all he doth, or can give up to the commonwealth, and by it to the legislative power, so that the legislative can have no more than this. Their power in the utmost bounds of it is limited to the public good of the society.[8]

The acts of the legislature, moreover, depended for their validity upon the free consent of the people by whom its members had been chosen. By way of example of his theories on this topic, Locke's views on the question of taxation may be quoted:

> It is true, governments cannot be supported without great charge, and it is fit every one who enjoys his share of the protection should pay out of his estate his proportion for the maintenance of it. But still it must be with his own consent—*i. e.*, the consent of the majority, giving it either by themselves or their

---

[4] Locke, *Two Treatises on Civil Government*, p. 256.   [5] *Ibid.*, p. 202.
[6] *Ibid.*, p. 261.   [7] *Ibid.*, p. 306.   [8] *Ibid.*, pp. 261–62.

representatives chosen by them; for if any one shall claim a power to lay and levy taxes on the people by his own authority, and without such consent of the people, he thereby invades the fundamental law of property, and subverts the end of government.[9]

But what if the legislature should presume to take action exceeding the bounds of the power entrusted to it? In Locke's state the "legislative" was the chief power, but it should remain, he insisted, subordinate to the will of the people. In his own words,

the legislative being only a fiduciary power to act for certain ends, there remains still in the people a supreme power to remove or alter the legislative, when they find the legislative act contrary to the trust reposed in them. For all power given with trust for the attaining an end being limited by that end, whenever that end is manifestly neglected or opposed, the trust must necessarily be forfeited, and the power devolve into the hands of those that gave it, who may place it anew where they shall think best for their safety and security. And thus the community perpetually retains a supreme power of saving themselves from the attempts and designs of anybody, even of their legislators, whenever they shall be so foolish or so wicked as to lay and carry on designs against the liberties and properties of the subject.[10]

Enlarging upon this theme, Locke added in a later passage:

Whenever the legislators endeavour to take away and destroy the property of the people, or to reduce them to slavery under arbitrary power, they put themselves into a state of war with the people, who are thereupon absolved from any farther obedience, and are left to the common refuge which God hath provided for all men against force and violence. Whensoever, therefore, the legislative shall transgress this fundamental rule of society, and either by ambition, fear, folly, or corruption, endeavour to grasp themselves, or put into the hands of any other, an absolute power over the lives, liberties, and estates of the people; by this breach of trust they forfeit the power the people had put into their hands for quite contrary ends, and it devolves to the people, who have a right to resume their original liberty, and by the establishment of a new legislative (such as they shall think fit), provide for their own safety and security, which is the end for which they are in society.[11]

In the annals of political science, however, it has been the executive rather than the legislative power which has most often abused its authority, interfering either directly or indirectly with the legislative body, or with the fundamental rights of the people. Therefore Locke provided at once for dealing with the chief magistrate who exceeded his lawful functions.

What I have said here concerning the legislative in general, holds true also concerning the supreme executor, who having a double trust put in him, both

---

[9] *Ibid.*, p. 266.   [10] *Ibid.*, p. 269.   [11] *Ibid.*, pp. 306–7.

to have a part in the legislative and the supreme execution of the law, acts against both, when he goes about to set up his own arbitrary will as the law of the society.[12]

If the chief magistrate sought to force his will upon his people, there was, in Locke's opinion, but one remedy:

> I say, using force upon the people, without authority, and contrary to the trust put in him that does so, is a state of war with the people, who have a right to reinstate their legislative in the exercise of their power.... In all states and conditions the true remedy of force without authority is to oppose force to it. The use of force without authority always puts him that uses it into a state of war as the aggressor, and renders him liable to be treated accordingly.[13]

There were those who argued against such a right as claimed by the people, notably Filmer; but by way of reply Locke posed a series of questions. The first of the series began with a premise so universally accepted that he apparently felt it required no argument in its support:

> The end of government is the good of mankind; and which is best for mankind, that the people should be always exposed to the boundless will of tyranny, or that the rulers should be sometimes liable to be opposed when they grow exorbitant in the use of their power, and employ it for the destruction, and not the preservation, of the properties of their people?[14]

The next question is: "Who shall be judge whether the prince or legislative act contrary to their trust?"[15] To this query Locke replied with further questions in which the answer is implicit:

> To this I reply, The people shall be judge; for who shall be judge whether his trustee or deputy acts well and according to the trust reposed in him, but he who deputes him and must, by having deputed him, have still a power to discard him when he fails in his trust? If this be reasonable in particular cases of private men, why should it be otherwise in that of the greatest moment, where the welfare of millions is concerned and also where the evil, if not prevented, is greater, and the redress very difficult, dear, and dangerous?[16]

The subject was so important that Locke restated his conception at some length and in terms which at once hark back to the theories of the schoolmen and look forward to the modern doctrine that the people have the right to make and unmake their government.

> If a controversy arise betwixt a prince and some of the people in a matter where the law is silent or doubtful, and the thing be of great consequence, I should think the proper umpire in such a case should be the body of the people. For in cases where the prince hath a trust reposed in him, and is dispensed

---

[12] Locke, *Two Treatises on Civil Government*, p. 307.
[13] *Ibid.*, pp. 272–73.
[14] *Ibid.*, p. 311.
[15] *Ibid.*, p. 318.
[16] *Ibid.*, pp. 318–19.

from the common, ordinary rules of the law, there, if any men find themselves aggrieved, and think the prince acts contrary to, or beyond that trust, who so proper to judge as the body of the people (who at first lodged that trust in him) how far they meant it should extend? But if the prince, or whoever they be in the administration, decline that way of determination, the appeal then lies nowhere but to Heaven. Force between either persons who have no known superior on earth, or which permits no appeal to a judge on earth, being properly a state of war, wherein the appeal lies only to Heaven; and in that state the injured party must judge for himself when he will think fit to make use of that appeal and put himself upon it.[17]

The doctrines proclaimed by Locke in England—which were a logical development of the earlier theories referred to in preceding chapters—were to receive their first application not in the Old but in the New World, where, as already mentioned, the thirteen English colonies of North America embarked upon a war against the mother country. The reasons for this action the representatives of the colonies set forth on the fourth day of July, 1776, in a Declaration of Independence, it being their view, as stated in the Declaration, that

When in the Course of human events, it becomes necessary for one people to dissolve the political bands which have connected them with another, and to assume among the Powers of the earth, the separate and equal station to which the Laws of Nature and of Nature's God entitle them, a decent respect to the opinions of mankind requires that they should declare the causes which impel them to the separation.

We are not here concerned with the actual enumeration of the causes which impelled them to rebellion, but rather with the fact that, as repeatedly remarked in these pages, they set forth a philosophy of government which, from whatever source or sources it may have been derived,[18] bears a marked similarity to the political philosophy of Locke. To begin with, they held certain "truths to be self-evident," and these were that "all men are created equal, that they are endowed by their Creator with certain unalienable Rights, that among these are Life, Liberty and the pursuit of Happiness." In substance, if not in exact phraseology, these were the rights which Locke ascribed to human beings in the state of nature. The signers of the Declaration of Independence then proceeded to proclaim "That to secure these rights, Governments are instituted among Men, deriving their just powers from the consent of the governed." This again, in summary form, is Locke's

[17] *Ibid.*, p. 319.
[18] The relation of American political theories to the doctrines of Bellarmine has been discussed in a previous chapter, *supra*, pp. 549–51.

conception of the purpose and nature of government. And finally the Declaration laid down a principle supported by Locke, that a people possessed the right to change a government which failed of the purpose for which they had established it—in the language of the Declaration:

> That whenever any Form of Government becomes destructive of these ends, it is the Right of the People to alter or to abolish it, and to institute new Government, laying its foundation on such principles and organizing its powers in such form, as to them shall seem most likely to effect their Safety and Happiness.

In due course, the erstwhile colonies, through their duly appointed representatives, proceeded to institute the "new government" to which their Declaration of Independence had referred, and the fundamental document of that government was a Constitution which, adopted in 1787 and ratified by the representatives of the people of the several states, became effective in 1789. Of this document, which has stood the test of a century and a half, the preamble reads:

> WE THE PEOPLE of the United States, in Order to form a more perfect Union, establish Justice, insure domestic Tranquillity, provide for the common defence, promote the general Welfare, and secure the Blessings of Liberty to ourselves and our Posterity, do ordain and establish this CONSTITUTION for the United States of America.

So successful was this government that the peoples of Europe from time to time appropriated a leaf from the American book of experience. No attempt will be made here to trace the subsequent development of these conceptions of law and government in the Old World, but it will be interesting to examine, as a European expression of them contemporary with their application in America, the views of a great political philosopher, statesman, and orator of the eighteenth century. Edmund Burke, of Irish birth and Irish parentage, and dealing with an Irish question, spoke in terms of universal application. Recording his convictions on the relation of law to what we of the Western World call the pursuit of happiness, he says:

> The happiness or misery of multitudes can never be a thing indifferent. A law against the majority of the people is in substance a law against the people itself: its extent determines its invalidity; it even changes its character as it enlarges its operation: it is not particular injustice, but general oppression; and can no longer be considered as a private hardship, which might be borne, but spreads and grows up into the unfortunate importance of a national calamity.[19]

---

[19] "Tracts Relative to the Laws against Popery in Ireland," published in *The Works of Edmund Burke*, V, 237–87, especially 254.

EPILOGUE 603

A so-called law of that nature had, in Burke's opinion, no actual authority: "Now, as a law directed against the mass of the nation has not the nature of a reasonable institution, so neither has it the authority."[20] This opinion he immediately substantiated by an argument which is thoroughly in harmony with the long development of democratic principles:

> In all forms of government the people is the true legislator; and whether the immediate and instrumental cause of the law be a single person or many, the remote and efficient cause is the consent of the people, either actual or implied; and such consent is absolutely essential to its validity.[21]

Now it is not in human nature for people to consent, expressly or tacitly, to laws which injure them, and hence legislation of that nature cannot "in propriety" be termed law. For the sake of argument, however, Burke assumes that the people give actual and direct consent to such legislation. "If we could suppose that such a ratification was made, not virtually, but actually; by the people, not representatively, but even collectively; still it would be null and void."[22]

Such a procedure on the part of the people would be contrary to the true nature of human beings, and to the higher law to which that nature conforms.

> They have no right to make a law prejudical to the whole community, even though the delinquents, in making such an act, should be themselves the chief sufferers by it; because it would be made against the principle of a superior law, which it is not in the power of any community or of the whole race of man to alter,—I mean he will of Him who gave us our nature, and, in giving, impressed an invariable law upon it.[23]

Laws must, above all else, be consistent with human nature and dignity. If they fail in that respect, then no matter how well they are framed or what arguments may be employed to support them, they are a menace to healthy society and sound government. Burke's warning against indiscriminate lawmaking is still very much to the point:

> It would be hard to point out any error more truly subversive of all the order and beauty, of all the peace and happiness of human society, than the position, that any body of men have a right to make what laws they please; or that laws can derive any authority from their institution merely, and independent of the quality of the subject matter. No arguments of policy, reason of state, or preservation of the constitution, can be pleaded in favor of such a practice. They may indeed impeach the frame of that constitution, but can never touch this immovable principle.[24]

[20] *Ibid.* [21] *Ibid.* [22] *Ibid.*, p. 255. [23] *Ibid.* [24] *Ibid.*

As one familiar with the classics, Burke here invokes the authority of Cicero[25] (upon whom as political philosopher, orator, and statesman he may well have patterned his own career), and then proceeds to set forth his own conception of the twofold foundation of law:

> In reality there are two, and only two, foundations of law; and they are both of them conditions without which nothing can give it any force; I mean equity and utility. With respect to the former, it grows out of the great rule of equality, which is grounded upon our common nature, and which Philo, with propriety and beauty, calls the mother of justice. All human laws are, properly speaking, only declaratory; they may alter the mode and application, but have no power over the substance of original justice.
>
> The other foundation of law, which is utility, must be understood, not of partial or limited, but of general and public utility, connected in the same manner with, and derived directly from, our rational nature; for any other utility may be the utility of a robber, but cannot be that of a citizen; the interest of the domestic enemy, and not that of a member of the commonwealth.[26]

Here is stated the familiar conception that the aim and purpose of laws must be the common welfare. And to support his argument on this point Burke[27] turned to *De legibus ac Deo legislatore* (I. vii, secs. 1, 4) of the Spanish theologian and jurist, Francisco Suárez, quoting in Latin a passage which, for present purposes, is reproduced in English. Discussing the question whether it is "inherent in the nature of law that it be enacted for the common good," Suárez himself supplied an unequivocal answer:

> With respect, then, to the question above set forth, there is no dispute among the various authorities; on the contrary, this axiom is common to them all: it is inherent in the nature and essence of law, that it shall be enacted for the sake of the common good; that is to say, that it shall be formulated particularly with reference to that good. . . . It would be contrary to every consideration of rectitude that the common good should be subordinated to the private good, or the whole accommodated to a part for the sake of the latter.

Those who are familiar with his magnificent speeches are aware of Burke's unequaled gift for logical, persuasive, and indeed convincing oratory. But he also possessed the gift of stating important truths with maxim-like brevity. In the present instance he declares "partiality and law are contradictory terms." Upon this maxim he makes certain forthright comments:

> Neither the merits nor the ill deserts, neither the wealth and importance, nor the indigence and obscurity of the one part or of the other, can make any alteration in this fundamental truth. On any other scheme, I defy any man living

---

[25] *De legibus* I. xv–xvi.   [26] Burke, *op. cit.*, V, 256.   [27] *Ibid.*, p. 258.

to settle a correct standard, which may discriminate between equitable rule and the most direct tyranny. For if we can once prevail upon ourselves to depart from the strictness and integrity of this principle, in favor even of a considerable party, the argument will hold for one that is less so; and thus we shall go on, narrowing the bottom of public right, until, step by step, we arrive, though after no very long or very forced deduction, at what one of our poets calls the enormous faith; the faith of the many, created for the advantage of a single person. I cannot see a glimmering of distinction to evade it; nor is it possible to allege any reason for the proscription of so large a part of the kingdom, which would not hold equally to support, under parallel circumstances, the proscription of the whole.

The purpose of the constitution must be to protect the interests of the people; and therefore Burke insists not only that "a constitution against the interest of the many is rather of the nature of a grievance than of a law," but also that "of all grievances it is the most weighty and important," and finally that "it is made without due authority, against all the acknowledged principles of jurisprudence, against the opinions of all the great lights in that science."[28] He then states in a few phrases his own conception of the true purpose of government: "that a conservation and secure enjoyment of our natural rights is the great and ultimate purpose of civil society; and that therefore all forms whatsoever of government are only good as they are subservient to that purpose, to which they are entirely subordinate."[29]

And by way of answer to those who opposed this conception Burke added a further statement as measured in form and wording as it is unanswerable in logic:

Now, to aim at the establishment of any form of government, by sacrificing what is the substance of it; to take away, or at least to suspend the rights of nature, in order to an approved system for the protection of them; and for the sake of that about which men must dispute for ever, to postpone those things about which they have no controversy at all, and this not in minute and subordinate, but large and principal objects, is a procedure as preposterous and absurd in argument, as it is oppressive and cruel in its effect.[30]

Yet though governments, one by one, slowly assumed a more democratic form, many of the social ills from which humanity suffered remained uncured. Indeed, with the advent of the industrial revolution these ills grew more acute until the appalling conditions of poverty and squalor in industrial centers again aroused the spirit of reform which—except in the political domain—had remained largely dormant since the great days of the Renaissance, when art and enlightenment had given to men a vision of happiness

[28] *Ibid.*, p. 263.   [29] *Ibid.*, p. 265.   [30] *Ibid.*

in a new order of civilization. For long decades that vision had faded in the turmoil of the modern world, but now it returned and, curiously enough, in one outstanding instance art and enlightenment were again joined in shaping the "form of things to come."

In the sixties of the last century the greatest of English art critics, a Londoner of Scottish parentage, having devoted no little attention to what he termed the political economy of art, became deeply interested in political economy in general. By way of preface to a brief consideration of John Ruskin's views, a few passages may be quoted from a distinguished modern historian of English letters:

> Political strife, in the ordinary sense, Ruskin did not touch. He was of no definable party, and though he called himself a Tory of the old school, and was full of feudal notions of paternal kingship and heaven-born aristocracy, he was also much too full of explosive material to be a Tory really; indeed, he attacked the assumptions of Tory, Whig, and Radical alike, at their roots, and by constant implication.[31]

To Ruskin the old laissez faire policy was simply another name for neglect on the part of the state of its obvious duty. It was his view, we are told, that

> The orthodox economy was only concerned with "certain accidental phenomena of modern commercial operations," and not with the total forces which really move, or ought to move, the whole body politic. "Wealth," hitherto defined in terms of the market, must be re-defined in terms of "life": and the science of political economy is meant for the furtherance of human life, understood in terms of virtue and happiness. On this showing, many alleged eternal necessities go by the board: the "laws" of supply and demand, the competitive system, the policy of non-interference. They are not eternal at all, said Ruskin, and moreover they are inherently poisonous, and ought to vanish. Wages, in particular, must be fixed, not by the law of the market, but by the law of justice. For Justice, to put the case no higher, pays, and a fixed minimum wage is good national economy.[32]

Others had expressed indignation over the abuses so characteristic of the existing industrial and social system; but Ruskin's approach to the problem was unusual. To quote again from the same authority, "he had approached the whole question, originally, from the artistic side, asking himself in what soil of character, and in what sunshine of welfare, the living art of a nation must be nourished, and thence proceeding to the economical social problem."[33] Moreover, while others inveighed against the evils of the day with anger or sorrow, Ruskin joined to these emotions the powerful weapon of reason. In due course he became convinced that human beings, not com-

[31] Oliver Elton, *A Survey of English Literature—1780–1880* (New York, 1920, 1927), III, 240–41.
[32] *Ibid.*, p. 241.
[33] *Ibid.*, p. 242.

modities, were the most important products of our civilization. In a series of essays which are gathered together under the title, *Unto This Last*, Ruskin set forth various conclusions which were the result of profound reflection. This book represents his innermost convictions, and indeed he preferred it above all of his other works. Time has shown that his vision was both penetrating and clear, and many of his ideas, considered revolutionary in his day, have now become, in whole or in part, accepted doctrines of current political and economic thought. It will be useful here to examine a number of his essays which embody the true spirit of reform.

Fundamental to Ruskin's theories was his conception of progress. It was his view that

> the science of nations is to be accumulative from father to son: each learning a little more and a little more; each receiving all that was known, and adding its own gain: the history and poetry of nations are to be accumulative; each generation treasuring the history and the songs of its ancestors, adding its own history and its own songs: and the art of nations is to be accumulative, just as science and history are; the work of living men not superseding, but building itself upon the work of the past.[34]

Carrying this conception a step further, Ruskin declared: "The whole nation is, in fact, bound together, as men are by ropes on a glacier—if one falls, the rest must either lift him or drag him along with them as dead weight, not without much increase of danger to themselves."[35] In other words, progress was not merely a matter of accumulation but of coöperation.

But was there any limit to the course of progress? To this question Ruskin's answer was that "there is as yet no ascertained limit to the nobleness of person and mind which the human creature may attain."[36]

This may be called a spiritual conception of progress. What is the true purpose of industrial and economic activities in relation to such progress?

> I leave to the reader's pondering [says Ruskin], whether, among national manufactures, that of Souls of a good quality may not at last turn out a quite leadingly lucrative one? Nay, in some far-away and yet undreamt-of hour, I can even imagine that England may cast all thoughts of possessive wealth back to the barbaric nations among whom they first arose; and that, while the sands of the Indus and adamant of Golconda may yet stiffen the housings of the charger, and flash from the turban of the slave, she, as a Christian mother, may at last attain to the virtues and the treasures of a Heathen one, and be able to lead forth her Sons, saying,—
>
> "These are MY Jewels."[37]

---

[34] Ruskin, *Unto This Last*, p. 43.
[35] *Ibid.*, p. 84.   [36] *Ibid.*, p. 199.   [37] *Ibid.*, p. 144.

Now Ruskin had very definite ideas as to the nature of political economy. It had been treated, so he considered, as "nothing more than the investigation of the phenomena of commercial operations."[38] Needless to say, this did not accord with his definition. His own view was that "political economy is neither an art nor a science, but a system of conduct and legislature, founded on the sciences, directing the arts, and impossible, except under certain conditions of moral culture." As domestic economy regulated the family, so the purpose of political economy was to regulate the "acts and habits" of society or the state with respect to "the means of its maintenance." And by "maintenance" Ruskin meant the "support of its population in healthy and happy life; and the increase of their numbers, so far as that increase is consistent with their happiness."[39] Again, "the real science of political economy, which has yet to be distinguished from the bastard science as medicine from witchcraft, and astronomy from astrology, is that which teaches nations to desire and labour for the things that lead to life; and which teaches them to scorn and destroy the things that lead to destruction."[40] On a later page Ruskin condenses his theory into a phrase, "true political economy is an ethical and by no means a commercial business."[41]

After these general definitions, it is easier to grasp Ruskin's views on the subject of wealth, which is regarded as the central element of political economy. We find that he has defined this element in terms which might well be printed on the first page of every treatise on economic questions:

THERE IS NO WEALTH BUT LIFE. Life, including all its powers of love, of joy, and of admiration. That country is the richest which nourishes the greatest number of noble and happy human beings; that man is richest who, having perfected the functions of his own life to the utmost, has also the widest helpful influence, both personal, and by means of his possessions, over the lives of others.[42]

Having thus defined wealth in terms of life, Ruskin proceeded to define "the aim of political economy" as "the multiplication of human life at the highest standard."[43]

Most economists in Ruskin's day, and not a few in our own, have placed the chief emphasis upon production. Some in the twentieth century, however, have flattered themselves upon the "discovery" that consumption is likewise important, and today there is an increasing tendency to stress this phase of economic life. But the "discoverers" of the fundamental importance of consumption would do well, before claiming title to their discovery, to examine certain doctrines which Ruskin laid down nearly fourscore years ago. It was his conviction that the

[38] Ruskin, *Unto This Last*, p. 197, n. [39] *Ibid.*, p. 197. [40] *Ibid.*, p. 168.
[41] *Ibid.*, p. 200. [42] *Ibid.*, p. 185.. [43] *Ibid.*, p. 199.

manner and issue of consumption . . . are the real tests of production. Production does not consist in things laboriously made, but in things serviceably consumable; and the question for the nation is not how much labour it employs, but how much life it produces. For as consumption is the end and aim of production, so life is the end and aim of consumption.[44]

Cherishing this view, it was but natural that he should also maintain "the final object of political economy" to be to furnish "good method of consumption, and great quantity of consumption: in other words, to use everything, and to use it nobly."[45] From that conception Ruskin advanced to a further conclusion on the definition of "value": that "the effectual value of a given quantity of any commodity existing in the world at any moment is therefore a mathematical function of the capacity existing in the human race to enjoy it."[46] This is a far cry from the definition of "value" in terms of the mere exchange of one commodity for another. Not that Ruskin would have denied the necessity of such exchange, nor the use of some monetary medium to facilitate it. It *was* his contention, however, that currencies should not have an intrinsic value. And again his statement has a prophetic ring:

> The use of substances of intrinsic value as the materials of a currency, is a barbarism;—a remnant of the conditions of barter, which alone can render commerce possible among savage nations. It is, however, still necessary, partly as a mechanical check on arbitrary issues; partly as a means of exchanges with foreign nations. In proportion to the extension of civilization, and increase of trustworthiness in Governments, it will cease.[47]

This statement may, in the view of many, brand Ruskin as a radical, but it is worthy of note that in recent years not a few doubts have been expressed as to whether gold should continue to be the basis of currencies, and indeed the present trend seems to be to separate the yellow metal more and more from the tokens with which men buy and sell.

There were certain other reforms advocated by Ruskin which would place him, in the opinion at least of conservatives, in the ranks of the socialists. Thus he advocated the establishment throughout the nation of training schools, at government cost and under government control, where the youth of the country should be taught rules concerning health, good habits—and particularly gentleness and justice—and a means of livelihood. He also proposed that there should be government factories and workshops for the production of any and all necessities, and the promotion of useful arts. These government undertakings were not to crowd out private industry but were to furnish a standard of quality and price to which private producers would have to conform. Futhermore, Ruskin suggested a cure

[44] *Ibid.*, p. 184. [45] *Ibid.*, p. 182. [46] *Ibid.*, p. 204. [47] *Ibid.*, p. 209.

for unemployment which, in simple terms, was that any person out of work should be admitted to the proposed government institutions and set to work at appropriate wages. And finally, he insisted that adequate provisions should be made for those incapacitated by age or otherwise rendered incapable of self-support. In his own way the laborer, like the soldier and statesman, serves his country and therefore should feel no hesitation, Ruskin considered, in accepting some form of pension. It need hardly be added that we have not yet completed the whole of this program.

But lest it be thought that, in making these proposals, Ruskin believed in the necessity of overturning the whole existing scheme of things, it should be added that he had definite views on the rights of property.

The first necessity of all economical government [he maintained] is to secure the unquestioned and unquestionable working of the great law of Property—that a man who works for a thing shall be allowed to get it, keep it, and consume it, in peace; and that he who does not eat his cake to-day, shall be seen, without grudging, to have his cake to-morrow. This, I say, is the first point to be secured by social law; without this, no political advance, nay, no political existence, is in any sort possible.[48]

So firmly did he hold these views that he deemed it the first duty of the nation's authorities to enforce the rights of property, to insure, as he puts it in figurative language, "that the cupboard door may have a firm lock to it, and no man's dinner be carried off by the mob, on its way home from the baker's."[49]

Ruskin shared, as might be expected, the view of Erasmus that the great cure for human ills was education. "There is," he declares,[50] "only one cure for public distress—and that is public education, directed to make men thoughtful, merciful, and just." As we have seen, he felt that provision of educational facilities was among the first duties of government, and he was also of the opinion that education should be practical in a twofold sense: that it should prepare the student to make his own way in the world and at the same time make the noblest use of such abilities as he possessed.

Needless to say, the government to which Ruskin refers from time to time is one which exists for the people and not for those who conduct it. In the following passage he pays his respects to selfish "kinghood":

I have no words for the wonder with which I hear Kinghood still spoken of, even among thoughtful men, as if governed nations were a personal property, and might be bought and sold, or otherwise acquired, as sheep, of whose flesh their king was to feed, and whose fleece he was to gather; as if Achilles' indig-

---

[48] Ruskin, *Unto This Last*, pp. 239–40. [49] *Ibid.*, p. 240. [50] *Sesame and Lilies*, p. 27, n.

nant epithet of base kings, "people-eating" were the constant and proper title of all monarchs; and enlargement of a king's dominion meant the same thing as the increase of a private man's estate! Kings who think so, however powerful, can no more be the true kings of the nation than gad-flies are the kings of a horse; they suck it, and may drive it wild, but do not guide it. They, and their courts, and their armies are, if one could see clearly, only a large species of marsh mosquito, with bayonet proboscis and melodious, band-mastered, trumpeting in the summer air; the twilight being, perhaps, sometimes fairer, but hardly more wholesome, for its glittering mists of midge companies. The true kings, meanwhile, rule quietly, if at all, and hate ruling; . . . who shall measure the difference between the power of those who "do and teach," and who are greatest in the kingdoms of earth, as of heaven—and the power of those who undo, and consume—whose power, at the fullest, is only the power of the moth and the rust? Strange! to think how the Moth-kings lay up treasures for the moth, and the Rust-kings, who are to their peoples' strength as rust to armour, lay up treasures for the rust; and the Robber-kings, treasures for the robber; but how few kings have ever laid up treasures that needed no guarding—treasures of which, the more thieves there were the better!"[51]

It was Ruskin's belief that the peace of the world depended in the final analysis upon the political economy of nations, and indeed he felt that the rules for the governing of individuals in their relations might equally apply to the relations of states. Thus he observed that "it would be well if a somewhat dogged conviction could be enforced on nations as on individuals, that, with few exceptions, what they cannot at present pay for, they should not at present have."[52] Moreover, he insisted that the characteristics of the nation were nothing more nor less than the sum total of the characteristics of its inhabitants.

Precisely according to the number of just men in a nation, is their power of avoiding either intestine or foreign war. All disputes may be peaceably settled, if a sufficient number of persons have been trained to submit to the principles of justice. The necessity for war is in direct ratio to the number of unjust persons who are incapable of determining a quarrel but by violence. Whether the injustice take the form of the desire of dominion, or of refusal to submit to it, or of lust of territory, or lust of money, or of mere irregular passion and wanton will, the result is economically the same;—loss of the quantity of power and life consumed in repressing the injustice, as well as of that requiring to be repressed, added to the material and moral destruction caused by the fact of war.[53]

[51] *Ibid.*, pp. 43–44.   [52] *Unto This Last*, p. 219, n.
[53] *Ibid.*, p. 200, n.
By way of comment on the views Ruskin here sets forth a few passages are quoted from one of his contemporaries, W. E. H. Lecky, a distinguished Irish historian and philosopher: "The conceptions that the interests of adjoining nations are diametrically opposed, that wealth

To illustrate his views, Ruskin here cited the "early civil wars of England" and the Civil War then raging in the United States, both of which he declared to be examples "of the results of the want of education of large masses of nations in principles of justice."

Not only war, but the fear of war, was and still is costly to nations, as we know to our sorrow: "the mere dread or distrust resulting from the want of the inner virtues of Faith and Charity among nations, is often no less costly than war itself." By way of illustration Ruskin adds: "The fear which France and England have of each other costs each nation about fifteen millions sterling annually, besides various paralyses of commerce; that sum being spent in the manufacture of means of destruction instead of

---

can only be gained by displacement, and that conquest is therefore the chief path to progress, were long universal; but during the last century political economy has been steadily subverting them, and has already effected so much that it scarcely seems unreasonable to conclude that the time will come when a policy of territorial aggrandisement will be impossible." (*The History of the Rise and Influence of Rationalism in Europe*, p. 226.)

"It can hardly be questioned that the advance of intellectual culture produces a decline of the military spirit. . . . But at the same time it is no less certain that the bond of intellectual sympathy alone is far too weak to restrain the action of opposing passions, and it was reserved for political economy to supply a stronger and more permanent principle of unity.

"This principle is an enlightened self-interest. Formerly, as I have said, the interests of nations were supposed to be diametrically opposed. The wealth that was added to one was necessarily taken from another; and all commerce was a kind of balance, in which a gain on one side implied a corresponding loss on the opposite one. Every blow that was struck to the prosperity of one nation was of advantage to the rest, for it diminished the number of those among whom the wealth of the world was to be divided." (*Ibid.*, pp. 354–55.)

"For this great evil political economy is the only corrective. It teaches, in the first place, that the notion that a commercial nation can only prosper by the loss of its neighbour, is essentially false. It teaches still further that each nation has a direct interest in the prosperity of that with which it trades, just as a shopman has an interest in the wealth of his customers. It teaches too that the different markets of the world are so closely connected, that it is quite impossible for a serious derangement to take place in any one of them without its evil effects vibrating through all. . . . Every fresh commercial enterprise is therefore an additional guarantee of peace." (*Ibid.*, pp. 355–56.)

"At the same time two kindred movements which I have already noticed—the recognition of the principle of the rights of nationalities as the basis of political morality, and the growing ascendency of intellectual pursuits diminishing the admiration of military glory—would consolidate the interests of peace. Many years must undoubtedly elapse before such a condition of society can be attained . . . but as surely as civilisation advances, so surely must the triumph come. Liberty, industry, and peace are in modern societies indissolubly connected, and their ultimate ascendency depends upon a movement which may be retarded, but cannot possibly be arrested." (*Ibid.*, p. 358.)

"Though concurrence of action based solely upon community of interests, considered in itself, has no moral value, its effect in destroying some of the principal causes of dissension is extremely important. And, indeed, human nature is so constituted, that it is impossible for bodies of men to work together under the sense of a common interest without a warm feeling of amity arising between them. Common aims and hopes knit them together by a bond of sympathy. Each man becomes accustomed to act with a view to the welfare of others, and a union of affections usually replaces or consecrates the union of interests. The sentiment thus evoked is undoubtedly a moral sentiment; and if it is not so powerful as that which is elicited by agencies appealing directly to enthusiasm, it is more general, more uniform, and perhaps, on the whole, not less beneficial to mankind." (*Ibid.*, pp. 362–63.)

means of production."[54] The applicability of these views to the present posture of international affairs requires no comment.

In the present chapter no more than a glance has been possible at a few phases of human progress which history has made visible to us. Even so hasty a survey reveals certain characteristics in the march—or, rather, the slow and painful ascent—of humankind. Progress is not a steady growth, but a series of advances and retreats in which, like the waves of the incoming tide, the sea of humanity gradually pushes forward. Discernible too, are recurring periods of reform in which the principles of future progress are laid down, although they may not be realized for years or even centuries to come. He who has studied the works of the leading reformers in which these principles are set forth will find in them some justification for optimism, for a belief in humanity as it exists, and especially in humanity as it will be.

It is not, however, within the province of this epilogue to attempt a prophecy. The present writer desires only to record his conviction that the path of the future will continue the path of the past; and that its guide-posts will in large measure be those supplied by the great reformers of ancient times, of the Middle Ages, and of the Renaissance, and by their modern successors in the English-speaking world—among them John Locke, an Englishman; Edmund Burke, an Irishman; and John Ruskin, a Scotsman born in London. In the fullness of time that path will lead to the realization of the dream of true democracy put into immortal verse by Robert Burns, the greatest poet of Scotland, whose songs are the songs of the world:

> A king can mak a belted knight,
> A marquis, duke, and a' that;
> But an honest man's aboon his might,
> Guid faith, he maunna fa' that!
> For a' that, and a' that,
> Their dignities, and a' that,
> The pith o' sense, and pride o' worth,
> Are higher ranks than a' that.
>
> Then let us pray that come it may,
> As come it will for a' that,
> That sense and worth, o'er a' the earth,
> May bear the gree, and a' that;
> For a' that, and a' that,
> It's coming yet, for a' that;
> That man to man, the warld o'er,
> Shall brothers be for a' that.

[54] Ruskin, *Unto This Last*, p. 201, n.